Innovative Strategies for Implementing FinTech in Banking

Yousif Abdullatif Albastaki
Ahlia University, Bahrain

Anjum Razzaque
Ahlia University, Bahrain

Adel M. Sarea
Ahlia University, Bahrain

IGI Global
PUBLISHER of TIMELY KNOWLEDGE

A volume in the Advances in Finance, Accounting, and Economics (AFAE) Book Series

Published in the United States of America by
IGI Global
Business Science Reference (an imprint of IGI Global)
701 E. Chocolate Avenue
Hershey PA, USA 17033
Tel: 717-533-8845
Fax: 717-533-8661
E-mail: cust@igi-global.com
Web site: http://www.igi-global.com

Library of Congress Cataloging-in-Publication Data

Names: Albastaki, Yousif, 1962- editor. | Razzaque, Anjum, 1973- editor. | Sarea, Adel M., 1979- editor.
Title: Innovative strategies for implementing FinTech in banking / Yousif Abdullatif Albastaki, Anjum Razzaque, and Adel M. Sarea, editors.
Description: Hershey : Business Science Reference, 2020. | Includes bibliographical references and index. | Summary: “”This book addresses key issues, challenges, opportunities, and implementation of FinTech in the banking sector”--Provided by publisher”-- Provided by publisher.
Identifiers: LCCN 2019049667 (print) | LCCN 2019049668 (ebook) | ISBN 9781799832577 (hardcover) | ISBN 9781799832584 (paperback) | ISBN 9781799832591 (ebook)
Subjects: LCSH: Banks and banking--Technological innovations. | Financial services industry--Information technology. | Financial engineering..
Classification: LCC HG1708.7 .I56 2020 (print) | LCC HG1708.7 (ebook) | DDC 332.1068--dc23
LC record available at https://lccn.loc.gov/2019049667
LC ebook record available at https://lccn.loc.gov/2019049668

This book is published in the IGI Global book series Advances in Finance, Accounting, and Economics (AFAE) (ISSN: 2327-5677; eISSN: 2327-5685)

British Cataloguing in Publication Data
A Cataloguing in Publication record for this book is available from the British Library.

For electronic access to this publication, please contact: eresources@igi-global.com.

Advances in Finance, Accounting, and Economics (AFAE) Book Series

Ahmed Driouchi
Al Akhawayn University, Morocco

ISSN:2327-5677
EISSN:2327-5685

Mission

In our changing economic and business environment, it is important to consider the financial changes occurring internationally as well as within individual organizations and business environments. Understanding these changes as well as the factors that influence them is crucial in preparing for our financial future and ensuring economic sustainability and growth.

The **Advances in Finance, Accounting, and Economics (AFAE)** book series aims to publish comprehensive and informative titles in all areas of economics and economic theory, finance, and accounting to assist in advancing the available knowledge and providing for further research development in these dynamic fields.

Coverage

- Finance
- Economic Downturn
- Corporate Finance
- Microfinance
- Economics of Innovation and Knowledge
- Auditing
- Economics of Migration and Spatial Mobility
- Investments and Derivatives
- Internet Banking
- Applied economics

IGI Global is currently accepting manuscripts for publication within this series. To submit a proposal for a volume in this series, please contact our Acquisition Editors at Acquisitions@igi-global.com or visit: http://www.igi-global.com/publish/.

The Advances in Finance, Accounting, and Economics (AFAE) Book Series (ISSN 2327-5677) is published by IGI Global, 701 E. Chocolate Avenue, Hershey, PA 17033-1240, USA, www.igi-global.com. This series is composed of titles available for purchase individually; each title is edited to be contextually exclusive from any other title within the series. For pricing and ordering information please visit http://www.igi-global.com/book-series/advances-finance-accounting-economics/73685. Postmaster: Send all address changes to above address.

Titles in this Series

For a list of additional titles in this series, please visit:
http://www.igi-global.com/book-series/advances-finance-accounting-economics/73685

Theory of Shocks and Self-Development Laws of Economic Systems Emerging Research and Opportunities
Olga Ivanovna Pilipenko (The Russian Presidential Academy of National Economy and Public Administration, Russia) Zoya Andreevna Pilipenko (Bank of Russia, Russia) and Andrey Igorevich Pilipenko (The Russian Presidential Academy of National Economy and Public Administration, Russia)
Business Science Reference • © 2021 • 250pp • H/C (ISBN: 9781799843092) • US $165.00

Handbook of Research on Emerging Theories, Models, and Applications of Financial Econometrics
Burcu Adıgüzel Mercangöz (Istanbul University, Turkey)
Business Science Reference • © 2020 • 300pp • H/C (ISBN: 9781799831969) • US $275.00

Circular Economy and Re-Commerce in the Fashion Industry
Archana Shrivastava (Jaypee Business School, JIIT, Noida, India) Geetika Jain (FMS, Amity University, Noida, India) and Justin Paul (University of Puerto Rico, Puerto Rico)
Business Science Reference • © 2020 • 204pp • H/C (ISBN: 9781799827283) • US $195.00

Mapping, Managing, and Crafting Sustainable Business Strategies for the Circular Economy
Susana Serrano Rodrigues (Polytechnic Institute of Leiria, Portugal) Paulo Jorge Almeida (Polytechnic Institute of Leiria, Portugal) and Nuno Miguel Castaheira Almeida (Polytechnic Institute of Leiria, Portugal)
Business Science Reference • © 2020 • 401pp • H/C (ISBN: 9781522598855) • US $195.00

Applied Econometric Analysis Emerging Research and Opportunities
Brian W. Sloboda (University of Phoenix, USA) and Yaya Sissoko (Indiana University of Pennsylvania, USA)
Business Science Reference • © 2020 • 264pp • H/C (ISBN: 9781799810933) • US $195.00

Handbook of Research on Accounting and Financial Studies
Luís Farinha (University of Beira Interior, Portugal) Ana Baltazar Cruz (School of Management, Polytechnic Institute of Castelo Branco, Portugal) and João Renato Sebastião (Polytechnic Institute of Castelo Branco, Portugal)
Business Science Reference • © 2020 • 487pp • H/C (ISBN: 9781799821366) • US $295.00

Emerging Tools and Strategies for Financial Management
Begoña Álvarez-García (Universidade da Coruña, Spain) and José-Pablo Abeal-Vázquez (Universidade da Coruña, Spain)
Business Science Reference • © 2020 • 357pp • H/C (ISBN: 9781799824404) • US $225.00

IGI Global
PUBLISHER of TIMELY KNOWLEDGE

701 East Chocolate Avenue, Hershey, PA 17033, USA
Tel: 717-533-8845 x100 • Fax: 717-533-8661
E-Mail: cust@igi-global.com • www.igi-global.com

Table of Contents

Detailed Table of Contents

There is a paradigm shift in the financial services industry. Combined with ever-changing customer expectations and preferences, emerging technologies such as artificial intelligence (AI), machine learning, the internet of things (IoT), and blockchain are redefining how financial institutions deliver services. It is an enormous task to remain competitive in this ever-changing environment. Financial institutions see FinTech as a major part of the digital future, and as proof of this, since 2015, financial institutions have invested over US$ 27 billion in FinTech and digital innovation. This chapter is an introductory chapter that explores FinTech in the literature. It focuses on how FinTech is reshaping the financial industry by describing FinTech phases and development process. The financial products and services using FinTech are also described with a highlight on Islamic FinTech. The chapter finally concludes by describing the future of FinTech.

The holistic approach of the phenomenon of expansion of financial innovations, respectively of current financial technologies, as otherwise abbreviated to FinTech, knows very specific elements and is adapted to the global financial context, and lately, the share of financial services in the virtual space is dominant compared to their traditional form. Moreover, this new financing instrument has arisen mainly due to the need to streamline the financing system, based on technology, either to provide financial services adapted to the current needs of consumers (especially those who are in need of financing, this is also the real reason for the FinTech coupling of the financial inclusion of the financially excluded), as well as the design of new financial products that are reliable and responsive to the market. The financial space is dual, presenting two often contradictory assumptions (all channels, stocks, and collection flow, on the one hand; and all entities, channels, stocks, and investment flows), and in the current context of digital financial technologies, this is in virtual space.

sandboxes differs from one jurisdiction to another. This topic is crucial to the banks as they need to understand further how regulatory sandbox may help them offer innovative financial products to level the competition with the fintech players in the market.

There has been an extensive boost in the use of FinTech in the Banking sector during the last few years. This chapter provides a comprehensive overview of the new opportunities offered by FinTech to the banking sector, its prospective risks, and the possible challenges to be faced in its adaptation. The authors propose that the new opportunities of FinTech include better digital banking experience, personalized customer services, high-level data security, cost-effective, and efficient services. On the other hand, FinTech results in risks such as security risk, technical risk, regulation risk, financial risk, and reputation risk. Finally, they suggest that the possible challenges of FinTech are a technological adaptation, risk reduction, regulations, and human capital employment.

Crowdfunding is a new form of both investment opportunities and source of raising capital. The aim of this chapter is to explore the understanding of the newly invented crowdfunding, types of the existing platforms of the industry. Authors investigated crowdfunding platforms that are registered in securities commission Malaysia and Kapitalboost platform of Singapore and their mode of investment. Authors also looked in depth and reviewed a current literature on crowdfunding. An investment model of crowdfunding that will be suitable for the Muslim investors who are looking into an ethical investment that will contribute to the wellbeing of the societies as whole through Mudharabah and Musharakah investment. The findings explored that equity crowdfunding could bring more benefit and less harm to entrepreneurs. Consequently, there are two types of models that are based on equity-in and equity-out; hence, the chapter recommends the equity crowdfunding over the debt-based through Islamic investment method of Musharakah and Mudharabah investment.

Fintech refers to the novel processes and products that become available for financial services due to the digital technological advancements. Fintech includes technologically enabled financial innovation leading to new business models, applications, processes, or products with an associated material effect on financial markets, institutions, and financial services. India is transitioning into a dynamic ecosystem

Financial technology (FinTech) has developed rapidly over the last decade. In the Kingdom of Bahrain, both public and private sectors have adopted FinTech in different ways. The objective of this research is to explore and assess Bahraini users' adoption of and satisfaction with FinTech services. A model was built to quantify FinTech users' satisfaction. and a questionnaire was used to collect data; 319 responses were returned. The outcome was that all the factors investigated, accessibility, ease of use, completeness, accuracy, security, reliability, responsiveness, service quality, system quality, and information quality, have a significant positive effect on user satisfaction. The contribution of this research is the model of satisfaction for FinTech that can be applied in different countries. The proposals recommended by the authors will also inform government and concerned organizations about FinTech in Bahrain for greater user satisfaction.

Chapter 12
The Impact of FinTech on Financial Services in India: Past, Present, and Future Trends 191
Gagan Kukreja, Ahlia University, Bahrain
Divij Bahl, Gulf International Bank, Bahrain
Ruchika Gupta, Amity Business School, Amity University, Greater Noida, India

Fintech is a new buzz word in the fourth industrial revolution environment. No financial services across the globe are left unaffected by the new technologies. Artificial intelligence, machine learning, blockchain, and data analytics have immensely influenced many aspects of financial services such as deposits, transactions, billings, remittances, credits (B2B and P2P), underwriting, insurance, and so on. Fintech companies are enabling larger financial inclusion, improvement of lives of humans, better decision-making, and lots more. This chapter covers the development, opportunities, and challenges of financial sectors because of new technologies in India. This chapter throws the light on opportunities that emerged because of demographic dividend, high penetration, and access to the latest and affordable technology, affordable cost of smartphones, and government policies such as Digital India, Startup India, Make in India, and so on. Lastly, this chapter portrays the untapped potentials of Fintech in India.

Chapter 13
Evaluating Mergers as a Tool to Strengthen and Modernize the Palestinian Banking System: An Analytical Study of Palestinian Local Banks 2010-2017 201
Azmi Wasfi Awad, Palestine Technical University, Palestine
Bahaa Subhi Awwad, Palestine Technical University, Palestine
Abdel-Aziz Ahmad Sharabati, Middle East University, Jordan

The study aims at evaluating the banking mergers as a tool to strengthen and modernize the Palestinian banking system by focusing on the national banks listed on the Palestine Stock Exchange using the descriptive-analytical approach as well as the inductive and deductive approaches. The study concludes that the circulars issued by the Palestine Monetary Authority mainly those which relate to the raising of the minimum capital of local banks, have a positive role, and were the main motivation towards these mergers. The mergers that took place in the Palestinian banking sector have resulted in a significant improvement in data and financial indicators as well as the competitiveness of domestic merged banks and reflected positively on the national economy. The study recommends the need to redouble the efforts of the Palestine Monetary Authority by using literary persuasion at certain times, and through the development of laws and regulations that encourage and stimulate mergers to create stronger banking entities that are capable of facing the challenges of competition and financial crises, and other banking risks, at other times. Moreover, national banks and large-scale expatriates must play a more active role in the process

of economic development and work to maximize their economic role and expand the value of productive projects that require large funding through granting syndicated loans and establishing joint ventures.

FinTech, a compound term for financial technology, signifies the usage of technology to provide financial assistance. Ever since its evolution FinTech has been growing tremendously, despite its positive and negative aspects. In the literature review, there are many factors affecting the adoption of FinTech. It was found that the ease of use of technology (Technology Acceptance Theory), investment decisions in crowdfunding (Decision Theory), and the risks involved in the adoption of FinTech (Prospect Theory) are the main factors that might affect the adoption of FinTech. However, there is a paucity of studies linking all these factors in the adoption of FinTech using these theories. This research project investigates the influence of these factors in the adoption of FinTech. In order to analyze these factors, a questionnaire was used. As a result, it was found that there is a positive relationship between the ease of use and FinTech's adoption; between FinTech's adoption and investment decisions in crowdfunding and between the level of risks when adapting to FinTech. Keywords: FinTech; Factors; Bahrain; Adoption; Financial Institutions

This chapter measures the attitudes of people residing in the Kingdom of Bahrain toward adopting mobile banking technology, also known as e-Wallets. The Technology Acceptance Model, the Unified Theory of Acceptance and Use of Technology, and the Diffusion of Innovations model were used to construct a questionnaire with the added focus on the promotional aspects. A total of 1,740 responses obtained from individuals in Bahrain revealed a high level of adoption rates. All dimensions measured were confirmed to have a significant impact on the adoption of e-Wallets, particularly those related to promotional benefits, which reveals a need for future studies to focus on the marketing approaches of mobile payment technologies. Studied factors were confirmed to have a significant impact on the usage and adoption of e-Wallets in the Kingdom of Bahrain. More focus is required from a benefits perspective rather than the technical perspective. Financial institutions need to pay more considerable attention to the changing mindsets of people toward making payments and the shift to new technologies.

The e-wallet is one of the successful innovative services that was launched in 2017. A quantitative survey approach based on a five-point Likert scale was used in this study. The sampling tool relies on the snowball and convenience sampling technique. The sample consisted of 660 users in Bahrain. This

Preface

In the interdisciplinary world of financial innovation, to comprehend how technology supports the financial system, FinTech has built new foundations for science. It is the role of digitization that influenced financial services significantly, with financial products being one of the most important areas of financial services. For instance, credit contracts, stock trading or online payments or payment transactions that contrast the purchase of a car, i.e., do not include physical or physical interactions. Digitization is realized through the advancement of IT for process automation, so that with new business models that automate IT-based financial services: "Financial" and "Technology" = FinTech. FinTech has led the evolution of new creative business concepts. For example, 2,000 + companies provided financial-technology-based services in 2017 across sixty-four countries. This is made possible by using technology innovatively to underpin new ways of banking, security trading, and various other financial services. Numerous FinTech companies range from microfinance, personal funding, investment and distributed ledge, equity financing, blockchain project platforms; just to name a few. FinTech encourages various new practices, such as reducing cash use in different countries, increasing mobile payment rates, new algorithms for and high-frequency trading across national borders, and so on. FinTech is paving the way for new technologies emerging in the IT scene, such as blockchain ledgers, machine learning, data mining, artificial intelligence, and knowledge discovery. Such new technologies combined with recent developments such as Internet of Things, Big Data, Social Computing and Cloud Computing; enable financial service firms to automate existing business processes so that new products, such as crowdfunding or peer-to - peer insurance platforms, can be offered: catering for hybrid customer engagement and self-service; thus shifting the environment by growing outsourcing to oriented specialization through resizing, leading to new ecosystems and new regulations to encourage fintech: including the 'sandbox' initiative introduced in Singapore and London, to facilitate fintech start-ups. Nevertheless, such new ecosystems are also accompanied by new challenges as also reported by scholars who have expressed challenges when it comes to deteriorating mobile payment system supported by Fintech, which bear the challenges that pertain to commercial factors (e.g., profitability and cost balancing), technical factors (e.g., technological solutions or security), and legal factors (e.g., audit, regulation, just to name a few).

FinTech encourages new practices, for example increasing mobile payment rates. Scholars have warned, however, that many mobile payment systems have been observed unsuccessful, while hundreds such systems were implemented worldwide: thus challenging the importance of mobile payment. Some instances like three mobile payment projects: conclude that mobile payment systems are complex systems that are not modular fashion creation but creation by instrument, law, mechanism, and actor service. This includes operationalizing electronic payments, including payment networks, distribution, and settlement processes, with banks and settlement officers, suppliers, regulators, technology partners being the lowest level. In short, mobile payment technology is applicable to fintech, in tandem with "dislocation and focus" as global banks expand regionally and globalize across borders internationally. Therefore, there is a literature-driven need to contribute an intellectual contribution like this book which can primarily serve as a guide to the mystified financially technological revolution. And hence mitigate the reported disruption while expedite the creativity and opportunity for FinTech. Through the contributions by leading thinkers in the academia and global investment room of FinTech, this book converges the diverse though processes of the academia and those practitioners well versed within their industry sectors, to contribute through as a singular and focused insight, so that traders, bankers, academics and investors are able to gain an insight, to quench their thirst for answers which they need for capitalizing on this lucrative market. Hence, the primary aim of this intellectual contribution (book) is to create an accessible and coherent Financial Technology (FinTech) book that will add value to current research (focusing on the remaining gaps) and lead to a deeper understanding of the factors affecting effective FinTech adoption in banking. As a result, this publication will play a significant role in addressing the key issues, challenges, and opportunities of FinTech by increasing its awareness in the banking sector in a systematic and holistic way for both individuals and the financial industry. It will also provide a clear direction for the effective implementation of FinTech initiatives/programmes for improving banking financial processes performance excellence.

Moreover, it will encourage managers of the financial world to assume a proactive role in FinTech, i.e., to actually make FinTech a reality; which contributed to superior decision-making capabilities that support financial institutions to become FinTech engines. Hence, publishing this book is of sheer interest to researchers, academics, students, and practitioners whose focus of expertise and research is within financial industries. This book is of a vital significance to those stakeholders within the banking sector. The prospective audience for this book are researchers, academics, and practitioners interested in: Fintech and digital banking, implementation of excellence banking, Total Quality Management (TQM) within the financial industry, financial administration. This book rises FinTech awareness by setting a clear direction for effectively implementing FinTech programs, to improve financial institutions through a culture of learning and an environment where stakeholders achieve performance excellence. In this sense, the intended audience are also from banking sectors, the government officials at various levels, the Chief Knowledge Officers (CKOs), managers and the policy makers who are enhancing the financial/banking sector, or also those considering entering the financial world.

There has been increased attention toward public administration degrees at universities and public administration institutes around the world. The number of students studying these disciplines/degrees is on a dramatic rise. Hence, this book is a useful academic source for students researching in the area of Knowledge Management System (KMS) design and developers. Such students will benefit from this book, as they will gain an understanding of the different KM elements needed to develop effective and efficient KMSs. The book bears implications for Financial Technology in general, and specifically for practitioners. This book expands on the current understanding of FinTech and its related technologies within the financial world by exploring and investigating various factors and how they relate to successfully implementing FinTech. Systematic and statistical research methods are applied, to overcome the missing elements in current literature, with a focus on validating the critical success factors (CSFs) within this research arena.

One of the main targeted aims is to form a new paradigm of FinTech in banking administrations; thus, FinTech adaptation strategies and frameworks would be included to overcome the limitations and challenges by guiding, controlling and sustaining financial organizational FinTech programs that encourage organizational learning and organizational wisdom. There is scant research examining the impact of FinTech on Financial organizations outcomes in the banking sector; this book will therefore examine its impact on the financial organizations outcomes, furthermore, determining most effective means to measure FinTech initiatives. The current research has failed to identify the exact relationship between FinTech and financial organizational services excellence; this proposed book will, therefore, provide insight into the impact and influence of FinTech on financial organizational excellence. Finally, the book will provide a scientific and practical guide for building a competitive financial organization sector.

Chapter 1 is an introduction illustrating how in the financial sector there is a paradigm shift, with a mix of ever-changing consumer perceptions and preferences which led to new emerging technologies like FinTech which is redefining how financial institutions offer services. The chapter also shows how to remain successful in this ever-changing world is an immense challenge, as result Financial institutions see FinTech as a major part of the digital future, and since 2015 financial institutions have invested more than US$ 27 billion in fintech and digital innovation as evidence of this. This chapter also collects and presents the added value of the visionaries, experts and writers contributing to the FinTech revolution and discusses FinTech in the literature, with a focus on how FinTech reshapes the financial industry by explaining phases of FinTech and the process of growth. The chapter also discusses global investments in FinTech, RegTech and FinTech and explains the financial products and services using FinTech with a focus on Islamic Fintech. Finally, the chapter concludes by discussing and describing what might be the future of FinTech.

Chapter 2 gifts the holistic approach of the phenomenon of expansion of financial innovations, respectively of current FinTech and knows very specific elements and how itis adapted to the global financial context, and recently, the share of financial services in the virtual space is dominant in comparison to their traditional form. Moreover, this chapter show how this new financing instrument arose mainly because of the need to streamline the technology-based financing system, either to provide financial services tailored to the current needs of consumers, particularly those in need of funding, the chapter also claims that this is also the real reason for fintech coupling the financial inclusion of the financially excluded, as well as the design of new financial products that are reliable and responsive to the market. This chapter also explains that the financial space is dual, offering two sometimes conflicting assumptions: all platforms, stocks, and collection flows, on the one hand, and all individuals, networks, stocks, and investment flows, and that is in virtual space in the current sense of digital finance technology. Finally, this chapter concludes that FinTech is at the crossroads of finance and technology, and the role of the human factor is much smaller compared to the role of technology in finance and main developments, such as the large volume of data and its availability, the exponential increase of computational capacity that allows for the analysis of increasingly large data sets, wider access and lower goods and services costs, growth disintermediation and remediation, and demographic and generational changes are all heading towards a crossroads of major technological changes in the provision of financial services.

Chapter 3 evaluates international FinTech instruments through the lens of the innovation diffusion theory (IDT) adoption strategies and the research work focused in helping to understand the ROA-related indicators for predicting the future of fintech implementations. The implications of the new Payment System Directive (PSD2) in Europe and blockchain applications are further discussed in the chapter with an emphases on how money transfer and payments, for example, have the highest ROA while insurance services have the highest rate of ROA growth due to relative advantages, high compatibility and trialability levels, and low complexity and uncertainty levels. This chapter also describes how a cross country comparisons conducted include descriptive statistics about FinTech deal value and volume, innovation rank, B2C commerce market, ROA and internet penetration and the results demonstrates that Germany is the only country listed in all of the top 10 ranking lists, followed by the U.S., the U.K., and France. This chapter is a study that reveals that China, India, and Canada have distinguished success in terms of fintech indicators while the growth in Japan is expected to be slow. Finally, this chapter concludes proof of Cancian theory that low-middle socio-economic status individuals are more creative than high-middle-class individuals because they have less to lose, particularly at the beginning of an innovation when there is a high degree of uncertainty

Chapter 4 claims that while the blockchain is still in its infancy stage, analysts have already considered its influence and effect as the start of a new technological revolution, which is especially important to the financial services industry. There are numerous institutions provided by Shari'ah, such as zakah, waqf, sadaqah, and qard hasan, that exist and founded, in Islamic legal literature and within the Muslim world. Due to various factors, however, the role of such institutions has been marginalized; therefore, they do not have a major impact at macro level. This chapter also critically examines FinTech's role in rejuvenating the blockchain and smart contracts of Islamic social financing goods and the work carried out discusses how blockchain and smart contracts are implemented and used in the sense of zakah, waqf and hasan qard. Finally, this chapter show how this research work serve as a comprehensive and crucial point of reference for the role of fintech, blockchain, and smart contracts with respect to Islamic social financing products.

Chapter 5 describes how Fintech emergence post-Global Financial Crisis puts the banking sector at risk and one of the banks' strategies to stay afloat and important in the digital age is by implementing regulatory sandboxes, which can be described as one of the tools opted by financial regulators in certain jurisdictions to regulate the rapid growth of fintech products within their financial sphere, the founder in which the Financial Conduct Authority (FCA) was the business and conduct regulator in the UK. This chapter claims that because of the basic structures in a sandbox is the eligibility requirements that the regulators draw for participation by the financial service provider in the sandbox, as a results this research work addressed how for both jurisdictions the entry criteria as the layout of the regulatory sandboxes vary from one jurisdiction to another and consequently, the topic is crucial to the banks as they need to understand further how regulatory sandbox may help them offer innovative financial products to level the competition with the fintech players in the market. Finally, this chapter concludes that banks which are participating in offering fintech products and regulated under the sandbox, the financial stability is ensured as systemic risks will be lesser by having the regulator's supervision and as consequence of this, the financial consumer may enjoy more efficient financial service options according to their financial appetite.

Chapter 6 is a comprehensive overview on the new opportunities offered by FinTech to the banking sector, its prospective risks, and the possible challenges faced during FinTech adaptation. This chapter demonstrates that new opportunities of FinTech include better digital banking experience, personalized customer services, high-level data security, cost-effective, and efficient services. The chapter also describes how FinTech results in risks such as security risk, technical risk, regulation risk, financial risk, and reputation risk. The chapter describes how FinTech can greatly improve the banks' operational performance, remain competitive, maintain sustainability, innovate new products and services, and enhance customer satisfaction levels. This chapter also illustrates how to implement FinTech successfully the banks need to strive hard to face the challenges and must try to overcome the hurdles in its pathway. Finally, this chapter concludes that FinTech is in its nascent stage, to revolutionize financial products and services being offered shortly. This chapter's research work is useful to academic, industrial practitioners and households in gaining an overview of the possible opportunities, risk, and challenges to be faced by banking institutions to put FinTech into practice.

Chapter 7 claims that Crowdfunding represents a new form of investment opportunities and a source of capital raising, and the chapter aims to broaden the perception of the newly developed crowdfunding, styles of the industry's current platforms. This chapter investigates crowdfunding platforms that are registered in securities commission Malaysia and Kapital boost platform of Singapore and their mode of investment. Additionally, this chapter performed an in-depth review of established crowdfunding literature. As a result, a model of crowdfunding that will be suitable for the Muslim investors who are looking into an ethical investment that will contribute to the wellbeing of the societies as whole through Mudharabah and Musharakah investment. Finally, this chapter concludes its findings through exploring that equity crowdfunding could bring more benefit and less harm to entrepreneurs and consequently two types of models that is based on equity-in and equity-out, hence recommending that the equity crowdfunding over the debt based through Islamic investment method of Musharakah and Mudharabah is better option.

Chapter 8 claims that FinTech includes technologically empowered financial innovation leading to new business models, technologies, processes, or goods with related material impact on financial markets, institutions, and financial services. This chapter also describes how India transitions to into a dynamic ecosystem offering Fintech start-ups a platform to grow into billion-dollar unicorns and Fintech in India pursues several goals, from targeting new segments to developing international markets; and how the historically cash-driven Indian economy responded well to the Fintech opportunity, primarily triggered by an rise in e-commerce and the penetration of smartphones. Additionally, this chapter demonstration how India 's growth, is still not comparable to its global counterparts in size, but is well stacked due to a strong tech workforce talent pipeline and therefore pursuing an exploratory approach based on an in-depth analysis of this research work which aimed to recognize the challenges and deliberate outlook for Fintech in India. This chapter stresses on the fast rate of Fintech evolvement, predicting that parts of Fintech's will slow down in coming years, going so far as to suggest a build-up in the Fintech bubble, to break out soon.

Chapter 9 demonstrates how Brazilian financial institutes facilitate the growth and advancement of new means of access and operation, these banks tried to implement friendly and efficient digital platforms so that they could accommodate FinTech advances. This chapter aims to describe how FinTech are defined as opportunities and challenges to large financial institutions in Brazil, despite this situation and to understand and analyze the aspects related to FinTech, the research approaches topics that are aligned with the theme, such as the current economic context, the National Financial System, and the start-up scenario in Brazil. This chapter adapts a descriptive and qualitative approach, in which the data were gathered from interviews with the financial institutions responsible and as a result the research has made it possible to identify that the great institutions are accepting to apply this FinTech model and the study revealed that that the sector needs to be regulated so that it can grow more freely and thus be able to add this technological wealth to the country, but it analyzes the need to be less bureaucratic, like the financial institutions operating in the market. This chapter also presented the limitations of a few cases in which more management could not be interviewed in other companies involved in the innovations of the organization in some way. Finally this chapter concluded by demonstrating how large companies already established in the financial market identify FinTech and their business models and suggested that other studies need to be carried out to cover other interesting points that concern the FinTech business model.

Chapter 10 sheds light on how new innovations and technologies affect practically all financial services in China, new technologies such as blockchain, artificial intelligence, machine learning, deep learning and data analytics have had a major impact on all aspects of financial services such as deposits, transactions, billings, credits underwriting and insurances and how Fintech companies are enabling larger financial inclusion, changing in lifestyle and expenditure behavior, better and fast financial services and lots more. This chapter covers the development, opportunities, and challenges of financial sectors when adopting new technologies in China. The chapter throws the light on opportunities that emerged because of large population of 1.4 billion people, high penetration, and access to the latest, user friendly and affordable technology, affordable cost of smartphones, and government policies and regulations. Thsi chapter concludes by demonstrating how FinTech has advanced the banking system and ensured new foundations of fragility, hence, China is becoming at the forefront of creating an inclusive platform that can offer essential solutions to financial and non-financial solutions to its clients by investing tremendously on the evolving technologies to better future financial services for instance works on artificial intelligence solutions. This chapter illustrates how China's FinTech, world leader, is exceptionally evolving at a fast speed as many of the international finance firms.

Chapter 11 describes how public and private sectors in kingdom of Bahrain adopted FinTech, aiming to explore and assessing user's adaptation and satisfaction with FinTech in both sectors. This chapter also proposes a model to quantify FinTech users' satisfaction by designing a questionnaire to collect data, were 319 responses summed. This chapter also illustrates the results of analyzing the data collected, which showed that all the factors examined, accessibility, ease of use, completeness, precision, health, reliability, responsiveness, quality of operation, quality of the system and quality of knowledge, had a major positive impact on user satisfaction. Finally, the chapter concluded by demonstrating the contribution of the research carried out as a proposed model of satisfaction for FinTech that can be applied in different countries and recommended engaging government and concerned organizations about FinTech in Bahrain for achieving a greater user satisfaction.

Chapter 12 begins with claiming that latest technology such as Artificial Intelligence, Deep Learning, Blockchain, and Data Mining, have profoundly impacted the financial services field, will not leave any financial institutions untouched worldwide. This chapter claims that Fintech is a community of well-established companies that offer a wide variety of financial services and operate internationally. Additionally, this chapter pronounces how Fintech firms are enabling greater financial inclusion, human life change, better decision-making, and companies adapting FinTech are achieving larger financial inclusion, improvement of lives of humans, better decision-making and as a result of this, the chapter attempts to evaluate how Fintech emerged in India in last couple of years, its present status and emerging trends and its impact on India's financial sector. Finally, this chapter sheds light on how Fintech will affect the future of Financial Institutions of India and concludes by showing how this research work will be useful for entrepreneurs, strategic advisors, investors, analysts, scholars, and large conglomerates to make informed decisions and gain a clear understanding of India's Fintech space & the unexplored opportunities.

Chapter 13 tests banking fusions as a method for improving and modernizing the Palestinian banking system by focusing on the national banks listed on the Palestinian Stock Exchange using a descriptive-analytical approach and inductive and deductive approaches. The chapter shows how the mergers that took place in the Palestinian banking sector, resulted in a significant improvement in data and financial indicators as well as the competitiveness of domestic merged banks and reflected positively on the national economy. This chapter concludes that the circulars issued by the Palestine Monetary Authority mainly those which relate to the raising of the minimum capital of local banks had a positive role in and was the main motivation towards these mergers and on the basis of these findings, this study recommended the need to redouble the Palestinian Monetary Authority 's efforts by using literary persuasion at certain times, and by developing laws and regulations that encourage and stimulate fusions to create stronger banking institutions.

Chapter 14 main explained the overall relationship between the adoption of FinTech in the current business and factors such as ease of use, risk of adoption and decision on investment in crowdfunds and the chapter further illustrated the connection between those two factors by taking into account the advantages and risks of FinTech activities. This chapter claims that since its evolution FinTech has grown tremendously, there are many factors affecting the adoption of FinTech, despite its positive and negative aspects and in the literature review and the ease of use of technology (Technology Acceptance Theory), investment decisions in crowdfunding (Decision Theory) and the risks involved in adopting FinTech (Prospect Theory) have been found to be the main factors that might affect the adoption of FinTech. Additionally, the chapter looks at the influence of these factors in FinTech 's adoption by distributing a questionnaire and the result analyzing the, questionnaire reveled that there is a positive relationship between the user-friendliness and the adoption of FinTech; between the adoption of FinTech and investment decisions in crowdfunding, and the level of risk when adjusting to FinTech. Finally, the chapter concluded by showing another positive relationship between FinTech's adoption and investment decisions in crowdfunding and a positive relationship was found between the levels of risks when adopting to FinTech.

Chapter 15 measures people living in the Kingdom of Bahrain 's attitudes towards the adoption of mobile banking technology, also known as e-wallets by adapting Technology Acceptance Model (TAM), the Unified Theory of Acceptance and Use of Technology (UTAUT), and the Diffusion of Innovations (DOI) model to construct a questionnaire with an additional emphasis on the promotional aspects. This chapter also Investigate the Performance Expectancy (PE), Efforts Expectancy (EE), Social Impact (SI), Perceived Value (PV), and Perceived Risk (PR) variables with the additional Promotional Benefits (PB) model through conducting a survey and collecting the data from 1,740 residents of four Kingdom of Bahrain governorates of various ages, incomes and educational backgrounds. The investigation of the research study in this chapter confirmed that all of the variables examined have been reported to have a substantial effect on e-Wallet use and adoption in the Kingdom of Bahrain and practical implications suggested Instead of the technical perspective, more focus is needed from a benefit perspective. This chapter demonstrated that the work carried out focused on the viewpoint of the customer, without taking into account the technological aspects of the service providers and in addition to an expanded sample size, further constructs should be explored in future studies to draw a conclusion about the subject. Finally, this chapter concluded with a strong recommendation that greater attention of financial institutions should be devoted to e-wallet technologies and applications as this will be a major trend in the coming decade that will reshape the economic industry.

Chapter 16 describes identifies factors affecting the use and continued use of e-wallets in the Kingdom of Bahrain and investigate the effect of demographic characteristics on the use of e-wallets. This chapter key emphasis is on the continuous usage of mobile payment services for daily settlement operations, rather than for initial acceptance and initial usage. This chapter's quantitative survey methodology was used in the analysis, based on a 5-point Likert scale and the sampling method relied on snowball and sampling technique for ease and the survey was made up of 660 Bahrain consumers. This chapter then reveals the results of the study which indicates that that the four predictor variables are statistically significant and supportive and compatibility variable is the leading factor in the analysis. Finally this chapter's findings revealed that the moderating variables were statistically insignificant, and findings contribute to the service providers and marketers, clearly comprehending the factors that affect e-wallets and continuance use.

Chapter 17 investigates the user friendly and user's satisfaction at Ministry of Works (MoW), Kingdom of Bahrain and it focused on Technology Acceptance Model (TAM), Perceived Ease of Use (PEOU) as tools which have a positive link to user friendly. The chapter demonstrated other potentials been observed during conducting the study and suggested to further integrate the SMART Help Desk Program with FinTech to further boost user-friendly and end-user acceptance, i.e. those users who belong to contractors, vendors, etc. involved in maintenance and construction projects. This chapter additionally, showed the results of the study and how that user friendly has a positive and significant impact on user satisfaction and the is empirically tested with a sample of 131 employees, a quantitative approach using SPSS Version 25; Pearson Correlation, Factor and Regression Analysis. Finally this chapter presented how the findings contributed to the existing body of knowledge in providing insights on factors influencing user's satisfaction and the limitation of studies showed to be the small sample size, convenience sampling and no interactive effects examined with a further recommendation to study and measure other variables such as user resistance to change and environmental factors.

Chapter 18 describes how FinTech is promoting numerous new activities, such as reducing the use of cash in different countries, rising the usage rate of mobile payments, implementing modern high-frequency trading algorithms across national boundaries, and thus gaining significant attention and nevertheless, scholars still doubt on the continued use of fintech. This chapter explains why it should be eager or reluctant to use FinTech to students of higher education who are potential entrepreneurs. This chapter additionally, describes how data from 350 university higher education students in Bahrain were collected and only those students who had prior experience with cashless online payment systems were the selected target population for this study's online survey. This chapter finally demonstrates the result of the analysis of the data which revealed that risk negatively effects the intent for the continence of using fintech, and convenience baring the strongest positive effect and the chapter concludes by recommending future studies using the time-analysis tools to measure the changes of students' awareness of the overtime in conjunction with the financial services developments done by the banks to determine how students' stereotypes have changed about using the e-financial technologies.

Yousif Albastaki
Ahlia University, Bahrain

Anjum Razzaque
Ahlia University, Bahrain

Adel Sarea
Ahlia University, Bahrain

Chapter 1
When Technology Meets Finance:
A Review Approach to FinTech

Yousif Abdullatif Albastaki
https://orcid.org/0000-0002-6866-2268
Ahlia University, Bahrain

ABSTRACT

There is a paradigm shift in the financial services industry. Combined with ever-changing customer expectations and preferences, emerging technologies such as artificial intelligence (AI), machine learning, the internet of things (IoT), and blockchain are redefining how financial institutions deliver services. It is an enormous task to remain competitive in this ever-changing environment. Financial institutions see FinTech as a major part of the digital future, and as proof of this, since 2015, financial institutions have invested over US$ 27 billion in FinTech and digital innovation. This chapter is an introductory chapter that explores FinTech in the literature. It focuses on how FinTech is reshaping the financial industry by describing FinTech phases and development process. The financial products and services using FinTech are also described with a highlight on Islamic FinTech. The chapter finally concludes by describing the future of FinTech.

INTRODUCTION

There is nothing new about the relationship between finance and technology. However, the global financial crisis of 2008 (GFC) was a pivotal moment separating prior phases of FinTech and Regulatory Technology growth from the current paradigm. Fintech is the term used to refer to financial and technology convergence space technologies and usually refers to companies or organizations that use software to provide businesses or customers with financial services. Fintech defines any company providing financial services through software or other technologies and encompasses anything from smartphone to cryptocurrency payment applications. Fintech specifically defines any business that uses internet, mobile devices, technology or cloud services to conduct or communicate with financial services. Most fintech

DOI: 10.4018/978-1-7998-3257-7.ch001

products are designed to link the finances of customers with easy-to-use software, although the concept often refers to Business-to-Business (B2B) innovations. Today, FinTech has entered a rapid development period marked by start-ups and other new entrants proliferating, such as IT and ecommerce companies that have disrupted the financial services sector. The new era presents new challenges to regulators and underlines why FinTech's development needs regulatory to evolve in parallel.

The word 'fintech' has recently appeared in the literature and related publications to describe the financial sector's revolutionary mission of providing quicker, cheaper and more human-cantered financial services. Accenture reported (Accenture, 2015) the term FinTech has become a motto for private and institutional investors who between 2010 and 2015 invested more than $50 billion in the sector. Bill Gates ' ground-breaking claim in 1994 that "banking is required, banks are not" has become a self-reinforcing prophecy, with 6,000 – 7,000 fintech firms around the world now trying to get a slice of the profitable business of the banking industry. Investment in financial technology (fintech) companies increased by 201 percent globally in 2014, compared to 63 percent growth in overall investment in venture capital, establishing this market as a hot ticket. Expectations for new digital start-ups in the industry continue to rise, with the amount of money alone flowing into first-round investments rising by 48%. In 2014, global investment in fintech companies tripled to $12.21 billion, clearly indicating that in the financial services sector, the digital revolution has arrived. It is still unclear whether this presents more of a challenge or an opportunity for the incumbents in the industry. Nevertheless, established players in financial services are beginning to take bold measures to engage with new technologies.

The financial ecosystem is rapidly changing due to increased use by financial institutions and new competitors of information technology. Broadly speaking, the word "financial technology," from the invention of digital money to double-entry bookkeeping, can refer to any advancement in how people transact business. Nevertheless, financial technology has grown explosively since the internet revolution and the mobile and smartphone revolution, and fintech, which originally referred to computer technology being applied to the back office of banks or trading firms, now represents a wide range of technical developments in personal and commercial finance.

According to Wordtracker, Fintech receives about 270'000 google searches worldwide on average on a monthly basis. What's more interesting, however, is the increase in Fintech's search popularity. We can see a large increase in interest in the term Fintech when normalizing the ratio between the fewest search entries and the most search demand over the past five years on a scale between 0 and 100

Fintech also defines a range of financial activities, such as money transfers, checking with your mobile, bypassing a bank branch to apply for credit, raising money for a start-up or managing your business. This chapter is an introductory chapter which attempts to highlight on how FinTech is reshaping and disrupting

Figure 1. FinTech Search Worldwide

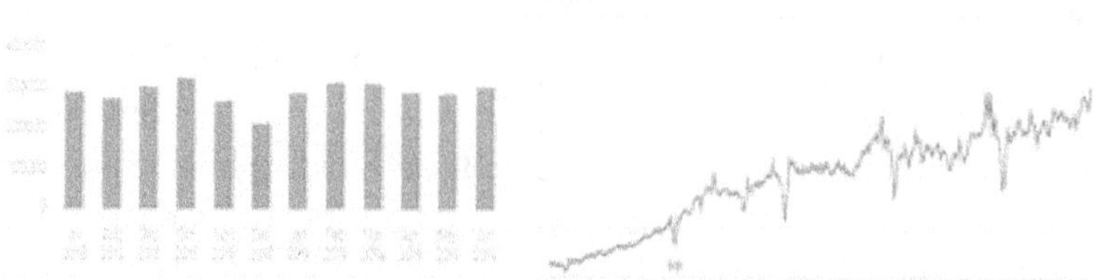

(a) Monthly Search for FinTech – Wordtracker Results

(b) FinTech Last 5 Years Interest over time – Google Trends Results

financial institutions. The remaining parts of the chapter will start by giving an appropriate definition of FinTech, discussing FinTech Phases and Development Process, presenting the main Financial products and services using FinTech and describing the Islamic FinTech concepts.

FINTECH DEFINITION

Once fintech appeared in the 21st century, the term was initially applied to the software used in existing financial institutions ' back-end systems and nevertheless, there has since been a shift towards more consumer-oriented products and thus a more consumer-oriented concept. Fintech also includes various markets and industries such as education, retail banking, crowdfunding and non-profit, and, to name a few, investment management. The following paragraph attempts to provide different views and different definitions of FinTech.

Since the mid-1980s, the term Fintech (or FinTech) has been included in the name for many businesses, services, events and newsletters. Lamagna reported that Fntech, a mixture of financial and "technology," may have been around for a while. One of this term's first uses goes back to the 1980s (Lamagna, 2018).

Clement Ancri, Board of Governors of the Federal Reserve System, Washington D.C. defined Fintech as "Fintech is an industry composed of companies that use technology to make financial systems and the delivery of financial services more efficient" (Ancri, 206).

European Central Bank (ECB) reported that the Financial Stability Board (FSB) defines fintech as "technology-enabled innovation in financial services that could result in new business models, applications, processes or products with an associated material effect on the provision of financial services". (ECB, 2017).

Leong and Sung provided a general definition for FinTech as "a cross-disciplinary subject that combines Finance, Technology Management and Innovation Management." (Leong and Sung, 2018). They further elaborated the FinTech definitions as "any innovative ideas that improve financial service processes by proposing technology solutions according to different business situations, while the ideas could also lead to new business models or even new businesses".

Gray and Leibrock of DTCC group defined FinTech as "technologically-enabled financial innovation that could result in new business models, applications, processes or products with an associated material effect on financial markets and institutions and the provision of financial services." (Gray and Leibrock, 2017).

Analysing the above given definitions of Fintech, it very clear that even technology has always been an integral part of the financial services sector, over the past few years the term FinTech has only become widely used. No matter how the term FinTech is used or defined, these and many other meanings give rise to two common characteristics:

- Fintech requires the use of innovative technology to provide financial services
- Fintech has the potential to improve, transform and/or disrupt business models, applications, regulatory oversight, processes or products substantially.

Having showed the importance of FinTech in the financial industry and the banking sector with different definitions for the term, the following section of the chapter will emphasis FinTech phases and development process.

FINTECH PHASES AND DEVELOPMENT

The term phrase can be traced back to the early 1990s, and now applies to a very rapidly growing industry. However, it is only since 2014 that regulators, industry members, customers and researchers have been focusing on the sector. However, when we look at the development process of FinTech in the literature, we come across different approaches for FinTech development process. In this chapter we tackle two different approaches described by (Buckley and Barberise, 2016) and (Leong and Sung, 2018). The following paragraph will briefly describe each of the two approaches.

Buckley and Barberise, 2016: In this article Buckley and Barberise distinguished three main eras of Fintech evolution. The financial services industry remained largely similar from around 1866 to 1967, despite being highly integrated with technology; this time was defined by Fintech 1.0. Due to the development of electronic communication and payment technologies, finance was gradually digitized from 1967 to 2008; we describe this time as Fintech 2.0. Since 2008, in the era we call Fintech 3.0, new start-ups and existing technology companies have started to offer financial products and services directly to enterprises, the public and banks. This development of FinTech is illustrated in figure 2.

Figure 2. FinTech Developments according to (Buckley and Barberise, 2016)

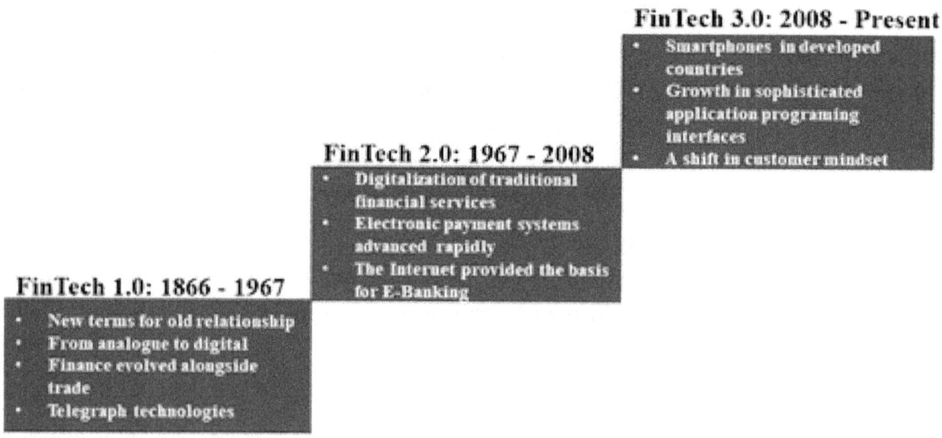

Leong and Sung, 2018: Leong and Sung reported that FinTech's growth is closely linked to the development of enabling technologies. Throughout FinTech 1.0, transmission cable and mainframe computers were the primary enabling technologies and such innovations breed financial technology related products, such as SWIFT and ATMs. The associated technologies included the Cloud and the Internet of Things during FinTech 2.0, while more and more information technology will be built during FinTech 3.0. Leong and Sung also reported that we are currently in the transition period from FinTech 2.0 to FinTech 3.0. This view of FinTech development is illustrated in figure 3.

Figure 3. FinTech Development according to (Leong and Sung, 2018)

GLOBAL FINTECH INVESTMENT

Attention around technology for financial services at all-time is high and interesting, and it is always hard not take part in this innovative technology which is reshaping the way we deal with the banking and the financial industries. In 2018, investments in FinTech's reached a new high. Consultancy.eu Europe reported that a huge amount of $112 billion has been poured into creative companies seeking technological innovation in the financial sector, a sharp increase over the previous year's $51 billion (Consultancy.eu, 2019). Globally, impressive growth is largely the result of three mega transactions of more than $10bn: Blackstone's $17bn investment in Refinitiv, Vantiv's $13bn purchase of UK's WorldPay, and Chinese company Ant Financials' $14bn equity funding. KPMG reported that during 2018, the growth agenda was a hot topic for FinTech's globally, with later stage FinTech's and unicorns raising large rounds, building international partnerships, and making their own acquisitions to drive global expansion activities and this was especially true of virtual challenger banks that have traditionally concentrated on their domestic markets (KPMG, 2019). Several challenger banks made huge investments in 2018 to expand beyond their borders such as Brazil's Nubank, Germany's N26, and several UK-based challenger banks. Funds raised by FinTech firms in Europe have hit a record high of $37.5 billion, up from the previous year's $12.2 billion. A proportional rise from $5.6 billion in 2017 to $24.1 billion in 2018, the United Kingdom accounted for most European FinTech investments, despite WorldPay being an attractive but inessential addition or enhancement. Powerhouses Germany and France, unlike the UK, saw a substantial drop in their FinTech spending last year. In Germany, over 57 deals in 2018, $1 billion was earned, compared with $1.7 billion in 88 transactions in 2017. France had 34 deals in 2016 for $294 million and this increased to 50 transactions worth $733 million in 2017. Figure 4 illustrates total FinTech investment activities from 2013 to 2018 as reported by KPMG report "The Pulse of FinTech 2018" (KPMG, 2019).

One clear finding from the data of Figure 1 is that large firms are growing their investments in FinTech firms and this can be explained by the increasing need for financial services institutions to increase their cost-effectiveness, service portfolios and customer experience, according to the authors. Technology and innovation are playing a significant key role in making such progress, and smaller, more agile companies are better able to mix the two into a value-adding proposition. Looking at year-over-year growth in both the size and total value of dollars invested in all private investment transactions, it is noteworthy how rapidly the sector has expanded. Nonetheless, 2018 was a strong high in both metrics, as incoming consolidation in the sector plus growing valuations of financial assets around the world led to the flat volume of transactions between 2017 and 2018. This year 2018 has been characterized by all kinds of mega-deals, from $14 billion in late-stage VC funding from Ant Financial to Worldpay's $12.8 billion acquisition; and 2019 may see more to come.

Figure 4. FinTech Investments
Source: Pulse of Fintech 2018, Global Analysis of Investment in Fintech, KPMG International (data provided by PitchBook) January 4, 2019.

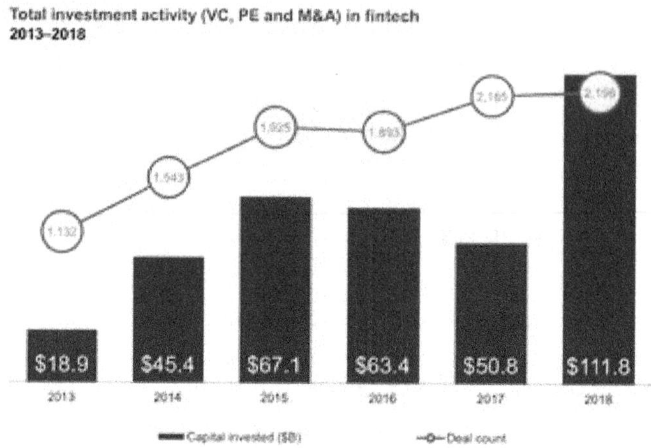

KPMG reported the breaking down the growth year-over-year shows the sheer scale, but quarterly figures show how much even one business can have an impact on the developments in fintech (KPMG, 2019). This braking down of the year-over-year is illustrated in figure 5.

Figure 5. Year-over-year FinTech Investments
Source: Pulse of Fintech 2018, Global Analysis of Investment in Fintech, KPMG International (data provided by PitchBook) January 4, 2019.

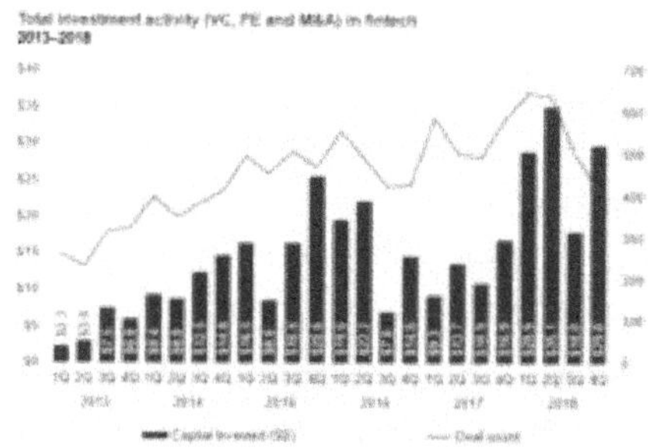

It obvious that, organizations will collect a multi-billion-dollar funding injection, but still the outer quarters in figure 5 are primarily driven by Ant Financial, which raised the largest investment round in history in Q2 2018; Worldpay, which was acquired for $12.9 billion; and last but not least, Refinitiv, which was purchased by a consortium in October for $17 billion.

The overall outlook for FinTech investments remains optimistic in coming years, according to the analysts at KPMG, but the possibility of global uncertainty and trade issues could jeopardize some of the increase in value and size of the contract. Ultimately, an increase in investment is likely to be based on approaches that address the needs of unbanked and underbanked people in the developing world, including Southeast Asia and Africa.

REGTECH AND FINTECH

Financial regulation is a form of regulation or supervision that subjects financial institutions to certain requirements, restrictions, and guidelines to maintain the financial system's integrity. This regulation is usually implemented by either a government or non-government organization. The ability of grasping the relationship between regulators and financial institutions makes it possible to develop solutions that balance regulatory and business needs and meet needs. The global financial crisis exposed significant financial regulation and supervision vulnerabilities and weaknesses(TC, 2017) and as a result, the Financial Stability Board (FSB) is undertaking a thorough and continuing reorganization of the global financial regulatory system, including traditional bodies such as the Basel Committee for Banking Supervision (BCBS). In addition to reacting to pressure to increase regulatory and supervisory efficacy, most financial regulators have also extended their roles to include obligations that some previously considered to conflict with the stability mandate, such as consumer protection, competition, and financial inclusion, which contribute to the difficulty of fair distribution of limited resources. As a result, authorities are stepping up their efforts to collect data and rethinking their overall supervisory approach.

Douglas Arner and his research team described RegTech as a technological solution that simplify regulatory processes and develop them and RegTech has developed in three stages, like FinTech (Arner et al., 2017). The first stage, RegTech 1.0, was led by large financial institutions which, as epitomized in the Basel II Capital Accord, integrated technology into their internal processes to combat rising compliance costs and complexity. The second stage, RegTech 2.0, was motivated by new regulatory standards for post-GFC and the cost of implementing them to the financial industry. Additionally, regulators try to replicate the increasingly digitized nature of the markets they track and improve their ability to analyse that data volumes produced by post-GFC reporting obligations. Arner also reported that RegTech will show its greatest potential in the third stage of its development of RegTech 3.0 in which technology will help us reconceptualize finance and its regulation: building a better financial system (Arner et al., 2017). Figure 6 illustrates the development process of RegTech as described by Douglas Arner and his research team.

Figure 6. RegTech Stages of Development

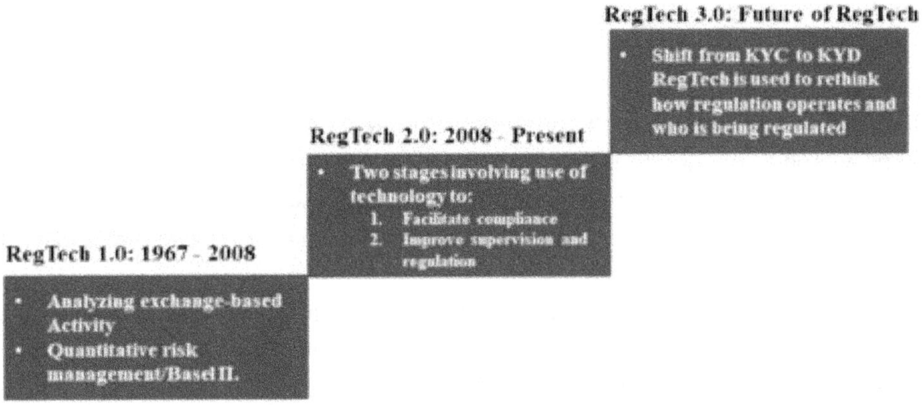

FINANCIAL PRODUCTS AND SERVICE USING FINTECH

Many innovations are observed around the globe in financial products and services, therefore, FinTech is viewed as a big and complex area. Consequently, over the past few decades, we have seen Fintech's recurrent area covering several different financial and banking domains. The FinTech domain describes changes affecting the financial sector, demonstrates the complexity of the payment infrastructure, identify and explain key payment instruments and how they work, understand the types of money exiting, and recognize changes in regulatory frameworks and how they inhibit or promote innovation. Therefore, it is essential to describe the domain of FinTech and how it encompasses different subdomains which allows a harmony when technology meets finance.

Many research works are published in the literature with an attempt to classify Fintech. Examples include Patrick Szakiel (Szakiel, 2018), Courtney Gakman (Gakman, 2019), Liudmyla Kyryliuk (Kyryliuk, 2019), McGuinness and Merrey (McGuinness and Merrey, 2017) and Salam Gateway (Salam, 2017). This chapter classifies FinTech based on the classification provided by Salam Gateway 2017. Figure 7 illustrates FinTech domain classification based on the classification of Salam Gateway.

Figure 7. Fintech Domain and Classifications

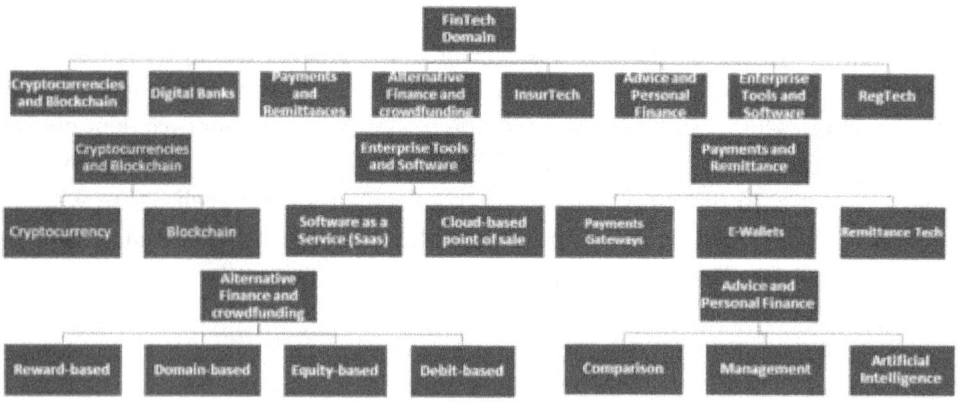

The following paragraph provides a summary for some of main FinTech types described in figure 7.

Payments and Remittances: It is reported by (Afi, 2018) that according to the World Bank global remittances totalled USD 595.7 billion in 20172, 75.6 percent ($450.1 billion) of which corresponds to remittance flows to low- and middle-income countries. This volume represents an increase of over 50% since 2007, and cross-border remittances now account for over 5% of GDP in 47 developing countries. The development of new communication and information technologies and innovative mechanisms for supporting the provision of financial services and products creates new opportunities allowing FinTech-based systems for cross-border transfers to get money into the hands of those who need it most, and ideally into the accounts. Payments and Remittances can further be classified into three different categories categories as follows:

Payment Gateways: While online transactions continue to grow and become a big part of the global economy, businesses' ability to accept online payments is becoming more important and Internet-based consumption spending is increasing at a significant rate. Lowry and his research team (Lowry et al.,

2006) and Rob (Rob & Opara,2003) reported that online spending has seen double-digit global growth of around 50 percent annually and spending alone in the United States is expected to reach $3.5 trillion. Global economic growth is behind these patterns. It can be expected that they will continue in the future. In the context of FinTech we can view Payment Gateways as an online seller service, usually provided by an e-commerce site or e-store enabler with authorized credit card and direct payments for companies online and offline, and individual merchants. It also can be thought of as an online point of sale terminal for your business.

E-Wallets: Electronic wallet also known as digital wallet or E-Wallets refers to an Internet-based electronic payment system that stores information related to financial and personal identity and it can be looked at as an app that allows smartphone and/or smart device users to store and spend money. The e-wallet is a payment system part. Jinimol described the term "payment system" which is characterized as enabling payment to be made between a payer and a recipient, any or all the services for clearing, compensation, or settlement (Jinmol, 2018). A user can link and top up their e-wallet from a bank account and it is increasingly used as tools for financial inclusion in emerging markets.

Remittance Tech: In many developing economies, the flow of funds from migrant workers back to their families in their home country is a major source of income. The beneficiaries also rely on remittances to cover day-to-day living expenses, to provide an emergency buffer and, in some cases, to fund small investments. Over the past decade, the total value of remittances has steadily increased, and it is reported by the (World Bank, 2007) that in 2005 the total worldwide volume of remittance reached the equivalent of USD 230 billion, affecting approximately 175 million migrants. In the Fintech context we can view Remittance Tech as a system that facilitates transfers of money between individuals across borders and tech firms are innovating to make remittances faster and more convenient at a fraction of the cost of banks and existing players.

Cryptocurrencies and Blockchain: The subject of cryptocurrency and blockchain is gigantic. There are several hundred cryptocurrencies and there are also numerous applications of blockchain technology (Houben & Synyers, 2018). Blockchain is a distributed platform for payment and data management, recognized as the technology behind the popularity of cryptocurrency such as Bitcoin. (Nakamoto, 2008). The main objective of Blockchain is to create an open system in which no third-party monitors transactions and data. Blockchain technology is now mainstream as it solves problems in a way that people could not before, generating an added business value that will reach around $176 billion by 2025 and $3.1 trillion by 2030 (Garriga et al., 2018). The rise of cryptocurrencies and blockchain technologies is part of a wider innovation movement which enables peer-to-peer (P2P) trading, consumer individualization and production methods versatility and this trend has gained traction after the global financial crisis a decade ago for a variety of reasons (World Bank, 2018).

Blockchain: Blockchain acts as an unchangeable ledger that allows transactions to take place in a decentralized way and Blockchain-based technologies are growing in many fields, including financial services, the reputation network and the Internet of Things (IoT), and so on. Zheng's research team reported that there are still many blockchain technology problems waiting to be addressed, such as scalability and security issues (Zheng et al., 2017). Blockchain is always related to Batticon, for example with a specially designed data storage system, Bitcoin network transactions will take place without any third party and the core technology for creating Bitcoin is blockchain, first introduced in 2008 and implemented in 2009 (Nakamoto, 2008). Therefore, Blockchain is the underlying technology upon which all cryptocurrencies are based and is looked at as a public online transaction ledger shared between different network nodes which can never be removed, making it easier to detect fraud and misuse. Blockchain has an ability to revolutionize several business sectors, not just FinTech. Blockchain further readings: (Holotesch, 2018), (Blechschmidt, 2018) and (Yaga et al., 2018).

Cryptocurrency: Cryptocurrency is the name given to a framework utilizing cryptography to facilitate distributed and decentralized safe transfer and exchange of digital tokens and these tokens can be traded at the fiat currency market rates. Dourado and Brito reported that Bitcoin was the first cryptocurrency that started trading in January 2009. Since then, many other cryptocurrencies have been developed using the same technologies pioneered by Bitcoin but modifying some of their governing algorithms ' specific parameters (Dourado and Brito, 2014). Over the past two years, an obscure technology once associated only with the Bitcoin virtual currency has become one of today's most important innovations. Cryptocurrency is viewed as a form of digital money that regulates the generation of currency units and verifies the transfer of funds, operating independently of the central bank. Regulators and central banks are trying to deal with cryptocurrencies differently from market to market with some such as China trying to ban them. In many countries such as the UAE, the central bank clarified regulations at the start of 2017, stating it does not outlaw cryptocurrencies. Recognizing a shared interest in helping to combat the criminal exploitation of this revolutionary technology, the blockchain and cryptocurrency industry proactively approached law enforcement and regulatory agencies and offered to help educate these agencies on how cryptocurrencies work, provide technical assistance, and foster an open dialog on issues of common concern (Dewey, 2019).

Alternative Finance or Crowdfunding: Crowdfunding is a collective effort of individuals who pool their resources to support other people or organizations ' initiatives. It is reported by UNDP that over the past decade, individuals and businesses have raised billions of dollars in debt, equity, and donations through social networks and the viral nature of online communication. (UNDP, 2017). Crowdfunding helps users raise capital from many individuals to fund business venture and projects. In summary crowdfunding is viewed as an innovative approach for projects, organizations, entrepreneurs, and start-ups to raise money for their causes from multiple individual donors or investors. Four models of crowdfunding exist: donations; reward; lending; and equity.

Rewards-based crowdfunding: The crowdfunder transfers funds with the expectation of a reward that may be in the form of a token gift or an early / exclusive release of a product or service offered by the start-up company. In exchange for a non-monetary cost, reward-based funding projects depend on investors to contribute money to their campaign (Tonttila, 2016). The value of the reward received normally increases by the amount pledged. This approach can be used as a perfect way to promote new products and ideas and to pre-sell them. It also serves as a perfect way to test the product's future demand and provides free access to a focus group that can contribute to the concept and develop this. In simple words rewards-based crowdfunding can explained as in exchange for money given by fans of the project, the business or organization will give some type of incentive for them to participate. Rewards can be anything, ranging from goods and services to discount and vouchers. Kickstarter (Kuppuswamy and Bayus, 2017) and indiegogo (Indiegogo, 2019) are among the most successful crowdfunding platforms built on rewards-based model of crowdfunding.

Donation-based crowdfunding: While anticipating any return, the crowdfunder donates funds. Usually, donations are used to fund disaster relief, poverty, health, etc. Crowdfunding based on donations is a way to fund a campaign by asking many contributors to contribute a small amount to it individually. In return, as the donation size increases, the backers can earn token bonuses that increase in prestige (Kenton, 2019). As a result, we can view donation-based crowdfunding as users find project that they wish to denote money to in exchange for nothing and often directly linked to charity or noble causes that the funders want to actively support.

Equity-based crowdfunding: The crowdfunder is buying equity in a business. Equity is a new, but rapidly growing, crowdfunding platform with investment in 2015 of over US$ 2.5 billion as reported by UNDP (UNDP, 2017). It is also reported by UNDP that equity-based crowdfunding could reach up to US$ 36 billion by 2020 and eventually surpass venture capital by value. In terms of the option between traditional bank financing and crowdfunding, the latter provides financial benefits such as customer reviews, product validation and public impacts. Other factors which also affect the choice of companies among the available crowdfunding business models are imperfect information and moral hazard. In the case of equity-based crowdfunding versus donation-based crowdfunding, financial return is critical for investors in addition to potential cash flow generation capabilities for businesses (Kuti, et al., 2017). Therefore, the equity-based crowdfunding can be viewed as where entrepreneurs and start-ups can find small investments from many backers in exchange for financial stake in their company or assets proportionate to the amount invested. The rights of the new shareholders may vary depending on terms and conditions

Debt-based crowdfunding: In this type of crowdfunding, individuals are lending money to businesses or other individuals with the expectation that it will be repaid along with added interest. Lending-based crowdfunding platforms, enabled by new information and communication technologies, represent a new mode of financial intermediation by connecting lenders and borrowers directly via internet platforms and when the first platforms appeared in the United Kingdom and the United States, they were called peer-to-peer (P2P) loan platforms (Havrylchyk, 2018). Debt-based crowdfunding has emerged in the United States as an investment vehicle in 2006 and a year earlier in the United Kingdom. Freedman and Nutting reported that crowdfunding debt version allows individual borrowers to apply for unsecured loans (not backed by collateral) and borrow money from "the crowd" if approved by the company and pay it back with interest (Freedman and Nutting, 2015). P2P platforms generate revenue by taking a one-time charge from investors a percentage of the borrower's loan amounts and a fixed annual fee or a one-time percentage of the loan amount as a loan service fee.

Digital Banks: Recent developments in IT empower consumers and contribute to a fundamental change in customer behaviour caused by digital natives which affects existing business models and leads to different expectations of financial service providers. Sundererarajan reported that the first area of transition is a general transformation in consumer behaviour, such as the move from ownership to existing, temporary use to the so-called "sharing economy" which affects all industries (Sundararajan, 2016). For example, in the banking industry, consumers share information on banking products on social networks and even share their assets to create new digital banking services without banks together. These developments not only enable new business processes, but lead to completely new business models and even indicate a complete change in the banking value chain in the same way that value chains have been radically transformed in other industries, such as the media or travel industry (Gasser, et al., 2017) and (Ito et al., 2017). Therefore, an online-only or a digital version of traditional banking emerged, which provides checking and saving accounts, with deposit, withdrawal and transfer facilities. Digital banking provides financial services to banks and their customers. However, the transition to digital banking as a result of changing customer behaviour is a challenge for banks, especially in the way services are provided. A digital bank provides contextualized, seamless experiences for customers that transform the customer journey. And becoming a digital bank means providing a compelling and relevant customer experience and execution through an open, integrated and flexible architecture. Many banks have introduced some form of digital transformation strategy and most of them start to see customer rewards using cheaper, self-service channels. It is possible to condense true digital banking into two main and distinct factors (Dickinson, D., (2019):

Customer Experience: The total experience that allows customers to self-serve through multiple devices in real time, with environmental contexts that result in a personal and relevant experience. In order to be able to provide relevant, contextualized and personalized content and offers at the right time and on the right device, this requires online access to all products and services as well as real-time customer intelligence.

Execution Experience: The overall experience that allows organizations to deliver on-demand services with minimal human involvement through straight-through processing while allowing internal bank users to serve customers through offline channels and continually enhance products and processes.

Insuretech: Fintech can also cover home insurance, car insurance, and data security, also known as insurtech. Fintech innovations have had an impact on the insurance industry through improved efficiency, cost reduction, improved risk assessment, and improved customer experience. inVerita reported that (inVerita, 2019) insurers pay more attention to insurtech, according to an Accenture study, with 86% believing that rapid innovation is a must if they are to maintain a competitive edge on the market. By improving insurance products, enhancing service compatibility and reducing regulatory costs, Insurtech will continue to optimize the insurance industry. Insurtech will thus build a rich and resourceful eco-system of "new insurance" (KPMG, 2019). Further readings on Insuretech can be found in (Holliday, 2019), (Pritchett, 2019) and OECD (2017)

Digital Finance Advice: A collection of mathematical rules that translates data entered a framework using techniques of financial modelling to generate financial advice. Financial advice using software which also widely known as robo-advice or robotic counselling. A robust governance and control system are applicable to digital financial advice as the software is focused on algorithms and assumptions that turn customer feedback into financial advice. Abraham and his research group reported that robo-advisors expand access to wealth management services by making opening investment accounts and receiving financial advice easier and less expensive, as well as planning and automating investment

Figure 8. Projected Assets Managed by Robo-Advisors in the United States, 2018–23
Source: (Abraham et al., 2019)

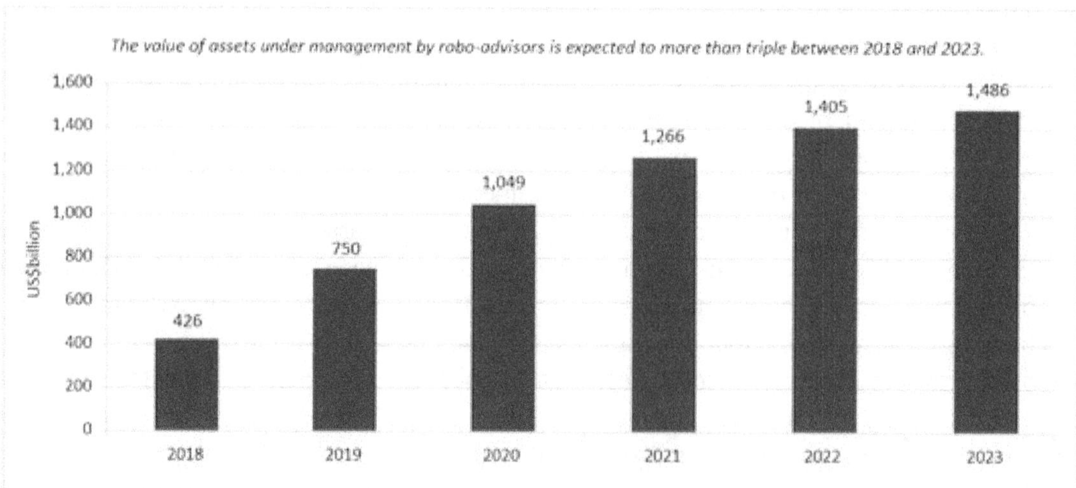

decisions (Abraham et al., 2019). The rise of robo-advisors, however, requires consumers to understand these services ' limitations and to receive proper financial education. Additionally, policymakers need to discuss the effect of robo-advice on the overall financial system and review their regulatory and supervisory activities. Abraham also reported that the United States is by far the leading robo-advisor market. Burnmark and CBInsights reported that as of 2017, United State had more robo-advisors than any other economy in the world (about 200) and captured 57 percent of all investments in robo-advisors (Burnmark, 2017) and (CBInsights, 2017). The estimated value of assets managed by robo-advisors in the United States exceeded US$ 400 billion in 2018 and is expected to grow at an average annual rate of 31% to nearly US$ 1.5 trillion by 2023. Figure 8 illustrates the projected assets managed by Robo-Advisors in the United States in the period between 2018 and 2023.

In 2018, Vanguard (US$ 112 billion), followed by Intelligent Portfolios (US$ 33 billion) and Betterment (US$ 14 billion) were the largest robo advisors for assets under management in the United States. Figure 9 illustrates the Largest Robo-Advisors in the United States in the year 2018.

Figure 9. Largest Robo-Advisors in the United States in 2018
Source: (Abraham et al., 2019)

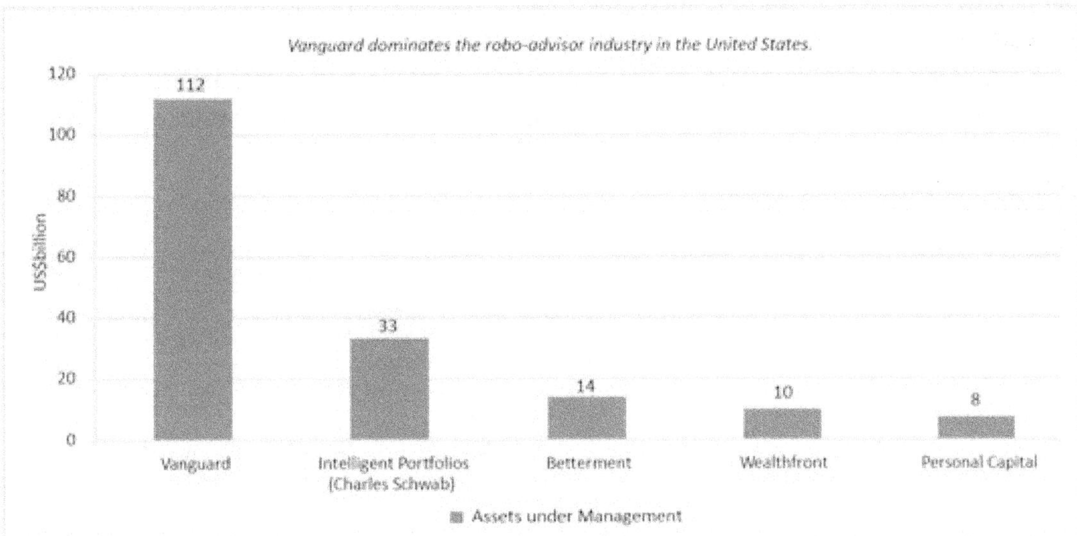

Using robo-advisors for wealth management services can offer several advantages over traditional services that rely on human consultants. One of the attractions of using robo-advisors is that they are easy to access. Instead of having to make an appointment with an advisor and attend a meeting at a physical location, robo-advisors offer clients the opportunity to get financial advice and manage investment from anywhere with an internet connection at any time. he cost of financial advice can also be reduced by robo-advisors. Unlike human consulting firms, robotic consultants can save on fixed costs, such as the wages of expensive financial consultants or the maintenance of physical offices.

ISLAMIC FINTECH

With around 1.8 billion population worldwide and one of the consequences of this rising population is the increasing demand for any products which are compliant to the sources of law of the Muslims, namely the holy Quran and hadith which is a collection of sayings of the prophet Muhammad which, with accounts of his daily practice (the Sunna), constitute the major source of guidance for Muslims apart from the Quran. Islamic finance (Fintech) is one of the developments in the field of Islamic finance, supported by advances in technology and internet. The Islamic Finance Industry has a lot of potential, with assets expected to reach $3.9 trillion by 2023, according to Thomson Reuters, but Islamic Fintech is at the very beginning of an exciting, disruptive industry journey, one that is still dominated by predominantly domestic and OIC-based financial institutions (DIEDC, 2018). Islamic Fintech is distinct from its traditional equivalent because it is open, beneficial to both parties and consistent with Islamic sharia law (Firmansyah and Anwar, 2019). Since 2010, the Islamic Fintech industry has grown robustly, mirroring the development of the wider Fintech global ecosystem, concentrating on sharia-compliant business and consumer financing. The Islamic finance industry was valued at $2.4 trillion in 2017 and is expected to grow at Compound Annual Growth Rate (CARG) 7.7 percent to $3.8 trillion in 2023. Thomson Reuters reported that the disruption and innovation that can be seen throughout the global financial industry also has an impact on Islamic finance, with significant developments in recent years (Thomson Reuters, 2018).

Islamic FinTech Key Drivers: There are many government initiatives for Islamic FinTech, for example Dubai International Financial Centre (DIFC) is planning a $100 million fund to invest in Fin-tech

Table 1. Select OIC FinTech initiatives

Country	Organization	Description
Kingdom of Bahrain	Bahrain Fintech Bay	Fintech Bay in Bahrain is a dedicated co-working space dedicated to attracting and developing Fintech and working with it in particular. Islamic Fintech in partnership with leading Islamic financial institutions operating in Bahrain and throughout the Gulf Cooperation Council countries (GCC).
Indonesia	Financial Services Authority (OJK)	While start-ups drive the growth of Islamic fintech in Indonesia government agencies realize their effect and begin to promote it. A regulatory structure for P2P lending platforms has been developed by the Financial Services Authority (OJK).
Malaysia	Malaysia Digital Economy Corporation	The Malaysian Digital Economy Corporation (MDEC) is a government-owned entity in charge of developing the digital business ecosystem in Malaysia. The organization also actively supports businesses in the halal economy by providing sharia certification and networking with venture capital investors
UAE	Dubai International Finance Centre	Dubai International Financial Centre (DIFC), a leading international financial hub, announced a FinTech-focused $100 million fund to invest from incubation to growth in Fintech start-ups.
Other countries	UK, Kazakhstan, IDB, Saudi Arabia	UK regulators supported their national Islamic Fintech Panel and start-up ecosystem. Astana International Financial Canter's launch is also aimed at expanding Islamic finance and fintech. Likewise, Fintech Saudi has recently been launched by the Saudi Arabian Monetary Authority. Finally, a Fintech Challenge has been launched by the multilateral Islamic Development Bank to support Islamic Fintech

Source: (DIEDC, 2018)

start-ups. The Kingdom of Bahrain and Malaysia have developed Fintech's regulatory sandbox. There are 93 Islamic FinTech players globally. The Organization of Islamic Cooperation (OIC) countries are demographically young countries, where 24 years median age of Muslims worldwide compared to 32 globally and 15 of top 50 countries with Smartphone penetration are Islamic economies. Additionally, 72% unbanked population in OIC member countries (core Islamic finance markets) compared to 49% worldwide.

The digital Islamic economy is a wider field of strategic importance prioritized by several OIC firms, with a special focus on Islamic Fintech. Table 1 illustrates selected OIC Islamic FinTech initiatives presented by Dubai Islamic Economy Development Centre in 2018.

Islamic FinTech Start-ups: Islamic Fintech start-ups were the first line of response with a rapidly evolving ecosystem to provide creative digital Islamic finance solutions. Start-ups, dedicated accelerators and incubators are emerging to support, offering the promise to catalyse funding and sharpen business proposals. Table 2 illustrates selected examples of start-up builders described by Dubai Islamic Economy Development Centre in 2018.

Table 2. Selected Examples of FinTech Start-Up Builders

Country	Organization	Description
Singapore	Islamic Fintech Alliance	The Islamic Fintech Alliance (IFT Alliance) was launched in 2016 as a global collaboration between Islamic Fintech start-ups to "facilitate the adoption of finance technology among Muslims."
Turkey	Al Baraka	Turkey's Albaraka Türk is targeting the large Muslim community across Europe with the launch of an interest-free digital banking app.
UAE	Goodforce labs	Goodforce Labs, founded in 2018, is the first foundry social impact in the MENA region and partners with and funds 10 Islamic and ethical economy start-ups

Source: (DIEDC, 2018)

The future of Islamic financial technology is bright, particularly in Muslim countries, seen from the rising number of customers and revenues of Islamic Fintech firms. For Islamic Fintech to thrive, the new growing trend in Islamic finance requires all stakeholders to support it. Cooper reported that Malaysia is the pioneer in this market, as in any field of Islamic finance. Malaysia has the bulk of Islamic Fintech firms, followed by London and Indonesia (Cooper, 2018). However, Dubai and the Kingdom of Bahrain both entered the race of FinTech pioneering.

THE FUTURE OF FINTECH

For bankers and traders, financial technology used to be the back-office support feature and the investment in this type of technology was very limited. However, private venture capital has risen suddenly and rapidly over the past decade and the share of investment dollars in fintech has risen from 5% to nearly 20% a level equal to the fair share of Gross Domestic Product attributed to the financial industry and in the innovation economy, Fintech has found its place. As fintech grew, telling the hype of reality became increasingly difficult.

In the past several years, chatbots and artificial intelligence, blockchain and crypto resources, robotic advisors and neobanks and countless other signs of digitization have become mouthpieces in the commercial media. Sokolin reported that large global banks are expanding business venture arms and online incubators, investing in, buying, or copying solutions from emerging firms (Sokolin, 2019). Sokolin also mentioned that globally, Eastern technology firms introduced super-app messaging with hundreds of millions of users and embedded financial services, outstripping Western-regulated jurisdictions' capacity. Singh reported that global FinTech sector funding rose to US$ 111.8 billion last year, up 120 per cent from US$ 50.8 billion in 2017. Similarly, America increased from $29 billion in 2017 to $54.5 billion last year; Europe increased from $12.2 billion in 2017 to $34.2 billion; and Asia Pacific increased from $12.5 billion in 2017 to $22.7 billion (Singh, 2019). These impressive statistics by Singh report bear witness to the sector's growth, which leverages technology to improve financial services and is divided into five broad categories — payments, clearing and settlement; deposit, borrowing and capital raising; insurance; investment management; and business support. Over the years, fintech has made the most payment inroads, due to the mobile and internet's international reach, and less so in the others.

Baker reported that FinTech has changed the way people think about money and value exchange in a real-time, "cashless" digital world that is popping up everywhere, forcing reluctant consumers to take the habit of digital transactions and governments to discuss whether it is discriminatory or just progress (Baker, 2019). The first move is to allow customers to pay for goods and services digitally instead of using money. Tech giant Amazon leads the way in merging an online shopping platform with a conventional brick and mortar experience to test their new model in nine cashier less convenience stores. Customers simply pick up what they need, leave the store, and their Amazon account will automatically charge the items. Concepts like these are likely to shape shopping's future.

Internet of Things (IoT), Artificial Intelligence (AI), blockchain and cloud computing are some of the innovations that drive changes in how customers communicate with buyers and how they manage their money. While traditional financial services players may see FinTech as a disruptor to their business, those who embrace technological advancement are disrupting the industry from the outside in and failing to thrive in traditional player areas. FinTech firms are now leading the industry, creating a wide range of new financial products and services to make money management easier and more efficient.

The FinTech industry is currently beginning to change how financial services are provided and customers can generally benefit immensely from not only user experience or comfort, but also from connectivity and cost savings. More than 2 billion people around the world are still completely unbanked. We have no access to a bank account or no means of saving money for college, and these are people for whom the only way to save money is to hide it under their bed and this perpetuates a system of violent deprivation. Good news is that we can give them access to financial services for the first time in history and that's just the start.

Pollari and Raisbeck reported that Fintech is our financial institutions' biggest disruptor of our time. It was ranked number one by 57% of our survey respondents, ahead of growing global regulatory complexity (51%) and new business models (46%) (Pollari and Raisbeck, 2017). Whether it provides new ways of enhancing customer experience, adapting to regulatory changes (such as open banking), underpinning new payments or digital delivery models, making service delivery quicker and more cost-effective, or improving the efficiency of back-office functions, the myriad fintech solutions that are now available or in progress help to reinvent the full value quickly. At the rapid rate the industry is developing, financial products and services and financial institutions' technical infrastructure will look remarkably different in a decade compared to how they look today. Tek Yew Chia Fintech Leader for KPMG in Singapore said that "In order to achieve the most from fintech opportunities, companies in financial services need to treat fintech innovation as a mainstream activity — and incorporate it within and across their entire organization". Figure 10 illustrates that nearly 90% of survey conducted by KPMG respondents either have a fintech strategy in place or are developing one now. But having a fintech strategy doesn't necessarily mean it's an organization's right strategy. In fact, less than half of these fintech-strategic organizations believe that their approach is well matched with current challenges and changes in fintech.

Figure 10. Where are financial institutions when it comes to having a fintech strategy?
Source: (Pollari and Raisbeck, 2017).

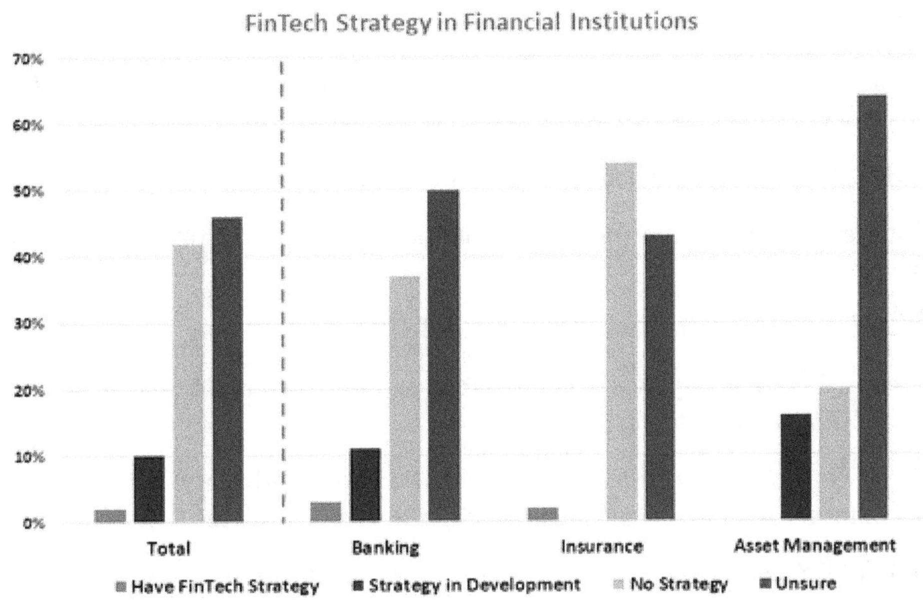

It is also important to remember that a complete plan is much more complex than getting a fund for venture capital or a list of FinTechs that the group has visited. Given that many financial institutions are still relatively early in their fintech journeys, we expect that a large proportion of them will still have to form a fully developed fintech strategy.

Fintech is also a potential disruptor to the labour market in financial services, accounting for 6–7% of U.S. jobs and Artificial Intelligence and Machine Learning erode many of these positions. Nevertheless, there is still a question about whether we will see the system progressing through intelligence increase (IA) or AI (artificial intelligence).

CONCLUSION

Technology and finance's long-standing relationship has been continually evolving. This chapter has gone through an introductory approach to FinTech and started by defining FinTech from different perspective and gave a special attention to the three stages of the evolution of FinTech and the two stages of the evolution of RegTech to date. It also tackled the different phases and development process of FinTech. The chapter attempted to define the overall FinTech domain by focusing on Financial products and services using FinTech. A brief description of Islamic Fintech is also introduced.

Although FinTech is viewed as the biggest disruptor of our time, this review reviled there has been no single way of defining how organizations should approach FinTech. Some different approaches are taken by leading financial institutions, including alliances, acquisition, procurement and investment strategies. When it comes to fintech today, there is no clear winner. Each organization has the chance to forge a new fintech future and win against its competition.

REFERENCES

Abraham, F., Schmukler, S., & Tessada, J. (2019). *Robo-Advisors: Investing through Machines*. Research & Policy Briefs from the World Bank Chile Center and Malaysia Hub. February.

Accenture. (2015). The Future of Fintech and Banking: Digitally disrupted or reimagined? Author.

Afi. (2018). Innovative Cross-Border Remittance Services: Experiences from Afi Member Countries. Guideline Note No. 30 August.

Ancri, C. (2016). *Fintech Innovation: An Overview.* IJTSRD.

Arner, G., Barberis, J., & Buckley, R. (2017). FinTech and RegTech in a Nutshell, and the Future in a Sandbox. *Research Foundation Briefs, 3*(4).

Baker, A. (2019). *FinTech and the future of finance.* The Global Advisory and Accounting Network. Retrieved from: https://www.hlb.global/fintech-and-the-future-of-finance/

Blechschmidt, B. (2018). *Blockchain in Europe: Closing the Strategy Gap*. Cognizant Report. Retrieved from https://www.cognizant.com/blockchain

Buckley, R., & Barberise, J. N. (2016). 150 Years of FinTech: An evolutionary analysis. *JASSA The Finsia Journal of Applied Finance, 3.*

Burnmark. (2017). *Digital Wealth.* Retrieved from: https://wealthobjects.com/ templates/protostar/images/Burnmark-April17.pdf

CBInsights. (2017). *A Wealth Tech World: Mapping Robo-Advisors Around the Globe*. Retrieved from: https://www.cbinsights.com/research/robo-advisor-global-fintech-map/

Consultancy.eu. (2019). *Global FinTech investment more than doubled to $112 billion.* Retrieved from: https://www.consultancy.eu/news/2390/global-fintech-investment-more-than-doubled-to-112-billion

Cooper, T. (2018). *The Race to Become the World's Leading Leading Islamic Fintech Hub - Raconteur.* Retrieved from: https://www.raconteur.net/finance/race-become-worlds-leading-leading-islamic-fintech-hub

Critical Issues to Consider by Small Merchants. (n.d.). *Human Systems Management, 22*(3), 133–142.

Dewey, J. (2019). *Blockchain & Cryptocurrency Regulation 2019* (1st ed.). Global Legal Group Ltd.

Dickinson, D. (2019). *Digital Banking. Temenos The banking Software Company*. Retrieved from: https://www.temenos.com/wp-content/uploads/2019/08/Digital-Banking-whitepaper-2019-Aug-21.pdf

DIEDC. (2018). *Islamic Fintech Report 2018 Current Landscape & Path Forward*. Dubai Islamic Economy Development Center. Retrieved from: https://www. dinarstandard.com/wp-content/uploads/2018/12/Islamic-Fintech-Report-2018.pdf

Dourado, E., & Brito, J. (2014). Cryptocurrency. The New Palgrave Dictionary of Economics, Online Edition (S. N. Durlauf & L. E. Blume, Eds.). Academic Press.

European Central Bank (ECB) (2017). *Guide to assessments of fintech credit institution licence applications*. Banking Supervision. European Central Bank.

Firmansyah, E. A., & Anwar, M. (2019). *Islamic Financial Technology (FinTech): Its challenges and prospect. Advances in Social Science, Education and Humanities Research* (Vol. 216). ASSEHR.

Freedman, D., & Nutting, M. (2015). *A Brief History of Crowdfunding Including Rewards, Donation, Debt, and Equity Platforms in the USA*. Retrieved from: https://www.freedman-chicago.com/ec4i/History-of-Crowdfunding.pdf

Gakman, C. (2019). *Understanding FinTech Categories*. IAN Martin. Retrieved from: https://ianmartin.com/understanding-fintech-categories/

Garriga, M., Arias, M., & Renzis, A. (2018). *Blockchain and Cryptocurrency: A comparative framework of the main Architectural Drivers*. CONF.

Gasser, U., Gassmann, O., Hens, T., Leifer, L., Puschmann, T., & Zhao, L. (2017). *Digital Banking 2025*. Retrieved from: https://xupery.com/wp-content/uploads/2017/08/Digital-Banking-2025.pdf

Gateway, S. (2017). *INFOGRAPH-What are the different types of fintech?* Retrieved from: https://salaamgateway.com/story/infograph-what-are-the-different-types-of-fintech

Gray, A., & Leibrock, M. (2017). *Fintech and Financial Stability Exploring How Technological Innovations Could Impact the Safety and Security of Global Markets*. DTCC Group.

Havrylchyk, O. (2018). *Regulatory framework for the loan-based crowdfunding platforms*. OECD. Economic Department Working Papers No. 1513.

Holliday, S. (2019). *How Insurtech Can Close the Protection Gap in Emerging Markets*. EM Compass Emerging Markets Note 70. Retrieved from: www.ifc.org/thoughtleadership

Holotesch, C. (2018). Understanding Blockchain Opportunities and Challenges. *The 14th International Scientific Conference eLearning and Software for Education.*

Houben, R., & Synyers, A. (2018). *Cryptocurrencies and blockchain: Legal context and implications for financial crime, money laundering and tax evasion. STUDY Requested by the TAX3 committee.* European Parliament. July.

Indiegogo. (2019). *The Essential Guide to Crowdfunding*. Retrieved from: https://learn.indiegogo.com/the-essential-guide-to-crowdfunding/

inVerita. (2019). *What is fintech? Uses and Examples in 2019*. Retrieved from: https://becominghuman.ai/what-is-fintech-uses-and-examples-in-2019-f8992d4fd2c2

Ito, J., Narula, N., & Ali, R. (2017). *The Blockchain Will Do to the Financial System What the Internet Did to Media*. Harvard Business Review, Digital Article. Retrieved from https:// hbr.org/2017/03/the-blockchain-will-do-to-banks-and-law-firms-what-the-internet-did-to-media

Kenton, W. (2019). *Donation-Based Crowdfunding*. Retrieved from: https://www.investopedia.com/terms/d/donationbased-crowd-funding.asp

KPMG. (2018). *The Pulse of Fintech 2018. Biannual global analysis of investment in fintech*. KPMG.

KPMG. (2019). *InsurTech: Infrastructure for New Insurance*. KPMG Advisory (China) Limited.

Kuppuswamy, V., & Bayus, B. (2017). Crowdfunding Creative Ideas: The Dynamics of Project Backers in Kickstarter. The Economics of Crowdfunding: Startups, Portals, and Investor Behavior. Academic Press.

Kuti, M., Bedő, Z., & Geiszl, D. (2017, December). Equity-based Crowdfundind. *Financial and Economic Review, 16*(4), 187–200.

Kyryliuk, L. (2019). *What are the different types of Fintech?* Retrieved from: https://www.quora.com/What-are-the-different-types-of-Fintech/answer/Liudmyla-Kyryliuk

Lamagna, M. (2018). *This 30-year-old financial term was finally added to the dictionary*. Retrieved from: https://www.marketwatch.com/story/this-finance-related-term-was-just-added-to-the-dictionary-do-you-know-what-it-means-2018-09-05

Leong, K., & Sung, A. (2018, April). FinTech (Financial Technology): What is It and How to Use Technologies to Create Business Value in Fintech Way? *International Journal of Innovation, Management and Technology, 9*(2), 74–78. doi:10.18178/ijimt.2018.9.2.791

Lowry, P., B., Wells, T., Moody, G., Humpherys, S., & Kettles, D. (2006). Online Payment Gateways Used to Facilitate E-Commerce Transactions and Improve Risk Management. *Communications of AIS, 17*.

McGuinness, C., & Merrey, P. (2017). *KPMG: Value of Fintech*. City of London Corporation.

Nakamoto, S. (2008). *Bitcoin: A peer-to-peer electronic cash system*. Retrieved from: https://bitcoin.org/bitcoin.pdf

Nino, J., L., Langthaler, J., Fabian, M., & Mayorga, J., (2017). *An Overview of FinTechs: Their Benefits and Risks Association of Supervisors of Banks of the Americas*. Academic Press.

OECD. (2017). *Technology and innovation in the insurance sector*. Retrieved from: https://www.oecd.org/pensions/Technology-and-innovation-in-the-insurance-sector.pdf

Pollari, I., & Raisbeck, M. (2017). *Forging the future: How financial institutions are embracing fintech to evolve and grow*. KPMG Report. Retrieved from: https://assets.kpmg/content/dam/kpmg/xx/pdf/2017/10/forging-the-future-global-fintech-study.pdf

Pritchett, W. (2019). *Insurtech 10: Trends for 2019*. KPMG International Cooperative. Retrieved from: https://assets.kpmg/content/dam/kpmg/xx/pdf/2019/03/insurtech-trends-2019.pdf

Rob, M. A., & Opara, E. U. (2003). *Online Credit Card Processing Models*. Academic Press.

Singh, B. (2019). *What the Future of Fintech Looks Like*. Retrieved from: https://www.entrepreneur.com/article/333891

Sokolin, L. (2019). *The Future of Fintech*. Retrieved from: https://www.investopedia.com/the-future-of-fintech-4770491

Sundararajan, A. (2016). *The Sharing Economy: The End of Employment and the Rise of Crowd-Based*. MIT Press.

Szakiel, P. (2018). *What Is Fintech: A Beginner's Guide to Financial Technology in 2019*. Retrieved from: https://learn.g2.com/fintech

TC -Toronto Centre, (2017). *FinTech, RegTech and SupTech: What They Mean for Financial Supervision*. Author.

Thomson Reuters (2018). *State of the Global Islamic Economy Report, 2018/19*. Author.

Tonttila, J. (2016). *Reward-Based Crowdfunding*. Thesis Spring 2016 Business and administration Oulu University of Applied Sciences.

UNDP. (2017). *Crowdfunding. Financing Solutions for Sustainable Development*. Retrieved from: https://assets.publishing.service.gov.uk/media/57a08a1540f0b652dd00055c/EoD_HD061_Jul2013_Review_CrowdFunding.pdf

World Bank. (2007). *General principles for international remittance services*. Committee on Payment and Settlement Systems. January.

World Bank (2018). *Cryptocurrencies and Blockchain*. Europe and Central Asia Economic Update. Office of the Chief Economist. World Bank Group.

Yaga, D., Mell, P., Roby, N., & Scarfone, K. (2018). *Blockchain Technology Overview*. . doi:10.6028/NIST.IR.8202

Zheng, Z., Xie, S., Dai, H., Chen, X., & Wang, H. (2017). An Overview of Blockchain Technology: Architecture, Consensus, and Future Trends. *IEEE 6th International Congress on Big Data*.

Chapter 2
Financial Technologies (FinTech), Instruments, Mechanisms, and Financial Products in the Current Context of Artificial Intelligence and Globalization

Otilia P. Manta
https://orcid.org/0000-0002-9411-7925
Romanian Academy, Romania

ABSTRACT

The holistic approach of the phenomenon of expansion of financial innovations, respectively of current financial technologies, as otherwise abbreviated to FinTech, knows very specific elements and is adapted to the global financial context, and lately, the share of financial services in the virtual space is dominant compared to their traditional form. Moreover, this new financing instrument has arisen mainly due to the need to streamline the financing system, based on technology, either to provide financial services adapted to the current needs of consumers (especially those who are in need of financing, this is also the real reason for the FinTech coupling of the financial inclusion of the financially excluded), as well as the design of new financial products that are reliable and responsive to the market. The financial space is dual, presenting two often contradictory assumptions (all channels, stocks, and collection flow, on the one hand; and all entities, channels, stocks, and investment flows), and in the current context of digital financial technologies, this is in virtual space.

DOI: 10.4018/978-1-7998-3257-7.ch002

INTRODUCTION

The advancement of financial technologies includes robotic financial trading, payments made through encrypted cashless platforms, crowdfunding financial platforms, financial consulting, technical and robotic assistance through virtual space, and last but not least virtual currencies so developed lately. "*The value of FinTech's global investment in 2015 increased by $ 22.3 billion by 75%. Corporations, venture capital and private equity firms have invested more than $ 50 billion in nearly 2,500 FinTech companies globally since 2010*"(Financial technology (FinTech): Prospects and challenges for the EU, EPRS, Cemal Karakas, Carla Stamegna - Graphics: Christian Dietrich, 2018). However, financial technologies (FinTech), although registering a rapid growth in the virtual space, have positive aspects, especially regarding the speed with which the financial services (adapted and flexible) reach the many financially excluded, but also have risks, challenges such as be particularly data related and of consumer protection, the risk of increasing financial volatility, as well as the alarming increase of cybercrime). The risks in particular attract the attention of the regulators of financial services, and a European Commission has been set up.

The defining elements for any financing model, regardless of whether we think of fintech or other types, are given by the following characteristics: digitization (artificial intelligence tools are crucial for digitizing services), mobilization (virtual space offers not only the possibility but especially the platform of realization of the mobility of people and services), disintermediation (virtual space offers the possibility of direct access without intermediaries), automation (through the financial services existing on

Figure 1. Representation of Financial Technologies (FinTech)
Source: Financial technology (FinTech): Prospects and challenges for the EU, EPRS, Cemal Karakas, Carla Stamegna, 2018

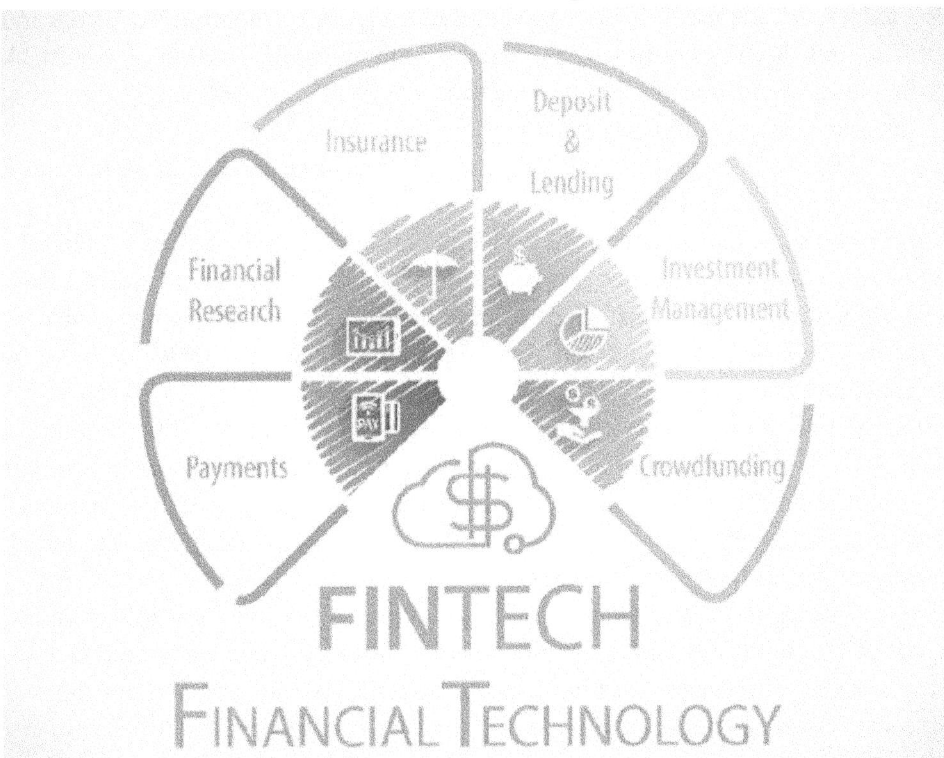

the online platforms, the client and the service provider optimize their time and cost in favor of making the service profitable).

Following the widespread use of FinTech, the authorities dealing with financial services regulation, may face a dilemma: one based on very clear but limited rules, the regulatory frameworks clearly establish the compliance obligations of the institutions involved in financial technologies, but these are often costly from the perspective of a start-up company and could be an obstacle to innovation and the creation of new jobs; Principle-based financial regulation is more flexible, but could create some uncertainty about exactly what is expected from the point of view of compliance by those who use the services of Fintech institutions.

Financial technology (FinTech) concepts defined in the *Prospects and challenges for the EU, EPRS, Cemal Karakas, Carla Stamegna, 2018*:

Blockchain: a decentralized digital ledger of economic transactions that can be programmed to record financial transactions (and more) by allowing digital information to be distributed but not copied or changed. Data packages, 'blocks', are stored in a linear chain. This technology was originally devised for the digital currency Bitcoin, but today presents other potential uses.

Crowdfunding: the use of capital from several individuals (via social media and specialized websites) to finance a business project. It allows start-up companies to raise money without giving up control to venture capital investors. In return, it often offers investors the opportunity to acquire an equity position. Critics of crowdfunding argue that funds may, for instance, be used for different purposes than those initially disclosed, or that tax laws governing e-commerce are not clearly defined, e.g. in the case of cross-border funding.

Distributed ledger: a database that is consensually shared and synchronized across multiple sites, institutions or locations. It allows transactions to have public witnesses, making cyberattacks more difficult. The participant at each node of the network can access the recordings shared. Changes or additions made to the ledger are copied to all participants.

Peer-to-peer (P2P) lending: a method of debt financing without the use of an official financial institution as an intermediary. It can also be described as 'social lending'.

Robo-advice: covers a broad spectrum of services, but essentially involves replacing face-to face investment advice with online, automated guidance and execution. It does not involve actual robots, but rather relies on algorithms or online offerings to invest money. Potentially, robo-advice could deliver financial advice in a more cost-efficient way, making it affordable for a wider range of investors and reducing the financial advice gap.

Robo-trading: a form of automated stock trading. The best known kind of robo-trading is algorithmic trading, also referred to as algo-trading and black box trading, which is a trading system that utilizes advanced and complex mathematical models and formulas to make high speed decisions and transactions in the financial markets. Algorithmic trading involves the use of computer programs and algorithms to determine trading strategies for optimal returns.

Virtual currencies: digital representations of value, issued by private developers and denominated in their own unit of account. They can be obtained, stored, accessed, and transacted electronically, and can be used for a variety of purposes, as long as the transacting parties agree to use them. The concept of virtual currencies covers a wider array, including internet coupons, airline miles, and crypto currencies such as Bitcoin.

The current process of financial technologies and the definition of financing models starts primarily with the contribution of digital technologies to the development of the financial industry as can be seen in the graph below. Figure 2 provides a clear picture of Industry 4.0 and digital technologies (including those that are digital tools for Fintech). Moreover, we consider that industry 4.0 and digital technologies will directly contribute to the branches of national economies, and in our case to the 17 branches of the Romanian real economy.

Figure 2. Industry 4.0 framework and contributing digital technologies
Sources: PwC report, 2018

The ***process of globalization*** inevitably leads to the reconsideration (conceptual reconstruction) of the paradigm of growth and economic development, and especially in financial technology (Fintech). The challenge, on the one hand, of the depletion and / or deterioration of resources (especially natural) and, on the other hand, of our optimization model - maximizing the objective functions of economic actors - is likely to require a radical change the options and the means by which we address this important activity of the individual and society: economic activity.

Literature Review

Among the remarkable personalities of the moment who have approached and tackle the phenomenon of globalization, I mention Joseph E. Stiglitz with the works: Globalization Mechanisms (2008): “In 2000, more than 150 Heads of State and Prime Ministers met in New York, at the Millennium Summit, committed to halving global poverty by 2015. Building on the author’s experience as an official of the

Clinton administration and the World Bank, the Globalization Mechanisms analyse the main obstacles to a fair globalization: the burden of national debt, the degradation the environment, the limits of liberalization, etc. The 10 chapters try to find solutions to these issues and provide a plan to restructure the global financial system. (George Soros), Globalization: Hopes and Disillusionments (2003), Globalization and its New Discontents, Aug. 5, 2016, The Globalization of Our Discontent Dec. 5, 2017 "Globalization, which should have benefited both developed countries and developing countries, is now criticized almost everywhere, as demonstrated by the political reaction in Europe and the US in recent years. The challenge is to minimize the risk that the reaction will intensify and that begins by understanding - and avoiding - mistakes of the past."

In the literature, FinTech has known different interpretations, as the name suggests, it is the fusion of finance and technology. Of course, technology has always influenced the financial industry, with advances that change the way the financial industry works. Consider, for example, the introduction of ATMs or the use of cable transfers as key innovations. So what's so special about the current FinTech revolution? First, the pace at which new technologies are being tested and introduced into finance is faster than ever in all industries. But more importantly, this FinTech revolution is unique in that much of the change is happening outside of the financial industry, as young start-ups and well-established technology companies try to disrupt those involved by introducing new products, and technologies, and providing a significant new dose of competition. You just have to step into a practitioner-oriented FinTech conference: with its audience mostly made up of people in their twenties from Silicon Valley and Silicon Alley, there is clearly something new (Goldstein I., Jiang W., Karolyi G., 2019).

New financial technologies (FinTech) have erupted around the world. Therefore, there has been a considerable increase in the academic literature on FinTech in the last five years. Research tends to be connected quite a bit with a coherent research agenda. Significant gaps in research and important questions remain. Much work needs to be done before this area becomes an established academic discipline (Kavuri AS, Milne A., 2019. At the same time, I believe that these financial technologies have emerged from the desire to create new financial instruments to support sustainable development in economies global.

Sustainable development (or growth) is a direct function of resources of the same category, i.e. sustainable resources, inclusive financial resources. The subject of this study is the research of a special resource, namely the financial technology (FinTech). Studying this resource from a sustainable development perspective will lead us to the proposal and the conceptual, methodological and technological development of what we will call a sustainable financial resource. For its part, the concept of a sustainable financial resource will generate some considerations about the sustainable sources of financial resources, including Fintech - our ultimate goal, on the other hand. As we develop more broadly at the right time, the financial sources for sustainable development are more sustainable financial sources for development (Manta O, 2017).

The Cobb-Douglas production function is often used to analyze the performance of supply and measure the productive potential of a country (in our case Romania). This functional form includes, however, the assumption of a constant share of labor in production, which may be too restrictive for a converging country (Hajkova D., Hurnik J., 2007). For example, the share of the labor force in Romania has gradually increased in the last decade. In this paper, we test whether this fact makes the application of the Cobb-Douglas production function unreliable for the Romanian economy. The authors apply a more general form of the production function and allow the development of the share of the workforce according to empirical data. The labor force is also the transmission channel, respectively absorption of financial technologies in the economies of each state.

METODOLOGY RESEARCH

The *methodology of the paper* will have as direct instruments the collection of data and information from the literature and from the existing practice in public and private institutions, but especially scientific articles published on specialized research networks (ResearchGate, Academia.edu), articles published in different journals, relevant books in the field of reference, legislation, analyzes and studies, official documents of various tax bodies, tax documents and interactive database of the Federal Banks and Central Banks, other relevant sources identified at the libraries Romanian Academy, National Bank of Romania, National and International Library..

In order to test the digital technologies at the level of the real economy, respectively of the branches and by regions, we analyzed at the level of the balance sheets of the active companies in Romania as of December 31, 2017, the ability to adapt to the current forms of financing used by the Romanian SMEs starting with more active with 2016, respectively, the following reference indicators were calculated, respectively: Evolution of the economic rate of return of the asset in the period 2007 - 2017 for the branches of the real economy (%) and by regions, The evolution of the labor productivity in the period 2007 - 2017 for the branches of the economy real *(RON /employee)*and by regions and Evolution of the average gross value added per employee in the period 2007 - 2017 for the branches of the real economy *(RON /employee)* and regions. From this result we can deduce that a large number of SMEs in Romania are financially excluded and therefore do not access loans from banking financial institutions, thus being potential direct beneficiaries of alternative financial solutions such as FinTech.

Starting from the analytical and predictive capacity of the theoretical methodological tools of production functions, in the present research we used one of the most used forms, namely the Cobb-Douglas production function, formulated in 1928 by American economist Paul Douglas, together with mathematician Charles W. Cobb. We used this function in its homothetic form and in the non-embedded technical progress, pursuing analytical and predictive purposes regarding the contribution of capital and labor factors to the economic growth.

The existing statistical information in Romania raises a series of problems regarding the availability of data necessary for *calculating the Cobb-Douglas production function*, especially for the capital production factor, with its usable variants - total fixed assets, fixed assets, gross investments - chronologically convenient as a number of observations or in a territorial profile. The greatest theoretical-methodological and practical interest in using the Cobb-Douglas production function at macroeconomic level is, in our opinion, the possibility to analyze the quality of Romania's economic growth, in terms of the *intensity of the use of capital and labor factors*, as determinants for level and structure of production and GDP.

In the analysis we started from the known form of the Cobb-Douglas production function:

$Y= A*K^{\alpha}*L^{\beta}$, with $\alpha, \beta >0$

where:

Y- output;
K - the capital production factor;
L - the labor factor;
A, α, β - constant.

Parameters α and β measure the proportion of total output that is generated by capital and labor. These two constants, in a certain sense, can also be assimilated to sui-generis elasticity coefficients.

If a + β = 1, the production function has a constant return to scale; for example, doubling the consumption of each factor, production will double. Constanta is not just a simple proportionality factor of economic significance that is more difficult to establish but can provide information on the full *efficiency of the factors of production.*

If the sum of exponents equals the unit ($\alpha + \beta = 1$), the Cobb-Douglas production function is linearly homogeneous, indicating constant returns to scale. If a + β> 1, the function expresses rising returns, and when a + β <1, the scale yields are decreasing.

The logarithmic transformation of the function Y = A * Kα * Lβ is frequently used in econometric analyzes, both for the estimation of the output function exponents and for the deepening of the analysis. Thus, by logging this function you get:

$$lnY = ln\,A + \alpha ln\,K + (1 - \alpha)ln\,L$$

Note that, with a one-percent increase in capital or labor, production Y increases with only α% or (1- α)%, i.e. by less than one percent, since α <1; Instead, the increase by one percent of the total productivity factor (parameter A) ensures the Y production also increases by 1%. Economic decision makers should consider this specific growth potential when assessing the likely impact of different economic policy measures.

The available statistical data on the Romanian economy do not allow the establishment of appropriate chronological series to perform analyses based on the *Cobb-Douglas production function*, which has led us to use the cross-section analysis method. In the absence of chronological data series we have an interesting substitute for them, adopting the working hypothesis that each company integrates into a group with a similar technological process. Moreover, using the balance sheets of all active companies in the real economy, the results are representative and can effectively serve decision-makers.

The Cobb-Douglas model, in its variant based on cross-sectional analysis, it is less or not applied in Romania. The cross-sectional analysis was completed with the introduction of analytical elements in two main directions:

1. Determining the Cobb-Douglas model parameters based on the cross-over method for several years and comparing the results obtained for different years;
2. Using chronological series (with a sufficient number of terms) for labor and capital production factors as well as for output.

SOLUTIONS AND RECOMMENDATIONS

Specifically, in order to estimate the parameters of the Cobb-Douglas production function for Romania's economy, the balance sheet data for the companies in some sub-branches of Romania's agriculture for the period 2008-2016 was used. In order to be conclusive, the sub- 2016 have at least 200 active companies (*see appendix no. 1*).

To estimate the Cobb-Douglas function parameters, the following were used:

1. the turnover achieved;
2. the value of fixed net assets;
3. labor costs (including contributions and tax).

These parameters analyzed in the Cobb-Douglas production function, respectively the turnover achieved, the value of net fixed assets and labor costs (including contributions and tax), were used to highlight the supply performance and measure the productive potential of the Romanian economy. Moreover, we consider the labor force as the transmission channel, respectively the absorption of financial technologies at the level of the Romanian economy.

The statistical analysis of the three data strings reveals a homogeneous distribution of the values of the statistical series terms, a conclusion validated by the values of the multiplication coefficients (*see annex no.2*).

Estimating the Cobb-Douglas production function parameters is typically done using the smallest square method. For the 12 sub-ranges selected from the agriculture of Romania, the results can be found in appendix no.2. Image of the evolution of the two parameters α and β from the Cobb Douglas production function and is illustrated in the following graphs.

What is of particular interest is the results obtained from the application of the model and the conclusions of economic policy that can be deduced from the analysis of the parameters of the production function. In this respect, the preliminary conclusions that can be highlighted from the application of the Cobb-Douglas production function with two factors - labor and capital - for the Romanian economy refer mainly to:

1. the labor factor has a significantly higher contribution than the capital in obtaining the total results (turnover);
2. the significant contribution of the labor force to the economic growth in the current stage of development of Romania, supports the positive economic evolutions of the last years.
3. Natural population growth is negative in the last 20 years, and the migration process is significant for Romania, with integration into the EU structures. In this respect, in the future, there will be a significant problem for the firms in the analyzed sectors, in the direction of rising labor costs, as the rarity of this resource rises.

The alternative appears to be: investment in fixed assets that ensure a significant increase in labor productivity and technical provision of labor.

Relevance of the two parameters of the production function for Romania in agri sector.

From the point of view of the strategy of sustainable development of the Romanian economy, the magnitude of these parameters offers elements of substantiation of the decision in support of the promotion of a high rate of gross fixed capital formation, under the conditions of their high efficiency. The experience of countries with strong economic start-up and lasting performance in the economic growth process (e.g. Japan, China, Norway) recorded a high rate of gross fixed capital formation over long periods, but this rate was accompanied during the respective coefficient periods sensitively raised micro and macroeconomic efficiency. Practically, it means the accumulation of new generations of technological breakthrough, strongly marked by cutting-edge technologies and the IT impact.

This information resulting from data processing can lead us to the dimensioning of the market for Fintech services in Romania. This model can be adapted for the sizing of markets and in other states,

size compared to the indicators of active companies. Further to identify the impact of current technologies in key branches of the real economy at national level, we have calculated the following reference indicators, respectively: *Evolution of the economic rate of return of the assets during 2007 - 2017 for the branches of the real economy* (%) and by regions, *Evolution of labor productivity in the period 2007 - 2017 for the branches of the real economy (RON /employee)*and by regions, and *Evolution of the average gross value added per employee in the period 2007 - 2017 for the branches of the real economy (RON /employee)* and regions.

Table 1. Evolution of the rate of economic return of the asset between 2007 and 2017 for the branches of the real economy (%)

No. crt.	Branches of the national economy	2007	2008	2009	2010	2011	2012	2013	2014	2015	2016	2017
1	Agriculture, forestry and fishing	3,31	2,70	3,04	2,68	2,72	1,74	2,86	3,84	4,10	5,69	6,97
2	Extractive industry	2,81	1,19	0,34	0,26	0,21	0,09	0,52	1,28	2,55	1,64	2,12
3	Manufacturing industry	2,60	1,54	1,07	1,38	0,72	0,70	1,68	2,67	4,52	4,98	5,27
4	Production and supply of electricity and heat, gas, hot water and air conditioning	1,38	0,43	0,66	0,47	0,09	0,06	0,05	0,00	0,03	0,01	-0,05
5	Water distribution, sanitation, waste management, decontamination activities	4,43	4,49	2,51	4,62	2,98	1,47	2,43	4,20	5,00	7,14	9,82
6	Constructions	11,73	5,26	2,26	1,86	1,35	1,24	3,21	5,16	9,09	9,82	11,60
7	Wholesale and retail trade, repair of motor vehicles and motorcycles	1,91	1,05	-0,18	0,06	-0,15	-0,13	0,12	1,25	4,20	5,47	5,72
8	Transport and storage	2,57	0,52	-1,74	-0,77	0,07	0,18	3,35	4,71	8,78	9,63	11,13
9	Hotels and restaurants	0,63	-0,11	-3,94	-4,78	-4,47	-6,28	-3,91	-0,86	5,63	7,03	7,87
10	Information and telecommunications	11,20	6,82	5,10	4,78	4,33	8,10	7,72	9,70	11,06	23,74	26,11
11	Real estate transactions, leasing and service activities mainly provided by companies	3,55	1,26	0,84	0,51	0,48	0,71	1,77	2,07	4,43	6,79	8,06
12	Professional, scientific and technical activities	15,54	13,37	9,24	7,37	7,60	6,74	10,67	12,90	16,59	22,65	25,50
13	Administrative service activities and support service activities	12,45	5,46	4,81	4,64	4,41	4,11	8,25	9,76	13,16	16,55	19,04
14	Education	4,71	2,11	-1,16	0,36	1,62	2,89	8,06	10,10	16,43	22,22	18,72
15	Health and social assistance	11,00	9,11	6,67	7,51	5,61	5,37	9,39	12,35	17,05	28,48	30,29
16	Entertainment, culture and recreational activities	5,52	6,81	5,37	5,27	5,49	0,08	9,48	11,65	15,62	15,19	18,86
17	Other activities of the national economy	-1,28	-5,97	-15,28	-13,05	-13,75	-3,16	-14,15	-7,64	1,16	7,11	7,28
	Total											

Source: calculated based on data provided by the Ministry of Public Finance
(annual financial statements of companies active in the real economy of Romania)

For the calculation of the *Indicator The rate of economic return of the asset* was used the formula:

$$R_e = \frac{Pbt}{At} * 100$$

where:

Pbt= gross profit;

At= total assets.

At the level of the real economy, during the period 2007-2017 there were significant increases in the value of the rate of economic profitability in the following branches of activity respectively: Agriculture, forestry and fisheries; Water distribution, sanitation, waste management, decontamination activities; construction; Professional, scientific and technical activities; Education and Health and social assistance (an increase of the rate of return from the real economy by approximately 3 times as of December 31,

Table 2. Evolution of the economic rate of return of the asset for the period 2007 - 2017 for the development regions in Romania (%)

No. crt.	Development regions	2007	2008	2009	2010	2011	2012	2013	2014	2015	2016	2017
1	NORTH-WEST	3,52	1,75	0,95	1,36	0,74	0,88	2,41	3,88	6,92	8,89	10,23
2	NORTH – EAST	2,66	1,60	1,56	1,66	0,76	0,92	2,11	3,39	6,19	8,17	9,37
3	SOUTH - WEST	3,29	2,48	1,52	1,96	1,04	1,03	2,12	4,11	7,33	9,25	10,54
4	SOUTH – EAST	3,45	2,12	0,56	1,15	0,76	0,62	2,16	3,69	7,70	9,20	10,05
5	SOUTH	4,11	2,82	1,81	2,07	1,07	1,02	2,32	3,54	6,69	8,64	9,23
6	CENTRE	3,60	2,08	1,23	1,52	1,13	1,11	2,88	4,41	7,80	9,71	11,01
7	WEST	2,97	1,68	0,39	0,90	0,66	0,57	1,87	3,68	7,12	9,14	9,76
8	BUCHAREST - ILFOV	9,17	5,60	1,90	1,18	0,78	0,48	2,46	4,11	8,43	12,48	14,81
	Total											

Source: calculated based on data provided by the Ministry of Public Finance
(annual financial statements of companies active in the real economy of Romania)

2017 compared to December 31, 2007). Moreover, at the regional level the breakdown by branches, for

Table 3. Evolution of labor productivity in the period 2007 - 2017 for branches of the real economy (RON[1] /employee)

No. crt.	Branches of the national economy	2007	2008	2009	2010	2011	2012	2013	2014	2015	2016	2017
1	Agriculture, forestry and fishing	6442650	6625400	8926050	9642000	11952500	15035850	12796050	14090250	13858350	17755850	17909400
2	Extractive industry	7823560	10133783	9527525	9561450	10345100	11160100	10139625	12532000	16308450	14976500	12923400
3	Manufacturing industry	4647900	6317550	6365700	5232375	5918500	5893675	5588725	7924800	8372900	8344433	8100633
4	Production and supply of electricity and heat, gas, hot water and air conditioning	10346256	23070010	11465850	10429550	10866550	16372650	28499900	57242800	79740200	91812500	53147700
5	Water distribution, sanitation, waste management, decontamination activities	9439200	14871333	16455550	12522967	9578250	11093467	9548933	10076533	9270267	10498533	12037567
6	Constructions	3808033	4690867	5227750	5922450	4700967	7401100	6954700	7529050	8822150	8739400	8946950
7	Wholesale and retail trade, repair of motor vehicles and motorcycles	5787700	9100000	12277600	6331750	6701050	6739150	6173350	13424300	15940700	17336100	18300800
8	Transport and storage	5505150	6849700	5722750	6633400	7407750	7494800	7521500	7887200	8526950	8549650	17217500
9	Hotels and restaurants	4477350	6102250	4618850	4437250	4816050	4826350	4585750	5119550	6654800	7470000	8381450
10	Information and telecommunications	7269500	11333800	8735600	8957800	9612000	10499000	9735400	9876300	10014100	11603800	11877600
11	Real estate transactions, leasing and service activities mainly provided by companies	7592800	10277300	8719500	8858100	9668300	9180100	9176700	10030400	9898600	11000000	11572300
12	Professional, scientific and technical activities	7329100	9583300	7788100	7597800	8563800	8691100	8570500	8985400	9507000	9739400	10255000
13	Administrative service activities and support service activities	6342800	4543150	3730750	4264350	4824750	5433750	5013000	10672800	11344300	12716700	12957000
14	Education	3458550	2750667	3001500	3775000	4067500	4025000	3871450	8154700	9163400	9450500	9047300
15	Health and social assistance	2586700	3805050	3451250	3559500	4094350	4421250	4520450	5070850	5843150	6102800	13509900
16	Entertainment, culture and recreational activities	6288400	9531300	7406100	7528600	8707500	6035800	9211100	9834000	9949900	6997700	7154300
17	Other activities of the national economy	1757700	2281600	1935750	1945850	2157200	2433100	1953100	2131050	2533800	5850000	6059400

Source: calculated based on data provided by the Ministry of Public Finance
(annual financial statements of companies active in the real economy of Romania)

the period 2007-2017, is presented in the table above, respectively the Bucharest-Ilfov region an increase from 9.17% in 2007 to 14.81% in 2017.

Table 4. Evolution of labor productivity in the period 2007 - 2017 for development regions in Romania (RON / employee)

No. crt.	Development regions	2007	2008	2009	2010	2011	2012	2013	2014	2015	2016	2017
1	NORTH-WEST	4949450	6652100	5087250	5432750	5876300	6202100	5941100	6381550	7187500	7341950	15048500
2	NORTH – EAST	4892300	6444000	5226650	5448900	5814150	6124200	5793950	6327800	7235000	7425100	15339900
3	SOUTH - WEST	4368700	6568350	9344600	4716300	5047450	5004000	9228900	10199400	11927900	12729700	13440100
4	SOUTH – EAST	4831050	6499150	4994850	5120700	5540050	5544600	5305300	5713350	13205900	13571600	14135700
5	SOUTH	5141900	7196400	5378100	5589150	5905900	6126500	5860000	6313950	7100000	7440200	15373200
6	CENTRE	5280000	7233350	5511300	5848150	6449400	6731250	6449700	7043500	7952000	8065700	16927100
7	WEST	4950350	6678250	5061950	5403200	5825750	6033750	5951400	6520500	7348050	7705400	15976500
8	BUCHAREST - ILFOV	6324700	9253950	12923300	6681750	7217150	7226150	13851200	14389900	15676800	16187000	16811500

Source: calculated based on data provided by the Ministry of Public Finance
(annual financial statements of companies active in the real economy of Romania)

The labor productivity indicator (in financial expression) is calculated according to the formula below, respectively:

$$W_f = \frac{Ca}{Ns}$$

where:

Ca= Fiscal value;
Ns= Number of employees.

Another relevant indicator regarding the competitiveness at the branches of the real economy is the labor productivity, during the period 2007-2017 there were important increases of the labor productivity in the following branches of activity respectively: Agriculture, forestry and fisheries, Extractive industry, Service activities administrative and support service activities Education and Health and social assistance (for example, labor productivity in the Administrative service activities and support service activities 48.95%). Moreover, at the regional level the breakdown by branches, for the period 2007-2017, there is an increase of labor productivity in each development region (see in the table above), but the largest increase is observed from the data presented in Bucharest-Ilfov region.

The VAB / employee indicator is calculated according to the formula:

$$Vab\ /\ s = \frac{Csa + Am + Pbt}{Ns}$$

where:

Table 5. Evolution of the average gross value added per employee in the period 2007 - 2017 for the branches of the real economy (RON / employee)

Nr. crt.	Branches of the national economy	2007	2008	2009	2010	2011	2012	2013	2014	2015	2016	2017
1	Agriculture, forestry and fishing	943500	1017233	1480150	1500700	1834250	2243650	1991100	2223950	2321750	2889500	3008100
2	Extractive industry	1478740	1730150	1905150	1845525	1985250	2339875	2292775	2124050	2900075	3254925	3283720
3	Manufacturing industry	846225	1260775	1471233	1085025	1267700	1261825	1208400	1688600	1872400	2091067	2238967
4	Production and supply of electricity and heat, gas, hot water and air conditioning	1666089	3504910	2315950	1363950	1423800	2055450	2032200	4010600	12147100	18652400	20841100
5	Water distribution, sanitation, waste management, decontamination activities	737500	1566867	1795600	1223233	1176400	1398400	1216533	1456567	1669500	1990867	2441733
6	Constructions	606033	884000	1170450	1093900	874467	1224450	1131900	1223800	1389050	1635100	1824500
7	Wholesale and retail trade, repair of motor vehicles and motorcycles	535300	938150	1447000	701900	820800	809950	788100	1619500	1825300	2252400	2660100
8	Transport and storage	928900	1341700	1348850	1290050	1259300	1168650	1094900	1116050	1246800	1434800	3246700
9	Hotels and restaurants	708750	1089500	934000	893400	1084650	1099500	1066950	1151800	1348350	1701200	2014150
10	Information and telecommunications	899000	1567100	1346200	1295500	1305000	1274600	1264000	1128700	1219700	1273600	1378900
11	Real estate transactions, leasing and service activities mainly provided by companies	1059500	2034400	1629800	1635600	1644200	1443900	1206500	1072500	1110400	1242100	1428800
12	Professional, scientific and technical activities	941300	1413700	1263100	1270900	1301500	1276900	1098800	1039500	1111100	1440300	1644600
13	Administrative service activities and support service activities	764800	878200	774900	835000	867400	866800	858250	1754000	1878400	2146800	2360100
14	Education	861050	813533	1040350	1200800	1131550	993800	885250	1758100	1747400	1795900	1741400
15	Health and social assistance	711250	1045850	1112150	1160000	1263100	1352700	1298000	1361950	1430300	1338650	2839700
16	Entertainment, culture and recreational activities	791500	1368900	1196000	1217000	1227100	1049400	1088700	1029900	970100	917200	882000
17	Other activities of the national economy	633700	873400	808400	789500	950550	767400	884700	928700	1022250	1857000	2120800

Source: calculated based on data provided by the Ministry of Public Finance
(annual financial statements of companies active in the real economy of Romania)

Csa= staff costs;
Am= expenses related to the depreciation of tangible assets;
Pbt= gross profit (profit-loss balance);
Ns= Number of employees.

From our point of view, the most relevant indicator is GVA / employee and reflects the competitiveness of the real economy, in the period 2007-2017, which leads us to say that there is a direct correlation between competitiveness and access to advanced technologies. Moreover, competitive firms are more open to adopt technologies both in terms of the technological process with a direct impact on the production process (implicitly using artificial intelligence such as robots in the automotive sector), and their openness to innovation such as Fintech-type financial solutions (Manta O., 2019). According to the data presented in the paper, among the branches with the highest growth and which have an impact on the real economy are the branch "Agriculture, forestry and fishing", the branch "Education" and the branch "Health" (aspect confirmed by a massive refurbishment starting with Romania's accession to the European Union, correlated with the infusion of non-reimbursable European funds in the form of direct subsidies or in the form of grants).Moreover, at the regional level the breakdown by branches, for the period 2007-2017, is observed an increasing evolution of the average gross value added per employee in the period 2007 - 2017 for the development regions in Romania (RON/ employee.) (See in table above), but the largest increase is observed from the data presented in the Center region. The above indicators confirm that the sectors in which the technology is present have a high level of performance and implicitly of the economic results.

Starting from the clear and detailed analysis of the situation of the companies that are active in Romania, and in conjunction with the needs and opportunities in financing, we can state that the current financial instruments and mechanisms of digital financial technologies correspond to those in real need of financing, i.e. microfinance, thus contributing to financial and economic inclusion at national and implicit European level.

Financial services do not only allow small investors to invest in their SMEs, they can help reduce liquidity constraints making it difficult for buyers to pay SMEs on delivery and force small-land owners to sell their crops at lower prices in exchange for a payment faster "(CGAP, 2018). Moreover, the applicability of financial innovations to the financing of agriculture using blockchain technology solutions appear to be particularly relevant for small non-bank farmers. However, while these technologies can help in authenticating, managing identity and controlling users, it is not enough as an independent solution to demonstrate identity. Indeed, a digital identity based on digital technologies still depends on a "reality" ID to which it is linked when it is created (Yaga et al., 2018). Therefore, the lack of formal identification may remain an obstacle in certain contexts.

In order to achieve the financial inclusion of many people in need, microfinance can be functionalized using tools and mechanisms that are tailored to the small farmer, and "collateralization of assets such as land, animals, cars, stored crops, or even payments to small owners for pledged or delivered products could allow small owners access to funding for inputs, working capital and post-harvest liquidity "(CGAP, 2018).

Policing the phenomenon of financial inclusion is trustworthy actors that ensure the smooth operation of the funding mechanism and their role is essential - even in a system designed to operate without third party intermediation. The CGAP found that on average only 5.5% of the small owners of the six markets surveyed had a smart phone (Anderson 2015, 2016).

In this context, FinTech covers a wide range of services and products, such as cashless payments, peer-to-peer (P2P) lending platforms, robotic trading, robo-advisory, crowdfunding and virtual platforms and is expected to be continues to expand in the coming years" (Financial technology (FinTech): Prospects and challenges for the EU, EPRS, Cemal Karakas, Carla Stamegna, 2018).

Increasing the accessibility of the population to Internet services, the introduction of mobile phones, online banking transactions and trading programs in the 1980s, were still important financial innovations. Indeed, the post-crisis financing gap, the growing distrust of beneficiaries (clients) in traditional financial institutions and following the RegTech regulations.

RegTech means "regulatory technology" - it was created to address the regulatory challenges in the financial services sector following the advent of innovative financial technologies. Based on data processing, RegTech allows companies to integrate compliance requirements into business processes, improve corporate governance and management. At the World Economy Forum, the presentation of the digitized economy and the society is presented according to the figure below with all the related connections starting from entrepreneurship and to artificial intelligence and robots, issues relevant to the current digital financial technologies.

FinTech today comprises five major areas, for which Arner et al. suggest the following topology:

(1) Finance and investment such as alternative financing mechanisms, particularly crowdfunding and P2P lending, but also robo-advisory services;
(2) Operations and risk management to build up better compliance systems (i.e. RegTech);
(3) Payments and infrastructure, such as internet and mobile payment systems, and infrastructure for securities trading and settlement and for over-the-counter (OTC) derivatives trading;

Figure 3. Digital Economy and Society

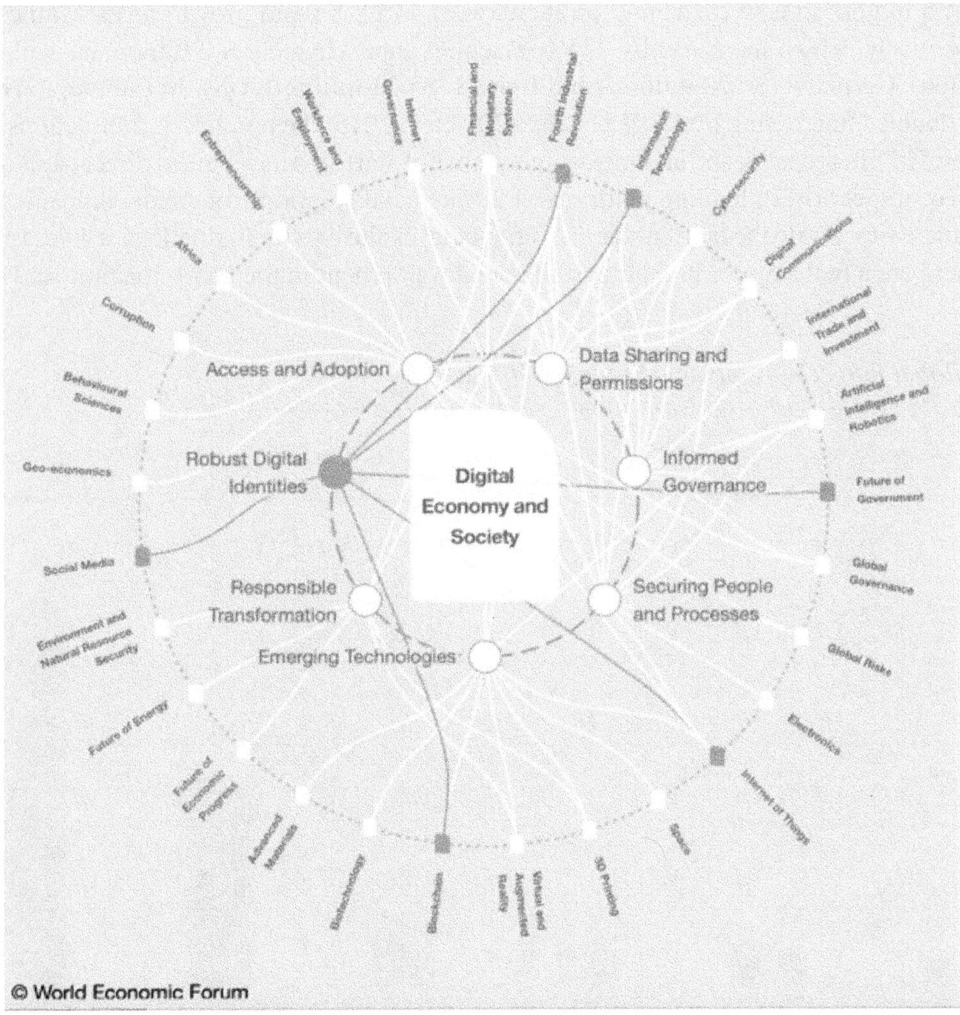

(4) Data security and monetisation to enhance the efficiency and availability of financial services (through the use of 'big data'), to better exploit the monetary value of data, and to tackle cybercrime and espionage;

(5) Customer interface such as online and mobile financial services.

Economic Prospects and Challenges According to Analysts, The Value of Global Fintech

Economic Perspectives and Challenges

According to analysts, the value of FinTech's global investment in 2015 increased by 75% to $ 22.3 billion and at present to nearly $ 40 billion. Corporations, venture capital firms and private equity firms have invested more than 50 billion dollars in nearly 2,500 FinTech companies globally since 2010. This trend was driven by a relatively moderate increase in the US FinTech sector (the largest in the world), which received $ 4.5 billion. in new financing (an increase of 44%); a rapid growth of the Chinese FinTech sector, respectively, which increased by 445%, reaching approximately $ 2 billion, as well as in India ($ 1.65 billion), Germany ($ 770 million) and Ireland ($ 631 million). US). In Europe, FinTech's total investment doubled, increasing by 120% between 2014 and 2015, the number of transactions increasing by more than 50%. In recent years, an increasing number of start-ups have raised direct capital instead of equity on peer-to-peer (P2P) lending platforms. P2P financial solutions for small companies have seen significant increases, due to the fact that for many financial exclusives these financial services are the most accessible and are a real support in their sustainable development in the short, medium and long term.

Figure 4. Global FinTech financing activity (2010 - 2015)
Source: Accenture, Fintech and the evolving landscape: landing points for the industry.

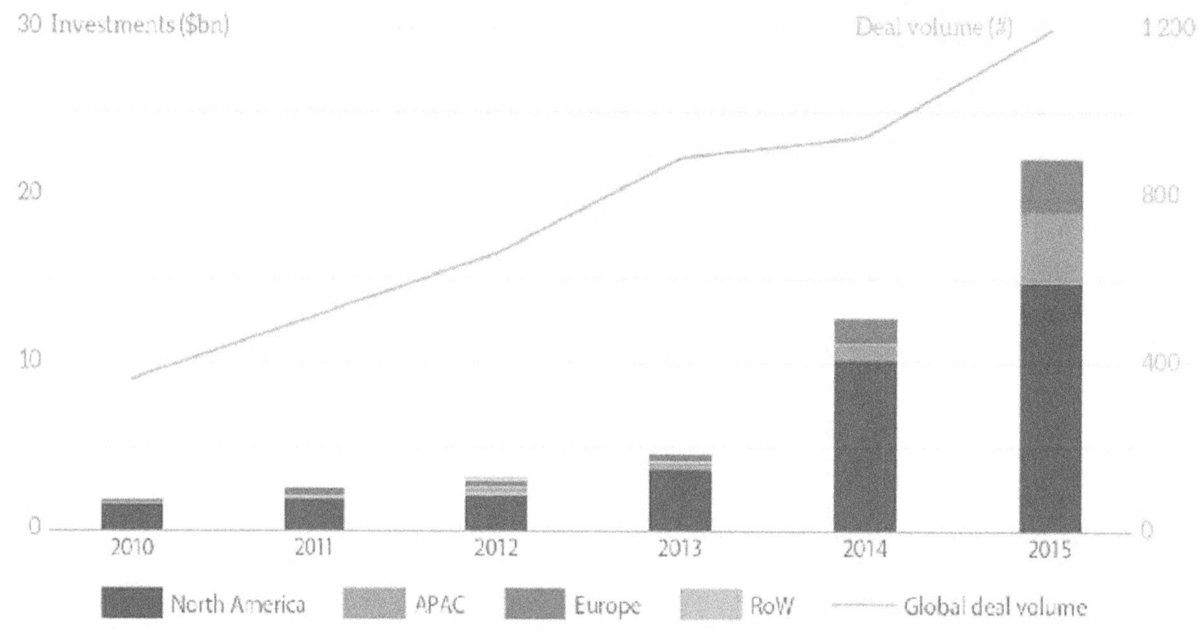

In 2012, the number of P2P financial services operators increased from ten in 2010 to 11 in 2015, the annual growth being 61.8%. Furthermore, there has been a potential growth of channels including student loans and securitization of P2P credits. By 2020, industry revenue is projected to grow 19.2% annually to $ 1.7 billion. All this being due to the interconnectivity shown in the figure below, according to Accenture the center is given by the digital competency framework.

In Asia, which is expected to account for 60% of the middle class by 2030, and here the market is growing rapidly, with rapid growth also in the FinTech and P2P.4 sectors.

The online payment provider Alipay, for example, had over 800 million accounts registered at the end of 2012 and recorded more than one million transactions per day. As far as Europe is concerned, new technologies can also contribute to overcoming it barriers that still impede the full integration of financial market infrastructures, which is one of the factors on which the success of the capital market

Figure 5. Digital competency framework

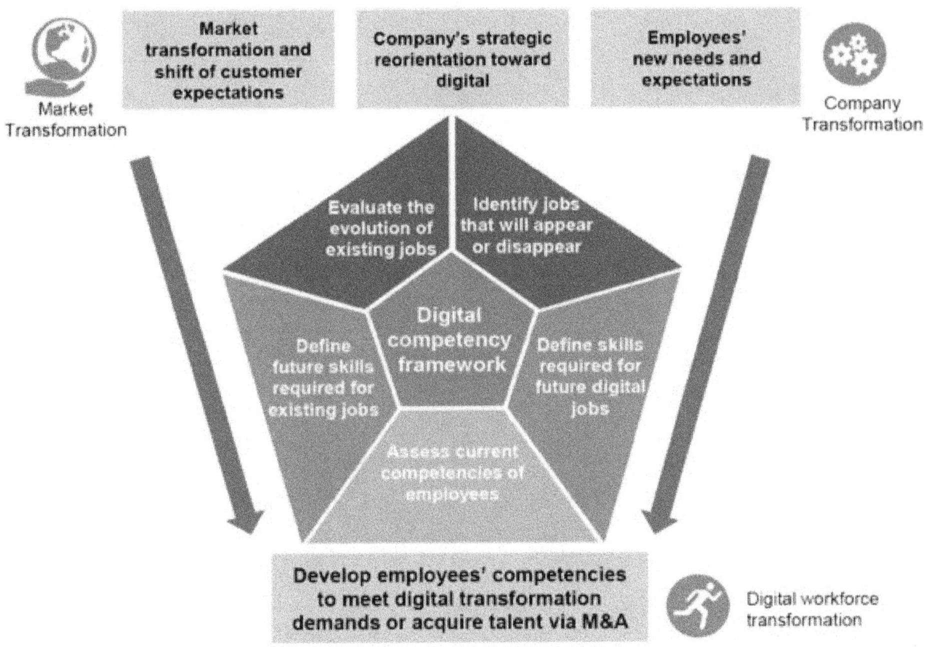

Source: Accenture

depends. Possible benefits (DLT) applied on securities markets are listed in a Consultation Document of the European Securities and Markets Authority (ESMA).

Regulations Related to FinTech Financial Technologies at EU Level

The Single European Act (1986) and the Maastricht Treaty (1992) set the framework for establishing a single market for financial services in the European Union and an increasing number of financial services directives and regulations. Michel Barnier, the Commissioner for the Internal Market and Services, at that time, justified the new rules by, inter moreover, the fact that fragmented rules in the EU payment industry creates costs more than 1% of EU GDP or 130 billion euros a year. According to Barnier, the implementation of PSD II could stimulate the European economy, as the proposal seeks "To promote the digital single market by making online payments cheaper and more secure, both for retailers and consumers.

The new directive is meant to respond to technological changes in the payments industry. Its purpose is to make payments and money safer and less expensive transfers. At the same time, they also address differences in the implementation of PSD I by Member States, which are perceived as distortion of competition.

Data and Consumer Protection

Some experts argue that the current EU data protection, competition and data protection legislation is clearly devoid of its definition of "big data", creating a on the spot, which needs to be addressed. The

Figure 6. Global FinTech financing activity by product segment, 2010-2015
Source: Accenture, Fintech and the evolving landscape: landing points for the industry.

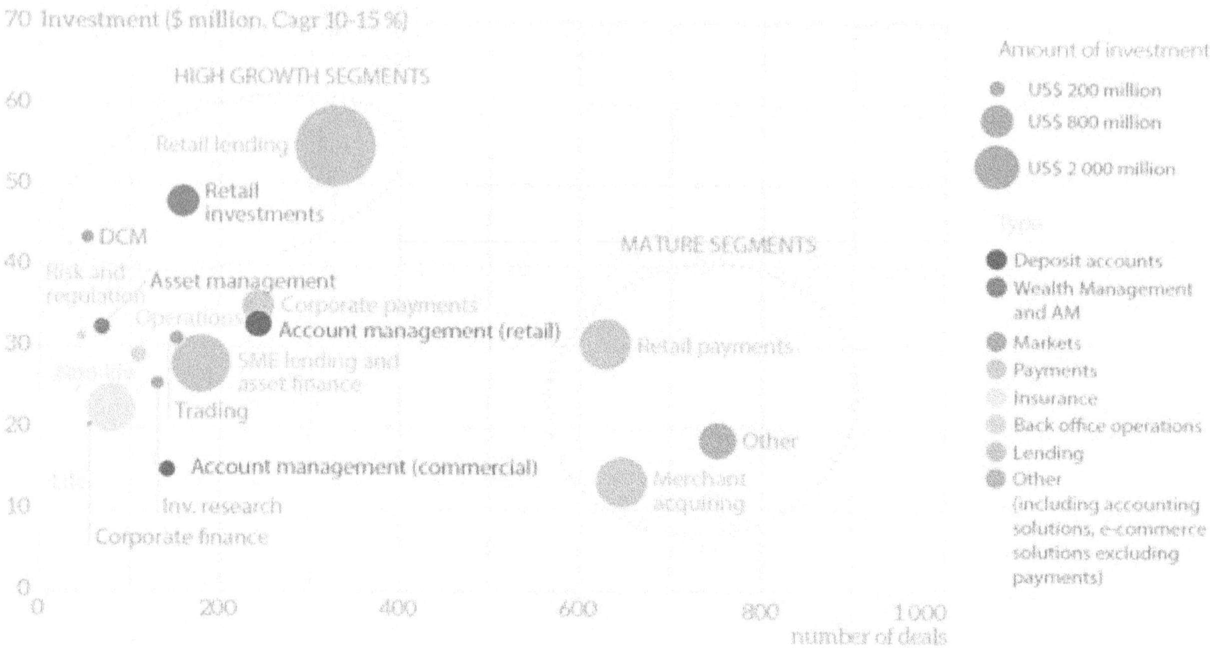

European Supervisory Authorities (ESAs) on financial issues are currently evaluating the specificity of FinTech, namely the application of the General Data Protection Regulation (GDPR) and / or other general provisions for consumer protection rules. On the issue of data protection (in the sense of "personal data protection"), the current legal framework is established by Directive 95/46 / EC on the protection of persons with disabilities regarding the processing of personal data and the free movement of such data.

In most countries, a consumer protection framework, which can be based on the internal market (national law/codes), regional (European) directives or international standards (OECD/G20 principles) is already in force. Even when such staff are present, the OECD/G20 High Level Principles on Financial Consumer Protection, developed by G20/OECD Task Force on Financial Consumer Protection, clearly sets out the key elements necessary for consumer protection. The G20 / OECD Action Group has identified FinTech is one of the key areas for examination.

FinTech Laws and Challenges for Regulators

In general, there are two approaches to the FinTech regulation: rule-based and basic principles. Rules based rules create clear rules and processes compliance obligations are clearly set, but this may limit the incentives for the supervised entity to do more, as the obligations are perceived to be sufficiently comprehensive. Model-based principles are flexible, but could create a degree of uncertainty about what exactly is expected compliance. Some experts argue that regulatory authorities should remain technologically neutral and focus on the outcome of a technology.

SUMMARY OF RESULTS AND ITS DISCUSSIONS

The results obtained both through empirical research on documented sources on fintech financial technologies in the current context of artificial intelligence and globalization, but especially through the parameters analyzed in the Cobb-Douglas production function, respectively the turnover achieved, the value of net assets fixed and labor costs (including contributions and tax), was used to highlight the performance of supply and measure the productive potential of the Romanian economy. Moreover, financial technologies (FinTech) as defined in the literature enter the sectors of activity at the level of state economies, through artificial intelligence resulting in tools, mechanisms, and financial products necessary for the sustainable development of economic branches at the state level.

Table 6. Regulations based on regulatory regimes

Rules-based regulatory regimes		Principles-based regulatory regimes	
Potential positives	**Potential negatives**	**Potential positives**	**Potential negatives**
Certainty and predictability, including with respect to future enforcement	'Check-box' forms of compliance that strategically evade the underlying purpose of the regulation	Executive-level management involvement in incorporating regulatory principles into business models	Uncertainty and the risk of unpredictable post hoc application or arbitrage
Clear communication of steps for compliance	High internal costs of compliance	Flexibility and innovation in the face of 'rapidly changing environments'	Concerns over fairness/bias in application
Ensures specific behaviour	Deterrence with respect to innovation	Speed in the regulatory process	Inadequate deterrence of specific problematic behaviour or activities
Uniform treatment of regulated entities	Frequent disconnect between the purpose of the regulation and the actual regulatory outcomes	The centrality of guidance and evolving norms/best practices	Over-reliance on current norms and practices
	Obsolescence		

Source: Brummer, Chris and Gorfine, Daniel: FinTech: Building a 21st-Century Regulator's Toolkit, Milken Institute – Center for Financial Markets, October 2014

FUTURE RESEARCH DIRECTIONS

Given the context of the topic of this chapter as part of the current global challenges (digitization of the economy, the emergence of financial technologies of the fintech type, etc.), we intend to continue the researches, respectively the proposal of new financing models / economic models of sustainable development for the real economy both at the level of Romania (based on analysis of indicators) and at global level.

CONCLUSION

Financial health globally is an increasingly important phenomenon with a direct impact on financial inclusion. Due to technological innovation, FinTech could bring banking services as close to people as small entrepreneurs or small farmers, and as close to their needs, actively contributing to the global financial inclusion of many non-banks. At the international level, the Financial Stability Board (FSB) of the G20 began in April 2016, examining the potential risks that FinTech could present for global financial stability. FSB is currently conducting a mapping exercise that focuses on the impact of digitization and FinTech in the banking sector and the possible implications for the banking sector, which is closely monitored. At the same time, there are attempts at EU level to collect the links between FinTech, information and data and to explore how FinTech companies can tackle the cross-border issue, namely taking over financial services and financial inclusion. In its first status report on (CMU), the Commission foresees, in its CMU action plan, a comprehensive assessment of European markets for retail investment products, including distribution channels and investment advice, by the end of 2018. The evaluation will was to be based on the contribution of experts and to consider "whether retail investors can have appropriate access to products on cost-effective and fair terms and if the potential offered by us the possibilities arising from online services and other technologies that services must perform more efficient financial systems (FinTech) are being exploited The representatives of the European Commission have expressed the aim of understanding the FinTech sector and its players better, as well as assessing its impact on the banking sector and the non-banking financial institutions sector, respectively the financial services sector and of its current players. As can be seen from the data of annex no.2, in most cases, $\alpha + \beta < 1$ which means the existence of decreasing yields. Moreover, with a one-percent increase in net fixed assets or labor costs, turnover increases by a%, respectively b%, i.e. by less than one percent. Instead, the increase by one percent of the total productivity factor (parameter A) ensures the increase of the turnover by more than 1%. Economic decision makers should consider this specific growth potential when assessing the likely impact of different economic policy measures:

- From what we know, for the first time in Romania, the calculation of the Cobb-Douglas model at the level of the significant sub-sectors of Romania's agriculture provides conclusive results that check all the usual statistical tests;
- The most dramatic conclusion resulting from the application of the model refers to the particular importance of capital (the technological level of machinery and equipment) that needs to be granted for economic growth, given that labor is becoming a rare resource for Romania;
- The contribution of unprompted technical progress (management and institutional efficiency of the economy) is still a factor with a very modest contribution to output growth, which is a challenge for the smooth functioning of our market economy in the future;
- Finally, but not least, the Cobb-Douglas production function could be a very useful tool for substantiating decision-making at different levels of economic aggregation, combining the static and dynamic analysis of the factors of influence considered, based on the hypothesis constant or variable substitution elasticity; of our research shows that the main part of this substitution is the cost of labor, supported by a higher technical endowment.

From the point of view of the sustainability of agricultural production in Romania, in the medium and long term, there is the problem of rising labor shortages and deficit coverage by measures to increase

Figure 7. The trend of the digital economy in Romania (2016-2025)
Source: Digital / McKinsey "The rise of Digital Challengers"

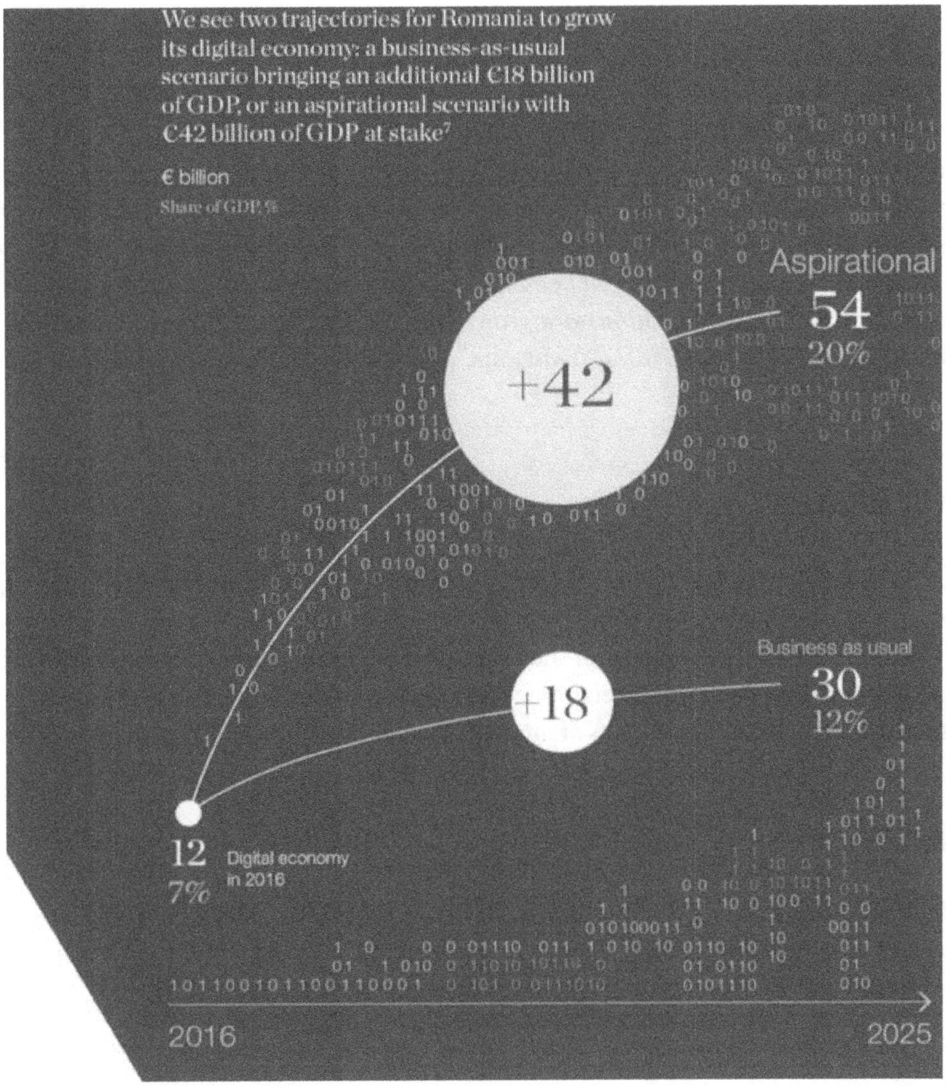

the capital contribution to the turnover. Or, this entails building an appropriate strategy to provide sub-sectors of long-term interest (agricultural sub-sectors with eco-production, for example), responsibilities for making important investments in agriculture (private investment, state aid, co- financial mechanisms to provide support to trigger an appropriate investment process.

Further, the strategy should be implemented consistently, irrespective of electoral cycles, in the economic policy mix, given the strategic importance of agriculture.

The most important aspect of our century is given by the fact that current digital financial technologies directly and positively influence the *17SDGs set out in the UN 2020 Agenda*, and this aspect will be dealt with especially in another future work of the author.

The current digitized financial technologies as can be seen through the indicators presented in the paper directly contribute to the development of innovation, technology transfer, entrepreneurship, but especially to the intelligent specialization in the financial field, as well as to the industrial transformation at global level. More, in conclusion with a work by Digital / McKinsey "*The rise of Digital Challengers*", within the detailed influences of digital technology in Central and Eastern Europe, and for Romania the trends can be found in the figure below:

As noted in the paper, Fintech is at the intersection of finance and technology, and the role of the human factor is much smaller compared to the role of technology in finance. More reflected key trends, such as the large volume of data and their availability,"*the exponential increase in computing power that allows the analysis of increasingly large data sets, wider access to and lower cost of goods and services, growth disintermediation and reintermediation and demographic and generational changes - all are heading towards a crossroads of significant changes determined by technology regarding the provision of financial services. Fintech applications are growing at an ever faster pace, creating new opportunities for better results for investors. At the same time, as with any change, new risks and vulnerabilities may arise*" [17].

ACKNOWLEDGMENT

This research received no specific grant from any funding agency in the public, commercial, or not-for-profit sectors.

Author Contributions: the structure of the real economy in the context of current fintech financial technology, developments, trends, and recommendations.

Conflicts of Interest: Declare conflicts of interest or state "The authors declare no conflict of interest."

REFERENCES

Anderson, C. R. J. (2013). *Segmentation of Smallholder Households: Meeting the Range of Financial Needs in Agricultural Families*. Focus Note 85. Washington, DC: CGAP. http://www.cgap.org/sites/default/files/Focus-Note-Segmentation-of- Smallholder-Households-April-2013.pdf

Arner D. W., Barberis J., & Buckley R. P. (2016). *The Evolution of FinTech: A New Post-Crisis*. Academic Press.

Brummer, C., & Gorfine, D. (2014). *FinTech: Building a 21st-Century Regulator's Toolkit*. Milken Institute – Center for Financial Markets.

Ferrell, O. C., Fraedich, J., & Ferrell, L. (2014). Business Ethics: Ethical Decision Making and Case (10th ed.). Academic Press.

Goldstein, I., Jiang, W., & Karolyi, G. (2019, May). To FinTech and Beyond. *Review of Financial Studies, 32*(5), 1647–1661. doi:10.1093/rfs/hhz025

Gravelle, H., & Ress, R. (1992). *Microeconomics*. Longman Group Limited.

Hajkova, D., & Hurnik, J. (2007). Cobb-Douglas Production Function: The Case of a Converging Economy. *Finance a Uver, 57*(9-10), 465–476.

Karagianis, G., Palivos, T., & Papageorgiou, C. (2004). *Variable Elasticity of Substitution and Economic Growth: Theory and Evidence*. Department of Economics, University of Macedonia.

Kavuri, A. S., & Milne, A. (2019). *Fintech and the Future of Financial Services: What Are the Research Gaps?* Centre for Applied Macroeconomic Analysis. https://papers.ssrn.com/sol3/papers.cfm?abstract_id=3333515

Klump, R., & de La Grandville, O. (2000). Economic Growth and Elasticity of Substitution. *The American Economic Review*, *90*(1), 282–291. doi:10.1257/aer.90.1.282

Lovell, C. A. K. (1973). CES and VES Production Functions in a Cross-Section Context. *Journal of Political Economy*, *81*(3), 705–720. doi:10.1086/260066

Manta, O. (2017). New challenges in economic science. LAP LAMBERT Academic Publishing.

Manta, O. (2019). Financial Market Trends, a Local Mission & a Global Vision. LAP LAMBERT Academic Publishing.

Manta, O. (2019). The instrument of globalization for the societal partnership (Sustainable Development Goals UN. *Global Economy Review: A Monthly Journal*. http://iige.co/global-economy-review-a-monthly-journal /

Marin, D. (1997). *Microeconomics*. ASE Publishing House.

Sato, R., & Hoffman, F. (1968). Production Functions with Variable Elasticity of Substitution: Some Analysis and Testing. *The Review of Economics and Statistics*, *50*(4), 453–460. doi:10.2307/1926813

Stancu, S., & Andrei, T. (1997). *Microeconomics*. All Publishing House.

Stefanescu, S. (2004). Solving a non-linear regression model used in the economy. *Economic Studies and Economic Cybernetics Studies and Research, 3*, 59-69.

Yaga, D., Mell, P., Roby, N., & Scarfone, K. (2018). *Blockchain Technology Overview*. Draft NISTR 8202. Gaithersburg, MD: National Institute of Science and Technology, U.S. Department of Commerce. https://csrc.nist.gov/CSRC/media/Publications/nistir/8202/draft/documents/nistir8202-draft.pdf

Zellner, A., & Ryu, H. (1998). Alternative Functional Forms for Production, Cost and Returns to Scale Functions. *Journal of Applied Econometrics*, *13*(2), 101–127. doi:10.1002/(SICI)1099-1255(199803/04)13:2<101::AID-JAE465>3.0.CO;2-V

ENDNOTE

[1] RON- is the national currency of Romania, 1 EURO = 4.76 RON

APPENDIX

Number of firms in agriculture in 2008 - 2016 which meet the conditions for determining the Cobb-Douglas function

No. crt.	Subsectors of agriculture	Period								
		2008	2009	2010	2011	2012	2013	2014	2015	2016
1	Cultivation of cereals (excluding rice), leguminous plants and oleaginous plants	3638	3603	3808	4071	4305	4556	4761	5222	5507
2	Cultivation of vegetables and melons, roots and tubers	274	280	304	350	381	378	367	391	435
3	Growing grapes	106	106	122	138	150	147	156	190	194
4	Growing fruit of berries, strawberries, nuts and other fruit trees	88	89	101	113	117	129	142	176	217
5	Breeding of dairy cattle	362	361	358	379	363	364	361	356	372
6	Pig breeding	158	203	236	274	296	272	291	293	294
7	Bird breeding	275	289	313	336	354	379	380	389	386
8	Activities in mixed farms (plant culture combined with livestock breeding)	536	552	557	591	619	627	649	681	716
9	Auxiliary activities for crop production	742	740	922	1197	1271	1265	1252	1230	1076
10	Forestry and other forestry activities	1232	1075	1022	1006	908	868	809	779	741
11	Forest exploitation	1228	1354	1447	1596	1689	1775	1828	1984	2041
12	Marine aquaculture and freshwater (321 + 322)	211	236	253	262	276	303	311	311	333
13	Total 1-12	8850	8888	9443	10313	10729	11063	11307	12002	12312
14	Total companies in agriculture	9835	9763	10297	11178	11594	11953	12242	13003	13399

Source: own processing

Variable:

A - proportionality factor;

α - the elasticity of the turnover figure relative to net fixed assets;

β - the elasticity of the number of factions in relation to the workforce;

R - multiple correlation coefficient

Evolution of the parameters of the Cobb-Douglas function for some sub-sectors of Romanian agriculture in the period 2008-2016

No.crt.	Subsectors of agriculture	variable	Period								
			2008	2009	2010	2011	2012	2013	2014	2015	2016
1	Cultivation of cereals (excluding rice), leguminous plants and oleaginous plants	A	3.503355	3.142805	3.910642	4.074577	4.123317	4.233467	4.351747	4.295940	4.070652
		α	0.269352	0.272219	0.254042	0.282997	0.298516	0.309074	0.293882	0.253938	0.255526
		β	0.578863	0.602622	0.573380	0.544053	0.519323	0.497604	0.503639	0.546969	0.565031
		α + β	<1	<1	<1	<1	<1	<1	<1	<1	<1
		R	0.766547	0.779036	0.760644	0.767691	0.771068	0.781150	0.778675	0.790400	0.799040
2	Cultivation of vegetables and melons, roots and tubers	A	2.436544	1.883064	2.450426	2.471397	2.750117	3.169149	2.430731	2.158436	3.320117
		α	0.219743	0.256507	0.266858	0.285863	0.172113	0.186825	0.170336	0.154885	0.161084
		β	0.679135	0.685827	0.625878	0.600952	0.705980	0.656617	0.739084	0.785656	0.671591
		α + β	<1	<1	<1	<1	<1	<1	<1	<1	<1
		R	0.700926	0.726046	0.656892	0.726003	0.695711	0.716214	0.720009	0.752571	0.742566
3	Growing grapes	A	2.392759	2.582836	3.502915	2.588047	1.190263	2.032747	1.562855	2.872166	2.151918
		α	0.081389	0.044069	0.100635	0.140219	0.011801	0.191150	0.183983	0.122553	0.108900
		β	0.798604	0.827594	0.696108	0.714892	0.985731	0.707561	0.742807	0.717629	0.788263
		α + β	<1	<1	<1	<1	<1	<1	<1	<1	<1
		R	0.736705	0.741183	0.760141	0.691066	0.702276	0.754673	0.799688	0.776608	0.819126
4	Growing fruit of berries, strawberries, nuts and other fruit trees	A	2.374139	2.978044	3.530354	3.865454	4.130157	4.649408	4.962325	3.289892	3.207984
		α	0.113226	0.090040	0.339975	0.219003	0.083878	0.039245	0.084432	0.058040	0.083374
		β	0.782938	0.724150	0.404934	0.513990	0.642437	0.647724	0.550886	0.739158	0.709978
		α + β	<1	<1	<1	<1	<1	<1	<1	<1	<1
		R	0.650478	0.666831	0.693044	0.705171	0.651256	0.595805	0.601513	0.609416	0.633171
5	Breeding of dairy cattle	A	3.331285	2.601502	3.669957	3.053176	2.888068	2.979584	2.026778	1.896132	1.851829
		α	0.278963	0.304162	0.345343	0.254872	0.251597	0.222484	0.190816	0.233280	0.255339
		β	0.556815	0.578152	0.437362	0.611180	0.624408	0.653482	0.781474	0.734544	0.702822
		α + β	<1	<1	<1	<1	<1	<1	<1	<1	<1
		R	0.766330	0.786609	0.751651	0.788743	0.790780	0.787557	0.822965	0.834312	0.804027
6	Pig breeding	A	1.519984	1.677368	2.407314	2.699576	2.398304	3.501806	2.680236	3.023193	2.528730
		α	0.367902	0.486112	0.400810	0.219192	0.335196	0.303675	0.237418	0.302782	0.193244
		β	0.644210	0.503439	0.539659	0.750424	0.640379	0.599265	0.737615	0.625802	0.789763
		α + β	>1	<1	<1	<1	<1	<1	<1	<1	<1
		R	0.827592	0.807704	0.797661	0.787018	0.759258	0.763128	0.773065	0.759161	0.804566
7	Bird breeding	A	3.047636	3.003382	3.364928	3.523115	2.279362	1.341092	2.405400	1.772141	1.931592
		α	0.260984	0.135266	0.201215	0.186883	0.147702	0.126296	0.126173	0.052565	0.102308
		β	0.658638	0.813702	0.694707	0.705156	0.858114	0.948334	0.869768	0.999281	0.924289
		α + β	<1	<1	<1	<1	>1	>1	<1	>1	>1
		R	0.855934	0.826673	0.828454	0.781087	0.821482	0.806556	0.831777	0.852176	0.869961
8	Activities in mixed farms (plant culture combined with livestock breeding)	A	2.764225	1.728132	2.487053	2.285855	3.058836	2.187890	2.335240	1.882091	2.188075
		α	0.218919	0.258754	0.272044	0.213373	0.242791	0.214695	0.271824	0.186147	0.253572
		β	0.674360	0.711472	0.636812	0.735580	0.633587	0.742126	0.662557	0.794955	0.686388
		α + β	<1	<1	<1	<1	<1	<1	<1	<1	<1
		R	0.749751	0.799107	0.760161	0.745319	0.733464	0.750872	0.786138	0.783564	0.792130
9	Auxiliary activities for crop production	A	2.616150	2.363838	3.030756	4.803998	4.895449	4.284594	3.896002	3.475820	1.960113
		α	0.380473	0.325464	0.197000	0.177316	0.150695	0.190080	0.192824	0.184818	0.233449
		β	0.501114	0.584058	0.660610	0.506703	0.528193	0.537568	0.571769	0.607348	0.700365
		α + β	<1	<1	<1	<1	<1	<1	<1	<1	<1
		R	0.701209	0.720815	0.646643	0.522841	0.547120	0.550565	0.582812	0.581394	0.647573
10	Forestry and other forestry activities	A	3.645020	3.462687	3.895880	3.706681	3.833022	4.183467	3.744406	3.940362	3.755674
		α	0.260118	0.232481	0.228278	0.193797	0.230976	0.191238	0.143722	0.117104	0.108523
		β	0.577677	0.610245	0.579115	0.636290	0.585539	0.600445	0.686290	0.692726	0.714351
		α + β	<1	<1	<1	<1	<1	<1	<1	<1	<1
		R	0.776865	0.784756	0.752763	0.781790	0.773606	0.775863	0.806315	0.788355	0.829097
11	Forest exploitation	A	3.117888	3.044019	3.252671	3.463774	3.248451	3.102388	3.021757	2.980746	2.187519
		α	0.246246	0.232286	0.244850	0.191510	0.182757	0.191501	0.149097	0.162104	0.158310
		β	0.650494	0.660365	0.644690	0.684926	0.710921	0.719811	0.771990	0.760624	0.825641
		α + β	<1	<1	<1	<1	<1	<1	<1	<1	<1
		R	0.823749	0.785400	0.796665	0.805819	0.785454	0.789368	0.808820	0.804317	0.819590
12	Marine aquaculture and freshwater	A	3.216120	2.547377	3.028152	3.401658	3.648661	4.111378	4.161632	4.171734	3.129802
		α	0.225283	0.061814	0.134544	0.242304	0.160370	0.077330	0.077797	0.055169	0.016612
		β	0.580602	0.796138	0.678487	0.521950	0.596114	0.627863	0.622543	0.669984	0.800460
		α + β	<1	<1	<1	<1	<1	<1	<1	<1	<1
		R	0.723352	0.645095	0.702384	0.610778	0.656898	0.592372	0.532784	0.598716	0.692872

Source: own processing

Chapter 3
An Overview of International Fintech Instruments Using Innovation Diffusion Theory Adoption Strategies

Ebru Saygili
Yasar University, Turkey

Tuncay Ercan
Yasar University, Turkey

ABSTRACT

The aim of this chapter is to evaluate and predict the future of international fintech instruments in the domain of innovation diffusion theory (IDT) adoption strategies. Further, the consequences of the new payments system directive (PSD2) in Europe and blockchain applications are discussed. For instance, money transfer and payments have the highest rate of adoption (ROA) while insurance services have the highest speed of growing ROA due to relative advantages, high compatibility and trialability levels, and low level of complexity and uncertainty. Cross country comparisons include descriptive statistics about fintech deal value and volume, innovation rank, B2C commerce market, ROA and internet penetration. Germany is the only country listed in all of the top 10 ranking lists, followed by the U.S., the U.K., and France. Also, China, India, and Canada have distinguished success in terms of fintech indicators while the growth in Japan is expected to be slow. Accordingly, ROA in five emerging markets is much higher than some of the developed countries which can be explained by the Cancian Theory.

DOI: 10.4018/978-1-7998-3257-7.ch003

INTRODUCTION

Financial technologies, such as ATMs, POS machines, payment and transaction systems, have been used since the 1960s. New financial technologies (fintech) have led to the growth of decentralized financial solutions and innovative new business startups. Currently, financial and non-financial businesses and individuals are trying to keep up with the accelerating number of fintech innovations. While new instruments are being formed, leading to further innovations, some existing business models are expected to disappear. Initial research indicates that some fintech innovations are challenged by rapid growth while the future of others remains uncertain. This chapter aims to evaluate fintech instruments in terms of innovation diffusion theory (IDT) strategies, developed by Rogers (1995) summarized in Figure 1.

Fintech startups are at the center of the fintech ecosystem (Lee and Shin, 2018). Based on prior research (Ernest and Young, 2017; Lee and Shin, 2018, CB Insights, 2018), the different fintech business models operating in various hubs are money transfer and payment, financial planning, savings and investments, borrowing, insurance, blockchain/crypto and regulation technologies (regtech). The chapter aims to provide a theoretical discussion of why the rate of adoption (ROA) of different fintech business models in a social system varies, and why the ROA of a single fintech instrument varies across different social systems. This study helps to understand the indicators related to ROA to predict the future of fintech instruments. Further discussions about block-chain applications and a revised directive on payment service (PSD2) in Europe are included. The research stream about fintech business models is accelerating so another aim of this study is to provide new research areas related to this.

Rogers (1962) in his book which holds the second most cited second book in the social sciences (blogs.lse.ac.uk, 2016), argued that innovation diffusion was a general process displaying patterns and regularities, determined by the adopters, places and/or cultures. Diffusion is a process where innovation is communicated through certain channels over time among the members of a social system (Rogers, 1995). This requires communication to exchange messages and information about a new idea to reduce uncertainty. The results of the invention, diffusion and adoption of innovation lead to social change. In the first part of the chapter, the IDT framework is summarized in five stages, adapted from Rogers' book "Diffusion of Innovations". The stages are explained with current examples from the international fintech instruments. The second part of the chapter evaluates and discusses the developments in the international fintech industry using IDT components. The discussion includes adoption rates of various innovative technologies, cross country comparisons, new payments system directive in Europe and blockchain applications.

FINTECH IMPLEMENTATIONS USING IDT ADOPTION STRATEGIES

IDT, developed by Rogers, covers a wide range of issues about the adoption strategies of innovations. This process is summarized in five stages in Figure 1. The stages, variables, assumptions, and explanations are adapted from his book "Diffusion of Innovations" to discuss different fintech instruments. Accordingly, an innovation is an idea, practice or object that is perceived as new by an individual or other units of adoption. Innovation development process starts with recognizing a problem or need by the innovator and ends with adoption of a commercial product to satisfy that need by the users (adopters). During the diffusion, the variables determining the rate of adoption affects the innovation decision process of the users leading to adoption or rejection decision. The first adopters in the society are innovators while the latest adopters are laggards. The diffusion process ends with rate of adoption and the related consequences.

Strategy Development Process for Fintech Implementations

The process starts recognizing a problem or a need and ends with adoption. At a certain point during diffusion, the rate of adoption (ROA) begins to increase exponentially, taking off at about 10 to 25 percent adoption, to form the S-curve of diffusion presented in Figure 2. Innovations in money transfers and payments emerged because traditional mobile and e-commerce products didn't answer consumer and merchant needs (Ernst and Young 2016). As nonbanks started to transfer money, it became possible to make payments with a mobile phone at checkout or with cryptocurrency (digital currency). Crowdfunding, which is a new form of saving and investment formation, emerged largely because of the difficulties after the 2008 financial crisis when banks became less willing to provide project financing loans to entrepreneurs and early-stage enterprises. Hence, entrepreneurs started to look elsewhere for raising funds, such as project financing by friends and family, extended through social networks and social profiles.

Individuals and companies have accessed funds in debt, equity and donations for projects over the past five years. (World Bank, 2013). Similarly, because of the high-interest rates and limited funds offered by traditional lending financial institutions consumers and corporations started to use Peer to Peer (P2P) fintech platforms to borrow from each other by matching lenders and borrowers. They offer low-interest rates and an efficient lending process using alternative credit models and data analytics in pricing risks. High tech industries pass through four stages of development (Rogers, 1995). At the innovation stage, the degree of uncertainty is high so few firms are founded. At the initiation stage, the degree of uncertainty decreases so more new firms enter the industry. In the third stage, technological competition starts, which makes it difficult for smaller firms to enter the industry. During the final stage, standardization, the ideal product has been found and price competition started.

Figure 1. Innovation diffusion theory
Source: Adapted from Rogers, 1995

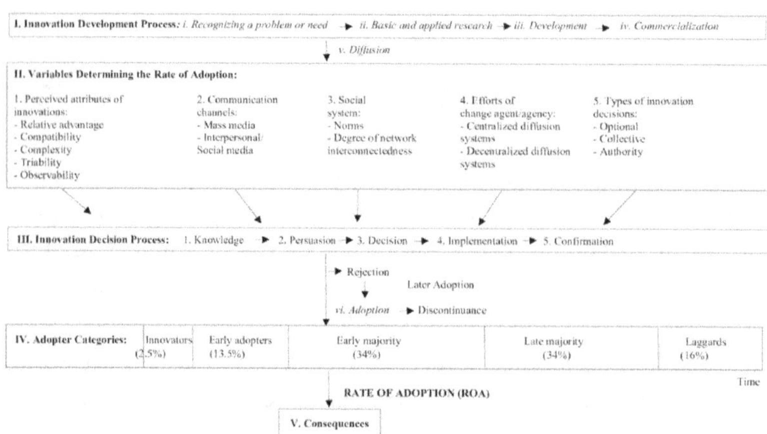

Figure 2. The diffusion process
Source: Rogers, 1995

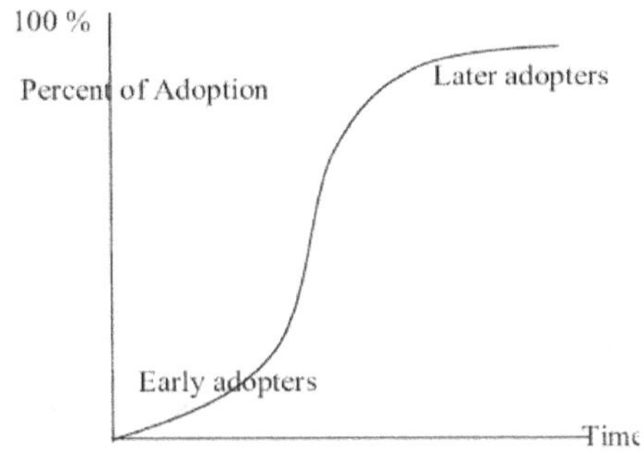

Variables Determining the Rate of Fintech Adoption in IDT

ROA is the number of members using innovation in a social system during a specified time interval. ROA is important in achieving success in IDT strategies. The five variables determining the rate of adoption are discussed below:

Perceived Attributes of Innovation: This consists of five components related to innovations: relative advantage, compatibility, complexity, trialability, and observability. One of the best predictors of ROA is a *relative advantage*, which indicates benefits like economic profitability, social prestige or other user gains and costs from preferring the new product. A majority of fintech innovations offer economic profitability, such as lower payment fees, lower borrowing interest rates, easy access to funds, higher investment returns and rewards. Other advantages include efficiency, and savings in time and effort, like shorter transaction periods. For instance, crowdfunding enables businesses and other organizations to raise money through donations or investments from multiple individuals (World Bank, 2013). Contributors have a wide range of reward, donation or equity-based project choices.

In the millennium era, many people gain social prestige by showing that they are closely following the latest technology and social media. Members of society seek to gain status by imitating the innovation behavior of others, as can be seen in the dramatic growth of social media. When individuals adopt an innovation that they should have rejected then over adoption occurs. Insufficient information, inability to predict the innovation's consequences or adopting it for status-seeking purposes may lead to over adoption. This is a major problem for many innovations, which sometimes happens when an attribute of an innovation is perceived as so attractive that people lose rationality. Past crises in financial markets taught that over adoption may cause huge losses to investors so regulations are necessary. In July 2015, there were 2,136 P2P lending platforms in China settling approximately U.S.$13.4 billion-worth of transactions, with 130 closed between January and March 2015, and more than 1,250 regarded as at risk by local credit rating agencies. The speed of the sector led to the enactment of new capital requirements by the Chinese Banking Regulatory Commission (Arner and Barberis, 2015).

The degree that innovation is perceived as consistent with current values, former experiences, ideas introduced already and the adopters' needs are the *compatibility* dimension. Compatible innovations are adopted faster and with a lower degree of innovativeness. However, even highly compatible innovations are useful for the adoption rates of future innovations. To achieve compatibility, innovations are presented as a bundle of new ideas called technology clusters (hubs) in which more distinguishable features are perceived as interrelated. Other factors affecting the compatibility of innovations are naming the innovation, positioning the innovation and indigenous knowledge systems. *Complexity* is the difficulty of using the innovation. According to IDT, ROA decreases as the degree of complexity increases. *Trialability* is the opportunity of experimenting with innovation. An innovation that is trialable is less uncertain for the adopter. The trialability of an innovation is positively related to its ROA. According to IDT, ROA increases as the degree of trialability increases. The final component, *observability*, represents how visible the innovation is to others. As the degree of observability increases, ROA increases.

Communication Channels: Communication is the information exchange, through communication channels, regarding an innovation between someone who has experience of the innovation and someone else who lacks any knowledge. Communication is essential for successful diffusion. Two major communication channels are mass media and interpersonal channels. Mass media channels (including social media, such as Facebook or Twitter) pass messages to large crowds through an intermediary. Interpersonal channels (including internal communication channels, such as WhatsApp, Facebook Messenger, Viber, SMS or e-mail) are direct exchanges between individuals.

Social System: Norms determine the behavior patterns of individuals living in the social system. Because norms guide individual behaviors, they can hinder change. Although all the system's members are not identical, a structure exists. The formal social structure is the patterned arrangements of individuals in a system that makes their behavior predictable whereas the informal social structure determines the level and timing of interactions in interpersonal networks. A communication network consists of individuals linked by patterned flows of information. An individual's network links affect ROA. Interconnectedness, which is the degree to which the units in a social system are linked by interpersonal networks, is positively related to the ROA of innovations (Rogers, 1995).

Change Agent's Efforts: Change agencies employ change agents to influence the clients' innovation decisions. An innovation's ROA is affected by the change agents' promotion efforts. According to IDT, change agents perform a variety of roles (Rogers, 1995), such as developing a need for change, informing the client, identifying problems, building intent and converting it into action, and making adoption permanent. A change agent's efforts include compatibility with the clients' needs and empathy. Are there any change agents in fintech implementations and, if any, who are they? Are the clients their change agents? In some cases, like blockchain and crowdfunding, the answer is yes. In others, because all the transactions are digital and take place through the internet, change agencies have direct contact with customers so there are no individuals employed as change agents. Due to recent developments in fintech, we believe that a change agent's role will be performed by artificial intelligence (AI). Companies in financial and e-commerce industries need to build new processes to perform the change agent's roles. Google, for instance, being aware of future demand for personal data to track individuals' needs, is the leading investor (Google Ventures – GV) in fintech startups. Other than Google, leading companies investing in fintech ventures in the U.S include Microsoft, Amazon, IBM, and Apple (CB Insights, 2017). As incentives increase, ROA increases. Amazon offers a certain percentage of cashback for store and credit cards. The company is attracting merchants to the Amazon Pay network through swipe fees, announcing that it will pass on the special card savings it receives from the card network to Amazon Pay using retailers. The company competes on fees by leveraging scale. It launched Amazon Cash in April 2017 to appeal to underbanked and unbanked households in and outside the U.S. In India, 190 million citizens are unbanked while just 37% of adults have a bank account in Mexico. Customers deposit cash, without a fee, into a digital account by showing a physically or digitally printed barcode at a partner brick-and-mortar retailer, such as CVS or 7-11 (CB Insights, 2018).

If innovation is decentralized, clients can become their change agents. Rogers suggests that decentralized diffusion systems are more suitable for diffusing innovations that do not require a high level of technical expertise where users have relatively heterogeneous conditions. In centralized diffusion systems, the direction of diffusion is from experts to local users of innovations where decisions are made by top managers and technical specialists. Innovations emerge from formal R&D activities that create a need for innovation where there is less local adoption and re-invention. In decentralized diffusion systems, there is peer diffusion through horizontal networks where adopters can make decisions about managing the diffusion. User participation solving problems and making modifications increases the adaptation of decentralized systems. Innovations come from local experimentation by non-experts who are often users with a high degree of local adaptation and reinvention. In situations that involve a high level of technical expertise and where homogenous conditions exist, centralized systems may fit better. A diffusion system contains components of both centralized and decentralized diffusion systems.

Types of Innovation Decisions: There are three types of decisions regarding adopting or rejecting an innovation. Optional innovation decisions are choices made by an individual free from the decisions of other members of the social system. Collective innovation decisions are made by consensus among the members of a system. Authority innovation decisions are made by a few individuals who possess power, status or technical expertise. For example, the European Union (EU) payment systems directive (PSD2) is an authority innovation decision. Finally, contingent innovation decisions are only made after a prior innovation decision. For instance, as the number of lending platforms increases, the number of credit risk monitoring and assessment platforms increases too.

The Decision Process in IDT Adoption Strategies

According to IDT, the innovation-decision process can lead to either adoption or rejection. Innovation-decision process is an information seeking and processing activity in which an individual obtains information in order to decrease uncertainty and it has five steps:

(1) Knowledge, when the customer is informed about an innovation's presence and how it works
(2) Persuasion, when the customer builds a favorable or unfavorable approach
(3) Decision, when the customer performs activities which lead to a choice to adopt or reject
(4) Implementation, when the customer starts using the new product
(5) Confirmation, when the reinforcement of the individual need to continue using the new product

Prior conditions like previous practice, felt needs and problems, innovativeness and the norms of the social system also affect the innovation-decision process. Identifying end users' perceptions of critical success factors affecting innovation decision process is important in achieving efficient results in technological innovation (Saygili et al., 2017a; Saygili and Saygili, 2017b). Prior conditions like previous practice, felt needs and problems, innovativeness and the norms of the social system also effect the innovation decision process.

Adopter Categories and Time

The members of the social system can be classified into different adopter categories based on innovativeness. Innovativeness is the extent to which an individual adopts new ideas earlier than other individuals of society. There are five adopter categories with different dominant attributes: innovators are venturesome, early adopters are respectable, the early majority is deliberate, the late majority are skeptical and laggards are traditional (Rogers, 1995). According to IDT, there are differences between earlier and later adopters of innovations in terms of socioeconomic status, personality variables and communication behavior. A selected of Rogers' generalizations about the characteristics of adopter categories are given

Table 1. Selected characteristics of adopter categories and their effects on innovativeness

Socioeconomic Characteristics	Expected effect on innovativeness	Personality variables	Expected effect on innovativeness	Communication Behavior	Expected effect on innovativeness
Age	not related	Empathy	positive	Social participation	positive
Education	positive	Dogmatism	negative	Interconnectedness	positive
Literacy	positive	Rationality	positive	Cosmopolitanness	positive
Higher social status	positive	Intelligence	positive	Change agent contact	positive
Upward social mobility	positive	Positive attitude toward change	positive	Mass media exposure	positive
Larger sized units	Positive	ability to cope with uncertainty	positive	interpersonal communication channels	positive

Source: (Rogers, 1996)

in Table 1. He concluded that earlier adopters have higher socioeconomic status than late adopters. On the other hand, the Cancian dip theory proposes that individuals of low-middle socioeconomic status are more innovative than individuals of high-middle status because they have less to lose, especially at the beginning of the diffusion of innovation, when there is a high degree of uncertainty (Gartrell, 1981). Cancian divides wealth into four ranks; low, low middle, high middle and high. He argues that individuals of high middle rank will risk less than individuals of low middle rank (Cancian, 1967) and he predicted a downward dip (Morrison et al.,1976).

According to the results of recent research analyzing global ROA for 20 markets (Ernst and Young, 2017), the global ROA average of 33%, with five emerging markets being above this average: South Africa (35%), Mexico (36%), Brazil (40%), India (52%) and China (69%). On the other hand, the ROA for developed countries like Belgium (13%), Japan (14%), Canada (18%) and the Netherlands (27%) is lower. Can this be explained by the Cancian dip theory? The same study also indicates that the highest ROA is observed at ages 25 to 34 (48%) while it is lower for older ages, 35 to 44 (41%), 45 to 54 (30%) and 55 to 64 (22%), and younger ages 18 to 24 (37%). Although IDT doesn't suggest any relationships between age and innovativeness, early evidence indicates that younger people use fintech more than the older ones.

Time: Time is an important dimension of IDT since ROA is measured in a given period. Taking time into consideration allows researchers to compare ROAs for different social, demographic and cultural groups. Recent technologies are diffusing faster than previous technologies. It took 75 years for telephones to reach 50 million users whereas Angry Birds was used by 50 million people within 35 days, Instagram was used by 300 million people within four years and WhatsApp had 700 million users within six years (CitiGPS, 2015). According to research covering the diffusion of 15 technologies in 166 countries in the past two centuries, it takes 45 years on average for countries to adopt new technologies, although this average varies significantly for particular technologies and countries. Overall, newer technologies have been adopted faster than older ones (Comin and Hobjin, 2010). The diffusion curve for proximity mobile transactions in Figure 3 exemplifies rapid adoption. By 2020, it is expected to have been adopted by 26% of the population using mobile phones, which means it will have reached the early majority stage (16%-50%).

Figure 3. Proximity mobile payment transaction curve in U.S.
The percentage of adoption is calculated by dividing the total number of mobile phone users by proximity mobile payment transaction users. Calculations for 2018, 2019 and 2020 are forecasts.
Source: (statista.com, 2018a); (statista.com, 2018b)

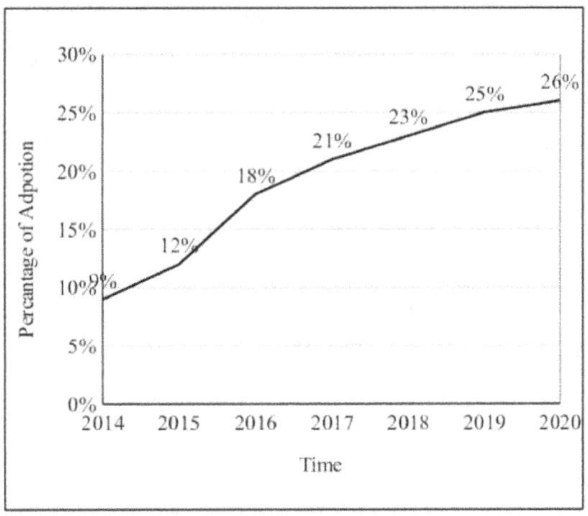

Consequences

Adoption of innovation leads to the following types of changes in the social system:

- **Desirable versus undesirable consequences**: Desirable consequences are the innovation's positive effects on the social system whereas undesirable consequences are its negative effects. For instance, the widespread usage of automation in banking generated cost savings whereas many middle-level workers lost their jobs. In the current unequal socioeconomic system, innovations usually increase inequality, as will be discussed below.

- **Direct consequences versus indirect consequences:** Direct consequences appear as soon as the innovation is adopted whereas indirect consequences appear later as a result of direct consequences. For example, Facebook, Apple, Microsoft, Google and Amazon (FAMGA) are making the majority of investments in fintech industry. This is the direct consequence of adopting fintech. On the other hand, through these new technologies, FAMGA companies will serve bigger markets within a very short period whereas small companies will not be able to enter the market, thereby creating more economic inequality (Rosen, 1981).
- **Anticipated consequences versus unanticipated consequences:** Anticipated consequences are the expected changes from the innovation whereas unanticipated consequences are the unexpected changes. For instance, approximately 50% of jobs in finance and insurance are expected to be at risk due to the adoption of fintech (CitiGPS, 2015).

EVALUATION OF INTERNATIONAL FINTECH INSTRUMENTS USING THE IDT STRATEGIES

Current digital and physical technologies that emerged in the Fourth Industrial Revolution have affected the financial sector including the following issues (Olsson, 2018):

- Automated and algorithm-driven services enable the creation, distribution, and storage of data.
- Blockchain and distributed ledger systems can provide transparency and security in regulatory compliance with the lower transaction and transfer costs through digital currencies.
- Advances in artificial intelligence will provide non-human investment, finance, and pension services.
- The widespread use of peer-to-peer computing has led to the development of direct financing platforms where the borrower and the saver meet.
- Another driving force has been the huge global losses in traditional financial markets during the past financial crises. Crowdfunding platforms offer alternative finance and investment opportunities, especially to younger generations.

In this section, various indicators related to the international fintech industry are discussed and compared using IDT components.

Comparison of Fintech Categories by Adoption Rates

This section discusses the underlying reasons for ROA variances in different fintech solutions in terms of the relative advantages introduced by IDT. Table 2, which compares fintech categories ranked by adoption rate in 2017, shows that money transfer and payments have the highest ROA while insurance services have the highest rate of ROA growth from 8% in 2015. The relative advantages of new payments and insurance services are ease of use, faster and more efficient services, and 24/7 accessibility (PwC, 2017). Uncertainty and risk levels are somewhat lower than the innovations in other categories. In contrast, borrowing services like P2P platforms have higher levels of uncertainty and risk so it is

Table 2. Comparison of fintech categories by adoption rates 2017

Type of Fintech	Rate of Adoption (%)
Money transfer and payments	50
Insurance	24
Savings and investments	20
Financial planning	10
Borrowing	10

Source: (Ernst and Young, 2017)

harder for borrowers to find funds if interest rates are not compelling. Regarding the compatibility and complexity dimensions, new payment solutions have become necessary due to the growth of global e-commerce. Users were already using credit cards, making money transfers through banks and buying insurance policies, which means payment and insurance innovations were consistent with current practices. The trialability of payment services is higher than other fintech innovations since adopters can use them in their everyday transactions, even for very small amounts. Observability was not so high in fintech innovations like mobile phones or tablets. Crowdfunding may have higher levels of visibility and effective use of communication channels due to the widespread use of social media platforms. The use of change agents may increase ROA for financial planning and borrowing services.

Table 3. Top ten countries in fintech deal value and deal volume

Fintech Deal Value (2017)		Fintech Deal Volume (2017)	
Country	($M)	Country	Num.
1. U.S.	7,053	1. U.S.	765
2. U.K.	1,783	2. U.K.	234
3. China	1,606	3. India	120
4. India	648	4. Germany	66
5. Hong kong	548	5. Canada	63
6. Sweden	478	6. France	47
7. Canada	444	7. China	39
8. Germany	331	8. Singapore	37
9. France	203	9. Switzerland	37
10. Singapore	130	10. Australia	31

Source: (InnovateFinance, 2017)

Cross-Country Comparison of Fintech Innovations

This section discusses cross-country indicators related to fintech within the IDT framework. Table 3, which presents the top ten country rankings for fintech deal value and volume in 2017, shows that the U.S. and U.K are the leading countries while 12 countries are ranked in the top ten for either fintech deal value or deal volume: U.S, U.K, China, India, Hong Kong, Sweden, Canada, Germany, France, Singapore, Switzerland, and Australia.

Table 4. Selected cross-country indicators related to fintech

Innovation Rank (2018)i		Countries with the Largest B2C Commerce Markets (2017) [ii]			FinTech Users' Adoption Rates (2017)[iii]		Internet Penetration (2017) [iv]	
Country Rank	Total Score	Country Rank	($bn)[ii]	Internet Users (M.)[iii]	Country Rank	%	Country Rank	%
1. S. Korea	89.28	**1. China**	682	772	**1. China**	69	**1. Germany**	97.3
2. Sweden	84.70	**2. U.S.**	438	312	**2. India**	52	**2. U.K.**	95.9
3. Singapore	83.05	**3. U.K.**	196	63	**3. U.K.**	42	3. Netherlands	95.9
4. Germany	82.53	**4. France**	95	60	4. Brazil	40	**4. the U.S.**	95.2
5. Switzerland	82.34	**5. Germany**	87	79	**5. Australia**	37	5. Japan	94.0
6. Japan	81.91	6. Japan	79	119	6. Spain	37	6. Spain	93.5
7. Finland	81.46	7. S. Korea	44	47	7. Mexico	36	7. S. Korea	93.0
8. Denmark	81.28	**8. Canada**	43	33	**8. Germany**	35	**8. France**	92.8
9. France	80.75	**9. India**	38	462	9. S. Africa	35	9. Italy	91.5
10. Israel	80.42	10. Italy	33	55	**10. U.S.**	33	**10. Canada**	89.4

Sources: [i] bloomberg.com; [ii] ecommercewiki.org; [iii] Ernst and Young, 2017 [iv] internetworldstats.com, countrymeters.info (countries with population over 10 million are included in internet penetration)

Table 4 presents the top ten countries using the Bloomberg innovation rank, largest B2C markets, fintech adoption rates and internet penetration for 2017. Bloomberg 2018 innovation index rankings are used because they are the results for the previous year. Countries also listed in Table 3 are shown in bold.

Comparing the countries listed in Tables 3 and 4 indicates the following:

- Only four countries (Sweden, Singapore, Germany, and France) from Table 3 are listed in the innovation ranking in Table 4.
- Seven countries (China, U.S., U.K., France, Germany, Canada, and India) from Table 3 are listed in the ten largest B2C commerce markets in Table 4.
- Six countries (China, India, U.K., Australia, Germany, and the U.S.) from Table 3 are listed in the fintech users' adoption rates in Table 4.
- Five countries (Germany, U.K., U.S., France, and Canada) from Table 3 are listed in the internet penetration rates in Table 4.

These results suggest that the fintech industry grows more rapidly in countries with a large B2C transaction volume than in more innovative countries. This raises the question of whether fintech is a diffusion of innovation or trade. The answer is both. The initial step in IDT is to recognize a problem or a need. Countries with high B2C volumes have a need or demand for fintech solutions. For the adopters in these countries, relative advantage, compatibility, and trialability levels are higher so fintech innovations diffuse faster. What about South Korea and Japan? Both are listed in the B2C commerce markets and Bloomberg innovation rankings, where South Korea has a leading position. Yet, it is not listed in the top ten fintech deal value or volume rankings. The reasons for the slow emergence of fintech ROA in Japan and South Korea, which may be social structure, norms, and the communication and decision behaviors of adopters, could be explored in future studies. The reasons may be social structure, norms, communication and decision behaviors of the adopters. For instance, Japan has the highest proportion of cash in circulation to GDP among developed countries and projects are underway to develop platforms using everything from QR codes to blockchain technology and digital currencies (Allan and Hagiwara, 2018). Even though, there is support from Japanese government, in terms of society acceptance and consumer awareness, the growth of fintech hubs in Japan is expected to be slow (Deloitte, 2017).

According to the results of recent research (Ernst and Young, 2017) analyzing global FinTech Users' Adoption Rates given in Table 4, China has a leading position with 69% ROA. The global ROA average is 33% where five emerging markets; South Africa (35%), Mexico (36%), Brazil (40%), India (52%) and China (69%) are above the global average of 33%. On the other hand, the same study indicates that ROA for developed countries like Belgium (13%), Japan is (14%), Canada (18%), Netherlands (27%) is lower. Can this be explained by Cancian dip theory? As stated in Table 1 in the previous section, according to IDT generalizations, early adopters are more literate and educated, with higher social status and larger-sized units (companies). These are the expected characteristics of adopters in developed countries that suit the countries in innovation ranking. While in fintech diffusion, ROA is much faster in some of the emerging countries like China, India, Brazil, Mexico, South Africa. The reasons may rely on under another IDT generalization which states that earlier adopters can cope with uncertainty

Table 5. A cross-country comparison of selected fintech indicators

	FinTech Deal Value (2017)	Fintech Deal Volume (2017)	Innovation Rank (2018)	Countries with the Largest B2C Commerce Markets (2017)	FinTech Users' Adoption Rates (2017)	Internet Penetration (2017)
1. U.S.	✓	✓		✓	✓	✓
2. U.K.	✓	✓		✓	✓	✓
3. China	✓	✓		✓	✓	
4. India	✓	✓		✓	✓	
5. Hong Kong	✓					
6. Sweden	✓	✓	✓			
7. Canada	✓	✓		✓		✓
8. Germany	✓	✓	✓	✓	✓	✓
9. France	✓	✓	✓	✓		✓
10. Singapore	✓	✓	✓			
11. Switzerland		✓				
12. Australia		✓			✓	

and risk. Additionally, they have a more favorable attitude towards borrowing money. Further research can investigate the issues related to fintech adoption in emerging markets.

Table 5 presents a combination of the results presented in Table 3 and Table 4 for 12 countries listed in Table 3. Germany is the only country listed in all top 10 rankings, followed by the U.S., U.K., and France listed in five of the top 10 rankings while Honk Kong is just listed in one ranking.

The Expected Consequences of the Payments System Directive (PSD2)

This section discusses the expected consequences of the revised Directive on Payment Service (PSD2). In 2018, EU member states are expected to implement PSD2 in their national laws. These rules apply to all payments and accounts in all currencies within the EU and European Economic Area (EEA) countries. Figure 4 presents the expected effects of PSD2 on the financial system, including the payments system, banks, fintech companies, and consumers. The directive's main objectives are to enhance integration, promote innovation, and increase transparency and efficiency with third party account access. The new directive expands the range of service providers, including non-banks, allowed to operate in the EU, which will encourage competition. For instance, in e-commerce payments, payment initiation service providers (PISP) establish a software bridge between a merchant's website and the online banking platform of the payer's account to initiate internet payments based on a credit transfer. Such services offer a low-cost solution for customers to shop without payment cards (EU Directive 2366, 2015). Account information service providers (AISP) will provide the user with aggregated online information on one or more payment accounts held with one or more payment service providers, and accessed via the online interfaces of the account servicing payment service provider. This will allow customers to view their financial situation in real-time (EU Directive 2366, 2015). Another objective is to improve customer protection, such as the Regulatory Technical Standards (RTS), which the European Commission adopted to strengthen the security of payment services across the EU.

PSD2 accelerates industry disruption by legalizing new forms of payment institutions and introducing new interaction models. According to the directive, banks have to share their application programming interfaces (APIs) with third parties (Turner and Hayer, 2018). PSD2 also enables consumers to use third-party providers for financial services so that customers may use Facebook or Google, for example, to pay bills, make transfers to their friends using their current bank account. (EVERY, 2018). Banks will be competing with every licensed third party, which will increase competition in the financial services market. Therefore, banks have to prepare for changing market conditions as well as the compliance requirements of PSD2 and RTS. They can create innovation and differentiation through collaboration with fintech companies.

Decentralized Fintech Innovation: Blockchain

Blockchain and distributed ledger systems and the underlined protocols proposed and designed by Satoshi Nakamoto provide a significant effect on the financial sector through Bitcoin cryptocurrency while handling transparency and security in regulatory compliance and enabling lower transaction and transfer costs (Nakamoto, 2008). Even though blockchain entered into economic life a little earlier, it is considered by some authors as a part of the industry 4.0 (Chunk and Kim, 2016). The photos or videos received by e-mail in the computer storage can easily be copied and send to other people. Unfortunately, IT technologies did not succeed in the same process in money transfer until 2008. This problem that is

Figure 4. Consequences of PSD2 on the financial system

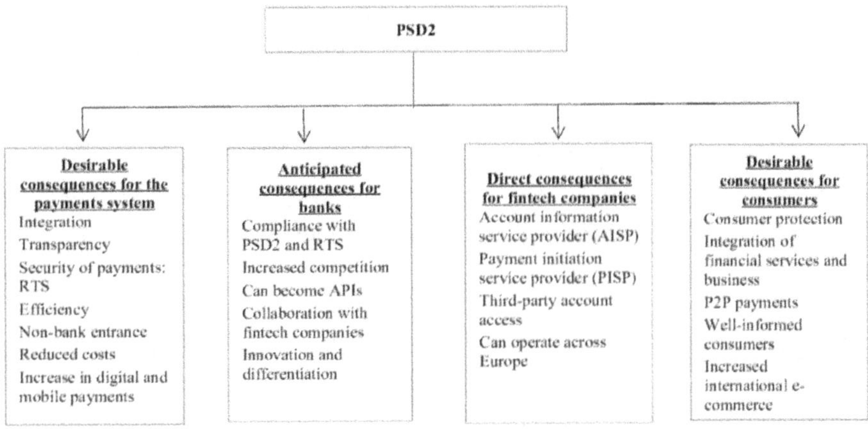

called money transfer without a banking system, which was supposed to be unresolvable in 2000 years, finally was enabled by Bitcoin, the first cryptocurrency, using the blockchain method. Collins (2016) stated that the society has become aware of the potential of blockchain technology not only cryptocurrency but also in many other areas.

Technical Background of Blockchain

Blockchains are digital books. Each page of this book is a "block", and these blocks are sorted without breaking the order in which they are created. It is not possible to change the order of a page, nor can it change the location of the block-chain rings linked to a common chain or root. The biggest reason of this usage reliable by the users, the information added to the system in some way is that it can never be changed or deleted because it is open to everyone in the system (Swan, 2015). Tschorsch and Scheuermann (2016) described the blockchain-based on Satoshi model as it is not a specific file, it is represented by transactions recorded in the chain itself blockchain. They also stated that it is a kind of spreadsheet to maintain and verify and each bitcoin transaction. It allows participants to secure the settlement of transactions, to achieve the transaction, and to transfer the assets at a low-cost. Especially transparency is one of the most important values of this system. Blockchain can work quickly on all computers that use public wallets and record all changes/transactions simultaneously. Therefore, the blockchain is highly resistant to manipulation and it is not possible to conceal any suspicious activity.

Palychata (2016) compared the blockchain structure with inventions that have made major changes in the industrial field, such as previous steam or combustion engines, and its potential for today's activities and business processes. A blockchain is a data structure that represents the record of each accounting move. Each account transaction is signed digitally to protect its authenticity and no one can intervene in this transaction. Smart contracts consisting of these different transactions are stored, reproduced and updated in the block chains distributed (Szabo, 1997). Since no manual action is required, both commercial banks and central banks believe that payments will become faster, more reliable and more controlled.

When a new account transaction order takes place in the system, or when an existing account transaction is modified, a certain algorithm will act on all records on the decentralized infrastructure to check the correctness of this new record. If most of the copies acknowledge the correctness of this record, a new blockchain is included in the system. If most of the user nodes in the system reject new recordings, this account movement cannot be recorded in the system. Smart contracts have gained a wide range of applications over time, from smart supply chains using Industrial Internet of Things, which are among the most technological terms of today, to all kinds of financial services (Hillbom and Tillström, 2016), Thanks to the distributed feature of the Blockchain system, the blockchain can operate effectively without having to be controlled from a single center.

Relative Advantages of Blockchain and Diffusion in Financial Services

The blockchain system, which also forms the infrastructure of Bitcoin, attracts the interests of large companies. This system as being faster and more secure works with the principle that the money transfers should be approved from many sources in different locations at the same time. For this reason, many different organizations from different industrial sectors have recently started to pay attention to this technology inspired by the distributed structure of the system. The following three benefits provided by blockchain technology make this system preferred;

- The lack of need for authority and intermediary systems reduces both costs and speeds up the transaction operations.
- The fact that many different points of control operations reduce the possibility of fraud in the system.
- A blockchain is an ideal platform for tracking where a financial entity/value comes from, which people pass through it and where it arrives.

When we look at emerging IT technologies, the only thing that is inevitable now is that new technologies in the world of the Internet are mostly related to the disciplines of electrical, computer or software engineering. No matter the resulting product is, the use of it by the public and its acceptance depend on these three components. According to (PwC., 2016), some of the technological innovations that financial institutions or organizations will not be able to avoid by 2020 and will have to adopt and implement is the blockchain for virtual currency systems, public cloud services for standard and public implementations and robotics and AI (Artificial Intelligence). These three systems will help diffuse new financial services.

Underwood (2015) discussed that distributed ledger technology (DLT) defined as the use of decentralized digital trust verification through encrypted digital signatures, will change the whole industry and trade and bring about an economical change globally by embedded reliable and secure features in private or public use. Economist (2015) made a positive assessment of blockchain technology as a trust machine.

We know that cash is still of vital importance for some people around the world. Those people who do not have bank accounts are automatically excluded from the financial system and e-commerce. Finally, thanks to virtual money systems in use, the only barrier between those and the system is that they have only one internet connectivity. This technology works and software developers are developing ways to use the blockchain for purposes beyond an alternative monetary system. Knezevic (2018) explained the impact of blockchain technology platform on the financial sector with cryptocurrency, and the impact on other industries. His studies show that it is still in the initial phase of changing many other industries, apart from the main impact in the financial sector. A significant number of organizations try to develop platforms based on blockchain technology according to Zheng et al. (2017). They listed some companies namely that integrated blockchain model to include identity and reputation systems and digital property management. There are some additional examples for blockchain inclusion in different industrial sectors like the music sector, medium-chain labs, and medical industry. Trustonic is a company developing a blockchain-based mobile operating system that can compete with Android and iOS. IBM provides block-chain services through its services which is a big opportunity for large companies to take a step in this area. Companies wishing to use block-chain technology will now be able to integrate this service into their systems by working with IBM. Master-chain and HyperLedger are two examples of blockchain platforms in use. However, both are used in different environments. The master-chain is designed for national or regional encryption standards and can be used for any kind of data. But the HyperLedger is open source and will be included in the global economic systems with Linux hosting and will be used by finance, banking, supply chain, IoT, manufacturing or technology companies (Kostin et al, 2017).

On the other hand, due to some of the disadvantages, blockchain is not widely adopted yet. The biggest disadvantage of the blockchain is that it is still quite slow. Every application built on a blockchain means that all changes to this blockchain are processed once every change is made. For example, Bitcoin can only process 8 transactions per second, while the Ethereum is 13. Visa, which is responsible for legally recognized current money transfers, performs 56,000 transactions and is fully centralized. Another problem with the system is that it is difficult to implement. Because this open-source system is designed and structured differently by different software groups, in the direction of different ideals. This prevents the establishment of a standard. The key issue in the different industrial monetary systems that use blockchain mechanisms is the ability to protect the standards between multiple interconnected systems (Golohvastov et al., 2016). Because evaluating the money transfer values in the blockchain platform and adapting them to the currently adopted standards requires a very clear, precise and common regulation. The powerful algorithms in blockchain and the complex contract systems in Ethereum have led to the development of common and unbiased regulating algorithms (Pokrovskaia, 2016). To find a solution to the standardization problem, large IT companies such as IBM, Cisco, Fujitsu, and Financial organizations like J.P. Morgan, Accenture aim to establish a system called Hyperledger. These companies set up a consortium to aggregate open-source block-chain implementations and want to create a large infrastructure to provide cross-sectoral money transfer. IBM company offered new blockchain services and standards working on Cloud and Docker platforms to ensure the security of these services (IBM Blockchain, 2018). Regulatory groups on tax and customs services work on analytical and intelligent algorithms for the transparency of all value transfers and the automatic determination of transfer fees within a controlled economic market (Alexankov et al., 2017).

CONCLUSION

The study aims to explain the reasons for divergent fintech innovation and country adoption rates in light of IDT introduced by Rogers. IDT has four main components which are; innovation, communication channels, social system and time. In the first part of the chapter, IDT is illustrated in five stages; innovation development process, variables determining the rate of adoption, the innovation-decision process, adopter categories, and consequences. Every stage is explained with current examples from fintech innovations. In the second part indicators related to the international fintech industry are evaluated with cross country descriptive statistics using the IDT framework. The evaluation included a comparison of adoption rates for different fintech innovations, expected consequences of PSD2 and blockchain applications. The divergence of fintech instruments' adoption rates can be explained with IDT which assumes relative advantages, higher compatibility and triability levels will increase ROA. Another assumption of IDT which expects a higher positive effect of social status conflicts with lower rates of fintech adoption in countries like Belgium, Canada and Netherlands and higher levels of fintech adoption in countries like China, Mexico, India and Brazil. This situation provides evidence for Cancian theory which argues that individuals of low-middle socioeconomic status are more innovative than individuals of high-middle status because they have less to lose, especially at the beginning of the diffusion of an innovation, when there is a high degree of uncertainty. The study has several implications for researchers and fintech industry innovators. According to the discussions covered throughout the study, the following propositions are suggested about fintech innovations:

- Innovations having direct economic significance and perceived as most rewarding while involving the least risks and uncertainty should be accepted most rapidly (Rogers, 1995). For instance, money transfer and payments have the highest ROA while insurance services have the highest speed of growing ROA due to relative advantages, high compatibility and trialability levels and low level of complexity and uncertainty.
- New communication channels are added to mass media channels (including social media such as Facebook, Twitter, etc.) and interpersonal channels (including internal communication channels such as WhatsApp, Facebook Messenger, Viber, SMS, e-mail, etc.).
- Almost all of the fintech transactions occur through the internet where the change agencies have a direct contact with customers and there are no individuals employed as change agents. Due to the recent developments in fintech it can be expected that a change agent's role will be performed by artificial intelligence (AI). Companies in financial and e-commerce industries need to build new processes to perform the roles of the change agent. For instance, Google, aware of the future demand for personal data to track individuals' needs, is the leading company (Google Ventures – GV) investing in fintech startups. The leading companies investing in fintech ventures in the U.S other than Google are; Microsoft, Amazon, IBM, and Apple.
- Even though IDT doesn't suggest any relationships between age and innovativeness early evidence indicates that younger people use fintech than the older ones.
- Newer technologies have been adopted faster than old ones. Developments on the internet and new communication platforms areare some of the main reasons which accelerate the speed of the diffusion. Diffusion curve for proximity mobile transaction in an example for the fast speed of adoption. By 2020 it is expected to be adopted by 26% of the population using mobile phones which means it will reach to early majority stage (16%-50%).
- The widespread use of automation in the banking industry which generated cost savings is an example of desirable consequences of a fintech innovation whereas many middle-level workers losing their jobs and increasing the level of inequality are undesirable consequences.
- The investments of Facebook, Apple, Microsoft, Google and Amazon in fintech industry are an illustration of the direct consequences of fintech innovation. This is the direct consequence of adopting fintech. Indirect consequences can be illustrated as; with new technologies, big companies will serve bigger markets in a very short period where small companies will not be able to enter the market creating more economic inequality.

- An exampleof an anticipated consequences is; approximately 50% of the jobs in the finance and insurance industry are expected to be at risk due to the adoption of fintech.
- Fintech industry grows more rapidly in countries that have large B2C transaction volume than that countries. So fintech phenomena are it a diffusion of innovation or trade? The answer is both. The initial stage of IDT is to recognize a problem or a need. Countries with high B2C volumes have a need or demand for fintech solutions. For the adopters in these countries' relative advantage, compatibility and trialability levels are higher so fintech innovations diffuse faster.
- S. Korea and Japan are the two countries are listed in both in B2C commerce markets top 10 and Bloomberg innovation top 10 rank where S. Korea has a leading position. But the countries are not listed in the top 10 fintech deal value or volume rankings. According to IDT, social norms are one of the main determinants of innovation diffusions. Japan has the highest proportion of cash in circulation to GDP. The slow emergence of fintech ROA in Japan and S. Korea can be explored in future studies.
- ROA in fintech innovations is much faster in some of the emerging countries like China, India, Brazil, Mexico, South Africa than developed countries like Belgium, Japan, and Canada. The reasons may rely on under another IDT generalization which states that earlier adopters can cope with uncertainty and risk. Additionally, they have more favorable attitude towards borrowing money. Further research can investigate the issues related to fintech adoption in emerging markets.
- The new payment systems directive (PSD2) is expected to have consequences on the payments system, banks, fintech companies, and customers.
- Blockchains are not centralized. This is also the biggest factor that makes them safe anyway. Besides the organizations like a central bank that affect countries' monetary systems from a single-center, this system is distributed all over the world. Therefore, even if security attacks affect only one region, it is not difficult to recover because trade and money transfers continue in other regions. The block-chain system is based on the principle that money transfer is approved by different sources.
- The new technology blockchain, which will impact the lives the many people in the coming years, is changing the lifestyles, especially in some financial services with different cryptographic currencies currently in use. However, although the blockchain is often associated with these virtual currencies, this technology has a wide range of uses in the global market.

REFERENCES

Alexankov, A. M., d'Ascenzo, F., & Pokrovskaia, N. N. (2017). The management for Cyber-physical systems in the context of Industry 4.0 and regulatory mechanisms. In *XXI Int. conf. "Systems analysis in engineering and control" (SAEC-2017)*. St.-Petersburg Polytechnic University.

Allan & Hagiwara. (2018). Available at, https://www.bloomberg.com/news/articles/2018-04-04/banks-rush-to-turn-japan-cashless-ahead-of-looming-tech-rivals

Arner, D. W., & Barberis, J. (2015). FinTech in China: From the shadows? *The Journal of Financial Perspectives*, *3*(3), 78–79.

BlockchainI. B. M. (n.d.). Available at, https://www.ibm.com/blockchain/hyperledger/fabric-support

Cancian, F. (1967). Stratification and risk-taking: A theory tested on agricultural innovation. *American Sociological Review, 32*(6), 912–927. doi:10.2307/2092845 PMID:5624925

Chung, M., & Kim, J. (2016). The internet information and technology research directions based on the fourth industrial revolution. *Transactions on Internet and Information Systems (Seoul), 10*(3), 1311–1320.

CitiGPS. (2015). *Technology at Work.* Available at, https://www.oxfordmartin.ox.ac.uk/ downloads/reports/Citi_GPS_ Technology_Work.pdf

Collins, R. (2016). Blockchain: A new architecture for digital content. *EContent (Wilton, Conn.), 39*(8), 22–23.

Comin, D., & Hobijn, B. (2010). An exploration of technology diffusion. *The American Economic Review, 100*(5), 2031–2059. doi:10.1257/aer.100.5.2031

Deloitte. (2017). *Japanese Fintech in the Global Context.* Available at, https://www2.deloitte.com/jp/en/pages/financial-services/articles/bk/jp-fi-fintech-in-japan.html

DirectiveE. U. (2015). Available at, https://eur-lex.europa.eu/legal-content/EN/TXT/PDF/?uri=CELEX:32015L2366 &from=EN

Economist. (2015, Oct. 31). *The promise of blockchain.* Author.

Ernst and Young. (2016). *UK Fintech on the Cutting Edge.* Available at, www.ey.com/Publication/vwLUAssets/EY-UK-FinTech-On-the-cutting-edge/%24FILE/EY-UK-FinTech-On-the-cutting-edge.pdf/

Ernst and Young. (2017). *Fintech Adoption Index 2017.* Available at, www.ey.com/Publication/vwLUAssets/ey-fintech-adoption-index-2017/%24FILE/ey-fintech-adoption-index-2017.pdf

EVRY. (2018). *White Paper: PSD2 – Strategic Opportunities Beyond Compliance.* Available at, https://www.evry.com/en/campaigns/white-paper-psd2/

Gartrell, J. W. (1981). Cancian. The Innovator's Situation: Upper-Middle-Class Conservatism in Agricultural Communities (Book Review). *Rural Sociology, 46*(2), 342.

Golohvastov, D. V., Pokrovskaia, N. N., & Snisarenko, S. O. (2016). InstitutionalConfidence and Economic Intelligence for the Performance at Macro and Micro Networks. *4th Conf. on Management, Leadership and Governance ICMLG 2016*, 255-263.

Hillbom, E., & Tillström, T. (2016). *Applications of Smart Contracts and Smart Property Utilizing Blockchains* (M.Sc. thesis in computer science). Chalmers, University of Technology and University of Gothenburg, Sweden.

InnovateFinance. (2017). Available at, https://www.innovatefinance.com/wp-content/uploads/2018/02/2017- vc-fintech-investment-landscape.pdf

InsightsC. B. (2017). Available at, https://www.cbinsights.com/research/google-amazon-microsoft-facebook-ibm-startup-funding/

InsightsC. B. (2018a). Available at, https://www.cbinsights.com/research/report/amazon-across-financial-services-fintech/

InsightsC. B. (2018b). Available at, https://www.cbinsights.com/research/report/fintech-trends-q1-2018/

Jamrisko, M., & Lu, W. (2018). *The U.S. Drops Out of the Top 10 in Innovation Ranking*. Bloomberg. Available at, https://www.bloomberg.com/news/articles/2018-01-22/south-korea-tops-global-innovation-ranking-again-as-u-s-falls

Knezevic, D. (2018). Impact of Blockchain Technology Platform in Changing the Financial Sector and Other Industries. *Montenegrin Journal of Economics*, *14*(1), 109–120. doi:10.14254/1800-5845/2018.14-1.8

Kostin, G. A., Pokrovskaia, N. N., & Ababkova, M. U. (2017). Master-chain as an intellectual governing system for producing and transfer of knowledge. *IEEE II International Conference on Control in Technical Systems (CTS)*. 10.1109/CTSYS.2017.8109491

Lee, I., & Shin, Y. J. (2018). Fintech: Ecosystem, business models, investment decisions, and challenges. *Business Horizons*, *61*(1), 35–46. doi:10.1016/j.bushor.2017.09.003

Morrison, D. E., Kumar, K., Rogers, E. M., & Fliegel, F. C. (1976). Stratification and risk-taking: A further negative replication of Cancian's theory. *American Sociological Review*, *41*(5), 912–919. doi:10.2307/2094742

Nakamoto, S. (2008). *Bitcoin: A Peer-to-Peer Electronic Cash System*. Available at: https://bitcoin.org/bitcoin.pdf

Olsson. (2018). *The Rise and Development of Fintech*. Routledge.

Palychata, J. (2016). *Bitcoin: What you didn't know but always wanted to ask*. Available at, http://securities.bnpparibas.com/quintessence/hot-topics/beyond/bitcoin-and-blockchain-what-you.html

Pokrovskaia, N. N. (2016). Neuro-communication and reverse rule of payment in the digital economy: the monetary evaluation of experience. In *2th Conf. Technological perspective within the Eurasian space, new markets and economic growth points*. St-Petersburg: Asterion.

PwC. (2016). *Financial services technology 2020 and beyond: Embracing disruption*. White paper. London: PwC.

PwC. (2017). *Global Fintech Report*. Available at, https://www.pwc.com/gx/en/industries/financial-services/assets/pwc-global-fintech-report-2017.pdf

Rogers, E. M. (1962). *Diffusion of innovations* (1st ed.). Free Press.

Rogers, E. M. (1995). *Diffusion of Innovations* (4th ed.). Free Press.

Rosen, S. (1981). The Economics of Superstars. *The American Economic Review*, *71*(5), 845–858.

Saygili, E. E., Ozturkoglu, Y., & Kocakulah, M. C. (2017a). End users' perceptions of critical success factors in ERP applications. *International Journal of Enterprise Information Systems*, *13*(4), 58–75. doi:10.4018/IJEIS.2017100104

Saygili, E. E., & Saygili, A. T. (2017b). Contemporary Issues in Enterprise Information Systems: A Critical Review of CSFs in ERP Implementations. In Enterprise Information Systems and the Digitalization of Business Functions (pp. 120-136). IGI Global. doi:10.4018/978-1-5225-2382-6.ch006

Swan, M. (2015). *Blockchain: Blueprint for a New Economy*. O'Reilly Media.

Szabo, N. (1997). The idea of smart contracts. In Nick Szabo's Papers and Concise Tutorials. Academic Press.

The World Bank. (2013). Available at, http://documents.worldbank.org/curated/en/409841468327411701/pdf/ 840000WP0Box380crowdfunding 0study00.pdf

Tschorsch, F., & Scheuermann, B. (2016). Bitcoin and beyond: A technical survey on decentralized digital currencies. *IEEE Communications Surveys and Tutorials, 18*(3), 2084–2123. doi:10.1109/COMST.2016.2535718

Underwood, S. (2015). Blockchain beyond Bitcoin. *Communications of the ACM, 59*(11), 15–17.

Zheng, Z., Xie, S., Dai, H., Chen, X., & Wang, H. (2017). An Overview of Blockchain Technology: Architecture, Consensus, and Future Trends. *2017 IEEE International Congress on Big Data (BigData Congress),* 557–564.

KEY TERMS AND DEFINITIONS

Blockchain: A blockchain is a data structure that represents the record of each accounting move. Each account transaction is signed digitally to protect its authenticity, and no one can intervene in this transaction.

Change Agent: Change agencies employ change agents to influence the clients' innovation decisions. An innovation's rate of adoption is affected by the change agents' promotion efforts. A change agent's efforts include compatibility with the clients' needs and empathy.

Crowdfunding: It is a new form of saving and investment formation, emerged largely because of the difficulties after the 2008 financial crisis when banks became less willing to provide project financing loans to entrepreneurs and early-stage enterprises. Hence, entrepreneurs started to look elsewhere for raising funds, such as project financing by friends and family, extended through social networks and social profiles.

Fintech: New financial technologies in money transfer and payments, insurance, savings and investments, financial planning and borrowing, regulation technologies (regtech) including blockchain.

Payment Systems Directive-2 (PSD2): In 2018, EU member states are expected implement PSD2 in their national laws. These rules apply to all payments and accounts in all currencies within the EU and European Economic Area (EEA) countries.

Peer-to-Peer (P2P) Financing: Platforms enabling consumers and corporations borrow from each other by matching lenders and borrowers. They offer low interest rates and an efficient lending process using alternative credit models and data analytics in pricing risks.

Rate of Adoption: It is the number of members using an innovation in a social system during a specified time interval.

Chapter 4
FinTech-Based Islamic Social Financing Products: A Critical Evaluation

Abu Umar Faruq Ahmad
https://orcid.org/0000-0003-1523-1883
King Abdulaziz University, Saudi Arabia

Farrukh Habib
https://orcid.org/0000-0002-3344-7154
Alif Technologies, UAE

ABSTRACT

Although the blockchain is still at its infancy stage, experts have already regarded its impact and effect as the beginning of a new technological revolution, particularly relevant to the financial services sector. There are various institutions offered by Shari`ah, like zakah, waqf, sadaqah, and qard hasan, which exist and are already established, not only in the Islamic juristic literature but also in the Muslim world. However, the role of such institutions has been marginalized due to various factors; hence, they fail to create a big impact at macro level. This chapter will critically analyse the role of fintech in rejuvenating the Islamic social financing products with the main focus on blockchain and smart contracts. It will explore the application and usage of blockchain and smart contracts in the context of zakah, waqf, and qard hasan. It will also serve the purpose of a comprehensive and crucial reference-point for the role of fintech, blockchain and smart contracts vis-à-vis Islamic social financing products.

DOI: 10.4018/978-1-7998-3257-7.ch004

INTRODUCTION

Giving charity is one of the noblest acts in Islam, for which the reward is immensely huge. The Prophet Muhammad (ﷺ) is reported to have said:

"When a man dies, his deeds come to an end except for three things: continuous charity (sadaqah jariyah); a knowledge which is beneficial, or a virtuous descendant who prays for him (for the deceased)." (Sahih Muslim, Book 13, hadith # 1383)

That is why, Islam encourages people to get involved in charity and altruistic acts, no matter big or small. And Sharī'ah provides a complete eco-system for Islamic philanthropy to ensure that wealth does not revolve among only the rich of a society.

There are various Islamic social institutions, like *zakah*, *waqf*, *sadaqat* and *qardh hasan* which are proposed by Islam. These institutions always played a pivotal role of sustainable economic development in a Muslim society throughout the history of Islam. The whole social ecosystem was an integral element of the financial empowerment program of the people which actively contributed in the financial inclusion, poverty alleviation and fruitful mutual community initiatives. However, recently, these important institutions have been generally failed to produce substantial impact within the Muslim society. There is an array of issues and challenges facing such institutions in the contemporary world, this paper explains how Blockchain and smart contract technologies can help these institutions for better governance, lower transaction cost, more transparency and higher trust; hence, enhancing the business flexibility and market accessibility. It also presents some related cases that are currently under development as an evidence for the practicality of these technologies in the Islamic social finance arena.

Key Concepts and Terms: It is crucial to have to have a clear understanding of the key Islamic charity concepts and terms, since these concepts are at the core of this chapter.

Zakah: The very word 'zakah' literally means purification and growth. However, in the Islamic law, zakah is defined as the act of placing one's wealth into the ownership of a specific deserving person given the fulfilment of certain conditions (Al-Jaziri, 2009).

The obligation of zakah has been mentioned in the primary sources of Sharī'ah, namely, the Qur'an and the Sunnah or the traditions of Prophet Muhammad (peace and blessings be upon him - pbuh). For example, the Qura'n says:

"Take, [O, Muhammad], from their wealth a charity [zakah] by which you purify them and cause them increase and invoke [Allah's blessings] upon them. Indeed, your invocations are reassurance for them. And Allah is Hearing and Knowing." (Al-Qur'an, Chapter al-Taubah, 9:103)

Abu Huraira narrated that Prophet Muhammad (pbuh) is reported to have said:

"If any owner of gold or silver does not pay what is due on him, when the Day of Resurrection would come, plates of fire would be beaten out for him; these would then be heated in the fire of Hell and his sides, his forehead and his back would be cauterized with them. Whenever these cool down, (the process is) repeated during a day the extent of which would be fifty thousand years, until judgment is pronounced among servants, and he sees whether his path is to take him to Paradise or to Hell. It was said: Messenger of Allah, what about the camel? He (the Holy Prophet) said: If any owner of the camel

does not pay what is due on him, and of his due in that (camel) is (also) to milk it on the day when it comes down to water. When the Day of Resurrection comes a soft sandy plain would be set for him, as extensive as possible, (he will find) that not a single young one is missing, and they will trample him with their hoofs and bite him with their mouths. As often as the first of them passes him, the last of them would be made to return during a day the extent of which would be fifty thousand years, until judgment is pronounced among servants and he sees whether his path is to take him to Paradise or to Hell. It was (again) said: Messenger of Allah, what about cows (cattle) and sheep? He said: It any owner of the cattle and sheep does not pay what is due on them, when the Day of Resurrection comes a soft sandy plain would be spread for them, he will find none of them missing, with twisted horns, without horns or with a broken horn, and they will gore him with their horns and trample him with their hoofs. As often as the first of them passes him the last of them would be made to return to him during a day the extent of which would be fifty thousand years, until judgment would be pronounced among the servants. And he would be shown his path-path leading him to Paradise or to Hell. It was said: Messenger of Allah, what about the horse? Upon this he said: The horses are of three types. To one than (these are) a burden, and to another man (these are) a covering, and still to another man (these are) a source of reward. The one for whom these are a burden is the person who rears them in order to show off, for vainglory and for opposing the Muslims; so, they are a burden for him. The one for whom these are a covering is the person who rears them for the sake of Allah but does not forget the right of Allah concerning their backs and their necks, and so they are a covering for him. As for those which bring reward (these refer to) the person who rears them for the sake of Allah to be used for Muslims and he puts them in meadow and field. And whatever thing do these eat from that meadow and field would be recorded on his behalf as good deeds, as would also the amount of their dung and urine. And these would not break their halter and prance a course or two without having got recorded the amount of their hoof marks and their dung as a good deed on his behalf (on behalf of their owner). And their master does not bring them past a river from which they drink, though he did not intend to quench their thirst, but Allah would record for him the amount of what they drink on his behalf as deeds. It was said: Messenger of Allah, what about the asses?, Upon this he said: Nothing has been revealed to me in regard to the asses (in particular) except this one verse of a comprehensive nature:" He who does an atom's weight of good will see it, and he who does an atom's weight of evil will see it"." (Sahih Muslim, Book 5, 2161)

Collection and Calculation of Zakah: There are certain principles and rules for zakah that are needed to be followed. For instance, there are certain conditions for the payers of zakah (Al-Jaziri, 2009) as they must be:

- Muslims
- Free
- Of sound mind
- Pass the age of puberty
- Have positive cash or goods flow
- Have a total personal wealth higher than the nisab (threshold) value.

Similarly, those who can receive zakah should also fulfil a specific criterion. They must be one of the following categories to receive zakah:

- Fuqara': the poor who have no or low income
- Masakin: the needy who do not have a day's food
- 'Amilun: those employed to distribute the amount or assets of zakah
- Riqab: to assist in freeing from slavery or captivity
- Gharimun: those are in unmanageable debts
- Fi sabillillah: to assist those struggle in the way of Allah
- Ibn al-Sabil: to assist stranded or struggling travelers
- Muallaf al-qulub: to assist those revert to Islamic faith, or friends of the Muslim community.

The above-mentioned categories of zakah receivers are mentioned in the Qur'an as:

"Zakah expenditures are only for the poor and for the needy and for those employed to collect [zakah] and for bringing hearts together [for Islam] and for freeing captives [or slaves] and for those in debt and for the cause of Allah and for the [stranded] traveler - an obligation [imposed] by Allah . And Allah is All Knowing and All Wise." (Al-Qur'an, chapter al-Taubah, 9:60)

Waqf: Literally, the word 'waqf' means to keep or to stop. In the Islamic legal terminology, waqf is defined as the act of keeping a property for Allah which can be used to derive benefits from without consuming itself by disconnecting the ownership rights of the giver (waqif) from it (Ibn Hubairah, 2009).

Allah allowed and encouraged waqf as a way to His blessings. Its jurisdictions are derived from the Qur'an and the Sunnah. In the Qur'an, the key verse encourage for charity and donation is as follows:

"Never will you attain the good [reward] until you spend [in the way of Allah] from that which you love. And whatever you spend - indeed, Allah is Knowing of it." (Al-Qur'an, chapter Al-Imran, 3:92)

The first Waqf in the history of Islam was that of `Umar ibn al-Khattab. Abdullah ibn `Umar reported:

"Umar acquired a land at Khaybar. He came to Allah's Apostle (صلى الله عليه وسلم) and sought his advice regarding it. He said: Allah's Messenger, I have acquired land in Khaybar. I have never acquired property more valuable for me than this, so what do you command me to do with it? Thereupon he (Allah's Apostle) said: If you like, you may keep the corpus intact and give its produce as Sadaqah. So 'Umar gave it as Sadaqah declaring that property must not be sold or inherited or given away as gift. And Umar devoted it to the poor, to the nearest kin, and to the emancipation of slaves, aired in the way of Allah and guests. There is no sin for one, who administers it if he eats something from it in a reasonable manner, or if he feeds his friends and does not hoard up goods (for himself). He (the narrator) said: I narrated this hadith to Muhammad, but as I reached the (words)" without hoarding (for himself) out of it." he (Muhammad' said:" without storing the property with a view to becoming rich." Ibn 'Aun said: He who read this book (pertaining to Waqf) informed me that in it (the words are)" without storing the property with a view to becoming rich."" (Sahih Muslim, Book 13, Hadith # 4006)

Qardh Hasan: The word '*qardh*' literally means to cut and disconnect, but its straight forward translation in English is loan. In the terminology of Islamic law, *qardh* means the act of giving one's property to another person upon his/her request (Ibn Hubairah, 2009). *Qardh Hasan* means an interest-free loan given out of benevolence.

Referring to *qardh hasan* the Qur'an mentions:

"Who is it that would loan Allah a goodly loan so He may multiply it for him many times over? And it is Allah who withholds and grants abundance, and to Him you will be returned." (Al-Qur'an, chapter al-Baqarah, 2:245)

FINTECH PHENOMENON

Fintech is part of the bigger phenomenon named as Industrial Revolution (IR) 4.0. The World Economic Forum (2017) has defined it as a "small, technology-enabled, new entrant to financial services" by. Similarly, McKinsey & Company (n.d.) defines fintech as "start-ups and other companies that use technology to conduct the fundamental functions provided by financial services, impacting how consumers store, save, borrow, invest, move, pay, and protect money". However, these definitions do not include big tech looking at financial services and financial institutions interested in using high-tech platforms. They indeed have a crucial role to play in promoting fintech.

Fintech in Islamic Finance: To the authors' view, fintech is a comprehensive phenomenon that can be described as the deep integration of cutting-edge technology into financial products and services to improve their overall efficiency, offering and consumption. From an Islamic finance perspective, it is more difficult to find a universally accepted definition of fintech. DinarStandard (2018) defines "Islamic" fintech as: *"fintech technologies exponentially enhancing and disrupting 20th century Islamic financial services, operations, business models, and customer engagement*". This seems to be the most suitable definition of Islamic fintech.

The Role and Functions of FinTech: There are mainly four major functions of fintech, such as: (1) automation; (2) digitalization; (3) decentralization; and (4) disintermediation.

Automation and digitalization are based on the cyber physical systems. These systems integrate computation, networking and physical processes (Schwab, 2016). Decentralization has been introduced through blockchain platforms which are digital and distributed (Ashraf & Adarsh, 2017). Similarly, the concept of disintermediation has become more viable in an advanced technological environment. Fintech is shifting the paradigm of traditional intermediary roles by making them obsolete. While financial institutions have acted as intermediaries in the financial system by providing an invaluable service to clients, their functions are being usurped by new technology-driven business models (PwC, 2017b).

The new incumbents of fintech, except traditional financial institutions, which are contributing to the technological disruption are: e-retailers, information and communications technology (ICT) and big-tech companies, social media platforms, telecom companies, financial infrastructure companies, and most importantly start-ups (PwC, n.d.). These incumbents are assuming various roles in different sectors of the financial sphere. For instance, the most affected areas by fintech are payments, remittances, fund transfers, personal finance, loans and debt transactions, deposit and savings mechanisms, insurance and wealth management (Opus, 2018; PwC, n.d.).

CONCEPTUAL FRAMEWORK OF BLOCKCHAIN

It is pertinent to understand a technology, its benefits, and limitations to truly appreciate and explore its full potentials and efficient implementation in any field. Similarly, this section will explore what blockchain is, and what it is not to offer an in-depth discussion regarding its implementation for Islamic social finance.

Definition of Blockchain: Blockchain is a distributed ledger technology which allows transactions to be recorded without the need for a central authority or any intermediary (Ashraf & Adarsh, 2017). In other words, it allows users to verify and store transactions/data, not on a certain server operated by a centralized body as usual, but on servers/computers (known as nodes) operated by various participants of the network. The challenge of having such a decentralized system through traditional technology was extremely difficult; blockchain technology found a way to synchronise the data/records among the users and to ensure that it is not manipulated.

Technically, blockchain is a database of immutable time-stamped information of every transaction that is replicated on servers across the network (Hansen, 2015). Enabled by an open-source software usually, the transactions are recorded in blocks after a verification process performed by 'full nodes'. The 'full nodes' is a term used in blockchain for those who are authorized to verify a transaction and participate in chapping the rules of a blockchain, like 'admin users'. In a public Blockchain, any user could be a full node, while it is restricted to certain users in a private blockchain. The blocks are generated according to the software protocols, recording the information about when and in what sequence the transaction took place. Each block is connected to the next block with a hash function, forming a chain of block, hence, the name - blockchain.

To add a transaction within a block, and the block into the chain, a consensus is required from most of the full nodes. Moreover, once a block is completed, it is verified by other full nodes, and subsequently, added to the chain. Once a block is added to the chain, all full nodes immediately update the copy of their ledger. With this setup, historical information cannot be altered or manipulated. Therefore, it is largely argued that blockchain offers higher degree of integrity without the need of a trusted intermediary or central authority.

Inception of Blockchain: Payment systems, or cryptocurrencies, are often cited as the primary product or use case for blockchain technology. It is because blockchain was first introduced to the world by the introduction of the famous cryptocurrency - 'Bitcoin'. Bitcoin was introduced as a peer-to-peer digital payment system; while the technology underneath was - what is now known as blockchain. Blockchain was used by Bitcoin as a platform to enable peer-to-peer transactions. Surely, Bitcoin is not the only cryptocurrency, there are 1993 different cryptocurrencies exist as of September 25, 2018 (Coinmarketcap.com). The differences between these cryptocurrencies lie mainly due to their different objectives, underlying technology, protocols and features.

Difference Between Cryptocurrencies & Blockchain: lthough blockchain and Bitcoin, or cryptocurrencies, were introduced jointly to the world, they are not the same thing. Marr (2018) tries to explain it in an intuitive way by saying:

"Blockchain is to Bitcoin, what the internet is to email. A big electronic system, on top of which you can build applications. Currency is just one." (Marr, 2018)

Cryptocurrencies are in principal the values stored on a distributed ledger. These entries show the amount of digital funds or value that each user owns. Being a product, they need to be analyzed from Sharī'ah perspective to be declared as compliant or non-compliant. In fact, any product offered through blockchain warrants Sharī'ah analysis for its compliance.

Beside cryptocurrencies, a blockchain platform can be used for other purposes, products, and services. In that sense, blockchain, being a digital technology platform, can be considered as neutral. It is up to the user of that platform to utilize such technology for either permissible purpose or otherwise. Or it can be safely said that since the hardware, software, and the resources required to operate a blockchain platform do not consist of any impermissible element from Sharī'ah perspective by default, it is Sharī'ah compliant.

Types of Blockchain: Based on permission or restriction protocols, there are mainly three types of blockchain: (1) private; (2) consortium; and (3) public blockchain.

Public Blockchain: Public blockchain is open source in which anyone can participate, without the need of permission. On such platform, anyone can download the code or software, and start running a full node on the local device, validating transactions in the network, thus participating in the consensus process. Due to the public nature, anyone can see or audit transaction on the public block explorer; however, the parties of a transaction remain anonymous.

There are few advantages of using public blockchain. It has a potential to disrupt current business models through disintermediation. Moreover, there is no need to maintain servers or system admins by the central authority, this radically reduces the cost of creating and running decentralized applications (DApps). Some examples of public blockchain are Bitcoin, Ethereum, and Litecoin.

Consortium Blockchain: It is also called federated blockchain. It operates under the control of a specific group of organizations which can perform the role of full nodes. As opposed to public blockchain, it is not allowed for any person with the access to internet to participate in the process of verifying transactions. The consensus process is controlled by a pre-selected set of nodes in which the protocol defines their minimum number to sign every block for the block to be valid. The right to read the blockchain can either be public or restricted to the participants only.

This type of blockchain has some specific advantages. For example, it reduces transaction costs; avoids data redundancies; and replaces legacy systems. It is also good for simplifying document handling and getting rid of semi manual compliance mechanisms. The transaction processing in such blockchain is faster than a public blockchain, which means there is a potential for higher scalability. It also provides more privacy, but at the cost of lesser transparency. Consortium blockchain can be suitable for the traditional banking sector. Some of the examples are: R3 Corda (for banks); EWF (for energy), B3i (for insurance).

Private Blockchain: Private blockchain can be defined as a platform controlled by a single or centralized organization with restricted number of nodes within that organization. It is valuable for solving efficiency, security and fraud problems within traditional institutions, but the most important feature of decentralization is not available for private blockchain.

It has same advantages as of the consortium blockchain, but it is different from it in the sense that it has more restriction and is not distributed.

Use Cases of Blockchain for Social Purposes: Blockchain has the potential to disrupt many industries and sectors. Social aid is among those sectors that could be reshaped by this innovative technology. In fact, few examples already exist. To appreciate the implication, one needs to understand the challenges that faces social-aid programs and non-government organizations (NGOs) as well as the issues that these programs and organizations try to address.

The most significant problem in helping poor and refugees is distribution of aid. While there are an estimated 766 million people under poverty line (World Bank, 2017) and 25.4 million refugees (UNHCR, 2018), distributing aids is very challenging. Daily supply of foods to a huge number of population is not an easy task. It requires many accountants, administrators and supervisors to keep track of all transactions from purchase to delivery. It requires time-consuming and costly processes to avoid mismanagement and ensure that the food reaches to the eligible person. Blockchain offers in this regard an important solution. There are a couple of experiments already implemented by UNHCR. Ethereum blockchain is used by The United Nations World Food Programme (WFP) to help Syrian refugees in Zatari Camp in Jordan. The solution offers unique electronic coupons (e-coupons) representing an undisclosed amount of money podcasted to the shops in the refugee camps. Using eye-scanning devices, refugees' identities is verified, and the aid is disbursed to the refugees by redeeming the e-coupons. The transaction is then recorded in the blockchain. This blockchain applications would minimize the traditional cost of sending money or food through a series of intermediaries. It could save up to 98% of the tradition fees of UN-HCR (Juskalian, 2018). Furthermore, such blockchain application may help solving another important challenge for refugees that is missing documentation. Blockchain would enable digitally-authenticated identification documents in which the refugees who have lost their passports or national identities can use the digital ID. 'Bitnation for instance is a blockchain start-up helping refugees to obtain digital ID documents, which host governments can use to verify their identity. To build trust in the blockchain identity, the service verifies a person's multiple social media accounts and links them to their social security number, passport, and other documents' (Bayram, 2018).

SMART CONTRACTS

Definition of Smart Contracts: Blockchain platform can also run smart contracts. Smart contracts are simply self-executing contracts. Kasri (2017) mentions:

"smart contract is a term used to describe a computer program code that is capable of facilitating, executing, and enforcing the negotiation or performance of an agreement (i.e. a contract) using block-chain technology. The entire process is automated and can act as a complement or substitute for legal contracts where the terms of the smart contract are recorded in a computer language as a set of instructions." (Kasri, 2017)

The idea behind them is to convert terms and conditions of a transaction into codes; if the conditions are met, the contract is immediately concluded. Previously, the challenge was to automatically ensure that conditions are met, and that this event automatically triggers the conclusion of the contract, and perhaps its execution. With blockchain, conditions - being written into lines of code – could exist across a distributed, decentralized blockchain network in which it could be verified against the pre-set conditions by anonymous parties without the need for a central authority, legal system, or external enforcement mechanism. This renders transactions traceable, transparent, and irreversible (Investopedia, n.d.).

Smart contracts can revolutionize trading. Such structure could provide an alternative to the traditional legal system. Being a new tool for solving the problem of trust between parties, trading can be made automatic. Furthermore, it enables machine to machine e-commerce without enforcement by legal entities (Stark, 2018). Khan (2017) explains the value proposition of smart contracts by stating:

"The main feature of smart contract technology is that it can reduce costs for financial transactions by circumventing regulatory infrastructures while simultaneously reducing risk through non-discriminatory execution. Greater efficiency is predicted in servicing markets on account of a lack of a central counterparty agent." (Khan, 2017)

Inception of Smart Contracts: Though the concept and idea of smart contract was not always attached to blockchain, in reality its application was facing technical challenges which could be solved today by blockchain. It is reported that in 1994, Nick Szabo, a legal scholar, and cryptographer, realized that the decentralized ledger could be used for smart contracts (Blockgeeks, n.d.). He was referring to a simple use for sale and purchase of securities. However, smart contracts were not able to find their place in the mainstream usage. Kasri (2017) mentions the reasons behind this situation as:

"However, smart contracts went through a long gestation period of inactivity and disinterest due to the non-availability of platform to enforce them. This changed when blockchain technology was introduced in 2009. Smart contracts then began to gain traction, which are now becoming a basic tenet of overall blockchain's power." (Kasri, 2017)

Smart Contracts: How it works? Smart contracts are basically just computer programs. The program code identifies parameters to play a role in triggering events in accordance to the terms and conditions of a contract. If certain conditions are fulfilled, then a specific pre-programed line of codes reflecting the contractual clause of the triggered condition will be executed. By this setup, the paper-based contracts are transferred into electronic format which anyone can see at real-time bases. This further allows a uniliteral application without a need of a trust.

These computer codes are not stored in a single database which could be manipulated by any party having control over it. Instead, it is replicated, stored and distributed over the network. This implies that there is no need to trust a centralized body as it is supervised by the network of computers that run the blockchain. It is also important to note here that the smart contracts allow an automatic enforcement of the penalties according to the predefined rules. With this technology, various complex problems can be solved. It is rightly stated that:

"Smart contract use-cases range from simple to complex. Time-stamping services like ascribe (art registry) or governmental and semi-governmental registries (land titles, birth certificates, school and university degrees) are examples for simpler technological use cases. The regulatory aspects might be more complex. Decentralized autonomous organizations, on the other hand, are the most complex form of a smart contract." (BlockchainHub, n.d.)

Use Cases of Smart Contracts for Social Purposes: According to Deloitte, though blockchain has a great potential in offering immutable data storing with transparency and traceability, smart contracts represent a next step of development in which the data not only stored efficiently, but it is also processed automatically in terms of execution of multi-party agreements. This automation does not just offer cheaper solution but also reduce human errors and risk of manipulation.

Smart contracts can help in creating endless scenarios in which organizations can collaborate to encourage charitable donations (Gengler, 2017). UNICEF is already working on this concept with a blockchain solution to digitize donations and create transparency in global aid (UNICEF, 2017).

SOLVING ISSUES WITH BLOCKCHAIN AND SMART CONTRACTS

The introduction of the blockchain has offered a ray of hope for the reinforcement of social financing products and institutions in the modern Islamic finance sphere. It possesses various attractive features that are naturally required by all the stakeholders of such products and institutions to establish trust and reliability. This section will investigate the general model of blockchain solution, as well as product or institution specific features of blockchain.

General Model of Blockchain Solution: Rightly called as 'trust machine', blockchain offers an array of general features which are equally desired by all the Islamic social financing products or institutions. Some of those prominent features will be discussed here.

Traceability: From *qard hasan* to *sadaqat, waqf* and *zakah*, all social financing instruments require traceability. Be it lenders or donors, they insist on receiving complete information about the utilization of their loan or charity. With limited capability of centralized governing bodies, there is always an issue of maintaining full records of all the transactions performed. Once the funds are received and commingled, it is almost impossible to track each and every amount of fund to be disbursed. Consequently, tracking mechanisms for funds have become a huge cost, contributing to further inefficiencies of such products. With built-in feature of distributed and decentralized ledger, blockchain provides an end-to-end tracking mechanism and complete history of a transaction.

Transparency and Public Disclosure: Blockchain-based ledgers are distributed among all the network nodes, or at least among the master nodes, from which transaction confirmation and block formation is required to obtain consensus. Therefore, all participating nodes at a blockchain network are able to scrutinise all the transactions; and they keep updating the copy of the ledger in almost real time with the addition of a new block. Moreover, all the public keys and their history of transaction is available in the ledger for the nodes to verify and confirm. This mechanism offers full transparency and public disclosure to all the stakeholders of the blockchain network.

Compliance and Audit: One of the main concerning issues with the Islamic social financing products or institutions is the lack of availability of complete data and reliable records to perform proper compliance review and audit. However, as mentioned earlier, blockchain can offer end-to-end traceability, transparency and public disclosure; subsequently, it is easy to perform a bona-fide compliance review and audit to identify and rectify any irregularities. This feature is very crucial for the regulatory and legal authorities as well as other stakeholders to gauge genuine overall performance of such institutions.

Security: Centralized databases are prone to security threats because they have single point of failure. On the contrary, blockchain ledger system is distributed in a decentralized manner. The whole network depends on a huge number of anonymous nodes which are sufficient to maintain the ledger, even in the situation where the security of a few nodes has been compromised. This added security feature reinsures safe working and viability of such products or institutions through digital channels.

Scalability: Although blockchain systems are currently facing the issue of further scalability, but even then, they are still comparatively more efficient than traditional databases in terms of scalability. Some blockchain systems have already achieved the equivalent speed of 'visa' for transaction processing. Moreover, they are less affected by the number of nodes as compared to the number of clients in usual databases. This factor of scalability has several advantages for such products and institutions as their users are individuals, who are large in numbers as well.

Prevention of Fraud: Due to the usage of unique hash function distributed ledger technique, once the data is entered in the blockchain ledger, it is immutable. Since the records at the blockchain are unalterable, it is very difficult to corrupt those records or data entries. Moreover, since all the nodes at the network maintain a copy of ledger for verification, the probability of double spending is zero. In fact, the problem of double spending, or making fake copies of an asset, is one of the biggest issues in the digital world which the blockchain has successfully solved. This strong security factor can ensure that once the data is securely input using predefined protocols, it cannot be manipulated either accidentally or maliciously. It will not only enhance reliability of records, but also prevent any fraud.

Product Specific Features: Blockchain not only has general characteristics to bolster Islamic social financing products or institutions, it is customizable according to the requirement to avail some specific benefits. However, these specific benefits are not mutually exclusive among such products; rather they are relevant to all of them.

Smart Contracts for *Waqf*: Smart contracts can be effectively used in *waqf*. For instance, a *waqf* deed can be converted into an algorithm or code. The algorithm can then be inserted in the blockchain platform in the form of a smart contract. The execution of the smart contract is automated, and it can prevent the *waqf* property being used outside of the stipulations of the *waqf* giver (*waqif*). In this way, the *waqf* deed can be protected and adhered to. This is a simple example of where *waqf* can benefit from the application of a smart contract. From the macro perspective, the use of smart contracts could further enhance the performance and efficacy of the *waqf* institution, due to improved compliance and audit mechanisms. Incorporating smart contracts could also reduce the cost, while further increasing the security, transparency and adherence to the *waqf* stipulations and traceability of the *waqf* funds.

Case Study: Finterra's Waqf Chain

Singapore-based fintech firm Finterra has developed a crowdfunding platform that uses blockchain to create smart contracts that would be tied to specific *waqf* projects. This can provide a more efficient way to raise money, manage and transfer ownership of *waqf*.

The *Waqf* Chain allows participants to create project proposals to develop and invigorate endowment properties. Others can fund these project proposals by contributing funds. If the project goals are met, the project proposal is accepted, and a certain number of endowment tokens are created and distributed to the participating funders. The tokens can be held to gain stakeholder rights and revenue sharing or transferred and exchanged in the wider Finterra ecosystem (and on other networks) through the Finterra Inter-Chain Protocol.

Among the key benefits that Finterra wants to achieve:

- Each project's 'real world' documentation is stored immutably and publicly for all stakeholder to see and review, ensuring safety and transparency of the project as it moves forward.
- Contribution, stakeholder voting, and special terms cannot be tampered with because they are enforced by blockchain consensus via smart contract.
- Token distribution and project revenue are handled automatically in the smart contract logic guaranteeing fairness and accounting accuracy for token holders.
- Specific project terms are encoded into (and enforced by) a smart contract in a tamper proof manner.

Transfer and Receipt of *Zakah:* One of the most important issues in *zakah* is to ensure that the ownership of *zakah* funds has been transferred to the rightful recipients (*mustahiqqun*). Through the traceability characteristic of blockchain, this objective can be easily achieved. Moreover, the procedures for on-boarding the recipients of *zakah* can be customized and automated through smart contracts. Their credentials can be cross verified through wider integration of application programming interfaces (APIs). Their data can be globally shared to utilize *zakah* funds effectively, while avoiding any wastage of resources.

Case Study: INCEIF-AidTech- IFRC project

The Global University for Islamic Finance (INCEIF), AidTech (fintech company) and the International Federation of Red Cross (IFRC) have come up with an Islamic social financing mobile application that leverages blockchain technology for *zakah* and *ṣadaqah*. The App provides the users with a choice of project. Once a project is selected and the payment is made, the transaction is registered on blockchain in which the disbursement to the end users is registered to. This structure allows the payer to get notifications once their *zakah/ṣadaqah* has reached the intended recipients. This offer higher transparency. The team is working now on developing a social scorecard to evaluate the projects. If it is implemented on blockchain, then users could see the evaluations which no one could manipulate.

Qardh Hasan: Several institutions and market players are already enthusiastic about building a system of *qardh hasan* (interest-free loan) through electronic crowdfunding platforms and peer-to-peer (P2P) systems. These platforms are active online through internet. After going mainstream, blockchain and smart contracts will become an inevitable part of such platforms. Currently, *qardh hasan* is not popular among Islamic finance players, due to its non-commercial nature; while social financial institutions also avoid it because of high administrative cost. However, with the usage of blockchain, it can be assumed that it will be perceived as a widely-used viable product for social finance.

ISSUES WITH BLOCKCHAIN AND SMART CONTRACTS AND THE WAY FORWARD

Despite several benefits and promising features, blockchain and smart contracts are facing serious issues and severe challenges. Although, the proponents of this technology are optimistic about its future implementation, it is not free from many pitfalls at present. Some of the concerns are stated as follows.

Immature Technology: Blockchain and smart contracts are still at their infancy stage. The technology is not matured enough now to be adopted for the mainstream application. That is why, most of the financial industry players are reluctant to consider this technological platform as a viable channel for offering their financial products.

Having said that, many market players are, currently, keen to test their proof-of-concepts (POCs) and hoping to roll-out their product when the time is right. This is only a matter of time, as the technology has already successfully received traction by the relevant industry players.

Lack of Human Talent: Due to the short history of this nascent technology, human expertise is lacking in programming and development; hence, its true potential is yet to be fully discovered and exploited. Meanwhile, developers who have achieved vast experience and skills are few and in high-demand. This situation has resulted in high price tag for acquiring such expertise.

It is recommended that the education and training of such an important technology should be conducted by mainstream educational institutions. There should be specialized programs and courses to fill up the dearth in the current human capacity development.

Governance Issues: Another problem is the governance of blockchain and smart contracts at an organizational level. This has raised issues of selecting among the types of blockchain solutions which are appropriate for an organization; permitting parties' involvement as nodes; choosing information to be input; and maintaining and sharing data.

Market players, particularly Islamic social finance institutions, should not adopt this technology because of the hype. They should carefully explore the technology and perform their own cost-and-benefit analysis before even having a pilot-project. They should not be carried away by the sentiments, rather they should base their decision on sound business logic.

Privacy and Security: Although transparency is a positive trait of this technology, at times, it poses real challenges regarding data privacy and security of people and transactions. It is argued that anonymity already exists to mask the information of the transacting parties; however, that can be easily breached by using meta-data collected through digital devices. The best thing is to strike a good balance between transparency and privacy by developing highest standards and regulations for data privacy and cyber security.

Inflexibility: Immutability is another strong feature of blockchain and smart contracts, however, it has appeared to be a double-edge sword. It makes this technology somewhat inflexible too. For example, if there are any bugs, they are not only visible to all the users, including hackers, due to open source code of smart contracts, but also, they cannot be immediately and easily fixed due to the requirement of majority consensus and distributed nature of the blockchain ledger.

This is purely a technical issue; and blockchain experts are working on it. The main concern is that there is a trade-off between flexibility and trust. It is possible for some market players to have customized blockchain solutions where there is a good mix of both.

Interoperability: Another major concern is integration of blockchain system with the current existing systems. Particularly, the financial institutions have already invested a huge amount of capital into their legacy systems. Moreover, the legacy systems are well-tested and widely used for the financial products; they have been considered as reliable technology for the financial sector. On the other hand, blockchain technology is not only unique, but also immature. Therefore, the blockchain technology cannot be adopted all at once.

Blockchain provides a completely independent eco-system and technology framework. This is not only unique, but also more advanced than other technologies. For this reason, a gradual approach is more appropriate which can be broken down into stages. At the first stage, the blockchain technology needs to be integrated with the current systems in order to further improve their efficiency. At the second stage, other technology infrastructure and supportive mechanisms should be devised and implemented. At the third stage, the whole blockchain framework should be tested and checked for any errors. At the fourth stage, an overall migration from the current system to the blockchain system should take place.

Regulatory and Legal Framework: Regulations and legal implications play an extremely crucial role in any sector. Their role is even stronger in the financial sector, as it is the highest regulated sector. Similarly, the blockchain and smart contracts technology requires a comprehensive regulatory and legal framework to support its adoption and implementation. The issues data privacy and its usage, legal status of smart contracts in courts, and others need to be examined and confidently responded.

Beginning 2018, regulatory and legal concerns regarding blockchain and smart contracts have been investigated with serious approach. It is indeed a good development; however, there is a lot to be done in terms of high standards, prudent guidelines, proper legislations, robust rules and regulations.

ISSUES OF FATWA AND ENDORSEMENT OF ISLAMIC FINANCING PRODUCTS

The Qur'an, the first and fundamental source of Sharī'ah says:

"And We sent not before you except men to whom We revealed [Our message]. So, ask the people of the message if you do not know." (Al-Qur'an, chapter al-Nahl, 16:43)

The above-mentioned verse of the Qur'an signifies the role of Islamic jurists and Sharī'ah scholars. According to Islamic Financial Services Board (IFSB), an adequate Sharī'ah governance system entails a set of institutional and organizational arrangements through which an institution offering Islamic financial products, whether it is social or commercial, oversees Sharī'ah compliance. It ensures that the products and operations under discussion are in accordance with Islamic principles and rulings. A logical requisite of such a system is the establishment of a Sharī'ah advisory board as well (IFSB, 2009).

Extending the same understanding and logic, Islamic social financial products which are driven by the latest technology should also go through the same scrutiny and examination. There should be a proper Sharī'ah governance system in place in order to approve and endorse such products as being compliant with the underlying principles of Sharī'ah. Adequate Sharī'ah boards consisting of competent Sharī'ah scholars as the board members should be part of that system where such committees/boards could advise and provide consultancy for developing fintech products for Islamic social finance.

CONCLUSION

The blockchain, though still in its infancy stage, has already proved itself as a game changing breakthrough for the global financial sphere. In fact, its utilization is not limited to only the financial sector, but it also affords promising features and usage for non-financial sectors.

Similarly, the Islamic social financing institutions could be invigorated with the innovative and efficient use of the blockchain and smart contracts. The blockchain technology and such institutions can indeed have a perfect natural match because, interestingly, the blockchain addresses many, if not all, of the issues and problems currently facing such institutions in the contemporary world.

It is strongly believed that with the firm *fiqhi* foundations of such institutions, an innovative approach consisting of technological advancements, like blockchain and smart contracts, towards their reinforcement will ensure that they could dynamically participate in the societal and economic development of the whole Muslim world. Such remarkable initiatives will also crystalize the ethical and social dimensions of Islamic finance in a robust manner.

This chapter has critically analyzed the role of fintech in rejuvenating the Islamic social financing products with the main focus on blockchain and smart contracts. It has explored the application and usage of blockchain and smart contracts in the context of *zakah*, *waqf* and *qardh hasan*. As a way forward, it is recommended that all the major Islamic social finance institutions among the Organization of Islamic

Cooperation (OIC) member countries should form a consortium to further research and build a global blockchain based platform for Islamic social finance products.

REFERENCES

Al-Jaziri, A. R. (2009). *Al-Fiqh 'ala al-Madhahib al-Arba'ah*. Fons Vitae.

Ashraf, S., & Adarsh, S. (2017). *Decentralized Computing Using Blockchain Technologies and Smart Contracts*. IGI Global. doi:10.4018/978-1-5225-2193-8

Bayram, A. S. (2018). *Here Are Three Ways Blockchain Can Change Refugees' Lives*. World Economic Forum. Available at: https://www.weforum.org/agenda/2018/06/three-ways-blockchain-change-refugees-lives/

BlockchainHub. (n.d.). *Smart Contracts*. Available at: https://blockchainhub.net/smart-contracts/

Blockgeeks. (n.d.). *Smart Contracts: The Blockchain Technology That Will Replace Lawyers*. Available at: https://blockgeeks.com/guides/smart-contracts/

DinarStandard. (2018). *Islamic Fintech Report 2018: Current Landscape and Path Forward*. Dubai, UAE: DinarStandard.

Gengler, E. B. (2017). Leveraging Blockchain Technology for Corporate Social Responsibility. *Payments Journal*. Available at: https://paymentsjournal.com/leveraging-blockchain-technology-for-corporate-social-responsibility/

Habib, F., & Ahmad, A. U. F. (2019). Using blockchain and smart contracts for waqf institutions. In Financial Technology and Disruptive Innovation in ASEAN. IGI Global. Doi:10.4018/978-1-5225-9183-2

HalalChain. (2018). *Halal-Chain White Paper*. Available at: http://www.halalchain.ae/whitepaper.pdf

Hansen, E. (2015). *The Blockchain, Explained*. Available at: https://medium.com/linkreply-blockchain/the-blockchain-explained-3300f4506890

Ibn Hubairah, Y. (2009). *Ijma' al-Aimmah al-'Arbaah wa Ikhtilafuhum*. Dar Al-Ola.

Investopedia. (n.d.). *Smart Contracts*. Available at: https://www.investopedia.com/terms/s/smart-contracts.asp

Juskalian, R. (2018). Inside the Jordan Refugee Camp That Runs on Blockchain. *MIT Technology Review*. Available at: https://www.technologyreview.com/s/610806/inside-the-jordan-refugee-camp-that-runs-on-blockchain/

Kasri, N. S. (2017). *Sharī'ah Compliance via Blockchain and Smart Contract – The Case for Islamic Credit Card*. Wahed Invest. Available at: https://journal.wahedinvest.com/Sharī'ah-compliance-via-blockchain-and-smart-contract-the-case-for-islamic-credit-card

Khan. N. (2017). *Smart Contracts - The Future of Islamic Banking*. Academic Press.

Marr, B. (2018). A Very Brief History of Blockchain Technology Everyone Should Read. *Forbes*. Available at: https://www.forbes.com/sites/bernardmarr/2018/02/16/a-very-brief-history-of-blockchain-technology-everyone-should-read/#5462f7f37bc4

McKinsey & Company. (n.d.). *FinTechnicolor: The New Picture in Finance*. Available at: https://www.mckinsey.com/~/media/mckinsey/industries/financial%20services/our%20insights/bracing%20for%20seven%20critical%20changes%20as%20fintech%20matures/fintechnicolor-the-new-picture-in-finance.ashx

Opus. (2018). *Fintech Outlook*. Available at: http://www.opusconsulting.com/wp-content/uploads/fintech-outlook-2018.pdf

PwC. (2017a). *Blockchain, A Catalyst for New Approaches in Insurance*. Available at: https://www.pwc.com/gx/en/insurance/assets/blockchain-a-catalyst.pdf

PwC. (2017b). *Global Fintech Report: Redrawing the Lines*. Available at: https://www.pwc.com/gx/en/industries/financial-services/assets/pwc-global-fintech-report-2017.pdf

PwC. (n.d.). *Global Fintech Report: Blurred-Lines*. Available at: https://www.pwc.com/gx/en/industries/financial-services/fintech-survey/blurred-lines.html

Sahabuddin, M., & Ahmad, A. U. F. (2020). Islamic finance in the fourth industrial revolution: Challenges and opportunities. *International Journal of Islamic Thought.*

Schwab, K. (2016). *The Fourth Industrial Revolution*. Penguin Random House LLC.

Stark, J. (2018). *Presentation at IIFM Seminar – Fintech, Smart Contracts and Blockchain, Kuala Lumpur*. Available at: https://www.iifm.net/sites/default/files/Session%206%20-%20Fintech%2C%20Smart%20Contracts%20and%20Blockchain%20-%20Nicholas%20Edmondes%20%28Trowers%20%26%20Hamlins%29.pdf

The World Economic Forum. (2017). *Beyond Fintech: A Pragmatic Assessment of Disruptive Potential in Financial Services*. Available at: http://www3.weforum.org/docs/Beyond_Fintech_-_A_Pragmatic_Assessment_of_Disruptive_Potential_in_Financial_Services.pdf

UNHCR. (2018). *Figures at a Glance*. Available at: https://www.unhcr.org/figures-at-a-glance.htm

UNICEF. (2017). *UNICEF to present 'Donercoin' at London Blockchain Week 2017*. Available at: https://un-blockchain.org/2017/01/09/unicef-to-present-donercoin-at-london-blockchain-week-2017/

World Bank. (2017). *No Poverty. SDG Atlas*. Available at: http://datatopics.worldbank.org/sdgatlas/archive/2017/SDG-01-no-poverty.html

Chapter 5
Regulating FinTech Through Sandboxes:
Entering the UK and Malaysian Regulatory Sandbox

Maryam Khalid
University of Malaya, Malaysia

Sherin Kunhibava
University of Malaya, Malaysia

ABSTRACT

Fintech emergence post-Global Financial Crisis puts a threat to the banking industry. One of the strategies for the banks to stay afloat and relevant in the current digital era is through regulatory sandbox. A regulatory sandbox is one of the tools opted by financial regulators in certain jurisdictions to regulate the rapid growth of fintech products within their financial sphere. The pioneer of which was the UK's market and conduct regulator, the Financial Conduct Authority (FCA). Bank Negara Malaysia (BNM) was also one of the first jurisdictions that followed suit. One of the basic structures in a sandbox is the eligibility criteria that the regulators draw for the financial service provider to participate in the sandbox. This chapter shall address the entry requirements in both jurisdictions as the structure of the regulatory sandboxes differs from one jurisdiction to another. This topic is crucial to the banks as they need to understand further how regulatory sandbox may help them offer innovative financial products to level the competition with the fintech players in the market.

INTRODUCTION

Financial regulation rests on the basis that financial regulators are mandated to regulate to ensure financial stability and provide adequate customer protection. The landscape of financial regulation has changed its course since the Global Financial Crisis (GFC) happened in 2007. Numerous reasons were cited (Arner, 2009), however, the main reason was due to a proliferation of financial innovations that

DOI: 10.4018/978-1-7998-3257-7.ch005

were unsupervised and coupled with de-regulation incentives. Thus, post-GFC, the financial regulators around the world are more cautious in dealing with financial innovations. The latest financial innovation that caught the regulators' eye is the emergence of fintech in the financial industry. Fintech is a combination of the words between finance and technology whereby the financial services provider leverage on technology to provide products that are cost-effective to the financial consumers. Although the relationship between finance and technology have been established since the 19th century during the introduction of pantelegraph and telegraph, (Arner, Barberis, & Buckley, 2016), it is only recently the financial industry has accepted the usage of the term fintech.

The emergence of fintech brings a challenge to the financial industry, especially in the banking sector. The financial markets have evolved to accommodate the growing demands of fintech products. At a glance, the fintech products have more advantage than the traditional banking industry on several points. Fintech products leverage technology; hence the products are more efficient and convenient especially in providing banking services to unbanked or underbanked financial consumers (Ajlouni & Al-Hakim, 2018). This is further supported by the survey conducted in 2019 stating that there was significant growth in the adoption of fintech by the consumers in the financial market especially in the payments and remittance sector (Young, 2019). Hence, fintech players are a definite contender for the traditional banking system (Ajlouni & Al-Hakim, 2018) post GFC. In responding to the threat that fintech has against the banking sector, the banks need to explore opportunities offered in the fintech scene. One of the strategies that the banking sector has already applied in widening its horizon in this current digital era is, by partnering with fintech players in offering innovative products to the financial consumers. Thus, such collaboration between the banks and fintech players (Juengerkes, 2016) offering innovative financial products may fall under the category of fintech as well.

Not only fintech disrupts the banking industry but it has also added a new regulatory burden towards regulators around the world. The regulators are now expected to regulate without hampering innovation. (Board, 2017) In effect, this means the regulators will not only need to ensure financial stability and provide adequate customer protection but nowadays the regulators are burdened with another mandate of promoting innovation. As fintech exponentially increases in meeting the demands in the market, there is a need to regulate them to ensure financial stability. Therefore, for the regulators to discharge its' duties in regulating this new type of financial innovation, the regulators turned to regulatory sandboxes. Similar to children's sandbox, regulatory sandbox creates a perimeter between the regulators, financial service providers and financial consumers to test. It is a pilot program where the regulators may supervise the financial service providers in a more relaxed environment of reduced regulations to serve the best innovative financial products to the consumers before the fintech products are released to the markets.

Regulatory sandboxes had been the talk of the town between international financial regulators since its inception in the United Kingdom's ('UK') financial sphere back in 2016. The primary purpose of a regulatory sandbox is for the regulators to supervise in an informative manner (Financial Conduct Authority, 2015) to ensure that it balances its' burden to regulate while promoting innovation. Others may argue that the original structure of regulatory sandbox originated from the United States' ('US') Consumer Financial Protection Bureau ('CFPB') under its Project Catalyst, where CFPB provided a friendly environment for the financial players to have a communicative relationship with the regulators (Bureau, 2016). Nevertheless, the structure of the regulatory sandbox initiated by the UK's market conduct regulator, Financial Conduct Authority ('FCA') is the one that the financial regulators from other jurisdictions are considering transplanting to their regulatory frameworks. At the time of writing, about 50 jurisdictions are adopting regulatory sandbox into their financial regulation and these numbers are increasing (Buckley, Arner, Veidt, & Zetzsche, 2019a) Thus, this signals that regulatory sandbox is accepted by the international financial regulators to function as one of the tools in regulating fintech.

Following the UK's footsteps, Malaysia also introduced its Financial Technology Regulatory Sandbox Framework in the same year (Malaysia, 2016). In Malaysia, the financial regulatory framework consists of two regulators; BNM and the Securities Commission (SC) (Commission, 2019). BNM regulates financial institutions, insurance, and takaful companies, payments system, and money service businesses. As the regulatory sandbox framework is under the purview of BNM, thus the scope of discussion with regards to Malaysia under this chapter shall be concerning the subject matter within BNM's supervision and powers.

A basic structure of a regulatory sandbox is; first, there must be a watchdog that is mandated with supervisory powers to monitor the sandbox. Secondly, there is a list of criteria that interested financial players need to meet to participate in the sandbox. Thirdly, the time frame for the sandbox a time that will apply to the players in testing their innovative business inside the sandbox. Fourthly, a useful consumer protection framework which includes a proper dispute resolution mechanism. Finally, a sandbox must be structured with exit strategies by the players during the test and after the testing stage. (Crane, Meyer, & Fife, 2018) In essence, this chapter will focus on the second basic structure of the sandbox. The main objective of this chapter is to examine and compare the legal requirements of the UK and Malaysian regulators in selecting the eligible participants to enter their respective regulatory sandboxes.

STRUCTURE OF THIS CHAPTER

Before going further to the discussion, it is essential to highlight that this chapter focuses on regulatory sandbox as part of fintech regulation. This topic is crucial as it disseminates knowledge to the banking industry especially those that offer fintech products that will be regulated through regulatory sandbox. Another vital point to note is the methodology used and the limitation of this chapter. This chapter uses comparative legal methodology coupled with doctrinal and document content analysis. The choice of jurisdiction is because there is little to none previous literature that has provided an analytical overview of the Malaysian and the UK regulatory sandbox legal structures. However, both jurisdictions are the firsts to implement sandbox in their fintech regulation. Hence, it is only relevant to the topic of this book that such analysis is made using the comparative-legal method to fill in the gap. Furthermore, the UK sandbox is the perfect fit to compare and benchmark against the Malaysian sandbox especially on how it operates since FCA is the pioneer in the sandboxing landscape.

In terms of document content analysis methodology, the information obtained is mostly from the publicly available primary and secondary sources of the regulators' and other websites, hence the chapter can only relate from whatever is available at the time of writing. Furthermore, the regulatory sandbox has only initiated since 2016 and therefore it is still a work in progress. It may take a longer time for any changes to be brought to the sandbox regime. Therefore this chapter provides its evaluation based on the information at the time of writing. In the following sections, this chapter will be discussed as follows:

As the topic chosen for this chapter may cover an extensive aspect in two different jurisdictions, this chapter will discuss three main points. Firstly, this chapter will compare between the UK and the Malaysian regulatory requirements on the eligibility criteria of financial service providers to be able to participate in their regulatory sandboxes. Secondly, this chapter will examine whether the UK and the Malaysian sandboxes provide a clear direction in determining what amounts to financial innovation in their financial industry. Thirdly, this chapter will discuss the legal issues of transparency in selecting the eligible financial service provider to enter the sandbox and how the regulators tackle the challenges in regulating without stifling innovation. Lastly, this chapter concludes on brief policy reflections for both regulators based on the impacts that regulatory sandbox has on the banking industry and what improvements that both of the sandboxes may need to work on.

ELIGIBILITY CRITERIA IN THE UK AND THE MALAYSIAN REGULATORY SANDBOX

Eligibility Criteria and Sandbox's Regulatory Objectives

When establishing a regulatory sandbox, the regulator is signalling to the market that they are open to innovation and will be flexible in their regulatory approaches. Nevertheless, too many applicants entering the regulatory sandbox may give a signal that the nation's financial framework needs a reform (Zetzsche, Buckley, Barberis, & Arner, 2017). It shows either the financial framework within that jurisdiction is too prescriptive and rules-based or no law regulates the business that intended players seek to venture into. Therefore, the regulators need to establish a borderline of flexibility in admitting financial service providers into the sandbox. Coloured with such background and juggling between the three regulatory objectives of financial stability, consumer protection, and promoting innovation, the regulators need to be mindful in crafting the requirements for the financial service provider to meet to play in the sandbox. As stated previously, the financial service provider will be given relaxed regulations when they entered the sandbox. Therefore, should there be a significant number of financial service providers allowed to play in the sandbox, it will be a trade-off to consumer protection (Buckley, Arner, Veidt, & Zetzsche, 2019b).

In developing the eligibility criteria, the FCA and BNM based their impositions on meeting the regulatory objectives of their regulatory sandboxes. Since FCA's inaugural introduction of sandbox back in 2016, FCA has numerously mentioned that the regulatory sandbox's objective is to drive competition in the financial markets for the benefit of the financial consumers (Financial Conduct Authority, 2015). The FCA took such an approach in meeting its regulatory burden of promoting innovation in today's evolving financial markets. This was further supported by the change of direction that the UK's government took in 2015 to align its policies focusing on raising productivity within its nation. The main idea is to instil competition in the markets to encourage growth within the financial services industry. This is with the hope that competition will foster efficiency in financial firms which will later oblige them to expand further in terms of novel financial products to be offered in the market. Getting the green light from the government and tremendous support in terms of new policies have therefore opened the gate to the regulatory sandbox to be implemented in providing the best regulatory environment for financial firms to compete (Treasury, 2011)

Whereas in Malaysia, when BNM first issued the regulatory sandbox framework in 2016, the objective stated was to provide a regulatory environment that supports the development of fintech (Malaysia, 2016). However, Malaysia explicitly states that it is one of the countries mandated by the United Nation's Secretary-General's Special Advocate for Inclusive Finance for Development in providing financial services that are inclusive and accessible to all (Malaysia, 2018). This might be because the financial inclusion as the regulatory sandbox' objective suits well for the Malaysian economy that is still in the pendulum of a developing nation.

ENTRY REQUIREMENTS IN THE UK AND THE MALAYSIAN REGULATORY SANDBOX

I. FCA Requirements for Sandbox Entry

In the FCA's website (Financial Conduct Authority, 2016), it itemizes the requirements and considerations that FCA will be guided by in determining whether a fintech player will be accepted in the cohort that they applied. The requirements are discussed as follows:

Eligibility Criteria

The interested fintech player must clarify to the FCA that it is eligible to enter the UK sandbox by proving firstly that its' business will be utilized within the UK financial services market. Secondly, the players must describe the innovativeness of its product to the FCA whereby the product is relatively new and the equivalent to it has not entered the market. Thirdly, the product must be proven to carry consumer benefits such as driving productivity or by giving a better competition than what the market already has. Fourthly, the players must clarify the need for their product to enter the sandbox. Lastly, the players must demonstrate to the regulator that they have all the resources to conduct the testing and have placed all the necessary safeguards for consumer protection.

Securing Partners

The interested players shall secure a partner if the testing requires them to do so.

Significant UK Presence

The guiding principle for the interested player to fulfil this requirement is to show that the headquarter of the player's business is in the UK and employees are handling the business there.

UK Bank Account

As the business requires a significant presence in the UK, the interested players may supply a UK bank account to prove the same.

ii. Malaysia's Requirements for Sandbox Entry

Under the Fintech Regulatory Sandbox Framework, the requirements listed by BNM are similar to the FCA's sandbox. However, there are several differences between the two. The requirements can be divided as follows:

Eligibility Criteria

Under BNM's eligibility requirement, it emphasizes that the interested financial service provider must show that the products or services are innovative by proving that the products will refine the accessibility, quality, security, and efficiency of the current products and services offered. BNM also looks at whether the products would increase the efficiency and effectiveness of Malaysian financial institutions' management of risks or address gaps in or open up new opportunities for financing or investments in the Malaysian economy (Malaysia, 2016).

Other Requirements

From the reading of BNM's regulatory sandbox's framework, it can be understood that the other requirements in entering the Malaysian regulatory sandbox replicate the FCA's sandbox's entry requirements. The interested players must show to the regulator that the intended products or services possessed all the required infrastructure and resources and are prepared to be tested in the sandbox. Similar to the requirements listed by the FCA, the interested players in Malaysia must also prove that the business has placed all the appropriate safeguards, especially on consumer protection. Furthermore, the players must show that the products and services intended to be tested are not in line with the laws and regulations issued by BNM for them to give leeway for the intended products or services to be tested. Apart from that, the players must show that the person managing the business is someone with integrity.

Table 1 below summarizes the comparison between the two jurisdictions.

Table 1. Comparison between the UK and Malaysian eligibility criteria based on their regulatory objectives

Sandbox's composition	Malaysia	UK
Eligibility criteria	The intended products or services to be tested shall prove that they: • will improve the current products and services offered in terms of accessibility, quality, security and efficiency; • increase the effectiveness of Malaysian financial institutions' management of risks; or • address gaps in or open up new opportunities for financing or investments in the Malaysian economy.	The intended products or services to be tested: • will be used for the domestic market; • are relatively new and any equivalence has not entered the market; • carry consumer benefit; • requires to be tested in FCA's sandbox; and • are in a business that has all the resources in place;
Regulatory Objective	• Deploy a friendlier regulatory environment with the financial service provider to improve financial services in light of technological advancement. • Financial inclusion.	• Increasing competition in the financial markets to promote innovation for the consumer's benefit.

Source: Authors' own

These entry requirements act as the guiding principle for both regulators and fintech in determining whether the intended products or services to be offered should be tested or not. The regulators of regulatory sandbox must pick and choose the products or services that are ready to be tested. Although the number of products or services applying to participate in the sandbox may possess innovativeness, the regulators cannot admit all of them to the sandbox. This is due to the size of the sandbox and one on one process that the regulators have to go through with the interested financial service provider (Zetzsche et al., 2017).

The early participants of regulatory sandboxes in the UK and Malaysia showed that the banks are interested in being part of the sandbox. In Malaysia, one of the largest banks, CIMB Bank Berhad partnered with Paycasso, a UK based fintech player that delivers a global customer identification platform to clients, was admitted to the sandbox in the early years of its operation (Singapore, 2017). A similar trend can be seen with the UK sandbox, where Barclays entered the sandbox in the third cohort to test its 'RegTech proposition which tracks updates to regulations within the FCA Handbook and aligns its implementation to Barclays' internal policies' (Financial Conduct Authority, 2017b).

Interestingly, BNM clearly stated in its regulatory sandbox framework that the priority would be given to financial institutions or fintech players that plan to collaborate with the incumbent financial institutions. (Malaysia, 2016). Arguably, FCA does not share the same view. Otherwise, it goes against their competition mandate. However, the percentage of large financial service providers (which include banks) participated in the sandbox comes second in terms of players' size in the UK sandbox (UK, 2017). Thus, this chapter asserts that the banking industry in both jurisdictions are taking the opportunity to synergize with fintech players in offering innovative products as part of their strategy to stay afloat and to ensure that they will not be massively disrupted by the newcomers in the current financial system.

By synthesizing from the entry requirements, the regulators' mandate of promoting innovation is assisted by the creation of regulatory sandbox. Although FCA sees sandbox as a driver of competition while BNM's objective of having a sandbox is financial inclusion, nevertheless the sandbox by itself promotes innovation. This means regulatory sandbox would also serve as a strategy for the banks in Malaysia and the UK to participate in competing with the emergence of fintech players by testing innovative financial products before they are released to the market. It can be concluded that from the regulations, BNM prefers to rope in the banks to participate in the sandbox due to the resources that they have and to serve BNM's regulatory burden of ensuring financial stability (by avoiding too much disruption by fintech as a financial innovation post-GFC) and at the same time promote innovation. The FCA has taken a different approach by allowing all sorts of players despite their sizes in the sandbox (UK, 2017). Banks might have the financial advantage to ensure that the financial products are ready to be tested especially in Malaysia as BNM favours the banks to participate.

Nevertheless, BNM's requirement is the same as FCA. Both focus on genuine innovation of the product before approving any players to enter their sandbox. Thus, it is crucial for banks in Malaysia and the UK to understand how FCA and BNM define genuine innovation.

Fintech Innovation in the UK and Malaysia

Both the FCA and BNM stated that for a financial service provider to enter the regulatory sandbox, they must prove that the intended products or services have genuine innovation. From the Oxford English Dictionary, innovation simply means the introduction of new things, ideas, or ways of doing something (Dictionary, 2019). John Schindler, Assistant Director of the Office of Financial Stability at the US Federal Reserve Board argued that financial innovation has started since time immemorial, and new changes brought to any type of products and services are accepted as innovation. Nevertheless, he further opined that genuine innovation is 'one that changes the fundamental nature of a product and thus introduces a genuinely new product or service' (Schindler, 2017). He gave the examples of credit default swaps which were the first product that allowed investors to value and hedge the credit default risk of a company.

This chapter asserts that the FCA and BNM's eligibility criteria of genuine innovation are mostly related to the theory introduced by Professor Clay Christensen in his best-known work of Innovator's

Dilemma (Christensen, 1997). Professor Christensen introduced the concept of "disruptive innovation" that has changed the way businessmen think about innovation. In his theory that was created in the 1990s, a disruptive innovation happens when an innovation transforms a product that was previously expensive and complicated that only caters for the customers at the higher end, to a more affordable and accessible product that a larger population will have access to it (Christensen, 2012).

Applying his theory of disruption to financial services, he opined that it occurs when an innovative company develops a product that is much simpler and more affordable than prior products and services in the marketplace. This allows the population that previously did not have money or skills to participate in the market to be part of the market. As such, disruptive innovation creates economic growth by enabling more people to do things that previously were in the realm of the rich. It is disruptive because when it occurs at the simple end of the market, the financial incumbents find it unattractive to go after that class of consumers given their business model. (Christensen, 2016)

In financial services, this type of innovation disrupts the financial incumbents, gives rise to systemic risks, and raises the need for greater consumer protections. The disruption may happen in banks, payments, remittance, and other services in the financial industry. Furthermore, this disruptive innovation in financial services is now increasingly growing through fintech. Although the theory of disruptive innovation does not apply entirely to the genuine innovation imposed by the FCA and BNM, this chapter argues that the FCA and BNM give focus on innovation that financial service start-ups will bring in targeting the financial consumers at the bottom end. This focus is to cater to them to have access to the financial services that they may not be able to or was not aware of previously. Such disruptive innovation brings enormous consumer benefits (the eligibility criteria emphasized by the FCA) and the inclusivity of the consumers to the financial system (the eligibility criteria emphasized by BNM).

This can be referred to as the genuine innovation brought by the successful fintech players exited from the FCA and BNM's sandboxes. In the UK, Luno (previously known as BitX), was one of the first fintech players that were successful in entering and exiting the FCA's sandbox. Luno is a company that offers cross-border remittance services enabled by blockchain utilizing digital currency. This is with the view to help to transfer money to other local currencies in lower cost and faster mode of remittance (Bellens & Pogson, 2017). Meanwhile in Malaysia, the only fintech player that has graduated from the Malaysian sandbox in 2019 was MoneyMatch Sdn. Bhd. It is a company that offers fully digital cross border remittance services with lower exchange rates and fees than the financial institutions. The genuine innovation brought by MoneyMatch was to utilize the peer to peer concept for remittance services coupled with electronic Know Your Customer for customer verification. (Fong, 2017). The combination of these elements was accepted as genuine innovation which allowed MoneyMatch to provide a comprehensive digital end to end experience for the consumer.

From the examples given above, the successful fintech players from both jurisdictions have met with the eligibility criteria imposed by the regulators. Nevertheless, the question remains. How do the financial regulators determine what amounts to innovation in financial services? This is because, in determining whether fintech products or services are innovative or not, it is not within the regulators' skill set. That is one of the reasons why the United States' financial regulators (both at the federal and state level, except for Arizona) refused to adopt the FCA's regulatory sandbox (Allen, 2019) although the US fintech market is getting larger by the day. Even if the regulators have tackled the gap in their knowledge in identifying what innovation is (via the learning process they go through in the regulatory sandbox), the question remains.

In essence, analyzing from the available information of each regulatory sandboxes, it is clear that the selection process of admitting financial service providers by the FCA and BNM is not fully transparent in informing the genuine innovation that financial service providers bring into the market. Thus, this chapter calls for more transparency for both the FCA and BNM in terms of the selection process for the financial service provider to enter into their regulatory sandboxes and information on the successful financial service provider that brought about genuine innovation. The need for such transparency is discussed further below.

TRANSPARENCY

Principles of Transparency

The regulatory sandbox rests on the principles-based approach to financial regulation that focuses on open communication between all stakeholders particularly the regulators and the regulated entities and the flexibilities it offers in regulating complex activities coming from the rapid growth of fintech products and services. (Awrey, 2011) The features in a principles-based approach to regulation are the values of consistency in regulating, openness, and communicative relationship between the regulators and the regulated entities and restraint in the implementation of enforcement. (Awrey, 2011) All of these features are within the structure and composition of the FCA and BNM's sandbox.

In the bigger picture, the basis for regulating the financial system is trust and confidence. Such trust will be further improved through the incorporation of transparency into regulation. The more transparent a regulation is the more precise direction of how the regulated entities should behave. This clear direction means legal certainty that is crucial in constructing an effective financial ecosystem based on the regulations imposed. The legal certainty necessitates the formation of rules (or in this regard principles) that are disseminated, exchanged, and accessible to all regulated entities and all other stakeholders (Kaufmann & Weber, 2010). Professor Mitchell in his research on the transparency of state policy regulations stated that in ensuring effectiveness in changing the conduct of the regulated entities the state (applying to this chapter would refer to the regulators) shall produce information on the affairs that they are pursuing to regulate and how the regulated affairs resulted on the ultimate objective of such regulation (Mitchell, 1998). In summary, it talks about the importance of transparency in regulation to produce effective results of having the regulation in the first place.

Applicability of Transparency to Regulatory Sandbox

The structure of the regulatory sandbox is based on the principles of the communicative relationship between the regulators and financial service providers as regulated entities. Having the ability to two-way communication would bring a collaborative learning process between the regulators and the players. In that sense, the financial service provider will be more comfortable in innovating products or services without fear of repercussion while the regulators will benefit in learning the technological advancement used in the financial sphere. The results of those exchanging lessons must be shared via information document that is accessible to the public to achieve an absolute legal certainty of having the regulatory sandbox as fintech regulation.

One of the drawbacks of the regulatory sandbox is the lack of transparency in terms of information disseminated to the financial community at large (Zetzsche et al., 2017). This is also due to the paradoxes that principles-based approach regulation had created, whereby even though the principles give room for flexibility, but it opens to different interpretations (Black, 2008). This brings to the subject matter of principles of transparency in the regulatory sandbox. How much do the regulators need to disclose? It is crucial to note that achieving total transparency is ideal. However, it is hard to accomplish. The focus then should be on the information that will be disclosed to the public for them to be able to assess the riskiness of financial products and services (Barth, Prabha, & Wihlborg, 2014) and to the other financial service provider to drive competition for better innovative ideas to multiply.

The call for transparency has been made since the inaugural introduction of the regulatory sandbox by the FCA (Zetzsche et al., 2017). However, currently, the FCA only published information on the accepted players and the products that they will be tested in the regulatory sandbox. In 2017, the FCA published its Regulatory Sandbox lessons learned report. Part II of the report reflects the innovations brought by the financial service provider to the market and how the consumer benefits from the products and services. However, the reports were based on the sector and technologies used. The latest report published by the FCA in April 2019, presented the impact and effectiveness that the regulatory sandbox has given to the financial system since the start of the testing (Financial Conduct Authority, 2019).

The report highlighted the work the FCA had done in the past in encouraging competition of the financial service provider and the benefits that financial consumers are reaping from the fintech products. Few fintech players have successfully exited the regulatory sandbox that was picked to illustrate the genuine innovation and consumer benefit that they bring to the sandbox such as Blink, Cavva, and Nivaura (Financial Conduct Authority, 2019). However, not all successful financial service providers who graduated from the sandbox were revealed. All in all, the FCA's websites do disclose information on the list of successful fintech players entering the regulatory sandbox (Financial Conduct Authority, 2015).

Perhaps FCA's interpretation of transparency is inclined towards optimal transparency rather than total disclosure, whereby FCA only disclose the relevant information that will not jeopardize the fintech players by putting them at a competitive disadvantage (Barth et al., 2014). It is comprehensible that the information on the innovative ideas brought by the fintech players is highly confidential and case sensitive. However, the reports published by the FCA show that it is possible to disclose without jeopardizing the fintech player's case sensitive information. Accordingly, this chapter argues that such information will not put the financial service provider at a competitive disadvantage but will only enhance FCA's credibility as a principles-based regulator. Hence, more elaboration is needed on the FCA's selection of genuine innovation especially after the success of the financial service provider exiting the regulatory sandbox.

Meanwhile, in Malaysia, such reports by BNM have yet to surface. Its official regulatory sandbox website previously published the name of the financial service provider admitted to the sandbox and their current status. However, the link to the approved financial service provider in BNM's sandbox is currently not accessible (Group, 2017). This website is handled by BNM's Financial Technology Enabler Group ('FTEG') which serves as the central bank's innovation hub. There was once the FTEG website published that one of the financial service providers, WorldRemit Ltd (a London based remittance service provider) was labelled as a discontinued project. (a London based remittance service provider) was labelled as a discontinued project.

Nevertheless, it became clear from the interview with En. Mohammad Ridzuan Abd Aziz the Malaysian Director and Head of ASEAN WorldRemit that it has exited the regulatory sandbox and currently improving the level of automation for the business process to make sure that the end to end experience will be automated. There were no official statements made since WorldRemit Ltd is taking a bit more time to restart its' business. He confirmed that BNM approved WorldRemit Ltd in June 2019 (Khalid, 2019). The discrepancy between the information obtained in the official Malaysian sandbox website concludes that BNM has not achieved even the optimal transparency provided by the FCA concerning the selection process of the financial service provider.

RECOMMENDATIONS

Therefore, from the analysis provided above, this chapter shall make several suggestions. Firstly, both the FCA and BNM may consider publishing the accepted financial service provider with their innovative business in the regulators' website together with the information on how they can achieve the eligibility criteria placed by the regulators. Further elaboration might be needed in terms of reasons as to how the accepted applicants of the sandbox possess competitive advantage than the rejected applicants, an innovation that they bring into the market, how the products and services will benefit the consumers in the market and how the innovative financial products and services will further the objectives in the regulatory sandbox.

Apart from that, the FCA and BNM may also consider listing out the reasons for not accepting the financial service provider in entering their sandboxes, without specifying the name of the company due to confidentiality in protecting their reputation. Both regulators did not disclose this information. In the UK's sandbox, FCA has revealed for each cohort the number of the financial service providers that applied to participate in the regulatory sandbox. In cohort two, where the application was closed in January 2017, the FCA stated that 77 applications were made to enter the regulatory sandbox and only 31 accepted possessing the eligibility criteria however seven were not ready to participate in the sandbox. The rejected applications were assumed that they do not possess the eligibility criteria. Nevertheless, FCA did not explain further (Financial Conduct Authority, 2017a). The same situation applies to the Malaysian regulatory sandbox. In 2017, there were 53 applications to enter its sandbox but, only seven were accepted to participate. There was no explanation as to the rejected financial service provider (Malaysia, 2017).

The regulators may also elaborate on whether the rejected financial service provider was not ready for sandbox in terms of infrastructure and resources or did not meet the eligibility criteria in terms of innovation. The information may also consist of the direction that the regulators feel that the financial service provider is better to be at such as being directed to informal steers or will be regulated under the existing regulations. Besides, this chapter further maintains that the information on the innovative fintech products or services that comes from the regulators will create awareness for the financial consumers in making an informed decision. This chapter asserts that transparency of information on the selection process will not only avoid accusations of selection biases, regulatory arbitrariness, and regulatory capture but will also help the regulators to serve their regulatory burden better. The table below illustrates the connection between the two.

Applying the connection tabulated above to the focus of this chapter, which is the UK and Malaysian regulatory sandboxes, it further suggests that transparency in the selection process will better serve the FCA and BNM to achieve their regulatory sandboxes' objectives. As mentioned earlier, the regulatory objective of FCA's sandbox is to heighten competition in the market. Thus, the disclosure of the selection process especially on the innovative idea will be a driving force for other financial service providers

Table 2. The connection between disclosure of transparency and regulators duties and objectives

Regulators objectives	Effects of transparency
Financial stability	• Track systemic risks. • Avoid the concentration of products and services.
Consumer Protection	• Creating financial customers' awareness. • Contribute to fintech literacy percentage.
Promoting Innovation	• By listing out all the innovative ideas that have successfully exited the regulatory sandbox and currently in the market together with the elaboration of reasons in choosing such innovation, it will encourage other players to innovate further with lesser financial and time costs spent on research.

Source: Authors' own.

to produce better and more innovative fintech products and services in the future. On the other hand, Malaysia's sandbox focusing on financial inclusion will be better achieved when the financial consumers are encouraged to participate in the market through the increase of fintech literacy among them. It will assist the Malaysian consumers on the types of products or services that are available and beneficial for them and most importantly increase their understanding of the risks associated with such products and services.

With more information disseminated across the board, it will bring legal certainty as to the reasons for allowing such financial service providers to enter the sandbox and provide clarity in terms of the procedures and decision making of the regulators in question.

FUTURE RESEARCH DIRECTION

As stated previously, the regulatory sandbox began only since 2016. Currently, it is still a work in progress. Hence there are several areas of research that should be undertaken in the future.

This chapter focuses on the transparency of the selection process made by the regulators in the regulatory sandbox. It must be emphasized that the call for transparency in the regulatory sandbox is not only limited to that. The lack of transparency in the regulatory sandbox can be said to be two folds. One is the information on the selection of the financial service provider to enter regulatory sandbox and another will be on the information with regards to the regulatory exemptions enjoyed by the players in the sandbox.

At the time of writing, both regulators have not published any information on the relaxations that the financial service provider enjoyed during the testing period in the regulatory sandbox. Having a regulatory sandbox as a fintech regulation creates different regimes for the financial service provider. The operation of the regulatory sandbox unintendedly generates different groups of regulated entities. The first group refers to the incumbents (financial institutions such as banks) that are subject to the existing rules and regulations. In contrast, the second group refers to the fintech players that entered the regulatory sandbox which will enjoy the regulatory exemptions while playing in the sandbox. Lastly, the third group refers to newly established fintech players that are not accepted in the regulatory sandbox (Lim & Low, 2019).

It is highly crucial to disclose the exemptions and relaxations enjoyed by the financial service provider in the sandbox to monitor systemic risks and to achieve the optimum level playing field between the financial service provider. Most importantly, the exemptions should not be treated as a regulatory holiday for the financial service provider which will compromise the stability of the financial system and give high risks to the financial consumers to go unprotected. The worst-case scenario will be to repeat the history of incentives that de-regulation provides which causes the global financial meltdown.

Thus, further research can be done on the compromise of the regulatory relaxation given to the financial service provider in the regulatory sandbox towards the financial regulatory system. However, this research, in particular, requires more time to study since none of the jurisdictions implementing regulatory sandbox has published the exemptions. Secondly, the principles elaborated on the protection of financial consumers in the BNM's Fintech Regulatory Sandbox Framework are quite vague hence further research should look at the extent of protection that financial consumers participating in the regulatory sandbox enjoy.

CONCLUSION

As stated previously, the banking industry must understand regulatory sandbox as one of fintech regulatory tools. Generally, fintech disrupts the financial industry. From the outset, there are both positive and negative impacts of fintech emerging in the financial industry. The bad news for the banking industry is that it needs to compete with more convenient and efficient financial providers (fintech players) at the core of its business such as payments, remittance, and credit. That is on top of banks being a highly regulated institution, unlike fintech players. On the positive side, regulatory sandbox exists to level the playing field where the banks may participate and offer innovative products in a more relaxed environment and still be able to compete or to an extent collaborate with the fintech players to keep up with the current financial market trends.

A regulatory sandbox would make regulation easier for the participants (which may include banks as well). However, this chapter highlights the importance of transparency in the regulatory sandbox selection process in the UK and Malaysia for the regulators to discharge their regulatory burden of balancing between financial stability, consumer protection, and promoting innovation. This chapter focuses on the policy reflections that the UK and Malaysia might consider in implementing their selection process of admitting the financial service provider into their regulatory sandboxes.

It must be noted that all sandboxes are not the same. The operation of the sandbox in each jurisdiction differs based on the structure of the national financial system, other regulatory frameworks that interconnect with the system, and the economic maturity of the jurisdiction. Since 2016, after the introduction of the UK's sandbox, its composition has been transplanted in most jurisdictions including Malaysia. However, based on the discussion above, it highlights that the FCA as the UK regulator is more transparent than BNM in disclosing information relating to the selection process of the financial service provider in the regulatory sandbox. This can be referred to as the FCA publishing its regulatory lessons learned report in 2017 and its impact assessment report in 2019.

However, the optimal transparency adopted by the FCA is insufficient to provide for information that would better serve the regulatory sandbox objectives. Therefore, more information on the selection process should be disclosed not only to the regulated entities but also to the public. Meanwhile, Malaysia has not even achieved the UK's transparency level. Therefore, for a start, Malaysia may learn the moves made by the FCA in terms of admitting interested financial service provider in the sandbox, by publishing lessons learned report since 1 of the fintech player has graduated from the sandbox in May 2019. This call for transparency as policy considerations by both regulators will magnify the FCA and BNM's credibility in admitting financial service providers that will enjoy regulatory exemptions in the regulatory sandbox. Such transparency will avoid accusations of selection biases that may, later on, evolve to accusations of arbitrariness and regulatory capture.

In essence, this chapter reiterates that regulatory sandbox as fintech regulation serves as a strategy for the banking industry to enhance their understanding of innovative products and widen their business horizon. In doing so, not only benefits the industry, but it will also benefit the regulators and financial consumers as stakeholders. With banks participating in offering fintech products and regulated under the sandbox, the financial stability is ensured as systemic risks will be lesser by having the regulator's supervision. Consequently, the financial consumer may enjoy more efficient financial service options according to their financial appetite.

REFERENCES

Ajlouni, A. T. A., & Al-Hakim, M. (2018). *Financial Technology in Banking Industry: Challenges and Opportunities.* Paper presented at the International Conference on Economics and Administrative Sciences ICEAS2018, Jordan. https://www.researchgate.net/publication/331303690_Financial_Technology_in_Banking_Industry_Challenges_and_Opportunities

Arner, D. W. (2009). The Global Credit Crisis of 2008. *Causes and Consequences The International Lawyer*, *43*, 91–136.

Arner, D. W., Barberis, J., & Buckley, R. P. (2016). The evolution of fintech: a new post-crisis paradigm. *Journal International Law*, 1271-1319.

Awrey, D. (2011). Regulating Financial Innovation: A More Principles-Based Alternative. Brooklyn Journal of Corporate. *Financial and Commercial Law*, *5*, 273–315.

Barth, J. R., Prabha, A. P., & Wihlborg, C. (2014). *Transparency of Financial Regulation.* Oxford University Press.

Bellens, J., & Pogson, K. (2017). *As FinTech Evolves, Can Financial Services Innovation Be Compliant?* Retrieved from UK: https://www.ey.com/cn/en/industries/financial-services/ey-as-fintech-evolves-can-financial-services-innovation-be-compliant

Black, J. (2008). *Forms and Paradoxes of Principles Based Regulation.* Academic Press.

Board, F. S. (2017). *Financial Stability Implications from FinTech: Supervisory and Regulatory Issues that Merit Authorities' Attention.* Academic Press.

Buckley, R. P., Arner, D., Veidt, R., & Zetzsche, D. (2019). Building Fintech Ecosystems: Regulatory Sandboxes, Innovation Hubs And Beyond. UNSWLRS, 72.

Bureau, C. F. P. (2016). *Project Catalyst Report: Promoting Consumer-Friendly Innovation.* Retrieved from United States: https://files.consumerfinance.gov/f/documents/102016_cfpb_Project_Catalyst_Report.pdf

Christensen, C. M. (1997). *The Innovator's Dilemma: When New Technologies Cause Great Firms to Fail.* Harvard Business School Press.

Christensen, C. M. (2012). Disruptive Innovation Explained/Interviewer: D. Dealov. *The Idea, Harvard Business Review*.

Christensen, C. M. (2016). *Disruption in Financial Services/Interviewer: A*. Rise Global, Barclays, New York.

CommissionS. (2019). *About the SC*. Retrieved from https://www.sc.com.my/about/about-the-sc

Crane, J., Meyer, L. M., & Fife, E. A. (2018). *Thinking Inside the Sandbox: An Analysis of Regulatory Efforts to Facilitate Financial Innovation*. Retrieved from Washington DC: https://www.regtechlab.io/report-thinking-inside-the-sandbox

Dictionary, O. L. s. (2019). *Oxford Learner's Dictionary*. Oxford UP.

Financial Conduct Authority. (2015). *Regulatory Sandbox*. Retrieved from https://www.fca.org.uk/firms/regulatory-sandbox

Financial Conduct Authority. (2016). *Eligibility Criteria*. Retrieved from https://www.fca.org.uk/firms/regulatory-sandbox/prepare-application

Financial Conduct Authority. (2017a). *Regulatory Sandbox Cohort 2*. Retrieved from https://www.fca.org.uk/firms/regulatory-sandbox/cohort-2

Financial Conduct Authority. (2017b). *Regulatory Sandbox Cohort 3*. Retrieved from https://www.fca.org.uk/firms/regulatory-sandbox/cohort-3

Financial Conduct Authority. (2019). *The Impact and Effectiveness of Innovate*. Retrieved from UK: https://www.fca.org.uk/publications/research/impact-and-effectiveness-innovate

Fong, V. (2017). *Malaysia's Fintech Sandbox Partcipant MoneyMatch Launches Transfer Portal*. Retrieved from https://fintechnews.sg/13658/malaysia/moneymatch-transfer-portal-launch/

Group, F. T. E. (2017). *List Of Approved Participants In Regulatory Sandbox*. Retrieved from https://www.myfteg.com/approved-participants-in-sandbox

Juengerkes, B. E. (2016). *Fintechs and Banks – Collaboration is Key*. Wiley. doi:10.1002/9781119218906.ch47

Kaufmann, C., & Weber, R. H. (2010). The Role of Transparency in Financial Regulation. *Journal of International Economic Law*, *13*(3), 779–797. doi:10.1093/jiel/jgq037

Lim, B., & Low, C. (2019). *Regulatory Sandboxes* (J. Madir, Ed.). Edward Elgar Publishing Limited. doi:10.4337/9781788979023.00028

Malaysia, B. N. (2016). *Financial Technology Regulatory Sandbox Framework*. Retrieved from http://www.bnm.gov.my/index.php?ch=57&pg=137&ac=533&bb=file

Malaysia, B. N. (2017). *Financial Stability and Payment Systems Report 2017*. Retrieved from http://www.bnm.gov.my/files/publication/fsps/en/2017/fs2017_book.pdf

Malaysia, B. N. (2018). *Financial Stability and Payments System Report 2018*. Retrieved from Malaysia: http://www.bnm.gov.my/files/publication/fsps/en/2018/fs2018_book.pdf

Mitchell, R. B. (1998). Sources of Transparency: Information Systems in International Regimes. *International Studies Quarterly*, *42*(1), 109–130. doi:10.1111/0020-8833.00071

Schindler, J. (2017). *FinTech and Financial Innovation: Drivers and Depth.* In Finance and Economics Discussion Series 2017-081. Washington, DC: Board of Governors of the Federal Reserve System.

Singapore, F. N. (2017). *Bank Negara Malaysia Approves 3 More Participants for Fintech Sandbox.* Retrieved from https://fintechnews.sg/13686/malaysia/bank-negara-malaysia-fintech-sandbox-approves-3-participants/

Treasury, H. (2011). *A New Approach To Financial Regulation: The Blueprint For Reform.* HM Treasury. Retrieved from https://assets.publishing.service.gov.uk/government/uploads/system/uploads/attachment_data/file/81403/consult_finreg__new_approach_blueprint.pdf

UK F. C. A. (2017). *Regulatory Sandbox Lessons Learned Report.* Retrieved from https://www.fca.org.uk/publication/research-and-data/regulatory-sandbox-lessons-learned-report.pdf

Young, E. (2019). *Global Fintech Adoption Index.* Retrieved from https://assets.ey.com/content/dam/ey-sites/ey-com/en_gl/topics/banking-and-capital-markets/ey-global-fintech-adoption-index.pdf

Zetzsche, D. A., Buckley, R. P., Barberis, J. N., & Arner, D. W. (2017). From regulatory sandboxes to smart regulation. *Fordham Journal of Corporate & FInancial Law*, *23*, 31–103.

ADDITIONAL READING

Alexander, K., & Dhumale, R. (2012). *Research Handbook on International Financial Regulation.* Edward Elgar Publishing Limited. doi:10.4337/9780857930453

Arner, D. W., Barberis, J., & Buckley, R. P. (2016). The evolution of fintech: a new post-crisis paradigm. *Journal International Law*, 1271-1319.

Arner, D. W., Barberis, J., & Buckley, R. P. (2017). Fintech, regtech and reconceptualization of financial regulation. *Northwestern Journal of International Law & Business.*, *37*, 371–414.

Black, J. (2010). The Rise, Fall and Fate of Principles Based Regulation. Retrieved from http://eprints.lse.ac.uk/32892/1/WPS2010-17_Black.pdf

Didenko, A. (2018). Regulating Fintech: Lessons from Africa. *San Diego International Law Journal*, *19*(2), 311–370.

Malaysia, F. N. (2018). *Malaysia Fintech Report 2018.* Retrieved from Malaysia: https://fintechnews.my/17922/editors-pick/fintech-malaysia-report-2018/

Malaysia, F. N. (2018). Fintech Influencers Malaysia: 14 Names You Should Know. Retrieved from https://fintechnews.my/15477/malaysia/fintech-influencers-from-malaysia-you-should-know/

Mitchell, R. B. (1998). Sources of Transparency: Information Systems in International Regimes. *International Studies Quarterly*, *42*(1), 109–130. doi:10.1111/0020-8833.00071

Treasury, H. (2018). *Regulatory Innovation Plan*. UK: HM Treasury Retrieved from https://assets.publishing.service.gov.uk/government/uploads/system/uploads/attachment_data/file/606953/HM_Treasury_Regulatory_Innovation_Plan.pdf

KEY TERMS AND DEFINITIONS

BNM: The Central Bank of Malaysia that acts as the financial regulator for financial institutions, insurance and takaful companies, payments system and money service businesses. The regulatory sandbox is under the purview of BNM.

FCA: Financial Conduct Authority is the United Kingdom's market conduct regulator that oversees the UK's financial system. FCA oversees the UK's regulatory sandbox.

Financial Innovations: The changes brought to the financial products or services to attract the financial consumers in the market.

Financial Service Provider: Incumbent banks and fintech players as participants in the regulatory sandbox.

Fintech: The combination of words of finance and technology that belongs to the type of financial innovation after the Global Financial Crisis.

Fintech Players: The financial innovators that develop disruptive innovation in the financial system, which ranges from start-ups, companies or collaboration with the incumbent financial institutions.

FTEG: Financial Technology Enabler Group held under BNM as part of its regulatory sandbox's initiatives to formulate regulatory policies to assist the adoption of financial innovations that leverage on technology in the current financial services industry.

GFC: Global Financial Crisis that occurred during 2008 which was mainly caused by proliferation of financial innovations that are unsupervised and coupled with de-regulation incentives.

Innovation Hub: The institution that is established in connecting the financial regulators and financial service provider for collaborative learning process.

Regulatory Capture: The regulators that are expected to act in the best interest of the public may be controlled by the industries that they are supposed to be regulating.

Regulatory Sandbox: A pilot program that creates a parameter for the financial service provider that are given regulatory relaxations, to test their fintech products with the financial consumers under the supervision of the regulators before releasing the fintech products in the market.

Systemic Risks: The possibility that when an event occurs, it will contribute to the collapse of an institution or in this case, the financial system at large.

Chapter 6
FinTech in Banks:
Opportunities and Challenges

Rabab Ebrahim
https://orcid.org/0000-0002-5081-0111
University of Bahrain, Bahrain

Sumathi Kumaraswamy
University of Bahrain, Bahrain

Yomna Abdulla
Univesity of Bahrain, Bahrain

ABSTRACT

There has been an extensive boost in the use of FinTech in the Banking sector during the last few years. This chapter provides a comprehensive overview of the new opportunities offered by FinTech to the banking sector, its prospective risks, and the possible challenges to be faced in its adaptation. The authors propose that the new opportunities of FinTech include better digital banking experience, personalized customer services, high-level data security, cost-effective, and efficient services. On the other hand, FinTech results in risks such as security risk, technical risk, regulation risk, financial risk, and reputation risk. Finally, they suggest that the possible challenges of FinTech are a technological adaptation, risk reduction, regulations, and human capital employment.

INTRODUCTION

The banking sector globally is witnessing a potential disrupt in terms of digital technology and FinTech evolution in the recent past. This change was driven by a host of factors including financial globalization, technological advancement, need for innovative business models, and the competition among service providers thrust to satisfy the rising customer expectations. The rapid rise of financial technology is driving the banking sector towards operational innovation in gaining a competitive sustainable advantage (Zhao, Tsai and Wang, 2019).

DOI: 10.4018/978-1-7998-3257-7.ch006

FinTech enables banks to revamp their traditional business model of brick and mortar business model to technologically revolutionized ones. Technologies like Big Data Analytics, Artificial Intelligence (AI), Machine learning, Cloud Computing, Blockchain, Fog Computing, Crowdfunding and the like are changing how the banks are operating today. These technological and digital innovations can provide new business opportunities, by transforming how financial institutions create value and deliver products and services. FinTech innovations in banks are expected to reach far more beyond than what most people thinking about online banking as technological advancement in banks. This chapter will contribute to the existing literature as to how the data collected from customers at large is expected to change the worldwide banking system shortly. The detailed analysis of the potential challenges, opportunities and risks of FinTech will help stakeholders to further improve and enhance this innovation. Furthermore, it will open more avenues for future research to investigate unexplored areas in FinTech. With this background, this chapter presents a detailed outlook on the new opportunities offered by FinTech to the banking sector, its potential risks in integrating the FinTech applications with the existing systems, and the possible challenges to be faced in its successful implementation are outlined below. The most eye captured fintech applications used in banks but not limited to be discussed below.

Artificial Intelligence

One of the most popular fintech application in financial services industry, AI includes chatbots and virtual assistants in enhancing customers banking experience, machine learning in anti-money laundering software, fraud detection and compliance. AI is expected to reduce the production cost and increase the revenue to a greater extent in banks.

Blockchain

The blockchain technology enables faster and accurate payment process including cross border payments, corporate payments, inter and intra bank transfers with minimal errors. Blockchain enhances data security, decreased cost and increase the efficiency of the transactions and the marginal profits.

Cloud Computing

Cloud computing solutions as a platform facilitates banks in storing, managing and accessing the data with high level data security. Cloud systems reduces infrastructure costs and helps banks to build resilient operations.

LITERATURE REVIEW

FinTech, in general, can be defined as "technologically enabled financial innovation that could result in new business models, applications, processes or products with an associated material effect on financial markets and institutions and the provision of financial services"(Navaretti et al.,2017). FinTech in banking can be understood as the process of integrating or employing technology in banking products and services.

It was often believed that the history of FinTech dates back to the 17th century when telegraphs, railroads and steamships were utilized as channels for cross border financial transactions. (Thakor,

2019).According to a report by Forbes FinTech started gaining its momentum with the introduction of credit cards in the 1950s and Automated teller machines that replaced bank branches and teller services in the 1960s. Introduction of automated electronic trading platforms in the 1970s, computerization of bank branches in the 1980s and initiation of Internet banking in the 1990s started revolutionizing the landscape of banking business. In addition to simple FinTech products like online banking, mobile banking, social media and networking, in recent times the banking sector is moving towards more advanced digital technologies like AI, blockchain and the like. Banks are integrating with FinTech firms in developing/offering innovative financial products and services to provide enhanced digital banking experiences to their customers. On the other hand, the banking customers are eagerly waiting on how the FinTech products are going to cater to their needs or affects or how they will perceive remains cloudy. According to Vasiljeva and Lukanova (2016) the FinTech activities can be divided into three groups. First, the service-oriented which are traditionally provided by financial institutions, such as fund transfers or card payments, lending and investment, P2P lending, crowdfunding, or foreign exchange. Second, data-oriented involving technologies of collecting, processing and analyzing information. Third, process-oriented which focuses on low-cost and efficient operating models.

Recently, a few papers have explore the adoption of FinTech in banks. Mulyani et al. (2020) find that Fintech represents a threat to the competitiveness of conventional banks. On the other hand, Sangwan et al. (2020) indicate that the FinTech provide various benefits to customers in terms of accessibility, costs, decision making and choice. At the same time, there are some challenges in the adoption of FinTech such as security and data protection.

Priya and Anusha (2019) accredits that in emerging markets like India, the huge unbanked population provides enormous potential for thriving fintech companies. The study highlighted that notwithstanding the fintech adoption rate of 52%, Indian markets is still facing hindrances in terms of regulatory framework, infrastructure, financial literacy and the like. Lin (2019) details how Singapore mitigated new risks of Fintech through institutional improvements and regulatory reforms, thereby practical implications to other countries in improving their regulatory environment for the successful implementation of Fintech.

OPPORTUNITIES AND CHALLENGES IN INTEGRATING ADVANCED TECHNOLOGY IN BANKS

The emergence of FinTech in banking industry has in store a wide array of best possible opportunities for banks to remain stable and sustain the high rising competition. Handro (2018) argue that the adoption of FinTech should be considered as an alarm for traditional financial institutions that need to adapt by further collaboration with the FinTech and regulatory bodies to better serve the customers. Banking institutions are required to adopt technologies in providing world-class automated digital banking experience to their customers in terms of product design and delivery. Tech firms in the global market place are competing with each other in developing the existing technologies that could transform how the banking services are offered today.

1. Enhanced Digital Banking Experience to Customers

Leading commercial banks around the world have embraced technological advancement by investing in AI mostly in the areas of customer service followed by regulatory compliances and risk monitoring.

The banking sector in all times which strives hard to meet the rising customer expectations remains itself as a challenge. Artificial intelligence is changing this landscape with Chatbots and Conversational Interfaces in customer support and front offices creating an exhilaration in the banking business. Introduced by Softbank Robotics in 2017, "pepper" the humanoid robot is one of its kind of chatbots that offers a new type of enhanced digital retail banking experience in U.S. Studies report that these chatbots have created excitements in public relations departments of banks and bank customers. This way the banking sector is attempting to utilize the cutting-edge technology for the convenience of the customers.

2. **Personalized Services to Clients with Big data and Fog computing**

Big data analytics refers to the computational process of collecting and analyzing large datasets that are more diversified to identify certain patterns (Riahi 2018). Banks are in general are already equipped with an immense volume of databases of their clients. These datasets provide an opportunity for banks to improve their operational performance by efficiently utilizing their database in new product development and service delivery. Big data allows banks to gain insights into the client's income levels, spending patterns and transaction behaviors and segment the customers accordingly. Based on this customer segmentation, relative personalized products that cater to their needs could be developed and marketed productively. In addition, fog computing technologies collects and analyse the data gathered from mobile devices. These technologies integrates predictive systems in the process of delivering personalized customer service and product recommendations. (Nieves et.al 2019). These tailor-made product offerings and service deliveries develop in earnest customer relationships and boost the overall profitability for banks.

3. **High-Level Data Security and Better Compliance with Cloud-Based Data**

Long term and loyal relationships in the banker-customer relationship are always built on the so-called factor of "trust". FinTech is giving diverse options to build and perpetuate trust in its customers. Dreaded data violations and threats, cyber and hackers attack to create a breach of trust in customers with their banks. IT security and compliance are the two major factors that make the banking sector being reluctant towards cloud computing according to the KPMG report on Cloud Monitor 2018. Towards that end FinTech companies are designing cloud computing models exclusively for financial institutions that provide high-level data security with updated, need-based technical infrastructures. Cloud technology with a high level of data security and better compliance with the banking supervision and regulation act will create a win-win situation for both customers and banks.

4. **Cost-Effective Financial Products and Services Using Blockchain Technology**

Blockchain technology is a distributed ledger that can chronologically and securely record and transmit data in real-time (Jani & Shah, 2018). Banks worldwide try to implement blockchain technology in promoting economic growth and green finance (Cocco et.al, 2017). Experts say that blockchain technology is expected to revolutionize the banking payment patterns soon. Blockchain has the potential in creating a global network that supports the bank in transforming cross border, interbank and corporate payments and minimizes failures. If implemented successfully, banks will able to process the payments quick and accurate with reduced transaction costs. This cost savings advantage.

5. **Higher Efficient Transactions with Financial Innovations**

With the rise of FinTech firms, innovation is the only key factor of survival for traditional financial institutions including banks. The PWC report highlights that on average 88 percent of banks have the threat of losing their income to FinTech firms in areas payments and personal loans. Another report by EY announces that 60 percent of consumers prefer a single platform to access financial services. This creates enormous opportunities for sectorial growth in banks by collaborating with FinTech firms which invests highly in developing banking products. Such collaborations will results in innovative, economical banking products and services offered through a single platform in real-time.

FinTech in Banks: New Challenges

Despite the benefits and opportunities of FinTech, this innovation suffers from several possible risks. The types of risks faced by FinTech can be divided into two groups, first are related to the technology itself, second, and are related to the nature of the financial service provided. This suggests that it is not straightforward to deal with these types of risks because of their diversity. Banks and FinTech companies need to be very cautious in their ways of mitigating these risks.

1. **Security risk**

In FinTech, similar to any IT tool, security and data privacy is always a concern especially that the dealing here is in funds. There are several examples of data security cases, for instance, in March 2016, the Consumer Financial Protection Bureau (CFPB) settled its first data security enforcement action against Dwolla, an online payment processing company that was found to provide misleading cyber-security. The company has to pay a penalty of $100,000 penalty as well enhance its data security practices for the next 5 years (Hayashi, 2016). Credit card fraud is another example of security risk which result in increasing concerns of people of using digital finance.

2. **Technical risk**

Some of the traditional banking operations may be incompatible with a new technology which is considered a deficiency in the process of complete digitalization of the banking system. Furthermore, like any IT-based technique, the risk of technical failure exists.

3. **Regulation risk**

Since many of the FinTech solutions are new to the banking industry, such as blockchain, crowdfunding, crypto currencies etc., central banks worldwide have been trying to cope with these innovations by providing them with the relevant regulations, the risk exists in case of the lag or inexistence of a regulation. For instance, in the case of a FinTech firm conducting P2P lending, lending regulations are usually based on the capital of financial institution, these regulations might not apply to them as it does not technically lend. The P2P lending is an online service of matching lenders with borrowers (Lee & Shin, 2018)

4. **Financial risk**

As FinTech is used to conduct financial transactions, financial risks will always exist. However, the type of financial risk will depend on the financial transaction (Lee & Shin, 2018). For instance, the recent trend of employing robot-advisors in wealth management had also a degree of financial risk exposure from an algorithmic failure of the robot-advisors. Lee & Shin (2018) indicate that there are recent lawsuits from faulty sales of derivate products caused by inaccurate robot-advisors' investment advice. Another example of financial risk is the counterparty risk faced by a Fintech offering financial services for student loans or mortgages.

5. **Reputation risk**

One of the main criteria for customer's bank selection is the reputation driven by the friendliness of bank staff. In Kuwait, businesses believe that the financial stability of a bank, efficiency, and helpfulness of bank staff help in financial emergencies (Edris, 1997). Similarly, Al-Mossawi (2001), reputation, friendliness of staff, and convenience are the main reasons for Bahraini students to choose banks. With the introduction of FinTech, many bank services are now carried out online or through a robot that removes the human element and emotions resulting in the risk of loss of reputation. It is challenging to provide customized digital services without increased cost. Lee & Shin (2018) argue that for FinTech companies to be successful, they should be very responsive to customer's concerns as well as provide enhanced accessibility, convenience, and tailored products.

As discussed above, FinTech offers a wide array of opportunities for banks to innovate, grow, compete and sustain the global market. At the same time the banking sector is forced to overcome the possible challenges in successfully integrating technology into the traditional business models. This section discusses the major challenges faced by the banking sector in the time of FinTech.

1. **Compatibility to adapt to new technological advancement**

Technology and digital innovations can provide new business opportunities, by transforming how financial institutions create value and deliver products and services. However, keeping up with technology innovations presents a challenge in itself. FinTech can ease the access to financial services, raising competition by new players. To survive, traditional firms will have to react, face rising competitive pressure and adopt new strategies. Furthermore, many FinTech are based on new technologies, and it is challenging to integrate FinTech applications with existing systems (Lee & Shin, 2018). However, without a sound integration plan and experience, traditional banking processes in many areas may become incompatible with new technology.

Outdated IT systems are a substantial concern for global bankers as they can create blind spots. Blind spots are areas in which IT does not have complete visibility regarding what is happening on the network or how applications are working. Failure to invest in secure, active systems can result in the significant loss while increasing the risk for cyber-attacks.

2. Risk reduction

As new technologies created new security risks which can cost financial institutions millions of dollars, solutions are needed to reduce security breaches and cyber theft. Jagtiani and Lemieux (2017) note that fintechs tend to use some data sources which are disposed to more errors and thus could potentially create further risks to consumers. Moreover, as trust represents an essential factor in adopting new technologies, FinTech should keep security as one of its main concerns. They need to reevaluate their old methods to protect themselves and their customers from cybercriminals. For example, FinTech may consider the use of dynamic security solutions such as a Moving Target Defense (MTD) which helps in disturbing attacks by constantly moving the points of attack and robbing hackers of the static targets they're familiar with breaching. Financial companies can also overcome the risk of cyber-attack by using several methods such as advances in biometrics, one-time and code-generated passwords which has been proven to be more secure than traditional passwords or security questions. Furthermore, following the trends in security breaches and ensuring employees are well trained to deal with sensitive data can help protect against cyber-attacks.

3. Regulatory environment

The regulatory environment also represents a major challenge for the different financial institutions. According to Rabbani et al. (2020), regulation is one of the biggest challenges for FinTech companies. Fintech firms are associated with interaction of functionalities, consumers, technological platforms, and emerging business models, which has challenged the regulators in many ways (Arner et al., 2015). Both traditional financial institutions and FinTech startups face regulatory challenges in terms of capital requirements, anti-money laundering, and privacy and security (Lee & Shin, 2018). Traditional financial institutions and FinTech start-ups face different regulatory requirements in terms of the type of financial services they provide. For example, according to the capital held, there are strict rules for what kind of lending can be done by a traditional financial institution that may not apply to a lending FinTech startup. As there is a lag between the regulatory and the innovation of the industry, FinTech firms need to be aware of any likely changes that may impact them and find ways to deal with those changes.

Since the financial crisis of 2008, banks have been subject to heavy financial regulations. Currently, the majority of financial regulations address traditional banking but as the world relies more on digital solutions, banks must apply the same regulatory standards to their digital banking practices as well or risk being out of compliance. A new derivative of FinTech called "Regulatory technology" can be used to digitize the regulatory risk management processes, saving time, money, and resources while ensuring greater accuracy than traditional processes (Arner et al. 2017). Many Regulatory technology solutions are making their way into the financial industry to handle Anti-Money Laundering and detect fraud.

4. Employability of highly specialized human capital

Today's financial firms not only find it challenging to attract and retain customers, but they are also finding it challenging to attract employees. Haddad and Hornuf (2019) highlight the importance of human capital for fintech firms. Institutions that want to attract and retain qualified employees must change their philosophy. No longer is it enough to offer good pay and benefits; workers now expect employers to nurture a culture that is accommodating to the values and lifestyles of the employee.

Most financial firms are seeking digital technologies to help them transform and innovate. However, many do not have the data scientists, developers or IT experts they need to build their solutions. Firms will need to continue investing in their digital talent pipeline and building the skills of their people, by giving employees access to training to reskill for the IT era. One good example of this is the In-Residence, which is a program launched by J.P. Morgan's Corporate & Investment Bank in June, 2016 for fintech startups to work side-by-side with its employees to develop innovations that enable banks to operate faster, safer, and at a lower cost.

FUTURE RESEARCH DIRECTIONS

This chapter provides an insight into the host of opportunities, risks, and challenges in administering FinTech in banks as a general perspective. FinTech has a broad research scope in various areas of interest. Extensive qualitative research studies could be conducted on the customers, FinTech firms and bankers' perspectives about FinTech in different markets around the world. Also, qualitative studies could analyze the impact of FinTech on the operational performance of the banks.

PRACTICAL IMPLICATIONS

It might be worth examining empirically whether Fintech firms are more efficient than traditional financial institutions. Furthermore, this chapter raises a question on whether Fintech firms generate further systemic risks that need to be addressed. Policymakers may consider the challenges identified in this chapter, to further support the development and incubation of FinTech. Bankers should recognize that we are moving towards a new generation of banking in which they need to cope and collaborate.

CONCLUSION

Overall, we believe that FinTech has wide array opportunities to offer in integrating technology into the banking business. This can greatly improve the banks' operational performance, remain competitive, maintain sustainability, innovate new products and services, and enhance customer satisfaction levels. To implement this successfully the banks need to strive hard to face the challenges and must try to overcome the hurdles in its pathway. Though FinTech in the banking sector is in its nascent stage it is expected to revolutionize the way the financial products and services are offered shortly. This chapter will be useful to academic, industrial practitioners and households in gaining an overview of the possible opportunities, risk, and challenges to be faced by banking institutions to put FinTech into practice.

REFERENCES

Almossawi, M. (2001). Bank Selection Criteria Employed By College Students in Bahrain: An Empirical Analysis. *International Journal of Bank Marketing*, *19*(3), 115–125. doi:10.1108/02652320110388540

Arner, D. W., Barberis, J. N., & Buckley, R. P. (2015). The evolution of Fintech: A new post-crisis paradigm. *Georgetown Journal of International Law*, *47*, 1271–1319. doi:10.2139srn.2676553

Arner, D. W., Barberis, J. N., & Buckley, R. P. (2017). *Fintech And Regtech in a Nutshell, And the Future in a Sandbox.* Retrieved from January 26, 2019, from https://www.cfainstitute.org/en/research/foundation/2017/fintech-and-regtech-in-a-nutshell-and-the-future-in-a-sandbox

Boustani, N. M. (2020). Traditional Banks and Fintech: Survival, Future and Threats. In *ICT for an Inclusive World* (pp. 345–359). Springer. doi:10.1007/978-3-030-34269-2_24

Cocco, L., Pinna, A., & Marchesi, M. (2017). Banking on Blockchain: Costs Savings Thanks to the Blockchain Technology. *Future Internet*, *9*(3), 25. doi:10.3390/fi9030025

Edris, T. A. (1997). Services considered important to business customers and determinants of bank selection in Kuwait: A segmentation analysis. *International Journal of Bank Marketing*, *15*(4), 126–133. doi:10.1108/02652329710189393

Haddad, C., & Hornuf, L. (2019). The emergence of the global fintech market: Economic and technological determinants. *Small Business Economics*, *53*(1), 81–105. doi:10.100711187-018-9991-x

Handro, P, O. (2018). The Role of Customer Experience in Retail Banking and the Rise of Fintech. *Annals- Economy Series*, (1), 175-185.

Hayashi, Y. (2016). CFPB fines FinTech firm Dwolla over data-security practices. *The Wall Street Journal*, p. C4.

Jagtiani, J., & Lemieux, C. (2017). *Fintech Lending: Financial Inclusion, Risk Pricing, and Alternative Information.* FRB of Philadelphia Working Paper.

Lee, I., & Shin, Y. J. (2018). Fintech: Ecosystem, Business Models, Investment Decisions, and Challenges. *Business Horizons*, *61*(1), 35–46. doi:10.1016/j.bushor.2017.09.003

Lin, L. (2019). *Regulating FinTech: The Case of Singapore.* NUS Law Working Paper Series 2019/028, November 2019, http://law.nus.edu.sg/wps/pdfs/028_2019_Lin%20Lin.pdf

Mulyani, S. R., Kadarisman, S., & Paramarta, V. (2020). Opportunities and threats of development of financial technologies (Fintech) against competitiveness of banks (at national conventional commercial banks). *Journal of Advanced Research in Dynamical and Control Systems*, *12*(3), 97–110. doi:10.5373/JARDCS/V12I3/20201171

Navaretti, G. B., Calzolari, G., Mansilla-Fernandez, J. M., & Pozzolo, A. F. (2017). *Fintech and Banking. Friends or Foes?* Retrieved January 26, 2019, from http://european-economy.eu/wp-content/uploads/2018/01/EE_2.2017-2.pdf

Nieves, E. H., Hernández, G., González, A. G., González, S. R., & Corchado, J. M. (2019). *Fog Computing Architecture for Personalized Recommendation of Banking Products.* Retrieved September 12, 2019 from https://www.sciencedirect.com/science/article/pii/S0957417419306189

Priya, P. K., & Anusha, K. (2019). Fintech Issues and Challenges in India. *International Journal of Recent Technology and Engineering*, *8*(3), 904–908. doi:10.35940/ijrte.C4087.098319

Rabbani, M. R., Khan, S., & Thalassinos, E. I. (2020). FinTech, Blockchain and Islamic Finance: An Extensive Literature Review. *International Journal of Economics and Business Administration*, *8*(2), 65–86.

Riahi, Y., & Riahi, S. (2018). Big Data and Big Data Analytics: Concepts, Types and Technologies. *International Journal of Research and Engineering*, *5*(9), 524–528. doi:10.21276/ijre.2018.5.9.5

Sangwan, V., Prakash, P., & Singh, S. (2020). Financial technology: A review of extant literature. *Studies in Economics and Finance*, *37*(1), 71–88. doi:10.1108/SEF-07-2019-0270

Shah, T., & Jani, S. (2018). *Applications of Blockchain Technology in Banking & Finance*. Retrieved January 26, 2019, from https://www.researchgate.net/publication/327230927_Applications_of_Blockchain_Technology_in_Banking_Finance

Thakor, A. V. (in press). Fintech and banking: What do we know? *Journal of Financial Intermediation.* https://www.sciencedirect.com/science/article/abs/pii/S104295731930049X

Vasiljeva, T., & Lukanova, K. (2016). Commercial Banks and Fintech Companies in the Digital Transformation: Challenges for the Future. *Journal of Business and Management*, *11*, 25–33.

Zhao, Q., Tsai, P. H., & Wang, J. L. (2019). Improving Financial Service Innovation Strategies for Enhancing China's Banking Industry Competitive Advantage during the Fintech Revolution: A Hybrid MCDM Model. *Sustainability*, *11*(5), 1419. doi:10.3390u11051419

Chapter 7 Crowdfunding:
New Form of Both Investment Opportunities and Source of Capital

Khaliq Ahmad Mohamad
https://orcid.org/0000-0001-8129-5178
College of Business and Economics, Qassim University, Saudi Arabia

Rizal Mohd. Nor
International Islamic University Malaysia (IIUM), Malaysia

Aimadhuddin Ahmad Kamely
International Islamic University Malaysia (IIUM), Malaysia

ABSTRACT

Crowdfunding is a new form of both investment opportunities and source of raising capital. The aim of this chapter is to explore the understanding of the newly invented crowdfunding, types of the existing platforms of the industry. Authors investigated crowdfunding platforms that are registered in securities commission Malaysia and Kapitalboost platform of Singapore and their mode of investment. Authors also looked in depth and reviewed a current literature on crowdfunding. An investment model of crowdfunding that will be suitable for the Muslim investors who are looking into an ethical investment that will contribute to the wellbeing of the societies as whole through Mudharabah and Musharakah investment. The findings explored that equity crowdfunding could bring more benefit and less harm to entrepreneurs. Consequently, there are two types of models that are based on equity-in and equity-out; hence, the chapter recommends the equity crowdfunding over the debt-based through Islamic investment method of Musharakah and Mudharabah investment.

DOI: 10.4018/978-1-7998-3257-7.ch007

INTRODUCTION

History is a witness as if human civilisations have relied on business and natural resources for economic development and to increase productivity. Economic development needs to find a virtuous cycle mode, be it the financial system or the physical/real economy. Every elements of the economic development process should be scrutinized rigorously with in-depth analysis of long-term consequences and their accompanying considerations.

Crowdfunding is an emerging internet-based type activity to raise capital by the collection of small amounts of capital from the crowd. One of the types of this newly invented technology is equity crowdfunding, which is a kind of entrepreneurial finance that has been quickly developing in the past couple of years throughout the world. It has given hope to newly established businesses that faced difficulties in raising capital from the traditional financial institutions. This phenomenon worsened in the wake of the financial crisis of 2008, where financial institutions decrease the advancement of loans and investments, consequently initiating the frustration of business owners and entrepreneurs on the access to capital.

Due to the newness of the equity crowdfunding in the world in general and Southeast Asia specifically, not much research been done on it. Although some studies have been made primarily aiming at describing these new types of financing and its contributions, the common focus has been other types of crowdfunding mainly on the donation-based crowdfunding and the reward-based financing.

In this chapter, authors explore the function of six existing platforms of crowdfunding that are registered under the Securities Commission of Malaysia, in addition to the assessment of the types mostly used, and whether it is debt financing or equity-based. Through our study, authors try to contribute to the previous works that have been done in the field by looking into new areas that have not been given any attention yet, which is on how Islamic investment can contribute to the currently practiced equity crowdfunding. The chapter analyzed the Malaysian equity crowdfunding and the Kapitalboost of Singapore and review their activity as the case study by studying their method of financing and assessing their methodology in financing start-up companies.

Mudharabah and *musharakah* are the most encouraged practice with regard to the investment behavior among people and it was even practiced in the early Islamic history. However, in the current worldwide Islamic banking system, this practice seems impossible to be implemented due to less concern given by the governments, central banks, and industry players even in Muslim countries. Islamic banks come into place as the alternative to the conventional banking system. Islamic banks perform the similar essential functions as banks do in the conventional system, except the need for them to carry out their transactions in compliance with the rules and principles of Islam (Dusuki & Abdullah, 2007). The selection of potential customers based on the creditworthiness also resulted in the existence of an un-bankable group of the community who were in need of capital assistance to start a business or improving day-to-day life. Due to this scenario, people are demanding for the establishment of a specific financial institution that can provide acceptable profit rate of financing, probably with no interest and profit at all.

Equity crowdfunding is one of the examples of a financial institution established with the purpose to provide capital to entrepreneurs and small businesses without charging any interest. It only charged a service fee, which is the main source of income to support the administration cost of the crowdfunding platforms. Therefore, there is a need to further study on this newly emerged equity crowdfunding platform to understand how feasible this kind of platform to be implemented here in Malaysia.

Objectives

The present chapter based on research and study has the following objectives:

i. The main aim of this study is to explore and expand the understanding of the newly-invented crowdfunding;
ii. To understand the scopes and types of the existing platforms of the industry in relation to crowdfunding.
iii. To engage in an unsearched area of crowdfunding platforms those are registered with the Securities Commission Malaysia and Kapitalboost platform of Singapore.
iv. To investigate the investment model and their (the Securities Commission Malaysia and Kapitalboost platform of Singapore) mode of investment.

Overall this chapter encompasses six crowdfunding platforms in Malaysia registered with the Securities Commission of Malaysia and one crowdfunding platform from Singapore.

BACKGROUND

Fintech

This section will highlight how fintech and crowdfunding can be introduced in more extensive strategies of corporate advancement by examining the characteristics of crowdfunding initiatives and how entrepreneurs may utilize these platforms.

As reported by BNY (2015), it is doubtless that the fintech is a great innovation and the banks should have a clear plan in place so that they can adopt and learn something from this growth of technology. The banking industry, on the other hand, is very conservative and for them to change will at least require some time. The report suggested that if banks were to delay the immediate change, they would have to pay a higher price because the technology will not only introduce new solutions but also compete with the banks' products and services.

It is clear that banks need to have closer cooperation with the fintech industry instead of competing with them. By doing so, this new technology would allow banks some advantages such as:

- Highly standardized and cheap financial services
- Lower risk compared to banks like the borrower default and maturity risk
- Being less geographically based and more internet based
- Lower regulation of financial services

The initiatives of the financial technology can be categorized into two, one that can work hand in hand with bank services and will likely support the bank's agenda, while another provides the same services that banks used to offer; hence competing with traditional banks and providing similar products.

The rapid growth of fintech is another obstacle to the banks, although most of the writers are somehow optimistic that the banks can take advantage of this opportunity and work closely with fintech. Romanova and Kudinska (2016) stated that banks have to start cooperating with fintech in business related products formerly controlled by banks, but recently provided by fintech. Immediate changes that allow banks to grow require the banks to invest in fintech, rethink service distribution, and integration between fintech and business into business.

Challenges Related to Fintech Development

In an era of digital economies today AI (Artificial Intelligence) appears to be everywhere nowadays and every member of the present and future societies have to live with it. Since AI found its role in human behaviour, its impact is first noticed to shake the most powerful institutions in any society, i.e. governments and political set up. Elections are now being campaigned online and electoral constituencies are fooled by AI, while law and legal documents are being prepared by automation, leading to the reduced need for lawyers. The massive open online course (MOOC) system is replacing traditional class room teaching methods, while bankers would not be needed in the future. The blockchain is a by-product with AI as the core, and these two underlying technologies show the promising application in the banking industry.

On the one hand, the banking industry in China is facing the impact of interest rate liberalisation and profit decline caused by the narrowing interest-rate spread. On the other hand, it is also affected by economic transformation, Internet development, and financial innovations. Hence, the banking industry requires urgent transformation and is seeking new growth avenues. As such, the blockchains could revolutionise the underlying technology of the payment clearing and credit information systems in the banks, thus upgrading and transforming them. The blockchain applications also promote the formation of "multi-centre and weakly inter-mediated" scenarios, which will enhance the productivity of the banking industry. However, despite the permission-less and self-governing nature of blockchains, the regulation and actual implementation of a decentralised system are problems that remain to be resolved and likely to create a jungle rule once left unchecked.

Therefore, the experts and industry both propose the urgent establishment of a "regulatory sandbox" and the development of industry standards. It will most likely solve the governance issue such as transparency, accountability, ethic violation and oversight issue. Romanova and Kudinska (2016) stated that banks have a long experience compared to fintech when it comes to financial services because they have been in the field for so long, along with different departments of the banks like wealth management, risk management and some more that needs bank managers who are qualified for that. The main advantage of banks over fintech is that of knowledge intensive services and customer-oriented services that allowed banks to understand better the satisfaction of their customers by applying the "know your customer" approach.

Moreover, the banks' highly regulated model enables their business to thrive, which is based on security and protection of data. The banks might change their behaviour towards their customer, although traditional banks predict that fintech will have more risk in that sense. From 2007, European Union provided a legal foundation, i.e. an EU-wide single platform for payments that will encourage lower prices for payments.

Besides recent challenges arise from new European Data Protection enactment or similar jurisdictional matter, Malaysia has its own data security system. The Personal Data Protection Act 2010 (PDPA) is the principle legislation in Malaysia. It regulates the processing of consumer personal data in commercial transaction and provides the protection to the privacy of customer.

The authority involved and responsible for data protection in Malaysia is the Personal Data Protection Commissioner who gets assistance by the Personal Data Protection Department established by the

Ministry of Communications and Multimedia in Malaysia. This is a game changer in local scenario that covers these platforms in securities and capital market locally.

However, PDPA does not cover to any personal data processed outside Malaysia except the data is intended to be further processed in Malaysia but PDPA still binding to those company established outside Malaysia where it uses equipment in Malaysia for processing the personal data.

Crowdfunding

Despite various definitions of crowdfunding, it can be said that it originated from crowdsourcing as mentioned by some experts as "the act of doing a job traditionally by a designated agent (an employee) and outsourcing it to an undefined, generally large group of people in the form of an open call".

According to Schwienbacher and Larralde (2010), crowdfunding is an open space with the help of the Internet that provides financial services in the form of helping others (donation) or in exchange for some form of payment (reward) or a right to vote to support start-ups for a specific purpose (Schwienbacher and Larralde, 2010).

The difference between crowdsourcing and crowdfunding that crowdsourcing mainly deals with knowledge and the consumer's preferences, while crowdfunding, on the other hand, can occur for different aims from artists who want support from funds, donation purposes, or disaster reliefs. Both depends much on the Internet and online communities. The crowd can suddenly form from different individuals around the globe who share the same interest in funding projects or campaign event.

The authors concluded that the similarity between innovation and crowdsourcing is that both use external individual instead of their employee to come up with new products and services or to solve a problem.

Three main players existed in crowdfunding as stated by Valanciene (2013);

1. Entrepreneurs who try to raise capital for different projects like community projects, producing new things and for a business venture.
2. Platforms that act as an intermediary between the crowd funders and entrepreneurs by bridging the gap and bringing them together.
3. General public or the crowd funders who are willing to invest their money into start-ups or entrepreneurial projects.

The Idea Behind Crowdfunding

Companies make this kind of crowd mainly for the sake of cost minimizing, whereby the crowd will participate and design the products, so the participators will add value to the company. This will help the company to reduce the cost as well as its product development. Schwienbacher and Larralde (2010) stated that in crowdfunding platforms, customers would offer the needed capital to the company that will facilitate the activity of the company like investing in new things or paying their workers, by which this cooperation will increase the customer's perception towards the company.

Another possible reason is that the crowd is more efficient compared to individuals. Whenever it comes to problem solving, the more diverse people involved, the more efficiency will be achieved because the solving solution from the crowd arrives from different minds who will measure the problem in different mentalities, thus leading to a better solution for the company. This is due to each of the crowd knows something different whereby, in the end, the knowledge becomes more useful when shared with the communities.

Crowdfunding can also be used by the companies to provide solutions to their problems, in the case where the company wants to launch a product, they can assess the marketability of the new product or service to see whether the new product will have a high demand in the society. This will guarantee the acceptance and purchasing ability of the public towards the products.

The Benefits of Crowdfunding

Unlike venture capital, crowdfunding entrepreneurs do not give away their rights, by which when companies raised money the entrepreneurs will make the decisions themselves. Also, raising fund in crowdfunding is easy and accessible, and crowdfunding solved the problem faced in most venture capitals. According to Sigar (2012), bank loans are denied because of the lack of collateral and proven track record, besides venture capital funding a small number of businesses. Sigar (2012) thinks that the advantage of crowdfunding is that it bridges the gaps between small businesses that are undermined and generally public.

Among the opportunities of crowdfunding as mentioned by the authors is the advancement of the technology should be utilized in line with the intensified usage of social media as the modern society mostly relies on the Internet. This led to accelerated web-based innovations and projects in crowdsourcing platforms. Social networks can act as the medium used to promote crowdfunding.

The economic growth can also be one of the benefits of crowdfunding as reported by Sigar (2012) since this innovation can create new jobs and help economic recovery. The governments in some countries approve bills like the job act in the United States for job creation; hence regarded as a great opportunity for the public.

We believe crowdfunding is a new method of raising capital and there will be no contradictions. Furthermore, he argued that crowdfunding would prove itself to be a help of all kind of start-ups that were not available for so long in the current ecosystem. Crowdfunding will also be favoured by those who are not able to invest in the stock market.

The Risks of Crowdfunding

As an innovation, some detriments will be expected due to the lack of experience in the field and having competitors in the ground. Even though current legal restrictions are not suitable and welcoming to equity crowdfunding, it is still illegal under many jurisdictions. However, some equity crowdfunding was registered in the securities commission of their respective countries recently. Experts are of the opinion that the equity crowdfunding that operates now in the United States do not offer the public to become the investor. Yet they pledged a small amount in return for the individual engagement with a project either in the form of pre order or a gift.

Sigar (2012) also thinks that small businesses can be considered risky, therefore he believed that start-ups companies are always riskier and have a higher rate of failure compared to the firm businesses, whereby uncertainty of unproven products may arise, which will lead to some of the crowdfunding investors being disappointed when the businesses they invested in failed.

The risk that results from start-ups and small businesses can also be higher because crowdfunding is a tool that only uses the Internet. The investors will invest in the businesses, but no one will advise them; what is needed as suggested is to have an insight that will help investors to be protected from the dangers of losing their capital. An idea that can solve this problem is agreed upon that the protection of crowdfunding means providing oversight of the outcome from the industry professionals that intermediate and facilitate these offerings.

Equity Crowdfunding

The biggest challenge faced by the entrepreneurs is the lack of capital, whereby most of them have brilliant ideas but not the money; because the mere idea does not help them to realize their potential. Accordingly in the time that financial institutions and banks are decreasing their loan amount, which became very popular in the 2008 financial crisis, entrepreneurs and small businesses have a lower chance of getting the capital from conventional financial institutions. This is due to the reduction of loans that were previously accessible to businesses. This scenario will later create many jobs for the society besides reducing the unemployment rate, and increasing innovations and economic development.

The financial crisis resulted in a decrease in saving accounts; hence these kinds of accounts are not attractive to small investors. For the investors to have a high return, they must invest somewhere else. He suggested another kind of investment platform can overcome the problem in the form of crowdfunding. Crowdfunding has the full advantage of having a high yield return compared to investment accounts. For that reason, crowdfunding has a better opportunity in this fintech era.

The outcomes showed that the venture's general impression, particularly perceived kindness, honesty and trustworthiness, is vital to decrease perceived information irregularities of investors in the equity-based crowdfunding. It is worth to be highlighted that crowdfunding should not be considered lightly and can be a considerable investment of resources to be successful.

Smart Contracts and Related Issues

A smart contract refers to any contract that does not require a third party when individuals are dealing with one another. The contracts are automatically enforced whereby the interesting part of this method is the written form of computer programming, unlike the traditional contract that is the formal language in a printed form of the document.

The emergence of this invention will cause some disruption to the traditional financial institutions which are very conservative when it comes to contracts. Smart contracts will not only challenge bankers but lawyers and *shariah* advisors in the Islamic banking industry. However, most of the crowdfunding platforms that function today still depend on human over the smartness of the technology.

MAIN FOCUS OF THE CHAPTER

According to the above details and the lack of further resources to be referred in the subject of smart contracts, some challenges to this innovation were identified:

- **Flexibility:** traditional contracts usually have better chances concerning the revocability of the contracts because people take some time to negotiate regarding the agreement before it was concluded. Smart contracts have no such mechanism that will allow amendment of the concluded contract.

- **Enforcement dilemma of real world:** usually if humans fail to understand commercially related issues, the court system can settle the disputed parties. On the other hand, smart contracts are an only software system that allows no court system interference.
- **Adoption**: it will take some time to be understood by the users since very few business entities are using this type of contract. Most people rely on traditional contracts; therefore, the usage of smart contacts is meant for multi-party interactions.

The authors decided to undertake a research to fill in the void as discussed above. This involves serious research and methods suitably used were as follows.

Research Design

With regards on how a fiat money had debased the value of what we consider 'currency' and how interest rates unjustly transferred wealth from the masses to the rich owners of capital. It is this seemingly contradictory situation that led us to embark on a search for a better alternative if any. While the theory on the virtues of Islamic finance is readily available, we wanted to know if there is a functioning financial institution that is able to positively impact the quality and financial wellbeing of its customers that can help young entrepreneurs and small businesses to grow without falling into banks debts and higher charges. It is in this quest that we stumbled upon the curious case of Malaysian-registered crowdfunding platforms under the securities commission and see how they can help grow young businesses that are looking for investment.

The paper utilized the case study of six platforms of crowdfunding, and we also looked in depth and reviewed the current literature on crowdfunding. This will establish an investment model of crowdfunding that will be suitable for Muslim investors and anyone who is looking into an ethical investment that will contribute to the wellbeing of the societies as a whole.

Case Studies

The collection of data from the case studies included different types of crowdfunding that have emerged since the first occurrence of crowdfunding in 1997, where donations were raised through a fan-based Internet campaign. Modern crowdfunding is a later phenomenon that mostly involves the use of social media. This study will also provide details about the six approved platforms of equity-based crowdfunding that began their operations in Malaysia under the approval of the Securities Commission Malaysia (Lee, 2015). In addition, this study will also include information on Kapitalboost, which one is a Singapore-based hybrid crowdfunding platform and its operation.

Here is a need of qualifying statement that there exists a limitation in this case studies approach. Most of the companies in this business are not public listed companies therefore the annual report cannot be obtained from public source. This necessitates a need of another study based on a special arrangement from university to conduct the research with the crowdfunding company because this will be beyond the scope of this study.

TYPES OF CROWDFUNDING

Crowdfunding is a platform where the finance is raised from a group of people or organizations that may contribute a small amount of money. The practice of funding a project or venture began in 1997. Since then, four distinct types of crowdfunding have emerged in the industry. What differentiate them are the platforms used. Each type of crowdfunding encompasses different terms and requirements that need to be carefully understood before selecting the type that is most suitable and relevant to one's needs, goals, and interests.

The four types of crowdfunding are equity-based crowdfunding, donation-based crowdfunding, lending-based crowdfunding, and reward-based crowdfunding.

Equity-Based Crowdfunding

This is a mechanism that enables the investors to pile up their capital for the entrepreneurs' interest and benefit. The finances can be raised by gathering a small amount of money from many people. Equity crowdfunding is on the rise after the signing of the Jumpstart Our Business Start-ups (JOBS) Act in April of 2012. The platform's concept is an exchange of ownership of a small piece of equity for capital. It enables a broad group of investors to fund start-up companies as well as small businesses in return for equity.

In equity-based crowdfunding, investors would normally fund a large portion of the money. It does not only fund a project or venture but sometimes a start-up company that needs fundraising. That is why it is not unusual for a start-up company to practice fundraising using equity crowdfunding. Simply put, the money is exchanged for shares or a small stake in the company, business, project, or venture. Depending on the project itself, if the project is successful, the value goes up as well as the value of a share in that project and vice versa.

There are a lot of equity platforms around the world which are being approached and regulated at an international level. For instance, the two most popular platforms in the United States are AngelList and Crowdfunder. Meanwhile, Fundable and EarlyShares are popular in both the United States and the United Kingdom (Fundable, n.d.). Concurrently in Malaysia, six organizations have been registered under the Securities Commission Malaysia (SC).

Donation-Based Crowdfunding

Donation-based crowdfunding is exactly what it sounds like; the campaign amasses and allocates some amount of donation that does not expect any kind of value in return except for the expression of satisfaction from contributing to a cause which the donors believe in. This type of crowdfunding helps charitable causes with the collective effort of individuals. The main objective of this platform is to contribute to a social cause as well as the public, which may benefit from the fundraising.

As mentioned, the only reward the donors will receive is gratitude and fulfilment of social service. It is clear that no shares or any form of tangible reward will be given as an exchange for the donations collected. It is commonly perceived that donation-based crowdfunding is where money is raised for non-profit causes such as building mosques, dams, or schools in underprivileged areas. Causes may also include personal campaigns such as paying a certain individual's medical bills. This type of crowdfunding also indirectly contributes to the microfinance sector as it serves as a social cause and expects zero return.

GoFundMe and Crowdrise are both popular donation-based crowdfunding platforms among many more in the industry. Anyone may participate in the donation-based crowdfunding within the guidelines of the platform itself. In Malaysia, a personal fundraising platform, generosity.com, an offshoot of a global fundraising site, Indiegogo, enables people to channel their donation towards needy persons, charity funds, projects for a public benefit like the building of overhead bridges and schools. However, it is proven in an article that donation-seeking crowdfunding campaigns in Malaysia have yet to grow as organizers have failed to attract the people's attention. Among the campaigns which have yet to take off are fundraisings for Refugee Aid in Malaysia, which has only received US$10 (RM39) in two months.

Lending-Based Crowdfunding

Lending-based crowdfunding is also known as debt-based crowdfunding and peer-to-peer (P2P) lending. Lenders within this platform lend their money for profit-making activities. The lenders are expected to get their money back with an expected interest from the borrower. This is somehow similar to a traditional bank's or financial institution's modus operandi, but what makes it different is that instead of borrowing a larger amount of money from the bank, one can borrow a smaller sum of money from multiple people.

The mechanism of lending-based crowdfunding is different from the other types of crowdfunding as it is not an exchange of shares in a company or reward for capital. It is not the backers or donors who will provide the capital, but it is the lenders who are also called investors. The lenders provide funding hoping and expecting to get back their principal together with interest. Normally the borrower will then pay back the amount of money that they have borrowed along with a profit over a pre-determined period.

When investors offer loans through the lending-based crowdfunding, it appears that the lenders will get a financial benefit as a return, but they indirectly contribute to the success of the project, business or venture that they believe in. The lending-based crowdfunding may somewhat contribute to the micro-finance sector as the lenders lent capital to financially challenged people, most often in the developing countries without charging any interest on the loan. The lenders are also rewarded as they provide a social service for those who need financial backing. In the case of Malaysia, P2P lending is ranked 18th on the World Bank's Ease of Doing Business league tables, positioning itself as the conduit for global players to set up in Kuala Lumpur as the gateway for serving P2P lending markets across Asia. This is initial equity-based crowdfunding that has received recognition as one of the six operators for peer-to-peer crowdfunding by the Malaysian Securities Commission in Asian region.

Reward-Based Crowdfunding

Reward-based crowdfunding is the most common platform that was made available. It is a mechanism where the backers contribute their money in exchange for a reward in return. The reward is often but not always, the merchandise that is being produced by the company, business or venture or may also be an item from any project such as a concert or theatre performance. In return, the investors may get a tangible item or service such as a watch, film screening, an album, or some other merchandise.

Kickstarter and Indiegogo are the two well-known reward-based crowdfunding platforms in the United States. Both favour reward-based crowdfunding for the public or intended persons that have promising ideas but are short of funds. This platform enables them to achieve their goals. The sites focus more on channelling funds through a project or venture in exchange for a gift rather than to offer a stake in the company or capital plus interest in return for the capital. In Malaysia, pitchIN is a platform registered under the Malaysian Securities Commission as a reward-based crowdfunding platform for public interest and those in need of funds. PitchIN focuses on both equity and reward-based crowdfunding.

EQUITY- AND LENDING- BASED CROWDFUNDING IN MALAYSIA

People are keen to get financing for specific reasons based on their needs and goals. Previously, people would obtain financing through traditional methods such as borrowing money from family members, friends or institutions such as the banks. Borrowing from family members and close friends may not encounter many problems, but it is substantially difficult for a borrower to obtain financing from investors who do not know who they are. On the contrary, banks are not concerned with who the borrower is if it does not affect their ability to pay back the principal borrowed.

The problem arises when an unknown individual intends to borrow money from a wealthy investor. The investor would surely have some reservations against investing their hard-earned money in an ambiguous activity. In modern times, equity and lending-based crowdfunding were adapted from previous crowdfunding activities with more advanced and sophisticated technology for more efficient handling of finances. Modern fintech has made the process of financing and funding much easier. Extensive documentation as needed by the bank, processing fees, charging fees and any other costs will no longer be the obstacles for entrepreneurs seeking funds for their ventures. The process of borrowing has become less complicated and this pleases the entrepreneurs. It is undeniable that crowdfunding platforms are some of the most popular platforms that adopt fintech mediums for their operations. This new method of raising funds works efficiently between both investors and entrepreneurs using the Internet and social media, allowing for investments in new start-ups and SMEs.

As previously stated, Malaysia is also one of the countries that practices crowdfunding as a form of raising funds and boasts the title of being the first country in ASEAN to introduce a regulatory framework to facilitate equity crowdfunding in 2015, with six registered equity crowdfunding (ECF) platform operators to be fully operationalized by the end of 2015.

The main objective of equity and lending-based crowdfunding is funding start-up companies, small businesses, or projects and ventures by individuals with high potential, but limited access to capital. The concept is relatively simple and easy to grasp where anyone who has a concept for a new venture or small trading or business may practice their entrepreneurship. Of course, they would have to provide a guarantee or pledge that their business or venture is going to be successful for there would be a lot at stake financially.

Below is a table (Table-1 List of Crowdfunding Platform) of the registered platforms that operate in Malaysia starting in 2015 sourced from the Securities Commission Malaysia official website (Securities Commission Malaysia, 2016). This paper will explain the mechanisms of each of the six registered platforms in Malaysia, all of which are in the form of equity-based crowdfunding.

Fundedbyme

FundedByMe is a private company that appears to be one of the first diversified crowdfunding platforms in the world to offer a one-stop-shop solution for equity and lending-based crowdfunding. It has come up with two different types of crowdfunding, which are lending-based crowdfunding and equity-based crowdfunding to be offered to both investors and entrepreneurs. FundedByMe is a global platform for the two parties to meet, specializing in cross-border investment. The relationship between investors and entrepreneurs are based on transparency and trust. Guidelines are provided at every step of the crowdfunding process as well as the social media integration, which makes the process even easier to be completed. When it comes to a cross-border transaction, equity crowdfunding campaign focuses on Europe whilst the lending-based crowdfunding (P2B) is only available to Swedish companies. The latest advancement in crowdfunding is reported in an article that iTalent Management-Enterprise Digital HR Automation campaign made its debut on October 7th, 2016.

Table-1 The Registered Platforms that Operate in Malaysia Starting since 2015

S.N.	Registered Platform Operators	Contact Person	Email	ECF Website
1	FundedByMe	Daniel Goettfert	admin@alix.my	www.fundedbyme.com
2	Ata Plus	Aimi Aizal	enquiry@ata-plus.com	www.ata-plus.com
3	Crowdo	Leo Shimada	enquiry@crowdo.com	investment.crowdo.com
4	Eureeca	Chris Thomas	contactus@eureeca.com	www.eureeca.com
5	Equity.pitchIN	Sam Shafie	equity@pitchin.my	www.equity.pitchin.my
6	Crowdplus.Asia	Bryan Chung	info@crowdplus.asia	www.crowdplus.asia

Source: Adapted by the authors

Typically, the amount of money invested was between €100 and €100,000, while the amount of money borrowed was between €25 and €25,000. FundedByMe has successfully operated locally in Sweden, Finland, and Malaysia; and partnered with Alex Global Sdn. Bhd. in Singapore.

The charges of services by the FundedByMe platform are different based on the type of the crowd-funding. For the equity campaign, a €1,000 listing fee goes to the campaign and an 8% success fee on the total amount of money is collected at the end of the campaign. This is solely chargeable to the entrepreneurs. As for the lending-based campaigns, 4% (2% is for FundedByMe, and 2% goes to handling payment services) will be charged on the success fee of the total amount of money raised for a successful campaign. An additional 1% administration fee will also be charged on repayments to the investors.

Ata Plus

This licensed online equity crowdfunding platform allows entrepreneurs to publicize and showcase their businesses opportunities to obtain funds from the investors. Entrepreneurs will pitch their business propositions through the Ata Plus portal to be screened and later to be listed in the portal. A crowd of potential investors may take a look at the listed businesses and engage with the entrepreneurs online and assess the deals before making a final decision. Once the target funding amount is met, the fund is then disbursed. The investors will be updated with business progression and performance. The amount of money to be invested varies; for a sophisticated investor, there are no restrictions on how much they can invest, while for an angel investor, a maximum of RM 500,000 is permitted within a 12-month period and a maximum of RM5,000 per issuer (entrepreneur) with a total amount of not more than RM 50,000 within a 12-month period for retail investors.

Processing fees are required for entrepreneurs to get their business listed. The first screening processing fee is RM500, whereas the next screening (My Pitch) processing fee is RM 2,500. As for the investors, all required government levies or taxes will be charged accordingly such as stamp duty etc.

Crowdo

Crowdo is a regional fintech company offering crowdfunding portfolios, equity-based and lending-based crowdfunding (P2B). Their fund raisings was meant to help connect high growth companies like start-ups and SMEs segments with the Global Smart Capital. The undertaking process will be assisted by Crowdo in customizing the entrepreneurs' marketing plan offers before they get published. Once the offers are successfully customized, they will be published on a membership-based newsletter. Investors may invest an amount that they are comfortable with. In addition, investors will need to abide by the investment limits imposed by the Securities Commission of Malaysia as follows: as a sophisticated investor, there is no investment cap; as an angel investor, RM500,000 per 12-months period (or its foreign currency equivalent), while as a retail investor, a maximum amount of RM5,000 per issuer and only up to RM5,000 per 12-months period (or its foreign currency equivalent). This easy-to-use platform is operated in three countries, which are Malaysia, Singapore, and Indonesia (Jakarta).

Basic fees will be charged to the entrepreneurs such as a processing fee of about RM999 (exclusive of disbursements and GST) for preparatory work and completion of statutory due diligence. The amount should be paid upon signing of the Engagement Letter immediately. An on-boarding fee of RM 7,000 (exclusive of disbursements and GST) will also be charged for on-boarding related services including business due diligence, form processing, consultation and offer marketing preparation work. The fees are payable in two tranches before the Offer's launch. In addition to those, administrative fees will either be charged between two fee schedules; fee schedule A: Offers a pre-committed Lead Investor/s: 4% on the Lead Investor contributed amount; 7% on the remaining raised balance amount (admin fee %s are exclusive of disbursements and GST), and Fee Schedule B: Offers NO pre-committed Lead Investor/s: 7% on the total raised amount (admin fee %s are exclusive of disbursements and GST). Additionally, a nominee service fee will be separately charged, while the membership and escrow account fee will be waived. On the investors' side, the payment processing fee will be borne due to specific scenarios.

Eureeca

Eureeca enables both members and investors to collaborate by buying shares and providing operational business. The entrepreneurs may apply to raise funds and subsequently go through the required processes such as rigorous screening. The entrepreneurs will then be able to launch their fundraising campaign on the provided platform. Eureeca provides an accessible, transparent, efficient, and cost-effective method of raising funds compared to the more traditional sources of capital. The minimum amount that can be raised for an SME is $250,000. For most jurisdictions, there is a zero limit on how much an SME can seek to raise. However, according to Malaysian SC regulations, the maximum amount an SME can raise is RM3 million within a 12-month period, which can be broken up over multiple rounds. This platform operates in Dubai, London, and Malaysia.

The entrepreneurs will be charged an application fee of $1,500; but if the assessment is not passed by the Investor Committee, the money will be fully refunded. Other charges such as success fees on the amount raised when the campaign is successful will be charged by Eureeca as much as 7.25%. There will also be an additional 3rd party legal fee, which is applicable during the closing process.

Equity-PitchIn

Since its inception in 2012, the pitchIN rewards venture has become the most successful rewards crowdfunding platform in Southeast Asia. It holds the record for the most funds raised and the greatest number of backers for a single project. The entrepreneurs have to provide information about their business or venture and the reason why they require funds. Depending on the number of funds being raised, SC guidelines mandates for various levels of audited or certified financial information. The minimum amount per investment is RM5,000, while the maximum is an investment of RM500,000 per annum in total. Investors also have the privilege of a cooling-off period of six business days.

The fees that are going to be charged include acceptance for full due diligence and listing processing for as much as RM888 administrative charges, 7% of success fee if the project is successfully funded, and as per nominee structure for extra shareholders charges will be charged starting from the second year onwards. Other than these, no fees are charged for the operation of the platform.

Crowdplus.Asia

This is an equity crowdfunding platform backed by the Netrove Ventures Group, a regional tech-based venture capital firm and Propellar Corporation Ltd., which is based in Hong Kong. Not only does the platform operate with a previously tested deal sourcing, but also launches a unique "QMI" feature that brings qualified and specialized mentors and investors across the region to achieve greater value creation as well as enhance the success level of the companies. No minimum investment is specified by the company, while the maximum investment is RM 3,000,000 in any 12-months. The minimum investment for an individual, however, is RM500 and the maximum investment is subject to the investor type. The platform operates in several countries like Malaysia, Thailand, China, Vietnam, and Hong Kong.

There will be a 5.5% to 7.5% fee charged on the total amount raised in a successful fund-raising campaign, whilst in the event of an unsuccessful campaign, zero fees will be charged. In addition, it is important to note that any cost associated with coaching, financial and legal due diligence, if required, is not refundable.

Kapitalboost

In addition to the previous crowdfunding platforms, this study will also include information on the Singapore-based hybrid crowdfunding platform, which allows investors to invest or donate in an ethical and *shariah*-focused way. Kapitalboost provides SME crowdfunding, donation crowdfunding, and private crowdfunding to the intentional entrepreneurs.

SME Crowdfunding

The capital is normally offered to small businesses for the purchase of assets. This is a cost-plus profit arrangement, which is also known as *murabahah* in the Islamic finance or sale base structure. The modus operandi is where the financiers buy assets for businesses and immediately sell to other businesses at a marked-up price on a deferred payment basis, in which the cost plus the profit is disclosed. For this platform, entrepreneurs face certain requirements for obtaining funds; their businesses would have to be operating for at least one year, they would have to achieve a revenue of at least SGD10.000 in the past financial year, they would also need to have a positive free cash flow in the past year and receivables from existing orders or sales contracts with fixed payment terms. The funds will be received in two to five weeks. Kapitalboost is operating in Singapore, Malaysia and Indonesia, but intends to expand its services to other ASEAN countries.

An administrative fee of 5% of the total funding amount will be charged on a successful campaign, while a fixed fee of $50 will be charged to cover the administrative costs on a failed funding campaign. The profit margin on asset sales will be determined by Kapitalboost with the business owner's consent and will depend on the repayment period and the risk profile of the business.

Donation Crowdfunding

Additionally, Kapitalboost also offers donation crowdfunding. In donation crowdfunding, funds will be channelled to any project which supports the less-privileged communities in Southeast Asia. This may include, but is not limited to, the building or renovation of schools or mosques and funding the development of infrastructures in lower-income communities. As is evident in its name, zero fees will be charged as it only offers services as a corporate social responsibility. The project's progress will be updated over a certain period accordingly via email.

Private Crowdfunding

Kapitalboost also assists fund transfers and preparation of legal funding agreements between parties, which aids in building trust between both contracting parties. It funds any kind of business that does not contravene with the Islamic rules and principles. The campaign will normally run for 30 days, but if the fund's target is not met, the campaign will be extended for another 15 days. In operating the private crowding, 3% of the total funding raised will be charged as an administrative fee.

FUTURE RESEARCH DIRECTIONS BASED ON FINDINGS

Equity-Based vs. Debt-Based Crowdfunding

In this chapter, we only focus on the two types of crowdfunding, which is the equity-based and debt-based. We can see that all the crowdfunding organizations that have been registered under Security Commission Malaysia are providing equity-based crowdfunding and only two out of six come out with an alternative type, which is based on debt. There are several advantages and disadvantages of using both types of the existing crowdfunding platform.

Firstly, equity-based crowdfunding could help in cutting the cost related to debt and other services such as the interest rate, processing fee and others. The entrepreneur does not have to think about making a fixed monthly loan payment to the debtors anymore. This is very important for the start-up business before they can have their first positive cash-flow. For some of the crowdfunding platform, they will provide only the capable business investors that have the knowledge, valuable skills, contact and experience as they can help entrepreneurs to grow and explore more on the nature of the project. In other words, investors could also become a consultant for the entrepreneur in directing their project. Investors will not let the project to run freely because they also have the right over it. Often, they will be a frequent follow-up to see the project's profitability, growth and increase in value. In addition, the entrepreneur also does not need to worry about the credit issues anymore. In equity financing, a poor credit history (having a bad debt or does not have any financial track record before this) is something immaterial to the investor. They only look at the prospect of the project and its growth opportunity. However, the good always comes with the bad. Accordingly one of the disadvantages of equity-based crowdfunding is the owner of the project could not be the only one who can decide in the business anymore. Moreover, a project manager will also have to invest their management time to provide information periodically to the investors because investors need to look comprehensively into the project that they are currently financing. Not to mention, the rate of return on equity financing could be much higher than a debt financing, but this is dependable on the policy of the business itself.

Debt-based crowdfunding also brings some advantages in helping out the entrepreneurs to raise their capital. Allen (2018) stated that the owner of the project would have the power to retain control over their ownership because as a borrower, the entrepreneur is only obligated to make payment of money plus an agreed level of interest only. Lenders do not obtain any rights regarding the ownership of the business. So, the entrepreneur has much more freedom in directing their business strategies and policies. Other than that, the significant attraction of debt-based crowdfunding is to have a tax deduction on the interest and principle paid by the borrower because it will reduce the net obligation of the business. In other words, the government is partially or fully eliminated (depending on the business tax rate) from the equation of expenses. Debt-based financing will also let entrepreneurs know in advance the amount of principle and interest they have to pay for a certain period. It helps them to plan their financial budget more efficiently. Unfortunately, debt-based crowdfunding also has a negative effect. The obligation to pay back the loan will always be continued even though the entrepreneur's project failed in the middle or a loss and it could lead to bankruptcy. The interest rate applied to the principle is much higher than the dividend that the owner of the project has to pay to the shareholders although the interest rate has been discounted from the tax deduction. Kunigis (2017) said that entrepreneurs need to be more disciplined to ensure the repayments to be made on time. This is because it could affect the credit rating of the business as investors will see them as a high-risk project in case of default. It is worth to note that the more debt an entrepreneur has, the higher the risk and the higher the interest rate they have to pay. Debt-based crowdfunding forced entrepreneurs to put up their assets as collateral in case of failure. In simple words, they have to personally guarantee the loan with putting their assets at a potential risk since the lenders will liquidate the assets to gain back their money if anything happens in the future.

Islamic Perspective of Equity Financing

First and foremost, it is agreed that the most important principle in Islam that must be upheld is *Adl* or Justice. That is why Prophet Muhammad (*saw*) has been sent down to mankind, as the messenger to this world and to teach the people on justice. As Allah the Almighty said in the Quran,

"We sent Our Messengers with clear signs and sent down with them the Book and the Measure in order to establish justice among the people" – Al-Hadid 57:25

In the context of economy, justice can only be established by adopting the *Shariah* law (code of divine law) in order to maintain and regulate activities of people in a fair state. As pointed out by Hassan (2014), the connection of justice and economy can be seen in a direct link to the Islamic belief in the Oneness of God and the role assigned to man. In the Quran, Allah has said that He appointed human as vicegerent on earth and trusted him with all of its resources. There should not be any dispute despite the differences in the human status because the privilege and responsibility are given to everyone and mankind should conduct justice in all their dealings. Therefore, either the rich or the poor should get an equal chance of using the available resources.

According to Yusof et al. (2009), debt-based financing does not provide equality in opportunity as there is a separation between the poor and the rich because the investors will give more concern to the collateral available for debt application, and because they do not expect profitability, no chance was given to the poor and middle income community to have a chance in developing their wealth. Debt financing is more likely to be driven by wealth protection in only one party and can cause wealth concentration. This is proven in the banking sector whereby they do not want to take a bigger risk in financing the poor people; therefore they only approve customers who have a stable and good credit rating. A study conducted by Ab Manan et al. (2011) stated that 75.8% of the established SMEs took both Islamic and conventional debt financing and the modes of financing that SMEs are using in the Islamic financing system is *qard hasan*, *murabahah*, *bay bithaman ajil*, *bay al-inah*, *ijarah*, and *bay al-dayn*. None of them took the institutional equity financing.

Therefore, an alternative mode of financing that can replace debt-based financing is by using equity financing whereby the emphasis is more on partnership and profit-loss sharing concept. As Allah said in the Quran, "If there be more (brothers and sisters of the same mother), they shall (equally) share a third of the estate, after payment of any bequest that may have been bequeathed or debt (incurred); the bequests made should not harm (the rights of the heirs)" – An-Nisa' 4:12.

Although this verse specifically underlines the rule of Islamic inheritance, Muslim jurist agreed that in a general term, the text is regarded as general permissibility of any form of partnership. Partnership or equity financing leads to more efficient and better use of resources because not all individuals have access to the same resources. Some individuals have the resources but do not have the time and expertise to manage it. Some of them have the expertise and time to manage the resources, but lack of resources. Pooling them together in partnership is a good move so that the resources could be used more efficiently and will circulate wealth in the economic cycle. However, the weakness of debt financing is that it depends solely on the credit worthiness of an individual regardless of the usage of funds. Other than that, equity financing also is a model that moves beyond the normal financial access because it addresses poverty alleviation by focusing on income generating activities and careful endorsement of entrepreneurial activity. These characteristics make equity financing to fulfil one of the *maqasid shariah*, which is the protection of life by uplifting social welfare issues. Abu-Joudeh (2011) said that most of the individuals that seek financing through equity financing were driven by the interest in improving their own quality of life (individuals that come from poor background income), thus enabling the entrepreneur to have a more ethical conduct in doing the business so that they can generate profit as they know how to appreciate the money.

Lack of Investment Account in Islamic Bank

Among the challenges of Islamic banks in Malaysia is using their investment account to cater the needs of customers. This phenomenon did not occur only in Malaysia but also affecting Islamic banks worldwide. Investment accounts in the Malaysian banking context refer to the *mudarabah* and *musyarakah* partnership contract that utilize the profit and loss sharing concept between the capital provider and the users of the fund (Bank Negara Malaysia, 2015). According to Abdul Rahman and Mohd Nor (2016), there are four challenges in the implementation of *mudarabah* and *musharakah* as contracts in the investment account. The four challenges are high risk, selection, demand, and capital security.

Firstly, Islamic bank classified investment account as high risk financing because of the high probability of failure influenced by some factors such as the entrepreneur's skills and experience in a business area. Banks do not favour high risk; hence they become very cautious in providing the financing because they have adverse risk appetite. Thus, only the entrepreneur identified as having a bigger potential to expand and have a long track record in financial performances will be approved in their financial application. This has somehow become the same as the debt financing requirement as they do not give a chance to new entrepreneurs. Secondly, the bank faces challenges in the selection process of their partner. The bank as a business organization needs to ensure they are consistently generating profit, so they will remain competitive in the market. The difficulty of the selection process is stressed in their review of a various aspect of risk related to the applicant's business condition. Nevertheless, it is done to protect the safety of the depositors' funds from loss and the bank need to compensate it later by subtracting the amount from the bank's other profit.

Secondly, banks are always sought out by applicants from the SMEs who lack in the capital to grow. In this case, most of them do not have any stable business track record and credit standing yet. Therefore, these applicants are largely exposed to the high risk of failure because of their unknown business potential. Referring to the risk factor, banks do not prefer to entertain high risk applicants who will contribute to their losses. Hence, although there is a higher demand from the SMEs, Islamic banks sometimes have to forgo this kind of application and will choose only well-established businesses. The final challenge is the capital security factor. A bank must protect the depositor's money by ensuring the safety of the capital in an investment account. Any investment contracts that are offered to the customers must have a capital guarantee in the form of collateral such as housing and land assets that have high value as an assurance in the case of losses in the future. Capital securitization is a very important element in protecting the bank if there is fraud or mismanagement by the partners. Unfortunately, not all partners can provide the capital guarantee since some of them does not have such privilege as they just started their business.

Islamic Equity-Based Financing

From the comparisons above, we found that equity-based crowdfunding could bring more benefits and less harm to the entrepreneur from both the conventional and Islamic point of view respectively. However, none of the models that have been used by the six organizations registered under the Securities Commission Malaysia is of the Islamic type model. In this chapter, authors proposed two types of models that are based on equity-in and equity-out as authors found that this is the best model to help investors invest in the project and dissociate debt from the entrepreneur.

Figure 1. First type of Musyrakah Crowdfunding Model Based on Equity-in and Equity-out

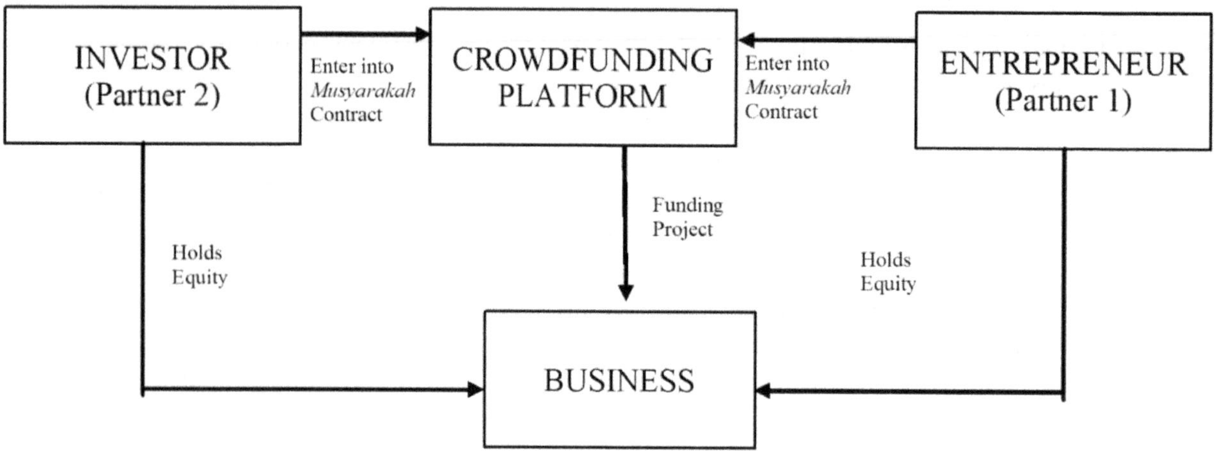

Musyarakah is a partnership between two or more parties and all contracting parties contribute capital to the *musyarakah* venture and share the profit and loss from the partnership. The relationship between partners is mainly on the principle of agency (*wakalah*).

- When the *musyarakah* contract emerges into the crowdfunding model, the entrepreneur (partner 1) in the *musyarakah* model will determine how many funds he or she need to raise after subtracting their capital contribution to fund the start-up business or to help existing business to grow further.
- Thereafter, they will go into the crowdfunding platform and run the campaign to raise money from the investors.
- They will also have to provide all the business and personal details to be evaluated by the investors and crowdfunding management and the evaluation must also include *shariah* elements such as the business must be free from *riba'*, *gharar*, *maysir*, and other haram elements.
- The projected campaign will go live on the Internet and attract investors to come in.
- The investors will invest their money into the project and become a partner to the entrepreneur.
- A pre-determined profit-sharing ratio is agreed between the investor and the entrepreneur upon the contract is concluded.
- When the period and goals of the campaign are achieved, all funds will be used in funding the project or business after deducting some fees to the crowdfunding organization.
- Each of the investor and entrepreneur will hold equity or shares according to their capital contribution.

- Any loss occurring in the future will be borne based on the ratio of the capital contribution to avoid the capital from being guaranteed as it is not permissible in Islam because it will create injustice to both parties.
- This type of model is suitable for a start-up entrepreneur with insufficient capital to run the project or well-established business that want to grow their business further.
- In the case where the entrepreneur does not have any capital but still want to proceed with the *musyarakah* contract, they may ask the investors to lend them some money based on the *qard al-hasan* contract. Then, they will use that money to proceed with the *musyarakah* contract with the same investors.

Figure 2. Second type of Mudarabah Crowdfunding Model Based on Equity-in and Equity-out

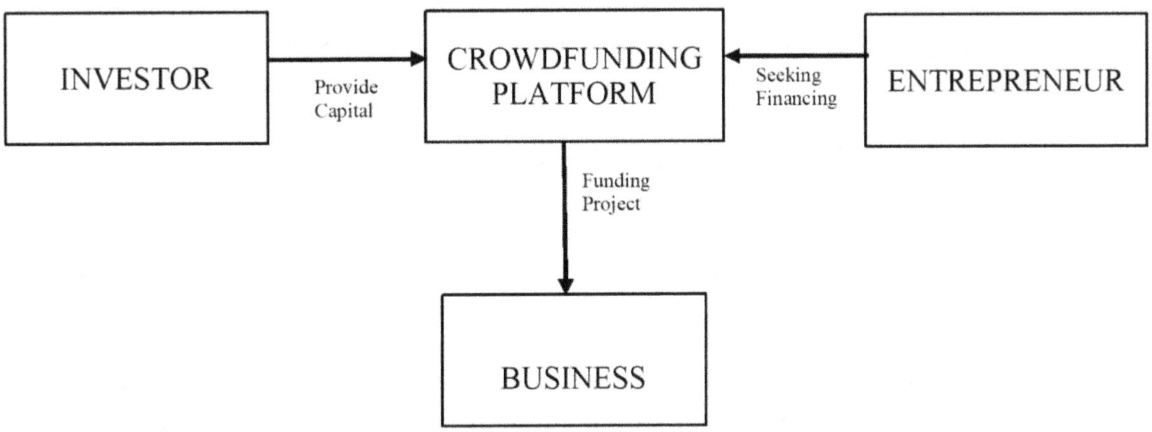

Mudarabah is the contract between a capital provider (*rabbul mal*) and an entrepreneur (*mudarib*) in which the *rabbul mal* provides the capital to be managed by the *mudarib* and any profit generated from the capital is shared between the *rabbul mal* and *mudarib* according to a mutually agreed profit-sharing ratio (PSR) while financial losses are borne by *rabbul mal*, provided that the losses are not due to the *mudarib's* negligence.

- When *mudarabah* emerges into the crowdfunding model, the entrepreneur will take the roll as the *mudarib* and the investor as the *rabbul mal.*
- In the beginning, the entrepreneur who does not have any capital will go into crowdfunding platform to fund their project.
- They will need to provide their business and personal details to be evaluated by the investors and crowdfunding management and the evaluation also must include shariah elements such as the business must be free from *riba'*, *gharar*, *maysir*, and other haram elements.
- The projected campaign will go live on the Internet and attract investors to come in.
- An investor who is interested to be involved in the project will then enter into the *mudarabah* contract with the entrepreneur.

- A pre-determined profit-sharing ratio is agreed upon the conclusion of the contract.
- After the period and goals of the campaign are achieved, all funds will be used in funding the project or business after subtracting some fees to the crowdfunding organization.
- Shares of the business are fully owned by the investors.
- Any loss occurring in the future will be covered by the *rabbul mal* provided that it is not due to the *mudarib's* negligence. This is because some scholar recognized the effort made by the entrepreneur as a form of capital.
- This contract is more suitable for a start-up entrepreneur.

Adaptation of the Smart Contract into Islamic Crowdfunding

The existing platforms will be a challenge for Islamic crowdfunding to attract potential users. Therefore, they must provide a unique feature to boost the performance of the conduct. In this paper, Islamic crowdfunding was suggested to adopt the smart contract approach to ensure the smoothness of a transaction. Accordingly a smart contract is a form of a legal clause or agreement that have been digitalized instead of using ink and paper where it combines the protocols with a user interface to formalize and secure relationship between parties involved over a computer network. It is used in facilitating the online transaction, particularly in online shopping over a decade ago because people are familiar with the terms and condition provided by those shopping websites. The smart contract also brings traditional contract a step further by transferring asset or currency running by encrypted data as it automatically determines where the asset or currency should be transferred between both parties when the terms and conditions are validated.

To ensure Islamic crowdfunding can compete with the existing platforms, it is recommended for them also to adopt smart contract in completing the transaction. The reason is that most of the legal fees imposed by the *shariah* experts in providing legal documentation for the contracting parties are too expensive. With the smart contract, the cost will be reduced as it is only a one-off fee in which the *shariah* expert will be involved only at the first time during the making of the contract (encryption of the contract information into computer code) instead of providing paper documentation every time there a transaction occurs. In addition, the transportation cost can also be eliminated from the chain of transaction fee because no travel expenses are needed for the signing of the contract. They would just need to digitally sign or click 'agree' on the pop-up box in the smart contract to accept the terms and conditions for the agreement. Any unnecessary delays between the contracting parties in achieving the goal of the contract will be cut off. This is important in strengthening the relationships of the parties involved

However, several challenges need to be considered before adopting a smart contract in the crowdfunding platform. It seems that the smart contract does not provide freedom in negotiating the term and condition of the agreement. As usually said for a human behaviour is unpredictable because they tend to find something that suits their needs. The flexibility in bargaining and avoiding rigid commitment and outcomes contained in the contract is one of it. Moreover, the smart contract also has the threat of confidential data exposure, it is also to be stated that although the smart contract has its miniature database accessible and controllable by only one party, it still does not solve the problem. This is because the data is still stored on every single node of the chain and the participants of the blockchain can just modify their blockchain software to retrieve the confidential information.

CONCLUSION

This study presents the power of fintech in developing the microfinance sector by using the crowdfunding model as a platform. Various types of crowdfunding model have been discussed such as the debt-based model, equity-based model, reward-based model, and donation-based model. However, in the case of developing the microfinance sector, only two out of four crowdfunding models have been emphasized, which is the debt-based and equity-based model.

During this research, the debt-based model was found to be of little help to entrepreneurs in terms of business growth. This is because of the interest rate imposed to the entrepreneur is expensive and by having debt, it will force them to put their assets as collateral to back the loan in which not everyone can afford it. The only closest model to the Islamic principle is an equity-based model, but none of the six-crowdfunding organization registered under the Security Commission Malaysia has adopted Islamic equity-financing contract in their model. In this paper, we have proposed two new crowdfunding models that are based on the *musyarakah* and *mudarabah* contract. New crowdfunding models provide a *shariah*-compliance platform either in terms of the contract and its business's substance.

In addition, Bank Negara Malaysia also has launched the Investment Account Platform (IAP) backed by six Islamic banks. This IAP function almost the same as the crowdfunding model but they aim to promote bank investment accounts. It does not portray the true functionality of crowdfunding in helping SMEs when banks used debt-based contract such as *murabahah* and *wakalah* with the entrepreneur while between the bank and investor are using equity contracts such as *mudarabah* and *musyarakah*. In simple words, the bank does not want to be involved in risky financing. IAP also charged a double profit for the entrepreneur and investor separately.

Hence, this research provided a solution on the best financing model that crowdfunding could adapt so that they could be used in the future to cater the Muslims need in this country. It is also hoped that the experts in *shariah* compliance will be involved in crowdfunding organization to ensure implementation of the *shariah* contract and close examination of the business proposal is done thoroughly.

Another dimension deals with scope of this study, is a limitation of this research that there might need a special arrangement from university as scope of a contract research to conduct the research with the crowdfunding companies elsewhere. Because this research has its limitation of time and resources and there is clear scope of limited jurisdiction of Malaysia including Singapore.

Recommendation for Future Research

We have found gaps in the current researches in this emerging discipline and innovation that is capable of a major disruption since most of the literatures reviewed only covered fintech's operation, risk related to the investment, type of crowdfunding and the pros and cons of the crowdfunding. However, none of them are touching on the *shariah* context of crowdfunding whereby the *shariah* context is the most critical part in determining the non-*shariah* investment for Muslims. This potential research area should be able to help other researchers to propose a new *shariah* based concept of crowfunding, measuring the performance of crowdfunding through different type of *shariah* compliance tools and determining the revenue generated from crowdfunding is either *shariah* compliant or otherwise. The current study provides evidence that the existing crowdfunding in Malaysia are successfully to offer equity crowdfunding platform to the public. Nevertheless, Islamic crowdfunding agencies are still very few, if none in number compared to the conventional ones. Therefore future research on the *shariah* context could help the industry to offer Islamic crowdfunding in the market later, is the strong recommendation for future researches.

REFERENCES

Ab Manan, S. K., Othman, J., & Shahadan, A. (2011, June 1–3). Descriptive analysis on the pattern of SME financing in Malaysia. In *3rd International Symposium & Exhibition in Sustainable Energy & Environment* (pp. 139-147). Melaka: Academia. 10.1109/ISESEE.2011.5977122

Abdul Rahman, A., & Mohd Nor, S. (2016). Challenges of profit-and-loss sharing financing in Malaysian Islamic. *Malaysian Journal of Society and Space*, *12*(2), 39–46.

Abu-Joudeh, B. (2011). *Exploring the potential for profit-loss sharing models in Islamic microfinance* (Working paper). Social Impact Research Experience (SIRE). University of Pennsylvania. Retrieved from http://repository.upenn.edu/cgi/viewcontent.cgi?article=1014&context=sire

Allen, S. (2018, December 24). *Pros and cons of debt financing for business owners*. The Balance Small Business. Retrieved from https://www.thebalance.com/debt-financing-pros-and-cons-1200981

Alois, J. (2015, June). *Fintech: FundedByMe is Approved to Operate Equity Crowdfunding in Malaysia*. Retrieved from Crowdfund Insider: https://www.crowdfundinsider.com/2015/06/69318-fundedbyme-is-approved-to-operate-equity-crowdfunding-in-malaysia/

Bank Negara Malaysia. (2015). *Mudarabah. Kuala Lumpur: Bank Negara Malaysia*. Retrieved from http://www.bnm.gov.my/guidelines/05_shariah/Mudarabah.pdf

Bank Of New York. (2015). *Innovation in payments*. BNY.

Bons, E., Daams, M., Neijnens, E., Ottenheym, D., Segeren, M., & Van der Sommen, G. (n.d.). *Open innovation: The benefits of crowdsourcing*. Tilburg University.

Fundable. (n.d.). *Crowdfunding101: Types of Crowdfunding. Fundable*. Retrieved from https://www.fundable.com/crowdfunding101/types-of-crowdfunding

Hassan, A. (2014). *The principles of Islamic economic justice and its sources*. Jubilee Australia. Retrieved from https://www.jubileeaustralia.org/page/about/Jubilee%20Islamic%20Economic%20Justice.pdf

Hebert, C. (2015, June 2). *Ask Clay: The Different Types of Crowdfunding*. Retrieved from Crowdfunidng Hacks: http://crowdfundinghacks.com/different-types-of-crowdfunding/

Hobbs, J., Grigore, G., & Molesworth, M. (2016). Success in the management of crowdfunding projects in the creative industries. *Internet Research*, *26*(1), 146–166. doi:10.1108/IntR-08-2014-0202

Hollas, J. (2013, December 15). *Blog: Three Types of Equity Crowdfunding*. Retrieved from Equity Net: https://www.equitynet.com/blog/three-types-equity-crowdfunding/

Hurst, S. (2016, October 13). *Fintech: FundedByMe Malaysia Debuts Second Equity Crowdfunding Campaign for iTalent Management.* Retrieved from Crowdfund Insider: https://www.crowdfundinsider.com/2016/10/91184-fundedbyme-malaysia-debuts-second-equity-crowdfunding-campaign-italent-management/

Karina, S. (2012). Inapplicability of Crowdfunding Concerns in The Internet Age and The Jobs Act's Safeguards. *Administrative Law Review, 64*(2), 474–505.

Kheong, K. C. (2016). *Publications: Joining The Crowd.* Retrieved from Skrine: https://www.skrine.com/publications/legal-insights/635-joining-the-crowd

Kunigis, A. (2017). *Advantages vs. disadvantages of debt financing.* The Hartford. Retrieved from http://www.thehartford.com/business-playbook/in-depth/debt-financing

Lee, L. (2015, June 11). *Malaysia's Securities Commission allows 6 players to launch equity crowdfunding services.* Deal Street Asia. Retrieved from https://www.dealstreetasia.com/stories/sc-announces-6-equity-crowdfunding-operators-for-malaysia-7680/

Lutz, A. M. J. B. E. (2015). Investor communication in equity-based crowdfunding: A qualitative empirical study. *Qualitative Research in Financial Market, 7*(3), 309–342. doi:10.1108/QRFM-07-2014-0021

Macht, S. A., & Weatherston, J. (2015). Academic research on crowdfunders: What's been done and what's to come. *Strategic Change, 24*(2), 191–205. doi:10.1002/jsc.2010

Romanova, I., & Kudinska, M. (2016). Banking and fintech: A challenge or opportunity? *Contemporary Studies in Economic and Financial Analysis, 98*, 21–35. doi:10.1108/S1569-375920160000098002

Ryan, C. (2012, May 10). *Navigation: 4 Types of Crowdfunding and What This Means For The Future Of Investment.* Retrieved from Under The Radar: https://utrconf.com/4-types-of-crowdfunding-and-what-this-means-for-the-future-of-investments/

Schwienbacher, A. (2007). A theoretical analysis of optimal financing strategies for different types of capital-constrained entrepreneurs. *Journal of Business Venturing, 22*(6), 753–781. doi:10.1016/j.jbusvent.2006.07.003

Schwienbacher, A., & Larralde, B. (2010). *Crowdfunding of small entrepreneurial ventures. Handbook of Entrepreneurial Finance.* Oxford University Press.

Securities Commission Malaysia. (2016). *Equity crowdfunding: List of registered market operators for ECF.* Retrieved from https://www.sc.com.my/digital/equity-crowdfunding/list-of-registered-market-operators-for-ecf/

Sigar, K. (2012). Fret no more: Inapplicability of crowdfunding concerns in the Internet age and the JOBS Act's safeguards. *Administrative Law Review, 64*(2), 473–506.

Valanciene, L., & Jegeleviciute, S. (2013). Valuation of crowdfunding: Benefits and drawback. *Economics and Management, 18*(1), 39–48. doi:10.5755/j01.em.18.1.3713

Venture Well. (2016). *Types of crowdfunding and regulations*. Retrieved from https://venturewell.org/types-crowdfunding-regulations/

Yusof, E., Fahmy, E., Kashoogie, J., & Anwar Kamal, A. (2009). *Islamic finance: Debt versus equity financing in the light of maqasid al-Shari'ah.* Munich Personal RePEc Archive. Retrieved from https://mpra.ub.uni-muenchen.de/20722/1 /MPRA_paper_20722.pdf

APPENDIX

Latest Literature can add value. Critical evaluation of available literature can be added

No	Author Name, Year, Title	Area	Issues	methodology used	results
1	Aishath Muneeza, Nur Aishah Arshad, Asma' Tajul Arifin, 2018, The Application of Blockchain Technology	Management and Applied Research	Benefits of integrating block chain to crowdfunding and how it varies in different economic and legal context.	Desk research where literature are reviewed to derive conclusion.	The result was in line with the current trends and issues are similar like other studies conducted in this emerging area of research.
2	Henry Sauemann, Chlara Franzoni, Kourosh Shafi, 2019, Crowdfunding Scientific Research: Descriptive Insights and Correlates of Funding Success	Crowdfunding	To measure the success of crowdfunding on the scientific research	Correlations. Descriptive Information. Empirical Evidence	Crowdfunding is different in from traditional funding mechanisms such as grants from government agencies: Success rates are comparatively high, junior scientists tend to be more successful than senior scientists, and female investigators are more likely to be funded than male investigators. Furthermore, the amounts raised with crowdfunding tend to be much smaller and funds are used primarily for materials and travel rather than salaries or tuition.
3	Ciro Troise, Mario Tani, Omella Papaluca, 2020, Equity and Reward Crowdfunding: A Multiple Signal Analysis	Economic and Finance	To analyze the success signals of initiatives through equity and reward crowdfunding, the two Typologies most used by start-ups and SMEs.	Samples construction and data collection	The success of the crowdfunding is determined by the influence to the investor and their decision making process. Consequently, it is able to influence the success of the campaigns.

Chapter 8
Fintech Challenges and Outlook in India

Neeta Baporikar
https://orcid.org/0000-0003-0676-9913
Namibia University of Science and Technology, Namibia & University of Pune, India

ABSTRACT

Fintech refers to the novel processes and products that become available for financial services due to the digital technological advancements. Fintech includes technologically enabled financial innovation leading to new business models, applications, processes, or products with an associated material effect on financial markets, institutions, and financial services. India is transitioning into a dynamic ecosystem offering Fintech start-ups a platform to grow into billion-dollar unicorns. From tapping new segments to exploring foreign markets, Fintech in India is pursuing multiple targets. The traditionally cash-driven Indian economy has responded well to the Fintech opportunity, primarily triggered by a surge in e-commerce, and Smartphone penetration. However, India's growth is still not comparable in scale to its global counterparts but is stacked well, due to a strong talent pipeline of the tech workforce. Hence, adopting an exploratory approach, based on in-depth literature review, the chapter aims to identify the challenges and deliberate on the outlook for Fintech in India.

INTRODUCTION

Fintech is an industry composed of companies that use technology to make financial systems and the delivery of financial services more efficient. Fintech refers to the novel processes and products that become available for financial services due to digital technological advancements. Thus, Fintech refers to technologically enabled financial innovation that could result in new business models, applications, processes or products with an associated material effect on financial markets and institutions and the provision of financial services. Nonetheless, the Fintech segment includes many elements, which according to Dorfleitner, Hornuf, Schmitt & Weber, (2017) can be loosely categorized into four main segments i.e. financing, asset management, payments and others. According to PwC (2016), 83% of financial institutions believe that various aspects of their business are at risk to Fintech startups. Due to

DOI: 10.4018/978-1-7998-3257-7.ch008

Fintech companies already having a significant impact on the financial industry, every financial firm needs to build capabilities to leverage and/or invest in Fintech in order to stay competitive. The growth of investment in Fintech has been phenomenal. According to Accenture (2016a), global investment in Fintech ventures in the first quarter of 2016 reached $5.3 billion, a 67% increase over the same period the previous year, and the percentage of investments going to Fintech companies in Europe and the Asia-Pacific nearly doubled to 62%. Hence adopting an exploratory approach based on secondary data the aim of this chapter is to identify the challenges and deliberate on the outlook for Fintech in India as India is a key player in the Asian Financial Market.

BACKGROUND

According to the report of (KPMG 2016), India is transitioning into a dynamic ecosystem offering Fintech start-ups a platform to grow into billion dollar unicorns. From tapping new segments to exploring foreign markets, Fintech start-ups in India are pursuing multiple aspirations. The forecast for Indian Fintech software market is approximate to the tune of USD 2.4 billion by 2020 from a current USD 1.2 billion, as per NASSCOM. The traditionally cash-driven Indian economy has responded well to the Fintech opportunity, primarily triggered by a surge in e-commerce, and Smartphone penetration. The transaction value for the Indian Fintech sector is estimated to be approximately USD 33 billion in 2016 and is forecasted to reach USD 73 billion in 2020 growing at a five-year CAGR of 22 percent.

However, India's growth wave may still not be of the scale when viewed against its global counterparts, but it is stacked well, largely due to a strong talent pipeline of the easy-to-hire and inexpensive tech workforce. From wallets to lending to insurance, the services of Fintech have redefined the way in which businesses and consumers carry out routine transactions. The increasing adoption of these trends is positioning India as an attractive market worldwide in general and specially for Fintech sector companies to develop, grow and attain competitive edge in the global financial market.

LITERATURE REVIEW

Financial markets worldwide were profoundly affected by the internet revolution in the early 1990s, with one of the major effects being that it lowered costs for financial transactions. Technological advances driven by the internet revolution changed the face of the financial services industry and led to the development of electronic finance (e-finance). E-finance refers to all forms of financial services such as banking, insurance, and stock trading performed through electronic means, including the internet and World Wide Web. E-finance allows individuals or businesses to access accounts, trans- act business, and obtain information on financial products and services without being in physical contact with financial firms. Many e-finance business models emerged in the 1990s, including online banking, online brokerage services, mobile payment, and mobile banking.

As with e-commerce, many of these changes have led to the downsizing and reduction of number in physical locations for banks. The impact of internet technology has been especially obvious in the banking industry. Information- intensive and time-sensitive in nature, virtually every component of the banking business' value chain benefitted from an innovative utilization of web technologies (Baporikar, 2019a; 2019b). From the bank's point of view, potential benefits of online banking include lower operational costs, shorter turnaround time, real- time managerial information, smoother communication within the organization, more convenient interaction with existing as well as prospective customers, and the provision of value-added services such as access to professional knowledge in financial management (Nielsen, 2002; Sathye, 1999). Online stock trading is another example of e-finance. It minimizes its operating costs by processing every stock transaction online. It achieves competitive advantage by providing differentiated services at the lowest feasible transaction fees. Some online stock brokers provide their clients free access to high quality research reports developed by reputed financial research firms. The growth of the Smartphone user base in the mid-2000s facilitated the growth of mobile finance, such as mobile payment and mobile banking, which is an extension of e-finance.

Financial institutions have allowed their customers not only to access bank account information, but also to make transactions, such as paying bills and remitting money, via their mobile device. With the advances in e-finance and mobile technologies for financial firms, Fintech innovation emerged after the worldwide financial crisis in 2008 by combining the e-finance, internet technologies, social networking services, social media, artificial intelligence, and big data analytics. Fintech startups differentiated themselves from traditional financial firms with personalized niche services, data-driven solutions, an innovative culture, and a nimble organization. While Fintech is generally considered a threat to traditional financial firms, it also provides ample opportunities for these firms to gain a competitive advantage over competitors. Most major financial firms have begun taking Fintech seriously and are developing strategies to compete, coexist, and collaborate with Fintech startups.

Understanding Fintech

Fintech brings about a new paradigm in which information technology is driving innovation in the financial industry. Fintech is touted as a game changing, disruptive innovation capable of shaking up traditional financial markets (Lee, & Shin, 2018). Yet, what is striking is that despite the consensus on the major impact that Fintech will have on the financial services industry; little academic literature has explored this area (Shim and Shin, 2016). Moreover, no common definition of Fintech still exists and there is a dire need for having a common ground understanding of what really Fintech means and constitutes (Schueffel, 2016).

Since, there is no universally accepted definition of the term "Fintech", the following section provides a brief survey of its use within existing scholarly literature. A definition is formed by means of a general description of the characteristics of Fintechs and an enumeration of the individual segments that make up the Fintech market (Dorfleitner, Hornuf, Schmitt & Weber, 2017). According to, the Oxford English Dictionary (2016), Fintech is computer program and other technology used to support or enable banking and financial services. In their 2015 research paper on the evolution of Fintech, Arner et al. (2015) state that "[t]he term's origin can be traced to the early 1990s and referred to the 'Financial Services Technology Consortium', a project initiated by Citigroup to facilitate technological cooperation efforts". Indeed, the source that the authors provide, an article published by the media outlet American Banker, mentions a project by the name of "Fintech" initiated by Citigroup in the early 1990s (Hochstein, 2015a).

Yet, the term Fintech was already used as early as 1972. In a scholarly article evidence exists that Mr. Abraham Leon the Vice President at the bank Manufacturers Hanover Trust detailed models on how analysis to solve daily banking problems encountered was done (Prabook, 2016). Bettinger (1972, p.72), defines Fintech as "an acronym which stands for financial technology, combining bank expertise with modern management science techniques and the computer." Warschauer (1974) furthermore proves that Bettinger's work did not go entirely unnoticed during his times. Thus, based on the evolution of financial technologies as described above, the term "Fintech" stands for all applications using analog and primarily digital IT to deliver financial solutions (Arner et al. 2016, p. 1272).

Fintech was originally also an expression describing banking backend technology, but widened over time to also encompass technological innovations in financial services and related areas (Investopedia, 2016).

Since the end of the first decade of the 21st century, the term has expanded to include any technological innovation in the financial sector, including innovations in financial literacy and education, retail banking, investment and even crypto-currencies like bitcoin, etc.

Fintech Ecosystem

To understand the competitive and collaborative dynamics in Fintech innovation, we must first analyze the ecosystem. A stable symbiotic Fintech ecosystem is instrumental in the growth of the Fintech industry. Diemers, Lamaa, Salamat, (2015) suggested that entrepreneurs, government, and financial institutions are the participants in a Fintech ecosystem.

In the Indian context, we have identified five elements of the Fintech ecosystem:

Figure 1. Elements of Fintech Ecosystem
Source: Self- Developed

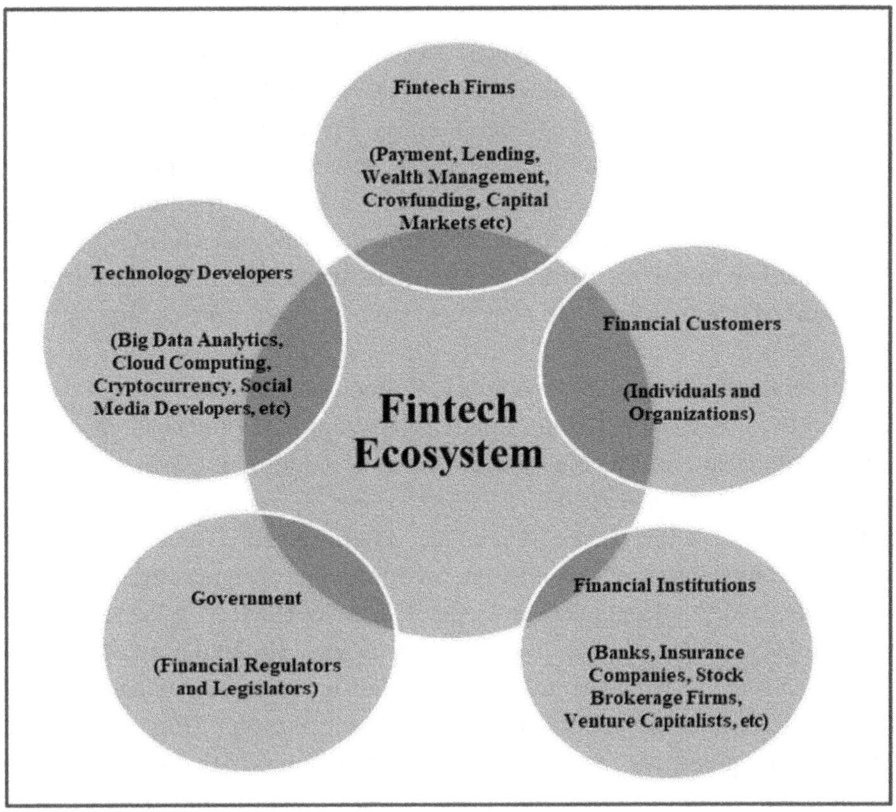

1. Fintech Firms (e.g., payment, wealth management, lending, crowdfunding, capital market, etc.);
2. Financial Customers (e.g., individuals and organizations);
3. Financial Institutions (e.g., traditional banks, insurance companies, stock brokerage firms, and venture capitalists, etc.).
4. Government (e.g., financial regulators and legislature);
5. Technology Developers (e.g., big data analytics, cloud computing, cryptocurrency, social media developers, etc.);

These elements symbiotically contribute to the innovation, stimulate economy, facilitate collabo-ration and competition in the financial industry, and ultimately benefit consumers in the financial industry. Figure 1 shows the five elements of the Fintech ecosystem.

These companies are mostly entrepreneurial and have driven major innovations in the areas of payment, wealth management, lending, crowd-funding, capital market, and insurances by incur-ring lower operating costs, targeting more niche markets, and providing more personalized services than traditional financial firms. They are driving the phenomenon of unbundling financial services, which has been highly disruptive for banks (Walchek, 2015). The ability to unbundle services is one of the major drivers of growth in the Fintech sector, as traditional financial institutions are disadvantaged in this situation. Consumers, rather than relying on a single financial institution for their needs, are beginning to pick and choose services they would like from a variety of Fintech companies. Venture capitalists and private equities are conducive to the creation of Fintech startups and the level of investments increased significantly over time as well.

Governments have been providing a favorable regulatory environment for Fintech since the 2008 financial crisis (Holland Fintech, 2015). Depending on the national economic development plans and economic policies, different governments provide different levels of regulation (e.g., licensing of financial services, relaxation of capital requirements, tax incentives) for Fintech startups to stimulate Fintech innovation and facilitate global financial competitiveness. For example, Singapore is changing online payment regulations to make the regulation friendlier to payment service providers and spur payment technology growth (Reuters, 2016). On the other hand, since 2008, traditional financial institutions have been subject to more rigorous regulation, capital requirements, and re-porting requirements from government regulators. The looser regulatory requirements imposed on Fintech startups allow them to provide more customized, inexpensive, and easy-to-access financial services to consumers than traditional institutions.

However, while certain regulations are favorable to Fintech startups, they still need to understand how regulations may affect their service provisions. LendUp, a payday loan Fintech Company, was fined $3.63 million for violations of consumer financial protection laws, including the Truth in Lending Act and the Dodd-Frank Wall Street Reform and Consumer Protection Act (Consumer Financial Protection Bureau, 2016). Financial customers are the source of revenue generation for Fintech companies. While large organizations are important sources of revenue, the predominant revenue source for Fintech companies are individual customers and small and medium-sized enterprises (SMEs). A survey found that the use of Fintech services is greatest among younger, wealthier customers (Holland Fintech, 2015). Early Fintech adopters tend to be tech-savvy, younger, urban, and higher-income individuals. Currently, millennial (people between the age of 18 and 34) constitute a significant portion of Fintech consumption in most countries. The future demographic is favorable to Fintech companies in that in the next few decades; the tech-savvy millennial will account for the largest part of the population and drive the growth of Fintech services in India. Traditional financial institutions are also a major driving force in the Fintech ecosystem. After realizing the disruptive power of Fintech and dwindling window of opportunities to blunt Fintech impact on the market, traditional financial institutions have been reevaluating their existing business models and developing strategies to embrace Fintech innovation. Traditional financial institutions have competitive advantages in economies of scale and financial resources over Fintech startups. However, traditional financial institutions tend to focus on bundled services, providing one-stop comprehensive financial products and services to consumers rather than unbundled specialized products and services. While traditional financial institutions initially treated these fast-growing Fintech companies as threats, they have shifted their focus to collaborating with Fintech startups with various funding provisions. In exchange for providing funding, they are able to draw on the insights of these startup companies in order to stay on the forefront of the technology (Yang, 2015).

Fintech Advantages and Disadvantages

According to a recent report by Accenture (2016a), more than $50 billion has been invested in almost 2,500 companies since 2010, as these Fintech redefine the ways in which people store, save, borrow, invest, move, spend, and protect money. According to Mellon (2015), consumer and retail payment Fintech include mobile wallets, peer-to-peer (P2P) mobile payments, foreign exchange and remittances, real-time payments, and digital currency solutions. These services improve the experience for customers who look for a streamlined payments experience in terms of speed, convenience, and multi-channel accessibility. Mobile payment services that can be conveniently and securely used on mobile devices are a popular business model. Approaches to mobile payments include but are not limited to: charging to a phone bill, near field communication (NFC), barcode or QR code, a credit card on mobile websites, a mobile phone card reader, and direct mobile payment without using credit card companies (Li, 2016). The most widely known NFC-based mobile payment applications are Google Wallet, Apple Pay, and Samsung Pay. Another popular payment business model is P2P payment services. Users are now able to reimburse each other with apps such as PayPal for free. Most prevalent Fintech business models implemented by the ever growing number of Fintech firms and startups in India currently include: payment, wealth management, crowd-funding, lending, capital market, and insurance services. Payment business model Payments are relatively simple compared to other financial products and services. Fintech companies focusing on payments are able to acquire customers rapidly at lower costs, and are one of the fastest moving in terms of innovation and adoption of new payment capabilities. The two markets of payment Fintech are (1) consumer and retail payment and (2) wholesale and corporate payment. Payments are one of the most used retail financial services on a day-to-day basis, as well as one of the least regulated financial services.

However, Webster and Pizalla (2015) point out that competition between Fintech and traditional banking services gets more intense every year due to continuing development of information technology. Simultaneously, Fintech increases the interest in modern financial services from progressive financial institutions that aim to maintain and strengthen their leading role in the field and provide modern services of high quality in a convenient and effective form for their clients anywhere, anytime. Recently the collaboration between traditional financial institutions and *Fintech* branch is growing as both parties see promising avenues for further development. A review of the areas in which the Fintech industry offers new technologies and traditional institutions of the financial sector, with which the Fintech firms

Table 1. Areas of Application of New Technologies, Advantages and Disadvantages of Fintech Services

Application Areas	Advantages and Disadvantages of Fintech Services vis-à-vis Traditional Services
Asset and Investment Management	Fintech companies have a very competitive value proposition in the new technology of robo-advising, when an individual's investment portfolio is selected by algorithms that offer clients an investment structure that corresponds to their investment preferences and risk profile; Annual maintenance costs are lower than those accepted in banks (1-2 percent), i.e., 0.3-0.5 percent; They allocate free assets of clients in deposits, convert currencies, bond and stock portfolios, seek to hedge risks and receive credit lines for these assets. Fintech firms make services that previously were only available to the wealthy accessible to the general population and SMEs (Baporikar, 2020a).
Digital Banks	Digital banks can provide convenient mobile services (settlement account, debit card, consumer loans, financial management tools, as well as the latest innovations in the field of mobile and p2p-payments) on the basis of the existing banking infrastructure, as well as create the infrastructure from scratch; Fintech companies use the flexibility of banking regulation and in many cases charges for services are lower and interest rates on savings products are higher.
Infrastructure and Support Services	Technologies related to security; work with large data, scoring mechanisms for borrowers, platforms, for example, on arranging loans or mobile payments.
Insurance	Fintech firms can offer new technologies in the insurance business instead of conservative distribution of products through the use of offline agent networks, charging up to 20 percent in the form of commissions and as a result services become cheaper.
Lending	Successful competition of Fintech firms with banks began after the crisis of 2008 due to the refusal by banks to lend to certain groups of borrowers like SMEs because of high risks. Fintech firms, working on the peer-to-peer (P2P) model, provide a platform for matching borrowers with lenders. However, banking competitors may charge much higher loans and commissions and the credibility still remains issue and the possibility of scandals cannot be ruled out. E.g. Bankruptcy of the P2P lending company Ezubao, China – major scandal in Fintech Industry.
Online Payments, Money Transfers and E-Commerce	Successful competition of Fintech companies with banks is manifested with large volumes of transactions in close cooperation with the world's largest trading platforms. However, bank competitors have much lower transaction costs.
Personal Finance, Planning and Analytics	Allow users to access their credit rating and credit history, as well as keep records of all client financial products - a free service in the field of personal finance management and in planning and analytics, Fintech firms offer an online platform for project managers to manage budgets, invoices and reports.

want to compete, as well as a description of the advantages and disadvantages of Fintech technology is given in Table 1.

As can be seen from Table 1, Fintech firms actively and successfully offer their technologies and services in all areas where traditional banks, insurance companies and other financial sector companies operate. At the same time banks, despite their inherent conservatism and caution, have already begun to actively recognize Fintech, understanding that the new technologies they offer in conjunction with banks' large client base, opportunities to attract low-cost resources and a robust regulatory system that ensures clients' trust, can lay the foundations of a new generation of digital financial institution. Thus, the larger Fintech firms become, the more they have been overlapping with traditional financial companies. In fact, in some cases it may be difficult to distinguish between a Fintech company and a traditional bank, for example, the so-called low-cost banks, which Hes and Jilkova (2016) define as "retail banking based on an Internet platform" effectively, combine the two. Such banks rapidly gained clients in Czech Republic and became profitable (Hes and Jilkova, 2016). Many experts note that the closer integration of Fintech start-ups with large traditional companies is inevitable and is, in fact, already starting a new stage in the development of the industry - Fintech 2.0.

CHALLENGES FACING THE FINTECH SECTOR

Currently, the financial industry is experiencing unprecedented change. A wide range of traditional banking products from payments to investment advice are being challenged by innovative Fintech products. Block chain technology is revolutionizing many traditional banking services with better trans-action security and faster exchanges of money at lower costs domestically and globally. Figure 2 gives the challenges for Fintech Sector. Fintech innovation has the ability to shake up the entire financial landscape in the coming years. As with any disruptive innovation, the disruptive power of Fintech innovations will manifest themselves clearly as the market evolves.

Figure 2. Fintech Sector Challenges
Source: Self- Developed

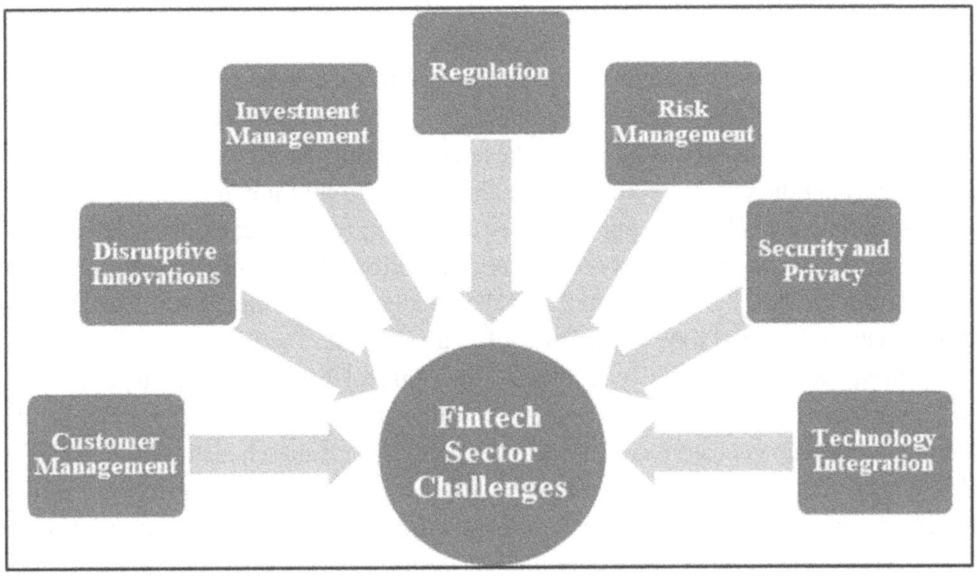

This section now deliberates the challenges facing Fintech in this time of global economic disruptions. These include customer management, disruptive innovations, investment management, risk management, security and privacy, technology integration.

Customer Management: As competition is high for customer acquisition and retention, customer management is crucial. Many customers use multiple services from different fin-tech firms for different needs. For example, customers may use PayPal for paying businesses online, while using Venmo for paying friends. Fintech need to understand the niche they are in and strive to provide the best possible service in that niche. High responsiveness and care to customer concerns is paramount, as word-of-mouth recommendations can be crucial for the success of a Fintech startup in this fast-paced environment. Robo advisors are designed to provide more personalized 24/7 service to a greater number of people with low fees. However, the human element is still important in investment services. Providing a personalized experience without a significant cost increase is challenging, but critical for customer acquisition and retention. As the clients from Generations X and Y are more tech-savvy, Fintech need to better address customer needs by offering enhanced accessibility, convenience, and tailored products. It will be more important to have an integrated client service management due to the addition of Fintech-based channels.

Disruptive Innovations: Disruption refers to a process whereby a smaller company with fewer resources is able to successfully challenge established incumbent businesses (Christensen, 2003). Disruptive Innovations on the other hand refer to innovation creates new market and value network and eventually disrupts an existing market and value network, displacing established market-leading firms, products, and alliances (Ab Rahman & Airini; et al. (2017). Christensen defines a disruptive innovation as a product or service designed for a new set of customers.

Generally, disruptive innovations were technologically straightforward, consisting of off-the-shelf components put together in a product architecture that was often simpler than prior approaches. They offered less of what customers in established markets wanted and so could rarely be initially employed there. They offered a different package of attributes valued only in emerging markets remote from, and unimportant to, the mainstream (Christensen, 1997 p. 15)

Further, the disruptive innovations can create a challenge to successful, well-managed companies that are responsive to their customers with excellent research and development as these companies tend to ignore the markets signals (Christensen, 1997). These companies adhere to the common business-world advice and focus only on the customer and stay so close to them that it can be strategically counterproductive. Though, Christensen (1997) argued that disruptive innovations can hurt successful, companies, Pett, Kristall & Mack (2017), feel that constructive integration of existing, new, and forward-thinking innovation could improve the economic benefits of these same well-managed companies, once decision-making management understood the systemic benefits as a whole.

Investment Management: The ability to assess the value of projects accurately will be critical in an increasingly competitive business environment. Without a proper portfolio management of Fintech projects, financial firms can get easily swamped in the plethora of Fintech technologies. The selection of promising Fintech projects is challenging. It is still early to predict the best portfolio of Fintech projects that will deliver the most competitive and profitable outcomes. Financial institutions may choose to invest in internal Fintech projects in competition with Fintech start-ups. Alternatively, financial institutions can use collaborative investments with Fintech startups as a means of remaining on the cutting edge of the technology without requiring internal innovation. For example, a Fintech startup may invest in a robo-advisor Fintech. The Fintech startup can benefit from the financial institution's expertise in modeling and analysis, while the financial institution can gain insight into what kind of Fintech services clients are looking for, as well as the cost structure and revenue streams.

Regulation: Both traditional financial institutions and Fintech startups face regulatory challenges in capital requirements, anti-money laundering, and privacy and security. For traditional financial institutions, the cost to meet regulatory requirements and compete against Fintech startups can be significant. Traditional financial institutions and Fintech start-ups face different regulatory requirements based on the type of financial services they provide. For example, most banks operate on some form of fractional-reserve banking system. There are strict and complex guidelines for what kind of lending can be done based on the capital held by a traditional financial institution that may not apply to a lending Fintech startup that does not technically lend (e.g., a P2P lending firm). As regulatory changes lag be-hind the innovation of the industry, Fintech firms need to be aware of potential changes that may impact them and find ways to handle those changes.

Risk Management: There are many risks for Fintech startups to deal with, including financial risk as well as regulatory risk, as mentioned above. The financial risk can vary based on what exactly the Fintech specializes in. For example, a Fintech offering financial services for student loans or mortgages may face counterparty risk that can be absorbed by a financial institution with large amounts of capital that a smaller startup would not be able to cover. Deploying robo-advisors for the wealth management of bonds, treasury bills, and stocks may expose customers to financial risk and the Fintech may have to take potentially serious responsibilities for any loss due to the algorithmic failure of the robo-advisors. Recent lawsuits and a number of settlements arising from the faulty sales of derivative products by top-tier banks indicate that Fintech will not be immune to the liability arising from robo-advisors' faulty investment advices. Overall, it is crucial for Fintech to have a focus on risk management in addition to the technology management of the firm. As many Fintech were created after the 2008 financial crisis, they need to fully understand their exposure to liquidity risk, as well their interest rate risk. The present lending environment is vastly different from before due to the current ultra-low interest rate environment in the financial market, so it is important for Fintech that are involved in lending to recognize how the current lending environment will impact them.

Security and Privacy: Government regulators that have been involved in privacy and security action include the Securities and Exchange Board (SEBI), the Department of Justice (DOJ), the Financial Industry Regulatory Authority (FINRA), Commodities Exchange Boards (CEB), and state attorney generals. For Fintech applications, critical information may be stored on mobile devices that oftentimes get lost or stolen. Security of mobile devices can also be compromised through payment applications such as Google Wallet and MasterCard PayPass. As consumers can easily file complaints related to data security and privacy breaches to regulatory agencies, Fintech companies need to develop appropriate measures to protect sensitive consumer data from unauthorized access. Furthermore, as trust plays an important role in the adoption of new technologies, it is in the Fintech's best interest to maintain security and privacy as one of its top priorities. It is expected that regulatory agencies, consumer protection organizations, and Fintech keep working together to make Fintech services a secure and value-adding experience for consumers.

Technology Integration: Technology integration is essential in providing seamless customers service (Baporikar, 2017a; 2014). Many Fintech are based on new technologies, and it is challenging to integrate the Fintech applications with existing legacy systems. In addition to the internal development of Fintech, banks need to create partnerships and joint ventures with Fintech startups via corporate venture funds and incubator programs (Drummer, Jerenz, Siebelt, & Thaten, 2016). These partnerships and joint ventures will allow tradition-al financial institutions to have a stake in an external source that will focus on new Fintech technology. However, without a sound integration plan and experience, traditional banking processes in many areas may become incompatible with new technology and business models that the financial institutions are interested in utilizing. The terms of opportunities, existing and new risks of FinTech are outlined in Figure 3.

OUTLOOK FOR THE FINTECH SECTOR

Financial subjects are also expected to find meaning, value and self-expression through their participation in financial activities. If they cannot than they are construed to be suffering from 'behavioral problems', issues of 'self-control' and shortages of 'cognitive resources' (World Bank 2015). Due to this, there

Figure 3. Fintech impact in terms of opportunities, existing risks and likely new risks
Source: Adopted from Technological Innovation and Dutch Financial Sector by Denetherlandsche Bank

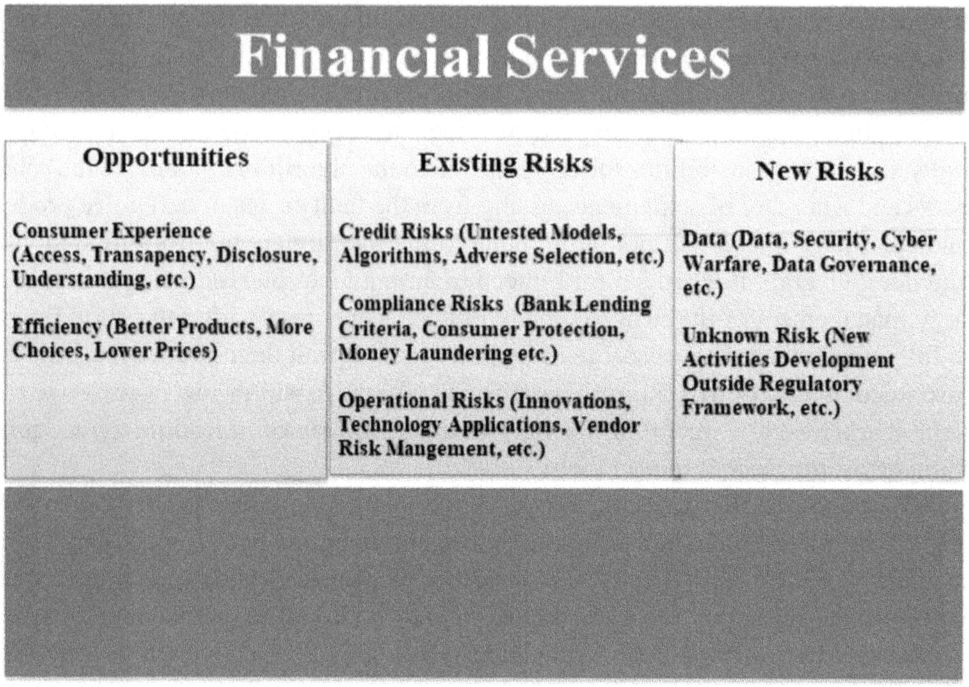

has been a convergence of policy and knowledge co-production, and in particular the employment of behavioralism as justification and guide to future development practice. However, these discourses of inclusion (and ‘access’) obscure the desire and momentum of financial capital to access high-risk/high return markets (Kaminska 2015).

The Global Financial Development Report (World Bank 2013) specifically downplays the role of financial actors in creating systemic instability, suggesting that financial institutions can only exploit consumers lacking financial capability. In Finance for All (World Bank 2008), the Bank side-stepped such pressing questions about the pitfalls of market-based financial sector development. It redirected attention from specialist MFIs to mainstream financial institutions, and to the broadening of the definition of ‘pro-poor’ financial services to include savings and payment services alongside lending, targeting both households and small businesses.

The Fintech industry is not a completely matured industry in India but it has brought the digital revolution in the financial service sector. The outlook is positive but much will depend on the ecosystem of Fintech industry which in turn is dependent on the government, regulator, users, universities and institution, and technology vendors. There is push by the government since past few years to promote digital payments and move towards cashless economy (Baporikar, 2017b). This is bound to have a multiplier effect and act as booster dose for the Fintech industry to mature in the coming decade. Further, individuals with appropriate financial literacy training make better financial decisions and manage money better that those without such training (Baporikar & Akino, 2020b). However, financial literacy must be augmented with proper financial services, which is possible only when there are robust policies and strategies for Fintech development. This holistic approach will ensure not only economic development and surge in financial sector development but also promote growth and inclusive society. Figure 4 provides a schematic influence of the Fintech multiplier effect on savings, investments and financial planning segment which will lead to optimum results when embedded with financial literacy drives.

Figure 4. Schematic Influence of Fintech on Savings, Investments and Financial Planning
Source: Self-Developed

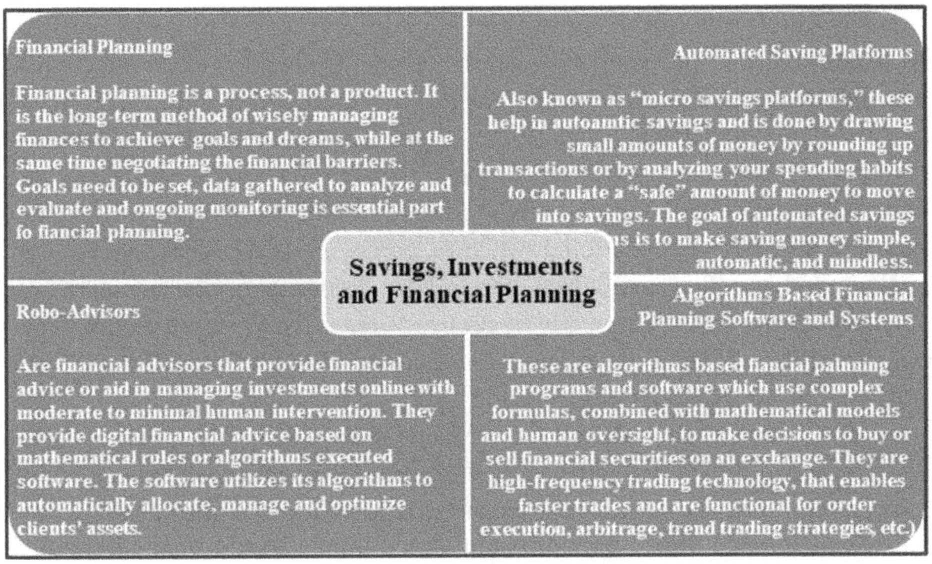

SOLUTIONS AND RECOMMENDATIONS

Some of the recommendations based on the deliberation in the preceding pages addressed to managers of Fintech enterprises include:

1. Excessively strict licensing regulations in India are one of the main drawbacks preventing Fintech development. Worldwide experience suggests that reinforcing lobbying and collaboration with State institutions has helped Fintech start-up enterprises to enter the market, gain consumers and regulators' trust and attract investors. This experience could prove useful in Indian circumstances.
2. Associations and Federations of Chamber of Commerce should inform the population about Fintech services that are already available for use.
3. Risk capital funds need to support new companies in this field because they have a large potential to develop and grow not only in India but also Asia and international markets;
4. Fintech firms have to create impactful marketing campaigns enhancing the public's awareness.

Finally, Indian government should stimulate the implementation of financial services at least in three directions:

1. By creating a platform (sandbox) allowing innovative financial technologies to enter the market and validating their safety;

2. By creating an understandable and transparent system of supervision over the activities of Fintech firms, especially the P2P and B2B lending platforms;
3. By creating a program of tax incentives stimulating investments in the financial sector.

FUTURE RESEARCH DIRECTIONS

From an academic point of view Fintech is still an untilled field. Hence, plentiful new research strands are perceivable. One of the most pressing one is surely the relationship between Fintech firms and incumbent players. Do they view each other as complements or competitors? Would mergers and acquisitions make sense or would strategic alliances yield more value? Another research question on industry level could be what sets apart Fintech firms from incumbent players. They oftentimes serve identical clients, yet Fintech firms and incumbent companies are in general fundamentally different. How do they differ in terms of vision and strategy, organizational structure, processes, and culture? Moving down the value chain, additional research questions arise from marketing and sales. How do Fintech firms approach clients? Which client segments are they typically targeting? What is their pricing model? Valuable insights could also result from investigating the support functions of Fintech firms: How is finance ensured? Which kind of HR model do Fintech firms pursue?

Fintech is poised for further growth. So far, we have been witnessing individual Fintech startups that have just begun seizing individual parts of the financial services value chain and optimizing them. This puts incumbent players in a difficult position as parts of their oftentimes most lucrative businesses are breaking away whilst they are left with the regulatory burden and the associated costs. At the same time, Fintech still needs to prove that it is not just a fleeting star. Despite its remarkable growth in the recent years, Fintech still needs to provide evidence that it is a sustainable phenomenon even in markets which are on the downturn.

CONCLUSION

There is no doubt that business innovations stimulate economic development on both micro and macro levels (Harrison, Jaumandreu, Mairesse & Peters, 2014). The application of information technology in the finance industry is a field with great potential for innovations; therefore, both enterprises and investors are highly interested in it. Fintech will have its impact on customer experience, meaning the entirety of all experiences the customer has with the service provider. Besides it will have its implications on business economics, i.e. revenue, costs, and margins. Last but not least the sector experts predict Fintech to alter the Industry dynamics altogether, causing changes in the competitive structure and ecosystem of financial services (Deloitte, 2016). Moreover, no type of financial services provider will remain unscathed as

Fintech will bring change to all types of banks, asset and wealth managers, fund and payment providers, brokers, exchanges, insurers alike (PWC, 2016). While the attention received in academia is nowhere close to the attention which is paid by practitioners, some scholars do perceive the phenomenon of Fintech as a fundamental shift. Kauffman & Ma, for instance, refer to the ongoing "global Fintech revolution" (Kauffman and Ma, 2015, p.261) and so does Mackenzie when heading her article on innovators in financial service "The Fintech revolution" (Mackenzie, 2015, p.50).

This chapter has provided an overview of the trends in the development of the Fintech industry in the Indian context. The development of Fintech was due to globalization giving a chance to small but sophisticated enterprises to develop financial services without the help of banks, by combining finance with IT, and offering consumers faster execution of typical banking processes. Therefore, the Fintech development is necessary for both global and Indian's financial sectors, since this will allow clients to use the opportunities and advantages of both the traditional banking system and Fintech companies. One can expect that Fintech technologies will change the traditional activity of banks - banks will adopt innovative IT technologies, and Fintech companies will have to work in conditions of more stringent supervision to ensure the safety of client operations. Such convergence will mark the beginning of a new era in the development of the financial industry. Because Fintech is such a recent development, there is still a paucity of studies on the social, regulatory, technological, and managerial aspects of Fintech. This makes it very challenging for financial firms to make informed decisions in regard to the investment in Fintech projects. Their development in India has been relatively slow, including due to credit constraints faced by all young businesses in India and the chapter posits a postulate that Indian society is not ready to use Fintech services preferring bank services instead.

On a final note, developing at a very high pace, it is safe to say that parts of current Fintech momentum will slow down in the years to come. Some market observers even go as far to say that there is a Fintech bubble building up which is likely to burst soon. However, the Internet and eCommerce did not disappear with the burst of the Dot-Com bubble. On the contrary, the innovations made in the years leading up to the bubble burst prevailed. Web technologies have never been as pervasively applied as today. A Web sales channel or at least an information outlet has become a standard for most enterprises in the western world. Hence, Internet technology did not disappear with the burst of the Dot-Com Bubble. Rather than that, it was absorbed, transformed, and adopted by the majority of firms in the western world and turned into a business standard. It is likely that similar things will happen to Fintech. Turning into an outcast in the eyes of investors in the event of a bubble burst, Fintech will then disappear as a label. However, a good share of the innovations brought forward by Fintech firms will then be absorbed by other players, such as by incumbent banks, insurers and software companies and be kept alive. In other words, even if the Fintech genie deflates it will still continue to live in its bottle. And this time we will be able to stick a proper label on it.

REFERENCES

Accenture. (2016a). *Global Fintech investment growth continues in 2016 driven by Europe and Asia, Accenture study finds*. Available at https://newsroom.accenture.com/news/ global-Fintech-investment-growth-continues-in-2016- driven-by-europe-and-asia-accenture-study-finds.htm

Accenture. (2016b). *Fintech and the evolving landscape*. Available at https://www.accenture.com/us-en/insight-Fintech-evolving-landscape

Arner, D. W., Barberis, J., & Buckley, R. P. (2015). The evolution of Fintech: A new post-crisis paradigm. *Geo. J. Int'l L., 47*, 1271. doi:10.2139srn.2676553

Baporikar, N. (2020a). Handbook of Research on Entrepreneurship Development and Opportunities in Circular Economy. IGI Global. http://doi:10.4018/978-1-7998-5116-5

Baporikar, N., & Akino, S. (2020b). Financial Literacy Imperative for Success of Women Entrepreneurship. [IJIDE]. *International Journal of Innovation in the Digital Economy, 11*(3), 1–21. doi:10.4018/IJIDE.2020070101

Baporikar, N. (2019a). E-Learning Strategies for Emerging Economies in the Knowledge Era. In J. Pelet (Ed.), *Advanced Web Applications and Progressing E-Learning 2.0 Technologies in Higher Education* (pp. 150–171). Hershey, PA: IGI Global; doi:10.4018/978-1-5225-7435-4.ch008

Baporikar, N. (2019b). Knowledge Management Dynamics and Public Sector Organization Development. In Y. Albastaki, A. Al-Alawi, & S. Abdulrahman Al-Bassam (Eds.), *Handbook of Research on Implementing Knowledge Management Strategy in the Public Sector* (pp. 55–71). Hershey, PA: IGI Global; doi:10.4018/978-1-5225-9639-4.ch003

Baporikar, N. (2017a). Strategies for Successful Implementation of Innovation. [IJIDE]. *International Journal of Innovation in the Digital Economy, 8*(2), 16–28. doi:10.4018/IJIDE.2017040102

Baragde, D., & Baporikar, N. (2017b). Business innovation in Indian software industries [JSTPM]. *Journal of Science and Technology Policy Management, 8*(1), 62–75. doi:10.1108/JSTPM-12-2015-0039

Baporikar, N. (2014). Information Strategy as Enabler of Competitive Advantage. [IJSITA]. *International Journal of Strategic Information Technology and Applications, 5*(1), 30–41. doi:10.4018/ijsita.2014010103

Bettinger, A. (1972). FINTECH: A Series of 40 Time Shared Models Used at Manufacturers Hanover Trust Company. *Interfaces, 2*(4), 62–63.

Christensen, C. M. (1997). *The innovator's dilemma: when new technologies cause great firms to fail.* Harvard Business School Press.

Christensen, C. M. (2003). *The innovator's solution: creating and sustaining successful growth.* Harvard Business Press.

Deloitte. (2016). *Disaggregating Fintech: Brighter shades of disruption.* Retrieved from https://www2.deloitte.com/content/dam/Deloitte/us/Documents/financial-services/us-fsi-dis-aggregating-Fintech-brighter-shades-of-disruption.pdf

Dictionary, O. E. (2016). *Definition of Fintech.* Author.

Dorfleitner, G., Hornuf, L., Schmitt, M., & Weber, M. (2017). Definition of Fintech and description of the Fintech industry. In *Fintech in Germany* (pp. 5–10). Springer. doi:10.1007/978-3-319-54666-7_2

Fetai, B. (2015). Financial Integration and Financial Development: Does Financial Integration Matter? *European Research Studies Journal, 18*(2), 97–106. doi:10.35808/ersj/447

Gabor, D., & Brooks, S. (2017). The digital revolution in financial inclusion: International development in the Fintech era. *New Political Economy, 22*(4), 423–436. doi:10.1080/13563467.2017.1259298

Harrison, R., Jaumandreu, J., Mairesse, J., & Peters, B. (2014). Does innovation stimulate employment? A firm-level analysis using comparable micro-data from four European countries. *International Journal of Industrial Organization, 35*, 29–43. doi:10.1016/j.ijindorg.2014.06.001

Hes, A., & Jilkova, P. (2016). Position of Low Cost Banks on the Financial Market in Czech Republic. *European Research Studies, 19*(4), 42–52. doi:10.35808/ersj/579

Hochstein, M. (2015a). *Fintech (the Word That Is) Evolves*. Accessed 19 July 2019. https://www.americanbanker.com/bankthink/Fintech-the-word-that-isevolves-1077098-1.html

Investopedia. (2016). *Fintech*. Accessed 19 July 2019. https://www.investopedia.com/terms/f/Fintech.asp

Jun, J., & Yeo, E. (2016). Entry of Fintech Firms and Competition in the Retail Payments Market. *Asia-Pacific Journal of Financial Studies, 45*(2), 159–184. doi:10.1111/ajfs.12126

Kauffman, R. J., & Ma, D. (2015). Special issue: Contemporary research on payments and cards in the global Fintech revolution. *Electronic Commerce Research and Applications, 14*(5), 261–264. doi:10.1016/j.elerap.2015.09.005

Kim, Y., Park, Y.-J., & Choi, J. (2016). The Adoption of Mobile Payment Services for "Fintech". *International Journal of Applied Engineering Research, 11*(2), 1058–1061.

Klapper, L., Lusardi, A., & Van Oudheusden, P. (2015). *Financial literacy around the world*. World Bank.

Lee, I., & Shin, Y. J. (2018). Fintech: Ecosystem, business models, investment decisions, and challenges. *Business Horizons, 61*(1), 35–46. doi:10.1016/j.bushor.2017.09.003

Mackenzie, A. (2015). The Fintech Revolution. *London Business School Review, 26*(3), 50–53. doi:10.1111/2057-1615.12059

Nielsen, J. F. (2002). Internet technology and customer linking in Nordic banking. *Internal Journal of Service Banking, 13*(2), 475–496.

Pett, J., Kristall, M., & Mack, D. (2017). Opportunity from disruption. *Internal Auditor, 74*(3), 57–60.

PwC. (2016, March). *Blurred lines: How Fintech is shaping financial services*. Available at https://www.pwc.de/de/

Ab Rahman & Airini. (2017). Emerging Technologies with Disruptive Effects: A Review. *PERINTIS eJournal, 7*(2).

Sathye, M. (1999). Adoption of internet banking by Australian consumers: An empirical investigation. *International Journal of Bank Marketing, 17*(7), 324–339. doi:10.1108/02652329910305689

Schneider, L. A., Shaul, M. A. X., & Lascelles, C. K. (2016). Regulatory Priorities for Fintech Firms—and Investors—in the Coming Year. *Journal of Taxation & Regulation of Financial Institutions, 29*(4), 5–14.

Schueffel, P. (2016). Taming the beast: A scientific definition of Fintech. *Journal of Innovation Management, 4*(4), 32–54. doi:10.24840/2183-0606_004.004_0004

Shen, Y., & Huang, Y. (2016). Introduction to the special issue: Internet finance in China. *China Economic Journal, 9*(3), 221–224. doi:10.1080/17538963.2016.1215058

Shim, Y., & Shin, D.-H. (2016). Analyzing China's Fintech Industry from the Perspective of Actor–Network Theory. *Telecommunications Policy, 40*(2–3), 168–181. doi:10.1016/j.telpol.2015.11.005

Vlasov, V. A. (2017). The Evolution of E-Money. *European Research Studies Journal, 20*(1), 215–224.

Warschauer, C. L. (1974). The financial programming of the financing companies, credit and investment. *Business Administration Journal, 14*(1), 33–57.

Webster, I., & Pizalla, J. (2015). *Fintech: Are banks responding appropriately?* Available at: https:// www.ey.com/

World Bank. (2008). *Finance for All? Policies and Pitfalls in Expanding Access*. The World Bank.

World Bank. (2013). *Global Financial Development Report: Financial Inclusion*. The World Bank.

World Bank. (2015). *World Development Report 2015: Mind, Society, Behaviour*. The World Bank.

ADDITIONAL READING

Alam, N., Gupta, L., & Zameni, A. (2019). Fintech Emergence and Global Evolution. In *Fintech and Islamic Finance* (pp. 11–35). Palgrave Macmillan. doi:10.1007/978-3-030-24666-2_2

Butt, M. W., & Butt, U. J. (2020). Digitalisation of the Global FinTech Industry. In *Handbook of Research on Innovations in Technology and Marketing for the Connected Consumer* (pp. 431–449). IGI Global. doi:10.4018/978-1-7998-0131-3.ch021

Chishti, S., & Barberis, J. (2016). *The FinTech book: the financial technology handbook for investors, entrepreneurs and visionaries*. John Wiley & Sons. doi:10.1002/9781119218906

Chuen, L. D. K., & Linda, L. (2018). *Inclusive Fintech: Blockchain, Cryptocurrency and ICO*. World Scientific.

Samaranayake, A., Tilakumara, S., Sripavan, T., & Withanawasam, R. (2019). Creative disruption in fintech from Sri Lanka. *Communications of the ACM, 62*(11), 56–57. doi:10.1145/3343458

Sironi, P. (2016). *FinTech innovation: from robo-advisors to goal based investing and gamification*. John Wiley & Sons. doi:10.1002/9781119227205

KEY TERMS AND DEFINITIONS

Banking: Is an industry that handles cash, credit, and other financial transactions.

Cashless Economy: Is a system where any type of money transactions are done through digital means like debit cards, electronic fund transfer, mobile payments, internet banking, mobile wallets.

Cashless Society: In which purchases of goods or services are made by credit card or electronic funds transfer rather than with cash or checks.

Digital Economy: Is a term for all of those economic processes, transactions, interactions and activities that are based on digital technologies.

Financial Services: Is a term used to refer to the services provided by the finance market. Financial Services is also the term used to describe organizations that deal with the management of money. Examples are the Banks, investment banks, insurance companies, credit card companies and stock brokerages.

Fintech: Refers to financial technology, and is technology and innovation that aims to compete with traditional financial methods in the delivery of financial services.

Technology: Is the application of knowledge for practical ends and it refers to practical application of science to commerce or industry. It is the discipline dealing with the art or science of applying scientific knowledge to practical problems.

Chapter 9
FinTech in Brazil: Opportunities or Threats?

Raphaela Godinho
University Center of Brasília, Brazil

ABSTRACT

To accompany the development and advancement of new means of access and service, banks have sought the adoption of friendly and efficient digital platforms so that they can contain the advances of fintechs. The research approaches topics that are aligned, such as the current context of the economy, the National Financial System, and the scenario of start-ups in Brazil. It was also observed that there is a need to regulate the sector so that it can grow with more freedom and thus be able to add to the country this technological wealth, but it analyzes the need to be less bureaucratic like the financial institutions that operate in the market. The study allowed the authors to understand how large companies already established in the financial market identify fintechs and their business models, identifying opportunities, threats, and how this understanding permits the fintechs to prepare for a competitive market, and for large companies to understand how this model can be characterized as an ally.

INTRODUCTION

With the technological advancement and the emergence of entrepreneurial ideas for new business models, innovative, creative, and profitable possibilities arise to facilitate the life of the consumer. In this scenario, startups, a model of companies that work with transformative activities and that seek a business that adds value to the customer are evidenced.

Startups are usually small companies that create a lean model, but that contribute with impact in the society, generating in the short term a profitable business. However, in order to do so, one must create a well-organized development planning, because, with a scenario where uncertainties are predominant, immediate success or failure cannot be predicted. This scenario of profitable and innovative new companies has been growing considerably in Brazil and in the world. Nubank exemplifies this situation. The company, successful in Brazil in the area of means of payments, which at first was considered an uncertainty, grew and attracted great results for both the company and its final consumer.

DOI: 10.4018/978-1-7998-3257-7.ch009

Among the startups are FinTech. A model that proposes to add technological innovations to companies of the financial area, arose to challenge the current financial model that is slow and bureaucratic.

According to the Brazilian Association of Fintecs - ABFintech, this model is growing in Brazil, having tripled in the last two years. Rodrigo Libaldo, president of ABFinTech, comments that there are 244 FinTech in the country (RODRIGUES, 2017).

In addition, these small organizations emerged to challenge large financial institutions already consolidated in the market as there were no new models that could compete with this system. With a modest beginning, the model achieved expressiveness in the financial market and became a bet for institutions interested in technological and social advancement.

The service brought by these FinTech tends to reach market with their products which can offer from credit card to personal loans without bureaucracy, challenging banks with their efficient business differentiation. These companies invest in technology and work more quickly and transparently.

In view of the above, the article seeks to answer the following research problem: Are FinTech configured as opportunities or as threats to large financial institutions in Brazil?

To respond to the proposed problem, the general objective of this research is to identify how FinTech constitute opportunities or threats for large financial institutions in Brazil. And as specific objectives: analyze the perceptions about FinTech; observe the partnerships that may arise between financial institutions and FinTech; identify the challenges of FinTech with the market; identify how is the fintech market in Brazil.

The academic relevance of this work is justified by the current relevance of the topic, by the small amount of research related to the subject and by the exponential growth of FinTech in the market. Therefore, research will add to the academic environment as an incentive to scientific study. Socially and economically the study will bring more knowledge to these types of organizations that seek to undertake through FinTech that are in great expansion.

Therefore, the following will be presented the theoretical reference and all its scientific base to reach the proposed objectives

THEORETICAL REFERENCE

Entrepreneurship

Entrepreneurship means willingness to add values, know how to identify and idealize opportunities (AURELIO, 2010). Maçães (2017) states that entrepreneurship is to plan projects to transform a profitable business economically and involves innovation and risk. However, for Dornelas (2016), entrepreneurship is the continuous search for development.

For Saraiva (2015), entrepreneurship is the description of processes, of creation and capture of new ideas and methodologies, in which the sources of inspiration can lead to the formation of new business models, thus generating a greater competitiveness.

Going further, Maçães (2017) explains that entrepreneurship is the process of seeking and reaching new opportunities, in which they are usually responses to market demands. Entrepreneurship is also linked to the process of starting a new business, where entrepreneurs take risks and analyze the benefits brought by their visionary and innovative ideas, with the production of new concepts of services and products.

In the twentieth century there were several transformations in a short space of time in which various inventions were created and they revolutionized the way of life of society.

Every day that the technological advance develops, more entrepreneurs are needed to bring new ideas or old ideas to renew themselves in order to recycle existing products and services (DORNELAS, 2016).

Donelas (2016) argues that undertaking is something that is aimed at the future and at building something innovative, realizing dreams and transforming ideas into opportunities for achieving goals. Every day it is necessary to renew and break paradigms that can advance economic and social development and thus generate new jobs. Entrepreneurs are meant to produce greater wealth for their business and society.

However, Tidd and Bessant (2015, p.4) argue that "innovation is driven by the ability to establish relationships, detect opportunities and take advantage of them." The understanding of innovation as an instrument of entrepreneurship creates a necessary and essential interconnection between the concepts in the elaboration of differentiated businesses with competitive potential.

Each entrepreneur has a creative and achiever profile, it is not usually characteristic of this professional to be in a bureaucratic and limiting environment, where formulations of new strategies are always being barred. This flexible profile that the entrepreneur contains is due to a characteristic also in start-up businesses, such as startups (TIDD and BESSANT, 2015).

All this interconnected potential between entrepreneurs and startups is of paramount importance to people with an innovative profile, as they help and sharpen creativity for new ideas. For Periard (2011), startups bring a concept of being an organization in the initialization phase that seeks to be repeatable and scalable.

By using this innovative creativity to modernize business models, their highest priority is the achievement of organizational success, in search of positive experiences or not, aim at an improvement to improve startups making them something repeatable able to lead to a product or service to a potential scale without limitation or large adaptations to profiles of different consumers.

Startup

The concept of startup is commonly related to the denomination of lean company. For Ries (2012), this is a low- and low-cost staff. Your goal is not just to manufacture or meet a demand. Startups also exist to power a sustainable business. They are companies that also look for investors to sponsor entrepreneurial ideas with the objective of making them increasingly competitive and differentiated.

Therefore, it is extremely important that from its embryonic form the startup bet on formulating actions that, with agility and improvement in the services and products offered, may be able to meet the demand that may increase with the time and success of it. And thus transmit to these new users their values, focusing on the way of dealing with the customer, offering quality and personalization no matter the amount of customers, because if the focus is lost the risk of that company to fail is great.

According to Blank and Dorf (2014), many startups begin with basic ideas and scribbled in their business plan. This will give rise to the first assumptions of how the service or product thought and structured will reach the customer's hands. It is necessary to discuss how all this may impact on their competitive advantages, their distribution channels and what costs are expected.

Once the initial stages of the business plan are defined, in which everything is described step by step of how each step will be done and thus demonstrated to investors. A description of the development of the product or service will be required. When you are delimited the positions and sectors then comes the time to put these ideas into practice. In Figure 1, Blank and Dorf (2014) suggest how the product can be developed to be worked on.

Figure 1. New product launch diagram, Source: Adapted from Blank and Dork (2014, p.3)

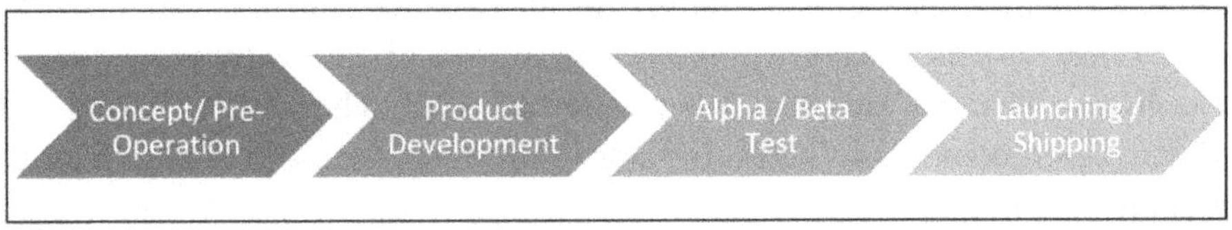

At this stage, the linking channels have already been defined and released to the target audience. For Blank and Dorf (2014), this operational model that focuses on the product and its processes is widely used by startups, to enter the market with their first products

Fintech

The so-called FinTech present many of the principles of strategy and innovation espoused by Porter (1979), Drucker (2002) and Christensen (2015). Many of these concepts are present in their new business models and have made it possible to create disruption and innovation in the financial industry. According to Rosemary (2017) and Horn (2015), the term fintech arises from a combination of the English words *financial* (finance) and *technology* (technology). The term, by itself, sums up the idea well, where fintech is every company that offers financial services that are differentiated by the facilities provided by technology and, indeed, by the internet.

According to Mayor and Gonzãlez (2017), FinTech is set of financial innovations that have the technical capacity to produce new business models, processes and products that are linked to financial markets and institutions and the provision of financial services.

In Ko theory (2017), executives of the financial service, featuring *FinTech* as the biggest disturbance in the next five years. With these large-scale companies advancing on the market, the traditional financial services create a strategy to deal with this the situation. Some *FinTech* beginners recognize that they can disturb the financial system, but they emphasize that their companies are collaborating to the system and not competitors.

In the view of Mayor and Gonzãlez (2017), although the fintech sector is still in development and has increased investments, this type of company has attracted the interest of the various national and international regulatory bodies, since all are aware of the potential that these companies have. Of course, these bodies have begun to study how these companies can offer risks and so the best way is to design projects for their regulation.

Similarly, Goeller and Shureen (2016), claim that this market is more associated with a broad market where competition and regulatory agencies are trying to tackle. The United States Department of the Treasury (2015 cited Goeller;. SHUREEM, 2016, p 5) defines the market as "financial services industry segment using online equity investment platforms based on data to lend to small businesses and consumers."

For Mayor and Gonzãlez (2017), markets that encompass the financial industry (banking services, investments and insurance) are affected by these innovative technologies. It is common that the term fintegration is mentioned as it refers to acquisition strategies and investments in startups by traditional financial institutions that acquire these companies to gain competitive advantage over other institutions and accelerate their digital transformation.

Mayor and Gonzalez (2017) further explain that FinTech are pushing the banking system to reinvent itself and become more digital every day. This development of the digitization market for money or payment services is of paramount importance. Adding this to the development of the internet and its impact on the daily lives of users are increasingly empowering the use of applications.

In fact, FinTech have been an area that has progressed a lot. The authors explain that the market has encouraged these entrepreneurs to invest in their innovative ideas and thus to become competitive companies that contribute in general to the development of the economy and society as a whole. These stimuli generate great impacts in the country providing economic and social benefits, making it favorable for the generation of new jobs and also obliges the institutions to give up the excessive bureaucracy they have in the search to continue attracting and retaining customers.

Mayor and González (2017) score, with the development and technological advancement of financial services, which will grow considerably, since its advantages are high and provide greater efficiency in the market.

Still, according to Mayor and González (2017), with the availability of these services, where communication is boosting the financial sector in a more efficient and personalized way, FinTech that are startups with digital content, start to become competitors of great potential of traditional and bureaucratic institutions that, in order to stay competitive, are seeking to acquire these companies every day with the objective of accelerating and expanding their digital transformation.

With the impact of these technological innovations it is important to observe if there is an excessive regulation of the sector, as this would imply unnecessary bureaucratization that hinders its development. The objective of promoting basic and uniform regulation affects all financial service providers. However, care should be taken in the consequences that can lead to errors, a security gap or a risk of investors error in understanding these products and services (MAYOR, GONZÁLEZ, 2017).

The authors further assert that in this way the last aspect to be addressed would be through monitoring compliance with the obligations on traditional financial institutions for these new financial services platforms. In addition, the regulation and supervision of companies called fintech must impose sufficient test requirements requiring that they corroborate the actual expression of contract consents and their scopes, the representation of money and financially non-existent financial instruments that are the object of this contract, as well as it is effective and effective existence.

Financial System and FinTech

In Brazil, the National Financial System (SFN) is composed of control entities, entities and operators, according to figure 2 and have the functions of determining general rules following the regulations used in the sector for the proper functioning of the SFN; to act so that the citizens and the members of the financial system follow the rules defined by the normative organs and to deal directly with the public in the role of financial intermediary (BACEN, 2017).

After the 2008 crisis, the reforms imposed on banks by regulators limited their ability to direct investments into the innovation process, opening space for the birth of Financial Technology (FinTech) and creating a context of difficult competition for banks. Another important point was the emergence

Figure 2. Composition and segments of the National Financial System, Source: Adapted from BACEN (2017)

	Moeda, crédito, capitais e câmbio		Seguros privados	Previdência fechada
Órgãos normativos	CMN – Conselho Monetário Nacional		CNSP – Conselho Nacional de Seguros Privados	CNPC – Conselho Nacional de Previdência Complementar
Supervisores	BCB – Banco Central do Brasil	CVM – Comissão da Valores Mobiliários	SUSEP – Superintendência de Seguros Privados	Previc – Superintendência Nacional de Previdência Complementar
Operadores	Bancos e caixas econômicas Administradoras de consórcios Cooperativas de crédito Corretoras e distribuidoras Instituições de pagamentos Demais instituições não bancárias	Bolsa de valores Bolsa de mercadorias e futuros	Seguradoras e resseguradoras Entidades abertas de previdência Sociedades de capitalização	Entidades fechadas de previdência complementar (fundos de pensão)

of new business models that still operate in many countries outside the regulatory model, such as loans between people directly (Arner, Barberi & Buckler, 2015).

In this context, but already in the regulatory environment of the SFN, Resolution no. 4,480, of the Central Bank of Brazil, regulated by the National Monetary Council (CMN), in April 2016, allowed Brazilians to open a checking account and savings account via the Internet. This move launched a new competitive landscape, taking the banks from a traditional performance and imposed a more aggressive performance. To keep pace with the development and advancement of the new means of access and service, the banks sought the adoption of friendly and efficient digital platforms so that they could contain the advances of FinTech.

METHOD

The study was descriptive, according to Gil (2017), to provide the researcher with a detailed description of the characteristics of the organization. Gil (2017) discusses that descriptive research has an objective in describing these characteristics that may be a pre-defined and structured conception.

The approach used was qualitative. According to Vergara (2016), the qualitative researches are not structured, because they are carried out based on small samples that allow a contextualized understanding of the problem.

The means used for the investigation and achievement of results were semi-structured interviews. Interviews have the ability to provide the necessary data even if flexibly (GIL, 2008).

The research was developed in three financial organizations of different segments: means of payment; financial institution; insurer. The means of payment company is currently one of the leaders in its global performance, with a strong presence in Brazil. The financial institution is the largest bank in Brazil when it comes to customer service network. As for the insurer, its results are the largest revenue generator in its follow-up in Brazil.

The procedures used to search the data were obtained through interviews with a representative of each company. The interviews were conducted in person and by telephone in the second half of September, with an average duration of thirty minutes. The interview script was based on questions pertinent to the study to meet general and specific objectives. Materials were also requested that could confirm the data reported in the interviews.

In the analysis of the data obtained, the technique used was content analysis, in which categories (Table 1) were raised that could respond to the research problem according to the subjects covered in theoretical reference and the questions asked in the interviews. According to Bardin (2010), this technique aims to obtain, through procedures and description of acquired content of the messages, indicators that grant the conclusion of knowledge correlated the variables acquired in the messages.

Table 1. Categories

	CATEGORIES
1	Perception
2	Actions of Partnerships between Financial Institutions and FinTech
3	Opportunities
4	Challenges

The category entitled "Perception of fintech" addresses the interviewees' understanding of the overall view of the presence of FinTech in the market. The category "Actions of Partnerships between Financial Institutions and FinTech" covers respondents' responses to the actions that financial institutions are taking to get closer to FinTech. The category entitled "Opportunities" addresses the respondents' considerations about the possibilities that FinTech can generate. The "Challenges" category seeks to present the considerations regarding the difficulties identified by financial institutions in relation to the performance of FinTech in the market.

DATA PRESENTATION AND DISCUSSION

In order to identify how is the FinTech market it is possible to notice that according to the BargainFox report of 2016, the main countries with this ecosystem are the United States (Silicon Valey, New York, Los Angeles and Boston), England (London) and Israel (Tel Aviv). Between 2010 and 2015, around US $ 50 billion were invested worldwide, with these investments concentrated in the United States (US $ 31 billion). The South American market, led by Brazil, received only US $ 100 million, showing that the ecosystem is still incipient in the region, as can be seen in figure 3.

Such scenario has been evolving with the number of FinTech that are appearing in the Brazilian market according to the last Fintechlab Radar (2017) that shows a 30% growth of FinTech in Brazil, as perceived in figure 4.

According to the Fintechlab Radar (2017) it was found that out of the total of 332 companies, 90 (27%) FinTech in Brazil, in 2017, are from the payments segment, 59 (18%) are financial management, 58 (17%) are credit and loans, 29 (9%) are investments, 27 (8%) are insurance, 19 (6%) are funding, 16 (5%) are debt collection, 15 (5%) are cryptocurrency and DTL, 9 (3%) are exchange, 10 (3%) are multiservice.

Figure 3. Global FinTech Investment, Source: Adapted from BargainFox Report 2016

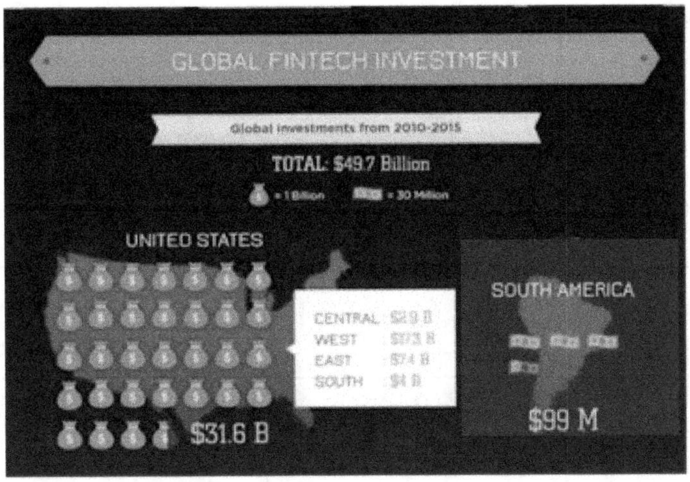

It is possible to observe that the segments that grew the most were insurance, with a 92% increase and loans, with a 75% increase. The segments that grew the most in absolute numbers were loans, with 25 more initiatives than the last radar that was conducted about nine months ago, and financial management, with 16 more initiatives.

According to the survey, the sum of the volume of FinTech with initiatives considered financial efficiency resulted in a number 40% higher than the previous study, going from 264 to 369. The new information bureau platforms are considered financial efficiency companies. fraud prevention solutions, biometrics, and analytics, as well as other technologies and services that support and bring greater agility and practicality to the financial market (Fintechlab Radar, 2017).

Figure 4. Map of FinTech in Brazil, Source: Adapted from Fintechlab November 2017

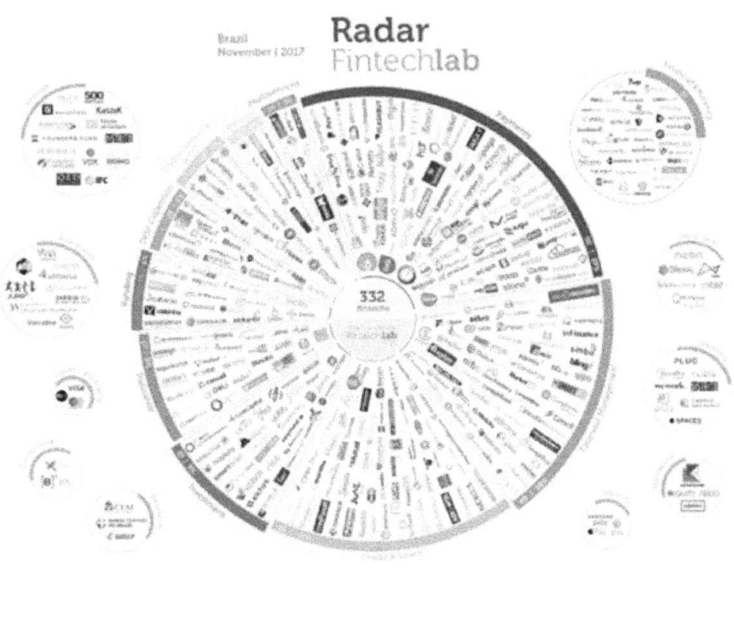

Table 2. Results of the categories

CATEGORIES	COMMENTS	
Perceptions Fintech	Payment options	"A vision I have, the FinTech have come to fight with the banks, banks do not like it, I think there is still some of this insecurity. At the same time we started to see many banks looking at FinTech as an opportunity."
		"I think I've already passed this stage of seeing FinTech as villains, I now see FinTech as a laboratory, as an experiment, as an opportunity that brings something different."
	Financial institution	"I approach these startups, I help put these ideas together, which are great, but often they do not have networking, they do not know anyone and they do not have an executive vision for the business."
	Insurance Company	"The FinTech market in Brazil is still incipient despite the fact that it already has more mature companies in the stage of investments and in the condition of being partners. But in terms of quantity they are small and few. " "Companies are being affected in the way they work because of these FinTech that are appearing."
Partnership actions between Institutions Financial and FinTech	Payment options	"The institution supports and mentors fintech programs such as Google Camp. We support and bring these FinTech into the company to carry out a mentoring and culture program."
		"The approach has already begun and is growing strongly, it brings this vision of fintech to the company with a more traditional vision of how the products are made, so that these traditional companies can take more risk, make a small business, as it happens, things will be adjusted throughout the process. "
	Financial institution	"An example of partnership, I know that the institution in which I work has already been talking with several FinTech in the search for possibility of adding efforts and making partnerships."
	Insurance Company	"What I have noticed is that it is starting to have this approach between FinTech and traditional banks." "I see FinTech now as opportunities to make any partnerships or make an acquisition."
Opportunities	Payment options	"Practical way, XP Investimentos was a Fintech that Itaú bought because it was troublesome, because that way it is not losing customers or even growing."
		"Nubank he came out with his digital card product that nobody believed and started making noise, without going into the discussion whether it is profitable or not, have a base of almost a billion customers, thus encouraging companies to want to do something. "
	Financial institution	"Banks have seen this as a kind of threat sprayed on some businesses they operate, but I have seen many banks approaching FinTech to learn and form partnerships."
		"Banks can use FinTech in the open banking concept to deliver that same experience through partnerships."
	Insurance Company	"The other thing I see in large segments, what is more latent is the issue of the digital bank, Original Bank, Nubank that will enter the area, We have received three requests, for the beginning of the year, more digital banks entering the market without agency, in this concept of digital bank that already begins to appear can not seem to exist. It is a reality. What starts to make banks look like their digital way of relating to customers, to make a chat as a customer service channel. I believe it has a digital banking influence on financial institutions. "
Challenges	Payment options	"I do not see the Central Bank regulating"
		"The market will not be more open but more regulated."
		"The gap that is emerging is with demand problems."
	Financial institution	"I still see little impact. I see more noise than impact itself. " "It's certainly a threat. We are being bitten by bees and these bites can be fatal to big business. " "The Central Bank has the function of maintaining the balance of the National Financial System. So he will always look at risk management and see if there is any movement affecting the stability of the system. "
	Insurance Company	"The Central Bank has a reactive stance. It comes to regulate what has already happened. The Central Bank is in his role. I think it will maintain the regulatory profile of the Brazilian financial market." "And it's always a safety case and it looks exemplary when compared to other markets."

Another strong move pointed out by FintechLab Radar (2017) was the increase in the intensity of integration and cooperation initiatives between the big financial companies, FinTech and startups. In this sense, the biggest examples were the expansion of Cubo, an initiative organized by Itaú Bank, the launch of Inovabra Habitat, an initiative organized by Santander Bank and the continuation of innovation programs such as B3, VISA and Porto Seguro / Oxygen.

On the other hand, the mapping also revealed the beginning of a natural selection process in the fintech segment. The closing movement of some initiatives was verified. During this period, it was notice that 18 companies are no longer active, most of them in the payments sector.

Still with the intention of reaching the objective of this research three representatives of financial organizations of different segments was interviewed: means of payment; financial institution; insurer. Based on the points covered in the theoretical framework, respondents were asked about startups and FinTech (Table 2). The data presented were classified into categories as shown in figure 3.

During the research it was found that the interviewees believe that FinTech represent a great growth of presence in the market although it is considered an underdeveloped market compared to

the most advanced countries. But still financial organizations are being affected in the way they work due to the FinTech that are emerging.

As for the actions of partnerships between financial institutions and FinTech the interviewees realize that it is a promising field that can be explored and is advantageous both for financial organizations and for FinTech. In the case of financial organizations mainly related to the specializations brought by FinTech and their way of thinking. For FinTech, the possibility of learning with large companies, through mentoring and the generation of business scale.

According to the interviewees, it is necessary to seek partnerships so that the market can always be updated dynamically and effectively. In this way, large institutions seek to acquire those startups that are troubling or are only causing a better partnership for their business, reducing the processes and expenses with the workforce. Ries (2012) affirms that it is necessary to seek to reduce risks and losses and to create new products and services, which is why it is the duty to analyze FinTech as partners and not as competitors.

Ries (2012) also states that it is necessary to use a set of tools with techniques of improvement, avoiding wastage and maximizing the chances of success, as the interviewees analyze the situations that are inevitable to the extent that large companies invest in the mentoring of these startups and FinTech, demonstrating how the steps will be analyzed and how they can be launched.

One highlight among the opportunities mentioned by the interviewees is the entry of fully digital banks. In this case, large institutions feel obliged to seek new digital tools that facilitate relationships with customers who are increasingly demanding the products and services they consume. Ries (2012) states that for success to be built one must follow a correct process, which allows for their learning, as banks seek in partnerships with FinTech.

Regarding the challenges listed by the interviewees, even with little impact on the results of financial organizations, FinTech are already a major threat, making them a current challenge for financial institutions to adapt and adapt.

In addition, to be analyzed as the best opportunities and partnerships that may arise in the future between traditional companies and FinTech, the interviewees put in discussion, as well as the authors Mayor and González (2017), that it is necessary to regulate these new companies. However, caution should be taken in order to ensure that there is no excess of bureaucracy that would hinder the growth of the sector.

FINAL CONSIDERATION

The present study had as general objective to identify how the FinTech constitute opportunities or threats for the big financial institutions in Brazil. And as specific objectives: analyze the perceptions about FinTech; observe the partnerships that may arise between financial institutions and FinTech; identify the challenges of FinTech with the market.

When analyzing the perceptions about FinTech, it was identified that they are present in the market and in constant growth. Although in a few expressive numbers, some FinTech are already developed enough to receive investments and to be bought by large financial institutions.

As for the partnerships that may arise between financial institutions and FinTech, the relevance of these new business models to the benefit of consumers through the combination of the modern and the traditional for the development of new products and services was noted. These partnerships also imply the possibility of generating customer facilities, less bureaucracy, more rapid credit opportunities for short-term investments, among others.

When identifying the challenges of FinTech with the market the main indication is the absence of regulation that permeates these new business models.

Finally, when analyzing the opportunities and challenges presented by the interviewees, it is concluded that FinTech can be considered an opportunity for institutions that are attentive to the emergence of new possibilities in the financial market. In view of the above, the objectives of this study were reached and the research problem was answered.

The limitations found to the research was the fact that it is a new topic and, consequently, the scarcity of information and research material.

For the future agenda, it is suggested that the subject be researched with a larger number of respondents and representatives of other financial institutions in Brazil. It is also suggested that a comparative study be carried out in order to identify if the perceptions presented in the Brazilian market are similar to those presented in other countries.

REFERENCES

Bardin, L. (2010). *Content Analysis* (70th ed.).

Blank, S., & Dorf, B. (2014). *Startup: Entrepreneur manual.* High Books.

Dornelas, J. C. A. (2016). *Empreendedorismo: transformando ideias em negócios. 6.* Atlas.

Ferreira, A. B. de H. (2010). *Webster's Basic Portuguese Language. 8.* Editora Positivo.

Gil, A. C. (2008). *Métodos e técnicas de pesquisa social.* Atlas.

Gil, A. C. (2017). *Como elaborar projetos de pesquisa.* Atlas.

Goeller, J. D., & Shureen, C. E. (2016). The top five federal tax issues for FinTech lenders. *Journal of taxation & regulation of Financial Institutions, 30*(1), 5-10.

Hail, P. M. (2015). *Entrepreneurship.* Press University of Coimbra.

Horn, W. (Ed.). (2015). *What is Fintech*. Finnovation. Available at: http://finnovation.com.br/o-que-e-fintech/

Ko, C. (2017, Apr.). Are FinTech startups eating traditional banks' lunch? *Computerworld.*

Maçães, M. (2017). *Entrepreneurship, innovation and organizational change. 3.* Actual.

Mayor, D. G. O., & González, I. A. P. (2017). Fintech: The Future of them servicios financieros. *Revista Española de Capital Riesgo, 1*, 19-28.

Periard, G. (2011). *What is a startup?* http://www.sobreadministracao.com/o-que-e-uma-startup

Ries, E. (2012). *The Lean Startup: How current entrepreneurs use continuous innovation to create highly successful businesses*. Paper Moon.

Rodrigues, R. (2017). *Brazilian FinTech boom provides new opportunities for investors*. https://www.istoedinheiro.com.br/boom-de-FinTechbrasileirasoferece- novas-oportunidades-para-os-investidores/

Rosemary, E. (2016). *What is FinTech?* https://www.infowester.com/fintech.php

Tidd, J., & Bessant, J. (2015). *Innovation management*. Bookman.

Vergara, S. C. (2016). *Projetos e Relatórios de Pesquisa em Administração* (16th ed.). Atlas.

Chapter 10
FinTech Adoption in China: Challenges, Regulations, and Opportunities

Gagan Kukreja
Ahlia University, Bahrain

ABSTRACT

Almost all financial services (especially digital payments) in China are affected by new innovations and technologies. New technologies such as blockchain, artificial intelligence, machine learning, deep learning, and data analytics have immensely influenced all most all aspects of financial services such as deposits, transactions, billings, remittances, credits (B2B and P2P), underwriting, insurance, and so on. Fintech companies are enabling larger financial inclusion, changing in lifestyle and expenditure behavior, better and fast financial services, and lots more. This chapter covers the development, opportunities, and challenges of financial sectors because of new technologies in China. This chapter throws the light on opportunities that emerged because of the large population of 1.4 billion people, high penetration, and access to the latest and affordable technology, affordable cost of smartphones, and government policies and regulations. Lastly, this chapter portrays the untapped potentials of Fintech in China.

INTRODUCTION

This chapter will cover the developments that had happened in financial institutions and in their products and services because of Fintech (Financial Technology) and How Fintech has been evolved in fast ever-changing environment in China over last decade? It will also cover trends and impact of Fintech on financial institutions and other stakeholders (particularly customers) of China in the future. Fintech looks like a promising solution to help the emerging economies such as China to try and reduce the gap between developed & developing countries to some extent. The principal tenacity of Fintech is not only to advance the quality of financial services, but to modify the way finance products and services serve the life of the people. In last decade, Ant Financial's Alipay, and Tencent's Wechat have revolutionize the way people of China spend on different services. These innovations in financial domain have be-

DOI: 10.4018/978-1-7998-3257-7.ch010

come ONESTOP solution from making payments to investments, loans, insurance, travel, remittance, communication and many more.

China has recently experienced a drastic growth in Fintech as compared to other parts of the world such as the U.S, Asia, and Europe. The value of fintech deals in China in 2018 was $25.5 billion which is far ahead of deals in other parts of the world. More than half of China's fintech investment came from a single deal. In May 2018, Hangzhou-based Ant Financial (spun off from the Alibaba Group), best known for its mobile payments service Alipay, raised $14 billion. This was also the largest fintech deal globally at that time. The second-largest capital raise by Du Xiaoman Financial, a spinoff of Chinese search engine giant Baidu, raised $4.3 billion in two separate transactions. Another large transaction of $1.3 billion was by wealth management platform Lufax. (Knowledge@Wharton, 2019, July 12). The reason behind China's success lies in the development and innovation of FinTech that has not only been obtained from the advantage of the technology revolution but the assimilation of its financial processes and the real-life prerequisites.

BACKGROUND

Upon the inception of the Alipay in 2003, China ventured into a regime of exceptional execution of technology in the broad financial segments (Chen, 2016). Because of the burgeoning development of e-commerce, rising demands for the financial services and surge in disposable income (over last two to three decades), China created a sound basis for the initiation of the fintech industry. In the 1990s, China escalated its investment and venture of the technology sector, commercial segment and public finances (Chen, 2016). Among the big Chinese companies such as Baidu, Tencent, Alibaba, and JD have been categorized to be the leading internet companies in the globe. Overall, the increasing growth in the fintech sector in China is due to the current government's supportive policies and the favorable regulatory environment. Recently, central bank of China brought 3 years development plan (2019-2021) for Fintech sector and addressing attached risks (Fintech Futures, 2019, August 23). Financial services industry in China has experienced fast growth over the past 5 years. According to the J P Morgan research, China's FinTech industry has seen an annual growth of 44% immediately after 2017. This has led to a projection of a whopping growth of $ 715 billion as gross yearly returns by 2020.

THE INFRASTRUCTURE OF FINANCIAL SERVICES

Before 2000s, China was operating on a cash basis until when it adopted digitization in handling financial products and services. This was after a massive manifestation of the internet, the evolution of the e-commerce, reasonable mobile data cost and availability of smartphones. As a result, the Chinese adopted the digital money transfer and payment programs and abolished cash payments. Further, it created solid platforms for e-commerce, alternative banking, banking the unbanked population (financial inclusion) and many more financial services. As of now, Chinese fintech are largely focused on the domestic payments space, mostly in retail. This is a space that many Chinese banks have ceded to the technology firms. In a very short span of time, these companies have built new ecosystem models around the smartphone and delivered this to consumers through super-apps that deliver a customer experience marked by usability, simplicity, and convenience.

There were online networks sites for most of the Chinese consumers like the Tmall, Taobao and the JD.com which were initiated because of the introduction of the internet and mobile technologies. The consumers within and outside China began shopping online aborting their offline retail infrastructure (Leong, Tan, Xiao, Tan & Sun, 2017). The e-commerce firms encouraged FinTech organizations to work on payments, insurance, financing, and third-party remittances.

GROWTH OF FINTECH

The rate at which China's FinTech sector has emerged simply groundbreaking. Tenpay is a payment branch of Tencent that entails the WeChat Pay, it was formed in 2013 to facilitate online financial services. By first quarter of 2019, WeChat had about 1.2 billion users. Its increased online ride-hailing compelled large organizations to join hands in forming Didi Chuxing, hence making its popularity rise at an even faster rate (Han, 2018).

Ant Financial was launched in 2014 after integration with Alipay that provided an array of services such as online gaming, credit, wealth management, and financing services. By March 2018, Ant Financial had 870 million active yearly users. FinTech companies of China include Didi Chuxing, Taobao, Ctrip, Tmall, Weibo among other Small and Medium Enterprises (SMEs) (Han, 2018). China has also invested heavily on advancing the financial services by adopting new technologies and digitization in financing and setting up alternative investment that ensures crowdfunding. Due to China's strong economic base, the US-based drive wealth has linked with credits to initiate a robot-advisory commodity ToumiRA for many investors to access the global equities effectively.

Most of FinTech companies in China are into online lending, consumer finance, online brokerage, online insurance, and personal financial management. Under online borrowing, there is a mobile payment system that is enhanced by the key players such as the e-commerce and the social media players Tencent and Alipay who are predominant in the market. Consumer finance allows borrowing and lending to the SMEs through capturing their critical data (Cortina Lorente & Schmukler, 2018). Regarding online brokerage, investor's data portals and the social network information in China which offers thematic investing through the mobile phones. E-insurance is also traded through wealth management platforms and e-commerce by firms such as the Ping An and the People's Insurance Company of China (Chen, 2016). The personal finance management has offered solutions by initiating access to the collective finds via the stock trading applications. Baidu is one firm that has adopted this technology.

REGULATIONS

Regulations, mainly for state-owned institutions, of the FinTech industry in China were initiated between 2013 and 2015 to provide a ground for robust growth. Initially, the financial institutions in China were focused on providing services for the state-owned enterprises, while limiting services to the retail clients and the SME (Fungáčová & Weill, 2015). The transition from the investment-led economy to the consumption-based economy influenced the companies to support the initiative that called for financial inclusivity through loosening regulatory measures to enhance conspicuous consumption.

In 2016, the Government formulated an inclusive policy that works effectively to regulate the internet finance industry on various areas of operations. Such areas encompass crowdfunding, lending, fund distribution, insurance, lending, and consumer finance. In March 2017, it put up an integrated clearing house known as "Wanglian" to provide services to third party payments which permitted supervisory oversight on the flow of funds (Vives, 2017). In May 2017, the central banks devised a FinTech committee that plays a role of coordinating all the FinTech policies. The regulatory policy ecosystem in China has acted proficiently to the many non-financial segments key players majorly on areas such as the mutual funds, the SME's, and the microfinance. Due to the massive financial crisis witnessed in the year 2015 when approximately 1600 P2P lenders exited the market, China through the People's Bank of China (PBOC) adopted a sequence of regulations to preside over a lending and online payment of the P2P (Ng, Muthukannan, Tan and Leong, 2017). The regulation-imposed credit restrictions and outlawed pooling and online borrowing of money by the P2P platforms. Recently, China has also been attributed to many data securities issues. The PBOC's has set up pre-requisites for the non-bank payments firms as enshrined around a more robust protective measure, risk control systems and the preservation of the more critical data.

In September 2019, the PBOC, the country's central bank, has released a three-year fintech development plan that aims to improve the quality of financial services, strengthen regulation on technology-driven innovations, and prevent financial risks. (Fintech News Hong Kong, 2019, September 6). The plan lays out six main tasks and priorities:

1. The need to strengthen the strategic deployment of fintech, improve forward-looking design, identify fintech development trends, and concentrate on coordinated planning, optimization of systematic arrangement and talent building.
2. Identifying proper fintech applications, key breakthroughs to drive development, and adequate regulation and control of key generic technologies.
3. Enhancing the quality and efficiency of financial services by diversifying financial service channels, enabling cost reduction, and optimizing financing services to benefit Chinese consumers and allow for the healthy and sustainable development of the real economy.
4. Enhancing technological capabilities to prevent financial risks, properly balance the relationship between security and development, leverage fintech to identify, curb and tackle cross-market, cross-industry and cross-regional financial risks, and strengthen control of cyber-security risks and the protection of financial information.
5. Strengthening fintech regulation by developing a system of fundamental regulatory rules, exploring innovative management mechanisms for fintech, facilitating integrated statistics for the financial sector, and making financial regulation "more professional, unified and penetrating". and
6. Consolidating basic support for fintech while improving the ecosystem, optimizing relevant governance systems, and taking appropriate steps in the fields of technology, laws and regulations, credit services, standards, and consumer protection.

Chang, Wong, Lee and Jeong (2016) concluded that the regulatory strategy in the FinTech purposes to help SMEs and retail clients. This dismisses the traditional organizational approach that only targeted the state-owned enterprises. The financial institutions among the technology companies in the Chinese FinTech industry are thriving due to the high technology that is associated with it. The evolution of financial digitization in the dimensions of active development, legislation and customer adoption are behind the finance growth in China. The commercial technology system in China has linked the banks, technology, retailers in the provision of financial services (Claessens, Frost, Turner and Zhu, 2018).

EMERGING TRENDS

China's established financial institutions are emerging as leading adopters of fintech, with an increasing number launching their own fintech subsidiaries. As of the end of the first half of 2019 at least ten Chinese banks had established their own fintech subsidiaries, including Ping An Bank, China Merchants Bank, China Everbright Bank, China Minsheng Bank, Huaxia Bank, Bank of Beijing, ICBC and Bank of China. This move will benefit companies in diversifying their risks and tapping the untapped and unbanked markets, but at the same time, these companies must deal with very diverse regulations and cultural diversity. Players in the Chinese fintech sector are increasingly setting their sights on opportunities in overseas markets, with payments companies taking the lead followed by developers of wealth management products.

In addition to the Chinese central bank, many other financial institutions and tech companies in China are making use of blockchain technology for cross-border payments and supply-chain financing, including Ant Financial and JD Data Science. Chinese banks are promoting open banking, domestically and abroad, which require special attention by the regulators. Chinese banks are making increasing use of big data, artificial intelligence and cloud computing to improve service levels at their bricks and mortar outlets.

With the emergence of 5G, it is expected to have drastic boost in existing fintech services. The new technologies will also promote Insurtech, Robo-advising, Wealthtech, Proptech, Regtech and many more services in future. It will further attract proactive attention of the regulators.

Chinese financial institutions are making increasing use of biometric technology including fingerprint identification, facial recognition, retina identification and voice recognition to improve security for clients. Internet giants such as Baidu, Alibaba, Tencent and JD.com are shifting the focus of their approach from being financial institutions to being tech providers, and concentrating their efforts on the B-end market to provide big data, artificial intelligence, Internet of Things and other tech services to traditional financial institutions. JD.com was one of the first to drive this trend, changing the official name of its subsidiary "JD Finance" to "JD Data Science" in September 2018.

China's online insurance market saw staggering growth during the five-year period from 2013 to 2018, growing from 1.17 billion yuan to 188.8 billion yuan, while the second half of 2018 saw Alibaba and Tencent launch their own insurance services. Regulators are adopting and embracing tech development against the background of Insurtech development.

Further, it is expected that post COVID 19 will bring paradigm shift in consumer behaviour. People will rely more on e products. Electronic payment, online remittance and new innovative products will be in high demand. Insurance policies would be bought more in online mode. Altogether, it will boost FinTech products and services (FinTech Futures, 2020 and Mohammad, 2020).

CHALLENGES

After COVID 16 pandemic, consumer behaviour and expectations about financial services will be changed; a more affordable infrastructure needs to be created by artificial intelligence (AI), cloud computing and big data; digital currencies have the potential to disrupt banking and credit; and mobile technologies have reduced the barriers to entry to the financial services industry. It is predicted that fintech of China continues to transform the global financial landscape in future. US-China trade tussle may have some impact on this move. In May 2020, China declared to issue digital currencies which will further escalate the tension between US and China which may lead to unpredictable impact on FinTech companies based in US and China. FDI from US and Europe might be affected which may hold ambitious projects of China's FinTeach companies (Gray 2020).

In recent two years, fraudulent fundraising activities have forced regulatory authorities to tighten regulations on emerging industries such as online P2P lending. Previously, a lack of oversight had been blamed for the rise of illegal lending platforms, including Ezubao, a Ponzi scheme that raised around $7.6 billion from 900,000 investors in 2017. Since then, Chinese regulators have launched an offensive against online lenders, which is expected to result in 70% all of P2P lending businesses being shut down by the end of 2019. China's crypto space has also been affected in last three years. After banning initial coin offerings in 2017, the PBOC in December 2018 warned the public against security token offerings (STOs), a new form of crypto fundraising in which tokens are backed by assets, saying that they are illegal (Jao, 2019, January 31).

CONCLUSION AND OUTLOOK

The FinTech has advanced the banking system and ensured new foundations of fragility. China is at the forefront of creating an inclusive platform that can offer essential solutions to financial and non-financial solutions to its clients. It has also invested tremendously on the evolving technologies to better future financial services for instance works on artificial intelligence solutions. China's FinTech, world leader, is exceptionally evolving at a fast speed as many of the international finance firms. It is essential that the FinTech companies should take a course of expanding beyond their territories to advance not only the domestic market but global market. Competition is also projected among the FinTech firms such as Google, Baidu, Facebook, Amazon, Alibaba and Tencent around the world (Xiang, Zhang and Worthington, 2018). Many Chinese companies are expanding their operations by acquiring local companies or establishing subsidiaries in other countries such as Hong Kong, Malaysia, Indonesia, South Africa, India and so on. With the existing FinTech in China, it is anticipated that the Fin-tech companies and incumbents will require to change and alter their activities to remain relevant in the contemporary dynamic world. Recommendations have been established for the risk management strategies, automating the wealth management and banking system and offering the international participants a viable opportunity to bridge gaps (Xiang, Zhang and Worthington, 2018). Such changes can provide a seamless performance experience across all the digital platforms putting into account full functionality in its trade cycles for cash stocks among many others. With the advent of new development plan of central bank, it is expected to be trajectory growth in Fintech. In future, Fintech may expand in InsurTech, Regtech, PropTech, WeathTech, and other fields. Post COVID 19 will bring some unique opportunities in this sector as people will prefer less human interactions which will encourage FinTech players to introduce new online financial products and services.

REFERENCES

Chang, Y., Wong, S. F., Lee, H., & Jeong, S. P. (2016, August). What motivates chinese consumers to adopt FinTech services: a regulatory focus theory. In *Proceedings of the 18th annual international conference on electronic commerce: e-commerce in smart connected world* (p. 40). ACM. 10.1145/2971603.2971643

Chen, L. (2016). From FinTech to Finlife: The case of Fintech Development in China. *China Economic Journal*, *9*(3), 225–239. doi:10.1080/17538963.2016.1215057

Claessens, S., Frost, J., Turner, G. & Zhu, F. (2018, September). FinTech credit markets around the world: size, drivers, and policy issues. *BIS Quarterly Review*.

Cortina Lorente, J. J. & Schmukler, S. L. (2018). The FinTech Revolution: A Threat to Global Banking? *World Bank: Research & Policy Briefs Paper*.

Fintech Futures. (2019, August 23). *People's Bank of China to issue fintech development plan*. Retrieved from https://www.fintechfutures.com/2019/08/peoples-bank-of-china-to-issue-fintech-development-plan/

Fintech Futures. (2020, February 26). *The impact of COVID-19 on the Chinese market*. Retrieved from: https://www.fintechfutures.com/2020/02/the-impact-of-covid-19-on-the-chinese-market/

Fintech News Hong Kong. (2019, September 6). *China Lays Out 6 Key Fintech Focus for the Next 3 Years*. Retrieved from https://fintechnews.hk/10032/fintechchina/china-fintech-plan/

Fungáčová, Z., & Weill, L. (2015). Understanding financial inclusion in China. *China Economic Review*, *34*, 196–206. doi:10.1016/j.chieco.2014.12.004

Gray, P. (2020, March 5). China too risky? Do you need a new strategy for your FDI in the face of COVID-19? Academic Press.

Han, H. (2018). *FinTech in China: An Introduction*. Retrieved from https://medium.com/wharton-fintech/fintech-in-china-an-introduction-6b11abd9cb64

Jao, N. (2019, January 31). China's P2P lending sector a 'disaster zone' of fraud: government official. Retrieved from https://technode.com/2019/01/31/china-p2p-disaster-zone/

Knowledge@Wharton. (2019, July 12). *Fintech in China: What Lies Ahead*. Retrieved from https://knowledge.wharton.upenn.edu/article/fintech-china-lies-ahead/

Leong, C., Tan, B., Xiao, X., Tan, F. T. C., & Sun, Y. (2017). Nurturing a FinTech ecosystem: The case of a youth microloan startup in China. *International Journal of Information Management*, *37*(2), 92–97. doi:10.1016/j.ijinfomgt.2016.11.006

Mohammad, M. (2020, April 27). *China to consolidate its claim for global leadership post COVID-19 crisis*. Retrieved from https://www.moneycontrol.com/news/business/markets/china-to-consolidate-its-claim-for-global-leadership-post-covid-19-crisis-5190411.html

Ng, Y. S. E., Muthukannan, P., Tan, B. & Leong, C. (2017). *FinTech Platform Development: A Revelatory Case Study of a Chinese Microloan Startup*. Academic Press.

Vives, X. (2017). The impact of FinTech on banking. *European Economy*, (2), 97-105.

Xiang, D., Zhang, Y., & Worthington, A. C. (2018, March). Determinants of the Use of FinTech Finance among Chinese Small and Medium-Sized Enterprises. In *2018 IEEE International Symposium on Innovation and Entrepreneurship (TEMS-ISIE)* (pp. 1-10). IEEE. 10.1109/TEMS-ISIE.2018.8478470

KEY TERMS AND DEFINITIONS

Blockchain: A blockchain, is a growing list of records, called blocks, that are linked using cryptography. Blockchain was invented to serve as the public transaction ledger of the cryptocurrency bitcoin.

InsurTech: Insurtech refers to the use of technology innovations designed to squeeze out savings and efficiency from the current insurance industry model. Insurtech is a combination of the words "insurance" and "technology," inspired by the term fintech.

Neobank: A neobank is a direct bank that is 100% digital and reaches customers on mobile apps and personal computer platforms only. Neobank does not operate traditional physical branch networks.

PropTech: PropTech is the use of information technology (IT) to help individuals and companies research, buy, sell and manage real estate. Like the way FinTech focuses on the use of technology in finance, PropTech uses digital innovation to address the needs of the property industry.

RegTech: Regtech is the management of regulatory processes within the financial industry through technology. The main functions of regtech include regulatory monitoring, reporting, and compliance.

Chapter 11
FinTech in the Kingdom of Bahrain:
An Investigation of Users' Adoption and Satisfaction

Hayat Ali
Applied Science University, Bahrain

Reem Al Kaabi
University of Bahrain, Bahrain

Hussain Mansoor Ali
University of Bahrain, Bahrain

Hussain Sami Ahmed
University of Bahrain, Bahrain

Mohammed Naser
University of Bahrain, Bahrain

ABSTRACT

Financial technology (FinTech) has developed rapidly over the last decade. In the Kingdom of Bahrain, both public and private sectors have adopted FinTech in different ways. The objective of this research is to explore and assess Bahraini users' adoption of and satisfaction with FinTech services. A model was built to quantify FinTech users' satisfaction. and a questionnaire was used to collect data; 319 responses were returned. The outcome was that all the factors investigated, accessibility, ease of use, completeness, accuracy, security, reliability, responsiveness, service quality, system quality, and information quality, have a significant positive effect on user satisfaction. The contribution of this research is the model of satisfaction for FinTech that can be applied in different countries. The proposals recommended by the authors will also inform government and concerned organizations about FinTech in Bahrain for greater user satisfaction.

DOI: 10.4018/978-1-7998-3257-7.ch011

INTRODUCTION

Since the financial crisis of 2008, FinTech has emerged and developed fundamentally. Fintech alludes to the novel procedures and items that wind up accessible for budgetary administrations on account of computerized mechanical headways. More precisely, the Financial Stability Board characterizes FinTech as "mechanically empowered financial development that could result in new business models, applications, processes or items with a related material impact on monetary markets and establishments and the arrangement of budgetary administrations" (Bates, 2017).

FinTech is an important tool for developing and supporting financial transactions in many sectors. Many countries around the world adopted this technology and employed it heavily in their transactions. FinTech in Kingdom of Bahrain has been started with many initiatives and support from different sectors including public and private. However, few studies have been conducted in the field of FinTech adoption and satisfaction since the beginning of FinTech adoption in Kingdom of Bahrain which raise the need for such kind of studies so that the factors affect both adoption and satisfaction can be investigated toward better satisfaction technology. Thus, this research is conducted.

AN OVERVIEW OF FINTECH

Definitions of FinTech

The term "FinTech" implies the use of technology inside the financial sector and covers a wide range of activities, including financing, instalments, frameworks, tasks and hazards of boards, information security and adaptation and client interface (Spain Financial Center, 2016).

As a specific technical term, FinTech is seen as a distinct scientific category which for the most part represents financial innovation in a wide area of activities by ventures or associations; fundamentally, it addresses improving the quality of administration by applying Information Technology (IT) (Gai et al., 2018).

FinTech Benefits and Challenges

The low-cost structure is one of the advantages of the FinTech solution, driving its future development. This takes into consideration potential risks from future data analysis by financial services. Reducing the cost to customers is a significant part of the FinTech solution, through complicated algorithms to analyze transactions and forecast future consumer needs (Andersson and Holmgren, 2017).

Martell (2018) predicted that providing better services to clients by streamlining them would become dependent on the Internet of Things (IoT). Banks can apply the benefits of FinTech and IoT to improve the security of the clients through sensors installed on-site and connected to FinTech applications, to confirm the identity of the client.

On the other hand, there are many challenges for FinTech adoption. Of the various challenges to FinTech (Lee and Shin, 2018), the most significant is the "Client Management Challenge", which addresses the acquisition of clients, fundamental to organizations in adopting the most proficient method of ensuring consumer satisfaction in the provision of financial services. Clients use a variety of FinTech services from different organizations, for example, using PayPal to pay online business fees. FinTech organizations must recognize and concentrate on opportunities to give their clients the best service. Although numerous FinTech services provide clients with constant coverage at low cost, the human element remains an essential factor in the provision of these services.

A second challenge is "Regulatory Challenge". Numerous considerations affect both FinTech start-up companies and traditional financial institutions, such as security and privacy, capital requirements, and money laundering. Financial institutions pay heavily to meet regulatory requirements, which makes it hard for them to compete with other FinTech companies in the market, as there are different requirements according to the services offered to clients. The laws and standards for loans are convoluted, related to the capital accessible to each financial institution, and this may not have a significant bearing on FinTech loan companies. FinTech companies are at last being required to know about potential changes in the regulatory framework, and to set up their business in the best way to manage possible future changes.

The "Challenge of Integration Technology" is third. The basis of this is the arrangement of FinTech services through numerous developing technologies and involves incorporating old systems into new FinTech applications.

The final challenge is "Security and Privacy". FinTech companies must establish standards and strategies to ensure the privacy of client information. They must prioritize security and protect the client's information if the client is to have confidence. in them. The issue of big data should be given extra consideration by government regulators, and raised to the business level, not exclusively to the level of individuals. Regulators should concentrate on three fundamentals: Do not violate the privacy of the customer's data; Non-classification of risks so that they are restricted in the market; and Individuals do not discriminate in the use of their data (Nicoletti, 2017).

FinTech Business Models

In this section, we will discuss different types of business model related to FinTech.

PAYMENT BUSINESS MODEL

FinTech organizations focusing on payment can secure customers at lower costs using one of the fastest moving technologies regarding the improvement and gathering of new payment capacities. The two markets for payments in FinTech are consumer and retail. Payments are among the most-used daily retail monetary transactions. According to BNY, purchaser and retail payment in FinTech consolidates flexible wallets, peer-to-peer (P2P) portable payments, outside trade and settlements, constant payments and advanced cash arrangements. These organizations upgrade the experience for customers who demand streamlined payment with speed, comfort, and multi-channel accessibility (Lee and Shin, 2018).

Lending Business Model

Loans and raising capital used to be the basic business model of banks. Generally non-banking business and the offer of low loan rates to SMEs has had widespread repercussions. With crowdfunding, money drifts, distributed loan stages, and credit correlation locales, national and independent ventures are empowered, as new ways are opened for those either wanting to contribute or to gather pledges (Wamda and Pay Fort, n.d.). The improvement in loans through FinTech is evident in the use of elective credit models, online information sources, information assessment to calculate risks, fast lending systems, and lower working costs. However, the success or failure of this strategy islargely dependent on how financing costs move, something that organizations have no control over. While the primary job of crowdfunding is financing specific endeavours, the essential job of P2P lending is commitment-cementing and charge-card renegotiating. FinTech lending services include Lending Club, Prosper, SoFi, Zopa, and Rate Setter (Lee and Shin, 2018).

Insurance Service Business Model

FinTech insurance strategies aim to strengthen the association between the sponsor and the customer. Information is examined to discover and guard againt risk; as the pool of potential customers broadens, customers are offered more facilities (e.g., car, life, healthcare or accident insurance). They also streamline social insurance charging structures. FinTech' insurance strategy is apparently the most widely adopted by traditional insurance providers. The innovation empowers safety-net suppliers to extend their data collection to non-ordinary sources to improve their traditional models, upgrading their danger assessment. FinTech insurance organizations include Censio, Cover Fox, The Zebra, Sureify Labs, and Ladder (Lee and Shin, 2018).

SATISFACTION AND E-SATISFACTION

Customer satisfaction is an essential and significant issue in all aspects of FinTech organizations. Satisfaction is defined as an effective state resulting from a procedure of viable and subjective assessment of a particular transaction. Oliver was the first researcher to defines satisfaction as "a synopsis mental state coming about when the feeling encompassing disconfirmed desires is combined with the customer's earlier emotions about the utilization experience" (Oliver, 1997).

Technology has an impact on satisfaction, and electronic services aim for E-satisfaction. Anderson and Srinivasan (2003) define E-satisfaction as "consumers' judgment of their Internet retail experience compared to their experience with other online or traditional retail stores", and Anand (2007) as "satisfaction based on relationship marketing with the use of media technology".

SATISFACTION MODELS

Various models have been designed to measure customer satisfaction DeLone and MacLean's (2003) information system success model measures customer satisfaction by three dimensions: information quality, service quality and system quality. Their measures of quality are ease of use, functionality, reliability, flexibility, data quality, portability, integration and importance.

Information quality is estimated by accuracy, timeliness, completeness, relevance, and consistency.

Service quality, as considered by the SERVQUAL model is measured by five quantifiable dimensions: tangibility, of materials, instruments, and some other physical offices; reliability; assurance and trust; security for purchasers; and empathy, an understanding of the shoppers' requirements (Shahin, 2006).

Chen (2010) investigated the effect of quality on taxpayers' satisfaction with an online tax-filing system, confirming the importance of information quality, system quality and service quality, building on the DeLone and McLean model, and using the SERVQUAL model to measure service quality. Information quality was dependent on accuracy, timeliness and completeness, but he combined the latter two as a single criterion called "informativeness". He measured system quality by accessibility, interactivity and ease of use, and service quality by responsiveness, reliability and empathy. He concluded that information, system and service quality positively affect satisfaction.

FINTECH IN BAHRAIN

In this section, we discuss different aspects of FinTech in the Kingdom of Bahrain: the partners, current situation, regulations, and the future. The Kingdom of Bahrain began to develop the financial sector in late 2016. On 6 November the Central Bank of Bahrain (CBB) established the Electronic Fund Transfer System (EFTS) to extend clients' financial transactions with banks throughout the country using electronic devices such as computers, smartphones and tablets. The system was set up in collaboration with BENEFIT company, enabling clients to complete their financial transactions between bank accounts in the shortest possible time. EFTS provides three services to clients: *fawri+* facilitates transfers up to BD1,000 a day; *fawri* pays salaries to a single or multiple beneficiaries within the same day or at a future date; and *father* enables clients to pay utility and other bills online (Central Bank of Bahrain, 2016).

The CBB in collaboration with the Bahrain Economic Development Board (EDB) continued the development of the national financial sector by organizing the first Middle East and NorthAfrican (MENA) FinTech forum in Manama, 3 April 2017, to discuss FinTech and it impact on banks. The CBB recognized the importance of FinTech to business models and jobs in the kingdom but recommended caution before adopting it (Central Bank of Bahrain, 2017).

In order to develop an environment to support the FinTech business, EDB entered into partnership with the FinTech incubator and ecosystem builder Singapore FinTech Consortium, and Dubai, to create a regulatory framework to support a commercial and legal infrastructure, enabling Bahrainto communicate with other FinTech companies around the Middle East (Central Bank of Bahrain, 2017). On 22 October 2017 the CBB announced the establishment of a FinTech Unit to guarantee the best services provided to individual and corporate clients. The Unit is responsible for processing practice in the Regulatory Sandbox, supervising the operations and activities of authorized organizations through cloud computing, payment and settlement systems, and monitoring technical and regulatory developments in the FinTech field.

On 13 December 2017 the CBB published the Bahrain FinTech Bay (BFB) with FinTech initiatives to support the development of a Bahraini FinTech ecosystem, guarantee involvement of financial firms to create and invest in FinTech and give BFB access to guide their framework (Central Bank of Bahrain, 2017). The BFB is a FinTech hub and corporate incubator for the MENA region, providing facilities that determine cooperative spaces, collective zones, workstations, and shared infrastructure. This hub is operated by the FinTech Consortium, a worldwide FinTech ecosystem developer and administrator, offering a set of conditions to attract local and international cooperate creative labs and FinTech startup; it involves creating, testing, scaling and sharing new technologies in the Kingdom of Bahrain and the Gulf Cooperation Council (GCC) region (Tech, 2017). The corporate partners in the BFB hub include Adsertor, Finastra, Mohammed Jalal & Sons (MJS), SICO and Simetric International; associate partners include Takaud Savings & Pensions and Travelex (Bahrain FinTech Bay, 2018).

FinTech Regulations

As part of CBB's strategy to maintain and control the financial sector, new regulations were introduced on 14 June 2017 to create a regulatory Sandbox that will empower startup companies and FinTech institutions to apply their financial ideas and make arrangements in a protected environment (Central Bank of Bahrain, 2017). The Sandbox permits existing authorized financial institutions and new entrants in the business sector to test and investigate financial services and products within a particular timespan. This will create opportunities for FinTech institutions around the world to enter the market and bolster the financial hub in the Kingdom of Bahrain, including both conventional and Sharia-compliant FinTech solutions.

The CBB made a firm decision to establish the regulatory Sandbox in order to promote effective challenge, trust new technologies, support finance-related considerations and improve client experience. These policies secure clients and anti-money laundering in the market. CBB set the term of the Sandbox as nine months with a maximum extension of three months, with the following qualification criteria:

Innovation: The solution ought to be truly creative, different from existing offerings or providing a new use for existing technologies; it must demonstrate that there are no identical offerings in the Bahraini market.

Customer benefit: The solution should offer recognizable direct or indirect advantages to clients, supported by quantifiable estimations.

Technical testing: The solution should be laboratory-tested with outcomes accessible to CBB or external validation.

Readiness for regulatory testing: The candidate should present regulatory testing plans and enough guarantees to protect customers. Risk identification and avoidance should be considered. A progress report incorporating achievements and target results should be submitted to the CBB.

Deployment post-testing: The candidate must share Sandbox products.

On 10 August 2017 the CBB published regulations for conventional and Sharia-compliant finance-based crowdfunding businesses. Additional requirements guarantee Sharia-compliance through a Sharia consultant or outsourcing to a third party.

The highlights of the crowdfunding regulations are as follows:

- Person to Business (P2B) lending/financing: the minimum capital requirement for crowdfunding platform operators is BD50,000.
- Small and medium businesses: the capital must not exceed BD250,000 raised by crowdfunding platforms.

Current State of FinTech

Bahrain has launched a significant regional FinTech hub to determine FinTech regulations and provide virtual space for local and global organizations to test and investigate their products and services with a predetermined number of consumers (Riyadh, 2017).

The financial services industry is the largest non-oil contributor to the Gross Domestic Product (GDP), with around 400 local and international institutions. These services have competitive advantages such as operating costs, an open market economy, and a skilled workforce of 14,000 employed in an industry growing at 3% per annum and focusing on hiring more Bahrainis (Bahrain FinTech Bay, 2018). The government is aiming to improve the financial sector by providing opportunities for undergraduates and new graduates to join a FinTech certificated programme by collaborating with the FinTech Consortium and Georgetown University's McDonough School of Business, providing access to global hubs in Singapore and Bahrain for researchers and academics (Zawya, 2018).

BFB launched its worldwide FinTech investment platform with InQvest Partners, helping FinTech institutions in Bahrain in their early stages. InQvest Partners have worldwide FinTech funds of around $100 million supported by local and international institutions and investor groups, including local institutional partners in Bahrain. Bahrain is the leading Islamic finance hub in the MENA region and the second biggest worldwide for Islamic finance. Islamic finance handles over 13% of the country's financial resources on a yearly basis (Economic Development Board Bahrain, 2017).

Future of FinTech

The Kingdom of Bahrain is anticipating further support for FinTech during the coming period by providing secure funding to meet business sector demand by focusing on attracting more investors and motivating financial institutions to share in the Bahraini FinTech ecosystem. It is also raising awareness of available investment channels to guide startups in applying their ideas (Bahrain FinTech Bay, 2018). The focus will be on the education sector, encouraging specialized abilities including FinTech in educational planning. Internationally, the vision of Bahrain for 2020 will focus on attracting worldwide players to the local market and building a regional bridge by exchanging knowledge and consultations between relevant associations, hubs and FinTech institutions (Bahrain FinTech Bay, 2018).

RESEARCH MODEL AND HYPOTHESES

The literature review identified some fifteen models related to customer satisfaction, eight of which were adopted to build the research model. The criteria for the selection of these models were the repetition of factors influencing customer satisfaction agreed upon by these models, as well as the fitness of the factors to the FinTech context. The research model consists of three parts: user satisfaction, the main factors, and the sub-factors. The main factors directly affect user satisfaction while the sub-factors influence the main factors. DeLone and McLean's IS Success model was the basis for the main factors, and other models for the sub-factors.

The research model consists of eleven factors and ten hypotheses, as illustrated in Figure 1. The factors, detailed below, are Accessibility, Ease of Use, Completeness, Accuracy, Security, Reliability, Responsiveness, System Quality, Information Quality, Service Quality, and Customer Satisfaction.

Accessibility

Chen (2010) defined accessibility as one of the key factors to measure system quality, determined by availability and timely access to the system. According to Zheng et al. (2009), accessibility is the degree to which the system can be accessed with minimal effort. Accordingly, the following hypothesis is postulated:

H1: *Accessibility has a positive effect on system quality.*

Figure 1. Research Model

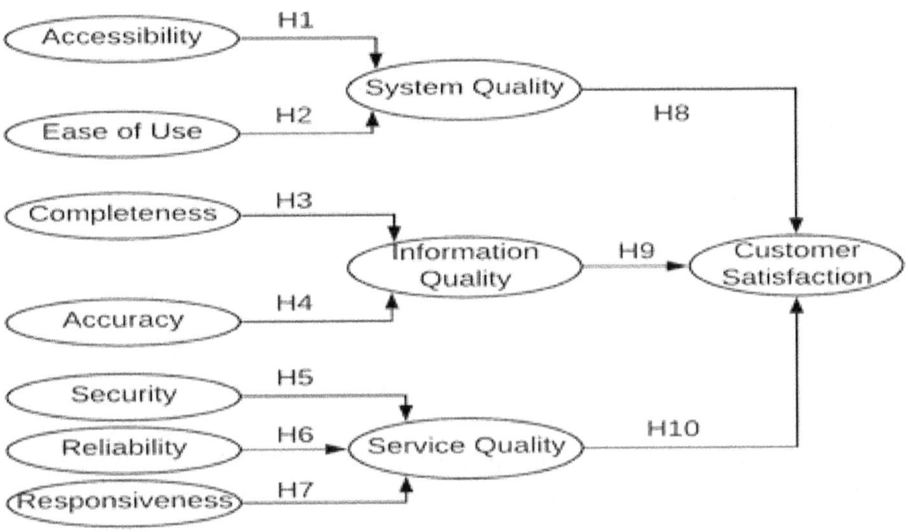

Ease of Use

Ease of use is defined as the belief that people can use the system without effort (Poon, 2007). Chen (2010) justified it as a critical factor to measure system quality. DeLone and McLean (2003), Chen (2010), and Yang et al. (2004) all agreed that ease of use affects system quality. Therefore, the following hypothesis is stated:

H2: Ease of use has a positive effect on system quality.

Completeness

Completeness supports information quality in identifying user satisfaction with the information system (Chen, 2010). DeLone and McLean,(2003) found several factors that impact information quality, and completeness is one of these. Accordingly, the following hypothesis is assumed:

H3: Completeness has a positive effect on information quality.

Accuracy

According to DeLone and McLean (2003), accuracy can be used to measure information quality. It is the extent to which information can represent reality (Alshikhi and Abdullah, 2018). Chen (2010), DeLone and McLean (2003) and Allen and Kishore (2006) all claimed that accuracy positively impacts information quality. Therefore, the following hypothesis is postulated:

H4: Accuracy has a positive effect on information quality.

Security

Choi and Sun (2016) defined security as an important criterion for service quality, ensuring that transactions in terms of exchange of funds are protected. According to Candra (2014) and Loonam and Loughlin (2008), security influences service quality. Accordingly, the following hypothesis is assumed:

H5: Security has a positive effect on service quality.

Reliability

Chen (2010) defined reliability as "ability to perform promised services dependably and accurately". DeLone and McLean (2003) referred to the SERVQUAL model and agreed that reliability impacts service quality. Choi and Sun (2016) defined reliability as overall consistency. The reliability factor directly impacts the service quality (Chen, 2010; DeLone and McLean, 2003; Shahin, 2006; Yang et al., 2004). Therefore, the following hypothesis is postulated:

H6: Reliability has a positive effect on service quality.

Responsiveness

According to Shahin (2006), DeLone and McLean (2003) and Chen (2010), responsiveness is related to willingness to help customers and provide them with a prompt response. Chen (2010), DeLone and McLean (2003), Shahin (2006), Choi and Sun (2016) and Yang et al., (2004) found that responsiveness affects service quality. Accordingly, the following hypothesis is assumed:

H7: Responsiveness has a positive effect on service quality.

System Quality

Chen (2010) defined system quality as the level of the appropriate characteristics of the information system, agreeing with DeLone and McLean (2003) that system quality affects customer satisfaction. Zheng et al. (2009) claimed that information quality represents the user's knowledge of the interaction of information technology of the system. System quality directly impacts customer satisfaction (Chen, 2010; Zheng et al., 2009; DeLone and McLean, 2003). Accordingly, the following hypothesis is assumed:

H8: System quality has a positive effect on customer satisfaction.

Information Quality

According to Chen, (2010), information quality depends on user perceptions of the value of the information system's output. Zheng et al. (2009), DeLone and McLean (2003) and Chen (2010) agreed that information quality impacts customer satisfaction. Therefore, the following hypothesis is stated:

H9: Information quality has a positive effect on customer satisfaction.

Service Quality

According to Shahin (2006), service quality is defined as the "extent to which a service meets customers' needs or expectations, or the difference between customer expectations of service and perceived service". Chen (2010) and DeLone and McLean (2003) agreed that service quality will positively affect customer satisfaction. Accordingly, the following hypothesis is assumed:

H10: Service quality has a positive effect on customer satisfaction.

Customer Satisfaction

According to DeLone and McLean (2003), customer satisfaction is "the extent to which an application helps the user create value for the firm's internal or external customers". Chen (2010) defined it as "an attitude that a user has toward the system".

RESEARCH METHODOLOGY

Instrument Development

In order to investigate the current users' adoption of FinTech in the Kingdom of Bahrain and evaluate their satisfaction with these services, quantitative research was conducted with data collected through a questionnaire. This consisted of three sections: the first section requested demographic information; the second related to the adoption of FinTech; and the third section to the factors that measure customer satisfaction with FinTech services. In the questionnaire, three types of question were adopted: multiple choice; "yes/no"; and Likert-type scale questions indicating users' satisfaction, from strongly agree = 1 to strongly disagree = 5. The items for each factor were derived from the literature. The questions for testing the research hypotheses were derived from the previous studies that investigated the particular factor included in the model where some of the questions were modified to be appropriated for the context of this research, and we modify these questions to be appropriate for our subject.

Data Analysis

The data were analyzed using the Statistical Package for Social Sciences (SPSS). Multiple regression analysis was conducted, in addition to reliability and validity tests. The results provide the foundation for accepting or rejecting the hypotheses and answering the research question.

Research Sample

The researchers followed the probability method for sampling the data; Bahraini FinTech users aged over 15 (totalling 1.2 million: Information & eGovernment Authority, 2018) were targeted, with an equal opportunity of being selected as a representative sample. Using the sample equation, with a confidence level of 95% and confidence interval of 5%, with a total population of 1.2 million, our required sample was 384; we reached more than 60% this figure, collecting 319 responses.

Validity and Reliability Test

Table 1 indicates that most exponents extracted have a value above 0.5, which indicates high internal consistency and proves that items are valid.

Table 1. Validity Testing

Factor	Item	Value
Accessibility	Access1	0.986
	Access2	0.987
	Access3	0.983
Ease of Use	Ease1	0.968
	Ease2	0.977
	Ease3	0.970
System Quality	SysQ1	0.989
	SysQ2	0.989
Completeness	Comp1	0.977
	Comp2	0.983
	Comp3	0.975
	Comp4	0.982
Accuracy	Acc1	0.966
	Acc2	0.959
	Acc3	0.964
Information Quality	InfoQ1	0.986
	InfoQ2	0.986
Security	Sec1	0.982
	Sec2	0.984
	Sec3	0.986
Reliability	Rel1	0.983
	Rel2	0.986
	Rel3	0.983
Responsiveness	Resp1	0.979
	Resp2	0.983
	Resp3	0.987
Service Quality	ServQ1	0.965
	ServQ2	0.981
	ServQ3	0.967
Customer Satisfaction	Cust1	0.978
	Cust2	0.977
	Cust3	0.980
	Cust4	0.976
	Cust5	0.974

Table 2 presents reliability testing based on the Cronbach Alpha, where all of the factors are more than 0.7.

Table 2. Reliability Testing

Factor	Cronbach Alpha	Number of Items
Accessibility	0.985	3
Ease of Use	0.985	3
System Quality	0.977	2
Completeness	0.985	4
Accuracy	0.981	3
Information Quality	0.972	2
Security	0.984	3
Reliability	0.984	3
Responsiveness	0.982	3
Service Quality	0.969	3
Customer Satisfaction	0.994	5

RESULTS ANALYSIS

Demographics Analysis

144 out of the 319 respondents were male (45.1%), meaning that 54.9% (175) were female. Ages were divided into six five-year groups; the majority of respondents were young people, aged 20-24 (61.4%). 273 (85.6%) responses were from Bahraini people. 232 participants (72.7%) already held a bachelor's degree. For current occupation, the highest number of responses were from students (188: 58.9%), with 89 (27.9%) employed, 34 (10.7%) unemployed, and 8 (2.5%) retired. 51.1% have a background in IT and 40.8% in business. Other fields include health, insurance and mass communication.

FinTech Adoption Analysis

Of the 319 respondents, 138 did not use FinTech, most because they worried that someone could access their financial information, and others because they preferred a human touch, cash transactions or because they lacked knowledge about FinTech services. Legal uncertainty was the least-stated reason for not using these serivces.

The most-used application of FinTech is SADAD (72.9%) followed by benefit pay (56.9%). Other applications include Bahrain Credit, Bahrain Commercial Facilities Company (BCFC), and the National Bank of Bahrain (NBB). The most-used type of service is payment (151, 83.4%), followed by shopping (122, 67.4%). Most of the respondents use FinTech services on a monthly or weekly basis.

Of FinTech's many benefits, availability and ease of use are the most commonly perceived. As to disadvantages, many respondents said that they never found any, although others referred to government regulation and fraud. These challenges should be considered as a field of study for the improvement of FinTech services in future.

Hypothesis Testing

To test the hypotheses, linear regression was employed to confirm the existence of relationships between the dependent and independent variables; the R-Square from each regression model summary was extracted to identify the percentage of variation of the dependent factor which was explained by independent factors.The research model has three main independent variables that affect customer satisfaction: system quality, information quality and service quality. At the same time, each of these factors is a dependent variable for other independent factors. Therefore, four linear regression models were established, three to test the main factors and the last one to test overall customer satisfaction based on the three main factors.

The first linear regression analysis was performed to determine the factors that made a significant contribution to system quality. Table 3 shows that accessibility and ease of use are positively and significantly associated with system quality, so these hypotheses are accepted. Table 4 shows the R-Square of system quality; 97.1% of the total variance in system quality is explained by accessibility and ease of use. Therefore, these two factors are important to the system quality factor; ease of use is the more important and critical factor because its Beta value is much higher than that for accessibility,which can be considered as a moderate factor.

The second linear regression analysis was performed to determine the factors that made a significant contribution to information quality. Table 3 shows that completeness and accuracy positively and significantly impact information quality, and the hypotheses are accepted. Table 4 shows that 96.9% of the variance in information quality is explained by completeness and accuracy, with similar Beta values.

The third linear regression analysis was performed to determine the factors that made a significant contribution to service quality. Table 3 shows that security, reliability and responsiveness are positively and significantly related to service quality, and the hypotheses are accepted. Table 4 indicates that 97.6% of the variance in service quality is explained by security, reliability and responsiveness, with similar Beta values.

The fourth linear regression analysis was performed to determine the factors that made a significant contribution to customer satisfaction. Table 3 shows that system quality, information quality and service quality are positively and significantly associated with customer satisfaction, and the hypotheses are accepted. Table 4 indicates that 94.6% of the variance in customer satisfaction is explained by system quality, information quality, and service quality. All three factors are important, with similar Beta values, but service quality is more critical.

Discussion

The research model contains many factors that affect satisfaction directly or indirectly.

To summarize the demographic results, 54.9% of the total sample were female and 58.9% were school or university students. The majority of respondents were employed in information technology and business, and most were Bahraini citizens. 56.7% of the respondents used FinTech services.

In 2016 an e-government survey found that 90% of the population where aware of electronic services, the highest figure recorded since the survey began. However, only 73% were satisfied with the electronic services provided by e-government (Bahrain.bh, n.d.).

Table 3. Hypothesis Testing Results of Research Model.

Hypotheses	Standardized Coefficient (B)	T Value	Significance P-Value	Status
Accessibility ® System Quality	0.371	8.081	0.000	Accept
Ease of Use ® System Quality	0.619	13.468	0.000	Accept
Completeness ® Information Quality	0.573	12.984	0.000	Accept
Accuracy ® Information Quality	0.418	9.475	0.000	Accept
Security ® Service Quality	0.376	11.132	0.000	Accept
Reliability ® Service Quality	0.305	8.135	0.000	Accept
Responsiveness ® Service Quality	0.321	9.293	0.000	Accept
System Quality ® Customer Satisfaction	0.262	4.476	0.000	Accept
Information Quality ® Customer Satisfaction	0.310	5.333	0.000	Accept
Service Quality ® Customer Satisfaction	0.411	6.832	0.000	Accept

Table 4 Explanation of Variance.

Variable	R-Square %
System Quality	97.1%
Information Quality	96.9%
Service Quality	97.6%
Customer Satisfaction	94.6%

We analyzed the data that we collected and found it to be reliable and valid. We performed four linear regression analyses to test the research hypotheses. The first found a positive impact of accessibility and ease of use on system quality. This supports the conclusion of Chen (2010) and Zheng et al. (2009), that accessibility is one of the system quality factors; and of Chen (2010), DeLone and McLean (2003) and Yang et al., (2004) that ease of use has a direct impact on system quality. Thus, a successful FinTech application must have a simple interface design that does not require a lot of effort to complete transactions quickly. FinTech applications should be useful to many categories of people, and accessible directly from any device at any time without restrictions on performing multiple transactions.

The second linear regression found a positive effect of completeness and accuracy on information quality. This supports the work of DeLone and McLean (2003) and Allen and Kishore (2006) for completeness DeLone and McLean (2003) and Chen (2010) for accuracy. Accordingly, users of FinTech need information to be at a high level of completeness, up-to-date and free from error if they are to be satisfied with it.

The third linear regression found a positive relationship between security, reliability and responsiveness with service quality, in line with the results of Candra (2014) and Loonam and Loughlin (2008) for security, Chen (2010) DeLone and McLean (2003), Shahin (2006) and Yang et al. (2004) for reliability and Chen (2010), DeLone and McLean (2003), Shahin (2006) and Yang et al. (2004) for responsiveness. Thus, to assure the quality of FinTech services, protecting personal information is important issue as it will increase users' trust in using FinTech applications. Repeating a similar transaction through FinTech without problem is another consideration to ensure service quality, as indication of reliability. Also, as users are not dealing directly with a human, response to problems should be immediate to resolve the issue

The fourth linear regression describes the three main factors that directly affect customer satisfaction: system quality, information quality and service quality. After testing, the hypotheses were accepted with a high significant and strong effect on customer satisfaction. For system and information quality, the results are consistent with those of Chen (2010), Zheng et al. (2009), and DeLone and McLean (2003), and for service quality with those of Chen (2010) and DeLone and McLean (2003). Customer satisfaction relies on all three of these factors, so the FinTech companies should provide strong systems, accurate information and effective service to covers all the needs of customers.

The variance of all the dependent factors was above 90%, which means that the factors used to measure them are very important, and critical in measuring the overall customer satisfaction of FinTech services.

CONCLUSION, RECOMMENDATIONs AND FUTURE WORK

Very little time has passed since the launch of FinTech in the Kingdom of Bahrain, but it is now widely deployed throughout the country, with people increasingly relying on the technology and moving away from traditional methods to carry out their transactions. This research focused on measuring the level of customer adoption and satisfaction with FinTech services, from different aspects. Factors believed to affect overall customer satisfaction are the components of the research model, based on that of DeLone and McLean. Furthermore; we study the state of FinTech in the Kingdom of Bahrain from several views. It was found that the number of FinTech users in Bahrain is high and increasing. FinTech-related organizations are planning for such growth in several ways, such as increasing the number of investors and providing FinTech-related courses and workshops.

Based on the results, the following recommendations are suggested:

- As the results show that most of the difficulties are related to security, financial institutions should improve this aspect of their systems with the approval of standards organizations, to increase existing customers' trust, attract new customers and enhance the company image.
- FinTech companies and financial institutions should focus on improving their system quality in order to keep their customers satisfied by providing applications that are accessible at any time and place. Also, in terms of ease of use, they should be understandable by all categories of people.
- FinTech companies and financial institution should focus on improving their information quality in order to keep their customers satisfied by providing the information they need to complete their transactions; at the same time, they should not give them irrelevant information. For accuracy, the information should always be up to date.
- FinTech companies and financial institutions should focus on improving their service quality by providing secure processing of user transactions. They should also provide reliable services by supporting the trouble-free multiple devices available to users. For responsiveness, they should carefully analyze customers' suggestions and feedback to improve and develop their services.

This research can be expanded to conduct a comparative study with other countries to investigate the gaps in improving FinTech adoption and satisfaction. Furthermore, this research could be a starting point for establishing an indicator of customer satisfaction for FinTech industries that will encourage competitiveness to produce better FinTech services.

REFERENCES

Akhsay, A. (2007). E-*Satisfaction: A Comprehensive Framework*. Presented in the International Marketing Conference on Marketing and Society.

Alshikhi, O., & Abdullah, B. (2018). Information quality: Definitions, measurement, dimensions, and relationship with decision making. *European Journal of Business and Innovation Research*, *6*(5), 36–42.

Anderson, R. E., & Srinivasan, S. S. (2003). E-satisfaction and e-loyalty: A contingency framework. *Psychology and Marketing*, *20*(2), 123–138. doi:10.1002/mar.10063

Andersson, O., & Holmgren, J. (2017). *Clients' lost interest in banks. The Business Model Development of a FinTech Start-Up*. Academic Press.

Bahrain FinTech Bay. (2018). *Bahrain FinTech Bay Manifesto 2020*. Retrieved from: https://www.bahrainfintechbay.com

Bates, R. (2017). *Banking on the future. An exploration of FinTech and the consumer interest*. Academic Press.

Candra, S. (2014). The service quality of Internet banking and impact to customer satisfaction: A preliminary finding. *International Journal of Applied Engineering Research*, *9*(22), 17963–17970.

Central Bank of Bahrain. (2016). *A noticeable increase in the usage of the Electronic Fund Transfer System within a year from launch*. Retrieved from: https://www.cbb.gov.bh/

Central Bank of Bahrain. (2017). *Regulatory Sandbox Framework*. Retrieved from: https://www.cbb.gov.bh/

Chen, C. W. (2010). Impact of quality antecedents on taxpayer satisfaction with online tax-filing systems—An empirical study. *Information & Management*, *47*(5-6), 308–315. doi:10.1016/j.im.2010.06.005

Choi, Y., & Sun, L. (2016). Reuse intention of third-party online payments: A focus on the sustainable factors of Alipay. *Sustainability*, *8*(2), 147. doi:10.3390u8020147

Delone, W. H., & McLean, E. R. (2003). The DeLone and McLean model of information systems success: A ten-year update. *Journal of Management Information Systems*, *19*(4), 9–30. doi:10.1080/07421222.2003.11045748

Economic Development Board Bahrain. (2017). *Bahrain for Islamic finance*. Retrieved from: https://bahrainedb.com

Economic Development Board Bahrain. (2018). *Bahrain FinTech Bay highlights launch with announcement of startups and founding partners*. Retrieved from: https://bahrainedb.com

Gai, K., Qiu, M., & Sun, X. (2018). A survey on FinTech. *Journal of Network and Computer Applications, 103*, 262–273. doi:10.1016/j.jnca.2017.10.011

Lee, I., & Shin, Y. J. (2018). Fintech: Ecosystem, business models, investment decisions, and challenges. *Business Horizons, 61*(1), 35–46. doi:10.1016/j.bushor.2017.09.003

Loonam, M., & O'loughlin, D. (2008). Exploring e-service quality: A study of Irish online banking. *Marketing Intelligence & Planning, 26*(7), 759–780. doi:10.1108/02634500810916708

Martell, J. (2018). *Advantages (and Disadvantages) of Fintech-Focused IoT*. Medium. Available at: https://medium.com/@jasonmartell/advantages-and-disadvantages-of-fintech-focused-iot-85aa72a7bd68

Nicoletti & Weis. (2017). *Future of FinTech*. Palgrave Macmillan.

Oliver, R. L. (1997). *Customer satisfaction: A behavioural perspective on the consumer*. McGraw-Hill.

Poon, W. C. (2007). Users' adoption of e-banking services: The Malaysian perspective. *Journal of Business and Industrial Marketing, 23*(1), 59–69. doi:10.1108/08858620810841498

Riyadh, E. (2017). *Largest Dedicated Fintech Hub in Mena Region to Launch in Bahrain*. [online] Available at: https://www.bahrainfintechbay.com/single-post/2017/11/06/Largest-Dedicated-Fintech-Hub-in-Mena-Region-to-Launch-in-Bahrain

23. Shahin, A. (2006). SERVQUAL and Model of Service Quality Gaps: A Framework for Determining and Prioritizing Critical Factors in Delivering Quality Services. In V. Partha Sarathy (Ed.), *Service Quality: An Introduction*. The ICFAI University Press.

Spain Financial Center. (2016). *Eu fintech regulatory framework*. Author.

Tech, T. (2017). *CBB teams up with Bahrain FinTech Bay*. Retrieved from: https://www.bahrainfintechbay.com/single-post/2017/12/14/CBB-teams-up-with-Bahrain-FinTech-Bay

Wamda and Pay Fort. (n.d.). *State of FinTech In Mena Unbundling the financial services industry*. Retrieved from: https://www.difc.ae/download_file/3081/

Yang, Z., Jun, M., & Peterson, R. T. (2004). Measuring customer perceived online service quality: Scale development and managerial implications. *International Journal of Operations & Production Management, 24*(11), 1149–1174. doi:10.1108/01443570410563278

Zawya. (2018). *FinTech Consortium and Georgetown university announce strategic partnership for global fintech innovation and education*. Available at: https://www.bahrainfintechbay.com/single-post/2018/04/18/FinTech-Consortium-and-Georgetown-university-announce-strategic-partnership-for-global-fintech-innovation-and-education

Zheng, Y., Zhao, K., & Stylianou, A. (2009). Information Quality and System Quality in Online Communities: An Empirical Investigation. SIGHCI 2009 Proceedings, 8.

Chapter 12
The Impact of FinTech on Financial Services in India:
Past, Present, and Future Trends

Gagan Kukreja
Ahlia University, Bahrain

Divij Bahl
Gulf International Bank, Bahrain

Ruchika Gupta
Amity Business School, Amity University, Greater Noida, India

ABSTRACT

Fintech is a new buzz word in the fourth industrial revolution environment. No financial services across the globe are left unaffected by the new technologies. Artificial intelligence, machine learning, blockchain, and data analytics have immensely influenced many aspects of financial services such as deposits, transactions, billings, remittances, credits (B2B and P2P), underwriting, insurance, and so on. Fintech companies are enabling larger financial inclusion, improvement of lives of humans, better decision-making, and lots more. This chapter covers the development, opportunities, and challenges of financial sectors because of new technologies in India. This chapter throws the light on opportunities that emerged because of demographic dividend, high penetration, and access to the latest and affordable technology, affordable cost of smartphones, and government policies such as Digital India, Startup India, Make in India, and so on. Lastly, this chapter portrays the untapped potentials of Fintech in India.

DOI: 10.4018/978-1-7998-3257-7.ch012

INTRODUCTION

Fintech is amalgamation of technology and finance. It is a new buzz word in business community; however, it has wide origins in the banking and finance industries for several decades. Early adopters of technology such as internet banking, utilizing ATMs, electronic banking, core banking systems and so on have mostly been the retail and finance industries. Technologies such as Fintech improve end-user experience, promote and simplify financial institutions operations. A lot of Fintech companies like Paytm (payment through mobile) have been trying to become a one stop solution for all the basic needs of an average customer. Fintech is also playing a pivotal role in fulfilling the Indian Governments agenda of financial inclusion, digital India & banking the unbanked.

India started walking on the road of globalization and liberalization in 1993, with several private-sector banks joining India and beginning operations. Before that, the major public sector banks including Punjab National Bank, State Bank of India, mainly dominated this market. With the increasing population, tech savvy people & high service cost, fintech started playing a crucial role to reach consumers through online financial mobile applications which the traditional banks could only dream off. New start up with new convenient and affordable services in Fintech were started with the help of venture capitalist and encouragement by government policies to tap new untapped opportunities in financial sector, particularly in banking sector.

Fintech appears to be a potential way to support the evolving Indian economy enjoy the advantages of digital technology and aim to reduce inequalities between industrialized and developing nations. According to India's Telecom Regulatory Authority (TRAI), in April 2109 there had been 1.16 billion mobile users. TRAI also states that the number of smartphone users in India has grown last year by leaps and bounds in India, culminating in the world's cheapest mobile data. The new entry of telecom operator, Reliance Jio, has changed the telecom market dynamics completely. This operator provides the telecom services in India which is the cheapest in the world (The Economic Times, 2018, September 6).

In India, there are around 1.17 billion phone subscribers which is second largest in the world after China with 1.30 billion (Wee, 2019). Further, a joint study by Associated Chambers of Commerce and Industry of India and PwC predicted that the number of smartphone users in India is expected to rise by 84% to 859 million by 2022 from 468 million in 2017 (Assocham & PwC 2019). Therefore, Fintech shall be having good penetration due to the increase in the number of people getting smart phone (even ordinary mobile phone) with cheap mobile services and data, young population, reducing gender disparities, government policies and accustomed to technology.

OBJECTIVES OF THE CHAPTER

The chapter aims to focus upon the fintech landscape of India. It will focus on the potential effects of technology in the financial space on the customers, financial institutions, businesses and society. The chapter will briefly discuss How India has changed over the last couple of years due to the disruption caused by the new technologies and How India became the fifth countries in world where the greatest number of start-ups have been founded between 2015 to 2018 (Papadopoulos, 2019, January 2). A lot of big tech giants have also shown keen interest in investing into India's Fintech start-ups & developing innovative products inhouse to cater to the changing demands of the Indian customers.

MANAGERIAL IMPLICATIONS

This chapter will be useful for entrepreneurs, strategic advisors, investors, researchers, academicians and big conglomerates for making informed decisions and developing a good sense of understanding of the Fintech space of India & the unexplored possibilities.

FINTECH IN THE PAST

During the last decade of the 18th century modern banking emerged in India. The fintech sector has undergone a major transition over the last two decades, struggling from the colonial and post-independence period and from nationalization and liberalisation (Agarwal, 2019). Indian economy was struggling back in the early 90s till the new globalisation & liberalisation policy came into effect in 1993, wherein a lot of multinational companies started stepping into the Indian Market. Indian Banking was still working on the old age paper-based ledger systems. This is when technology a.k.a. financial technology first started to make disruptive changes with the launch of Finacle by the Tech Giant Infosys.

Finacle became a huge success, and was considered as the backbone of core banking systems of most of the banks in India and abroad. The banks were able to reduce the time taken to do various task by over 90%. Each branch has accessibility of the customer accounts which help the customers to get services from anywhere. But this wasn't the end to the dilemmas that the consumer had to face to make payments for various activities through Cheque's where the receiver had to visit the bank to deposit the cheque he collected from the payer. In addition, customer has to do every transaction by visiting his own branch.

ICICI Bank, however, launched Net Banking in India in 1998 for the first time and shortened payment periods from 3-5 days to only a few hours, resulting in savings of thousands of man hours and relieving some of the worries of companies operating in India. Since then, Fintech has begun to expand slowly with digitization beginning after 2010, contributing to the introduction of mobile banking apps and offering consumer banking comfort at their convenience & improved user interface through their personal computers, laptops and smartphones.

The cash-obsessed Indian economy has responded well to the fintech boom, which is basically triggered by a flood in the e-commerce industry and penetration of mobile phones. The market volume for the Indian fintech sector is projected to be approximately USD 33 billion out of 2016 and is anticipated to rise to USD 73 billion in 2020 at a CAGR of 22 per cent five years.

Government pro-digitization policies, policy reforms, structures such as the introduction of Digital India, Start-up India Scheme, eKYC standards, UPI, Financial Inclusion, Unique Identification (Aadhar) and Bharat QR etc, placed the Indian financial sector at the global epicenter and built a sound forum for fintech firms and services.

Another big drive came when the Indian government declared on November 8th, 2016, the demonetization of 500- and 1,000-rupee notes and people had no option to follow wallet or card or bank channel payments that gave a massive boost to the digital payment industry. Paytm has been one of the big winners of this government change. This went from 125 million wallet customers to 185 million three months later before demonetization, and it has continued to expand, reaching 280 million users by November 2017. It had gained five million merchants with acceptance of the QR code in one year, and the company had processed $1.6 billion of transactions three and a half times a year (Wright, 2017, November 29). Back in 2014, central bank Reserve Bank of India released draft guidelines for a new type of organization called a payment bank. Such banks could take small deposits (no more than 100,000 Indian rupees per customer, equal to roughly $1,530) and did not offer loans or credit cards but could run current and savings accounts, offer ATMs and debit cards and operate net banking. Forty-one organisations have requested, among them was Paytm, and in August 2015 Paytm was one of 11 companies to be issued in principle licenses. (Wright, november 29, 2017). Millions of Indians started to use mobile payments and become conscious (99.5 per cent) of them for the first time in their lives within a few days.

The financial specialist consideration has been concentrated towards hitech urban areas in 2015, with Bengaluru seeing eleven VC (Venture Capital) backed venture arrangements of USD 57 million, followed by Mumbai and Gurgaon with nine and six arrangements, separately. Bengaluru, the start up capital of India has profited by the equivalent and is positioned 15 among the world's significant beginning up urban communities.

India's development wave may in any case not be of the scale when seen against its worldwide partners, yet it is stacked well, to a great extent. From wallets to insurance, the administrations of fintech have re-imagined how organizations and customers do routine exchanges. The expanding reception of these patterns is situating India as an alluring business sector around the world.

INDIAN FINTECH MARKET: PRESENT SCENARIO

India is transitioning into a competitive environment providing a forum for fintech start-ups to eventually develop into unicorns worth billions of dollars. Fintech entrepreneurs in India are following various goals, from entering new sectors to targeting international markets. Adoption of Indian Fintech has grown rapidly in recent years. For Fintech India has now become Asia's market leader. In establishing their dominance over Asia's Fintech markets, India has defeated fast competitor China. India has recently earned US$ 286 million in venture capital funding. Fintech companies in China, on the other hand, obtained an investment of USD 192.1 million over the same period (Fig.1). According to NASSCOM, the Indian fintech app industry is projected to hit USD 2.4 billion from a estimated USD 1.2 billion by 2020.

Figure1. Top Fintech Start-ups of India with Total Investments
Source: World Fintech Report:2019-20

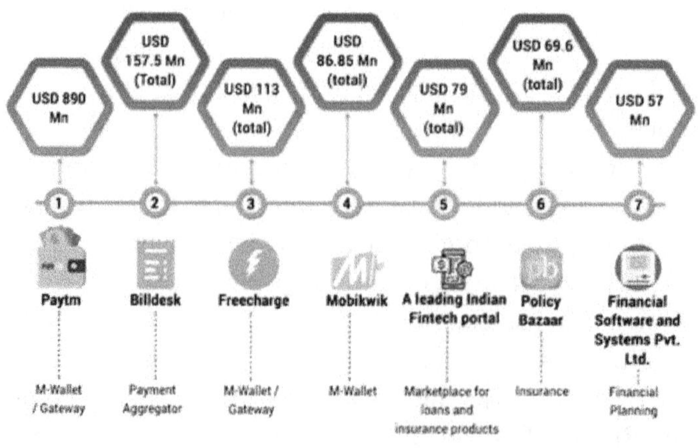

The main driver of Indian Fintech Market's unprecedented growth has been its robust fintech ecosystem, where multiple players are increasingly supportive both in terms of providing funds and building technological and entrepreneurial skills. One of the most desirable trends in the nation is a deep innovation pool with affordable and easy-to-hire tech workers (Fig.2).

Figure 2. Focused Market Adjustment Stage
Source: Internal KPMG Analysis, 2016

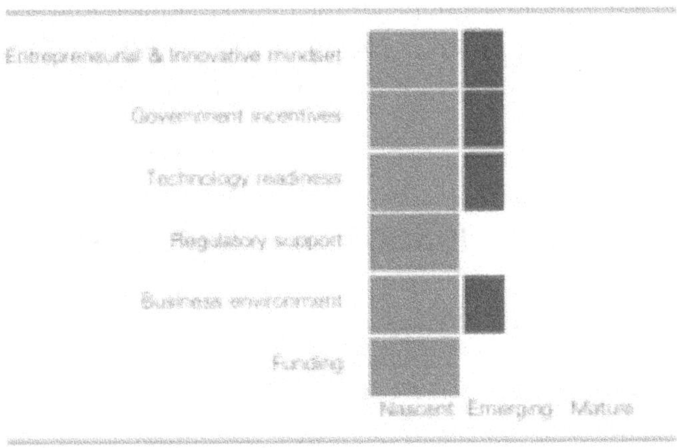

The companies that come up in this room can be mainly divided into 4 industries, i.e. Payments, insurance, lending and management of wealth. Payment market can be subdivided into Mobile wallets, Mobile POS, Payment Gateways are only a few groups where much of the activity takes place. Citrus Pay, PayUBiz India, CCAvenue, Direcpay, Instamojo, Zaakpay, Bill Desk, PayUMoney, Atom Paynetz, ePaisa, Airpay, JusPay, Emvantage, and Transecute are major players in this region. Loans can be categorized into Digital loans, P2P loans and SME financing, etc. Wealth management is one of the main sectors that several businesses are coming up with creative ideas as the per household, disposable income has dramatically risen over the years. Therefore, people need help to make informed investment decisions.

India has always been a country of economies of scale, wherein a lot of new companies / start-ups are running the race to accumulate maximum data possible. For example, a new company called Cred has been giving huge cashbacks and discounts to people who are paying credit card bills through that financial technology start-up based out of Bangalore in India. A lot of people in the Industry have been wondering why? The answer is simple that after the company has good amount of data they shall be able to sell relevant products to their data base without any difficulties, they would know which bank has maximum credit card, high net individual customers etc in turn they will be pitch & position their products, loans, offers from the partners effectively.

Therefore, Fintech is now an option to conventional banks and procedures; they offer digital solutions to conventional cash management. Banks are starting to come up with things such as api banking, automated cash management, e-collections etc. Many of these items address millennials who believe fintech is better than conventional banking. For example, with virtual account management a company will be able to have multiple account numbers which can be shared with different clients. However, the funds will be parked in one main account, hence the customer will be able to reconcile the funds easily by bifurcating the virtual account numbers, whilst keeping a single main account for easier book-keeping.

Also, the government has started to take some measures to improve Fintech's penetration by ordering banks to build more and more POS terminals. As India currently has the lowest number of POS terminals, i.e. 1 POS per 500 citizens, among the BRICS countries, this demonstrates that companies in the financial technology sector such as Mobile POS (paytm, mobikwik etc) do have a large reach here. The government has set up a body named India's National Payment Council that introduced a digital portal for domestic payment named Rupay. The primary goal of launching this was to make money and in-house control of the transactions being routed through international players such as Visa or Mastercard. Governments have taken many steps to promote it in India and beyond. Indian government signed separate Memorandum of Understanding with Singapore, Bhutan, Maldives, United Arab Emirates, Kingdom of Bahrain.

FINTECH: IMPACT ON INDIAN FINANCIAL SERVICES INDUSTRY

With customized solutions, foundational support and notable developments in all-encompassing sectors including education, insurance and credit management, Fintech has cautiously yet beneficially reshaped the entire financial services and payments space. According to the Vision 2020 study by Deloitte & CII, India is increasingly becoming a digital economy of over one billion cell phones, 330 million internet users (about 94 percent on cellular devices), and 240 million smartphones.

India is evolving into a vibrant ecosystem that provides a forum for fintech start-ups to expand into unicorns of billions of dollars. Fintech companies in India follow various goals, from entering new sectors to targeting international markets. In the last few years, the growth of Indian Fintech has grown exponentially. According to NASSCOM, the Indian fintech software market is expected to reach USD 2.4 billion from a current USD 1.2 billion by 2020.

Indian Fintech firms could address a portion of the basic issues influencing Indian money related administrations — expanding effort, improving client experience, decreasing operational grating, and empowering advanced channel reception and use. Heritage inclined structures and higher fixed cost models of conventional banks and financial institutions should offer a preferred position for new Fintech firms as banks play find these increasingly adaptable and innovative new businesses. Fintech \'s possibility is to extend the market, shape client conducts and impact long haul changes in the monetary business. Some of Fintech \'s worthwhile segments for extension are given:

Indian Fintech firms can reshape the financial services industry in the accompanying three different ways:

- Fintech ought to create exceptional and innovative hazard evaluation systems. Utilizing huge information, profound learning, and elective information to guarantee credit and construct FICO ratings for customers with poor credit foundation would increment financial services entrance in India.
- Fintech organizations are relied upon to decrease costs and lift the financial services proficiency. The advantages of less fatty working models can be given to clients not being troubled with inheritance tasks, IT frameworks and costly physical systems.

Figure 3. Lucrative Sectors
Source: World Fintech Report:2019-20

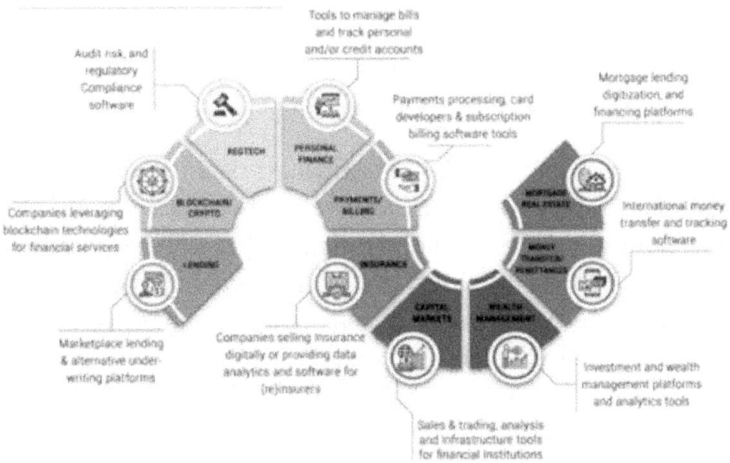

- Fintech can make an increasingly powerful, safe, and proficient biological system of financial services. Fintech firms are less homogeneous than existing banks and offer extraordinary learning formats to improve abilities just as culture.

FUTURE TRENDS

The World Bank estimates that over 1.7 billion individuals globally do not constitute and are inaccessible as a member of the formal financial system. We don't have bank accounts because we don't have enough funds (over 60 percent), they don't need it (30 percent), and the accounts are too costly (26 percent) according to the study. The report also states that there is at least some kind of insurance in just two percent of the population in India, and this is where fintech take the lead. Not the only approach that decides the direction of fintech 2020 and beyond is going out to the unbanked. Some of the other future fintech trends that will reshape the financial services industry are given:

Digital Banks

Visiting a bank branch today is a mere echo of the past, and the future of fintech and finance can simply be named smartphone phones. Industry estimates claim digital solutions' prominence will continue to rise, and by 2024 the proportion of internet users will hit 71 per cent. The key factors guiding this trend 's development are a large-scale adoption of mobile apps in financial services, comfort and general access, and reduced usage prices.

Mobile Payments

Some of fintech's most important "huge stuff" is the rise of the mobile payment industry. Consumers want instant, invisible and free (IIF) payments. Mobile payment technologies might also break our conventional wallets because global customers become less cash reliant. Google, Apple, Tencent and Alibaba now have their own payment systems and are starting to carry out innovative technologies like biometric access control, fingerprint activation and facial recognition.

Blockchain

Blockchain, a modern, transparent and distributed permanent data ledger, is threatening financial institutions. Blockchain will make things in the financial services industry more effective. Because fraud and identity theft cost trillions of dollars annually to financial companies, blockchain has the ability to stop business from suffering such major losses. Fintech network is projected to cross US $6,700 million by 2023. Blockchain can be used by financial companies for smart contracts, automated transfers, identification protection and stock exchange.

Public Cloud Implementation

This was expected that the usage of a software-as-a-service cloud infrastructure will more definitely become a standard among financial companies across the world by 2020. Also today, financial organizations are deliberately utilizing a shared data infrastructure system, CRM systems and HR administration. The reach of the digital cloud will begin to expand over the coming years, adding easy payment allowing, payroll, and loan management. Rather of utilizing inflexible equipment, Fintech businesses can settle for cloud infrastructure accessible everywhere-anytime.

Artificial Intelligence and Big Data

With AI and Big Data that lets us collect, store and push data knowledge, hyper-personalization on an unparalleled scale, is feasible. Financial firms also have details on the actions of their clients and the background of surfing and social habits. AI allows real-time omnichannel convergence with these experiences to provide their clients a customized one-to-one communication interaction while the knowledge is most important and usable.

Growth of Neobanking and BaaS platforms

In partnership with neobanks and banking-as-a-service (BaaS) networks, the banks and payment service providers can develop next-generation consumer applications with the government planning to embrace more transparent banking standards. Established companies like Kotak Mahindra Bank, Paytm, Bharti Airtel and DBS have already made the first step for the Indian market to launch digital-only banking services.

Robotic Process Automation

Even though fintech firms may not have enough in-house capital to develop unique AI technologies, they are searching for alternate solutions-the best choice is collaboration with a supplier of technology. In 2018-2019, AI was a strategic edge in that the length of the operations-a way to stand out from the market. According to Accenture report, banking customers accept digital support systems, as long as they offer tailor-made and customized services that suit their needs. As many as 71 percent of consumers were able to provide computer-generated assistance.

We've seen strong increase in fintech adoption thus far and would also improve in the future. New businesses including insurtech, wealthtech, proptech and regtech will acquire expertise from established goods and services in fintech. Such sectors can likely combine with each other and introduce new creative products and services in the package. Fintech 's potential looks promising particularly in developing & populated economies like India, where 65 percent of the population is below the age of 35 with a dependence level of only 0.4. It obviously shows the need for new advanced and package goods and services would be strong for successful workforce.

CONCLUSION

Fintech developments caused a change in conventional paradigms in financial services and led major financial companies to reassess how they do business. Over the years, the outsized influence fintech have made on the sector was not only destructive, but quantifiable.

Fintech grew gradually in the initial years but in the last few years this room has seen a sudden accelerated development thanks to the Indian government's pro-digitization initiatives. In the next 2 decades, it will continue to rise at an accelerated pace due to the growth in India's active population & growing literacy levels. India, a nation of 1.3 billion people, demand and supply will still remain an obstacle, the business that must excel in fulfilling the demands of a greater proportion of the populace. Although this would not mean that the niche goods would struggle, they will have to decide whether their market would be able to accept the price at which they plan to sell or whether they would decline shortly after launch.

Fintech businesses will need to work on creating mobile-first approach goods relative to other platforms because most Indians invest more time on their smartphone compared to the rest of their digital gadgets. Mobile data would be cheaper. Transition from 4 G to 5 G, latest corporate tax cut, policy boost to start-ups, and affordable handheld apps in this field would improve pace and ease in the future. As India has the lowest price for one giga byte of data around the globe, mobile first solution would be simpler to accomplish. If the Fintech firms can still cope with the language barrier, this will be another move for the nation with several official languages.

REFERENCES

Agarwal, M. (2019, October 30). *What Impact Has India's Fintech Ecosystem Created on Banking?* Retrieved from https://inc42.com/features/what-impact-has-indias-fintech-ecosystem-created-on-banking/

Assocham & PwC. (2019). *Emerging technologies disrupting the financial sector.* Retrieved from https://www.pwc.in/assets/pdfs/consulting/financial-services/fintech/publications/emerging-technologies-disrupting-the-financial-sector.pdf

EY. (2019). *Global FinTech Adoption Index 2019.* Retrieved from https://assets.ey.com/content/dam/ey-sites/ey-com/en_gl/topics/banking-and-capital-markets/ey-global-fintech-adoption-index.pdf

Ghai, R., Tyagi, M., & Gupta. (2020). Leveraging Technology for Robust Financial Facilities: A Comparative Assessment of BRICS Nations. In *ICCAKM 2020*. IEEE Xplore.

Papadopoulos, A. (2019, January 2). *Most Start-up Friendly Countries in The World, 2019*. Retrieved from https://ceoworld.biz/2019/01/02/most-startup-friendly-countries-in-the-world-2019/

Sahni, A. (2019 October 7). *Which Are The Most Successful Fintech Startups In India?* Retrieved from https://inc42.com/features/which-are-the-most-successful-fintech-startups-in-india/

The Economic Times. (2018, September 6). *The Jio effect: Consumers have been the absolute winners*. Author.

The Economic Times. (2019, August 30). Retrieved from https://economictimes.indiatimes.com/markets/stocks/news/mega-bank-merger-pnb-obc-and-ubi-to-be-merged-to-form-2nd-largest-bank/articleshow/70909726.cms?from=mdr

Wee, R. Y. (2019, March 13). *Which Country Has the Largest Number of Cellphones?* Retrieved from https://www.worldatlas.com/articles/10-countries-with-the-highest-rates-of-cell-phone-subscriptions.html

World Fintech Report: 2019-20 – Indepth Analysis for Fintech Sector. (n.d.). Retrieved from https://enterslice.com/learning/wp-content/uploads/ebook/fintech-report-2020.pdf

Wright, C. (2017, November 29). *How Paytm went big on Indian demonetization*. Retrieved from https://www.euromoney.com/article/b15ts6qpxvj51d/how-paytm-went-big-on-indian-demonetization?copyrightInfo=true

KEY TERMS AND DEFINITIONS

Artificial Intelligence: It is the simulation of human intelligence processes by machines, especially computer systems. These processes include learning (the acquisition of information and rules for using the information), reasoning (using rules to reach approximate or definite conclusions) and self-correction.

B2B: B2B is abbreviation for "business to business." It refers to sales you make to other businesses rather than to individual consumers.

B2C: Sales to consumers are referred to as "business-to-consumer" sales or B2C.

BFSI: Banking, financial services, and insurance (BFSI) is an industry term for companies that provide a range of such financial products or services. It includes universal banks as well.

Machine Learning: ML is a method of data analysis that automates analytical model building. It is a branch of artificial intelligence based on the idea that systems can learn from data, identify patterns, and make decisions with minimal human intervention.

P2P: Peer-to-peer lending, abbreviated as P2P lending, is the practice of lending money to individuals or businesses through online services that match lenders with borrowers. The lender's investment in the loan is not normally protected by any government guarantee.

Unicorn: A unicorn is a privately held start-up company valued at over $1 billion.

Chapter 13

Evaluating Mergers as a Tool to Strengthen and Modernize the Palestinian Banking System:
An Analytical Study of Palestinian Local Banks 2010–2017

Azmi Wasfi Awad
https://orcid.org/0000-0003-2061-1434
Palestine Technical University, Palestine

Bahaa Subhi Awwad
Palestine Technical University, Palestine

Abdel-Aziz Ahmad Sharabati
Middle East University, Jordan

ABSTRACT

The study aims at evaluating the banking mergers as a tool to strengthen and modernize the Palestinian banking system by focusing on the national banks listed on the Palestine Stock Exchange using the descriptive-analytical approach as well as the inductive and deductive approaches. The study concludes that the circulars issued by the Palestine Monetary Authority mainly those which relate to the raising of the minimum capital of local banks, have a positive role, and were the main motivation towards these mergers. The mergers that took place in the Palestinian banking sector have resulted in a significant improvement in data and financial indicators as well as the competitiveness of domestic merged banks and reflected positively on the national economy. The study recommends the need to redouble the efforts of the Palestine Monetary Authority by using literary persuasion at certain times, and through the development of laws and regulations that encourage and stimulate mergers to create stronger banking entities that are capable of facing the challenges of competition and financial crises, and other banking risks, at other times. Moreover, national banks and large-scale expatriates must play a more active role in the process of economic development and work to maximize their economic role and expand the value of productive projects that require large funding through granting syndicated loans and establishing joint ventures.

DOI: 10.4018/978-1-7998-3257-7.ch013

INTRODUCTION

The safety of the banking system, in general, and the avoidance of any banking shocks, in particular, may weaken trust and confidence if some institutions are left alone to meet and confront bankruptcy or liquidation. These strong motives urge the monetary authorities to persuade and, sometimes, force such institutions to merge because the safety of banking is a vital guarantee to support the national economy. Therefore, the main task of monetary authorities is to ensure and continuously validate the banking structure. Moreover, monetary authorities have to assess the banks in a way that gives the correct answer to whether there is a need to move toward merger as an important tool to strengthen the banking system or use other means of integration that may be more useful and more convenient in terms of application[1] (Abdelfattah, 1992).

There is no doubt that some of the banks operating in Palestine suffer mainly from weakness in their financial indicators and from the small size of their capital especially those which do not meet the requirements of the Palestine Monetary Authority regarding raising their capital to reach the minimum required capital. In 2003, the Palestine Monitory Authority planned carefully to promote the idea of a merger to build strong Palestinian banking entities capable of coping with the challenges facing the Palestinian economy. Consequently, mergers and/or acquisitions between banks operating in Palestine became necessary. This allows for the formation of large banking entities that are capable of absorbing and confronting the expected and unexpected risks, as well as, to meeting the requirements of the Palestinian economy. Before 2004, there were no mergers in the Palestinian banking sector. In 2005, the Palestine Monetary Authority (PMA) announced the signing of an agreement between the Islamic Bank of Palestine and branches of Cairo-Amman Islamic Bank to sell the net assets of all transactions to Palestine Islamic Bank in a process known as banking consolidation in the form of acquisition.

The demand for mergers has increased, especially for small banks, which have taken this approach as a necessity to increase their competitiveness and to establish the principle of presence and continuity in the banking sector due to two main variables[2] (Yasin and Matay, 2008):

1. The Agreement on Liberalization of Banking Services that comes within the framework of the World Trade Organization Agreement which would increase the competition in the global banking market.
2. The capital adequacy standard should be at least 12% of the value of the banking obligations towards any bank in addition to other variables such as technological progress, the development of informatics and the consolidation of the phenomenon of giant economic blocs.

Statement of the Problem and Study Questions

The current study aims to highlight mergers as a way to strengthen and modernize the Palestinian banking system. This will be done by analyzing and evaluating the indicators for the local Palestinian banks which were merged during the period 2010-2017. The main problem of the study can be formulated in the following question: What is the importance of mergers as a tool to strengthen and modernize the banking system in Palestine? The researchers' aim to answer the following set of questions:

1. Have the instructions issued by the Palestine Monetary Authority after 2010 regarding the raising of paid-up capital led to further mergers with local banks in Palestine?

2. What are the most important drivers of mergers in the Palestinian banking sector after 2010?
3. Do mergers strengthen and modernize the Palestinian local banks?

Study Hypotheses

The following hypotheses have been developed to answer the above stated questions:

H01: There is no significance for the instructions issued by the Palestinian Monetary Authority after 2010 regarding raising the paid-up capital and granting incentive benefits for mergers with local banks in Palestine.

H02: There is no significance for motives that call for mergers in the Palestinian banking system?sector after 2010.

H03: There is no significance for mergers in strengthening and modernizing the local Palestinian banks.

Importance and Objectives of the Study

The current study intended to achieve the following objectives:

1. Determine the need for banks mergers in the Palestinian banking sector.
2. Illustrate the important role played by the process of banking mergers and integration to build a strong and effective banking system.
3. Identify the most important motives that drive the mergers among national banks operating in Palestine.
4. Evaluate the results of the Palestinian banks' mergers that carried out after 2010 to strengthen and modernize the system of the Palestinian banking sector. The reasons for the interest of local banks in the recent mergers, in particular, as one of the phenomena that has been developed in the Palestinian banking arena, and finally the benefits gained by the local Palestinian banks in the framework of these mergers.

The study also aims to formulate a set of conclusions and recommendations that will help banks and decision makers in the banking field to work on expanding bank mergers or integrations and understanding how to manage them efficiently and effectively by Palestinian national banks.

BACKGROUND

This part of the study presents the concept of bank mergers, the development of the Palestinian banking sector and the measures of promotion and motivation; the researchers then review the relevant literature on mergers in the banking sector.

The Concept of Bank Mergers

In the field of banking economics, there are many definitions of banking mergers. For example, Abdul Hamid (2001) argued that a merger is "an agreement that leads to the union of two or more banks and their voluntary solubility in one banking entity, so that the new entity has a higher and more effective ability to achieve objectives that could not have been achieved without the consolidation of the new bank[3]. Some also believe that bank merger is the financial process that leads to the acquisition of one or more banks by another financial or banking institution, whereby the merged/consolidated bank usually abandons its independence and enters into the merging bank and both become one. The new bank takes a new name; it is usually the name of the merging/consolidating institution or a common name that combines or integrates both names. The expansion of bank mergers and the formation of giant banks is one of the most important features of modern banking in the context of financial globalization. Hammad (1999) defined mergers as a union of interests between two or more companies or institutions; it is a combination of the assets and liabilities of two or more banks. Such a union may take place through two or more companies or banks for the emergence of a new entity or the incorporation of one or more companies/banks into it. The merger may be wholly or partially and the process may be fully or partially controlled or carried out voluntarily or involuntarily[4].

There are many other definitions for bank mergers; most of them vary according to the perspective of content, composition, effects, or whether legal or illegal. The following are the most important definitions[5] (Matai, 2010) stated merger is:

- An agreement between two or more banks; it is an administrative liability in one single banking entity so that the new entity becomes highly capable and effective to achieve objectives that cannot be achieved before the completion of the process of consolidating the new banking entity.
- Furthermore, merge can be defined as a bank joins another bank or more; they are usually of equal importance and size. The two of them disappear individually and a new independent entity with a new name emerges.

The Development of the Palestinian Banking Sector

Despite the challenges and obstacles that face the Palestinian economy, the Palestinian banking sector, which is particularly important in economic activity as the main component of the financial system, has continued to grow and can deal with many local and regional risks; it has established itself as one of the most important pillars that support the Palestinian economy. The number of licensed banks in Palestine was (15) in 2017 including seven local banks and eight foreign commercial banks. These banks have (332) branches with (204) branches for local banks and (128) branches for foreign banks with an increase of (10%) from the last year according to the (The Annual Report of Palestine Monitory Authority, 2017)[6]. The following tables (1 and 2) show developments in the banking indicators of the Palestinian banking sector.

Measures of the Palestinian Monetary Authority to Strengthen the Palestinian Banking System

Since its establishment in 1994, the Palestinian Monetary Authority has worked to strengthen the status of the Palestinian banking sector by issuing laws and regulations to monitor and control the banking industry. To enhance this trend, the Palestinian Monetary Authority has given great importance to dealing with weak banks and encouraging them to merge to raise the level of competitiveness in the Palestinian banking sector. It also put into force several resolutions and circulars to determine the minimum paid-up capital for Palestinian banks. In 2008, they issued instructions No. (5) to raise the paid-up capital from

Table 1. The Main Financial Statements for the Palestinian Banking Sector during 2010-2017 (USD Million)

Item	2010	2011	2012	2013	2014	2015	2016	2017
Total Assets	8,555.7	9,076.9	9,663.8	10,783.8	11,416.7	12,271.0	13,765.1	15,376.4
Total Liabilities	7,461.4	7,891.8	8,405.7	9,422.2	9,949.1	10,271.0	12,093.8	13,623.5
Total Equity Capital	809.6	874.6	894.7	928.1	976.0	961.3	1,021.7	1,082.6
Total Reserves	110.2	199.2	241.8	288.2	306.8	346.0	377.7	420.9
Total Property Rights	1,094.2	1,186.5	1,258	1,361.5	1,467.4	1,467.6	1,601.8	1,752.9
Total Customer Deposits	6,778	6,945.8	7,460.1	8,277.0	8,906.4	9,627.8	10,586.7	11,948.8
Total Facilities	2,820.5	3,487.0	4,117.9	4,404.3	4,816.6	5,736.7	6,765.4	7,900.2
Total Interest & Commission Income	285.7	344.32	376.4	423.4	443.6	460.9	492.4	580.1
Total Revenue	396.9	416.1	434.3	479.3	514.5	530.6	569.7	680.6
Total Net Profit	138.7	,128.6	123.5	143.4	146.9	132.8	149.3	168.5
Total Retained Earnings	94.3	87.8	106.4	121.8	159.6	129.6	136.4	170.8

Source: Financial statements issued by the Association of Banks in Palestine 2010-2017

Table 2. The Main Financial Indicators for the Palestinian Banking Sector during 2010-2017 (Percentage)

Capital Structure Index	2010	2011	2012	2013	2014	2015	2016	2017
Liabilities / Assets	87.4	86.9	87.0	87.4	87.1	88.0	88.3	88.6
Facilities / Equity	257.8	293.9	327.4	323.5	328.2	390.9	422.4	450.6
Property Rights / Assets	12.7	13.0	13.0	12.6	12.8	11.9	11.7	11.4
Retained Earnings / Equity	8.6	7.5	8.4	9.0	10.9	8.8	8.5	9.7
Liquidity Index	2010	2011	2012	2013	2014	2015	2016	2017
Customer Deposits / Assets	79.2	76.6	77.2	76.7	78.1	78.5	77.3	77.7
Facilities / Assets	33.0	38.4	42.6	40.8	42.2	46.8	49.4	51.4
Facilities / Customer Deposits	41.6	50.1	55.2	53.2	54.0	59.6	63.9	66.1
Profitability Index	2010	2011	2012	2013	2014	2015	2016	2017
Net Interest Income & Commission / Total Income	72.0	82.8	86.8	88.3	86.2	86.8	86.4	85.2
Return on Assets	1.6	1.4	1.3	1.3	1.3	1.0	1.0	1.1
Return on Equity	12.75	10.8	9.8	10.5	10.0	9.1	9.3	9.6

Source: Financial indicators issued by the Association of Banks in Palestine 2010-2017[7]

$ 10 million to $ 35 million. In 2009, it also issued instructions on the forms, conditions and procedures of mergers and acquisitions. Consequently, the banks began to prepare the necessary plans for mergers and integration to continue to grow and strengthen their financial positions. The restructuring policy of the banking sector resulted in the acquisition of Al-Aqsa Islamic Bank by the Palestine Islamic Bank in 2009. In 2010, the Palestinian Monetary Authority issued instructions to raise the paid-up capital from $ 35 million to $ 50 million. This led Al-Quds Bank to acquire Palestine International Bank at the end of 2010 and Palestine Welfare Bank to merge with the Arab Investment Bank and make National Bank at the end of 2012. The Palestinian Monetary Authority issued its instructions No. (5) to raise the minimum paid-up capital from $ 50 million to $ 75 million to strengthen the Palestinian banking sector and protect it from the risks and financial crises. This led to the acquisition of Jordan Union Bank by the National Bank, on the one hand, and the Bank of Palestine acquired Palestine Commercial Bank at the end of 2015, on the other hand. Moreover, there was the acquisition of a controlling stake in the Arab Islamic Bank by the Bank of Palestine in 2016. Likewise, National Bank acquired a controlling stake in the Palestine Islamic Bank in 2018.[(8)]

All of these measures have strengthened the system of local Palestinian banks because some of those banks were suffering from weak capital, which forced them to merge to meet the requirements of the Palestinian Monetary Authority for the minimum capital. The capitals of these banks did not correspond to the challenges that the banking industry was passing through such as its incapability to meet the requirements of the Palestinian Monetary Authority concerning raising their paid capital to the minimum or its inability to achieve growth in their capital to match the growth of the capital of other working banks. Therefore, the strengthening of the Palestinian banking system requires banks capable of creating balance and building strong Palestinian banking entities that can cope with the foreign banks so that they could face the challenges that beset the Palestinian economy. This is a necessity for conducting interbank mergers to create banking entities that can absorb expected and unexpected risks and meet the requirements of the Palestinian economy[9] (Zaida, 2006).

The Motives for Integration in the Palestinian Banking Sector

Since the establishment of the Palestinian Monetary Authority in 1994, no special draft law that may encourage banking mergers and integration has been submitted except that which was incorporated in Chapter 11 of the Palestinian Banking Law No. (2) of 2002. This chapter contains several merger items that are characterized by a lack of clarity and void of incentives and encouraging features that can be presented to the banks operating in Palestine for mergers or integration. There is only one item (i.e., No. 6) that states that the Monetary Authority can offer some benefits and incentives to banks, to encourage them for mergers, as provided by the Banking Act without clarifying those benefits and/or incentives. Banking Law No. (2) for the year 2002 was then amended, and a new law for banks (No. 9) of 2010 was issued; explained the instructions and provisions on the benefits and incentives for mergers. The most important provisions are:

- The bank may be granted a loan or loans for different periods with the interest rates as defined by the Monetary Authority and based on its instructions.
- Granting tax exemptions to the bank resulting from the merger in coordination with the Council of Ministers regarding the value and period of these exemptions.
- The bank shall be exempted from part of the license fees and the annual fees for one year renewable by a decision of the Monetary Authority.

Finally, in addition to the above motives that stimulate banks to merge, there are many other reasons such as weakness of capital in some national banks and their inability to meet the requirements of the

Palestinian Monetary Authority regarding the minimum capital. Moreover, the small size of the Palestinian banks compared with foreign banks were among the main reasons and motives that led to more mergers and acquisitions that may develop the Palestinian banking sector, which is reflected eventually on the Palestinian economy as a whole as the banking sector is one of the main pillars of the Palestinian economy. Consequently, many mergers and acquisitions in the bank industry took place in Palestine after the year 2010.

Previous Related Studies

Several studies have been conducted to analyze and evaluate the importance of banking mergers in strengthening the financial sector in various Arab countries. For instance, Abdul Nabi (2011) carried out a study to clarify the importance of banking integration or mergers in Iraq. The researcher followed an analytical-descriptive approach to find out the reasons for mergers in Iraqi banks and found that mergers are a necessity for economic reform and to achieve the objectives of the bank to provide broader and better services to increase the public's confidence to maintain their savings and eventually offer them the best facilities. The study indicated that the central bank should explain and clarify the process of bank integrations and mergers in Iraq. Moreover, it is important to create an appropriate environment for these mergers within a certain transitional period; grant a time limit for the bank to resolve its problems; finally grant soft loans using secondary means of credit which can be provided by the Central Bank of Iraq under Law (No. 56) of 2004.[(10)]

Mohammed (2015) conducted a study to investigate the need for bank mergers in Sudan using the inductive and deductive approaches. The researcher stressed the need for the banking sector in Sudan to provide large capital and high cash liquidity to be able to carry out its functions. The study findings showed that some Sudanese banks opted for mergers with other banks to form new ones with larger financial capacities; this led to increasing the size of the investment activity of the Sudanese banking sector and improving banks liquidity and profitability.[(11)]

Omar Jahmani (2002) evaluated the mergers that had already taken place in the Jordanian banking sector and the resulting financial and economic results that affected the banking sector. The researchers collected data on commercial banks in which actual mergers took place and resulted in public shareholding companies during the period 1985-1997. The results of this study were based on a period of two years before the merger, the merger year, and two years after the merger. The researchers aimed at identifying the impact of mergers among Jordanian banks on a range of financial ratios. These ratios included expenditure rates, cash flow ratios and income ratios. The study examined the effect of these ratios on the merged banks and compared them with the rates achieved before the merger at individual banks. The study concluded that there is a positive effect of banking merger or integration on these ratios in these merged banks.[(12)]

At the local level, Rihan(2006) carried out a study to evaluate the experience of Palestine Islamic Bank's acquisition of the three branches of Cairo-Amman Bank mainly those that are classified as Islamic whose focus is religious transactions and were operating in Palestine in 2005. The study adopted a descriptive-analytical approach. The study findings showed that the merger was a successful operation as the assets of the Palestinian Islamic Bank increased by 342%, the volume of deposits by 233% and the volume of profits by 32%. The Palestinian Islamic Bank obtained incentive benefits and encouragement from the Monetary Authority including approval of these new branches. Therefore, the researcher recommended that the other banks operating in Palestine, particularly the weak ones should follow the example of Palestine Islamic Bank to think about mergers and integrations as tools to solve some of their problems. The Monetary Authority should work on the development of regulated mechanisms for bank mergers and integrations. Finally, to identify the advantages and incentives that can be offered to banks in Palestine to encourage them to integrate and merge.[13]

Zaideh Mahaib (2006) followed an analytical-descriptive approach as well as the inductive and the deductive methods to examine the various motives of the banking industry to integrate and merge and its determinants that hinder or block such integration and mergers, whether they are internal determinants- resulting from the internal environment of national banks- or external determinants. The researcher aimed also to determine the various attitudes of the employees working in both the Palestine Monetary Authority and the high-ranking administrative staffs of the national banks operating in Palestine towards the nature of the motives and determinants of achieving such mergers or integrations. The results of the study showed that the national banks are concerned and worried about the small size of its entities and its limited activity in the Palestinian banking market, which is dominated by foreign banks. Consequently, these national banks must merge and form large and strong banking entities that capable of meeting the challenges and confronting the crises they are likely to face.[9]

STUDY METHODOLOGY

Study Design, Population, and Sample

This study is based on the analytical-descriptive approach in addition to the inductive and deductive approaches. The researchers used the data and financial indicators of the banks operating in Palestine, as well as the available literature, and previous research on the subject of banking mergers and integration.

The population and sample of the study consisted of all the banks that merged during the period 2010-2017, namely the National Bank (Arab Bank for Investment, Al Rafah Bank, Union Bank of Jordan), Palestine Commercial Bank and Bank of Palestine, which have all the necessary financial data.

Mergers and Acquisitions in the Palestinian Banking Sector After 2010

The following are the mergers that took place in the Palestinian banking sector after 2010, which came as a natural result of the new Palestinian Banking Law No. (9) of 2010, which included several incentives for the processes of the mergers:

First: National Bank (of Palestinian Origin)

The National Bank was established in 2012 from the Palestinian Welfare Bank and the Arab Palestinian Investment Bank merger. The National Bank is currently considered as one of the most important commercial banks in Palestine. It is the second largest bank in terms of the paid-up capital ($ 75 million). In addition to providing investment services, treasury and financing of small and medium enterprises, which have the lion's share in the Palestinian banking market; the National Bank is the fastest growing Palestinian bank and the second largest banking group providing comprehensive, integrated financial services for the corporate, retail, investment and microfinance sectors. With over 9,000 shareholders, The National Bank commands the largest shareholder base within the Palestinian banking sector and attracts the most respected and successful companies to its board. Some of these companies include Massar International Investment Company, Pal-Tel Group, Birzeit Pharmaceutical Company and Mashareq for Investment & Development. The bank offers its banking services to its customers the various Palestinian geographic regions through its scattered (17) branches in the West Bank to provide its unique banking services to more than 80,000 customers.

In addition, the bank offers banking services to its customers outside the geographic regions where its branches are located through electronic services such as electronic banking and mobile banking. The National Bank operates through an ATM network located in various vital and strategic locations in the West Bank. Although the National Banks the most recent bank in the Palestinian banking market, it has been able to demonstrate its financial performance and prove that it is a Palestinian bank over the past years. The bank has been recognized as the fastest growing bank in Palestine in 2013,2016, and 2017 by CPI Financial / Banker Middle East, the leading bank rating company in the Middle East; the CPI Financial has been ranked the bank as the fastest growing bank in the Middle East in terms of assets and liabilities[14](The annual National Bank). The National Bank was able to win the best treasury management prize among banks in Palestine Prize offered by the Banker Middle East magazine in 2014. Below are the mergers and acquisitions that took place in the Palestinian banking sector after 2010; the most important merger was the National Bank merger:

The Merger Between Al Rafah Microfinance Bank and the Arab Palestinian Investment Bank in 2012

At the end of 2012, a merger agreement was announced between Al Rafah Microfinance Bank and the Arab Palestinian Investment Bank to invest in one bank under the name of the National Bank (Palestinian origin) with a paid-up capital of ($ 50 million) in the first stage. The paid-up capital will be raised to ($ 75 million) in 2013. The agreement provides for the acquisition of the Arab Palestinian Investment Bank's assets and liabilities by the National Bank (formerly known as Al-Arabi). In return for the value the of Arab Investment Bank's net assets, its shareholders receive shares in the National Bank. The Arab Palestinian Investment Bank was established in 1996 as a limited public shareholding company. In 1997 it started to provide services according to the laws and regulations that are put in force in Palestine with a capital of ($ 15 million) in partnership with Arab Bank, International Financing Corporation and the Deutsche Bank to be the first Palestinian bank specialized in investment banking services. Since its inception until the end of 2010, the Arab Palestinian Investment Bank's management did not comply with the instructions of the Monetary Authority to increase the paid-up capital to a minimum of ($ 50 million) at the end of 2010 as per the requirements of the Palestinian Monetary Authority. On the other hand, Al-Rafah Microfinance Bank was established in 2005- to finance micro-enterprises with an authorized and subscribed capital of US $ 30 million; however, 25% of the subscribed capital was paid in 2005. Since 2006, the Bank has not taken any action to increase the paid-up capital. The Bank's management did not comply with the Monetary Authority's resolution (No. 5/2008) which called for raising the paid-up capital to $ 35 million or resolution (No. 7/2009) which stated that the minimum capital required for the practice of banking was set at $ 50 million. This had encouraged the two banks to sign a memorandum of understanding to reach an agreement leading to the formation of a Palestinian banking entity integrated into the name of the National Bank. The memorandum explained the basic requirements and ability to meet the needs of the local market for different types of financial services and all segments of society and its economic sectors, and can stand all various types of crises and meet

Table 3. The most important financial indicators for Al-Rafah Bank and Arab Palestinian Investment Bank (%)

Year	2010	2011	2010	2011
Indicators	Al Rafah Bank		Arab Palestinian Investment Bank	
	Capital Structure Index		Capital Structure Index	
Liabilities / Assets	81.8	88.2	3.1	3.8
Facilities / Equity	149.6	260.8	0.3	0.2
Retained Earnings / Equity	(7.3)	(7.3)	1.3	2.3
Capital Adequacy	33.6	19.0	27.9	228.8
Capital / Liabilities	23.0	13.6	305.4	244.4
Liquidity				
Customer Deposits / Assets	50.38	52.4	0.9	0.9
Facilities / Assets	27.2	30.8	0.3	0.2
Facilities / Customer Deposits	53.6	58.8	32.0	27.2
Profitability				
Interest Income and Commissions / Total Income	91.7	84.6	87.4	96.0
Return on Assets	0.1	0.2	0.5	1.3
Return on Equity	0.7	1.9	0.5	1.3
Return on Capital	0.7	1.9	0.5	1.4

Al Rafah Bank				Arab Palestinian Investment Bank		
Year	Paid-up Capital	Minimum Amount	Disability Amount	Paid-up Capital	Minimum Amount	Disability Amount
2005	7.8	20	(12.2)	15	20	(5)
2006	28.8	20	8.8	15	20	(5)
2007	29.8	20	9.8	15	20	(5)
2008	29.8	35	(5.2)	15	35	(20)
2009	29.8	35	(5.2)	15	35	(20)
2010	29.8	50	(20.2)	15	50	(35)
2011	29.8	50	(20.2)	15	50	(35)
2012	29.8	50	(20.2)	15	50	(35)

Source: Financial indicators issued by the Association of Banks in Palestine 2010-2017

the requirements of the Palestinian Monetary Authority. The following are the most important financial statements of the two banks before the completion of the merger:

The Motives for the Merger of the Arab Investment Bank With Al Rafah Bank for the Formation of the National Bank in 2012

According to the financial statements of the banks in Table (3) above, the most important motives and reasons for the merger was the inability of the two banks to meet the requirements of the Palestinian

Monetary Authority and to raise capital despite the increase in the size of deposits in the Al Rafah Bank from ($ 80 million) in 2010 to ($ 129 million) with a growth rate of 61%. As a result, direct credit facilities increased from ($ 42 million) to ($ 76 million), an increase of (81%). However, the bank's retained losses remained negative at ($ ⁻2.1 million). When a shallow comparison of the most significant bank indicators with the financial indicators of the banks operating in Palestine in as shown in Table (2) during the same period, it can be noticed that they are weak and below the required level of growth. Similarly, we find that the indicators and data of the Arab Palestinian Investment Bank are below the required level of growth.

National Bank's Acquisition of the Branches of Al Etihad Jordan Bank Operating in Palestine in 2015

The growth of National Bank after the merger in 2012 is shown in Table (4) which assess the performance of the National Bank, the National Bank acquired the assets and liabilities of Al Etihad Jordan Bank that was operating in 2015 in Palestine by combining its assets and liabilities to the assets and liabilities of the National Bank. The partnership agreement was the entry of Al-Etihad Jordan Bank as a new strategic partner in the National Bank with 10% of the paid-up capital which was($75 million). The portfolio of Al Etihad Jordan Bank that was working in Palestine will be transferred to the National Bank's portfolio. It was also agreed to choose a member of its Board of Directors to represent it in the new bank's Board of Directors. The following table shows the most important financial indicators of the Al Etihad Bank from 2010 until the year of acquisition 2014.

The Motives for the Al Etihad Jordan Bank to Merge With the National Bank in 2014

Referring to the most important financial indicators of Al Etihad Jordan Bank as shown in Table (3) above and in comparison with the most significant financial indexes compiled for the banks operating in Palestine as shown in table (2) and during the same period, it can be notices they are weak and below the required level. The bank's capital structure index shows a drop in most indicators compared to the capital structure of the banks operating in Palestine; the same is true for to the liquidity index and the profitability index. Most of the reasons that prompted the bank to get involved in the partnership deal with the National Bank are attributed to its inability to meet the requirements of the Palestinian Monetary Authority. The data in Table (3) of the bank indicate that there is a deficit in the payment of the capital from 2011 until 2013; however, the deficit was resolved when the transaction was concluded in 2014 and the paid-up capital was raised to ($ 50 million).

Assessment of the Importance of Mergers on the Performance of the National Bank

The National Bank was able to demonstrate that it is a strong banking entity which develops steadily. Its financial results show a growth of (207%)to reach ($ 1,079.3 million) at the end of 2017. This represents (7%) of the total assets of the Palestinian banking sector compared to ($ 350.8 million) at the end of 2012; moreover, its liabilities increased by (227%) to reach ($ 299.5 million) in 2012 and rising to ($981.8 million) in 2017 representing (7.2%) of the total liabilities of the Palestinian banking sector. On the other

Table 4. The most important financial indicators for Al Etihad Jordan Bank

Year	2010	2011	2012	2013	2014
Capital Structure Index					
Liabilities / Assets	56.8	56.3	54.5	45.3	34.3
Credit Facilities / Equity	30.4	31.4	49.3	25.5	20.0
Property Rights / Assets	43.1	43.7	45.4	54.6	65.6
Retained Earnings / Equity	11.5	11.8	11.4	8.2	6.6
Capital Adequacy	92.3	77.7	83.8	101.0	108.1
Capital / Liabilities	65.1	66.1	71.1	107.8	175.1
Liabilities / Assets					
Liquidity					
Customer Deposits / Assets	55.8	55.0	53.2	43.9	33.2
Credit Facilities / Assets	13.1	13.7	22.4	14.0	13.2
Credit Facilities / Customer Deposits	23.5	24.9	42.1	31.8	39.7
Profitability					
Direct Revenue / Total Revenue	81.3	88.0	87.7	93.7	94.2
Return on Assets	1.0	0.2	-0.002	0.4	0.39
Return on Equity	2.4	0.5	-0.004	0.8	0.6
Return on Capital	2.8	0.6	-0.005	0.8	0. 6

Al Etihad Jordan Bank

Year	Paid-up Capital	Minimum Amount	Disability Amount
2010	23	50	(27)
2011	23	50	(27)
2012	23	50	(27)
2013	36.5	50	(13.5)
2014	50	50	0

Source: Financial indicators issued by the Association of Banks in Palestine 2010-2014

hand, its deposits grew by (274%)and became ($ 808.7 million) instead ($ 216.1 million) at the end of the year 2012. These figures represented (6.7%) of the total deposits of the Palestinian banking sector. As for the direct credit facilities portfolio, it reached ($ 653.8 million) at the end of 2017 compared to 142.7% in 2012 with a growth rate of (358%). Net profit also witnessed some changes; it increased from ($ 2 million) in 2012 to ($ 9.2 million) in 2017. The total equity raised from ($ 51.3 million) in 2012 to ($ 97.5 million) in 2017 and a growth rate was (90%) compared to the growth rate of the total equity of the Palestinian banking sector for the same period which was (39%). It is a clear crystal indication of the rapid growth of the bank in a short period (less than 6 years when it was established in 2012 until 2017).

As a natural result of the rapid development and growth of the National Bank and within a short time it was able to acquire a significant, controlling stake in Palestine Islamic Bank in March 2018[15] by purchasing 31,300 million shares of the Palestine Investment Fund and transferring other shares to its own. In other words, the National Bank acquired (45%) of the total shares of the bank in a deal worth

Table 5. The most important financial indicators of the National Bank (previously Al Rafah Bank & Arab Palestinian Investment Bank) (%)

Year	2012	2013	2014	2015	2016	2017
Capital Structure Index						
Liabilities / Assets	85.4	89.6	88.2	89.1	89.5	91.0
Credit Facilities / Equity	278.2	415.3	373.2	447.3	561.5	670.1
Property Rights / Assets	14.6	10.3	11.7	10.9	10.5	9.0
Retained Earnings / Equity	0.5	0.9	4.8	7.1	6.9	7.6
Capital Adequacy	20.5	16.3	20.4	17.5	14.3	14.4
Capital / Liabilities	16.3	10.3	11.8	10.2	9.4	7.6
Liquidity						
Customer Deposits / Assets	61.6	57.1	60.9	65.7	74.1	74.9
Credit Facilities / Assets	40.7	43.1	43.9	49.0	58.7	60.0
Credit Facilities / Customer Deposits	66.1	75.4	72.1	74.6	79.2	80.8
Profitability						
Direct Revenue / Total Revenue	74.9	85.1	84.5	87.0	87.0	85.4
Return on Assets	60.0	0.7	0.65	0.66	0.8	0.9
Return on Equity	80.8	6.5	5.5	6.1	8.0	9.4
Return on Capital	74.9	7.2	6.2	7.2	9.8	12.2
The National Bank						
2017	Paid-up Capital		Minimum Amount		Amount of Surplus	
	75		75		0	

Source: Financial Indicators issued by the Association of Banks in Palestine 2010-2017

up to ($ 70 million). The merits of the deal resulted in the fact that a consortium of shareholders led by the National Bank established the Islamic National Company for Investments, which bought 22 million shares of the total shares of the Islamic Bank of Palestine – which at that time was owned by the Investment Fund. A group of investors had invested their share(about 9 million shares) in the National Bank. Consequently, consortium became the dominant stake in the Palestinian Islamic Bank as it accounts for 45%. The Islamic Bank of Palestine remained an independent bank, maintaining its identity as an Islamic bank, to continue its business under the provisions of Islamic Shari'a. The change was only relevant to the Bank's shareholders and the rights of shareholders in the Palestine Islamic Bank; and the rights of customers and employees were maintained. This transaction had a positive impact on both the National Bank and the Palestinian Islamic Bank[16]. Furthermore, this transaction resulted in two entities that are mutually integrated, strong and reinforcing that aim at serving the Palestinian national economy which will positively affect the customers and the quality of banking products and performance. In total, the mergers and acquisitions that the National Bank had been involved in since its inception have led to the growth of the bank and the rise of its financial indicators; this has strengthened its position and competitiveness and has become one of the leading national banks in the banking industry.

Second: Bank of Palestine

Bank of Palestine was established in 1960 as a financial institution that sought to improve the level of banking services in Palestine, finance various projects and meet the financial and banking needs. Bank of Palestine is one of the largest and most popular national banks in terms of number of branches and offices; it has the most widely-spread branches (network) in Palestine (74 branches), a paid-up capital of ($200 million), assets of over ($ 4.76 billion), with (1,731) employees serving more than (917,076) customers. The Bank has adopted a holistic, sustainable growth strategy which focused on modern banking, technology and information automation through the continuous development of services, expansion and empowerment, and the establishment of new departments to achieve this purpose. It has a long-embedded presence and experience; it is constantly growing to be financially inclusive. In recognition of the role and achievements of Bank of Palestine, it keeps continuously receiving local and international awards, most notably the award of the "Best Bank in Palestine Award" given by several prestigious international institutions. The Shareholders Relations Association Middle East also awarded the Best Bank in the field of Investor Relations in Mashreq it in 2017, and the following are the mergers and acquisitions carried out by the Bank of Palestine to enhance its financial and competitive position:

The Merger of the Palestine Commercial Bank With the Bank of Palestine in 2016

In the middle of 2016, the Board of Directors of Commercial Bank of Palestine unanimously approved the merger with the Bank of Palestine through an exchange of shares in which every three shares in the Commercial Bank of Palestine are equivalent to one share in the Bank of Palestine. Alternatively, under this agreement, the deposits of the customers of the Commercial Bank of Palestine and its facilitation and assets will be added to the financial indicators of the Bank of Palestine. The shareholders of the Palestine Commercial Bank became an essential part of the investors and shareholders of Bank of Palestine. This partnership was reflected positively in the performance of Bank of Palestine in various fields of the Palestinian economy[17](Bank of Palestine Annual Report, 2016). This merger was in line with the policy adopted by the Palestinian Monetary Authority to enhance the solvency and financial stability of the Palestinian banking sector and to enhance its ability to cope with the obstacles and risks that may strike the banking industry. The merger intended to prove that Palestine is the only investment compass of the two banks; it aimed also to enhance the trust in the Palestinian economy as well as contribute to the development of the banking industry. Finally, the merger was carried out to strengthen the capital adequacy.

By referring to financial indicators of Palestine Commercial Bank, its total assets increased from ($ 279.3 million) in 2014 to ($ 282.8 million) at the end of 2015, with a growth rate of (1.2%). The total value of the assets of the Palestinian commercial banking sector increased from ($ 243 million) in 2014 to ($ 244.8 million) in the year 2015 with a growth rate of (0.7%). The growth rate of the aggregated liabilities of the Palestinian banking sector for the same period was (3%), while the total commercial equity increased from ($ 36.3 million) in 2014 to ($ 38 million) in 2015 with a growth rate of (4%) whereas the total equity in the Palestinian banking sector increased by (0.2%). When considering the Palestine Commercial Bank net profit after tax, it had increased from ($ 1.1 million) in 2014 to ($ 1.3 million) in 2015 with a growth rate of 18%. The net profit of the Palestinian banking sector decreased by (9.6%).

The bank's financial statements showed that it is growing at a low rate compared to the growth of other banks[18] (Commercial Bank Annual Reports 2010-2015).

Motives for the Merger of Palestine Commercial Bank With the Bank of Palestine

By referring to the data and financial indicators of Palestine Commercial Bank, it can be noticed that it had faced an average loss of ($ 4.5 million) between 2010 to 2015 and that the bank's capital adequacy ratio had declined from (26.1%) in 2010 to (15.7%) in 2015, see table (6) below for the most important indicators of the bank. The Commercial Bank of Palestine faced a decline in all its main indicators, including the return on equity, return on capital and return on assets and from 2010 to 2015; weakness in the indicators of profitability and liquidity are below the required level compared with the indicators of the banking sector in Palestine. The Bank was unable to meet the requirements of the Palestinian Monetary Authority to raise the paid-up capital. For example, the bank was facing a deficit in completing the paid-up capital of $ 20 million from 2010 until the year of the merger in 2015; consequently, the deficit increased to ($ 45 million). The Commercial Bank of Palestine has approved the merger with Bank of Palestine in the middle of 2016 through an exchange of shares in which every three shares in the Commercial Bank of Palestine are equivalent to one share in the Bank of Palestine. The following are the main financial indicators of Commercial Bank:

Evaluation of Bank of Palestine Performance After Mergers of 2010

By referring to the financial indicators of the Bank of Palestine, it can be noticed that there has been constant development; its assets have increased from ($ 4.1 billion) in 2016 to ($ 4.8 billion) in 2017 with a growth rate of (18.5%) that represents(31%) of the total assets of the banks operating in Palestine while the growth of assets of the banks operating in Palestine was (11.7%). Concerning the liabilities, they increased from ($ 3.7 billion) in 2016 to ($ 4.4 billion) with a growth rate of (19%); it constitutes (32.5%) of the total liabilities of the Palestinian banking sector. The volume of credit facilities increased in 2017 to reach ($ 2.51 billion) while it was ($ 2.21 billion) at the end of 2016 representing an increase of (13.7%). It constitutes (32%) of the total facilities granted by the Palestinian banking sector. Furthermore, customers' deposits increased by(19.9%) from ($3.1 billion) in 2016, to ($ 3.7 billion) in 2017. This represents (36%) of the total deposits of the Palestinian banking sector, while the total property rights increased from ($403.5 million) in 2016 to ($ 449.9 million) in 2017 and at a growth rate of (11.4%) constituting (25.6%) of the banking sector's total equity which grew by (9%)during 2016.The Bank achieved a net profit of ($ 54 million) in 2017 compared to ($ 53 million) in 2016. By looking at the Bank's financial indicators in depth as shown in Table 7 below, it can be noticed that the Bank of Palestine is one of the leading banks in Palestine[19] (Annual Reports, 2010-2017).

As a natural result of the rapid development and growth of the Bank of Palestine, it managed to acquire a controlling stake in the Arab Islamic Bank by getting about 52% stake in March 2016. The total assets held by the Bank of Palestine within the Arab Islamic Bank were 39 million shares. This was the largest controlling share that came after an additional purchase of (31%) of the bank's stake; it was around (21%) of the Bank's shares up to 2015. As a result, the bank witnessed a significant change in the structure of its shareholders' when the ownership of the Al Fakhouri Group was transferred to the Bank of Palestine and the Palestine Investment Fund. There the share of the Bank of Palestine was about

Table 6. The most important financial indicators of Palestine Commercial Bank (%)

Year	2010	2011	2012	2013	2014	2015
Capital Structure Index						
Liabilities / Assets	83.7	83.4	84.9	88.0	87.5	86.5
Credit Facilities / Equity	177.5	201.1	263.1	350.0	354.7	397.5
Property Rights / Assets	15.7	16.6	15.0	12.9	12.9	13.4
Retained Earnings / Equity	(16.5)	(15.4)	(16.7)	(19.1)	)12.9(	(9.5)
Capital Adequacy	26.1	24.2	24.5	16.6	17.1	15.7
Capital / Liabilities	21.0	21.4	19.0	14.4	12.3	12.2
Liquidity						
Customer Deposits / Assets	64.6	68.3	66.1	65.8	60.7	66.0
Credit Facilities / Assets	28.9	33.4	39.7	41.9	46.1	53.5
Credit Facilities / Customer Deposits	44.7	49.0	60.1	63.7	76.0	81.0
Profitability						
Direct Revenue / Total Revenue	74.0	88.2	94.8	86.5	82.8	91.2
Return on Assets	1.0	0.3	0.03	0.05	0.4	0.5
Return on Equity	6.4	2.1	0.2	0.4	3.3	3.7
Return on Capital	6.0	2.0	0.2	0.3	3.9	4.6
Palestine Commercial Bank						
	Paid-up Capital		**Minimum Amount**		**Disability Amount**	
2010	30		50		(20)	
2011	30		50		(20)	
2012	30		50		(20)	
2013	30		50		(20)	
2014	30		50		(20)	
2015	30		75		(45)	

Source: Financial Indicators issued by the Association of Banks in Palestine 2010-2015

(52%) and the share of the Palestine Investment Fund was about (35%). This change has influenced the structure, number and composition of the Board of Directors. The Arab Islamic Bank was established in 1995 and started its banking activities in early 1996. It was meant to carry out banking and investment according to Islamic Shari.

When the Bank of Palestine has acquired a controlling stake in the Arab Islamic Bank, it was hoped to become a strong strategic partner that intends to work hard to achieve qualitative additions to Arab Islamic Bank. This agreement will have a positive impact on both the Bank of Palestine and the Arab Islamic Bank. This transaction will result in and constitute two mutually supportive entities that serve the Palestinian national economy. Again, this would be reflected in customers and banking products. On the other hand, the Bank of Palestine's acquisition of a controlling stake in the Arab Islamic Bank would be a major lever for the Arab Islamic Bank. This was reflected in the paid up share capital of the Arab Islamic Bank, as shown in Table 8 below. The Bank's capital increased in 2016 to ($ 62.5 million) after it had a deficit of ($ 25 million) in 2015. However, in 2017, the bank increased the paid up capital to ($

Table 7. The most important financial indicators of Bank of Palestine (%)

Year	2010	2011	2012	2013	2014	2015	2016	2017
Capital Structure Index								
Liabilities / Assets	**89.4**	**88.2**	**89.0**	**89.3**	**88.4**	**89.0**	**90.2**	**90.8**
Credit Facilities / Equity	**332.6**	**370.5**	**441.9**	**437.9**	**411.2**	**454.2**	**548.5**	**504.6**
Property Rights / Assets	**10.5**	**11.7**	**11.0**	**10.7**	**11.5**	**10.9**	**9.8**	**9.2**
Retained Earnings / Equity	**12.8**	**12.0**	**12.5**	**9.5**	**12.8**	**10.0**	**9.0**	**11.4**
Capital Adequacy	**13.6**	**13.6**	**13.2**	**13.9**	**13.0**	**14.56**	**14.7**	**14.44**
Capital / Liabilities	**7.2**	**8.2**	**7.5**	**7.1**	**7.4**	**7.0**	**5.2**	**4.5**
Liquidity								
Customer Deposits / Assets	**81.2**	**78.4**	**77.6**	**74.3**	**85.1**	**80.5**	**76.3**	**77.1**
Credit Facilities / Assets	**35.3**	**43.5**	**48.7**	**47.0**	**47.5**	**49.9**	**53.7**	**51.6**
Credit Facilities / Customer Deposits	**43.5**	**55.5**	**62.8**	**63.2**	**55.8**	**61.9**	**70.4**	**66.8**
Profitability								
Direct Revenue / Total Revenue	**78.2**	**85.6**	**82.2**	**88.4**	**85.2**	**84.6**	**84.0**	**82.7**
Return on Assets	**1.9**	**2.1**	**1.9**	**1.7**	**1.7**	**1.5**	**1.3**	**1.1**
Return on Equity	**18.4**	**17.5**	**17.4**	**16.0**	**14.4**	**14.1**	**13.1**	**12.0**
Return on Capital	**30.1**	**28.2**	**28.5**	**26.9**	**25.0**	**24.5**	**27.1**	**27.0**
The National Bank								
2017	Paid-up Capital		Minimum Amount			Amount of Surplus		
	200		75			125		

Source: Financial Indicators issued by the Association of Banks in Palestine 2010-2017

69 million). As a result, the acquisition had influenced the financial performance of 2017; it increased from ($ 794.1 million) in 2016 to ($ 1,041 million) in 2017 with a growth rate of (31%). Concerning the liabilities, they increased from ($ 718.9 million) in 2016 to ($ 934.1 million) in 2017 with a growth rate of (29%).Moreover, the property rights increased from ($ 75.2 million)in 2016 to ($ 106.9 million) in 2017 with a growth rate of (42%), and consequently, the bank gained a profit of ($ 6.4 million) in 2017.

CONCLUSION

Through the study, many results can be drawn; the most significant findings were:

1. The study showed that the circulars issued by the Palestine Monetary Authority concerning raising the minimum capital have had a positive impact and the main motivation for mergers and acquisitions. The gradual increase in the minimum capital from ($10 million) in 2008 to ($35 million) on the one hand, and from ($ 35 million) to ($ 50 million) in 2010, and then from ($ 50 million) to ($ 75 million) in 2015, on the other hand, had a positive impact on mergers and acquisitions in

Table 8. The most important financial indicators of Arab Islamic Bank (%)

Year	2010	2011	2012	2013	2014	2015	2016	2017
Capital Structure Index								
Liabilities / Assets	83.2	81.1	84.8	86.7	87.9	89.4	90.5	89.7
Credit Facilities / Equity	162.4	234.3	300.2	307.0	364.9	451.3	558.0	524.2
Property Rights / Assets	16.8	18.9	15.3	13.2	12.0	10.6	9.5	10.3
Retained Earnings / Equity	)4.3(	(1.4)	0.4	2.5	7.1	5.4	8.9	3.1
Capital Adequacy	20.2	24.2	21.6	18.9	15.5	12.4	14.1	15.9
Capital / Liabilities	16.8	19.9	14.9	11.7	10.1	8.6	6.9	8.0
Liquidity								
Customer Deposits / Assets	81.31	78.6	77.4	74.8	75.8	79.5	78.6	76.0
Credit Facilities / Assets	27.3	44.4	45.8	40.7	44.0	47.9	54.2	53.9
Credit Facilities / Customer Deposits	33.6	56.5	59.2	54.4	58.0	60.2	68.9	70.9
Profitability								
Direct Revenue / Total Revenue	85.5	77.1	88.1	83.6	83.1	85.4	87.1	86.0
Return on Assets	(0.8)	0.3	0.2	0.7	0.7	0.8	0.8	0.6
Return on Equity	(4.7)	1.6	1.1	5.6	6.1	7.5	8.3	6.0
Return on Capital	(5.6)	1.9	1.4	7.1	8.2	10.4	12.4	8.5

Arab Islamic Bank			
	Paid-up Capital	**Minimum Amount**	**Disability Amount**
2011	**47**	**50**	**(4)**
2012	**50**	**50**	**(3)**
2013	**50**	**50**	**(0)**
2014	**50**	**50**	**(0)**
2015	**62.5**	**75**	**(25)**
2016	**69**	**75**	**(12.5)**
2017	**46**	**75**	**(6)**

Source: Financial Indicators issued by the Association of Banks in Palestine 2010-2015

Palestine. The incentives and benefits offered by the Monetary Authority had significantly contributed to mergers and had a positive effect on them.

2. The study showed that mandatory circulars for capital support were in line with the decision of the Monetary Authority in 2009 that entails the necessity of not transferring any profits outside Palestine, or to distribute them in cash; instead, they have to be capitalized or retained amount of profits in circulation with the banks. Finally, they should also be consistent with the instructions on the forms, conditions, terms, and procedures of mergers and acquisitions.
3. The study revealed that most of the banking mergers were carried out in the Palestinian banking sector according to an integrated voluntary negotiation process between the Palestinian banks to improve their competitive position The mergers which aimed to achieve high growth rates that

enable the banks to survive and to form large-scale banking units that can participate significantly in the financing of economic development plans.

4. The study showed that the mergers that took place in the Palestinian banking sector resulted in a significant improvement in the data and financial indicators of the local banks. This was reflected positively on the national economy.
5. The study showed that bank mergers and acquisitions protect banking institutions from bankruptcy or liquidation, thus reducing the banking crises, and consequently, stabilizing the banking system as well as the national economy as a whole.
6. The increase in the productivity of integrated/merged banks, the great development in their performance, and increase the quality and efficiency in the services provided to customers after these mergers played had positive impacts on the performance and productivity of the Palestinian banking system compared to foreign banks.

RECOMMENDATIONS

In light of these findings, the researchers recommend that the efforts of the Palestinian Monetary Authority should be intensified to stimulate mergers to create banking entities capable of facing the competitive challenges, financial crises and banking risks. It is also required to raise awareness of the importance of banking mergers and/or integration in Palestine and clarify the side effects of them. Large-scale national banks side by side with expatriate banks must play a more active role in the economic development process; they should work hard to maximize the economic development and expand the establishment of productive projects that need large funding that might be obtained through the granting of syndicated loans.

It is necessary to assess the performance and indicators of the banks operating in Palestine periodically, especially the weak ones, and to come up with decisions that ultimately contribute to the development of the Palestinian banking system. There are instances of banks that are weak financially and competitively in the Palestinian banking sector, the need to be strengthened through more mergers and acquisitions. Consequently, the safety of banking is a necessary guarantee to support the national economy. Therefore, the monetary authorities must ensure and continuously validate the banking structure and assess them in a way that ensures whether there is a need to move towards mergers and consolidation to strengthen the banking industry or not.

REFERENCES

Al-Toni, M. A. (2007). *Banking Integration (Origination and Development of Motivations, Justifications and Implications) with a view on the experiences of global, Arab and Egyptian integration* (1st ed.). Dar Al Fajr Publishing and Distribution.

Bushlagh, F., & Zakiq, H. (2015). *Banking Integration and a Course in Improving the Competitiveness of Banks: Case Study of Algeria* (Master's thesis). University of AkliMohandOulhaj, Bouira, Algeria.

Hamid, A. (2001). *Abdulmutallab*. Globalization and Banking Economics. University House.

Hammad, A.-A. T. (2017). *The Integration and Privatization of Banks Part IV*. Commercial Banking Series, University House.

Jahmani, O. I. (2002). Integration into Jordan: A Field Study on Commercial Banks. Journal of Public Administration, 42(3).

Judge, N. (2017). Research entitled Banking Integration and Acquisitions in Arab Countries. *Journal of Administrative Sciences*.

Matai, A. (2010). *Banking Integration as a Modern Approach*. Administrative and Economic Research, Mohammed Khader Biskra University.

Mohamed. (2005). *Integration and its impact on the financial performance of commercial banks* (PhD thesis). Sudan University of Science and Technology, Khartoum, Sudan.

Nabi, A., & Eide, W. (2011). *Banking Integration in Iraq as a Need for Banking Reform*. Central Bank of Iraq.

Rihan, K. (2006). *Banking Integration of Banks Operating in Palestine (Evaluation of the Experience of the Integration of Cairo Amman Bank - Islamic Transactions in the Palestinian Islamic Bank)*. Presented to the Conference of the Development of the Gaza Strip, Gaza.

Shalaby, M. A. (2003). *Banking Integration as a Tool for Market Access and Enhancing Competitiveness in an Era of Giant Clusters and Entities. Saleh Saleh Kamel Center for Islamic Economics, Al-Azhar University*.

Yassine, E.-T., & Abdelkader, M. (2008). The Importance of Banking Integration as a Tool to Enhance the Performance of the Algerian Banking System. *Introduction to the Second International Scientific Conference on the Reform of the Algerian Banking System*.

Zaideh, M. M. (2006). *The Motivation of Banking Consolidation in Palestine and Its Determinants. Introduction to Master's Degree in Accounting and Finance from the Islamic University*.

ENDNOTES

1. Abdel Fattah, Ahmed (1992). Extrapolating the results and future of banking integration. Union of Arab Banks, Beirut.
2. Yassin, al-Tayeb, and Matai, Abdelqader (2008). "Banking Integration as a Tool for Improving the Performance of the Algerian Banking System".
3. Abdul Hamid, Abdulmutallab (2001). Globalization and Banking Economics, University House, Egypt.
4. Hammad, Abdel Aal Tariq(1999). The Integration and Privatization of Banks", Part 4, Commercial Banking Series, University House, Alexandria.
5. Matai, Abdelqader (2010). Banking Integration as a Modern Approach to the Development and Modernization of the Banking System, University of Mohammed KhaderBiskra, Issue 7.
6. Palestinian Monetary Authority (2017). Annual Report, Monetary Research and Policy Department, Palestine.

(7)Association of Banks in Palestine (2017. "Statistical Reports issued by the Association of the year 2010 -2017".

(8)Bank Al Quds, Reports issued by the Bank, 2010-2017

(9)Zaideh, Mahaib Mohamed (2006). "The Motivation of Banking Mergers in Palestine and Its Determinants". Master Thesis. Islamic University, Gaza, Palestine.

(10)Abdul Nabi, Walid Eide (2011). Banking Integration in Iraq as a Need for Banking Reform, Central Bank of Iraq.

(11)Sherif Mohamed (2015). "Integration and its impact on the financial performance of commercial banks". Doctoral Dissertation. Sudan University of Science and Technology, Khartoum, Sudan.

(12) Jahmani, Omar Issa (2002). "Mergers in Jordan: A Field Study on Commercial Banks", Journal of Public Administration, Yarmouk University, Jordan, Vol. 42, No. 3, pp. 575-628.

(13) in Gaza.

(14) National Bank, Reports issued by the Bank, 2012-2017.

(15) The National Bank: https://www.tnb.ps

(16) The National Bank: https://www.tnb.ps

(17) Bank of Palestine, Annual Report, 2016.

(18) Commercial Bank of Palestine, Annual Report of the Bank, 2010-2015.

(19) Bank of Palestine, Annual Reports of the Bank, 2010-2017.

Chapter 14
Investigation of Factors Affecting Adoption of FinTech in Financial Institutions

Subhashini Sailesh Bhaskaran
https://orcid.org/0000-0003-0517-9866
Ahlia University, Bahrain

ABSTRACT

FinTech, a compound term for financial technology, signifies the usage of technology to provide financial assistance. Ever since its evolution FinTech has been growing tremendously, despite its positive and negative aspects. In the literature review, there are many factors affecting the adoption of FinTech. It was found that the ease of use of technology (Technology Acceptance Theory), investment decisions in crowdfunding (Decision Theory), and the risks involved in the adoption of FinTech (Prospect Theory) are the main factors that might affect the adoption of FinTech. However, there is a paucity of studies linking all these factors in the adoption of FinTech using these theories. This research project investigates the influence of these factors in the adoption of FinTech. In order to analyze these factors, a questionnaire was used. As a result, it was found that there is a positive relationship between the ease of use and FinTech's adoption; between FinTech's adoption and investment decisions in crowdfunding and between the level of risks when adapting to FinTech.

Keywords: FinTech; Factors; Bahrain; Adoption; Financial Institutions

INTRODUCTION

Financial Services or "FinTech" has attracted increasing attention in recent years. The term comes from the contraction of the words finance and technology. It refers to technology startups that take advantage of the most modern technologies to create innovative digital financial services. In other words, the term FinTech is also applied to describe these financial services. It is a revolution of the customer experience, in some cases creating new unique services, in others improving or disrupting existing ones. It all depends

DOI: 10.4018/978-1-7998-3257-7.ch014

on the type of technological financial products used in a company. (Bradley Rice, 2018).FinTech services are aimed at final customers, whether individuals, professionals or companies, excluding intermediaries. Societal conduct and organizational activities are fundamentally being affected by technology and the digital revolution. The very essence of our lives is always being influenced by connectivity.

According to the statistics recorded in 2016, at least 95% of the businesses prevalent in OECD 'Organization for Economic Co-operation and Development' initiated in 1961 to stimulate economic development and the global trades, had internet connectivity and more than 75% were found to be operation online. The monetary industry has always been influenced by technology at large; resulting in it being the first to adopt every new technological aspect that comes in the market (Gurria, 2008).

The very first Automated Teller Machine (ATM) was set up in 1967 in London at a branch of Barclays bank. From that point forward customers have demanded proximity in response to which many automated services have been introduced; Point-Of-Sale (POS) systems, debit card, credit card, virtual trade, banking services, and many other services (Panetta, 2018).

The practice of digitalized financial services is set to rise, inspired by customer expectations, the extent of the reach of the internet, smartphones, tablets, and the stable drop in data storage costs and the upgrade in the capacity of systems.

The development documented in the preceding years is outstanding; for instance, the total amount of data exchanged across international borders reached over 45% in 2005, while the subsequent cost of data storage is 10 times less than what it used to be. In response to the contradiction of this situation's setting that "FinTech" came into the picture. Though it has been known only since 2014, it started attracting responsiveness from managers, industry participants, and clients (Arner, 2015). An industry that had previously been deemed stable over the course of decades was suddenly threatened with new emerging market entrants influenced by digital innovation. A stream of new companies emerged providing digitized financial solutions, promising to transform the entire industry.

BACKGROUND

Origin and Definition

FinTech, a compound term for financial technology, signifies the usage of technology to provide financial assistance. The term was first heard in the 1990s, where it began from a project started by Citigroup to enable the technical assistance activities, "Financial Services Technology Consortium". A number of varied views are available upon the definition of FinTech:

- Since the first establishment of FinTech in Bahrain in 2016, FinTech has been able to define itself as a distinct segment within the financial services industry. The key components of this segment are the corporations and startups that provide services similar or identical in nature to those being provided by traditional financial institutions and intermediaries. Although, in contrast with the traditional financial service providers, companies might fall within the FinTech segment could be inclined towards using the latest technology and internet-based software, in order to reach clients satisfaction (PwC, 2016).

- The term FinTech is unlimited to certain clear segments that prevail in countries' economies (e.g. financing) or business models (e.g. peer-to-peer lending), but instead includes the complete range of facilities and products conventionally provided by the financial services industry (Arner, 2015).
- The financial revolution came with critical aspects which include producing and spreading new financial instruments, new financial technologies, institutions, and markets. It also includes unique innovations at institutes, products and process levels (Varga, 2017).
- Financial technology companies (known as FinTech) are broadening access to a range of services that they claim can help us manage our spending, save more money, and make investments in our long-term financial security simultaneously. FinTech offers users an array of financial services from transactions to underwriting that was once almost exclusively the business of banks (Kagan, 2019).

(I) FinTech's Eras and Evolution

(1) FinTech's Eras

- FinTech 1.0 (1866-1967):

From the establishment of the principal transoceanic link to the creation of the main ATM, money and innovation were consolidated to deliver the primary time of budgetary globalization. Innovations, for example, money related between linkages crosswise over fringes, permitting the transmission of monetary data, exchanges, and payments.(Bates, 2017)

- FinTech 2.0 (1967-2008):

At the point when FinTech stayed interior to the part and was vanquished for the most part by the conventional money related administrations industry that was utilizing innovation to give monetary items and administrations. This time saw the presentation of electronic installments and clearing frameworks, ATM machines and internet banking. During the mid-1990s, the money related administrations industry turned into its single biggest buyer – a position which stays to this day.(Bates, 2017)

- FinTech 3.0 (2008-present):

As far back as the worldwide money related emergency finished, troublesome new companies and recently settled innovation organizations have started to convey budgetary items and administrations straightforwardly to organizations and the overall population and where new contestants will in general spotlight on a solitary reason arrangement, intended to offer an improved involvement in only one item or service.(Bates, 2017).

(2) Evolution of FinTech

The primary usage of technologies that are being used by banks and trading corporations was dependent on the physical resources of transportation and storage. Moreover, markets were mainly restricted to a local scope. These limitations were increased with the rise of information and communications technology. As a result, the visual and the electric telegraph allowed the information to be transferred over larger areas; which led to neglecting the location. The telegraph's economic impacts were vital since it became well-known for its industrial development of modern societies(Thomas W. Malone, 1987). These relatable technologies lasted for the better part of the 20th century. Therefore, the rise of technological communication in the late 20th century lead to the foundation of the financial technologies phase. It started depending on the electronic transactions between customers, markets, and financial institutions on an international level. The technology also spread towards the banking sector, which affected the banking value chain that progressed to four groups(Rainer Alt, Roman Beck, Martin Smits, 2018):

1- Customers (Retail, Commercial, Investment)
2- Channels (Branches, Brokers, Social, Mobile)
3- Financial service providers (Banking and Non-Banking Institutions)
4- Interbank providers (Exchanges, Networks, OTC's)

(II) FinTech's Industry

Figure 1. Evolution of financial technologies
Adapted from (Rainer Alt, Roman Beck, Martin Smits, 2018)

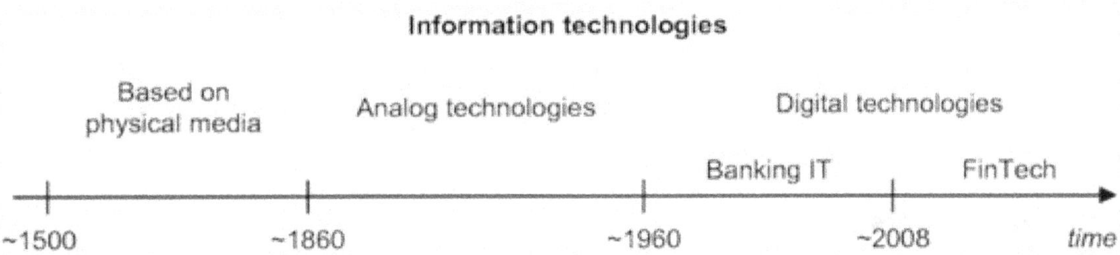

FinTech industry in the present consists of five major segments:

A) Finance and investment:

On one hand, finance and investment is a greater part of the public, investors and regulatory authorities that focus on the substitutive methods of finance. Particularly, crowdfunding and peer to peer lending. On the other hand, FinTech's reach is extended beyond this limited scope of financial technology (venture capital, private equities, Over the Counter, public offerings, etc.). From a different point of view, one example of the finance and technology period is NASDAQ (National Association of Securities Dealers Automated Quotations), which has caused the securities exchange and related sector to replace their physical records with advanced computerized systems. In addition, they have continued to develop substitutive financial mechanisms, as they are looking to be involved in areas like robotic advisory services (Rainer Alt, Roman Beck, Martin Smits, 2018).

B) Financial operations and risk management:

One of the main activities that have influenced the overall IT' One of the main activities that have influenced the overall IT's s budgeting is caused by operations and risk management sectors. Thus, financial institutions are building better compliance systems to control immense regulations.(Schilder, 2005)

C) Payments and infrastructure:

The internet and cellular phone systems are crucial for FinTech's infrastructure. The governing bodies are focusing on expenses since the 1970s, causing both local and cross-border payment systems to grow enormously. Today, they are supporting 5.4 US$ trillion worth global market on a daily basis. Similarly, the mechanism of securities trading and the Over-The-Counter derivative exchange remains a key facet of the FinTech landscape.(McKinsey, 2018)

D) Data security and monetization:

Data security and monetization are the focus of FinTech nowadays. The digital nature of the finance industry has been in a vulnerable position about cybercrime and surveillance; as this industry is fixated on providing solutions that limit this risk to the maximum level. (Ismail, 2018)

E) Consumer interface:

Consumer interfaces mostly focus on virtual and cellular financial services as it continues to be the main influencer for attention. Especially the attention towards conventional financial services and non-conventional FinTech progresses (Courbe, 2016).

(III) Positive Aspects of FinTech

FinTech can offer solutions that are efficient and effective even in less widespread use. This will give small businesses better access to a variety of financing options, such as peer-to-peer finance or e-commerce. Both of which are extremely relevant and trending nowadays. Not forgetting to mention that innovative financing solutions can significantly help small businesses by providing better cash flow, improved working capital management, and more stable or secure financing. Finally yet importantly, FinTech can help companies with improved payments using their access to their capital, customer relationship management, billing, and debt collection systems. Finally, FinTech solutions include e-invoice management portals and supply chain finance solutions.(Carpenter, 2017)

To elaborate, there are several advantages to FinTech such as:

- Ability to provide real-time data collection, technologies can remotely measure and evaluate gathered information. For instance, sensors systems can provide detailed coverage information, options, and updates through a smartphone application that would be accessible anytime anywhere by the client.(Martell, 2018)
- Enhanced customer service, the internet of things (IoT) based solutions in banking words to streamline and personalize the customer experience. Moreover, IoT and FinTech can work on

speeding customer service and ensuring the security of data. For example, banks can automate service requests and can install onsite sensors that connect with a mobile application to authenticate customers' identities.(Martell, 2018)

- Quick decision, with the availability of customers data including financial history, habits and risk factors it can help to generate better decisions. Through FinTech tools, analytics tools and IoT sensors can examine customers' credit histories and social media activities to determine customer creditworthiness and provide institutes like banks with the ability to generate ideal offers (Martell, 2018).

(IV) Negative Aspects of FinTech

The majority of the corporations working under the FinTech sector are not recognized as traditional financial institutions since most of the international laws under the respective legislations concerning financial institutions of their countries are not applicable to these organizations. This presents a big loop in the legislative structure, which can be used against them (Munteanu 2016, Nathan Associates India 2017).

The potential risks related to the processes of FinTech companies are; threats to cybersecurity, violation of information confidentiality and the potential of the FinTech facilities or products being utilized for unlawful tenacities such as money laundering, contraband transactions and tax evasion (Vardi 2017, Dodgson et al. 2015, Campenon 2016, Nakaso 2016, Athey et al. 2016).

Therefore, it is essential that FinTech companies' existence is "legitimized" and that a certain ruling authority, like all other sources of financial services (Mirmazaheri 2016, Brunsden 2016), guarantees them. Or else, the absence of rules may boost dangerous behavior and become a fraction of a prevailing "shadow banking" procedure (Panckhurst 2017, Munteanu 2016). FinTech credit is expanding rapidly on an international scale over the recent years, but its size still varies a lot depending on the savings. These differences reflect the structure development of financial markets: the higher the income of a country and the lower its banking system is competitive, plus, FinTech's credit activity is crucial. The volumes FinTech credits are also more developed in countries where banking regulations are not strict. FinTech credit, a source of alternative financing for companies and households, could improve access to credit for some underprivileged segments. This could further enhance the effectiveness of financial intermediation. Nevertheless, as shown by certain failures and behavioral problems, FinTech credit also poses certain challenges to regulatory authorities, particularly in regard to ensuring adequate protection of consumers and investors (Ernst and Young, 2017) (Pejkovska, 2018).

How does FinTech make payments easier for companies?

The FinTech upheaval changes the business scene and alters how clients oversee and use installments. The installment business has encountered significant changes over the most recent couple of years, principally because of the insurgency of FinTech. As far back as the presence of the principal bank in the nineteenth century, the way wherein we make installments has been continually developing. During those days, the development of banks was conceivable gratitude to the cash we know (Banknotes and coins). Securities exchanges and checks have likewise added to this advancement. Alongside the fast development of the financial division, governments chose to force stricter guidelines. Up to this point, banks and monetary foundations managed the money related condition. In spite of the fact that, in the present setting where FinTech altered the financial business as we probably am aware it, everything will soon change (EDB Bahrain, 2017).

Just, FinTech is a mix of money and innovation. The principal slants in the division showed up in 2007 after the monetary emergency. In this circumstance, organizations entering the market looked for new and less expensive methods for offering monetary administrations. The least demanding and quickest approach to accomplish this objective was to consolidate money related administrations, online exchanges, and cutting edge diagnostic abilities. At present, FinTech totally adjusts the manner by which shoppers oversee and bolster installments. Albeit most Business-to-Business shoppers appear to comprehend what the term FinTech implies, private customers still don't have any broad information about it. Be that as it may, before proceeding onward to how FinTech organizations encourage making installments to organizations, we have to discover what the FinTech customer condition looks like (EDB Bahrain, 2017).

MAIN FOCUS OF THE CHAPTER[1]

Issues, Controversies, Problems

From the above background and literature review discussion, it can be seen that factors like ease of use, investment decisions in crowd funding and risk in adoption of FinTech seem to have an impact on the adoption of FinTech. Hence as literature points out there is a need to investigate and understand the effect of these factors on adoption of FinTech.

Figure 2. Adoption of FinTech Research Model
Adapted from (In Lee and Yong Jae Shin, Business Horizons - 2018)

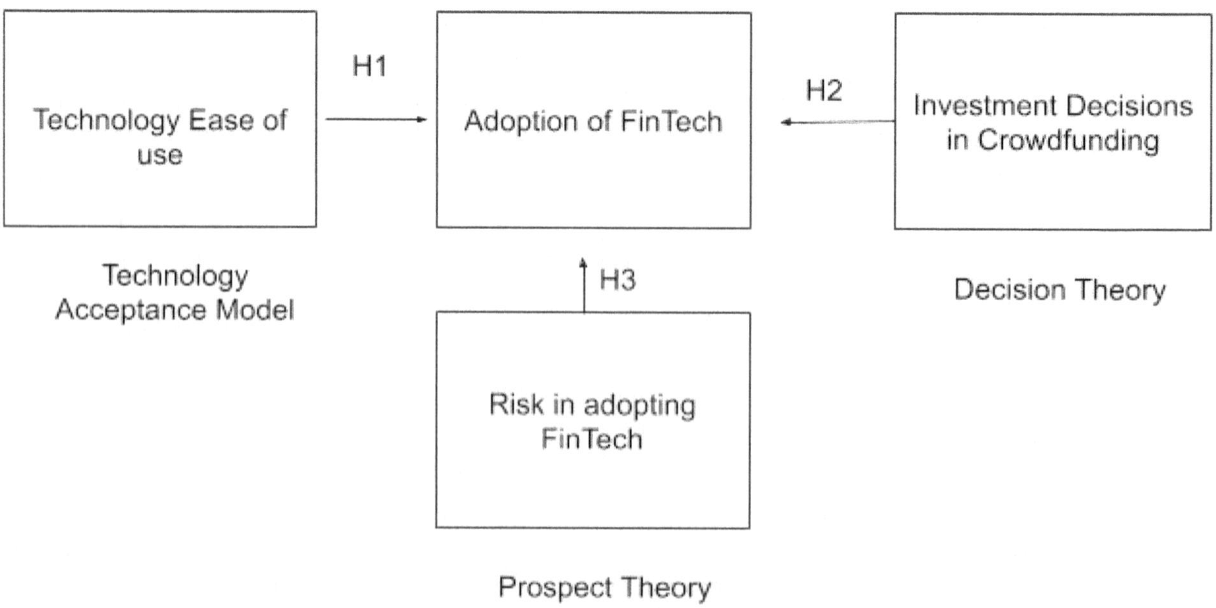

Three hypotheses emerge from the literature which is detailed as follows.

H1: There is a positive relationship between the ease of use and the adoption of FinTech (Technology Acceptance Theory).

Perceived usefulness is a contributing factor that is constantly being used in the process of adopting information systems. As for the ease of use, it is considered as another important yet contributing factor. It is defined as the degree of effort that is involved in using this new technology. Many scholars have demonstrated a significant correlation between perceived ease of use and new technology adoption attitudes, it was considered by researchers that perceived usefulness highly affects organizations attitudes and their willingness to adopt FinTech.

In this research, perceived usefulness refers to organizations adopting FinTech's services and explains the various methods of how they adopt FinTech. As for its relation to the ease of use of technology, it clarifies the extent to which organizations or customers feel at ease and comfortable while using FinTech's services.

H2: There is a positive relationship between the adoption of FinTech and investment decisions in crowdfunding (decision theory).

Crowd funding is a noteworthy financing cause that every year subsidizes around a large portion of a million European activities that would some way or another never get the chance to see the sun. FinTech is the principle idea here as it has as of late entered the language of the matter of banking. FinTech is one of the most energizing occasions of the previous couple of years when it began giving money related administrations and items utilizing modern data innovation.

Crowd funding is a technique for joint effort between a network of people who largely utilize their assets to advance the endeavors of people and associations on Internet destinations. A descending advancement includes microfinance that prepares people and assets. It can apply to ventures from any industry, from the subsidizing of a business dare to design and social inheritance to inventive organizations and logical research. Mechanical advancement has empowered working expenses to be decreased, which brought about advancing a decrease system. FinTech's accomplishment and crowd funding have opened crisp monetary outlets and empowered clients to deal with their tasks a lot swifter with the aftereffect of the ensuing crossing out of pointless administration costs.

H3: There is a positive relationship between the level of risks and the adoption of FinTech (prospect theory).

Perceived risks refer to the financial and technological facets; these are the main factors that negatively affect the adoption of technology. On one hand, financial risk is the risk that consumers take regarding the property damage of their assets and properties. On the other hand, privacy risk refers to the personal data of the consumers and the security of their transactions.

Moreover, the main concern of most organizations is the misuse of personal information when using FinTech services. Based on these risks and their impacts, there is a negative relationship between the levels of risks when businesses adapt to FinTech.

Table 1.

Variables	Definition
Dependent variable	The adoption of FinTech, the rise of digitization and financial innovations shall be measured through this research.
Independent variable	The ease of use of Technology (FinTech Technology), Investment decisions in crowdfunding, risks in adopting FinTech are all dependent variables that might affect the adoption of Fintech.

Hypothesis: The Advancement of FinTech positively enhances the work of current businesses.

As is widely recognized, each project, whether small or big, would experience certain setbacks or problems before or after implementation. The challenges in FinTech's implementation are the entrepreneurs wanting to see themselves less and less as rivals with respect to large financial institutions, rather than seeing themselves as collaborating partners when it comes to a heavily controlled marketplace. Both of these divisions are all intended to obtain the appropriate interaction in order to benefit as much as possible. The rapid pace of technological development only underlines the significance of correcting FinTech adoption (FinTech Innovation Lab, 2018).

As for the three hypotheses and their interconnected concepts, the first is the ease of use of technology. Ease of use is a simple notion–it is a measure of how simple it is to use the completed item by the individuals who intend to use it. Design is often a struggle between attempting to offer features and attempting to achieve ease of use. It is essential to recognize the ease of use during the design, planning and implementing stage. Where it is possible to be feasible, in order to satisfy the need for the comfort of use (Cockton, 2013). Ease of use is related to the Technology Acceptance Model (TAM). It is considered one of the most important research models in accepting determinants of data systems/information systems (Information Systems/ Information Technology) studies. TAM has demonstrated to be a helpful theoretical model in assisting to comprehend and clarify the behavior in Information Systems application. It has been investigated that in various empirical research and the instruments used with the model have demonstrated to be of value and produce statistically accurate outcomes. Seeing, as the purpose is to clarify the use of use, higher emphasis should be placed on the metric. Another significant restriction of TAM is to consider Information Systems as an autonomous problem in organizational dynamics (Chu, 2015; Lai, 2017).

As for the second hypothesis, investment decisions are linked to the participants ' choice or the highest-level leadership regarding the number of resources to be utilized in equity possibilities. There are two classifications; the first is the long-term capital budgeting category. While the other is the short-term classification, which serves for working capital management (Jargons, 2017). Investment decisions are directly related to decision theories. As there are many different ways to theorize about decisions, and therefore also many different research traditions. It is defined as the mathematical review of ideal decision-making approaches, it is focused directly on various risk, expectations or return perceptions, based on the result (Hansson, 2005).

As for the third and last hypothesis, it was decided to research the risk occurring when adopting FinTech. Customers may often experience some amount of danger or uncertainty when making choices. FinTech's opportunities for economic failure is almost in all financial and economic transitions. Specifically, apparent financial risk is the most coherent predictor of the internet and mobile user behaviors. (Ryu, 2018) The theory that relates to it is called the prospect theory. Kahneman and Tversky (1988,

1981) created a prospect hypothesis to clarify the results of studies with the decision problems that were indicated in aspects of currency outcomes and meaningful probabilities. Its primary characteristics are generally applicable to decision-making. Prospect theory differentiates from most other decision-making theories by being "unrepentantly concise" and making "no prescriptive allegations" (Hansson, 2005).

SOLUTIONS AND RECOMMENDATIONS

This section is intended to expose the methodological choices of research. In addition, the focus will be on the main epistemological examples, which were addressed in the literature. In addition, there will justification for the epistemological positions adopted and the methodological frameworks that are relevant to the study. Moreover, the choices made to measure the variables of the research theoretical models from the quantitative survey perspective.

This research will conduct primary research in the form of a questionnaire. This research method will measure the effect of FinTech on current businesses. The population taken for this research will focus on individuals with knowledge in the banking and finance sectors. Therefore, the target group consists of employees working in the banking and finance sectors, university doctors and students majoring in the same field. The sampling method chosen for this research is cluster sampling, which is dividing the population into units then randomly selecting from these units. Therefore, the participants have been acknowledged depending on their level as employees, students, doctors, and unemployed individuals all with knowledge in the banking and finance sector. In addition, the variation of the degree level among participants has been taking under consideration to understand the level of knowledge that they obtain.

The questionnaire contains 17 questions that will help test the assumption of FinTech enhancing the work of current businesses. There are several types of questions that have been used in this survey such as rating scale questions, multiple-choice questions, and checkboxes questions. However, in the multiple-choice questions and checkboxes questions, the participants have the option to add (others), if there is another point that they think answers the question better. (WomenInFinTech, 2019).

To analyze the results of the questionnaire, the responses will be viewed through a Google survey. The responses will be viewed based on how much percentage the answer is repeated. Furthermore, the data will be systematically analyzed through IBM SPSS Statistics where the mean, standard variation and percentages will be shown. In order to understand the relationship between the two variables.

The epistemological stance of research Epistemology is "the critical study of knowledge, its foundations, its principles, its methods, its conclusions and the eligibility conditions of its proposals". In the study 'The Adoption of FinTech in current businesses' presents the study of knowledge in technology. In other words, to obtain the knowledge that forms the sciences in asking how this technology emerges and evolves. This step is an essential part of the research "The specification of the epistemological framework in which the researcher registers his research project is a founding act, which has consequences for the whole of the research". Confirming the remarks "The epistemological reflection is consubstantial to the research that takes place" and "In every day of the researcher, it is simply able to legitimize at any moment his research on the phenomenon studied ". The explanation of the chosen method makes it possible to control the research approach, in order to increase the validity of the knowledge derived from it and to discuss it cumulatively. Moreover, epistemological questioning aims at "Clarifying the conception of knowledge on which research work will rest and how knowledge will be justified which will be developed" (Ichikawa, 2017).

How is scientific knowledge generated?

The study aims to explain 'The adoption of FinTech in current businesses', the relationship established in the post-adoption phase. The phase also works independently on the basis of a questionnaire validated measurements. It is mainly about discovering an underlying structure of reality.

What is the value of knowledge?

The validation of the research will be carried out by the confrontation of the hypotheses with the facts. It is driven by a derivable logic considered as "The reasoning that concludes from premises and assumptions to the truth of a proposition, or to its reputation in using inference rules". From these responses, it appears that the perspective chosen in the context of the research is in a positive position. It's about discovering an underlying structure of reality to discover the causes of customers' adoption of technology. Moreover, it also explains the consequence of this adoption in terms of the relationship established between the technology and its customers' adopters (Scotland, 2012).

In this case, the positivist posture that is ours leads us to respect the criteria related factors: verifiability and confirmability. In the next paragraph, the compatible methodological approach with the epistemological choice "the positivist posture" is discussed (Scotland, 2012).

The expected effort represents in these articles presents the degree of ease associated with the use of technology in the financial sector. It was previously mentioned that its familiar to the facility perceived usage, which was defined in the theory of acceptance and use of Micro Assembly Technologies. In the literature review, computer-human interaction and studies of customer-to-business focus on ease navigation, speed of response as functional factors that are needed to create beneficial and usable trade sites for customers. In these studies, ease of use emerges as the fundamental characteristic in the efficiency of a merchant site. Therefore, the literature shows the system must be both easy to learn and easy to use. In other articles, there are numerous studies to measure the expected effort (Nadim Jahangir, Noorhajan Begum, 2008).

Convenience has been highlighted in the literature as a motivating factor for consumers to use automated services. Certainly, there are consumers motivated by the cost (saving money) and the ease of collecting information, on the other hand, others are motivated by convenience. In the study, the adoption of FinTech in current businesses convenience has several aspects such as the degree of flexibility the use of technology in financial sector, the possibility of doing business in financial sector in terms of lifestyle (use these services in the workplace, at the home, travel, not having to wait), and ease of use (physical effort and mental necessary) (Nadim Jahangir, Noorhajan Begum, 2008).

Data Analysis

Instrument Used

The survey link to employees working in both sectors, university doctors and to students who are majoring in banking or finance. As a result, 222 responses were collected and analyzed.

The questionnaire had 17 questions of three different types. The first three questions were asking about general information. The next 3 questions were introductory questions regarding FinTech, the participants were asked if they have ever heard of FinTech, the source of their knowledge and their level of

		Frequency	Percentage	Mean	Standard Deviation
1- Age Group	18-25 Years	65	29.3%	2.14	0.844
	26-33 Years	60	27%		
	34 & above	97	43.7%		
2- The Highest level of degree	Secondary Education	11	5%	3.82	1.110
	Diploma	8	3.6%		
	Bachelors	69	31.1%		
	Masters	55	24.8%		
	PHD	79	35.6%		
3- Occupation Status	Student	56	25.2%	1.78	0.493
	Employee	158	71.2%		
	Unemployed	8	3.6%		
4- Concept of FinTech	Yes	210	94.6%	1.05	0.227
	No	12	5.4%		
5- Where?	Newspaper	17	8.1%	1.642	0.427
	Social Media	145	69.0%		
	Banks	56	26.7%		
	School/University	115	54.8%		
	Family/Friends	64	30.5%		
6- Level of FinTech understanding	Extremely knowledgeable	104	46.8%	1.59	0.601
	Slightly knowledgeable	105	47.3%		
	Not at all	13	5.9%		
7- The extent of how financial services will be replaced by humans	1	1	0.5%	3.65	0.808
	2	10	4.5%		
	3	88	39.6%		
	4	89	40.1%		
	5	34	15.3%		
8- Preference of using mobile applications over visiting the bank itself	Using mobile applications	214	96.4%	1.04	0.187
	Visiting the bank	8	3.6%		
9- Preferred methods to complete financial matters:	Cash	58	26.1%	2.43	1.215
	Debit Card	63	28.4%		
	Credit Card	75	33.8%		
	Cheque	0	0.0%		
	Mobile applications	26	11.7%		
10- The preferred method to pay when using FinTech	Mobile applications	94	42.3%	2.17	1.037
	Portable payment station (Sadad)	5	2.3%		
	Banking applications	114	51.4%		
	PayPal	9	4.1%		
11- Most used FinTech services	Money transfer and payments	85	38.3%	3.07	1.819
	Financial planning	17	7.7%		
	Insurance	3	1.4%		
	Borrowing and lending	31	14.0%		
	Saving investments	86	38.7%		
12- The sector that will be affected by financial tools	Banking	110	49.5%	2.72	1.853
	Insurance	11	5.0%		
	Securities	11	5.0%		
	Assets management	13	5.9%		
	Crowdfunding	76	34.2%		
	Start-ups	1	0.5%		
13- The key strengths of FinTech's value propositions	Ease of use	143	64.4%	1.512	0.426
	Lower cost	148	66.7%		
	Faster service	171	77.0%		
	Better client experience	48	21.6%		
	Wider variety of features	31	14.0%		
14- The opportunities related to the rise of FinTech	Expanding products/services	93	41.9%	1.658	0.456
	Leveraging existing analytics	83	37.4%		
	Increasing customer base	101	45.5%		
	Faster response to competition	113	50.9%		
	Reducing headcount cost	52	23.4%		
	Improving Retention of Customer	68	30.6%		
	Decreasing IT infrastructure costs	24	10.8%		

continued on following page

Table 2. Continued

		Frequency	Percentage	Mean	Standard Deviation
15- The financial activities that will be at risk when moving to a FinTech company within 5-10 years	Insurance payments	65	29.3%	1.673	0.449
	Personal loans	87	39.2%		
	Funds transfer	48	21.6%		
	Wealth management	38	17.1%		
	Personal finance	69	31.1%		
	Saving accounts	129	58.1%		
	None	1	0.5%		
16- The greatest challenges for FinTech companies	Achieving the scale	125	56.3%	2.2	1.565
	Talent recruitment	18	8.1%		
	Funding	23	10.4%		
	Gaining visibility and awareness	26	11.7%		
	Technological innovation	26	11.7%		
	Retention competition	4	1.8%		
17-The risky monitory issues if firms collaborated with FinTech	Customer-data privacy	58	26.1%	2.31	1.297
	Anti-money laundering compliance	100	45.0%		
	Risk of fraud	31	14.0%		
	Consumer protection	14	6.3%		
	Intellectual property rights	8	3.6%		
	Mis-selling of financial advice	11	5.0%		

understanding of the required topic. The final 10 questions were all FinTech related questions, targeted specifically for the banking experts (WomenInFinTech, 2019). Here are all the questions with the results:

Data Analysis and Statistics

The total number of respondents was 222, SPSS version 23.0 was used to analyze all the data. However, before conducting the analysis, the data was adjusted to adapt to the research requirements of students, employees and Ph.D. doctors who have a background in either banking or finance.

Table 2.

Hypothesis 1: A positive relationship exists between the ease of use in technology and the adoption of FinTech.

Hypothesis 2: A positive relationship exists between investment decision in crowdfunding and the adoption of FinTech

Hypothesis 3: A positive relationship exists between the level of risks and the adoption of FinTech.

Technological evolution in the financial sector is very fast, new corporations who offer financial services at low costs are emerging (PwC, 2016). These companies aren't included in the conventional

Table 3. Findings

Model	*Relationship between variables*	*F*	*t*	R^2	*B*
H1	Ease of use => Adoption of FinTech	232.159	15.237	0.513 ~ 51.3%	1.207
H2	Crowdfunding => Adoption of FinTech	96	9.752	0.351 ~ 35.1%	1.075
H3	Level of Risk =/> Adoption of FinTech	359.705	18.966	0.620 ~ 62%	1.301

Table 4.

	Synchronous eLearning	Asynchronous eLearning
When	• Discussing less complex issues. • Getting acquainted. • Planning tasks.	• Reflecting on complex issues. • When synchronous classes cannot be attended due to illness, work, family or other commitments.
Why	• Students become more committed and motivated due to getting quick response.	• Students have more time to reflect as the quick response is not immediately expected.
How	• In addition to face-to-face class, various synchronous means including video conferencing, instant messaging and conversation (chat) are used.	• Various asynchronous means such as e-mail, discussion boards, and blogs are used.
Online	Synchronous means: • Virtual Classroom. • Video/teleconferencing. • Conversation (chat) rooms/instant messaging.	Asynchronous means: • Web-based teaching/ computer based teaching. • Threaded discussion groups. • Recorded live events. • Online documents/ e-mail/global announcement.
Offline	Synchronous means: • Face to face classroom. • Hands on laboratory practices. • Field trips, field work.	Asynchronous means: • Bound books/ learning resources. • Videos/Echo360/Lectopia. • Audio tapes.
Examples	• Students work in groups and can use instant messaging as a support for getting to know each other, exchanging ideas, and planning tasks. • A teacher who wants to present concepts from the literature in a simplified way might give an online lecture by video conferencing.	• Students expected to reflect individually on course topics may be asked to maintain a blog. • Students are expected to share reflections regarding course topics and critically assess their peers' ideas. They may be asked to participate in online discussion on a discussion board.

financial service contributors primarily because they utilize progressive technology and internet to placate the ever-changing and developing needs of their consumers. Thus, they are put in a separate segment of the financial services, called FinTech. FinTech has been growing rather fast as a segment and has been able to sustain $27.4 billion in funds in 2017 (Accenture 2018). The USA sits as the undisputed front-runner where venture capital investments are concerned. Nevertheless, conventional financial services providers need to watch out for the development of FinTech, because it is occurring rapidly and if they fall behind in improving their policies and procedures as they will not be able to retain their market share and FinTech corporations could cause the effectiveness of the segment to decline.

DISCUSSION

This research is a brief study of the effectiveness of adopting FinTech's services for financial institutions in Bahrain. One correlation of quality can be observed in this paper is the Technology Acceptance Theory and the adoption of FinTech. Three other moderating variables can also be observed, they were tested to see the effect of the ease of use, crowdfunding in investment decisions and the level of risks in regard to the adoption of FinTech. This paper will focus on the effectiveness of adopting FinTech on the Technology Acceptance Theory, Decision Theory, and Prospect Theory.

Firstly, there was a positive relationship between the ease of use and the adoption of FinTech, as evident in the data analysis, (B= 1.207, $P <= 0.05$). Which means that the ease of use of FinTech increases the chances of financial institutions in adopting to FinTech. Adjusted R^2 was .513 referring to 52.3% of variation of ease of use affected the adoption of FinTech. Therefore, the relationship is significant and the hypothesis is accepted.

Secondly, there was a positive relationship between the adoption of FinTech and investment decisions in crowdfunding, as evident in the second hypothesis data analysis (B= 1.705, P <= 0.05). This concludes that the higher the investment decision in crowdfunding, the higher the acceptance of adopting FinTech in financial institutions. The adjusted R^2 was 0.351 referring to 35.1% of variation of investment decisions in crowdfunding in the adoption of FinTech. Therefore, the relationship is significant and the hypothesis is accepted.

Thirdly, there was a positive relationship between the level of risks and the adoption of FinTech, as shown in the third and last hypothesis data analysis (B=1.301, P <= 0.05). This theory has led us to believe that the higher the level of risks related to FinTech and its implementation, the less the effectiveness of adopting FinTech. The adjusted R^2 was 0.620 referring to affects the adoption of FinTech. Therefore, the relationship is significant and the hypothesis is accepted.

FUTURE RESEARCH DIRECTIONS

Nevertheless, like any other research paper, this research has a couple of limitations. A research method like surveys is great to enable a large number of responses while being cost-effective at the same time. Yet, this survey lacked sufficient response rate although it got distribution through WhatsApp and face to face, the respondents of (222) are considered low. This is due to the common fact that people lacked interest or did not feel the urgency to answer the online survey. Other than that, the consistency of the survey results cannot be ensured. As online surveys do not allow for interpreting body language and facial expressions. Therefore, participant's dishonesty might affect the credibility of the results. In order to overcome those limitations, the suggestion for conducting further research on the topic in the form of a questionnaire. This can be conducted with the same set of questions after a short amount of time to check the conformity and consistency of the participant's responses.

Furthermore, for future research method implementation aside from surveys, using the interview or focus group methods keeping in mind that it is time-consuming and costly. However, those types of research methods will provide the conformity aspect in the research by acknowledging and interpreting participant's body language and facial expressions. Hence, it will provide enhanced results that are valid and reliable more than surveys.

CONCLUSION

With FinTech being the new trend in the business world, many do not understand whether it is actually beneficial or not. The main purpose of this research is to understand the overall relationship between the adoption of FinTech in current business and the factors like ease of use, risks in adoption and investment decision in crowdfunding. Further, the research highlighted the correlation between those two variables by considering the benefits and risks of FinTech activities.

In the literature review, there are many factors affecting the adoption of FinTech. It was found that the ease of use of technology (Technology Acceptance Theory), investment decisions in crowdfunding (Decision Theory) and the risks involved in the adoption of FinTech (Prospect Theory) are the main factors that might affect the adoption of FinTech. However, there is a paucity of studies linking all these factors in the adoption of FinTech using these theories. This research investigated the influence of these factors in the adoption of FinTech. In order to analyze these factors, a questionnaire was used. Financial experts or those who are currently pursuing their finance or banking degree mostly answered the survey. As a result, it was found that there is a positive relationship between the ease of use and FinTech's adoption. It was also found that there was another positive relationship between FinTech's adoption and investment decisions in crowdfunding. Lastly, a positive relationship was found between the levels of risks when adopting to FinTech.

REFERENCES

A Google trend search reveals that the interest over time for the word "Fintech" increased exponentially in 2014. (n.d.). https://www.google.com/trends/explore#q=fintech

Accenture. (2018). *Global Venture Capital Investment in Fintech in 2017.* https://newsroom.accenture.com/news/global-venture-capital-investment-in-fintech-industryset-record-in2017-driven-by-surge-in-india-us-and-uk-accenture-analysis-finds.html

Alt, Beck, & Smits. (2018, August 13). FinTech and the transformation of the financial industry. Springer Berlin Heidelberg. doi:10.100712525-018-0310-9

Bahrain, E. D. B. B. (2017, June). *Invest in experience. Financial services in Bahrain.* Retrieved from Economic Development Board: https://bahrainedb.com/app/uploads/2017/06/Financial-Services-A4-Brochure-Jun2017.pdf

Bates, R. (2017, July). *Banking on the Future: An Exploration of FinTech and The Consumer Interest.* Retrieved from Consumers International: https://www.consumersinternational.org/media/154710/banking-on-the-future-full-report.pdf

BBC News. (2015). *Why do many Americans mistrust the Federal Reserve?* https://www.bbc.com/news/business-35079495

Bradley Rice, L. J. (2018, February). *Implications of fintech developments for banks and bank supervisors.* Retrieved from Bank for International Settlement: https://www.bis.org/bcbs/publ/d431.pdf

Brunsden, J. (2016). *New EU laws legitimize fintech challengers.* https://www.ft.com/content/3803914a-6eba-11e6-a0c9-1365ce54b926

Bugrov, D., Dietz, M., & Poppensieker, T. (2017). *A brave new world for global banking.* McKinsey & Company https://www.mckinsey.com/industries/financial-services/our-insights/abrave-new-world-for-global-banking

Carpenter, C. (2017, May). *FinTech, Green Finance, and Developing Countries.* Retrieved from Green-Invest: http://unepinquiry.org/wp-content/uploads/2017/06/Fintech_Green_Finance_and_Developing_Countries-input-paper.pdf

Chu, P. Y. (2015). An Empirical Assessment of a Modified Technology Acceptance Model. *Journal of Management Information Systems*, 185–204.

Cockton, G. (2013). *The Encyclopedia of Human-Computer Interaction*. Interaction Design Foundation.

Courbe, J. (2016). *Financial Services Technology 2020 and Beyond: Embracing disruption*. Retrieved from Pricewaterhousecoopers: https://www.pwc.com/gx/en/financial-services/assets/pdf/technology2020-and-beyond.pdf

Deloitte. (2017). *Regulatory Sandbox – Making India a Global Fintech Club*. https://www2.deloitte.com/content/dam/Deloitte/in/Documents/technology-media-telecommunications/intmt-fintech-regulatory-sandbox-web.pdf

Deloitte. (2017). *Fintech by numbers*. https://www2.deloitte.com/content/dam/Deloitte/us/Documents/financial-services/us-dcfs-fintech-by-thenumbers-web.pdf

Douglas, W., & Arner, J. B. (2015, October 20). *The Evolution of FinTech: A New Post-Crisis Paradigm?* Retrieved from University of Hong Kong: https://hub.hku.hk/bitstream/10722/221450/1/Content.pdf

FinTech Innovation Lab. (2018). *Mind the gap: Addressing challenges to FinTech adoption*. Retrieved from Accenture: https://www.accenture.com/t00010101T000000Z__w__/gb-en/_acnmedia/PDF-74/Accenture-FinTech-Challenges-Adoption.pdf

Gurria, A. (2008, January). *Organization for Economic Co-Operation and Development Annual Report*. Retrieved from Organisation for Economic Co-operation and Development: https://www.oecd.org/newsroom/40556222.pdf

Hansson, S. O. (2005, January). *Decision Theory: A Brief Introduction*. Retrieved from Royal Institute of Technology: https://www.researchgate.net/publication/210642121_Decision_Theory_A_Brief_Introduction

Hochstein. (2015). *Fintech (the Word, That Is) Evolves*. The American Banker at https://www.americanbanker.com/bankthink/fintech-the-word-that-is-evolves-1077098-1.html

Ichikawa, J. J. (2017, March 7). *The Analysis of Knowledge*. Retrieved from Stanford Encyclopedia of Philosophy: https://plato.stanford.edu/entries/knowledge-analysis/

Ismail, N. (2018, April 17). *The cybersecurity challenges facing emerging fintech startups*. Retrieved from Information Age: https://www.information-age.com/cyber-security-challenges-emerging-fintech-startups-123471506/

Jahangir, N., & Begum, N. (2008, January 28). *The role of perceived usefulness, perceived ease of use, security, and privacy, and customer attitude to engender customer adaptation in the context of electronic banking*. Retrieved from African Journal of Business Managemen: https://academicjournals.org/article/article1380536538_Jahangir%2520and%2520%2520Begum.pdf

Jargons, B. (2017, January). *Investment Decision*. Retrieved from Business Jargons: https://businessjargons.com/investment-decision.html

Kagan, J. (2019, May 17). *Financial Technology & Automated Investing*. Retrieved from Investopedia: https://www.investopedia.com/terms/f/fintech.asp

Lai, P. (2017). The literature review of technology adoption models and theories for the novelty technology. *Journal of Information Systems and Technology Management*, *14*(1), 21–38. doi:10.4301/S1807-17752017000100002

Martell, J. (2018, August 20). *Advantages & Disadvantages of FinTech-Focused IoT*. Retrieved from A Medium Corporate: https://medium.com/@jasonmartell/advantages-and-disadvantages-of-fintech-focused-iot-85aa72a7bd68

McKinsey, C. (2018, October). *Global Payment 2018: A dynamic industry continues to break new ground*. Retrieved from Global Banking: https://www.mckinsey.com/~/media/McKinsey/Industries/Financial%20Services/Our%20Insights/Global%20payments%20Expansive%20growth%20targeted%20opportunities/Global-payments-map-2018.ashx

Moody's: Threat of Cyber Attack on US Utilities cushioned by the likelihood of government support. (2015). https://www.moodys.com/research/Moodys-Threat-of-cyber-attack-on-US-utilities-cushioned-byPR_336640

Panetta, F. (2018, May 12). *FinTech and Banking: Today and Tomorrow*. Retrieved from Harvard Law School Bicentennial: https://www.bis.org/review/r180515d.pdf

Pejkovska, M. (2018, April 24). *Potential negative effects of FinTech on the financial services sector*. Retrieved from Helsinki Metropolia University of Applied Sciences: https://www.theseus.fi/bitstream/handle/10024/148416/Maja_Pejkovska_Theseus.pdf?sequence=1&isAllowed=y

PwC. (2016). *Financial Services Technology 2020 and Beyond: Embracing Disruption*. Retrieved from PwC: https://www.pwc.com/gx/en/financial-services/assets/pdf/technology2020-and-beyond.pdf

Ryu, H.-S. (2018). *Understanding Benefit and Risk Framework of Fintech Adoption: Comparison of Early Adopters and Late Adopters*. Retrieved from 51st Hawaii International Conference on System Sciences: http://hdl.handle.net/10125/50374

Schilder, A. (2005, April 29). *Compliance and the compliance function in the banks*. Retrieved from Bank for International Settlements: https://www.bis.org/publ/bcbs113.pdf

Scotland, J. (2012, May 27). *Exploring the Philosophical Underpinnings of Research: Relating Ontology and Epistemology to the Methodology and Methods of the Scientific, Interpretive, and Critical Research Paradigms*. Retrieved from Canadian Center of Science and Education: https://pdfs.semanticscholar.org/f24f/1d16645ee19b0263f4c377d9e086ed277a3c.pdf

Srivastav, S. (2019, January 9). *The Fintech Effect: What it Would Mean for Your Business in 2019?* Retrieved from AppInventiv: https://appinventiv.com/blog/impact-of-fintech-on-your-business/

Thomas, W., & Malone, J. Y. (1987, June). *Electronic Markets and Electronic Hierarchies*. Retrieved from Communications of the ACM: https://www.researchgate.net/publication/220425850_Electronic_Markets_and_Electronic_Hierarchies

Varga, D. (2017, November). *FinTech, The New Era of Financial Services.* Retrieved from Budapest Management Review: https://core.ac.uk/download/pdf/132273819.pdf

WomenInFinTech. (2019, May 26). *Understanding the role of women in the emerging industry.* Retrieved from Bahrain Women in FinTech: https://bahrainfintechbay.us10.list-manage.com/track/click?u=ede0050de3961e3f5d090d405&id=741989aef6&e=3d358071f2

APPENDIX

The Institute of Museum and Library Services has collected some interesting statistics indicating that despite the sharp decline in library usage over the last ten years, libraries have actually seen an *increase* in the number of people who come through their doors annually since the beginning of the current recessionary period in 2008. Was this a contradiction, or some kind of error? Table 5 shows the data in question.

Table 5. Visits to public libraries (Data source: National Center for Education Statistics, 1998-2007)

Year	Per Capita Visit to Public Library	Year	Per Capita Visit to Public Library
1998	4.2	2003	4.6
1999	4.3	2004	4.6
2000	4.3	2005	4.7
2001	4.4	2006	4.8
2002	4.4	2007	5.0

Chapter 15
The Adoption of E-Wallets:
Current Trends and Future Outlook

Adel Ismail Al-Alawi
https://orcid.org/0000-0003-0775-4406
University of Bahrain, Bahrain

Ali H. Al-Hammam
University of Bahrain, Bahrain

S. Sadiq Al-Alawi
University of Bahrain, Bahrain

Ebtesam Ismaeel AlAlawi
University of Bahrain, Bahrain

ABSTRACT

This chapter measures the attitudes of people residing in the Kingdom of Bahrain toward adopting mobile banking technology, also known as e-Wallets. The Technology Acceptance Model, the Unified Theory of Acceptance and Use of Technology, and the Diffusion of Innovations model were used to construct a questionnaire with the added focus on the promotional aspects. A total of 1,740 responses obtained from individuals in Bahrain revealed a high level of adoption rates. All dimensions measured were confirmed to have a significant impact on the adoption of e-Wallets, particularly those related to promotional benefits, which reveals a need for future studies to focus on the marketing approaches of mobile payment technologies. Studied factors were confirmed to have a significant impact on the usage and adoption of e-Wallets in the Kingdom of Bahrain. More focus is required from a benefits perspective rather than the technical perspective. Financial institutions need to pay more considerable attention to the changing mindsets of people toward making payments and the shift to new technologies.

DOI: 10.4018/978-1-7998-3257-7.ch015

INTRODUCTION

In recent years, technology has been advancing payment systems at an unprecedented level, especially through mobile devices. Consequently, methods of making payments through smartphones have been studied over the past two decades. Mallat (2007) listed several characteristics that make smartphones unique for making payments. They are widespread, they can be carried in people's hands, unlike fixed-line phones and computers, and they rely on well-established telecom infrastructures to facilitate micropayment transactions. Another study done by Dahlberg Mallat and Ondrus (2008) confirmed how mobile phones transformed the telecom industry, which allowed it to capitalize on new technologies by incorporating value-added services such as e-commerce and payment tools. The usage of mobile phones far exceeds other technical devices that could also be used to market, sell, produce, or deliver products and services to consumers. These developments open lucrative opportunities to merchants and service providers (Dahlberg, Mallat, Ondrus, & Zmijewska, 2008; Al-Alawi & Al-Bassam, 2019).

In a study conducted by de Lunaa, Cabanillas, & Fernándezb (2018), the researchers noticed that payment systems have changed and evolved from simple methods of cash and credit payments to more advanced payment methods that use mobile devices. Increasingly, transactions performed with the most recent technologies of mobile payment systems. On the other hand, the study tried to provide reasons for such developments by clarifying that "this transition has taken place due to changes in the economy, technological developments on the internet, the proliferation of social networks, and increased use of mobile devices." (de Lunaa, Cabanillas, & Fernándezb, 2019).

In addition, Oliveira, Tomas, Babpista & Campos (2016) elaborated that the improvements in technology have supported the economy through improved smartphone payment methods. They added that "advance in technology have enabled a broad range of new functionalities for mobile devices, supporting several mobile financial services, such as bill payment, account transfers, person to person transfers, proximity payments at the point of sale, remote payments to purchase goods and services, as well as other kinds of services such as location-based, mobile marketing, ticketing, discounts, or coupons" (Oliveira et al. 2016).

According to a recent study by Rolfe (2019), "Mobile wallets are still in early development in most countries, where some areas are starting to see an uptick in success. Worldwide, 2.07 billion consumers will use a mobile wallet to [purchase] in 2019; this is up nearly 30 percent from the 1.6 billion consumers recorded at the end of 2017. China is currently the largest adopter of mobile payments, but other countries are starting to catch up."

Several models have been developed and tested to measure how people respond to different technologies. In this study, we will first cover the most commonly reviewed and tested models and shed light on studies done in other countries on adoption rates of mobile banking applications, or e-Wallets.

The purpose of this study is to measure the attitudes toward the adoption of the different e-Wallets available in the Kingdom of Bahrain. It has been built on a combination of models with an additional construct focusing on Promotional Benefits. Therefore, this study aims at exploring the engagement level of people in Bahrain with regards to e-Wallets in their financial activities. In addition, the motivational factors, as well as the risks associated with the concept of e-Wallets, have been elaborated and empirically tested.

Based on the quantitative measurements provided throughout this paper, this study will provide empirical evidence that will test the adoption level of e-Wallets in the Kingdom of Bahrain. Also, this study will provide a basis for business practitioners to understand better consumer perspectives on using e-Wallets in terms of the incentives and associated risks. Furthermore, the recommendations proposed in this study will shed light on the crucial aspects of e-Wallets that service providers should focus on when promoting the use of e-Wallets.

The evolution of e-Wallet concepts in the world since 1997, combined with the enhancement of related technologies, gives this topic increased attention and continuous focus to support the economy and facilitate the financial payments of consumers. Accordingly, taking into consideration the lack of studies in the Kingdom of Bahrain, this study meets the need for empirical evidence to understand the adoption level of e-Wallets among people in the Kingdom of Bahrain.

LITERATURE REVIEW

Several studies have investigated how individual people respond to new technologies; as a result, several models have been suggested by different researchers. Lai (2017) published *The Literature Review of Technology Adoption Models and Theories,* which discussed several models such as:

- Theory of Diffusion of Innovations (DOI) (Rogers, 1995),
- Theory of Reasonable Action (TRA) (Fishbein and Ajzen, 1975),
- Theory of Planned Behavior (TPB) (Ajzen, 1985, 1991),
- Decomposed Theory of Planned Behaviour (Taylor and Todd, 1995),
- Technology Acceptance Model (TAM) (Davis, Bogozzi and Warshaw, 1989),
- Technology Acceptance Model 2 (TAM2) (Venkatesh and Davis, 2000), and
- Technology Acceptance Model 3 (TAM3) (Venkatesh and Bala, 2008).

The Technology Acceptance Model is one of the most commonly used and tested models among different researchers and studies since Fred Davis first introduced it in 1986 for his doctoral proposal. The model was an extension of the Theory of Reasonable Action, and it was tailored specifically for measuring how people respond to new information systems (Lai, 2017). Davis further developed the model in 1989, and it has since gone through a series of developments and improvements (TAM2 and TAM3). TAM and its extensions have been widely tested and compare favorably to other models partly due to the extensive attention it has received (Venkatesh, Davis, & Morris, 2007).

On the other hand, as illustrated in Figure 1 below, some technology adoption theories focused on studying the readiness of people to accept and adopt new technology. By classifying them into five stages, starting with innovators, early adopters, and an initial majority, followed by those coming late called late majority and finally laggards, who wait until the end to adopt new technology (Rogers, 1983). In their book *Techno-Ready Marketing: How and Why Customers Adopt Technology*, Parasuraman, and Colby (2001) defined Technology Readiness (TR) as "people's propensity to embrace and use of new technologies for accomplishing goals in home life and at work, and based on individual's technology readiness score and the technology readiness," and classified technology consumers into five Technology Readiness categories: explorers, pioneers, skeptics, paranoids, and laggards.

Therefore, our study has adopted a combined model of Technology Acceptance Model (TAM), Unified Theory of Acceptance and Use of Technology (UTAUT), and Diffusion of Innovations (DOI) models with an additional construct focusing on Promotional Benefits.

History of e-Wallets

As indicated by Inuit Inc. (2017), the history of making payments through mobile devices and mobile commerce originated in 1997 when "Coca-Cola set up several vending machines that accepted payment through text messages." Later on, "in 1998, the online payment system PayPal was established, by 2015, it was the biggest online payment system in the world, with more than 4 billion payments," which was elaborated on by Mercer (2015). To show the progress of e-Wallets and mobile payments, (Blockchain. info (2017) stated that "in 2017, PayPal had nearly 10 million monthly transactions."

Figure 1. Diffusion of Innovation Model, adopted from (Rogers, 1983)

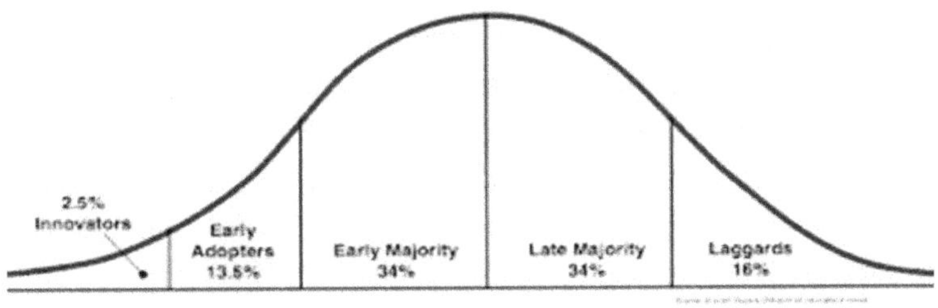

Practical Cases From Several Selected Countries

Technology acceptance and adoption tests have been executed in several countries around the world. The following is a discussion of sample cases that includes a summary of how the tests were done in addition to the results concluded by the researchers. In a recent study conducted in Malaysia, a total of 300 students and workers aged between 18 and 39 years were asked about their intentions to adopt mobile payment technologies using an adopted TAM model consisting of four constructs: perceived usefulness, perceived ease of use, perceived credibility, and social influence (Mun, Khalid, & Nadarajah, 2017). The study found a significant positive relationship between the four measured dimensions and the intention to use mobile payment services in Malaysia (Mun, Khalid, & Nadarajah, 2017).

Another study done in Portugal surveyed 301 students and alumni from universities in Portugal, aged from 18 to 66 years with a median of 29 years. It tested customers' intentions to use new payment technologies and recommend it to others (Oliveira et al. 2016). The researchers used a combined model of UTAUT2 and DOI in addition to perceived technology security. The constructs used were Performance Expectancy, Efforts Expectancy, Social Influence, Facilitating Conditions, Hedonic Motivation, and Price Value from UTAUT2, and Compatibility and Innovativeness from DOI, with an additional construct representing Perceived Technology Security. The study found a significant relationship between compatibility, innovativeness, perceived technology security, performance expectation, and social influence, and the adoption of mobile payments and intention to recommend it to others. On the other side, the study did not find a significant relationship between Facilitating Conditions, Hedonic Motivation, or Price Value, and customer adoption of new payment technologies and their intention to recommend it to others. The study made some practical and theoretical recommendations for practitioners and researchers. For practical implications, the study found that well-informed customers are more likely to adopt mobile payment and accordingly recommended advertising through different tools to explain the main benefits of usage in addition to available security features, which lead to higher usage rates. Target marketing focusing on a user's lifestyle revealed from compatibility construct results will improve usage rates. On the security side, the study recommends higher investments into having sufficient resources to ensure the most secure environment possible. To capture potential users' attention, promotional benefits should be advertised in marketing campaigns focusing on faster shopping, productivity gains, security, and the ability to conduct payments anywhere and anytime. The study emphasizes the influence of social networks and their potential to help marketers reach a wider audience. For theoretical recommendations, the study showed the power of their combined model, showing a predictive power of 61.3% (versus 42% in other sample studies) (Oliveira, Thomas, Baptista, & Campos, 2016).

Another study conducted by Madan & Yadav (2016) covered a sample of 210 postgraduate students and working professionals from the Delhi National Capital Region (Delhi NCR) in India who were likely to have an internet-enabled smartphone and bank account, mainly focusing on people under 30 years old (81.4%). The study used TAM and UTAUT in their second extensions (TAM2 & UTAUT2) and added Perceived Regulatory Support (PRS) and Promotional Benefits (PB), which resulted in a model consisting of 9 constructs: Performance Expectancy (PE), Effort Expectancy (EE), Social Influence (SI), Facilitating Conditions (FC), Perceived Value (PV), Perceived Risk (PR), Perceived Trust (PT), Perceived Regulatory Support (PRS), and Promotional Benefits (PB).

The results of the study confirmed a significant impact of all factors considered in the study except for Efforts Expectancy (EE), which had no significant effect on users. The researchers explained this with two main issues that had arisen previously but have both been resolved with advancements in technology. Previously, the small screen sizes of mobile phones along with lower bandwidth and slower connectivity could both negatively impact a user's intention to adopt mobile technologies. Still, with the introduction of smartphones and larger screen sizes (compared to screens available before smartphones) in addition to the introduction of speedy 3G and 4G mobile internet connections, those issues have been eliminated.

The study referred to several limitations, one of which was the focus on measuring only customers' points of view and ignoring the ecosystem that surrounds the process, including different stakeholders like mobile wallet service providers, merchants, technology providers, and financial institutions, as well as governments (Madan & Yadav, 2016).

Kingdom of Bahrain Cases

Although the Kingdom of Bahrain is a pioneer country in the Middle East with regards to the adoption of mobile payment technologies, there is a significant shortage in studies conducted in this area. However, several studies discussing advanced mobile technologies and e-commerce applications have been conducted and performed.

In their study about e-commerce in Bahrain, Henary & Mahboob (2008) evaluated the level of awareness about the different e-commerce applications and the level of usage among the participants. With a sample size of 500 university students from Bahrain, only 18% participated in e-commerce activities. The main constraint found by the authors was security: "Even though it being the electronic age with internet usage growing at a tremendous rate, but when it comes to ordering online, organizations and individuals still face resistance" (Henary & Mahboob, 2008). Furthermore, Al-Alawi & Al-Ali (2015, p. 5) stated that "e-Commerce is not just about using new technologies. E-Commerce offers a wide range of services and opportunities for electronic trading in the international marketplace".

There have also been multiple types of research conducted on mobile banking that examine the current and future advances in the use of the Internet and the latest technologies in the banking industry. Awadhi (2013) conducted a study with over 360 participants to measure the level of adoption and acceptance of mobile banking in the Kingdom of Bahrain. The study concluded that around 76% of participants have a positive behavioral intention towards mobile banking concerning the comfort level of the tasks being handled by mobile banking.

Another study measuring the critical determination factors that affect the attitudes of customers toward mobile banking in the Kingdom of Bahrain was conducted by Mashhour & Saleh (2015). With a total of 246 banking customers, the study concluded that participants have an outstanding level of awareness of mobile banking. However, 68.4% of respondents reported that they do not trust the services provided through mobile banking.

Even though there are plenty of international e-Wallets that offer their services worldwide, like ApplePay and PayPal, there are many domestic e-Wallet options in the Kingdom of Bahrain. The main advantages of those e-Wallets over international applications are the promotional benefits and associated services. Below is a summary of these e-Wallets and a brief description of each one:

- *Benefit-Pay* is the national e-Wallet application in the Kingdom of Bahrain that has enabled mobile payment systems. It allows consumers to use all Electronic Fund Transfer System (EFTS) services.
- *B-wallet* is an e-Wallet system provided by Bahrain Telecommunications Company (Batelco). It has been introduced as a mobile e-wallet application that enables consumers to conduct their daily consumption trends digitally in a comfortable and secure manner.
- *Max-Wallet* is a virtual e-Wallet application introduced by CrediMax, a credit card company owned by the Bank of Bahrain and Kuwait that enables consumers to conduct purchases and payments using their mobiles and smart tablets in an easy and convenient way.
- *STC Pay Wallet*, which is offered by the Bahraini branch of the Saudi Telecom Company STC, has provided support for various merchants' payments with plenty of promotional offers. It has empowered consumers to control their purchases and payments with secure and efficient procedures.

Model Constructs

To analyze the conceptual framework of the study, the following section explains in detail the relationships between the constructs and the corresponding hypotheses tested in our study, followed by a summary of the relationships in Figure 2.

Performance Expectancy

To thoroughly examine this construct, it would be beneficial to present the different definitions of Performance Expectancy. To start with, Venkatesh et al. (2012) argued that the customer would view Performance Expectancy as the extent to which using the technology will provide additional benefits to them while performing different activities. Additionally, they emphasized that from this perspective, it is the most influential construct on Behavioral

On the other hand, and in the context of this paper which has been established from the e-Wallets aspect, Madan and Yadav (2016) defined Performance Expectancy as "the degree to which consumers perceive that using it as an alternative technology for making payments will improve and speed up their performance while conducting their daily sales and purchasing transactions."

In addition, Lee et al. (2004) discussed the role of technology and various social elements in adopting mobile payment technologies. They emphasized the importance of Performance Expectancy as a significant constituent of the Behavioral Intention toward the successful movement to the adoption of these technologies.

Moreover, Shine (2009), Kim et al. (2010), Wang and Yi (2012), Pham and Ho (2014), and Slade et al. (2015) have adopted the theory explained and emphasized by Venkatesh et al. (2003), which holds that four major elements directly determine the intention to use technology and the Behavioral Intention, namely: "performance expectancy, effort expectancy, social influence, and facilitating conditions."

Similar concepts have been integrated previously in other conceptual frameworks developed by Davis (1989). Consistent with the Performance Expectancy construct, Davis (1989) built the Technology Acceptance Model (TAM) on a construct called Perceived Usefulness (PU). Davis (1989) defined Perceived Usefulness (PU) as "the degree to which a person believes that using a particular system would enhance his or her job performance" (320).

After the initial adoption of the Technology Acceptance Model, several models have been extended from and enhanced the initial model developed by Davis. The importance of Performance Expectancy as a significant construct in the developed models has been reaffirmed by Venkatesh and Davis (2000) in the Technology Acceptance Model 2 (TAM2) as well as by Venkatesh and Bala (2008) in the Technology Acceptance Model 3 (TAM3).

In his theory of diffusion, Rogers (1995) states: "One of the main reasons for the slow diffusion of mobile applications in general and mobile payment, in particular, could be a failure in communicating a clear benefit to potential users. According to diffusion theory, users are only willing to accept innovations if those innovations provide a unique advantage compared to existing solutions." Based on the previous argument, it is hypothesized that:

H1. The higher the Performance Expectancy is, the higher the Behavioral Intention to adopt a mobile wallet will be.

Effort Expectancy

While discussing the acceptance of customers and the impact on technology, Venkatesh et al. (2012) defined Effort Expectancy based on the consumer's point of view. Their definition of Effort Expectancy is "the degree of ease associated with consumers' use of technology" (Venkatesh et al., 2012, 159). Another definition comes from Madan and Yadav (2016), who developed a model to determine the constructs that lead to the Behavioral Intention to adopt the new technology of mobile wallets. In their conceptual model, they have defined Effort Expectancy as "the extent to which consumers expect mobile wallet technology to be free from effort and easy enough to learn, to be adopted in their daily lives" (Madan and Yadav, 2016).

A similar concept had been used in the Technology Acceptance Model developed by Davis, but it fell under the construct Perceived Ease of Use (PEOU). PEOU was defined by Davis (1989) as "the degree to which a person believes that using a particular system would be free of effort" (320).

Venkatesh et al. (2003) emphasized the relevance of Effort Expectancy to the Unified Theory of Acceptance and Use of Technology (UTAUT). Thus the model was constructed from the perspective of the information systems of the organization.

Additionally, when Lee et al. (2004) and Schierz et al. (2010) examined the role of technology and other social influences on behavioral intentions and the adoption of mobile payment tools, they accepted Effort Expectancy as one of the constructs that will determine the level of adoption by end-users.

Dahlberg et al. (2003) conducted an empirical study on 61 consumers of different ages and professions. By analyzing group interviews, they identified the significant factors that contribute to consumers' acceptance of various systems of mobile payment. Using special coding to analyze the comments and feedback from the participants, the researchers identified three major factors that should be considered while studying the level of acceptance of using mobile payment tools, namely: "perceived ease of use, perceived usefulness, and trust" (Dahlberg et al., 2013). This has generally been explained by the fact that there is a level of satisfaction with the adoption of new technologies for mobile payments.

Research conducted by Pagani & Schipani (2005) criticized the importance of this factor for mobile payment services. One of the essential aspects that must be considered to allow new mobile payment technologies to compete with traditional means of payment is the level of effort consumers expect to perform. For this reason, Pagani and Schipani (2005) identified that "important aspects related to mobile payment services ease of use include, for example, clear symbols and function keys, few and simple payment process steps, graphic display, and help functions." Therefore, we hypothesize that

H2. The higher the Effort Expectancy is, the higher the Behavioral Intention to adopt a mobile wallet will be.

Social Influence

Venkatesh et al. (2012) defined Social Influence as "the extent to which consumers perceive that important others (e.g., family and friends) believe they should use a particular technology" (159).

Riquelme and Rios (2010) conducted research to identify factors that impact the adoption of mobile banking in Singapore, focusing on the moderating consequences of certain demographic factors. The study collected opinions from over 600 mobile banking users regarding "their intention to use mobile banking, perceptions of the relative advantage of the mobile device, perception of risk, social norms, ease of use and usefulness of the device for banking purposes" (Riquelme and Rios, 2010). Even though the sample selected is biased toward people who are current users of mobile banking, the findings of the research can be used and discussed for further analysis and study. Social Influence, as represented by social norms and social risk, has been identified in the study as an influential construct that will impact the intention to adopt mobile banking. As stated by Riquelme and Rios (2010), "[u]sefulness, social norms and social risk, in this order, are the factors that influence the intention to adopt mobile banking services the most."

Social Influence has been embedded in several papers that have analyzed the adoption of mobile payments, e.g., by Amoroso and Magnier-Watanabe (2012). By using the Unified Theory of Acceptance and Use of Technology (UTAUT), Shin (2009) examined the adoption of mobile wallets. The paper has proposed four constructs, including Social Influence. The research found that two factors, security, and trust, influence the customer's intention to use mobile wallets, which will contribute to the determination of the actual behavior of the potential user. Importantly, the research suggested that Social Influence will enhance those two factors.

Emphasizing the importance of Social Influence on the adoption of the technological solutions of wireless finance, Kleijnen et al. (2004) concluded in his study that there is a significant role for the Social Influence on the adoption of these technologies. The empirical study collected responses from 203 mall shoppers and reached the outstanding finding that "social influence offers challenging opportunities to mobile services providers. The results suggest that advertising should focus more on situational contexts rather than on the functional aspects of mobile services. Moreover, positive word of mouth seems more important than ever, bearing in mind that friends or colleagues might play a key role in persuading consumers to use mobile services" (Kleijnen et al., 2004). Based on the statements above, the following hypothesis is formed:

H3. The higher the degree of Social Influence is, the higher the behavioral intention to adopt a mobile wallet will be.

Perceived Value

One of the main definitions of Perceived Value was explained by Zeithaml (1988) as a "trade-off between what customers are receiving (in the form of quality, benefits, and utilities) and what they are sacrificing for it (mainly in the form of price)."

To examine the Behavioral Intention among consumers to adopt the technological advancements represented by the mobile wallet, Madan and Yadav (2016) conducted a study to identify and understand the various factors that will impact the Behavioral Intention of consumers to adopt alternative methods to process day-to-day purchases, namely mobile wallets. The research was conducted on a sample of 210 mobile users. It characterized the adoption of mobile payments with many constructs, including Perceived Value, which they defined as "the value that consumers perceive they are to receive in exchange for the price that they pay to avail any product or service" (Madan and Yadav, 2016). The final findings of the study were that "performance expectancy, social influence, facilitating conditions, perceived risk, perceived value, PRS, as well as PBs, [were] significant factors in predicting behavioral intentions to adopt mobile wallet solutions" (Madan and Yadav, 2016).

A remarkable qualitative study was conducted by Slade et al. (2015) on the adoption level of consumers for new electronic payment mechanisms, focusing on mobile payments. The researchers generated empirical data from six focus groups to analyze and interpret. The study found that various applications of Perceived Value are behind the level of consumer's adoption of mobile payments. The study stated that "[t]he results suggest that the relative advantages of mobile payments include time and place independence, availability, possibilities for remote purchases, and queue avoidance. The interviewees found mobile payments to be mostly compatible with digital content and service purchases and to complement small value cash payments" (Slade et al., 2015).

Different applications have been generated from the enhanced technologies in the last decades. E-Wallets, online banking, and other mobile commerce technologies are clear examples of internet-based technologies. Among the different constructs, Perceived Value is an integral part of the adoption process of those new technologies. This finding can be found clearly in several papers like those by Pagani (2004),; Al-Alawi (2005); Amoroso & Magnier-Watanabe (2012; Al-Alawi (2018).

Perceived Value has been identified as one of the important constituents that shape consumers' intention to adopt new technologies. Such findings can be identified in the Unified Theory of Acceptance and Use of Technology 2 (UTAUT 2) model adopted by various studies, like Venkatesh et al. (2012).

With that abovementioned statements, the following hypothesis is formed:

H4. The higher the Perceived Value is, the higher the Behavioral Intention to adopt a mobile wallet will be.

Perceived Risk

Wu and Wang (2005) conducted an empirical study to evaluate the revised Technology Acceptance Model (TAM) by integrating diffusion theory and two other dominant constructs: Perceived Risk and Associated Cost. The paper defined Perceived Risk concerning online transactions performed through mobile payments and mobile commerce. The definition is comprehensive and can be referenced: "The definition of perceived risk has changed since online transactions became popular, in the past, perceived risks were primarily regarded as a fraud and product quality, today, perceived risk refers to certain types of financial, product performance, social, psychological, physical, or time risks when consumers make transactions online" (Wu and Wang, 2005). The study found that Perceived Risk has a significant positive influence on the behavioral intention to use online transaction technology.

Hence, the Perceived Value and Perceived Risk in online stores have been emphasized and investigated in several studies. Vila and Kurster (2011), in their paper about the consumer's feelings and their consequent behavior on websites, have criticized that the Perceived Risk can be identified as a driven factor and a significant predictor of the consumer's behavior in the online environment. Zha et al. (2013) have concluded that the Perceived Risk will harm the online experience of customers.

Another aspect of risk has been mentioned and evaluated by Madan and Yadav (2016), where they have shined a light on the risk driven by the use of mobile phones to make online payments. In their study, they drew attention to the risk embedded in the usage of mobile phones: "Mobile phones usually store important personal information, which gives rise to the issues of security and privacy risks that are involved in making any transaction via a mobile wallet" (Madan and Yadav, 2016).

Concerning the different dimensions of Perceived Risk in the process of mobile payments and e-Wallet experiences, several studies have demonstrated a wide variety of aspects that should be considered and evaluated to minimize the negative consequences attached to mobile payments and therefore enhance the behavioral intention to adopt e-Wallets. Kim et al. (2005) illustrated many dimensions and aspects in their model of the different types of Perceived Risk and associated risk reduction strategies to improve and enhance high-tech services and technologies, such as "financial, performance, psychological, physical, and social risk."

Based on the abovementioned literature, the following hypothesis is formed:

H5. The lower the Perceived Risk is, the higher the behavioral intention to adopt a mobile wallet will be.

Promotional Benefits

To elaborate on this construct based on the literature reviews conducted by several studies, it is important to consider that this particular research has been established to examine the adoption of the e-Wallets from a consumer perspective. Therefore, the perception of the benefits provided by the service provider has significance for the Behavioral Intention of the users. In defining the nature of Promotional Benefits Madan and Yadav (2016) clarified that the "Promotional Benefits may include various kinds of benefits such as app download cash rewards, coupon codes, cash discounts, loyalty points and other freebies which are offered by companies involved in providing mobile wallet services."

H6. The higher the Promotional Benefits are, the higher the Behavioral Intention to adopt a mobile wallet will be.

Conceptual Framework

Based on the above demonstration of the factors below and reviewing the research background, the conceptual research framework was formulated in Figure 2 to illustrate in detail the relationships between the constructs and the corresponding hypotheses tested in this study. It is expected that all the key elements in the conceptual model have a positive impact on customer behavior

Figure 2. Conceptual Framework of the Study

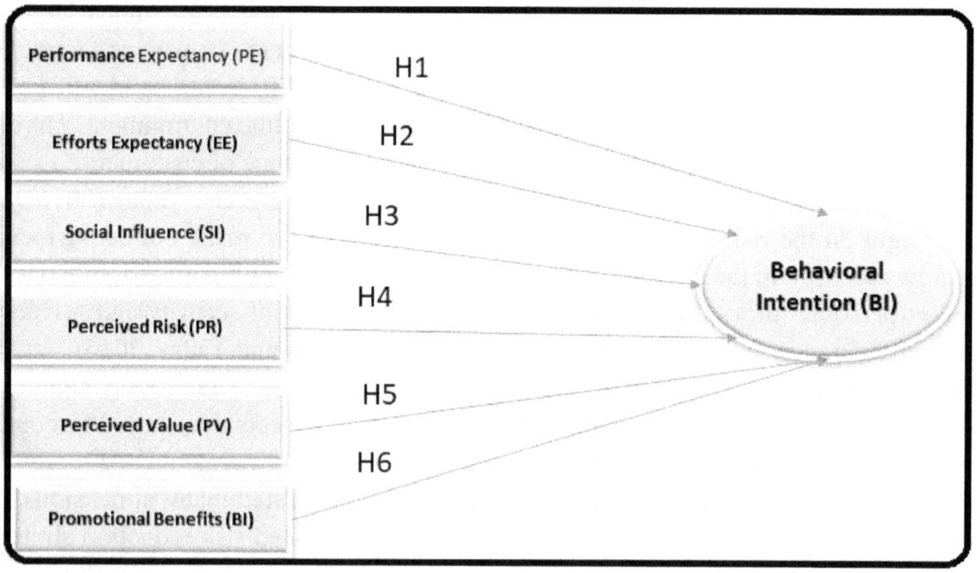

METHODOLOGY

To achieve the objectives of this study, a structured questionnaire was developed and disseminated among people in the Kingdom of Bahrain. Through a convenient sampling, face-to-face interviews in four governorates of the Kingdom of Bahrain were conducted by a trained team. The exercise resulted in a total of 1,740 complete responses obtained from a variety of people from different demographic groups. Accordingly, the results were analyzed with the SPSS application to evaluate the responses obtained.

The Sample Characteristics

Table 1 below shows deep insight into the static details of the respondents analyzed in the study. The following characteristics can be concluded:

- Males respondents represented 55% of the total versus 45% for females.
- Respondents in the age group between 20 and 29 years represented more than half of the sample (52.6%), while individuals between 30 and 39 years old came next with 26.3%. The majority of the responses were obtained from the young working generation representing Generation Y, which represents the demographic cohort of people born in the 1980s and 1990s.
- More than 80% of respondents were Bahraini people versus the remaining who are expats living in Bahrain.
- Marital status was fairly distributed between single and married people. Single people represented 48%, and married represented 44%.
- People with BSc degrees represented 45% of responses, and those with High School only represented 25%.
- More than 57% of respondents were employed, while students represented 22%. Business owners represented 8%, and the remaining were retired and unemployed.
- When grouped by income, respondents with income between BD100 and BD500 represented 31%, while people with income between BD500 and BD899 came next with 22%. One-third of the respondents had income above these two categories.

FINDINGS

Exploring the findings of the survey has led to a concrete conclusion about the future of the e-Wallet in the Kingdom of Bahrain. Initially, the results showed that 93.3% of the respondents are familiar with e-Wallet applications and technology, or they know little about the technology, as explained in Figure 3.

Such a result takes deep attention toward the future application of e-Wallet technologies in the Kingdom. Moving forward, by using the Statistical Package for the Social Sciences (SPSS), several tests have been conducted to elaborate on the constructs and dimensions of e-Wallet adoption in the Kingdom.

With the One-Sample T-test, the findings showed a significant rate of adoption of e-Wallet applications among respondents with a confidence level of 95%, as seen in Table 2.

Although the results in Figure 4 show that a very high percentage of respondents have actually adopted e-Wallet technologies, 26% of respondents do not use it.

The high percentage of adoption may be attributed to many reasons: the well-developed infrastructure in the Kingdom, which allows easy access to the internet anytime and anywhere, the education level of the residents, and the stability of the economy.

Performance Expectancy

Considering the theoretical studies conducted and the practical implications of Performance Expectancy for the adoption of the e-Wallet applications, the results showed that around 65.1% of respondents have an

Table 1. Static details of the study respondents

Governorate Responses Distribution	Capital	26.3%
	Muharraq	25.1%
	Northern	30.0%
	Southern	18.7%
Responses By Gender	Female	45.4%
	Male	54.6%
Responses By Age Group	Below 20	6.6%
	20 – 29	52.6%
	30 – 39	26.2%
	40 – 49	8.5%
	50 – 59	5.5%
	60 and above	0.7%
Responses By Nationality	Bahraini	82.5%
	Non-Bahraini	17.5%
Responses By Marital Status	Single	48.1%
	Married	44.0%
	Divorced/Separated	6.5%
	Widow	1.4%
Responses By Highest Educational Level	Lower than high school	3.3%
	High school Cert. /Dip	24.0%
	Associate Diploma	8.1%
	Post-Graduate Diploma	7.3%
	HND	0.6%
	BSc./BA	45.9%
	MSc/MA/MBA	8.9%
	PhD	1.4%
	Others	0.5%
Responses By Working Status	Student	22.8%
	Business Owner	8.3%
	Employee	57.8%
	Retired	2.8%
	Unemployment	7.1%
	Others	1.3%
Responses By Income Group	Below 100	12.2%
	100 - 499	31.4%
	500 - 899	22.4%
	900 - 1299	9.9%
	1300 - 1699	3.2%
	1800 - 2199	3.6%
	2200 - 2599	0.8%
	2600 - 2999	0.5%
	3000 - 3699	0.5%
	3700 - 4099	0.2%
	4100 - 4499	0.1%
	4500 and above	0.5%
	Prefer not to answer	14.7%

interest in opening an e-Wallet account to avail of the performance benefits of the technology. Therefore, the results showed that Performance Expectancy is an important construct that affects the Behavioral Intention toward the adoption of mobile wallet technologies. This finding is in line with other studies conducted by Shine (2009), Kim et al. (2010), Wang and Yi (2012), Pham and Ho (2014), and Slade et al. (2015). Accordingly, we can accept the hypothesis (H1) and conclude that the higher the Performance Expectancy is, the higher the behavioral intention to adopt a mobile wallet will be.

Figure 3. Responses Familiarity with the term e-Wallet App

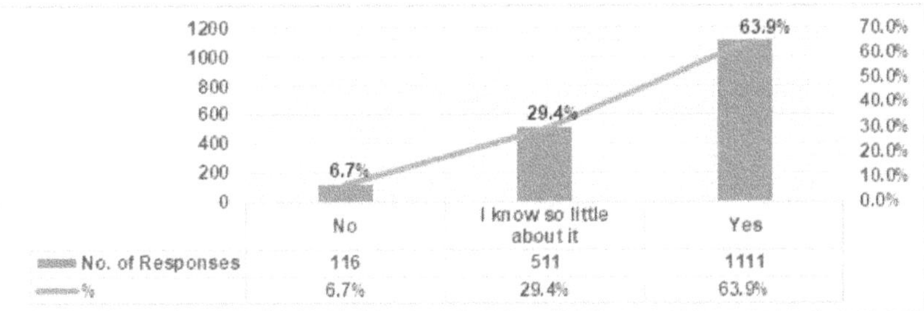

Table 2. One-Sample Statistics, general

	N	Mean	Std. Deviation	Std. Error Mean		
Adopt	1740	1.7282	.45652	.01094		
	Test Value = 1.5					
	t	Df	Sig. (2-tailed)	Mean Difference	95% Confidence Interval of the Difference	
					Lower	Upper
Adopt	20.848	1739	.000	.22816	.2067	.2496

Figure 4. Individuals currently using or have any e-Wallet Accounts

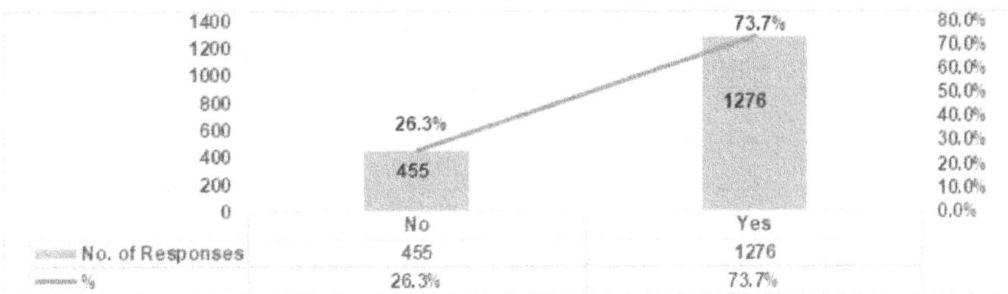

Effort Expectancy

Examining the ease of using mobile wallets in daily life and conducting day-to-day transactions, the results in Table 3 show a high mean of 1.975 toward the adoption of the mobile wallets due to the Effort Expected in using e-Wallets. With a confidence level of 95%, the analyst can accept the hypothesis (H2) that the higher the Effort Expectancy, the higher the Behavioral Intention to adopt a mobile wallet will be. An important implication that can be conveyed to service developers and providers is to keep the application user-friendly and easy to apply to daily life as the Effort Expectancy construct plays an important role in shaping the future of mobile wallets applications.

Table 3. One-Sample Statistics, Effort Expectancy

	N	Mean	Std. Deviation	Std. Error Mean		
EE	1740	1.9753	1.07508	.02577		
	Test Value = 3					
	t	df	Sig. (2-tailed)	Mean Difference	95% Confidence Interval of the Difference	
					Lower	Upper
EE	-39.759	1739	.000	-1.02471	-1.0753	-.9742

Social Influence

The extent and degree of social relationships in Islamic and Arab countries give this construct additional importance and existence. While examining the degree of the importance of Social Influence on the behavioral intention toward the adoption of e-Wallets, the majority of the respondents agreed that they would recommend the application to their families and relatives. In Table 4, with a mean of 1.8, the construct can be validated at a 95% confidence level. Accordingly, the hypothesis (H3) that the higher the Social Influence is, the higher the behavioral intention to adopt a mobile wallet will be, is accepted and validated.

Table 4. One-Sample Statistics, Effort Expectancy

	N	Mean	Std. Deviation	Std. Error Mean		
SI	1740	1.8023	.46745	.01121		
	Test Value = 1.5					
	t	df	Sig. (2-tailed)	Mean Difference	95% Confidence Interval of the Difference	
					Lower	Upper
SI	26.976	1739	.000	.30230	.2803	.3243

Perceived Value

Another dimension that was considered and evaluated is the Perceived Value since the consumer is behaviorally yielding toward the greater benefits obtained with the lowest efforts and costs paid. This kind of trade-off will result in a Perceived Value construct. To evaluate this construct, the respondents were asked about their concerns about not using the new technology and its implications. The outcome of the question revealed that only 166 (9.5%) of the respondents had not been convinced of the value provided by e-Wallet applications. Therefore, the study can conclude that over 90% of the respondents perceive the importance of the value provided by the e-Wallet, which will lead to the acceptance of the hypothesis (H4) that the higher the Perceived Value is, the higher the behavioral intention to adopt a mobile wallet will be.

Perceived Risk

The inherent risk in any new technology is usually the most influential factor that may prevent the acceleration of the adoption of technology. This concept is highly applicable in this study and can be found in many papers like those by Wu and Wang (2005), Vila and Kurster (2011), Zha et al. (2013), and Madan and Yadav (2016). Incorporating this construct in the survey showed that 1079 of the respondents (61%) have concerns about security, and it highly impacts their intention to adopt and use e-Wallets, as seen in Figure 5. Moreover, the results showed that the respondents have concerns about how complicated the applications may be, which represents a risk that developers need to consider and mitigate. Therefore, the hypothesis (H5) that the lower the perceived risk is, the higher the behavioral intention to adopt a mobile wallet will be.

Figure 5. Responses Regarding Major Concerns about e-Wallets

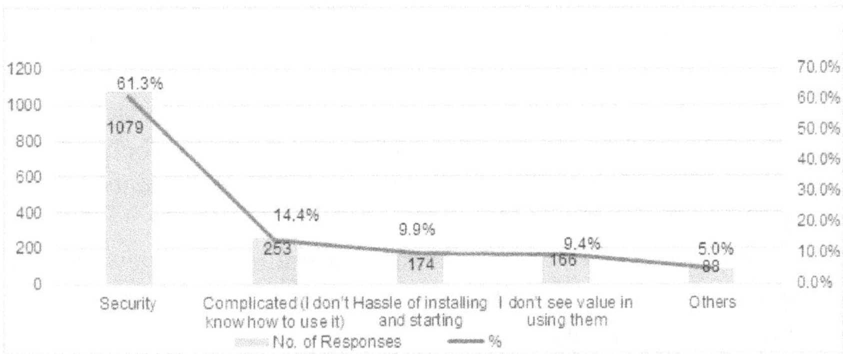

Promotional Benefits

Service providers have incorporated a wide range of promotional benefits into their applications to advocate for the acceptance and accelerate consumers' intentions to adopt their e-Wallet technologies. Consumers have greatly appreciated the influence of those attractions and advantages. Specifying the type of promotional benefits that have a strong influence on the adoption, as detailed in Figure 6, has shown that discounts, with 50% of the sample size, are the most influential type of promotional benefit that affect the intention to adopt e-Wallet applications. In addition, "buy-one-get-one-free" offers have the second highest attractiveness factor of the Promotional Benefits, with 25.8% of the respondents. Such findings lead to the acceptance of the hypothesis (H6) that the higher the promotional benefits are, the higher the behavioral intention to adopt a mobile wallet will be.

CONCLUSION

The research found a high level of usage and intention to use e-Wallets among people in the Kingdom of Bahrain. It was a supportive study with evidence that Performance Expectancy is a major factor represented by a high rate of people interested in opening e-Wallets. The Efforts Expectancy factor

Figure 6. What would encourage you to use an e-Wallet?

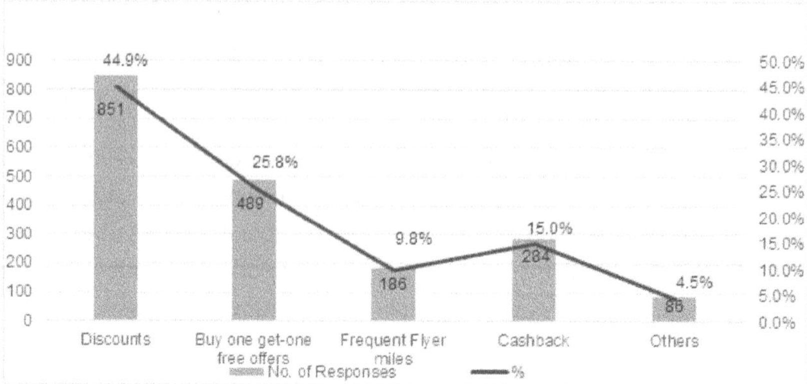

also recorded an outstanding usage rate, confirming that more than 80% of respondents were either natural adopters or interested in keeping themselves up to date with technological developments. The study also confirmed Social Influence as a significant factor, with 83% of respondents confirming their willingness to recommend e-Wallet for others to use. The Perceived Value factor was also found to be a considerable element of the study, where more than 90% confirmed the belief of the value provided by e-Wallets. Security represented the major concern among the respondents from different concern dimensions examined in the study.

The Promotional Benefits factor, which is found in other studies, was shown to be a significant element of e-Wallet adoption in the Kingdom of Bahrain. The respondents confirmed their attraction to use e-Wallets is mainly due to the availability of different promotions packaged with the usage of e-Wallets. This has major implications for the development of e-Wallets that will be discussed in the final section.

Overall, the study confirmed a high tendency among respondents in the Kingdom of Bahrain to use e-Wallets, showing a high level of interest in new technologies, which implies a larger market potential for these new tools in the near future. These findings will be of high interest to telecom companies, banks, and new FinTech companies entering the market.

Research Limitations

The main limitation of this study is the point of perspective, as the study has analyzed the outcomes and consequences of the practical factors that affect the adoption of e-Wallet technologies from the consumer's perspective only without taking in consideration the technical aspects from the service provider's point of view that may also affect the level of adoption. Future researchers are encouraged to give this topic additional attention and to include other factors that may have a significant impact, such as government support and the readiness and availability of infrastructure in the Kingdom of Bahrain. Although the sample size was large enough to draw conclusions, global and national recommendations to the industry should require a larger sample size that can truly represent the population. Furthermore, there is a need to study the impact of COVID-19 on the adoption intention of e-Wallet as an area for future research.

Recommendations and Practical Implications

The main practical implication of this research reveals the need for the service providers of e-Wallet applications to focus more on promotional benefits. A further focus on benefits will bring an increase in the number of users as per the outcomes of the research. Discounts packaged through the usage of e-Wallets makes the major attracting factor for consumers. Additionally, a greater focus on security is crucial as it represents the main concern for e-Wallet users, especially with increasing cybersecurity attacks around the world. Telecoms and financial institutions are also expected to pay increasing attention to social factors and word of mouth, and the study reveals that this is a major influencer on the wide or narrow usage of any e-Wallet launched in the market. (Al-Alawi, Al-Bassam & Mehrotra, 2020; Al-Alawi & Al-Bassam, 2020).

This study strongly recommends the great attention of financial institutions that should be devoted toward e-Wallet technologies and applications, as this is going to be a significant trend that will reshape the financial industry in the coming decade. Financial institutions are expected to work proactively in dealing with the shift in the payments market, which will generate an essential source of revenue for banks. Further studies should be devoted to the detailed examination of e-Wallet applications from the different service providers in Bahrain to produce a comprehensive analysis of the adoption of e-Wallets in the Kingdom of Bahrain. In addition, the detailed study of each e-Wallet application in Bahrain will help the researchers to understand better the acceptance level among users and the most influential factors in determining the adoption level.

REFERENCES

Al-Al-Alawi, A. I., & Al-Bassam, S. A. (2020). Study of the Cybercrime Cost and the Risk of Criminal Threats to the Banking Sector. *Xi'an Jianzhu Keji Daxue Xuebao/Journal of Xi'an University of Architecture & Technology, 12*(4), 252-270. Doi:10.37896/JXAT12.04/770

Al-Alawi. (2018, August). Using Balanced Scorecard in Measuring the Performance of Online Banking: Cultivating Strategic Model Map in Financial Sector- Case of Bahrain. *Journal of Internet Banking and Commerce*, *23*(2).

Al-Alawi, A. I. (2005). Adoption and Awareness of Online Banking Issues among Mature Users. *Asian Journal of Information Technology*, *4*(9), 856–860.

Al-Alawi, A. I., & Al-Ali, F. M. (2015). Factors affecting e-commerce adoption in SMEs in the GCC: An empirical study of Kuwait. *Research Journal of Information Technology*, *7*(1), 1–21. doi:10.3923/rjit.2015.1.21

Al-Alawi, A. I., & Al-Bassam, S. A. (2019). Evaluation of telecommunications regulatory practice in the Kingdom of Bahrain: Development and challenges. *International Journal of Business Information Systems*, *31*(2), 282–303. doi:10.1504/IJBIS.2019.100282

Al-Alawi, A. I., Al-Bassam, S. A., & Mehrotra, A. A. (2020). Critical Cybersecurity Threats: Frontline Issues Faced by Bahraini Organizations. In Implementing Computational Intelligence Techniques for Security Systems Design (pp. 210-229). IGI Global.

Amoroso, D. L., & Magnier-Watanabe, R. (2012). Building a research model for mobile wallet consumer adoption: The case of mobile Suica in Japan. *Journal of Theoretical and Applied Electronic Commerce Research, 7*(1), 94–110. doi:10.4067/S0718-18762012000100008

Blockchain.info. (2017, February). *Total number of transactions*. https://blockchain.info/charts/n-transactions-total?timespan=30days

Dahlberg, T., Mallat, N., Ondrus, J., & Zmijewska, A. (2008). Past, Present and Future of mobile payments research: A literature review. *Electronic Commerce Research and Application*, 165-181.

Dahlberg, T., Mallat, N., & Öörni, A. (2003). Consumer acceptance of mobile payment solutions. *mBusiness 2003 – The Second International Conference on Mobile Business*, 211–218.

Davis, F. D. (1989). Perceived usefulness, perceived ease of use and user acceptance of information technology. *Management Information Systems Quarterly, 13*(3), 319–339. doi:10.2307/249008

de Luna, I. R., Liébana-Cabanillas, F., Sánchez-Fernández, J., & Muñoz-Leiva, F. (2019). Mobile payment is not all the same: The adoption of mobile payment systems depending on the technology applied. *Technological Forecasting and Social Change, 146*, 931–944. doi:10.1016/j.techfore.2018.09.018

Inuit Inc. (2017). *The history of money and payments*. https://payments.intuit.com/history-of-money-and-payments

Kim, C., Mirusmonov, M., & Lee, I. (2010). An empirical examination of factors influencing the intention to use mobile payment. *Computers in Human Behavior, 26*(3), 310–322. doi:10.1016/j.chb.2009.10.013

Kim, H. K., Lee, M., & Jung, M. (2005). Perceived risk and risk-reduction strategies for high-technology services. *Asia Pacific Advances in Consumer Research, 16*(2), 171–179.

Kleijnen, M., Wetzels, M., & de Ruyter, K. (2004). Consumer acceptance of wireless finance. *Journal of Financial Services Marketing, 8*(3), 206–217. doi:10.1057/palgrave.fsm.4770120

Lai, P. (2017). The literature Review of Technology Adoption Models and Theories for Novelty Technology. *Journal of Information Systems and Technology Management, 14*(1), 21–38. doi:10.4301/S1807-17752017000100002

Lee, C. P., Warkentin, M., & Choi, H. (2004). The role of technological and social factors on the adoption of mobile payment technologies. AMCIS 2004 Proceedings, 333.

Madan, K., & Yadav, R. (2016). Behavioural intention to adopt mobile wallet: A developing country perspective. *Journal of Indian Business Research, 8*(3), 227–244. doi:10.1108/JIBR-10-2015-0112

Mallat, N. (2007). Exporing Consumer Adoption of Mobile Payments. *The Journal of Strategic Information Systems*, 413–432. doi:10.1016/j.jsis.2007.08.001

Mercer, C. (2015). *History of PayPal: The history of the biggest online payment system in the world*. From https://www.techworld.com/picture-gallery/e-commerce/history-ofpaypal-1998-now-3630386/

Mun, Y. P., Khalid, H., & Nadarajah, D. (2017). Millennials' Perception on Mobile Payment Services in Malaysia. *4th Information System International Conference 2017, ISICO 2017*.

Oliveira, T., Tomas, M., Babpista, G., & Campos, F. (2016). Mobile Payment: Understanding the determinants of customer adoption and intention to recommend the technology. *Computers in Human Behavior*, *61*, 404–414. doi:10.1016/j.chb.2016.03.030

Pagani, M. (2004). Determinants of adoption of third generation mobile multimedia services. *Journal of Interactive Marketing*, *18*(3), 46–59. doi:10.1002/dir.20011

Pagani, M., & Schipani, D. (2008). Motivations and barriers to the adoption of 3G mobile multimedia services: An end user perspective in the Italian market. In End-User Computing: Concepts, Methodologies, Tools, and Applications (pp. 2329-2340). IGI Global.

Parasuraman, P. A., & Colby, C. (2001). *Techno-Ready Marketing: How and Why Customers Adopt Technology*. The Free Press.

Pham, T. T. T., & Ho, J. C. (2014). What are the core drivers in consumer adoption of NFC-based mobile payments?: a proposed research framework. *Management of Engineering & Technology (PICMET), 2014 Portland International Conference*, 3041-3049.

Riquelme, H. E., & Rios, R. E. (2010). The moderating effect of gender on the adoption of mobile banking. *International Journal of Bank Marketing*, *28*(5), 328–341. doi:10.1108/02652321011064872

Rogers, M. E. (1983). *Diffusion of Innovations* (3rd ed.). The Free Press.

Rolfe, A. (2019). *Payments (Cards & Mobile)*. Retrieved from Payments Industry Intelligence: https://www.paymentscardsandmobile.com/mobile-Wallet-trends-annual-report-2019/

Schierz, P. G., Schilke, O., & Wirtz, B. W. (2010). Understanding consumer acceptance of mobile payment services: An empirical analysis. *Electronic Commerce Research and Applications*, *9*(3), 209–216. doi:10.1016/j.elerap.2009.07.005

Shin, D. H. (2009). Towards an understanding of the consumer acceptance of mobile wallet. *Computers in Human Behavior*, *25*(6), 1343–1354. doi:10.1016/j.chb.2009.06.001

Slade, E., Williams, M., Dwivedi, Y., & Piercy, N. (2015). Exploring consumer adoption of proximity mobile payments. *Journal of Strategic Marketing*, *23*(3), 209–223. doi:10.1080/0965254X.2014.914075

Venkatesh, V., & Bala, H. (2008). Technology acceptance model 3 and a research agenda on interventions. *Decision Sciences*, *39*(2), 273–315. doi:10.1111/j.1540-5915.2008.00192.x

Venkatesh, V., Davis, F., & Morris, M. G. (2007). Dead or alive? The development, trajectory and future of technology adoption research. *Journal of the Association for Information Systems*, *8*(4), 1. doi:10.17705/1jais.00120

Venkatesh, V., & Davis, F. D. (2000). A theoretical extension of the technology acceptance model: Four longitudinal field studies. *Management Science*, *46*(2), 186–204. doi:10.1287/mnsc.46.2.186.11926

Venkatesh, V., Morris, M. G., Davis, G. B., & Davis, F. D. (2003). User acceptance of information technology: Toward a unified view. *Management Information Systems Quarterly*, *27*(3), 425–478. doi:10.2307/30036540

Venkatesh, V., Thong, J. Y., & Xu, X. (2012). Consumer acceptance and use of information technology: Extending the unified theory of acceptance and use of technology. *Management Information Systems Quarterly*, *36*(1), 157–178. doi:10.2307/41410412

Vila, N., & Kurster, I. (2011). Consumer feelings and behaviours towards well-designed websites. *Information & Management*, *48*(4-5), 166–177. doi:10.1016/j.im.2011.04.003

Wang, L., & Yi, Y. (2012). The impact of use context on mobile payment acceptance: An empirical study in China. In *Advances in computer science and education* (pp. 293–299). Springer. doi:10.1007/978-3-642-27945-4_47

Wu, J. H., & Wang, S. C. (2005). What drives mobile commerce?: An empirical evaluation of the revised technology acceptance model. *Information & Management*, *42*(5), 719–729. doi:10.1016/j.im.2004.07.001

Zeithaml, V. A. (1988). Consumer perceptions of price, quality, and value: A means-end model and synthesis of evidence. *Journal of Marketing*, *52*(3), 2–22. doi:10.1177/002224298805200302

Zha, X., Li, J., & Yan, Y. (2013). Information self-efficacy and information channels: Decision quality and online shopping satisfaction. *Online Information Review*, *37*(6), 872–890. doi:10.1108/OIR-09-2012-0156

Chapter 16
Identifying Factors That Influence the Use of E-Wallets and Its Continuance:
An Empirical Investigation

Muwafaq Al Kubaisi
University of Bahrain, Bahrain

Nedaa Ali Ahmed Naser
University of Bahrain, Bahrain

ABSTRACT

The e-wallet is one of the successful innovative services that was launched in 2017. A quantitative survey approach based on a five-point Likert scale was used in this study. The sampling tool relies on the snowball and convenience sampling technique. The sample consisted of 660 users in Bahrain. This study found that the four predictor variables are statistically significant and supportive. The compatibility variable is the leading factor in the analysis. However, the study's results indicated that the moderating variables were also found to be statistically insignificant. The research findings contribute to the service providers and marketers with a clear understanding of the factors that affect the use of e-wallets and continuance use. Also, there was an addition to the theoretical implications indicated by the significant direct relationship between continuance use and compatibility.

INTRODUCTION

E-wallets are a kind of electronic card that is used generally for business transactions made online through a smartphone or a computer. Its value is the same as a bank's credit or debit card. An E-wallet needs to be connected with the user's bank account to make any payments. Through continuous innovations, payments become more efficient and convenient for buyers using online platforms.

DOI: 10.4018/978-1-7998-3257-7.ch016

The growing number of smartphone users eventually would shift the mobile from being accessory to necessity. Although there are several approaches to encourage an individual to adopt new technology, the decision to continuance use of technology relies more on the post-adoption behavior factors that affect the individual continuance intention to use rather than on the initial adoption decision (Venkatesh & Thong 2012). In order to succeed and gain competitive advantage among others, the technology provider company needs to identify the benefits of the technology owned by an in-depth understanding of user behavior (Tam et al. 2018). According to Albashrawi & Motiwalla (2019), the technology provider companies need to focus primarily on understanding the continuance intention factors to broaden their services in order to sustain and retain users in the long term.

The overall trend moves towards using electronic wallets (e-wallets), which is a mobile application. E-wallet is equivalent to the physical wallet that holds the money. It is defined as a virtual wallet that allows users to place any information in the mobile wallet, such as identification cards, student IDs, credit cards, debit cards, and driver licenses. In other words, secure storage includes personal information, bank information, payment history, and shopping details on the mobile to be used to manage, review, and completely different transactions such as paying bills, transferring funds, and shopping (Singh et al. 2017).

The e-wallet service activation is done by installing the application to the mobile set. It is followed by applicant registration, which requires the name and phone number, copy the Postal Index Number (PIN) code, that is received through Short Message Service (SMS), to the application, and enter card details in the application.

Globally, Apple Pay is the pioneer in e-wallet business that launched in 2014, followed by Google Pay and Samsung Pay to enable users to pay to the shops securely. However, the forecasted adoption of the e-wallet was higher than the actual users. The users of smartphones are expected to increase by 7% every year; China, India, and the US are the countries with the highest smartphone users with 1.3 billion, 530 million, and 229 million users, respectively. Moreover, the mobile payment volume was expected to be one trillion US dollars in 2019.

According to Singh et al. (2017), Indian youth are attracted to e-wallet and prefer to use it more than paying in cash because they enjoy the use of new mobile technologies. The competition is intense between the providers of the e-wallets service due to the low switching cost (Cao et al. 2018); thus, investigating the factors that affect the use and continuance use of e-wallet is essential.

Bahrain is considered as the regional leader in the banking and finance sector (Benefit, 2017). The global trend towards cashless measures has motivated the Kingdom of Bahrain to move forward and introduce the Electronic Fund Transfer System (EFTS) by the Benefit Company in 2015 (CBB, 2019). Nevertheless, the EFTS enables individuals to perform transactions and provide fast and secure fund transfer; the ability to pay bills immediately, almost with no mistakes, occurs throughout three services available, which are Fawri+ Fawri and Fawateer (CBB, 2019).

E-wallet is defined as a service that enables the occurring purchase or transfer of the fund (Kumar et al. 2018). According to Singh et al. (2017), the e-wallets service is gaining ground in the developing markets. The continuance collaboration between telecommunication companies and institutional banks aimed to provide payment solutions services, which are e-wallets, as well as maintaining continuance use of e-wallets. For example, Batelco collaborated with Arab Financial Services (AFS) and launched a digital mobile wallet called bWallet (Batelco, 2018). Moreover, Viva cash or as called now STC pay BH launched as the collaboration with SADAD (STC, 2019).

Kingdom of Bahrain is heading to become a Financial Technology (FinTech) center in the region (CBB, 2019). Central Bank of Bahrain (CBB) in October 2017 has established a FinTech unit to proceed towards FinTech, which is responsible for the quality of the services provided to clients, which include providing approval to participants in the FinTech as well as monitoring and supervision responsibilities. Moreover, the CBB has issued several guidelines, regulations policy, and a series of measures to regulate and facilitate the implementation of FinTech. The FinTech unit helps develop the existing financial environment by attracting national, regional, and international FinTech companies to the Kingdom of Bahrain (CBB, 2019).

One of the highlighted developments of FinTech is the successful launched of the e-wallet in the Kingdom of Bahrain. The use of e-wallets will change how individuals interact with money (CBB, 2019) as the physical cards and actual cash is replaced by e-wallets that enable users to settle their payments and transfers funds electronically by waving or scanning the codes via smartphones. The digital society provides a network of connected and collaborated entities that are CBB, bank entities, telecommunication companies, shopping stores, and individuals (CBB, 2019).

The below table 1 is extracted from the Central Bank of Bahrain (CBB); it shows that the volume of transactions in the second quarter of 2018 increased from 0.166 million to almost 1.4 million in the second quarter of 2019. The amount of value (BD) dramatically increased from almost BD 2.8 million in the second quarter of 2018 to almost reached BD 66 million in the second quarter of 2019.

Table 1. **Volume of Transactions in Bahrain,** *Source: CBB*

Period		Volume	Value (BD)
2018	Quarter 1	56,438	474,199
	Quarter 2	165,869	2,795,996
	Quarter 3	340,411	8,070,273
	Quarter 4	571,939	18,072,712
2019	Quarter 1	955,540	31,899,530
	Quarter 2	1,382,762	65,981,116

The significant growth in the quarterly volume of transactions, as well as the amount of value (BD) in 2019 compared to 2018, is due to the widespread acceptance in going cashless and the launch of e-wallets in 2017 (CBB, 2019).

The success of e-wallets in the kingdom of Bahrain can be reviewed in numbers, for example, BenefitPay, which is one of the e-wallets in the Kingdom of Bahrain. The volume of transactions recorded in the first half of 2018 was almost 12 thousand, while the volume reached 806 thousand in the first half of 2019. Moreover, the amount of value (BD) dramatically increased from BD 0.7 million in the first half of 2018 to BD 55.2 million in the first half of 2019 (CBB, 2019).

According to CBB (2019), simplicity, quick, and easy to conduct transactions in one place is the reason for e-wallet usage growth. The e-wallet forced to enhance user experience as the kingdom of Bahrain is progressing towards the cash-less and card-less approach.

This study is conducted in order to identify factors that affect the use of e-wallet and its continuance usage in the Kingdom of Bahrain and to investigate the effect of demographical characteristics on e-wallets usage. The primary focus is toward using mobile payment services continuously for everyday settlement activities rather than for initial adoption and initial intention to use. Also, based on the volume and the value of transactions in Bahrain, it is expected that the current tendency to use mobile payment services in a broader range beyond the traditional transactions through mobile.

BACKGROUND

Based on the focus area presented in the introduction, e-wallet service is viewed as an innovative idea (Singh et al., 2017). It is defined as secure storage of bank card information on the mobile to be used to complete different transactions such as paying bills, transferring funds, and shopping (Singh et al. 2017). Moreover, users can place any information in the mobile wallet, such as identification cards, student IDs, credit cards, debit cards, and driver licenses.

E-wallet service was newly launched in the Kingdom of Bahrain by Benefit company in May 2017 (CBB, 2019). In the Kingdom of Bahrain, payment solution services continue to grow through expanding services, upgrading the features, enhancing position in the market, and adding new service to e-wallet. For example, in 2019, a new partnership between VIVA and National Bank of Bahrain (NBB) to launch a new service that enables the user to withdraw cash from the STC wallet (STC, 2019).

The below table 2 presents e-wallets that were introduced in the kingdom of Bahrain from 2017 up to 2019. Also, the table presents a comparison of services provided by each e-wallet. However, the services provided are quite the same for all the wallets as the primary services, such as paying at the retail stores and promotional offers are available in all e-wallets.

Table 2. Available e-wallets in Bahrain

E-wallet name	Launch date	Add cards/ cash	Add bank account	wallet to wallet transfer	Scan and pay at the retail	View merchants list	Pay service bills	View transaction history	Withdraw cash	Offers
BenefitPay	May 2017	Ö	Ö	Ö	Ö	Ö	Ö	Ö	-	Ö
Max Wallet	Jul 2017	Ö	-	-	Ö	Ö	-	Ö	-	Ö
bWallet	Jan 2018	Ö	-	Ö	Ö	Ö		Ö	-	Ö
STC pay BH	Mar 2018	Ö	-	Ö	Ö	Ö	Ö	Ö	Ö	Ö

Mobile payment services enable users to perform financial transactions anytime and anywhere, using their smartphone devices (Tam et al. 2018; Chen & Wu, 2017). The mobile payment transactions that can be performed in stores or even out stores consist of paying for purchasing goods and services, paying bills, and instantly transferring funds (Chen & Wu, 2017).

According to Cao et al. (2018), there are two types of mobile payment services concerning the place of origin of the service. The first type of mobile payment service is the service that was already available on computers such as AliPay.com, which become AliPay wallet on the mobile version. In contrast, the second type is mobile payment service that initially launched from mobile, such as WeChat payment, the social network service provider. In the Kingdom of Bahrain, bWallet is an example of the first type of mobile payment service that was already available on computers as batelco.com. However, BenefitPay is an example of the second type of mobile payment service that was initially launched from the mobile device.

The preference towards using an e-wallet is more than the traditional method, and e-wallet is convenient to users as they are satisfied with the easiness of using e-wallet and the transaction speed (Singh et al., 2017). The phenomena of using the new advanced technology that allows user to access their financial and perform transactions quickly. This was illustrated earlier in the table 1, as there were significant growth in the volume of transactions and the amount of value (BD) in 2019 compared to 2018, the reasons mentioned by the CBB (2019) are the widespread acceptance in going cashless, and the launched of e-wallets in 2017.

The use of e-wallet seems to be attractive to users, and they prefer to use it instead of another mode of payment due to the facilities provided, such as promotional offers, loyalty points, cash back benefits, and other benefits (Singh et al., 2017). Also, individuals feel more convenience and efficiency when using mobile payment instead of online payment (Cao et al., 2018).

Several models and theories investigate the continuance use of e-wallet such as the Technology Acceptance Model (TAM) and Expectancy-Confirmation Model (ECM), below are an in-depth discussion of the post-adoption theories and models.

Technology Acceptance Model (TAM) is a widely used framework for understanding and exploring how new technology is adopted and used by end-users. According to Alaeddin et al. (2018), this is due to its simplicity (Tam et al. 2018; Chen & Wu, 2017).

Initially, this model focus on technology adoption as it was implemented by Akturan & Tezcan (2012). Also, TAM indicates the actual use, which is determined by consumer intention; Yuan et al. (2016) implemented it. However, the implantation of TAM is very generic, as Alaeddin et al. (2018) applied TAM to investigate the users switching intention and behavior. Moreover, Chang applied TAM to investigate continuance use.

TAM used in almost 67% of research published in 2017 that studied users' behavior in adopting electronic payments (Alaeddin et al., 2018). Prior studies that have used TAM to examine the factors that affect the post-adoption usage concluded that the usefulness and ease of use are either directly or indirectly affect the post-adoption usage, especially in mobile banking. (Avornyo et al., 2019; Yuan et al., 2016).

Figure 1 below shows the TAM model that consists of perceived ease of use and perceived usefulness; these two constructs are serving as a determinant of individual attitude and behavioral intention towards using the technology (Venkatesh & Davis, 1996).

Figure 1. Technology Acceptance Model (Source: Venkatesh & Davis, 1996)

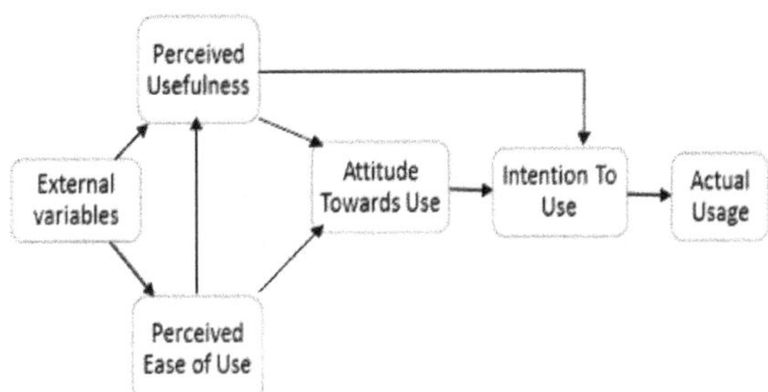

Figure (1) Technology Acceptance Model

In this research, incorporate the two primary constructs to the research model to gain a better understanding of the factors affecting the continuance use of e-wallet.

Oliver (1980) developed a consumer behavior model called Expectancy–Confirmation Theory (ECT) that is widely used to explain consumer satisfaction. According to Kumar et al. (2018), ECT is an extension of the TAM model; it proves the ability to investigate continuance use. In ECT, consumer satisfaction is determined by both expectation and perceived performance. The confirmation is an indication of the degree to which the expectation is confirmed by comparing it to the performance.

The Expectancy–Confirmation Model (ECM) introduced in the spot of ECT by Bhattacherjee (2001a). The ECM is useful in understanding the continuance use factors in the technologies related to the mobile (Avornyo et al., 2019). The ECM was recognized as the most suitable model to investigate the post-adoption intentions and continuance usage to sustain and retain users in the long term (Tam et al., 2018). Also, it is noticed as the dominant model to investigate the continuance usage of mobile banking services (Avornyo et al., 2019).

As shown in figure 2 below, Consumer satisfaction is determined by both perceived usefulness and confirmation (Yuan et al., 2016). The confirmation is the usage benefits that users expected to obtain through technology experience (Tam et al., 2018). The expectations and experience determine the user confirmation of expectations. Thus, the positive effect on user satisfaction is determined by both the confirmation of expectations and the positive effect on the perceived usefulness. The confirmation of expectations is the usage benefits that users anticipated to gain; thereby, it positively affects the perceived usefulness and user satisfaction.

Figure 2. Expectancy-Confirmation Model (Source: Bhattacherjee, 2001a)

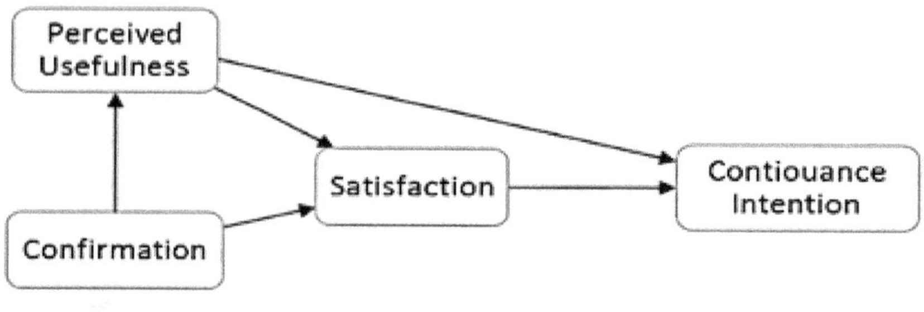

Figure (2)Expectancy-Confirmation Model

In the spotlight of the ECM model, this research adopts the relationships that exist in the model as follows: First, the direct relationship between usefulness and continuance use. Second, the indirect relationship that exists between usefulness and continuance use through satisfaction. Last, the direct relationship between satisfaction and continuance use.

The theories that were set together, the TAM that recognized as the widely used model (Alaeddin et al., 2018) and the ECM that recognized as the most suitable method to investigate the post-adoption intentions and continuance usage. (Tam et al., 2018; Kumar et al. 2018). The ECM assumes a change in initial expectations after adoption (Avornyo et al., 2019).

The integration of both TAM and ECM has formed the bases for this study, and they were widely used to investigate the continuance usage intention (Yuan et al., 2016). However, TAM and ECM are functioning better when they are implemented separately (Avornyo et al., 2019).

The ECM suggests that continuance use is determined by consumer satisfaction and both perceived usefulness and confirmation. However, the ECM is not comprehensive as more factors are affecting the continuance use (Yuan et al., 2016). TAM was integrated into the ECM to investigate more factors. Consequently, this research model and hypotheses were develop based on the integration of both TAM and ECM.

Most of the previous studies' emphasis was concentrated on investigating the factors that affect the mobile adoption intention of banking services, while less emphasis on investigating the factors that affect the continuous use (Avornyo et al., 2019). Moreover, the use of technology is relying on proper security, usefulness, ease to use, as indicated by Devaraj et al. (2002).

This study tries to examine the dependent variable (continuance use) as well as the mediating variable (user satisfaction) by constructing concepts for the independent variables: ease of use, compatibility, usefulness, and security based on the above studies.

Several studies considered the continuance usage of mobile banking as a dependent variable in their studies (Yuan et al., 2016; Gumussoy, 2016). According to Cao et al. (2018), key elements to maintain continuance use is by enhancing user satisfaction level. The results of several studies concluded that there is a significant effect of satisfaction on the continuance use, whereas continuance use is impacted by the user satisfaction level (Singh et al., 2017; Chen & Li, 2017). The satisfied individual is anticipated to adopt and use mobile banking services more frequently (Cao et al., 2018).

Previous studies set the ease of use as a predictor of continuance use (Albashrawi & Motiwalla, 2019). The ease of use directly affects the user satisfaction of mobile payments (Chen & Wu, 2017). However, Avornyo et al. (2019), the result showed that the ease of use indirectly affects user satisfaction through the usefulness, and it has an insignificant direct effect the continuance use.

Avornyo et al. (2019) went to suggest that the e-wallet "usefulness" significantly affects both user satisfaction and continuance use. The usefulness of mobile payments effects directly on user satisfaction (Chen & Li, 2017; Chen & Wu, 2017) and effects directly on continuance use (Chen & Li, 2017; Yuan et al., 2016). The attractive rewards or promotional benefits are considered as one of the factors of e-wallets continuance use, as indicated by Bagla & Sancheti (2018). The relationship between promotional benefits and continuance use is determined as positive relation (Kumar et al., 2018; Singh et al., 2017).

E-wallet "compatibility" is one of the essential factors related to using technology (Bagla & Sancheti, 2018). Nevertheless, compatibility has no role in adoption decisions. However, an individual is challenging to adopt technology if the technology is incompatible and does not meet the new trends in lifestyle.

E-wallet "security" is recognized as an essential consideration (Chen & Wu, 2017) and primary concern when it comes to dealing with financial transactions (Kumar et al., 2018). Security was added to the research model due to the importance of capturing the use of mobile banking services, and it is a critical concern to the user to perform financial transactions via mobile. E-wallet security is a critical factor in using any technological system, and it is indirectly affecting satisfaction through mediator variables (Kumar et al., 2018). However, the more security the users feel about the technology, the higher the satisfaction (Chen & Wu, 2017; Chen, 2012).

The factors that affect the e-wallets continuance use, as indicated by Bagla & Sancheti (2018), are attractive rewards, ease of use, and security. However, some studies indicated that the security issue only matters at the initial stage of adopting the technology. Furthermore, since the user assumes that banks are providing a high level of security in order to protect the financial information of all users, therefore, it has no direct effect on satisfaction.

RESEARCH MODEL

The study's proposed model is based on the integration of both ECM and TAM. ECM is widely used to explain user satisfaction. In contrast, TAM is widely used for many purposes, such as explaining the adoption of technology (Alaeddin et al., 2018), indicate the actual usage (Yuan et al., 2016), and investigate continuance use of technology.

The integration of both models was designed to identify which of the below factors (figure 3) are influencing user satisfaction (actual usage) and continuance use of e-wallet in the Kingdom of Bahrain. The combination of ECM and TAM represents the variable relationships used to answer these research questions.

The extracted variables from the integration of ECM and TAM are the "ease of use," "usefulness," "user satisfaction," and "continuance use." The "continuance use" is predicted by the overall satisfaction level (Kumar et al., 2018). The research model supports that satisfaction is a predictor of the "continuance use," and there is a positive association between satisfaction and e-wallet continuance use.

Moreover, the addition of the two new constructs to this research model was aimed to test the significance of the constructs on satisfaction and continuance use of e-wallet. The two constructs are compatible, which is one of the essential factors when it comes to using technology (Bagla & Sancheti, 2018) and security constructs, which is the primary concern and critical factor when it comes to dealing with financial transactions (Kumar et al., 2018).

The moderating demographic variables that consist of age, gender, educational qualification the and employment status were added to the model. It is used to test the moderating role of user demographic

Figure 3. Research Model

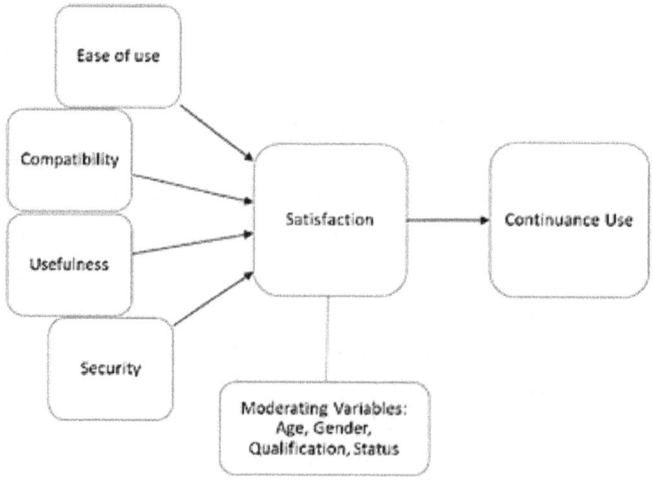

Figure (3) Research Model

characteristics in the relationship between the satisfaction concerning the use of e-wallet and the four predictor variables (ease of use, compatibility, usefulness, and security).

The research model is derived from the focused research objectives and research questions. The research model is presented below (figure 3).

STUDY HYPOTHESES

After the stage of setting the research objectives, research questions, and the research model, the researcher formulates the research hypotheses that initially explain the situation or interpret variables or describe cause and effect relationships.

The research hypotheses below are developed based on the proposed research model that is under scrutiny. The research questions were presented earlier, which is based on the research objectives to identify the possible factors that significantly affect the use of e-wallets in the Kingdom of Bahrain, which also presented in detail in the introduction.

Research hypotheses were derived based on the research questions, research objectives, and research proposed model that is under scrutiny stipules the following hypotheses with a brief explanation for each hypothesis.

H_1: The ease of use of e-wallet is directly affected the users' satisfaction concerning the use of e-wallet.

The individual who finds the use of e-wallet is a straightforward application is more satisfied to use it. This hypothesis assumes there is a significant direct effect of ease of use on the users' satisfaction. In other words, does ease of use of e-wallet has a significant direct role in deciding the user level of satisfaction?

H_2: The ease of use of e-wallet is indirectly affected the users' continuance use through the satisfaction concerning the use of e-wallet, as being a mediator.

An individual who finds the use of e-wallet is a straightforward application, is intended to continue using e-wallets only if they are satisfied. This hypothesis assumes there is a significant indirect effect of ease of use on the users' continuance use through users' satisfaction level as a mediator. In other words, does ease of use of e-wallet has a significant indirect role in deciding the user continuance use through satisfaction as being a mediator?

H_3: The compatibility of using an e-wallet is directly affected the users' satisfaction concerning the use of e-wallet.

An individual who finds the use of e-wallet is compatible and meets the new trends in lifestyle are more satisfied. This hypothesis assumes there is a significant direct effect of compatibility on the users' satisfaction. In other words, does the compatibility of e-wallet have a significant direct role in deciding the user level of satisfaction?

H_4: The compatibility of using an e-wallet is indirectly affected the users' continuance use through satisfaction concerning the use of e-wallet, as being a mediator.

An individual who finds the use of e-wallet is compatible and meets the new trends in lifestyle are intended to continue using e-wallets only if they are satisfied. This hypothesis assumes there is a significant indirect effect of compatibility on the users' continuance use through users' satisfaction level as a mediator. In other words, Does the compatibility of e-wallet have a significant indirect role in deciding the user continuance use through satisfaction as being a mediator?

H_5: The usefulness of e-wallet is directly affected the users' satisfaction concerning the use of e-wallet.

An individual who finds e-wallet is useful are more satisfied. This hypothesis assumes there is a significant direct effect of usefulness on the users' satisfaction. In other words, Does the usefulness of e-wallet has a significant direct role in deciding the user level of satisfaction?

H_6: The usefulness of e-wallet is indirectly affected the users' continuance use through satisfaction concerning the use of e-wallet, as being a mediator.

An individual who finds e-wallet is useful is intended to continue using e-wallets only if they are satisfied. This hypothesis assumes there is a significant indirect effect of usefulness on the users' continuance use through users' satisfaction level as a mediator. In other words. Does the usefulness of e-wallet have a significant indirect role in deciding the user continuance use through satisfaction as being a mediator?

H_7: The security of e-wallet is directly affected the users' satisfaction concerning the use of e-wallet.

An individual who finds e-wallet is secured and safe, are more satisfied. This hypothesis assumes there is a significant direct effect of security on participant satisfaction. In other words. Does the security of e-wallet have a significant direct role in deciding the user level of satisfaction?

H_8: The security of e-wallet is indirectly affected the users' continuance use through satisfaction concerning the use of e-wallet, as being a mediator.

An individual who finds e-wallet is secured and safe, is intended to continue using e-wallets only if they are satisfied. This hypothesis assumes there is a significant indirect effect of security on the users' continuance use through users' satisfaction level as a mediator. In other words. Does the security of e-wallet have a significant indirect role in deciding the user continuance use through satisfaction as being a mediator?

H_9: The users' satisfaction of e-wallet is directly affected the continuance use concerning the use of e-wallet.

The satisfied individual is anticipated to continue using the e-wallet. This hypothesis assumes there is a significant direct effect of users' satisfaction on the users' continuance use. In other words, Does the level of satisfaction of e-wallet has a significant direct role in deciding the user continuance use of e-wallet?

H_{10}: The users' demographic characteristics play a moderating role in the relationship between the satisfaction concerning the use of e-wallet and the four predictor variables (ease of use, compatibility, usefulness, and security).

TARGETED POPULATION

The targeted population generally defined as the number of people living in a particular area. On the one hand, the below table 3 shows the targeted population in the Kingdom of Bahrain as obtained from The Information & eGovernment Authority (IGA). The latest data, published in the middle of the year 2018, sorted by gender, age groups, and nationality.

Table 3. Bahrain Population

Age group	Bahraini		Non-Bahraini		Total
	Males	Females	Males	Females	
Below 14	110,199	105,556	41,242	39,891	296,888
15 – 19	31,889	30,035	8,836	7,238	77,998
20 - 24	30,591	28,932	37,636	15,380	112,539
25 – 34	55,896	54,014	227,037	68,198	405,145
35 – 44	43,354	42,779	169,733	49,466	305,332
Above 45	77,732	78,737	112,719	36,001	305,189
Total	349,661	340,053	597,203	216,174	1,503,091

As shown in the table 3 above, the total population is exceeding 1.5 million. However, the individuals belonging to the age group between 0 to 14 years are excluded from the population because it contains both infancy and minority. This age group (0 – 14) are either do not have a bank account. If they have a bank account, it is controlled by their parents or their custody, therefore unable to review their experience in using e-wallets application, and it is excluded from the e-wallet population. Accordingly, the e-wallet population shrinks to almost 1.2 million.

SAMPLING FRAME

The sampling frame is known as the representative of the population units; it is defined as the list of the actual users of e-wallets from which the selected representative of the population will be derived. In an attempt to obtain a list of the actual users of e-wallets in order to determine the sampling frame of this study, the e-wallets population could be extracted from the e-wallet provider companies in Bahrain.

In an attempt to capture the targeted population units with regards to the number of smartphone subscribers in Bahrain, the data were extracted from the report published by the Telecommunications Regulatory Authority (TRA) in Bahrain at the end of the first quarter of 2018. The report stated that out of 2.2 million mobile subscribers, 1.8 million were mobile data subscribed (mobile internet). However, not all subscribers are using e-wallets, and no report was found that statistically shows the number of users of e-wallet applications. Thus, the actual e-wallets population remains unknown to the researcher.

Since the study is focusing on the Kingdom of Bahrain to identify factors that affect the use and the continuance use of e-wallets, therefore, the targeted population is considered for this study are all e-wallets users in the Kingdom of Bahrain. Accordingly, the e-wallets population and sampling for this study are controlled by the inhabitants in Bahrain and the number of smartphone users who use e-wallets application.

RESEARCH SAMPLING TECHNIQUE

After careful consideration of the non-probability sampling techniques, respondents will be selected through snowball (chain-referral) and convenience sampling techniques. The previously conducted studies in this type of research gave given the authors a piece of handy information on how a similar sampling method, either one sampling technique or combination of sampling techniques. For example, Kumar et al. (2018) used a convenience sampling technique, while Madan & Yadav (2016) used a combination of snowball (chain-referral), convenience, and judgmental sampling technique.

The reasons for combining two types of non-probability sampling methods, which are convenience and snowball sampling, are due to several reasons. The convenience sampling technique used because it provides members that are readily available and easily known, such as friends and family. This type of sampling technique is considered as inexpensive, least time consuming, and most convenient method.

The snowball (chain-referral) sampling technique is used due to several reasons. Firstly, due to difficulties in framing the sampling because of the inability to reach the targeted population list from the concerned authorities. The data considered a sensitive and closed nature. Secondly, the sample members do not come together, and it is challenging to locate users. Third, there is no other way to access the sample because of failure in determining the sample representatives, so the first selected members of the sample will refer to other members.

The sample size calculation is determined based on Krejcie & Morgan (1970). They set a rule of thumb, which stated that if the population is 1 million and above, the sample size is 384 participants based on confidence level 95% (degree of accuracy). This rule was adopted for this study due to the unknown population size to the researcher.

Survey respondents (units) are defined as members of a sample drawn from all users of local e-wallets in Bahrain. Careful considerations were taken to guarantee the selection of the variety of participants' characteristics to consist of mixed gender, age, educational background, and employment status of the participants. The respondents received an electronic questionnaire. The data collected through Survey Monkey, the participants, shared the website among their friends and family that are using e-wallets, 889 responses collected. However, out of 889 responses collected, 660 completed the questionnaire, which is considered a quite large sample size for any statistical analysis. The participants were given ten days' duration to complete the survey.

QUESTIONNAIRE DESIGN

The voluntary participants have been requested to fill-out a well-designed questionnaire divided into three sections. The first section is general information about the usage of e-wallet and consists of 6 questions. The second section of the questionnaire contained 26 multiple statements of a 5-point Likert scale. This section was built to assess user satisfaction by indicating the level of agreeing or disagreeing on four factors (variables) that have an impact on the continuance use of e-wallets. The indication of number "1" strongly disagrees while strongly agree reflected by number "5". The final section is related to demographical background and consists of 4 questions which are related to gender, age, and education.

The questionnaire was written in both languages, Arabic and English. The reason for establishing the Arabic version is to make sure that all people with different educational backgrounds can participate in this study.

The process applied in distributing the self-administered questionnaire using an exponential non-discriminative snowball and convenience sampling technique. The convenience sampling technique is used first because it provides members that are readily available and easily known, such as friends and family. The convenience method can connect family, friends, and any volunteer through social media applications to fill the online survey (electronic form using Survey Monkey website). Also, we can ask the respondents to forward the survey to their connections who use the e-wallets, which led us to employ exponential non-discriminative snowball sampling technique.

It was helpful to use social networks in distributing the questionnaire to collect a large number of responses. Consideration is given to the inclusion of age, gender, education to show the trends by diversity. The message contains information about the usage of the survey as it is intended for study purposes only, ensuring the personal data of participants will be protected, and they have the right to withdraw from the research's sample at any time if requested. Additionally, upon the participant's request, a copy of the final research study will be provided.

ANALYSIS AND FINDINGS

The selected sample consists of 660 respondents, and each one answered the survey of 36 close-ended questions in total.

Reliability Scale

Reliability was defined roughly as the precision of scale scores; it means the degree to which scores accurately reflect some actual state of the variable in a given sample. The need to check the scale reliability is to ensure that the instrument produces an accurate and consistent measurement. A reliable instrument called on an instrument that works consistently and predictably.

The most popular measurement of internal consistency is Cronbach Alpha, which is varied between 0 and 1. Cronbach Alpha is an "item-level" internal consistency approach, using inter-item associations to estimate the reliability of scale scores, it describes to what extent all items in the test measure the construct.

The Cronbach Alpha was used in this study to measure the reliability of the instrument used. If the score of Cronbach Alpha is 0.7 and more, then it would indicate the reliability of high internal consistency, which means that the reliability of scale has been achieved.

The study comprises six scales (variables), of which all showed an excellent reliability index on Cronbach's Alpha except for the "Usefulness" scale, which was suboptimal (as it below 0.7). All items in these scales contributed well to their scales' overall reliability as the Corrected Total-Item correlation ranged between 0.32 to 0.67. The following table 4 shows more detail about Cronbach's alpha for the dependent and independents variables.

Table 4. Reliability Scale

Scale	Items	Cronbach's Alpha
Ease of use	5	0.841
Compatibility	5	0.780
Usefulness	4	0.667
Security	3	0.778
Satisfaction	4	0.853
Continuance use	5	0.892

Respondents Demographic Characteristics

The demographic characteristics that were preset as moderating variables are gender, age, educational level, and employment status. The respondent's demographic characteristics are shown below.

Gender

The sample consists of 660 participants, of which the majority were male (n=405, 61.4%). The following table 5 shows gender details with obvious male superiority use over female:

Table 5. Gender

Gender	N	%
Male	405	61.4%
Female	255	38.6%

Age Group

Users aged between 26 and 35 years formed more than half of the sample (n=346, 52.4%). Out of 660 participants, only two belong to the group of 18 years and below (n=2, 0.3%). The following table 6 shows age group details. More than 75% of total users are aged between 26 and 45 years:

Educational Level

Respondents who hold Bachelor and higher academic degrees make the vast majority (n=504, 76.3%). The following table 7 shows educational level details:

Table 6. Age Group

Age Group (Years)	N	%
Less than 18 years	2	0.3%
18-25 years	81	12.3%
26-35 years	346	52.4%
36-45 years	154	23.3%
Above 45 years	77	11.7%

Table 7. Educational Level

Highest Educational Level	N	%
High school or less	55	8.3%
Diploma	101	15.3%
Bachelor degree	381	57.7%
Master degree and higher	123	18.6%

Table 8. Distribution of Age and Educational level

Age Group	High school or less	Diploma	Bachelor degree	Master degree and higher	Total
Less than 18 years	2(0.3%)	0(0%)	0(0%)	0(0%)	**2(0.3%)**
18-25 years	9(1.4%)	4(0.6%)	64(9.7%)	4(0.6%)	**81(12.3%)**
26-35 years	23(3.5%)	64(9.7%)	**203(30.8%)**	56(8.5%)	**346(52.4%)**
36-45 years	11(1.7%)	23(3.5%)	80(12.1%)	40(6.1%)	**154(23.3%)**
Above 45 years	10(1.5%)	10(1.5%)	34(5.2%)	23(3.5%)	**77(11.7%)**
Total	**55(8.3%)**	**101(15.3%)**	**381(57.7%)**	**123(18.6%)**	**660(100.0%)**

Distribution of Age and Educational Level

Table 8 below shows the sample distribution across their age groups and educational level. Those who ages are between 26 and 35 years and hold bachelor's degrees represented one-third of the sample (n=203, 30.8%), which makes it the dominant group relative to the rest.

Employment Status

Three-quarters of the participants are employed (n=496, 75.2%), and the rest are equivalently divided into the other employment groups. The below table 9 shows the status in detail:

Table 9. Employment Status

Employment Status	N	%
Student	21	3.2%
Employee	496	75.2%
Self-Employed	38	5.8%
Unemployed/Homemaker	44	6.7%
Retired	61	9.2%

Table 10. E-wallet usage

Question / Response	N	%
What kind of e-wallet(s) have you used?		
BenefitPay (Alone)	388	58.8%
BenefitPay (With other e-wallets)	251	38%
bWallet (Alone)	10	1.5%
bWallet (With other e-wallets)	210	31.8%
Viva Cash (Alone)	10	1.5%
Viva Cash (With other e-wallets)	81	12.2%
Max wallet (Alone)	0	0%
Max wallet (With other e-wallets)	76	11.5%
The most frequent e-wallet application I use is:		
BenefitPay	599	90.8%
bWallet	41	6.2%
Viva Cash	18	2.7%
Max Wallet	2	0.3%

Respondents e-Wallets Usage

Application Used

The vast majority of the participants (n=639, 96.8%) use the BenefitPay e-wallet either alone (58.8%) or with other e-wallets (38%), and they reported that it is the most frequent e-wallet application used (n=599, 90.8%). See the below table 10 for more details:

Purpose

The most reported reason for using e-wallets was for transferring funds (n= 442, 67%) followed by paying bills (n=127, 19.2%). See the below table 11 for more details:

Structural Equation Modeling Analysis

Table 11. Purpose of using an e-wallet

Most frequently, I use e-wallet for the purpose	N	%
Fund Transfer	442	67%
Pay bills	127	19.2%
Shopping	78	11.8%
All	9	1.4%
Pay bill & Fund transfer	2	0.3%
Fund transfer & Shopping	2	0.3%

Structural Equation Modeling (SEM) is a multivariate statistical analysis technique that is used to analyze structural relationships. This technique is a combination of factor analysis and multiple regression analysis. It is used to analyze the structural relationship between measured variables and latent constructs. Latent constructs are the variables that are neither directly observed nor measured. The observed variables are measured during the data collection process, and latent variables are the variables measured by connecting to the observed variables as they cannot be measured directly.

However, to understand relationships in a complex model that contain many path relationships and consists of latent variables and constructs, it is necessary to employ sophisticated multivariate analysis such as Structural Equation Modeling.

The Proposed Model

Direct Constructs Relationships

Figure 4 below shows the proposed model structure based on the partial least square structural equation modeling. All the hypothesized relationships were estimated and turned to be statistically significant as the p-value of each factor is less than 0.05, this is consistent with studies conducted earlier (Albashrawi & Motiwalla, 2019; Tam et al., 2018; Kumar et al. 2018; Chen & Wu, 2017; Singh et al., 2017).

Among the four factors, the weakest relationship is identified between usefulness and satisfaction as the beta equals +0.091. Collectively, ease of use, compatibility, usefulness, and security exerts a considerable effect on satisfaction as it reflected by a sizeable adjusted $R^2=0.642$.

The most significant effect on the participants' satisfaction with the use of e-wallets came mainly from Security (beta=+0.337, p<0.0001) and ease of use (beta=+0.336, p<0.0001). The following table 12 shows the direct effects flowing in the model:

Figure 4. Direct Construct Relationships

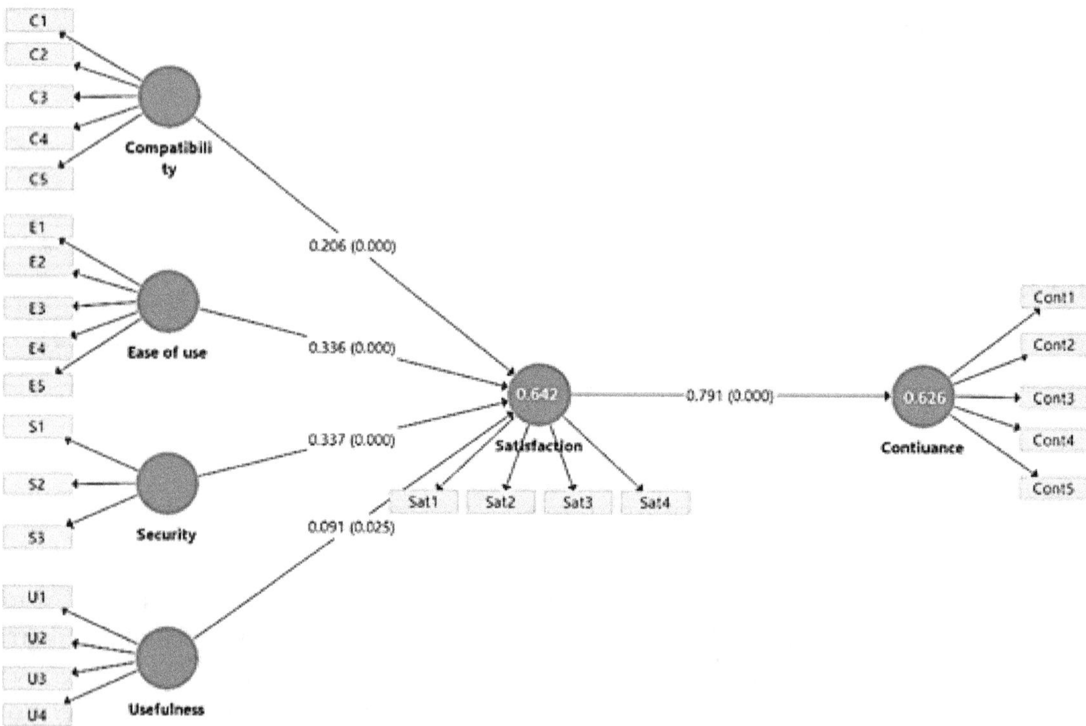

Figure (4) Direct Construct Relationships

Table 12. Direct constructs relationships

Path of a direct relationship	Beta*	p-value
Compatibility → Satisfaction	+0.206	<0.0001
Ease of use → Satisfaction	+0.336	<0.0001
Security → Satisfaction	+0.337	<0.0001
Usefulness → Satisfaction	+0.091	0.025
Satisfaction → Continuance	+0.791	<0.0001

The analysis's results go along with previous studies of (Chen & Wu, 2017; Singh et al., 2017) that the e-wallets "ease of use" has a direct effect on user satisfaction concerning the use of e-wallet. The use of e-wallet to perform transactions was founded to be much easier and faster compared to the traditional method as e-wallet shorten the process of conducting the transactions (Madan & Yadav, 2016).

The research of Chen & Wu (2017) indicates that the usefulness of mobile payments directly affects user satisfaction, while the compatibility of mobile payment effects indirectly on satisfaction through usefulness and ease of use. However, both "compatibility" and "usefulness" variables are found in this study significant predictors that directly affect user satisfaction.

Kumar et al. (2018) emphasized that security indirectly affects satisfaction through mediator variables. However, this study is consistent with the earlier study of Chen & Wu (2017) that founded the more security the users feel about the technology, the higher the satisfaction and direct relationship exist.

Demographic Variables

The four factors are grouped in one indicator in order to test whether the relationship is strengthening if introducing the demographic variables between the factors and user satisfaction. As shown in figure 5 and table 13 below, the moderating variables are statistically insignificant as the p-value is above 0.05. Based on several studies (Singh et al. 2017) that consider the demographic characteristics as significant variables in determining the satisfaction level of the e-wallet usage. However, in this study, the demographic variables have no significant effects on the relationships that exist between the satisfaction and the four predictors (ease of use, compatibility, usefulness, and security). It is consistent with Avornyo et al. (2019) which found that gender, education, and occupation has an insignificant effect on continuous use. Also, Cao et al., (2018) which found that age has insignificant effects on the continuance intention use.

Table 14. Demographic variables

Path of moderating relationship	Beta	p-value
Age moderating effect → Four predictors/Satisfaction	-0.057	0.149
Gender moderating effect → Four predictors/Satisfaction	+0.024	0.510
Education moderating effect → Four predictors/Satisfaction	-0.022	0.326
Emplomen moderating effect → Four predictors/Satisfaction	+0.036	0.326

Indirect Constructs Relationships

As being proposed in the model, satisfaction has a relationship with continuance which turned to be a powerful and statistically significance (beta=+0.791, R^2=0.626, p<0.0001), as shown in figure 4 above. However, the four stated factors do have indirect effects on continuance via the mediating variable "satisfaction," and this is consistent with prior studies conducted (Albashrawi & Motiwalla, 2019; J; Chen & Li, 2017; Yuan et al., 2016). The largest observed indirect effects were exerted by ease of use (beta=0.266, p<0.0001) and security (beta=0.267, p<0.0001). The following table 14 delineates the magnitude of the four factors' indirect effects on continuance:

Figure 5. Demographic Variables

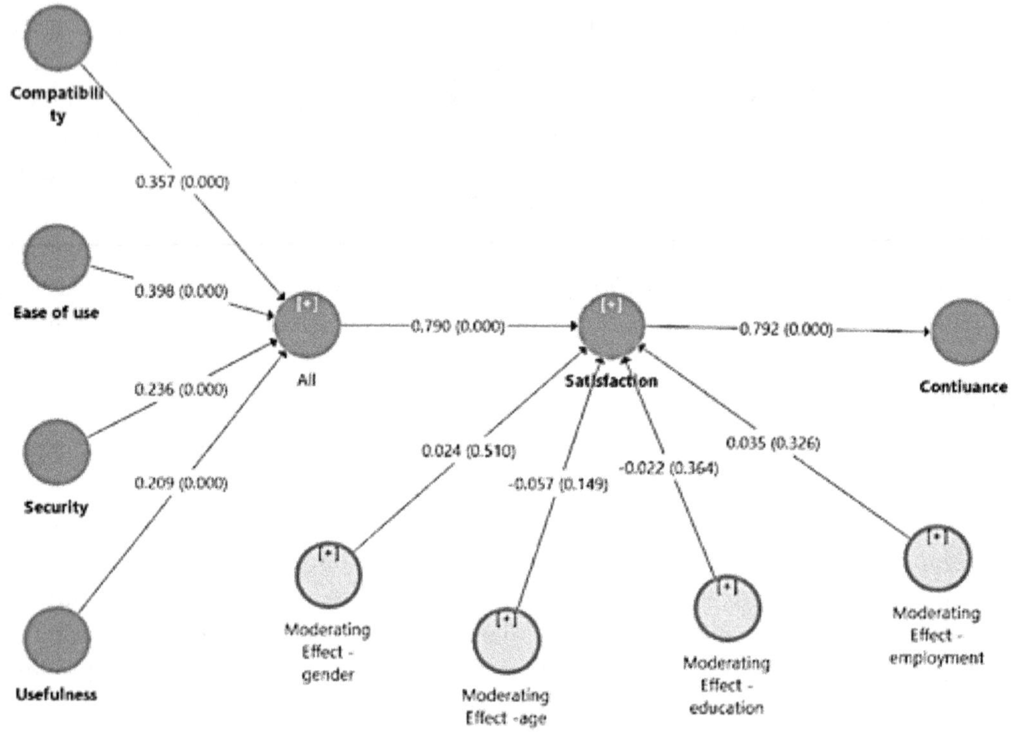

Figure (5) Demographic Variables

In summary, the above hypotheses are tested and concluded that all hypotheses are accepted except the moderating variables hypotheses. The below table 16 shows in detail:

Table 15. Indirect constructs relationships

Path of indirect relationship	Indirect Beta*	p-value
Compatibility → Continuance	0.163*(0.206*0.791)*	<0.0001
Ease of use → Continuance	0.266*(0.336*0.791)*	<0.0001
Security → Continuance	0.267*(0.337*0.791)*	<0.0001
Usefulness → Continuance	0.072*(0.091*0.791)*	<0.0001

*The indirect effect is the product of multiplying the direct effect between the factor and the mediator (satisfaction) and the direct effect between the mediator and the dependent variable (continuance) – based on T statistic

The Saturated Model

Figure 6 below shows the saturated model based on the partial least square structural equation modeling that outlines all possible relationships that may exist between the construct variables. On the one hand, the ease of use (beta=-0.079, p=0.082) and security (beta=0.043, p=0.220) are recognized as statistically

Table 16. Hypothesis summary

Hypothesis	Findings
H_1: Ease of use → Satisfaction	Supported (significant)
H_2: Ease of use → Satisfaction → Continuance	Supported (significant)
H_3: Compatibility → Satisfaction	Supported (significant)
H_4: Compatibility → Satisfaction → Continuance	Supported (significant)
H_5: Usefulness → Satisfaction	Supported (significant)
H_6: Usefulness → Satisfaction → Continuance	Supported (significant)
H_7: Security → Satisfaction	Supported (significant)
H_8: Security → Satisfaction → Continuance	Supported (significant)
H_9: Satisfaction → Continuance	Supported (significant)
$H_{10.1}$: Age moderation → Four predictors → Satisfaction	Unsupported (insignificant)
$H_{10.2}$: Gender moderation → Four predictors → Satisfaction	Unsupported (insignificant)
$H_{10.3}$: Education moderation → Four predictors → Satisfaction	Unsupported (insignificant)
$H_{10.4}$: Employment moderation → Four predictors → Satisfaction	Unsupported (insignificant)

insignificant relationships with the continuance use. On the other hand, compatibility (beta=+0.282, p<0.0001) and usefulness (beta=+0.152, p=0.001) are recognized as statistically significant relationships with the continuance use.

The Improved Model

Figure 7 below shows the improved model structure based on the partial least square structural equation modeling that outlines the statistically significant relationships that exist between the construct variables.

As shown below, in figure 7, the model is improved to include the direct path of the statistically significant relationships that are proved in this study. The new adjusted R^2 is 0.699 while previously adjusted $R^2$was 0.626 in the proposed model, since adjusted R^2 has the ability to quantify the percentage of explanation in the continuance use by the four factors in the model [ease of use, compatibility, security, usefulness]. Therefore it is a good indicator to determine the optimal model. This noticeable improvement in adjusted R^2 means that almost 70% of continuance use is well predicted by the four factors, which is mean it is an instrumental model. The ease of use, compatibility, usefulness, and security exert an enormous effect on continuance use as it reflected by a sizeable adjusted R^2=0.699. The total effect on the continuance use is shown in the table 17 below in detail:

RESEARCH DISCUSSION AND CONCLUSION

The results are discussed with the comparison of previous literature findings and interpreted to satisfy the research questions and hypotheses in the following sections. This research aimed to identify the main factors that have a significant impact on the e-wallet usage and its continuance use. The study success-

Figure 6. The Saturated Model

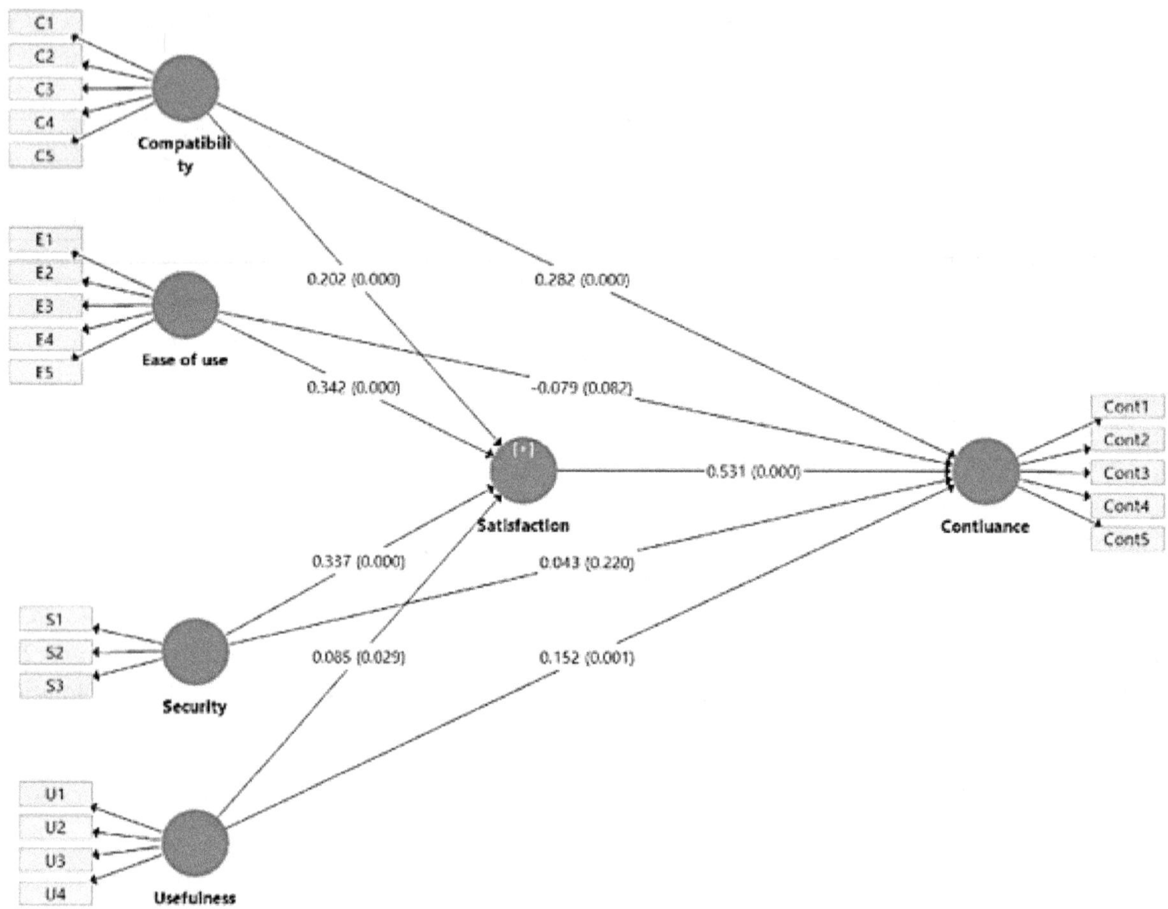

Figure 6 The Saturated Model

Table 17. Beta Coefficients

Relationship	Indirect Beta*	Direct Beta	Total Beta**
Compatibility → Continuance	0.105(0.202*0.520)	0.267	0.372
Ease of use → Continuance	0.178(0.342*0.520)	-	0.178
Security → Continuance	0.177(0.340*0.520)	-	0.177
Usefulness → Continuance	0.044(0.084*0.520)	0.147	0.191

*The indirect effect is the product of multiplying the direct effect between the factor and the mediator (satisfaction) and the direct effect between the mediator and the dependent variable (continuance).

**The total Beta is the sum of indirect beta and direct beta.

Figure 7. The Improved Model Variables

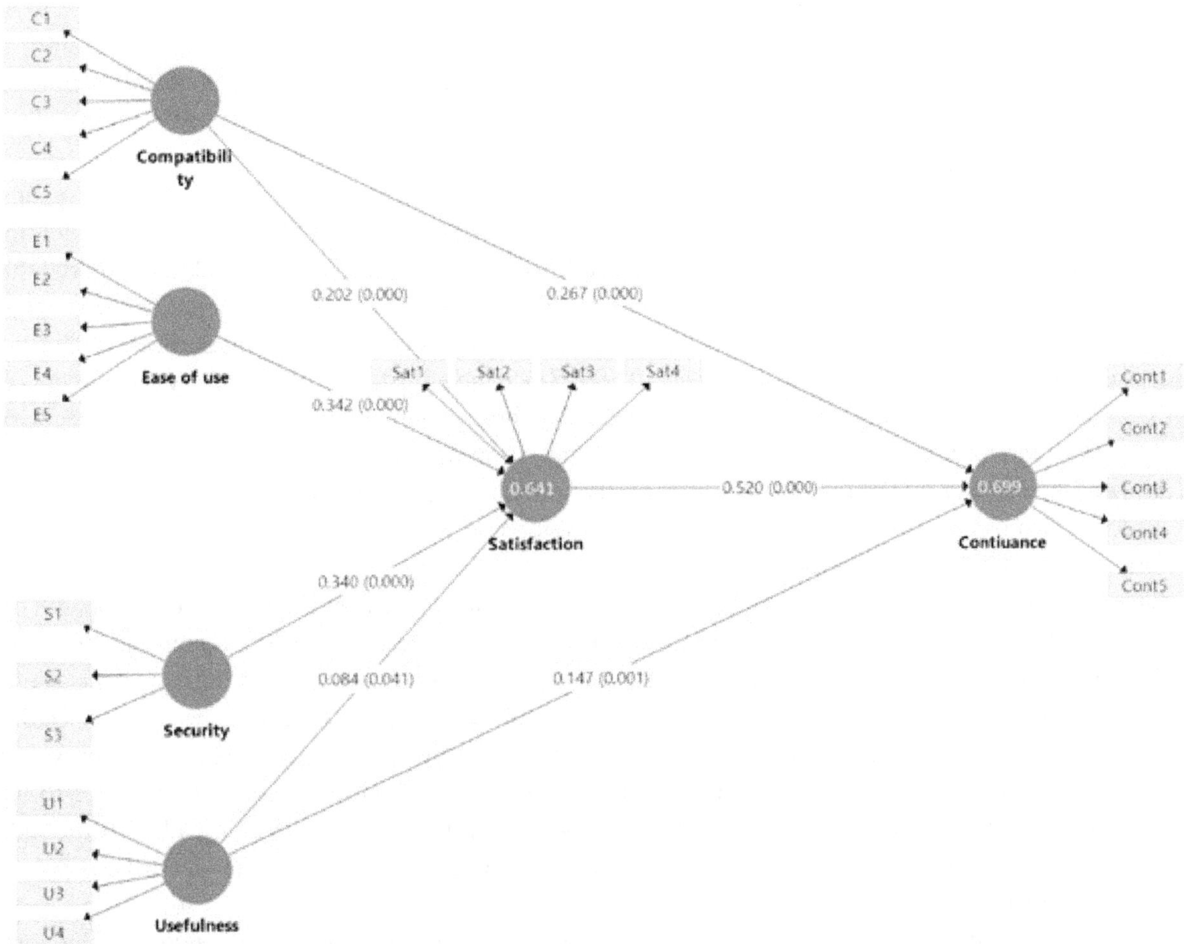

Figure 7 The Improved Model

fully merged the elements of the Technology Acceptance Model (TAM) and Expectancy-Confirmation Model (ECM).

Also, this study successfully extended the research model to include two new predictor variables that were previously examined (Chen & Wu, 2017; Kumar et al., 2018). Furthermore, the study introduced the moderating effect of the demographic characteristics on the relationship between the satisfaction of e-wallet and the four variables that were previously examined (Singh et al., 2017).

The empirical results of this study demonstrated that direct relations are statistically significant between satisfaction concerning the e-wallet use, and the four predictors (ease of use, compatibility, usefulness, and security). Also, the relation between continuance usage and satisfaction concerning e-wallet use is statistically significant.

Moreover, the results show that continuance usage is indirectly and significantly influenced by the four predictors (ease of use, compatibility, usefulness, and security). However, the moderating variables were found to be statistically insignificant (demographic variables) in the relationship between the satisfaction and the four predictors (ease of use, compatibility, usefulness, and security).

This study presents a proposed research model that is under scrutiny. However, in an attempt to discover all possible relationships that may exist between the construct variables, the saturated model introduced. The saturated model outlines the comprehensive relationships that may exist in the entire model. The findings of the saturated model will be discussed below.

First, the adjusted R^2 value is considered as a valuable indicator of the goodness of any mathematical model; the higher the value of the adjusted R^2, the better. The adjusted R^2 was 0.626 in the model that is under the scrutiny of this study, the proposed model. However, in the saturated model, the model that outlines all possible relationships that may exist in the model, the new, improved adjusted R^2 value is 0.699.

The ease of use, compatibility, usefulness, and security variables exert a substantial effect on continuance use, as reflected by a sizeable adjusted R^2=0.699. Since the adjusted R^2 can quantify the percentage of explanation in the continuance use by the four factors in the model [ease of use, compatibility, security, usefulness]; therefore, it is a good indicator to determine the better model. The noticeable improvement in adjusted R^2 means that the four factors well predict almost 70% of continuance use.

Second, two of the model factors have a direct relationship with continuance use, while two of the factors have no direct relationship with continuance use.

The compatibility and usefulness variables are recognized as significant direct relationships with the continuance use. The direct relationship between usefulness and the continuance use is consistent with the ECM model and Chen & Li, (2017) findings. This means that if an individual finds the e-wallet is useful and compatible with their needs and wishes, they will continue using it even if they are not satisfied.

However, the ease of use and security variables have shown insignificant direct relationships with the continuance use variable (Avornyo et al., 2019). This means that if an individual continues to use an e-wallet, then he/she should be satisfied concerning ease of use and security of e-wallet. If the individual is unsatisfied with the e-wallet ease of use and unsatisfied with the e-wallet security, they will not continue using it.

Third, as an indication of the leading factor that affects the use and the continuance use, the comparison is made by identifying the highest number of total Beta figures. Among the four predictors (ease of use, compatibility, usefulness, and security), the results indicate that the compatibility is the leading factor that exerts the highest effect on continuance use, as reflected by the total Beta =0.372 as shown in table 17 above.

RESEARCH CONTRIBUTIONS

The research contribution can be summarized in the following two points when considering the theoretical implications. First, the essential contribution is the combination of the Technology Acceptance Model (TAM) and Expectancy-Confirmation Model (ECM) to provide an extensive scope of the continuance use factors. The basis for this research is the ECM model, as it measures the level of an individual's satisfaction and expectation.

Moreover, the TAM model is widely used for measuring the initial adoption; the constructs identified for initial adoption factors are also identified for the continuance usage factors. Therefore, the TAM model indicates the initial adoption and continuance usage factors. Theoretically, this study results concluded that the proposed model constructs that extracted from TAM and ECM are significant.

Second, the proposed model has been further tested for any possible relationships that may exist. The findings of this research indicate that there were significant direct relations between the continuance use and both compatibility usefulness, the direct relationship between usefulness and the continuance use consistent with findings of the study conducted by Chen & Li, (2017). Moreover, the ECM model state this relationship. This means that, if the individuals find e-wallet is useful, they will continue using it, even if they are not satisfied with e-wallet. Therefore, it is not necessary to be satisfied with the usefulness of e-wallet to continue using it.

Furthermore, if the individuals find e-wallet is compatible with their needs and wants, they will continue using it, even if they are not satisfied with e-wallet. In other words, it is not necessary to be satisfied with the compatibility of e-wallet to continue using it.

However, the ease of use and security are recognized as insignificant direct relationships with the continuance use. This means that to continue using an e-wallet, the individual should be satisfied with the ease of use and the security of e-wallet. Once the individual is not satisfied with the e-wallet ease of use and not satisfied with the security of the e-wallet, then they will not continue using it. In other words, it is necessary to be satisfied with the ease of use and security of e-wallet in order to continue using it.

RESEARCH LIMITATIONS

This research analysis is classified as an inferential statistics analysis exercise conducted to discover the factors that affect the use of e-wallet in the Kingdom of Bahrain. Data was collected through an online questionnaire. This study managed to collect 660 completed responses that gave a much more excellent opportunity to draw a more accurate conclusion and reflect the real position of factors that gauge the e-wallet usage. However, this study has experienced many limitations. First, the study was limited to the users in the Kingdom of Bahrain with a relatively small sample size. The source of satisfaction may differ among countries (Zhang et al., 2012); therefore, the identified factors that affect the individual satisfaction and usage of e-wallet may differ from country to country. Thus, the study results cannot be generalized outside Bahrain.

Second, this research designed to identify the significance of four factors only. However, there may be other important factors, such as the social influence on the e-wallets usage that were not investigated due to the time limitation of the study. Third, the lack of previous researches poses a challenge in selecting the optimal theoretical model to investigate the driven factors towards the new concept of using e-wallets. However, the selected two models to this study were TAM and ECM models that were used by the previous research work in investigating new technology.

Forth, the lack of direct interaction with the participants poses limitations as the data collected using a self-administered survey. The study conducted a pilot study to gauge the level of respondent's understanding. The outcome of this pilot study showed adequate understanding and clarity of the survey's questions. Nevertheless, the researcher cannot verify the level of actual understandability of all participants in case of ambiguities. Fifth, this study identified the factors that affect the use of e-wallet in Bahrain regardless of the e-wallet providers. The data collected were analyzed and generalized with all e-wallet providers in Bahrain. In other words, individuals may be satisfied with regards to the security of specific e-wallet while not satisfied with other e-wallet providers. Future studies may be conducted to identify the variances among e-wallet providers.

RECOMMENDATIONS FOR FUTURE RESEARCH

Finally, there are several highlighted points to be taken into consideration for future researches. The identified factors that affect the individual satisfaction and usage of e-wallet may differ from one country to another. Therefore, the satisfaction construct needs to be further investigated to obtain the significant factors that affect the use of e-wallet. Thus, enhancing the understandability of e-wallet usage. Moreover, the theoretical implications of this study are recommended to further expand in future research in order to validate the study results.

This study aggregates the results and recommendations of all involved factors among all e-wallet providers in Bahrain. These recommendations can be used to build upon for future researches and to analyze the factors that affect the use of each e-wallet provider separately, to provide a meaningful comparison on the strengths of each provider, as the strength of a specific provider may be a weakness for other providers.

REFERENCES

Akturan, U., & Tezcan, N. (2012). Mobile banking adoption of the youth market: Perceptions & intentions. *Marketing Intelligence & Planning*, *30*(4), 444–459. doi:10.1108/02634501211231928

Alaeddin, O., Rana, A., Zainudin, Z., & Kamarudin, F. (2018). From physical to digital: Investigating consumer behavior of switching to a mobile wallet. *Polish Journal of Management Studies, 17.*

Albashrawi, M., & Motiwalla, L. (2019). Privacy & Personalization in Continued Usage Intention of Mobile Banking: An Integrative Perspective. *Information Systems Frontiers*, *21*(5), 1–13. doi:10.100710796-017-9814-7

Avornyo, P., Fang, J., Odai, R. O., Vondee, J. B., & Nartey, M. N. (2019). Factors Affecting Continuous Usage Intention of Mobile Banking in Tema and Kumasi. *International Journal of Business and Social Science*, *10*(3). Advance online publication. doi:10.30845/ijbss.v10n3p11

Bagla, R. K., & Sancheti, V. (2018). Gaps in customer satisfaction with digital wallets: A challenge for sustainability. *Journal of Management Development*, *37*(6), 442–451. doi:10.1108/JMD-04-2017-0144

Batelco. (2018). *Batelco and Arab Financial Services Partner to launch bWallet: A new FinTech Service.* Retrieved from http://batelco.com/news-media/batelco-and-arab-financial-services-partner-to-launch-bwallet-a-new-fintech-service/

Benefit. (2017). *The Benefit Company introduces the National E-Wallet by the 4th of July 2017.* Retrieved from https://www.benefit.bh/events/2017/NationalEWallet.aspx?monthNo=6

Bhattacherjee, A. (2001a). Understanding information systems continuance-An expectation-confirmation model-. *Management Information Systems Quarterly*, *25*(3), 351–370. doi:10.2307/3250921

Cao, X., Yu, L., Liu, Z., Gong, M., & Adeel, L. (2018). Understanding mobile payment users' continuance intention: A trust transfer perspective. *Internet Research*, *28*(2), 456–476. doi:10.1108/IntR-11-2016-0359

CBB. (2019). *Financial Stability Report.* Retrieved from https://www.cbb.gov.bh/ar/publications/

Chen, L. Y., & Wu, W. N. (2017). An exploration of the factors affecting user satisfaction with mobile payments. *International Journal of Computer Science & Information Technology.*, *9*(3), 97–105. doi:10.5121/ijcsit.2017.9308

Devaraj, S., Kohli, R., & Fan, M. (2002). Antecedents of B2C channel satisfaction and preference: Validating e-commerce metrics. *Information Systems Research*, *13*(3), 316–333. doi:10.1287/isre.13.3.316.77

Gumussoy, C. A. (2016). Factors affecting users' decision to continue using mobile banking in Turkey. *International Journal of Mobile Communications*, *14*(4), 411. doi:10.1504/IJMC.2016.077341

Krejcie, R. V., & Morgan, D. W. (1970). Determining sample size for research activities. *Educational and Psychological Measurement*, *30*(3), 607–610. doi:10.1177/001316447003000308

Kumar, A., Adlakaha, A., & Mukherjee, K. (2018). The effect of perceived security & grievance redressal on continuance intention to use M-wallets in a developing country. -. *International Journal of Bank Marketing*, *36*(7), 1170–1189. doi:10.1108/IJBM-04-2017-0077

Madan, K., & Yadav, R. (2016). Behavioral intention to adopt mobile wallets: A developing country perspective." -. *Journal of Indian Business Research*, *8*(3), 227–244. doi:10.1108/JIBR-10-2015-0112

Oliver, R. L. (1980). A cognitive model for the antecedents and consequences of satisfaction. *JMR, Journal of Marketing Research*, *17*(4), 460–469. doi:10.1177/002224378001700405

Punch, K. F. (2003). Survey research: The basics. *Sage (Atlanta, Ga.)*.

Singh, N., Srivastava, S., & Sinha, N. (2017). Consumer preference & satisfaction of M-wallets: A study on North Indian consumers. *International Journal of Bank Marketing*, *35*(6), 944–965. doi:10.1108/IJBM-06-2016-0086

STC. (2019). *VIVA Cash launch*. Retrieved from https://www.stc.com.bh/content/cash_launch

Venkatesh, V., & Davis, F. (1996). A Model of the Antecedents of Perceived ease of use-: Development and test. *Decision Sciences*, *27*(3), 451–481. doi:10.1111/j.1540-5915.1996.tb01822.x

Venkatesh, X., Thong, & Xu. (2012). Consumer acceptance and use of information technology: Extending the unified theory of acceptance and use of technology. *Management Information Systems Quarterly*, *36*(1), 157–178. doi:10.2307/41410412

Yuan, S., Liu, Y., Liu, J., & Yao, R. (2016). An investigation of user's continuance intention towards mobile banking in China. *Journal of Information Development*, *32*(1), 20–34. doi:10.1177/0266666914522140

Zhang, L., Liu, Q., & Zhu, J. (2012). A meta-analysis of mobile commerce adoption and the moderating effect of culture. *Computers in Human Behavior*, *28*(5), 1902–1911. doi:10.1016/j.chb.2012.05.008

KEY TERMS AND DEFINITIONS

Compatibility: The degree of consistency of e-wallet with the user's lifestyles and needs.

Continuance Use: Users desire to use e-wallet continuously.

E-Wallets: Electronic Wallets are a kind of electronic card that is used generally for business transactions made online through a smartphone or a computer.

Ease of Use: The level of easiness and user-friendliness in using e-wallets, the volume of effort need it to perform transactions.

Satisfaction: The degree of positive feeling the users feel when they use the e-wallet.

Security: The extent to which users' belief that is using an e-wallet is secured. The security consists of authentication, confidentiality, non-repudiation, and data integrity.

Usefulness: The degree to which the e-wallets are useful and provide benefits to help users facilitate particular activity.

Chapter 17
User Friendly and User Satisfaction Model Aligned With FinTech

Khalid Ahmed Al-Emadi
Arab Open University, Bahrain

Zorah Abu Kassim
Arab Open University, Bahrain

Anjum Razzaque
https://orcid.org/0000-0002-7455-4175
Ahlia University, Bahrain

ABSTRACT

This chapter investigates user friendliness and user satisfaction at Ministry of Works (MoW), Kingdom of Bahrain. Literature is focused on Technology Acceptance Model (TAM), Perceived Ease of Use (PEOU) as having a positive link to user friendliness. Findings show that user friendliness has a positive and significant impact on user satisfaction. This is empirically tested with a sample of 131 employees, a quantitative approach using SPSS Version 25, Pearson Correlation, Factor and Regression Analysis. Findings contribute to the existing body of knowledge in providing insights on factors influencing user satisfaction. Limitation of the study include small sample size, convenience sampling, and no interactive effects examined. Further studies should measure other variables such as user resistance to change and environmental factors. Other studies on user confidence level could also be investigated. User confidence has a major role in improving customer satisfaction.

DOI: 10.4018/978-1-7998-3257-7.ch017

INTRODUCTION

Ministry of Works, Bahrain, is a government entity, involved with public works in Kingdom of Bahrain. In 1992, Ministry of Works (MoW) is known as Public Works and Electricity & Water Authority. By year 2001 this government organization was re-named as Ministry of Works (MoW). The ministry's major functions are construction and maintenance of roads, bridges, flyovers, construction of governmental buildings such as public schools and government buildings. IT Helpdesk system (aka SMART Service desk System) plays a chief role in delivering a simple and efficient means to provide IT support to users. IT Helpdesk System is an ITIL (IT Infrastructure Library) system, offers an all-in-one, effective IT process, and helpdesk support.

The SMART Help Desk System has been in the market since 2007 (Smart Service Desk System, n.d.). The current IT Helpdesk system in MoW requires improvements and enhancements to improve IT services efficiency and effectiveness. There are users' complaints on system's interface being not user-friendly such as difficulties in searching for tickets, and inability to use the back button of webpages. User friendly is defined as being easy to use and learn. User friendly involves systems, applications, equipment, and processes (Bashir & Madhavaiah, 2014) from computers or in the field of IT, with a clear interface, easy navigation, and is well organized (Sönmez, 2018, & Mai, Tuan, Yoshi, 2013). Moreover, a user-friendly interface is concise and well-built so that users will feel comfortable using the system (Mai, et.al., 2013).

Another opportunity observed by the scholars of this study is to further align the SMART Help Desk System with FinTech to further improve user friendly and acceptance from the end-user point of view, i.e., those users who pertain to the contractors, suppliers etc., involved in the maintenance and construction projects within the Kingdom of Bahrain. As a result, the aim of this study is also to provide a review of literature to comprehend what is FinTech and how the Ministry of Works of Bahrain can indulge using this for improving the end-user acceptance of the SMART Help Desk System.

TAM (Technology Acceptance Model): TAM (Technology Acceptance Model) by Davis, (1989) has two beliefs; Perceived Usefulness (PU) and Perceived Ease-of-Use (PEOU) for user's acceptance. Davis, (1989) defines PEOU as the measure to which the potential user expects the system to be effort-free. Thus, there is a positive link between Perceived Ease of Use (PEOU) and user friendly, which leads to customer's satisfaction. Therefore, it is probable to determine a cause and effect relationship between User Friendly and User Satisfaction. TAM is particularly tailored for modeling users' acceptance of information systems or technologies (Abdul Nasser & Prabhakar, 2017). TAM is renowned for applicability across various situations. TAM was primarily meant to explain the impending user's behavioral intentions while using a technological innovation such as information systems (Bashir & Madhavaiah, 2014).

In addition, this model includes five factors: perceived ease of use, perceived usefulness, behavioral intention, attitudes, and actual usage (Alsamydai, 2014). TAM demonstrates that perceived usefulness, perceived ease of use as per user acceptance is directly linked to user-friendly, as whenever these elements exists, a system is user-friendly, hence, users will feel comfortable and happy to use it (Davis, 1989). Moreover, according to TAM, these two beliefs Perceived Usefulness (PU) and Perceived Ease-of-Use (PEOU) are primary significance for user's acceptance and can improve the level of confidence towards information system (such as a Helpdesk System). Nevertheless, PU refers to the potential user's subjective likelihood that the use of a certain application will increase his or her performance. Davis, (1989) defines PEOU as the measure to which the potential user expects the system to be effort-free. There is a positive link between Perceived Ease of Use (PEOU) and user friendly, which leads to customer's satisfaction. According to Lim & Ting (2012), PEOU is a major determinant of attitude towards user's behavior. Online retailers for example, are recommended to make digital marketplace simple to learn and easy for consumers to be skilled in using the user's interfaces, i.e. as user friendly as possible in order to increase users' satisfaction.

Benefits of User-Friendly: A user-friendly interface enables users to understand how to operate a system without the need to refer to a user manual. In addition, the flow of actions is short and fast, so that users will not go through many steps and not waste time to perform a task (Scholtz, & Mahmud, 2016). User-friendly interface is created in a way that enables customers to revert in case of errors and offers correction alternatives. Moreover, the user-friendly interface is concise and well-built that users will feel comfortable using it (Mai, et.al, 2013). Another important benefit of a user-friendly interface is that customers can customize how it "looks" and "feels". For example, a customer can change the interface color to the color he/she likes, and to change the fonts and backgrounds (Mai, et.al., 2013). User friendly concept is also used in mobile banking (Ahmadi, Bahrami, & Ahmad, 2016). TAM model assists in formulating the theoretical foundation for determining the important factors, which contribute to consumers' usage of the Internet as a distribution channel for Financial Services (McKechnie, Winklhofer & Ennew, 2006). A user-friendly system encourages participation of citizens and organizations in e-government acceptance (Olushola & Abiola, 2017). Moreover, banks must design user-friendly websites to reduce the technophobia of customers (Agha & Saeed 2015). According to Intana & Chansa-ngavej, (2010) banks should ensure that customer user-interface toward the online banking application to be user-friendly and understandable. The terminologies used within the web site must be self-descriptive and allows the users to benefit from the desired service without external assistance from bank's personnel. Banks further need to streamline mobile banking features to design additional user-friendly system interface (Abadi, Kabiry, & Forghani, 2013).

Studies on User Friendly: Mohan, Ahmad, Kong, Yew, Liew & Mat, (2013), concludes that the internet-banking portal should be user-friendly, because not many users are familiar with computer and the Internet especially demographically aged users. User-friendly allows internet-banking services to have operational simplicity, and ease of use to manage transactions between banks and customers. E-banking service is focused on building an agile and simple experience, from the perspective of the user. User-friendly dimension simplifies the operation, which leads to a better banking experience (Intana & Chansa-ngavej, 2010). In addition, enhancing the security for online transactions and motivating customers to perform internet banking is needed. Consumer acceptance or adoption of e-banking services, accessibility, convenience, design, and content of e-banking portal are sources of satisfaction (Tan, Chong, Ooi & Chong, 2010). From students' perception of the use of Table Desktop (TPC) is easy to use (user-friendly) will certainly affect attitude towards TPC (El-Gayar, Moran, & Hawkes, 2011). Programs aiming at positively influencing students' attitude (and thus acceptance) should aim at performance and effort expectancy.

In another study, Bogart & Wichadee, (2015) concluded that perceived ease of use, vastly stimulates the acceptance of a system because as a user-friendly tool enabling users to establish voice-calls and send messages instantly. As such, this system can be applied to create many classroom activities. User friendly is also applied in the context of e-learning (Al-Rahmi, Othman, & Yusuf, 2015, Nuamah, & Darko, 2016). Mavroidis, Karatrantou, & Koutsouba, (2013) study that by using analytical and systematic directions, technical support and the use of a helpdesk have a significant impact on perceived ease of use. User friendly as a feature is paramount to usage of a system in three different contexts of internet banking, E-Learning, and use of national Databases.

Aligning FinTech with Technology Acceptance: It is important to understand how FinTech facilitates the philosophy of this study. Advances in technological spawned innovations in financial services: in the emergence of FinTech, which integrates technology with finance with a view to providing payment services regarded as highly utile for consumers (Chang et al., 2016). FinTech is a financial service that integrates finance and technology. FinTech is not a new concept. Such a service was initially termed as "financial technology" in the 1990s and "digital finance" or "e-finance" in the 2000s. The investment in FinTech arose from 4.05 billion USD in 2013 to 122 billion USD in 2014in the USA, where, in 2016, more than 7 trillion USD worth of FinTech transactions occurred in the US. In China, in the same year, up to 4 trillion USD worth of transactions were reported (Razzaque et al., 2019; Chang et al., 2016). The high rate of adoption of FinTech has been attributed to transparency and cost effectiveness in as much as FinTech eliminates financial "middlemen" in the financial intermediation process. FinTech firms leverage disruptive business models enabling, in the latter example, investors to self-manage their investment portfolios without brokers resulted in reduced transaction costs (Kim et al., 2016; Zavolokina et al., 2016).

Ample literature explains consumers' motivation for using a product/service through the intrinsic and extrinsic factors. Intrinsic factors drive activity performance involving achievement of desired objectives/goals without any tangible incentive/s. Extrinsic factors drive activity performance under conditions in which there are tangible incentives for achieving objectives/goals. External factors are the causes to the extent to which individuals lack intrinsic motivation (Hur, 2017; Vallerand & Reid, 1984). There are three suggested external factors driving FinTech adoption and continued use: cost savings, customer friendliness and ease of access (Leonga et al., 2017; Lee & Shin, 2015). Seamless transactions, from which consumers derive benefit in the form of speedy transactions, involve employment of innovative customer-friendly financial service platforms reshaping the financial ecosystem i.e., the interstices between financial and IT firms is blurring (Zavolokina et al., 2016). Convenience of using FinTech stems from ubiquity in access given that consumers can execute financial transactions using mobile platforms (Leonga et al., 2017; Hung & Luo, 2016; Lee & Shin, 2015) anywhere in terms of location. As a result, it is the opinion of the scholars of this study to incorporate the features of user friendly as antecedent in determining user satisfaction. Ministry of Works IT HelpDesk scenario can be a reflection on the adoption of FinTech within government organizations in Bahrain.

METHODOLOGY

The target population is 1000 employees who work at MoW in different directorates. Total sample size is 623 users (employees) who use a computer, and who are employees of directorates at MoW. Convenience sampling was used. Respondents are employees preselected from respective directorates. 131 employees (users) of MoW responded to the self-administered questionnaire. Measures of items were from published sources. The following table contains the respondents' details:

Analysis of the total Respondents: SPSS Version 25 was used. Data were analyzed by use of descriptive, Pearson Correlation, Factor and Multiple Regression. From the sample size, males are in the majority of respondents(68.7%), relatively younger (mean=37.5 years), relatively educated (70.2% with a bachelor's degree) with an educational background predominantly in engineering . Respondents are having the job designation of technical and Senior in the Ministry of Works. Overall, sample consist predominantly of younger men from an engineering background who hold the positions of Technicians and Senior in the Ministry of Works. Their educational background and age could have an effect on their

Table 1. Respondents details

Respondents		*Frequency*	*Percent*	*Cronbach's α*
Gender	Female	41	31.3	
	Male	90	68.7	
Age	18 –27 years old	19	14.5	
	28 –37 years old	54	41.2	
	38 –47 years old	36	27.5	
	48 –58 years old	18	13.7	
	Above 58 years old	4	3.1	
	Age Mean is 37.5, SD is 9.98			
Highest Level of Education	Bachelors	92	70.2	
	Diploma	20	15.3	
	Masters	16	12.2	
	PhD (Doctorate)	2	1.5	
	Secondary	1	.8	
Educational Background	Architecture, Building Environment, Urban Planning & related	16	12.2	
	Business Management, Commerce, & Social Sciences	33	25.2	
	General Engineering, Civil & related	59	45.0	
	IT & related	18	13.7	
	Sciences & Mathematics	5	3.8	
Current Job Position	Chief	8	6.1	
	Director & Above	6	4.6	
	Head	15	11.5	
	Senior	53	40.5	
	Technician	49	37.4	
	User-friendly			0.9
	Level of user-satisfaction			0.84

N=131

awareness level on the functions and usage of the IT HelpDesk. To assess the accuracy of measures used, Cronbach's α reliability analysis is executed to test reliability and internal consistency of user friendly and user satisfaction. Pearson Correlation analysis was conducted between User Friendly (Independent Variable, IDV) and Users' Satisfaction (Dependent Variable, DV). Findings show 0.76. Hence, the correlation between both variables is significant.

A Factor analysis is conducted to analyze responses by using Varimax rotation and extraction method. Factor analysis is done on ten items that measures User-Friendly. Eight items were retained because of a higher factor loading of more than 0.6 and labeled as Ease of Use according to literature. Eigenvalue is 4.7, which is 58.8 percent explained the variance. KMO is 0.87 and Cronbach reliability (α) is 0.90 indicating that items are reliable. User Satisfaction had five items retained because a high factor loading of more than 0.6. The factor is labeled into Satisfaction according to literature. Eigenvalue is 3.1, which is 61.6 percent of the variance. This indicates that satisfaction accounts for the 61.6% of the variable. The KMO is 0.85 and Cronbach's α reliability is 0.84; indicating that items responses is reliable. To test the hypotheses, a regression analysis further conducted on these variables as shown below:

Table 2. Results of Regression Analysis of Ease of Use on Satisfaction

Independent Variables	Beta	t	Sig
Ease Of Use	.46	6.72	.000*
R^2			.62
Adjusted R^2			.61

a. Dependent Variable: Satisfaction
*sig. $p<0.05$

Regression analysis indicates that the significance level of Ease of Use is 0.00 (i.e. <0.05), hence, a positive and significant impact on user's satisfaction. The findings indicate that a user friendly that is ease of use could be for example, having a friendly and captive design style, helps the users of the organization feel at ease in using the system. This will naturally enhance utilization of the system.

CONCLUSION

The study concludes the following answers to the research questions. A user-friendly interface which focuses on ease of use provides user satisfactions. The finding of this study gives a strong indication that adoption of technology needs to embed ease of use as a dominant feature in being user friendly. This means that any new technology if there is a high probability that users will adopt the technology then user friendly remains a key factor in determining user satisfaction. A new technology may be technically sophisticated but not be easy to use will probably result in non-adoption of such technology. In relation to FinTech, being ease of use will improve the probability that a user will be well-versed to using FinTech on the Internet. As a result, this poses a better likelihood of user satisfaction is assured to adopt the FinTech products and services online. In relation to the Kingdom of Bahrain, the public in this country is quite aware and knowledgeable in using the Internet and the devices that are integrated on the Internet. Therefore, this indicates that aligned with findings of this study, the public in Bahrain are ready to adopt FinTech if the products and services comply with the human computer interaction standards and are easy to use.

IMPLICATIONS

User experiences have five characteristics (utility, usability, aesthetics, identification and value) have an impact on customer satisfaction (Badran & Al-Haddad, 2018). Users are satisfied with a system that provides them with a friendly interface with features and tools. Similarly, in a study conducted by Seraj &Wong (2014), users were satisfied using tablet devices than mobile phones because of tablets' larger screen size and clarity of information presented. Baabdullaha, Alalwanb, Ranac, Kizginc, & Patilc, (2019), indicate a strong relationship exists between actual usage behavior and customer satisfaction. Customer loyalty shows that a strong prediction by both usage behavior and users' satisfaction. Findings of this study contribute to the existing body of knowledge by providing awareness on factors that influence users' satisfaction in addition what was investigated the knowledge management research topic, e.g., (Razzaque et al., 2020; Razzaque, et al., 2019; Razzaque, 2019; Razzaque & Eldabi, 2018; Razzaque et al., 2012; Razzaque & Alalawi, 2015; Razzaque & Karolak, 2010). A user-friendly system interface will also have a positive impact on users' satisfaction.

Other implications findings of this study will benefit government sectors with IT HelpDesk systems. Generally, users are impatient when it comes to browsing for services and are reluctant to use it if too cumbersome. Therefore, it is essential that managers ensure IT Helpdesk system include a User-friendly graphical user interface (GUI) (Zanjani, Edwards, Nykvist & Geva, 2015) to encourage users to utilize it. Management should aim at ensuring when users report an incident, users are able to use the system with a modern and easy-to-use interface. Financial Institutions such as banks can benefit by improving current online banking systems to make it easier to use by customers enabling them to contact support personnel if need to. The overall implication is that system quality and user satisfaction should be maintained and enhanced to achieve positive benefits to the business.

LIMITATIONS OF THE STUDY

Sample size is small due to low response rate (21%). 623 users were chosen because they were employees who used computers daily in their work. Pilot testing was done that resulted in a reduction of items in the questionnaire to enable a higher response rate. However, data collection period was only done for 2 months. A prolonged data collection period could have resulted in a higher response rate.

Convenience sampling used because being relatively inexpensive and an easy option but affected generalizability of results of the study. Only one independent variable and one dependent variable investigated. No interactive effects as only linear relationships were examined. This is because statistically analysis employed is linear multiple regression.

Another limitation of the study is there could be a lack of awareness of the IT HelpDesk among the users in terms of fully utilizing the system and enhanced features such as raising complaints through the Help Desk. Therefore, there is a need to provide intensive training to users on utilization of features so that the HelpDesk can be effective.

FURTHER STUDIES

Future research can measure other factors; customer or user resistance to change and environmental factors. Quality of services could also be investigated. User satisfaction is influenced by perceived benefits and service quality (Philip & Zake, 2017); especially within the FinTech perspective, i.e., by considering the role and integration of FinTech. Further studies can be conducted on users' confidence level. Confidence factor had a large role in improving consumer satisfaction, trust and satisfaction variables simultaneously affecting consumer loyalty (Daud, Farida, Andriya & Razak, 2018). A longitudinal assessment can be taken understand consideration, as this study's data collection was cross sectional.

REFERENCES

Abadi, H., Kabiry, N., & Forghani, M. (2013). Factors Affecting Isfahanian Mobile Banking Adoption Based on the Technology Acceptance Model. *International Journal of Academic Research in Business and Social Sciences.*, *5*(3), 611–623.

Abdul Nasser W. & Prabhakar K., (2017). Technology Acceptance Model (TAM): Design of Work Life Balance Practices. *International Journal of Research in Management & Business Studies, 4*(1).

Agha, S., & Saeed, M. (2015). Factors Influencing Customer Acceptance of Online Banking in Pakistan and the Moderating Effect of Technophobia. *Journal of Marketing and Consumer Research,* 12.

Ahmadi, K., Bahrami, Y., & Ahmad, M. (2016). Studying and developing a model for mobile banking adoption in Iran banking system. *International Journal of Humanities and Cultural Studies, 1*(1), 2195–2207.

Al-Rahmi, W., Othman, M., & Yusuf, L. (2015). Exploring the Factors that Affect Student Satisfaction through Using E-Learning in Malaysian Higher Education Institutions. *Mediterranean Journal of Social Sciences,* (6), 4. doi:10.5901/mjss.2015.v6n4s1p299

Alsamydai, M., (2014). Adaptation of the Technology Acceptance Model (TAM) to the Use of Mobile Banking Services. *International Review of Management and Business Research, 3*(4).

Baabdullaha, A., Alalwanb, A., Ranac, N., Kizginc, H., & Patilc, P. (2019). Consumer use of mobile banking (M-Banking) in Saudi Arabia: Towards an integrated model. *International Journal of Information Management,* 44.

Badran, O., & Al-Haddad, S. (2018). The Impact of Software User Experience on Customer Satisfaction. *Journal of Management Information and Decision Sciences, 21*(1).

Bashir I. & Madhavaiah C. (2014). Determinants of Young Consumers' Intention to Use Internet Banking Services in India. *The Journal of Business Perspective. Sage Publications, 18*(3), 153-163.

Bogart W. & Wichadee S., (2015). Exploring Students' Intention to Use LINE for Academic Purposes Based on Technology Acceptance Model. *International Review of Research in Open and Distributed Learning, 16*(3).

Chuang, L.-M., Liu, C.-C., & Kao, H.-K. (2016). The Adoption of Fintech Service: TAM perspective. *International Journal of Management and Administrative Sciences, 3*(7), 1–75.

Daud, A., Farida, N., Andriya, A., & Razak, M. (2018). Impact of customer trust toward loyalty: The mediating role of perceived usefulness and satisfaction. *Journal of Business and Retail Management Research,* 2(13), 235–241. doi:10.24052/JBRMR/V13IS02/ART-21

Davis F., (1989). Perceived Usefulness, Perceived Ease of Use, and User Acceptance of Information Technology. *MIS Quarterly, September, 13*(3), 319-340.

El-Gayar, O., Moran, M., & Hawkes, M. (2011). Students' Acceptance of Tablet PCs and Implications for Educational Institutions. *Institutions. Journal of Educational Technology & Society, 14*(2), 58–70.

Hung, J.-L., & Luo, B. (2016). FinTech in Taiwan: A case study of a Bank's strategic planning for an investment in a FinTech company. *Hung and Luo Financial Innovation*, *2*(1), 2–16. doi:10.118640854-016-0037-6

Hur, D. (2017). Buyer power and supplier relationship commitment: A cognitive evaluation theory perspective. *The Journal of Supply Chain Management*, *53*(2), 39–60. doi:10.1111/jscm.12138

Intana, M., & Chansa-Ngavej, C. (2010). An extended technology acceptance model for internet banking adoption. *Asian Journal of Management Research*, *5*(1).

Kim, Y., Choi, J., Park, Y.-J., & Yeon, J. (2016). The Adoption of Mobile Payment Services for "Fintech". *International Journal of Applied Engineering Research*, *11*(2), 1058–1061.

Lee, I., & Shin, Y. J. (2015). Fintech: Ecosystem, business models, investment decisions, and challenges. *Business Horizons*, *61*(1), 35–46. doi:10.1016/j.bushor.2017.09.003

Leonga, C., Tan, B., Xiao, X., Tan, F. T., & Sun, Y. (2017). Nurturing a FinTech ecosystem: The case of a youth microloan startup in China. *International Journal of Information Management*, *37*(2), 92–97. doi:10.1016/j.ijinfomgt.2016.11.006

Lim, W., & Ting, D. (2012). E-shopping: An Analysis of the Technology Acceptance Model. *Modern Applied Science*, *6*(6), 4. doi:10.5539/mas.v6n4p49

Mai, N., Tuan, N., & Yoshi, T. (2013). Technology Acceptance Model and the Paths to Online Customer Loyalty in an Emerging Market. *Market- Tržište Journal*, *25*(2), 231 – 248.

Mavroidis I., Karatrantou A., & Koutsouba M., (2013). Technology Acceptance and Social Presence in Distance Education – A Case Study. *European Journal of Open, Distance and e-Learning*, *16*(2).

McKechnie, S., Winklhofer, H., & Ennew, C. (2006). Applying the Technology Acceptance Model to Online Retailing of Financial Services. *International Journal of Retail & Distribution Management*, *34*(4/5), 388–410. doi:10.1108/09590550610660297

Ministry of Works. (n.d.). *About Us*. Retrieved from https://www.works.gov.bh/English/Pages/home2.aspx

Mohan, H., Ahmad, N., Kong, O., Yew, C., Liew, J., & Mat, N. (2013). Determinants of the Internet Banking Intention in Malaysia. *American Journal of Economics*, *3*(3).

Nuamah, P., & Darko, A. (2016). University Students' Perceptions on the Adoption of Electronic Voting. *Global Journal of Interdisciplinary Social Sciences*, *6*(5), 7–13.

Olushola, T., & Abiola, J. (2017). The Efficacy of Technology Acceptance Model: A Review of Applicable Theoretical Models in Information Technology Researches. *Journal of Research in Business and Management*, *4*(11).

Philip, E., & Zake, S. (2017). The role of user satisfaction in implementing a Business Intelligence System. *South African Journal of Information Management*, *1*(19), 1–8.

Razzaque, A. (2019). Organizational learning through Knowledge sharing in Virtual Communities thru Learner readiness and their Social Capital. In *Implementing Knowledge Management Strategy in the Public Sector*. IGI Global Publications. doi:10.4018/978-1-5225-9639-4.ch008

Razzaque, A., Al-Hashimi, M., Hamdan, A. M., Musleh, A., Ahlam Hassan, E. S., Aldahean, B. A., & Reyad, S. (2019). *Learning readiness when sharing knowledge while e-learning*. Option Journal. doi:10.33965/el2019_201909F007

Razzaque, A., & Alalawi, M. (2015). Knowledge Sharing And Positive Emotions In Virtual Communities: The case of the Healthcare sector. In *KS Global Research International Conference on Emerging Trends in Multidisciplinary Research (ETMR-2015)*. Istanbul, Turkey: KS Global Research.

Razzaque, A., Aldahean, E. S., Al-Hashimi, M., Hamdan, A. M., & Musleh, A. (2020). Learning readiness when sharing knowledge while e-learning. *International Journal of Computer Aided Engineering and Technology*.

Razzaque, A., & Eldabi, T. (2018). Assessing the impact of Physicians' Virtual Communities on their medical Decision Making quality. In *51st Hawaii International Conference on System Sciences - HICSS-51*. University of Hawaii at Manoa. 10.24251/HICSS.2018.397

Razzaque, A., Eldabi, T., & Jalal-Karim, A. (2012). An integrated framework to classify healthcare virtual communities. *European, Mediterranean & Middle Eastern Conference on Information Systems 2012*.

Razzaque, A., Hamdan, A., & Cummings, R. (2019). The Propensity to Use FinTech: Input from bankers in the Kingdom of Bahrain. *Journal of Information & Knowledge Management*.

Razzaque, A., & Karolak, M. (2010). Knowledge Management and Electronic Heath Record Facilitate Clinical Support to Improve Healthcare Quality. In *International Conference on E-business, Management and Economics (ICEME 2010)*. Hong Kong.: IEEE Press.

Scholtz & Mahmud, (2016). Does Usability Matter? An Analysis of the Impact of Usability on Technology Acceptance in ERP Settings. *Interdisciplinary Journal of Information, Knowledge, and Management, 11*.

Seraj, M., & Wong, C. (2014). Impacts of Different Mobile User Interfaces on Student Satisfaction. Learn. *International Journal of Information Management*, (8), 4.

Smart Service Desk. (n.d.). *About Us*. Retrieved from https://smartservicedesk.com/company.html

Sönmez, F. (2018). Technology Acceptance of Business Intelligence and Customer Relationship Management Systems within Institutions Operating in Capital Markets. *International Journal of Academic Research in Business and Social Sciences*, *8*(2), 400–422. doi:10.6007/IJARBSS/v8-i2/3882

Tan, G., Chong, C., Ooi, K., & Chong, Y. (2010). The adoption of online banking in Malaysia: An empirical analysis. *International Journal of Business and Management Science*, *3*, 169.

Vallerand, R. J., & Reid, G. (1984). On the Causal Effects of Perceived Competence on Intrinsic Motivation: A Test of Cognitive Evaluation Theory. *Journal of Sport Psychology*, *6*(1), 94–102. doi:10.1123/jsp.6.1.94

Zanjani, N., Edwards, S., Nykvist, S., & Geva, S. (2017). The Important Elements of LMS design that Affect User Engagement with e-learning tools within LMSs in the higher education sector. *Australasian Journal of Educational Technology*, *33*(1).

Zavolokina, L., Dolata, M., & Schwabe, G. (2016). FinTech – What's in a Name? In *Thirty Seventh International Conference on Information Systems* (pp. 1-19). Dublin, Ireland: Association for Information Systems.

Chapter 18
Adoption of FinTech by Students in Higher Education Institutions

Sakeena Ebrahim Traif
Ahlia University, Bahrain

Ibrahim Ehsan Alshihabi
Ahlia University, Bahrain

Abdulrahman Ajlan
Ahlia University, Bahrain

Abdulqader Bubshait
Ahlia University, Bahrain

Anjum Razzaque
Ahlia University, Bahrain

ABSTRACT

Financial technology is encouraging various new practices, such as diminishing of the use of cash in different countries, increasing the rate of use of mobile payments, introducing new algorithms for high-frequency trading across national boundaries, etc., hence attracting significant attention. However, the continues use of fintech is still doubted by scholars. As a result, this chapter aims to comprehend whether, and why, higher education students, who are future entrepreneurs, would be willing, or hesitate to utilize fintech. Data was collected from 350 higher education students from universities in Bahrain. Only those students who had prior experience with cashless online payment systems were the selected target population for this study's online survey. The findings confirmed that risk negatively effects the intent for the continence of using fintech, and convenience baring the strongest positive effect. This study contributes to theoretical and practical implications for future and budding entrepreneurs graduating from the higher education sector of Bahrain.

DOI: 10.4018/978-1-7998-3257-7.ch018

INTRODUCTION

In the age of modern technology, the world has been competing for the best technological instruments, which have contributed greatly to improving living conditions and providing excellent services to consumers and businesses at the same time."Fintech" Finance technology is a description of a modern technology that aims to develop the delivery of financial services in automated and critical methods with a huge capability that can reduce the time and effort and saves a lot of the costs that were previously used (Bell, D. R., Gallino, S., & Moreno, A, 2014). The exploitation of finance technology helps companies, banks, business owners, and consumers, in particular, to manage financial services through pre-developed algorithms managed through computers and electronic clouds that allow consumers to access financial services data anytime, anywhere. Moreover, fintech emerged in the last few years, initially was applied to the technologies used at the back-end systems for the financial companies and especially for the banks. Nowadays, fintech has been expanded to cover wider technological innovations and automation processes include the front-end side which helps the consumers to manage and operate all the financial services provided by the financial sector. (Lamb Jason & Polverini Sacha, 2015).

The proliferation of the new mobile services contributed significantly to make an easy payment, easy transfer funds between account to account as well as account balances, and much more professional services (Ernst and Young, 2014). Therefore, Fintech has unsettled just about every area of the world financial, the traditional bankers began to work on establishing electronic databases to cope with the great development of financial technology due to the reluctance of consumers to traditional banks that do not provide modern fintech services that facilitate time and effort besides that the fintech has become one of the pillars of competitive advantages that banks (Sofia, 2016). The issue is that scant research assessed what is the view of higher education students on the adoption of FinTech, and it is the observation of the scholars of this study that students are merely pushed into using this technology without really wondering whether they This aims of this study were to assess the effect of higher education students' perception of the benefits and risks of Fintech on Fintech continuation intention.

Statement of the problem: The rapid development of financial technology (Fintech) coupled with acceptance and rejection by a segment of university students who make up a large proportion of the population. Therefore, the study of students' acceptance and perception of financial technology, as well as the extent of use of the available services, provides in this area. Therefore, the research will investigate variables and factors that increase or weaken student acceptance of Fintech in the kingdom of Bahrain. This problem of the study will be concentrated on measuring students' acceptance of the use of financial technology services in Bahrain. The main objectives of our study were to (1) To examine the economic benefit of FinTech, (2) To examine the perceived benefits of FinTech, (3) To determine the most potential risks facing the FinTech, and (4) To analyze the perception of higher education students' in terms of the benefits and risks of Fintech. These objectives were proposed to help in answering three research questions: (1) What is the Economic Benefit of Fintech? (2) What are the Perceived Benefits of Fintech? (3) What are the most potential risks facing the FinTech? And (4) What is the effect of higher education students' perception of the benefits and risks of Fintech? This study is very important for investigating the effect of (Fintech) financial technology on student's higher education students' as well as examining the students' perception, awareness, expected benefits, and acceptance.

BACKGROUND

Financial technology (fintech) is transforming the delivery of financial services across the Middle East. Fintech sandboxes and Government driven initiatives support a growing base of fintech startups. Regional and international banks are developing digital platforms and smart solutions and are coming together to create projects such as the Batelco Wallet etc.

In this chapter The Researchers will present the most valuable literature relevant to the subject of the study. The literature review has been taken from multiple studies, journals and previous articles. All literature has been documented with original references and sources.

Concept of Fintech: Sofia (2016) Fintech is an acronym for two words, "financial" and "technology," which is relatively new that applies to any emerging technology that helps consumers or financial businesses deliver more advanced financial services using the most modern technologies, with new faster ways than was traditionally available. (Nicoletti, B, 2014) There is a huge change between walking into a bank to request for a sample balance report and the ability to pull up that information in real-time on customer phone which is the concept and idea of fintech's impact. (Desai, F. 2015). Moreover, Fintech is a term used to and describe and define financial technology, an industry surrounding any kind of technology in financial services using business to customer method. Fintech describes any company that provides financial services through software or other technology, and includes anything from mobile and web payment applications. (Yuen, Yeow & Lim, 2015).

Economic benefit of Fintech: According to Juwaheer TD, Pudaruth S, Ramdin P. (2012) Fintech has been used for many banks over the world and considered a competitive strategy for banks using the newest technological developments from payment applications through the smartphones and the online services provides by the commercial banks. Moreover, combining the latest technological developments with financial services, fintech has helped businesses and provide a lot of benefits largely start-ups disrupt the industry and provide better financial services to businesses and individuals at the same time. (Accenture. 2014). Hochstein, M. (2015) Fintech is allowing consumers to take charge of their financial activities, leading to much better financial services than ever before. Fintech is changing the old financial school practice and helping to advance the customer's financial situation and outcomes by promoting more advanced technologies. (Zimmerman, J, 2014) Furthermore, the concept of fintech combines traditional financial services with the latest in digital and online technologies services with smart data to make end consumer users the financial and banking services cooler and better.

Perceived benefit: Venture KPMG and Matchi (2016) most fintech organizations interrelate with their consumers through modern and advanced platforms that are accessible through internet browsers and smartphone applications such as Android and Apple platforms. The developments and operations of such platforms depend on advanced information technologies and data mining techniques. The newest technologies supporting the concept and idea of fintech services are machine learning, cloud computing, and data mining technology though widely used, these technologies remain highly incomprehensible to a large segment of society. (Lin, K.Y. and Lu, H.P., 2011)

B. Nicoletti (2017) The main benefit from the financial company's customers' point of view is a weighty saving of time by the automation of banking services processing and introduction of easy maintenance tools for managing customer's money. The main advantages of E-banking for corporate customers are the reduction of costs in using the E-banking services, increasing comfort and timesaving, transactions can be made at any time anywhere without requiring the physical interaction with the bank, quick and continuous access to information, they can check on multiple accounts at the click of a button, fintech facilities speed up cash cycle and increase the competence of business processes as a huge variety of fund and cash management instruments are available on internet sites of banks, private customers seek slightly different kinds of benefit from the financial technology services. (Chuen, D. K., & Teo, E. G., 2015).

Convenience: Shen, Y., & Huang, Y. (2016) A lot of financial organizations are using fintech technology mainly for the provision of payments and settlement services to create easy and convenient communication between the finance company and the customers. One of the top aims of fintech is to place the innovation in providing the financial services, as the traditional payment processing models and have become incompatible with the current situation of a major development in electronic infrastructure.

Financial risk and Legal risk: Gawer, A. (2014) Banks are using E-channels to do banking operations with both domestic and international customers. Currently, financial companies are using E-channels to receive instructions and deliver their products and services to their consumers. Although the ranges of services provided by financial companies over the online electronic infrastructure vary widely in content between the financial companies, then the nature of the financial risks may vary. Zott, C., Amit, R., & Massa, L. (2011) stated that especially with the latest development of electronic fraud techniques by professional hackers that belong to the organized transnational crime. Therefore, such products and services can include deposit-taking, lending, account management, the provision of a financial device, electronic bill payment, and the provision for other products and services such as electronic money, which means more financial risks that require complex methods to prevent these unexpected risks. (Xie, P., & Zou, C., 2013)

Azouzi D. (2019) Fintech progresses a bank's performance and competitiveness so that existing consumers can be benefited from a greater level of convenience with one-click transactions. However, the banks are facing with different levels of risks and expectations arising from the online banking services as compared to traditional banking services. Several risks are involved in online financial services. (Shrier, D., Canale, G., & Pentland, A, 2016) It has sole distinctiveness that may expand an institution's overall hazard profile and the level of risk associated with usual financial services, strategic, operational, reputation, and legal risks. Due to the starter of fintech technology, operational risks are on the rise and should be maintained in an appropriate method. Furthermore, Supervisory agencies may choose to ban or regulate the use of cryptocurrencies in their jurisdiction. Then, users within these jurisdictions are exposed to asset losses. Also, the recognition of the electronic signature is still in its infancy which may be creating a problem in the financial transactions. Therefore, it is considered major legal risks of fintech. (Rechtman, Y., & O'Callaghan, S., 2014).

Security risk: Van Alstyne, M. W., Parker, G. G., & Choudary, S. P. (2016) First, due to the open architecture of mobile devices and their susceptibility to malware, unencrypted confidential and personal information data can be compromised or leaked, and funds could be stolen through hacking activities. Transaction authorization, card authentication, transaction performance, and the security of the payment system must be addressed by regulators. Also, while blockchain is not prone to be attacked, some platforms must suspend activities when they are victims of hacking attacks, which can lead to financial theft which a real problem facing fintech services. (Insurtech, 2017)

Operational risk: Al-Debei, M. M., & Avison, D. (2010) Operational risk is the most significant risk type as it is strongly correlated with other risks. Operational risk results from inadequate or failed internal processes, people, and systems, or external events. Three main operational breakpoints are identified in the failure of a digital payment process. The financial provider needs to manage these risks in the areas of security, data confidentiality, data system integrity, system availability, and outsourcing. These risks are closely linked to reputation risks and legal risks for banks as if the security breaches than it will have damaging effects on the reputation of the financial company which could have the legal magnitudes also. (Insurtech, 2017).

Technology Failure: It includes transaction delays due to the poor or lack of internet signal, or due to agents' devices not working, which might result in wrong data entry, error in systems maintenance, execution failures, delivery failures, and process management failures. With increasing atomization of processes, the number of technology-linked breakpoints may grow if there is not a comprehensive classification and understanding of them. (Insurtech, 2017)

Human Error: It includes issues such as an agent or customer inputting the wrong account number, selection of services (paying and insurance were not wanted) or providing the wrong amount. Most of the client's error might be caused by poor process design, as also in the case if other sectors such as the healthcare sector, as there is not standardized and functional guidance to provide the service (Insurtech, 2017; Razzaque, Eldabi, Jalal-Karim, & Karolak, 2013; Razzaque, Eldabi, & Jalal-Karim, 2012).

Frauds: Includes fraudulent or illicit activities in payment processes, such as draining of funds in the relation costumers-agents or by a third party (Insurtech, 2017)

Summary: Fintech continuation intention depends on the benefits and risks of FinTech, while both sides contain several factors, such as the Economic benefit, seamless transactions, convenience, Security, legal Risk, Financial Risk, operational risk, and others. where these things must be considered while adopting Fintech services by the providers and clients as well.

DATA COLLECTION

In this part of the study, the methodology is exhibited including every one of the strategies assembling the research. The aim of the approach part is to describe, Identify and interpret study on the procedures and strategies utilized for each segment of the study. Research system is a comprehensive description of all chapters and describes the technique and every segment and unveils the ethical norms that went with the information gathering process. In addition, explanations of the research analysis and statistical tools were utilized in analyzing the raw data to achieve the research aim and objectives.

Study Design and Approach: The structure of the study has been used the descriptive research design, based on cause-effect relationships between the higher education students' and the Fintech variables and factors. The primary data has been analyzed statistically to investigate the relationship between the independent and dependent variables. The primary data has been collected from reliable sources to obtain accurate data on the effect ratio. The survey has been distributed using Google survey tools. The population has covered all the higher education students' by collecting a certain percentage of the total population using the sample size calculator.

Data Sources: The researchers used two sources for the collection of data by using the "primary and secondary data," as stated by Rabianski, J.S. (2006). The primary data collection aims to survey the population based on the study to obtain accurate data on the status of the target population by using the quantitative approach.

Quantitative Approach: The study has made use of the quantitative approach to quantify and generate numerical data through the population-based survey. This approach allows us to use analyze the numerical data and measure the real effective factor about the study problem and the primary role of adopting of FinTech by students in Bahrain Higher Education Institutions.

Research Instruments: For testing the hypothesis and measuring the research variables, researchers made a questionnaire based on Likert five selections scales. The first part will consist of demographic description about the firm, such as Gender, Status, Level of student in higher education and university enrolled. The second part has been designed according to five selection scales: (Strongly agree, Agree, Neutral, Disagree, strongly disagree) which will be related to the study variables and linked to the hypothesis.

Research Hypothesis and framework: The following hypothesis has been formulated to prove the variables of the study as follows:

Ha: There is a significant impact of Perceived benefit on Fintech Continuance intention.
H1: There is a significant impact of Economic benefit on Perceived benefit.
H2: There is a significant impact of Seamless transaction on Perceived benefit.
H3: There is a significant impact of Convenience on Perceived benefit.
Hb: There is a significant impact of Perceived risk on Fintech Continuance intention.
H4: There is a significant impact of financial risk on perceived risk.
H5: There is a significant impact of Legal risk on Perceived risk.
H6: There is a significant impact of Security risk on Perceived risk.
H7: There is a significant impact of Operational risk on Perceived risk.

Sample size calculator and distribution method: As observed from (Razzaque, Eldabi, & Jalal-Karim, 2012), the distribution is oriented to universities in Bahrain, all accounting and finance students can participate in the questionnaire. Every student can participate in one questionnaire. The online survey

Figure 1. Conceptual model framework

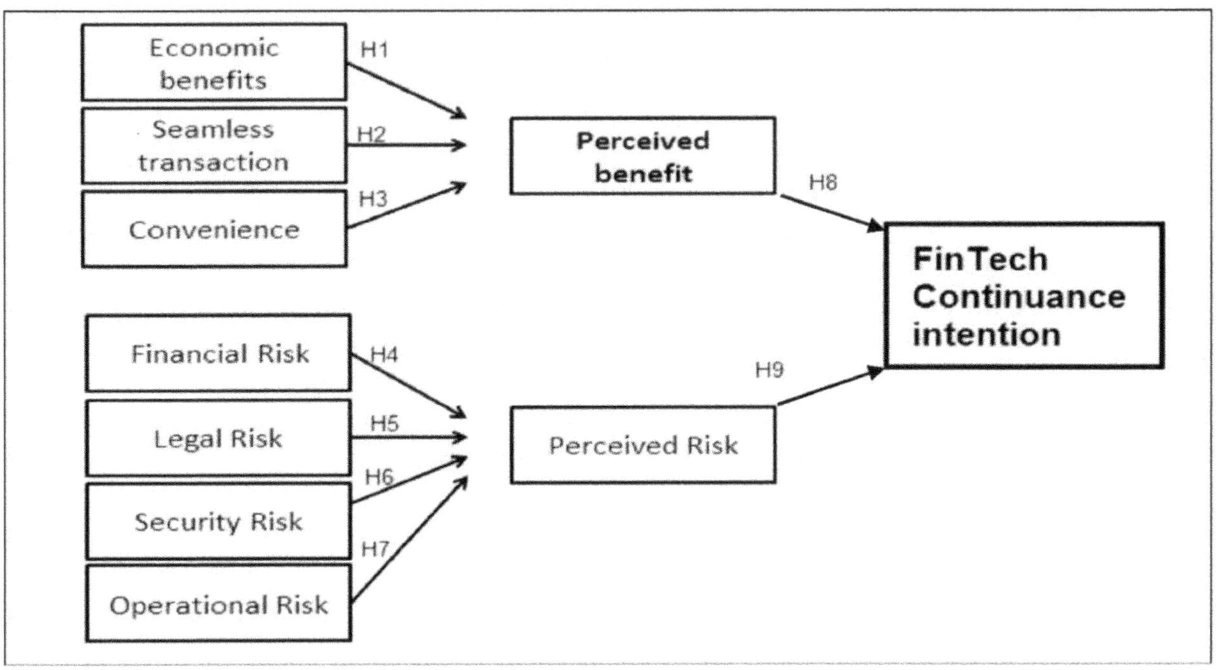

link will be distributed to the students of all the universities in Bahrain. The E-link will be generated using the Google survey tool. The sample size has been selected according to the following calculator:

Figure 2. Sample size calculator https://www.surveysystem.com/sscalc.htm

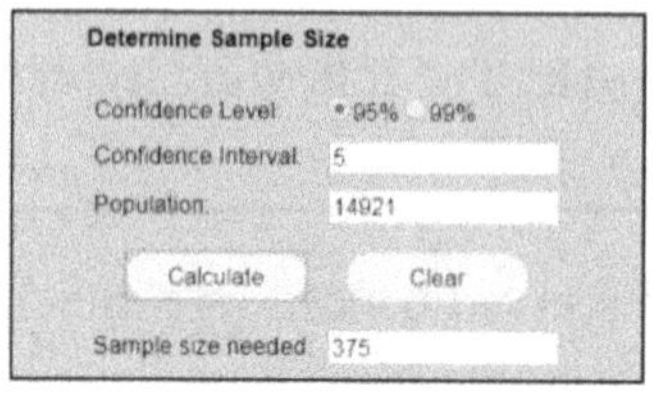

The total students in the universities of Bahrain excluded the higher studies programs will be 14921 according to the published statistics of the ministry of education in Bahrain. Therefore, the total population targeted is 14921 with confidence interval 5% and 95% confidence level, the sample size needed shows that The Researchers need to reach to 375 of the students in the universities of Bahrain.

Distribution Survey: The distribution is oriented to universities in Bahrain, all accounting and finance students can participate in the questionnaire. Every student can participate in one questionnaire. The online survey link will be distributed to the students of all the universities in Bahrain. The E-link will be generated using the Google survey tool.

Questionnaire Design: The design of the questionnaire will be based on the Likert Five pointer scales, which consists of five selections. The design will be as follows: (1) Strongly agree, (2) Agree, (3) Neutral, (4) Disagree, and (5) Strongly disagree.

Analysis of the Data: In analyzing the data that will be obtained from the questionnaires, mean score, T-tests, frequencies counts. Correlations and percentages and CFA will be applied especially in describing the focal variables of the study. SPSS statistical tools will be used to analyze the primary data previously collected from the research samples, while R software has been used for CFA analysis. SPSS statistical tool and R software will be utilized in this study due to its efficient data management, a wide range of options, better output organization.

Reliability and Validity: The constructs adopted are validated and reliable which were tested by their original We. As observed from (Razzaque, 2019a, 2019b) the Cronbach Alpha was used to measure the internal consistency or reliability of responses. The coefficient was obtained and proved that the research constructs and variables had reliable results across all its independent variables along with overall reliability. The reliability test was conducted separately for each construct and an overall test was made. (Refer 4.4/4.5, Reliability test).

Ethical issue: The credibility of this study will depend on how the rights are protected while addressing this research which makes the ethical issue very crucial. This study obtained its survey by keeping the respondent anonymous which will ensure confidentiality. Also, the literature review is well-cited that will give credit to the writers.

DATA ANALYSIS

This chapter address the data analyzed and the interpretation done by the data. In other words, the results or outcome of the survey. It begins with survey data presentation or demographic descriptive test and the reliability testing. Then comes the descriptive test for each construct following each reliability test, respectively. Furthermore, hypothesis testing is made using linear regression analysis to test whether the hypothesis set is accepted or rejected. Then, the Second type of analysis "CFA". Also, to the discussion section which will be presented in this chapter.

Response Rate: "370" questionnaires were distributed, and "357" returned, that means the Response Rate is 96.49%.

Distribution of the Sample: Data on four demographic variables namely, Gender, Student Status, Student Level, and University. Following are the details:

Gender: Table 1 indicates that the respondents, who participated in the survey regarding gender, are mostly males with 66.4% of the respondents, then females with 33.6%. As shown in the following.

Table 1. Frequencies and Percentages for Gender categories

Categories	Frequencies	Percent
Male	237	66.4%
Female	120	33.6%
Total	**357**	**100%**

Student Status: Table 2 indicates that the respondents who participated in the survey regarding the student status, were mostly full-time student with 66.7% of the respondents, then the part-time student with 33.3% of the sample. As shown in the following.

Table 2. Frequencies and Percentages for Student Status categories

Categories	Frequencies	Percent
Full-time student	238	66.7%
Part-time student	119	33.3%
Total	**357**	**100%**

Student Level: Table 3 indicates that the respondents who participated in the survey regarding the Student Level, were mostly fourth-year students with 40.9% of the respondents, then first-year students with 21.3% of the respondents, as well as third-year students with 18.5%, finally second-year students with only 18.5%. As shown in the following.

University: Table 4 indicates that the respondents who participated in the survey regarding to the University that enrolled in, in the first-place were Ahlia University students with 32.2% of the respondents, followed by Arab Open University with 14.0%, and the University of Bahrain with the percentage

Table 3. Frequencies and Percentages for Student Level categories

Categories	Frequencies	Percent
Fourth Year student	146	40.9%
First Year student	76	21.3%
Third Year student	69	19.3%
Second Year student	66	18.5%
Total	**357**	**100%**

Table 4. Frequencies and Percentages for University categories

Categories	Frequencies	Percent
Ahlia University	115	32.2%
Arab Open University	50	14.0%
University of Bahrain	41	11.5%
Gulf University	35	9.8%
Kingdom University	33	9.2%
AMA International University of Bahrain	25	7.0%
Arabian Gulf University	18	5.0%
University College of Bahrain	14	3.9%
Royal University for Women	13	3.6%
Applied Science University	8	2.2%
Bahrain Institute for Banking and Finance	3	0.8%
Royal College of Surgeons in Ireland - Medical University of Bahrain	2	0.6%
Total	**357**	**100%**

of 11.5% of the sample, then Gulf University with 9.8% of the respondents, as well as Kingdom University with 9.2%, as then comes AMA International University Bahrain with 7.0%, followed by Arabian Gulf University with the percentage of 5.0%, the University College of Bahrain with 3.9%, next, comes Royal University for Women with the percentage of 3.6%, as well as Applied Science University with 2.2%, and Bahrain Institute for Banking and Finance as well with 0.8%, as finally the Royal College of Surgeons in Ireland - Medical University of Bahrain represent only 0.6% of the respondents. As shown in the following.

Reliability and Internal Consistency: The reliability test was carried out on the constructs identified for this research the list of which is provided in Tables 5. The Table provides the figures for Cronbach's alpha for the sample responses derived from SPSS version 20.

Table 5. Reliability and Internal consistency – main sample

Construct	No. of questions	Cronbach's alpha (Reliability measure)
Perceived benefit	4	0.725
Perceived risk	3	0.776
Economic benefit	3	0.741
Seamless transaction	3	0.862
Convenience	3	0.811
Financial risk	3	0.806
Legal risk	4	0.798
Security risk	3	0.754
Operational risk	3	0.822
Continuance intention	4	0.725

DISCUSSION

Table 5 indicates that Cronbach's alpha for the questionnaire's constructs exceed 0.7 with the minimum being 0.725 and maximum being 0.862, as well as all questionnaires' Cronbach's alpha value was 0.904. Thus, it can be said that the internal consistency of the items was achieved, and the data are reliable.

Analysis methods: Cronbach's alpha was used to test the validity and internal consistency of study instruments. Then, the study used means and standard deviation to descriptive sample data. Finally, the hypotheses tests depended on the Simple Linear Regression model.

Sample Responses: First, the researchers are going to explore sample responses that respondents answered on the section's questions, using Means, Standard Deviations, and sorted in descending. The results were as shown at the following since:

Perceived benefit: The responses on this section as the following:

Table 6 indicated that the general mean of the section was (2.77), since at the first place was "Using Fintech yields a more superior outcome quality than traditional financial services" with mean equals to (2.82), followed by "Using Fintech is useful for me" with mean equals to (2.78), then "I can easily and quickly use Fintech" with mean equals to (2.75), and finally "Using Fintech has many advantages" with mean equals to (2.73).

Table 6. Frequencies for Perceived benefit

Question	Mean	Std
Using Fintech yields a more superior outcome quality than traditional financial services	2.82	1.18
Using Fintech is useful for me	2.78	1.17
I can easily and quickly use Fintech	2.75	1.19
Using Fintech has many advantages	2.73	1.27
Average Section	**2.77**	**1.08**

Perceived risk: The responses on this section as the following:

Table 7 indicated that the general mean of the section was (2.53), since at the first place was "Overall, I think that there is little benefit to use Fintech compared to traditional financial services" with mean equals to (2.56), followed by "There is a high level of uncertainty using Fintech" with mean equals to (2.55), and finally "Using Fintech is associated with a high level of risk" with mean equals to (2.48).

Table 7. Frequencies for Perceived risk

Question	Mean	Std
Overall, I think that there is little benefit to use Fintech compared to traditional financial services	2.56	1.17
There is a high level of uncertainty using Fintech	2.55	1.04
Using Fintech is associated with a high level of risk	2.48	1.12
Average Section	**2.53**	**0.97**

Economic benefit: The responses on this section as the following:

Table 8 indicated that the general mean of the section was (2.80), since at the first place was equally both "I can save money when I use Fintech" and "I can use various financial services with a low cost when I use Fintech" with mean equals to (2.85), and finally "Using Fintech is cheaper than using traditional financial services" with mean equals to (2.71).

Table 8. Frequencies for Economic benefit

Question	Mean	Std
I can save money when I use Fintech	2.85	1.13
I can use various financial services at a low cost when I use Fintech	2.85	1.19
Using Fintech is cheaper than using traditional financial services	2.71	1.17
Average Section	**2.80**	**1.02**

Seamless transaction: The responses on this section as the following:

Table 9. Frequencies for Seamless transaction

Question	Mean	Std
I can use various financial services at the same time (e.g., one-stop processing) when I use Fintech	2.78	1.10
I can have the peer-to-peer transactions between providers and users without middle man when I use Fintech	2.76	1.16
I can control my money without the middleman when I use Fintech	2.70	1.22
Average Section	**2.75**	**1.03**

Table 9 indicated that the general mean of the section was (2.75), since at the first place was "I can use various financial services at the same time (eg one-stop processing) when I use Fintech" with mean equals to (2.78), followed by "I can have the peer-to-peer transactions between providers and users without middle man when I use Fintech" with mean equals to (2.76), and finally "I can control my money without the middleman when I use Fintech" with mean equals to (2.70).

Convenience: The responses on this section as the following:

Table 10 indicated that the general mean of the section was (2.88), since at the first place was "I can use financial services anytime anywhere when I use Fintech" with mean equals to (2.94), followed by "can use financial services easily when I use Fintech" with mean equals to (2.90), and finally "I can use financial services very quickly when I use Fintech" with mean equals to (2.78).

Table 10. Frequencies for Convenience

Question	Mean	Std
I can use financial services anytime anywhere when I use Fintech	2.94	1.16
can use financial services easily when I use Fintech	2.90	1.22
I can use financial services very quickly when I use Fintech	2.78	1.23
Average Section	**2.88**	**1.09**

Financial risk: The responses on this section as the following:

Table 11 indicated that the general mean of the section was (2.63), since at the first place was "Financial losses due to the lack of the interoperability with other services are likely when I use Fintech" with mean equals to (2.69), followed by "Financial fraud or payment frauds are likely when I use Fintech" with mean equals to (2.68), and finally "Financial losses are likely when I use Fintech" with mean equals to (2.52).

Table 11. Frequencies for Financial risk

Question	Mean	Std
Financial losses due to the lack of interoperability with other services are likely when I use Fintech	2.69	1.18
Financial fraud or payment frauds are likely when I use Fintech	2.68	1.16
Financial losses are likely when I use Fintech	2.52	1.13
Average Section	**2.63**	**1.03**

Legal risk: The responses on this section as the following:

Table 12 indicated that the general mean of the section was (2.67), since at the first place was "It is not easy to use Fintech due to the government regulation" with mean equals to (2.70), followed by "My use of Fintech is uncertain due to many regulations" with mean equals to (2.68), then "There is a legal uncertainty for Fintech users" with mean equals to (2.66), and finally "It is difficult to use various Fintech applications due to the government regulation" with mean equals to (2.63).

Security risk: The responses on this section as the following:

Table 12. Frequencies for Legal risk

Question	Mean	Std
It is not easy to use Fintech due to government regulation	2.70	1.11
My use of Fintech is uncertain due to many regulations	2.68	1.14
There is a legal uncertainty for Fintech users	2.66	1.12
It is difficult to use various Fintech applications due to government regulation	2.63	1.11
Average Section	**2.67**	**0.96**

Table 13 indicated that the general mean of the section was (2.68), since at the first place was "My financial information is not secure when I use Fintech" with mean equals to (2.71), followed by "I worry that someone can access my financial information when I use Fintech" with mean equals to (2.68), and finally "worry about the abuse of my financial information (e.g. transaction and private information) when I use Fintech" with mean equals to (2.64).

Table 13. Frequencies for Security risk

Question	Mean	Std
My financial information is not secure when I use Fintech	2.71	1.14
I worry that someone can access my financial information when I use Fintech	2.68	1.20
worry about the abuse of my financial information (e.g. transaction and private information) when I use Fintech	2.64	1.16
Average Section	**2.68**	**1.03**

Operational risk: The responses on this section as the following:

Table 14 indicated that the general mean of the section was (2.61), since at the first place was "I worry about the way Fintech companies respond to financial losses or financial information leakages" with mean equals to (2.69), followed by "The organizational responses of Fintech companies are too slow when financial losses or financial information leakages occur" with mean equals to (2.66), and finally "Fintech companies are not willing to solve the issues when financial losses or financial information leakages occur" with mean equals to (2.50).

Table 14. Frequencies for Operational risk

Question	Mean	Std
I worry about the way Fintech companies respond to financial losses or financial information leakages	2.69	1.13
The organizational responses of Fintech companies are too slow when financial losses or financial information leakages occur	2.66	1.13
Fintech companies are not willing to solve the issues when financial losses or financial information leakages occur	2.50	1.11
Average Section	**2.61**	**0.99**

Continuance intention: The responses on this section as the following:

Table 15 indicated that the general mean of the section was (2.89), since at the first place was "I would prefer Fintech" with mean equals to (2.94), followed by "I will use Fintech in the future" with mean equals to (2.91), then "I would positively consider Fintech in my choice set" with mean equals to (2.87), and finally "I intend to continue to use Fintech" with mean equals to (2.84).

Table 15. Frequencies for Continuance intention

Question	Mean	Std
I would prefer Fintech	2.94	1.14
I will use Fintech in the future	2.91	1.26
I would positively consider Fintech in my choice set	2.87	1.21
I intend to continue to use Fintech	2.84	1.18
Average Section	**2.89**	**1.07**

Hypothesis Test:

Hypothesis (1): There is a significant impact of Economic benefit on Perceived benefit.

To test the hypotheses, the researchers have used a simple linear regression model. Since:

- *The economic benefit* is the independent variable.
- *Perceived benefit* is the dependent variable.

The following table shows the regression results:

Table 16 indicated that the F value was 384.94, and Beta was 0.766 referring to positive and significant Impact (Beta p-value lesser than 0.05), as well as the adjusted R^2 was 0.519 referring to good explanation value for the model and means that 51.9% of variation of perceived benefit was explained by the variation of economic benefit. Therefore, the relationship is significant and the hypotheses are accepted, as the researchers state that the economic benefit has a significant impact on the Perceived benefit.

Table 16. Simple Linear Regression Model Summary

Model F	Adjusted R^2	β	P-value (β)
384.94	0.519	0.766	0.000

Hypothesis (2): There is a significant impact of Seamless transaction on Perceived benefit.

To test the hypotheses, the researchers have used a simple linear regression model. Since:

- *The seamless transaction* is the independent variable.
- *Perceived benefit* is the dependent variable.

The following table shows the regression results:

Table 17 indicated that the F value was 429.38, and Beta was 0.778 referring to positive and significant Impact (Beta p-value lesser than 0.05), as well as the adjusted R^2 was 0.546 referring to good explanation value for the model and means that 54.6% of variation of Perceived benefit was explained by the variation of Seamless transaction.

Table 17. Simple Linear Regression Model Summary

Model F	Adjusted R^2	β	P-value (β)
429.38	0.546	0.778	0.000

Therefore, the relationship is significant, and the hypotheses afore mentioned are accepted, as the researchers state that the Seamless transaction has a significant impact on the Perceived benefit.

Hypothesis (3): There is a significant impact of Convenience on Perceived benefit.

To test the hypotheses, the researchers have used a simple linear regression model. Since:

- *Convenience* is the independent variable.
- *Perceived benefit* is the dependent variable.

The following table shows the regression results:

Table 18 indicated that the F value was 422.25, and Beta was 0.735 referring to positive and significant Impact (Beta p-value lesser than 0.05), as well as the adjusted R^2 was 0.542 referring to good explanation value for the model and means that 54.2% of variation of Perceived benefit was explained by the variation of Convenience. Therefore, the relationship is significant and the hypotheses are accepted, as the researchers state that the convenience has a significant impact on the perceived benefit.

Hypothesis (4): There is a significant impact of financial risk on perceived risk.

Table 18. Simple Linear Regression Model Summary

Model F	Adjusted R^2	β	P-value (β)
422.25	0.542	0.735	0.000

To test the hypotheses, the researchers have used a simple linear regression model. Since:

- *Financial risk* is the independent variable.
- *Perceived risk* is the dependent variable.

The following table shows the regression results:

Table 19 indicated that the F value was 187.45, and Beta was 0.557 referring to positive and significant Impact (Beta p-value lesser than 0.05), as well as the adjusted R^2 was 0.344 referring to good explanation value for the model and means that 34.4% of variation of perceived risk was explained by the variation of Financial risk. Therefore, the relationship is significant and the hypotheses are accepted, as the researchers state that the financial risk has a significant impact on the Perceived risk.

Table 19. Simple Linear Regression Model Summary

Model F	Adjusted R^2	β	P-value (β)
187.45	0.344	0.557	0.000

Hypothesis (5): There is a significant impact of Legal risk on Perceived risk.

To test the hypotheses, the researchers have used a simple linear regression model. Since:

- *Legal risk* is the independent variable.
- *Perceived risk* is the dependent variable.

The following table shows the regression results:

Table 20 indicated that the F value was 180.49, and Beta was 0.586 referring to positive and significant Impact (Beta p-value lesser than 0.05), as well as the adjusted R^2 was 0.335 referring to good explanation value for the model and means that 33.5% of variation of perceived risk was explained by the variation of Legal risk. Therefore, the relationship is significant and the hypotheses are accepted, as the researchers state that the Legal risk has a significant impact on the Perceived risk.

Table 20. Simple Linear Regression Model Summary

Model F	Adjusted R^2	β	P-value (β)
180.49	0.335	0.586	0.000

Hypothesis (6): There is a significant impact of Security risk on Perceived risk.

To test the hypotheses, the researchers have used a simple linear regression model. Since:

- *The security risk* is the independent variable.
- *Perceived risk* is the dependent variable.

The following table shows the regression results:

Table 21 indicated that the F value was 193.74, and Beta was 0.562 referring to positive and significant Impact (Beta p-value lesser than 0.05), as well as the adjusted R^2 was 0.351 referring to good explanation value for the model and means that 35.1% of variation of perceived risk was explained by the variation of Security risk.

Table 21. Simple Linear Regression Model Summary

Model F	Adjusted R^2	B	P-value (β)
193.74	0.351	0.562	0.000

So, the relationship is significant and the hypotheses are accepted, as the researchers state that the Security risk has a significant impact on the Perceived risk.

Hypothesis (7): There is a significant impact of Operational risk on Perceived risk.

To test the hypotheses, the researchers have used a simple linear regression model. Since:

- *Operational risk* is the independent variable.
- *Perceived risk* is the dependent variable.

The following table shows the regression results:

Table 22 indicated that the F value was 131.26, and Beta was 0.510 referring to positive and significant Impact (Beta p-value lesser than 0.05), as well as the adjusted R^2 was 0.268 referring to reasonable explanation value for the model and means that 26.8% of variation of perceived risk was explained by the variation of Operational risk. Therefore, the relationship is significant and the hypotheses are accepted, as the researchers state that the Operational risk has a significant impact on the Perceived risk.

Hypothesis (8): There is a significant impact of Perceived benefit on Continuance intention.

Table 22. Simple Linear Regression Model Summary

Model F	Adjusted R^2	B	P-value (β)
131.26	0.268	0.510	0.000

To test the hypotheses, the researchers have used a simple linear regression model. Since:

- *Perceived benefit* is the independent variable.
- *Continuance intention* is the dependent variable.

The following table shows the regression results:

Table 23 indicated that the F value was 386.13, and Beta was 0.712 referring to positive and significant Impact (Beta p-value lesser than 0.05), as well as the adjusted R^2 was 0.520 referring to good explanation value for the model and means that 52% of the variation of continuance intention was explained by the variation of Perceived benefit. Therefore, the relationship is significant and the hypotheses are accepted, as the researchers state that the Perceived benefit has a significant impact on the Continuance intention.

Hypothesis (9): There is a significant impact of Perceived risk on Continuance intention.

Table 23. Simple Linear Regression Model Summary

Model F	Adjusted R^2	β	P-value (β)
386.13	0.520	0.712	0.00

To test the hypotheses, the researchers have used a simple linear regression model. Since:

- *Perceived risk* is the independent variable.
- *Continuance intention* is the dependent variable.

The following table shows the regression results:

Table 24. Simple Linear Regression Model Summary

Model F	Adjusted R^2	β	P-value (β)
129.03	0.265	0.567	0.000

Table 24 indicated that the F value was 129.03, and Beta was 0.567 referring to positive and significant Impact (Beta p-value lesser than 0.05), as well as the adjusted R2 was 0.265 referring to reasonable explanation value for the model and means that 26.5% of the variation of continuance intention was explained by the variation of Perceived risk. Therefore, the relationship is significant and the hypotheses

Table 25. Parameters measure

Symbole	Definition	Latent Variable
PB1	Perceived benefit (PB) [Using Fintech has many advantages]	PB
PB2	Perceived benefit (PB) [I can easily and quickly use Fintech]	
PB3	Perceived benefit (PB) [Using Fintech is useful for me]	
PB4	Perceived benefit (PB) [Using Fintech yields a more superior outcome quality than traditional financial services.]	
PR1	Perceived risk(PR) [Using Fintech is associated with a high level of risk]	PR
PR2	Perceived risk(PR) [There is a high level of uncertainty using Fintech]	
PR3	Perceived risk(PR) [Overall, I think that there is little benefit to use Fintech compared to traditional financial services]	
EB1	Economic benefit (EB) [Using Fintech is cheaper than using traditional financial services]	EB
EB2	Economic benefit (EB) [I can save money when I use Fintech]	
EB3	Economic benefit (EB) [I can use various financial services with a low cost when I use Fintech]	
ST1	Seamless transaction (ST) [I can control my money without the middleman when I use Fintech.]	ST
ST2	Seamless transaction (ST) [I can use various financial services at the same time (e.g. one stop processing) when I use Fintech.]	
ST3	Seamless transaction (ST) [I can have the peer-to-peer transactions between providers and users without middle man when I use Fintech]	
CV1	Convenience (CV) [I can use financial services very quickly when I use Fintech]	CV
CV2	Convenience (CV) [I can use financial services anytime anywhere when I use Fintech]	
CV3	Convenience (CV) [can use financial services easily when I use Fintech]	
FR1	Financial risk (FR) [Financial losses are likely when I use Fintech]	FR
FR2	Financial risk (FR) [Financial fraud or payment frauds are likely when I use Fintech]	
FR3	Financial risk (FR) [Financial losses due to the lack of the interoperability with other services are likely when I use Fintech]	
LR1	Legal risk (LR) [My use of Fintech is uncertain due to many regulations.]	LR
LR2	Legal risk (LR) [It is not easy to use Fintech due to the government regulation]	
LR3	Legal risk (LR) [There is a legal uncertainty for Fintech users]	
LR4	Legal risk (LR) [It is difficult to use various Fintech applications due to the government regulation.]	
SR1	Security risk (SR) [worry about the abuse of my financial information (e.g. transaction and private information) when I use Fintech]	SR
SR2	Security risk (SR) [My financial information is not secure when I use Fintech]	
SR3	Security risk (SR) [I worry that someone can access my financial information when I use Fintech]	
OR1	Operational risk (OR) [Fintech companies are not willing to solve the issues when financial losses or financial information leakages occur.]	OR
OR2	Operational risk (OR) [The organizational responses of Fintech companies are too slow when financial losses or financial information leakages occur.]	
OR3	Operational risk (OR) [I worry about the way Fintech companies respond to financial losses or financial information leakages]	
CI1	Continuance intention (CI) [I would positively consider Fintech in my choice set.]	CI
CI2	Continuance intention (CI) [I would prefer Fintech]	
CI3	Continuance intention (CI) [I intend to continue to use Fintech]	
CI4	Continuance intention (CI) [I will use Fintech in the future]	

are accepted, as the researchers state that the Perceived risk has a significant impact on the Continuance intention.

" CFA" Analysis

Second Method analysis " CFA": As mention before, the researchers surveyed to measure and investigate the effect of higher education students' perception of the benefits and risks of Fintech on Fintech continuation intention. Besides, the researchers measure the higher education students' awareness and acceptance of the Fintech continuation intention. Indeed, The researchers elaborate a survey in which The researchers measure the following parameters as shown in table 25:

The above-mentioned items have been adopted from Razzaque, Hamdan and Cummings (2019) and Razzaque, Hamdan and Cummings (2019)

The collect of data has reached more than 350 surveys in which our peoples target was higher education student in kingdom of Bahrain. Moreover, the figure 3 presents the different affiliation of the target students.

Figure 3. Distribution of the students' affiliation

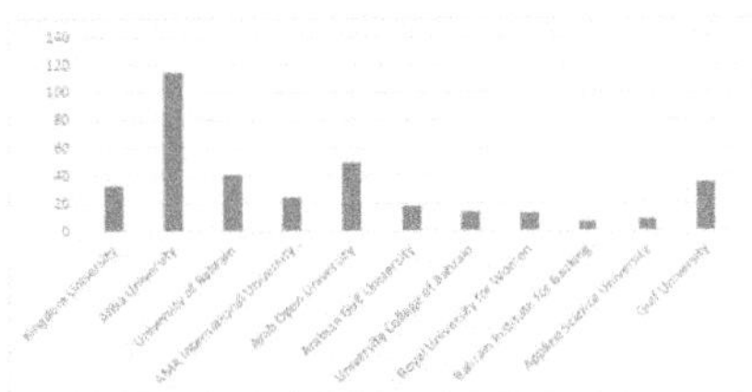

The descriptive statistical results of 357 questionnaires that analyzed the demographic characteristics of the respondents, such as gender, education level, are shown in Table 26.

Results analysis: In the design of the questionnaire, the researchers focus our work to investigate and measure the higher education students' acceptance of the Fintech continuation intention. As mention

Table 26. Demographic Characteristics

demographic characteristics		Frequency
Gender	Male	237
	Female	120
education level	First Year student	76
	Second Year student	66
	Third Year student	69
	Fourth Year student	146
status	Full time	238
	Part Time	119

in the research methodology chapter, perceived benefit and risk were understood as multi-dimensional constructs in this study. The three major dimensions of perceived benefit developed in this study are as follows: economic benefit, convenience, and transaction process. Moreover, the four major factors employed to measure perceived risk are financial, legal, security, and operational risks. The collected data has been analyzed using univariate, bivariate, and multivariate analysis techniques. Specifically, descriptive statistics have been assessed to examine the basic characteristics of the sample data. CFA with maximum likelihood criteria has been adopted for the measurement and validation of various constructs. To satisfy this study. The study used R software, which is open-source software. Particularly, use the Lavaan package to elaborate on the CFA model.

Second Discussion

Confirmatory factor analysis: The analysis was performed in R and following is the summary statistics of exploratory CFA:

- Optimization method NLMINB
- Number of free parameters 96
- Number of observations 357
- Estimator ML
- Model Fit Test Statistic 745.672
- Degrees of freedom 369
- P-value (Chi-square) 0.000

The CFA model used in this work are dived in two as shown in Table 27. First, the researchers study the relation between the Perceived benefit, economic benefit, Continuance intention and Convenience. Second, the researchers study the relation between the various risks.

First CFA model: In the first study, the researchers focus about the CFA model between the following latent variables:

Table 27. CFA Model

First study	Perceived benefit	PB
	Economic benefit	EB
	Continuance intention	CI
	Convenience	CV
Second study	Perceived risk	PR
	Financial risk	FR
	Legal risk	LR
	Security risk	SR
	Operational risk	OR
	Seamless transaction	ST

Benefit of FinTech in higher education + Perceived benefit = ~PB1 + PB2 + PB3 + PB4 + Convenience = ~CV1 + CV2 + CV3.

The running of the first model CFA with the R software the results presented and divided as follow:

- Latent Variables
  ~= PB
  PB1 … 1.000
  PB2 … 0.936 … 0.040 … 23.673 … 0.000
  PB3 … 0.891 … 0.040 … 22.102 … 0.000
  PB4 … 0.904 … 0.040 … 22.355 … 0.000
  ~= EB
  EB1 … 1.000
  EB2 … 0.999 … 0.061 … 16.397 … 0.000
  EB3 … 1.068 … 0.064 … 16.744 … 0.000
  ~= CI
  CI1 … 1.000
  CI2 … 0.993 … 0.049 … 20.367 … 0.000
  CI3 … 1.036 … 0.050 … 20.530 … 0.000
  CI4 … 1.054 … 0.055 … 19.257 … 0.000
  ~= CV
  CV1 … 1.000
  CV2 … 1.072 … 0.059 … 18.062 … 0.000
  CV3 … 1.066 … 0.061 … 17.461 … 0.000
- Covariance
  ~~PB
  EB … 0.829 … 0.084 … 9.842 … 0.000
  CI … 0.941 … 0.091 … 10.299 … 0.000
  CV … 0.688 … 0.076 … 8.996 … 0.000
  ~~EB
  CI … 0.809 … 0.082 … 9.893 … 0.000
  CV … 0.597 … 0.068 … 8.766 … 0.000
  ~~CI
  CV … 0.660 … 0.073 … 8.998 … 0.000
- Variances:
  PB … 1.246 … 0.119 … 10.476 … 0.000
  EB … 0.847 … 0.098 … 8.617 … 0.000
  CI … 1.040 … 0.109 … 9.504 … 0.000
  CV … 0.837 … 0.093 … 8.981 … 0.000

The figure 4 presents the CFA model graph in which it presents the different relation between the latent variables.

Second CFA model: In the second study, the researchers focus about the CFA model between the following latent variables:

Figure 4. first CFA model

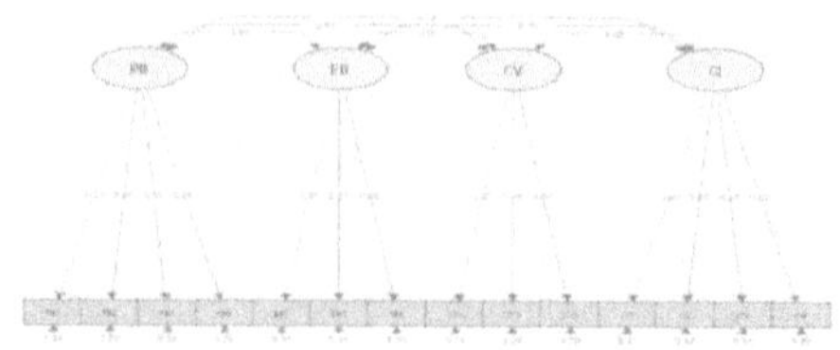

Risk of FinTech in higher education + Perceived risk = ~PR1 + PR2 + PR3.

The running of the first model CFA with the R software the results presented and divided as follow:

- Latent Variables
  ~=PR
  PR1 … 1.000
  PR2 … 1.014 … 0.018 … 57.660 … 0.000
  PR3 … 1.023 … 0.020 … 50.950 … 0.000
  ~=ST
  ST1 … 1.000
  ST2 … 1.015 … 0.017 … 59.183 … 0.000
  ST3 … 1.013 … 0.018 … 57.457 … 0.000
  ~=FR
  FR1 … 1.000
  FR2 … 1.008 … 0.017 … 58.707 … 0.000
  FR3 … 0.990 … 0.018 … 55.412 … 0.000
  ~=LR
  LR1 … 1.000
  LR2 … 1.009 … 0.019 … 52.552 … 0.000
  LR3 … 1.035 … 0.019 … 55.948 … 0.000
  LR4 … 1.023 … 0.020 … 51.278 … 0.000
  ~=SR
  SR1 … 1.000
  SR2 … 1.058 … 0.019 … 56.130 … 0.000
  SR3 … 1.069 … 0.019 … 56.987 … 0.000
  ~=OR
  OR1 … 1.000
  OR2 … 1.021 … 0.015 … 66.199 … 0.000
  OR3 … 0.996 … 0.015 … 64.297 … 0.000
- Covariance
  ~~ PR
  ST … 0.603 … 0.061 … 9.849 … 0.000
  FR … 0.547 … 0.058 … 9.366 … 0.000
  LR … 0.551 … 0.057 … 9.625 … 0.000

SR ... 0.470 ... 0.055 ... 8.619 ... 0.000
OR ... 0.520 ... 0.061 ... 8.591 ... 0.000
~~ST
FR ... 0.631 ... 0.064 ... 9.931 ... 0.000
LR ... 0.548 ... 0.060 ... 9.170 ... 0.000
SR ... 0.541 ... 0.059 ... 9.143 ... 0.000
OR ... 0.702 ... 0.069 ... 10.223 ... 0.000
~~ FR
LR ... 0.737 ... 0.065 ... 11.418 ... 0.000
SR ... 0.655 ... 0.061 ... 10.670 ... 0.000
OR ... 0.677 ... 0.067 ... 10.167 ... 0.000
~~ LR
SR ... 0.712 ... 0.062 ... 11.456 ... 0.000
OR ... 0.625 ... 0.064 ... 9.818 ... 0.000
~~ SR
OR ... 0.638 ... 0.064 ... 10.031 ... 0.000

- Variances:
  PR ... 0.777 ... 0.071 ... 10.996 ... 0.000
  ST ... 0.896 ... 0.080 ... 11.203 ... 0.000
  FR ... 0.837 ... 0.076 ... 11.057 ... 0.000
  LR ... 0.800 ... 0.071 ... 11.213 ... 0.000
  SR ... 0.775 ... 0.070 ... 11.103 ... 0.000
  OR ... 1.022 ... 0.086 ... 11.858 ... 0.000

The figure 5 presents the CFA model graph in which it presents the different relation between the latent variables.

Figure 5. the second CFA model

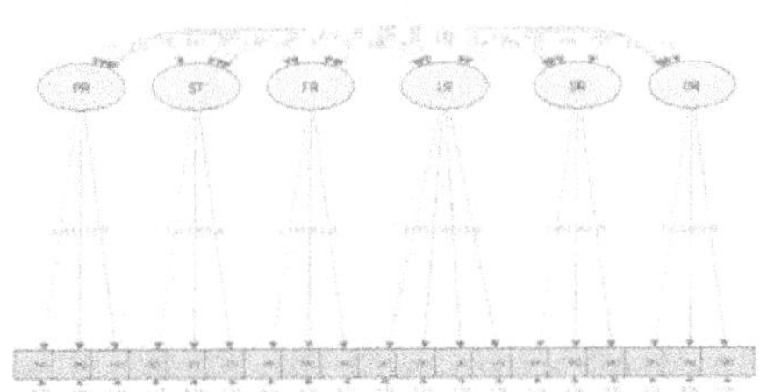

CONCLUSION

This study provides a conceptual and practical understanding of the concept of the adaption of FinTech by students in higher education institutions in Bahrain. Despite the significant development of financial

IT, which targets users of all ages, a state of rejection and acceptance prevails in the student community at universities. Furthermore, to investigate the existence of this phenomenon and to measure the extent of acceptance or rejection, in this study the statistical analysis tools and population-based survey has been used to obtain accurate feedback from the selected samples in universities in the Kingdom of Bahrain.

A large proportion of the 357 respondents, most are males in the fourth academic year, emphasize the importance of using financial technology and perceived benefits, which confirms and reflects the economic benefit they receive from using the financial technology, which has led the majority to adopt FinTech as a major tool for financial transactions. Moreover, the huge developments in the financial services have contributed heavily to the success and spread of the financial technology in Bahrain and the entire world through a major change in user's awareness in this regard which is one of the key factors for success of FinTech.

This study fills a gap prevalent among academic circles and the degree of acceptance or rejection of university students who are considered the important category of the society in the kingdom of Bahrain, which reflects the extent of awareness of using the financial technology. The study, through several variables and hypotheses designed to measure the level of awareness among university students in Bahrain, proved that Fintech is a great benefit for students and high acceptance proved the success of financial companies in exploiting modern technology that provides all the financial services needed by people from all social groups especially university students. Subsequently, several variables and factors have contributed significantly to elevating the success FinTech among students, such as the high convenience and ease of use and nonfinancial risk, low legal risk, secure connectivity, and perfect operational risks using flexible phone applications.

The success of the Fintech companies in raising awareness among members of the society reflects a real desire to move to electronic transactions and provide easy-to-use solutions using the virtual world, which proved to be a great success in achieving many gains. This led most respondents to confirm that FinTech is a key financial transaction, helping financial companies to move forward with more effort in developing more advanced financial services for young people and students in Bahrain.

The study concluded that the ongoing changes in the Fintech landscape are affecting the consumer behavior and global trends and make all financial companies offer all financial solutions as an end-to-end process through the Internet, which is consistent with the customer's behavior and non-stereotype of using e-financial services and make them widely spread among members of society and replaced the old stereotype of previous traditional services.

RECOMMENDATIONS

The researchers recommend future studies using the time-analysis tools to measure the changes of students' awareness of the overtime in conjunction with the financial services developments done by the banks to determine how students' stereotypes have changed about using the e-financial technologies. The financial companies to support further studies on the best electronic solutions suitable for university students which will enhance the level of awareness and usage level among students. Future research should involve the financial companies in the questionnaire to measure their strategies in providing the best FinTech solutions for students. This model to be executed at FinTech Bay in Bahrain. Also, this model could be applicable in the e-health industry as observed from Razzaque and Karolak (2013, 2011) and Razzaque, Mohiuddin and Jalal-Karim (2011).

SCOPE AND LIMITATIONS

This study researches the impact of the Adoption of Fintech by Higher Education Students in the Kingdom of Bahrain to optimize the understanding of this phenomenon. This includes the process of collecting and analyzing the data regarding the demographic profile and Educational Level. The limitation of this study is the lack of available resources regarding the research area. Also, the obstacles faced by receiving enough responses in the limited time frame and many students do not know about FinTech. Moreover, the study is concentrated on university students in Bahrain only which might limit the study in one area only.

The study was about technology which is to open changes and development every period (quickly), so it needs further studies. The study is concentrated on university students in Bahrain only which might limit the study in one area only. No qualitative study was done due to the limited available time.

This study benefits students who are studying business studies. Also, it can benefit companies who are planning to apply it, along with universities who would like to apply it/teach it in their programs, and the individuals who would like to keep up with where the latest technology has reached. Also, technicians who would like to improve and develop technology, as well as the banks who are willing to implement it.

REFERENCES

H2 Ventures. KPMG and Matchi. (2016). *Fintech 100. Leading Global Fintech innovators, Report 2015.* Retrieved July 31, 2016, from https://www.kpmg.com/FR/fr/IssuesAndInsights/ArticlesPublications/Documents/Etude-Fintech100-2015.pdf

Accenture. (2014). *The rise of Fintech: New York's opportunity for tech leadership*. Retrieved July 31, 2016, from http://pfnyc.org/wp-content/uploads/2014/06/NY-fintech-Report-2014.pdf

Al-Debei, M. M., & Avison, D. (2010). Developing a unified framework of the business model concept. *European Journal of Information Systems, 19*(3), 359–376. doi:10.1057/ejis.2010.21

Azouzi, D. (2009). The adoption of electronic banking in Tunisia: An exploratory study. *Journal of Internet Banking and Commerce, 14*(3), 1–11.

Bell, D. R., Gallino, S., & Moreno, A. (2014). How to win in an Omni channel world. *MIT Sloan Management Review, 56*(1), 1–45.

Chuen, D. K., & Teo, E. G. (2015). *Emergence of Fintech and the LASIC principles.* doi:. doi:10.2139srn.2668049

Ernst and Young. (2014). *Landscaping UK Fintech.* UK Trade and Investment.

Gawer, A. (2014). Bridging differing perspectives on technological platforms:Toward an integrative framework. *Research Policy, 43*(7), 1239–1249. doi:10.1016/j.respol.2014.03.006

Hochstein, M. (2015). *Fintech (the Word, That Is) Evolves.* Accessed 19 October 2016. https://www.americanbanker.com/bankthink/fintech-the-word-that-is-evolves-1077098-1.html

Insurtech'. (2017). *Investopedia*, accessed March 21, 2017 https://www.investopedia.com/terms/i/insurtech.asp

Juwaheer, T. D., Pudaruth, S., & Ramdin, P. (2012). Factors influencing the adoption of internet banking- A case study of commercial bank in Mauritius. *World Journal of Science. Technology and Sustainable Development*, *9*(3), 204–234.

Lamb & Polverini. (2015). *Assessing risk in digital payments*. Bill & Melinda Gates Foundation.

Lin, K. Y., & Lu, H. P. (2011). Why people use social networking sites: An empirical study integrating network externalities and motivation theory. *Computers in Human Behavior*, *27*(3), 1152–1161. doi:10.1016/j.chb.2010.12.009

Mackenzie, A. (2015). The Fintech Revolution. *London Business School Review*, *26*(3), 50–53. doi:10.1111/2057-1615.12059

Nicoletti. (2017). *The Future of FinTech*. DOI doi:10.1007/978-3-319-51415-4_1

Prabook. (2016). *Abraham Leon Bettinger*. Accessed 25 October 2016. https://prabook.com/web/person-view.html?profileId=669232

Razzaque, A. (2019). Multicultural teaching-learning model for Western Higher Education Institutions. *International Journal of Electronic Banking*, *2*(1), 358. doi:10.1504/IJEBANK.2019.10022931

Razzaque, A. (2019). Virtual learning enriched by social capital and shared knowledge, when moderated by positive emotions. *International Journal of Electronic Banking*, *1*(4), 77–95.

Razzaque, A., & Eldabi, T. (2018). Assessing the impact of Physicians' Virtual Communities on their medical Decision Making quality. In *51st Hawaii International Conference on System Sciences - HICSS-51*. University of Hawaii at Manoa. 10.24251/HICSS.2018.397

Razzaque, A., Eldabi, T., & Jalal-Karim, A. (2012). Knowledge Sharing for Medical Decision-Making in an E-Health Virtual Community of Practice. *2012 Annual Conference of Asian Group for Public Administration (AGPA)*.

Razzaque, A., Eldabi, T., Jalal-Karim, A., & Karolak, M. (2013). E-Health Collaborative Knowledge management facilitates medical decision making supported by Culture. In *Hawaii International Conference on System Sciences (HICSS-46)*. Grand Wailea Maui, HI: University of Hawai'i at Manoa, IEEE computer society. Retrieved May 1, 2012, from http://www.hicss.hawaii.edu/

Razzaque, A., Hamdan, A., & Cummings, R. (2019). The Propensity to Use FinTech: Input from bankers in the Kingdom of Bahrain. *Journal of Information & Knowledge Management*.

Razzaque, A., Hamdan, A., & Cummings, R. (2019). *The Propensity to Use FinTech: Input from bankers in the Kingdom of Bahrain. In The International Conference on Intelligent Systems and Data Analytics Applications - ICSDAA 2019*. Jordan University. Retrieved from https://icsdaa.com/

Razzaque, A., & Karolak, M. (2011). Building a Knowledge Management System for the e-Health Knowledge Society. *Journal of Economic Development, Management, IT. Finance and Marketing*, *2*(2), 23–40.

Razzaque, A., & Karolak, M. (2013). *Trends and Future Research in innovative and collaborative e-Health. 2013 IIAS-IASIA Joint Congress*. IIAS-IASIA.

Razzaque, A., Mohiuddin, Q., & Jalal-Karim, A. (2011). Semantic Web Based Tacit Knowledge Reshapes E-Health to improve Healthcare Decision-Support. *The International Conference and Exhibition on Knowledge-Based Business, Industry and Education, Management and Economics (KBIE 2011).*

Rechtman, Y., & O'Callaghan, S. (2014). Understanding the Basics of Crowdfunding. *The CPA Journal, 84*(11), 30.

Shen, Y., & Huang, Y. (2016). Introduction to the special issue: Internet finance in China. *China Economic Journal, 9*(3), 221–224. doi:10.1080/17538963.2016.1215058

Shrier, D., Canale, G., & Pentland, A. (2016). Mobile money & payments: Technology trends. MIT Connection Science's series on financial technology.

Sofia. (2016). *26 FinTech Companies Powering Institutional Investments and Trading*. Let's Talk Payments. Accessed March 24, 2017,https://letstalkpayments.com/26-fintech-companiespowering-institutional-investments-and-trading/

Van Alstyne, M. W., Parker, G. G., & Choudary, S. P. (2016). Pipelines, plat-forms, and the new rules of strategy. *Harvard Business Review*, 1–18.

Xie, P., & Zou, C. (2013). The Theory of Internet Finance. *Chinese Economy, 8*(2), 1–15.

Yuen, Y. Y., Yeow, H. P., & Lim, N. (2015). Internet banking acceptance in the United State and Malaysia: Cross-cultural examination. *Marketing Intelligence & Planning, 28*(3), 443–448. doi:10.1108/MIP-08-2013-0126

Zimmerman, J. (2014). *The emergence of responsible digital finance*. Centre for Financial Inclusion. Retrieved August 24, 2016, from https://cfi-blog.org/2014/07/21/the-emergence-of-responsible-digital-finance/

Compilation of References

23. Shahin, A. (2006). SERVQUAL and Model of Service Quality Gaps: A Framework for Determining and Prioritizing Critical Factors in Delivering Quality Services. In V. Partha Sarathy (Ed.), *Service Quality: An Introduction*. The ICFAI University Press.

A Google trend search reveals that the interest over time for the word "Fintech" increased exponentially in 2014. (n.d.). https://www.google.com/trends/explore#q=fintech

Ab Manan, S. K., Othman, J., & Shahadan, A. (2011, June 1–3). Descriptive analysis on the pattern of SME financing in Malaysia. In *3rd International Symposium & Exhibition in Sustainable Energy & Environment* (pp. 139-147). Melaka: Academia. 10.1109/ISESEE.2011.5977122

Ab Rahman & Airini. (2017). Emerging Technologies with Disruptive Effects: A Review. *PERINTIS eJournal, 7*(2).

Abadi, H., Kabiry, N., & Forghani, M. (2013). Factors Affecting Isfahanian Mobile Banking Adoption Based on the Technology Acceptance Model. *International Journal of Academic Research in Business and Social Sciences., 5*(3), 611–623.

Abdul Nasser W. & Prabhakar K., (2017). Technology Acceptance Model (TAM): Design of Work Life Balance Practices. *International Journal of Research in Management & Business Studies, 4*(1).

Abdul Rahman, A., & Mohd Nor, S. (2016). Challenges of profit-and-loss sharing financing in Malaysian Islamic. *Malaysian Journal of Society and Space, 12*(2), 39–46.

Abraham, F., Schmukler, S., & Tessada, J. (2019). *Robo-Advisors: Investing through Machines*. Research & Policy Briefs from the World Bank Chile Center and Malaysia Hub. February.

Abu-Joudeh, B. (2011). *Exploring the potential for profit-loss sharing models in Islamic microfinance* (Working paper). Social Impact Research Experience (SIRE). University of Pennsylvania. Retrieved from http://repository.upenn.edu/cgi/viewcontent.cgi?article=1014&context=sire

Accenture. (2014). *The rise of Fintech: New York's opportunity for tech leadership*. Retrieved July 31, 2016, from http://pfnyc.org/wp-content/uploads/2014/06/NY-fintech-Report-2014.pdf

Accenture. (2015). The Future of Fintech and Banking: Digitally disrupted or reimagined? Author.

Accenture. (2016a). *Global Fintech investment growth continues in 2016 driven by Europe and Asia, Accenture study finds*. Available at https://newsroom.accenture.com/news/ global-Fintech-investment-growth-continues-in-2016-driven-by-europe-and-asia-accenture-study-finds.htm

Accenture. (2016b). *Fintech and the evolving landscape*. Available at https://www.accenture.com/us-en/insight-Fintech-evolving-landscape

Accenture. (2018). *Global Venture Capital Investment in Fintech in 2017.* https://newsroom.accenture.com/news/global-venture-capital-investment-in-fintech-industryset-record-in2017-driven-by-surge-in-india-us-and-uk-accenture-analysis-finds.html

Afi. (2018). Innovative Cross-Border Remittance Services: Experiences from Afi Member Countries. Guideline Note No. 30 August.

Agarwal, M. (2019, October 30). *What Impact Has India's Fintech Ecosystem Created on Banking?* Retrieved from https://inc42.com/features/what-impact-has-indias-fintech-ecosystem-created-on-banking/

Agha, S., & Saeed, M. (2015). Factors Influencing Customer Acceptance of Online Banking in Pakistan and the Moderating Effect of Technophobia. *Journal of Marketing and Consumer Research,* 12.

Ahmadi, K., Bahrami, Y., & Ahmad, M. (2016). Studying and developing a model for mobile banking adoption in Iran banking system. *International Journal of Humanities and Cultural Studies, 1*(1), 2195–2207.

Ajlouni, A. T. A., & Al-Hakim, M. (2018). *Financial Technology in Banking Industry: Challenges and Opportunities.* Paper presented at the International Conference on Economics and Administrative Sciences ICEAS2018, Jordan. https://www.researchgate.net/publication/331303690_Financial_Technology_in_Banking_Industry_Challenges_and_Opportunities

Akhsay, A. (2007). E-*Satisfaction: A Comprehensive Framework.* Presented in the International Marketing Conference on Marketing and Society.

Akturan, U., & Tezcan, N. (2012). Mobile banking adoption of the youth market: Perceptions & intentions. *Marketing Intelligence & Planning, 30*(4), 444–459. doi:10.1108/02634501211231928

Alaeddin, O., Rana, A., Zainudin, Z., & Kamarudin, F. (2018). From physical to digital: Investigating consumer behavior of switching to a mobile wallet. *Polish Journal of Management Studies, 17.*

Al-Al-Alawi, A. I., & Al-Bassam, S. A. (2020). Study of the Cybercrime Cost and the Risk of Criminal Threats to the Banking Sector. *Xi'an Jianzhu Keji Daxue Xuebao/Journal of Xi'an University of Architecture & Technology, 12*(4), 252-270. Doi:10.37896/JXAT12.04/770

Al-Alawi, A. I., Al-Bassam, S. A., & Mehrotra, A. A. (2020). Critical Cybersecurity Threats: Frontline Issues Faced by Bahraini Organizations. In Implementing Computational Intelligence Techniques for Security Systems Design (pp. 210-229). IGI Global.

Al-Alawi. (2018, August). Using Balanced Scorecard in Measuring the Performance of Online Banking: Cultivating Strategic Model Map in Financial Sector- Case of Bahrain. *Journal of Internet Banking and Commerce, 23*(2).

Al-Alawi, A. I. (2005). Adoption and Awareness of Online Banking Issues among Mature Users. *Asian Journal of Information Technology, 4*(9), 856–860.

Al-Alawi, A. I., & Al-Ali, F. M. (2015). Factors affecting e-commerce adoption in SMEs in the GCC: An empirical study of Kuwait. *Research Journal of Information Technology, 7*(1), 1–21. doi:10.3923/rjit.2015.1.21

Al-Alawi, A. I., & Al-Bassam, S. A. (2019). Evaluation of telecommunications regulatory practice in the Kingdom of Bahrain: Development and challenges. *International Journal of Business Information Systems, 31*(2), 282–303. doi:10.1504/IJBIS.2019.100282

Albashrawi, M., & Motiwalla, L. (2019). Privacy & Personalization in Continued Usage Intention of Mobile Banking: An Integrative Perspective. *Information Systems Frontiers, 21*(5), 1–13. doi:10.100710796-017-9814-7

Al-Debei, M. M., & Avison, D. (2010). Developing a unified framework of the business model concept. *European Journal of Information Systems, 19*(3), 359–376. doi:10.1057/ejis.2010.21

Alexankov, A. M., d'Ascenzo, F., & Pokrovskaia, N. N. (2017). The management for Cyber-physical systems in the context of Industry 4.0 and regulatory mechanisms. In *XXI Int. conf. "Systems analysis in engineering and control" (SAEC-2017)*. St.-Petersburg Polytechnic University.

Al-Jaziri, A. R. (2009). *Al-Fiqh 'ala al-Madhahib al-Arba'ah*. Fons Vitae.

Allan & Hagiwara. (2018). Available at, https://www.bloomberg.com/news/articles/2018-04-04/banks-rush-to-turn-japan-cashless-ahead-of-looming-tech-rivals

Allen, S. (2018, December 24). *Pros and cons of debt financing for business owners*. The Balance Small Business. Retrieved from https://www.thebalance.com/debt-financing-pros-and-cons-1200981

Almossawi, M. (2001). Bank Selection Criteria Employed By College Students in Bahrain: An Empirical Analysis. *International Journal of Bank Marketing, 19*(3), 115–125. doi:10.1108/02652320110388540

Alois, J. (2015, June). *Fintech: FundedByMe is Approved to Operate Equity Crowdfunding in Malaysia*. Retrieved from Crowdfund Insider: https://www.crowdfundinsider.com/2015/06/69318-fundedbyme-is-approved-to-operate-equity-crowdfunding-in-malaysia/

Al-Rahmi, W., Othman, M., & Yusuf, L. (2015). Exploring the Factors that Affect Student Satisfaction through Using E-Learning in Malaysian Higher Education Institutions. *Mediterranean Journal of Social Sciences*, (6), 4. doi:10.5901/mjss.2015.v6n4s1p299

Alsamydai, M., (2014). Adaptation of the Technology Acceptance Model (TAM) to the Use of Mobile Banking Services. *International Review of Management and Business Research, 3*(4).

Alshikhi, O., & Abdullah, B. (2018). Information quality: Definitions, measurement, dimensions, and relationship with decision making. *European Journal of Business and Innovation Research, 6*(5), 36–42.

Alt, Beck, & Smits. (2018, August 13). FinTech and the transformation of the financial industry. Springer Berlin Heidelberg. doi:10.100712525-018-0310-9

Al-Toni, M. A. (2007). *Banking Integration (Origination and Development of Motivations, Justifications and Implications) with a view on the experiences of global, Arab and Egyptian integration* (1st ed.). Dar Al Fajr Publishing and Distribution.

Amoroso, D. L., & Magnier-Watanabe, R. (2012). Building a research model for mobile wallet consumer adoption: The case of mobile Suica in Japan. *Journal of Theoretical and Applied Electronic Commerce Research, 7*(1), 94–110. doi:10.4067/S0718-18762012000100008

Ancri, C. (2016). *Fintech Innovation: An Overview*. IJTSRD.

Anderson, C. R. J. (2013). *Segmentation of Smallholder Households: Meeting the Range of Financial Needs in Agricultural Families*. Focus Note 85. Washington, DC: CGAP. http://www.cgap.org/sites/default/files/Focus-Note-Segmentation-of- Smallholder-Households-April-2013.pdf

Anderson, R. E., & Srinivasan, S. S. (2003). E-satisfaction and e-loyalty: A contingency framework. *Psychology and Marketing, 20*(2), 123–138. doi:10.1002/mar.10063

Andersson, O., & Holmgren, J. (2017). *Clients' lost interest in banks. The Business Model Development of a FinTech Start-Up*. Academic Press.

Arner D. W., Barberis J., & Buckley R. P. (2016). *The Evolution of FinTech: A New Post-Crisis*. Academic Press.

Arner, D. W., Barberis, J. N., & Buckley, R. P. (2017). *Fintech And Regtech in a Nutshell, And the Future in a Sandbox.* Retrieved from January 26, 2019, from https://www.cfainstitute.org/en/research/foundation/2017/fintech-and-regtech-in-a-nutshell-and-the-future-in-a-sandbox

Arner, D. W., Barberis, J., & Buckley, R. P. (2016). The evolution of fintech: a new post-crisis paradigm. *Journal International Law*, 1271-1319.

Arner, G., Barberis, J., & Buckley, R. (2017). FinTech and RegTech in a Nutshell, and the Future in a Sandbox. *Research Foundation Briefs, 3*(4).

Arner, D. W. (2009). The Global Credit Crisis of 2008. *Causes and Consequences The International Lawyer*, *43*, 91–136.

Arner, D. W., & Barberis, J. (2015). FinTech in China: From the shadows? *The Journal of Financial Perspectives*, *3*(3), 78–79.

Arner, D. W., Barberis, J. N., & Buckley, R. P. (2015). The evolution of Fintech: A new post-crisis paradigm. *Georgetown Journal of International Law*, *47*, 1271–1319. doi:10.2139srn.2676553

Ashraf, S., & Adarsh, S. (2017). *Decentralized Computing Using Blockchain Technologies and Smart Contracts*. IGI Global. doi:10.4018/978-1-5225-2193-8

Assocham & PwC. (2019). *Emerging technologies disrupting the financial sector*. Retrieved from https://www.pwc.in/assets/pdfs/consulting/financial-services/fintech/publications/emerging-technologies-disrupting-the-financial-sector.pdf

Avornyo, P., Fang, J., Odai, R. O., Vondee, J. B., & Nartey, M. N. (2019). Factors Affecting Continuous Usage Intention of Mobile Banking in Tema and Kumasi. *International Journal of Business and Social Science*, *10*(3). Advance online publication. doi:10.30845/ijbss.v10n3p11

Awrey, D. (2011). Regulating Financial Innovation: A More Principles-Based Alternative. Brooklyn Journal of Corporate. *Financial and Commercial Law*, *5*, 273–315.

Azouzi, D. (2009). The adoption of electronic banking in Tunisia: An exploratory study. *Journal of Internet Banking and Commerce*, *14*(3), 1–11.

Baabdullaha, A., Alalwanb, A., Ranac, N., Kizginc, H., & Patilc, P. (2019). Consumer use of mobile banking (M-Banking) in Saudi Arabia: Towards an integrated model. *International Journal of Information Management*, 44.

Badran, O., & Al-Haddad, S. (2018). The Impact of Software User Experience on Customer Satisfaction. *Journal of Management Information and Decision Sciences, 21*(1).

Bagla, R. K., & Sancheti, V. (2018). Gaps in customer satisfaction with digital wallets: A challenge for sustainability. *Journal of Management Development*, *37*(6), 442–451. doi:10.1108/JMD-04-2017-0144

Bahrain FinTech Bay. (2018). *Bahrain FinTech Bay Manifesto 2020*. Retrieved from: https://www.bahrainfintechbay.com

Bahrain, E. D. B. B. (2017, June). *Invest in experience. Financial services in Bahrain*. Retrieved from Economic Development Board: https://bahrainedb.com/app/uploads/2017/06/Financial-Services-A4-Brochure-Jun2017.pdf

Baker, A. (2019). *FinTech and the future of finance*. The Global Advisory and Accounting Network. Retrieved from: https://www.hlb.global/fintech-and-the-future-of-finance/

Bank Negara Malaysia. (2015). *Mudarabah. Kuala Lumpur: Bank Negara Malaysia*. Retrieved from http://www.bnm.gov.my/guidelines/05_shariah/Mudarabah.pdf

Bank Of New York. (2015). *Innovation in payments*. BNY.

Baporikar, N. (2020a). Handbook of Research on Entrepreneurship Development and Opportunities in Circular Economy. IGI Global. http://doi:10.4018/978-1-7998-5116-5

Baporikar, N. (2014). Information Strategy as Enabler of Competitive Advantage. [IJSITA]. *International Journal of Strategic Information Technology and Applications*, *5*(1), 30–41. doi:10.4018/ijsita.2014010103

Baporikar, N. (2017a). Strategies for Successful Implementation of Innovation. [IJIDE]. *International Journal of Innovation in the Digital Economy*, *8*(2), 16–28. doi:10.4018/IJIDE.2017040102

Baporikar, N. (2019a). E-Learning Strategies for Emerging Economies in the Knowledge Era. In J. Pelet (Ed.), *Advanced Web Applications and Progressing E-Learning 2.0 Technologies in Higher Education* (pp. 150–171). Hershey, PA: IGI Global; doi:10.4018/978-1-5225-7435-4.ch008

Baporikar, N. (2019b). Knowledge Management Dynamics and Public Sector Organization Development. In Y. Albastaki, A. Al-Alawi, & S. Abdulrahman Al-Bassam (Eds.), *Handbook of Research on Implementing Knowledge Management Strategy in the Public Sector* (pp. 55–71). Hershey, PA: IGI Global; doi:10.4018/978-1-5225-9639-4.ch003

Baporikar, N., & Akino, S. (2020b). Financial Literacy Imperative for Success of Women Entrepreneurship. [IJIDE]. *International Journal of Innovation in the Digital Economy*, *11*(3), 1–21. doi:10.4018/IJIDE.2020070101

Baragde, D., & Baporikar, N. (2017b). Business innovation in Indian software industries [JSTPM]. *Journal of Science and Technology Policy Management*, *8*(1), 62–75. doi:10.1108/JSTPM-12-2015-0039

Bardin, L. (2010). *Content Analysis* (70th ed.).

Barth, J. R., Prabha, A. P., & Wihlborg, C. (2014). *Transparency of Financial Regulation*. Oxford University Press.

Bashir I. & Madhavaiah C. (2014). Determinants of Young Consumers' Intention to Use Internet Banking Services in India. *The Journal of Business Perspective. Sage Publications, 18*(3), 153-163.

Batelco. (2018). *Batelco and Arab Financial Services Partner to launch bWallet: A new FinTech Service*. Retrieved from http://batelco.com/news-media/batelco-and-arab-financial-services-partner-to-launch-bwallet-a-new-fintech-service/

Bates, R. (2017). *Banking on the future. An exploration of FinTech and the consumer interest*. Academic Press.

Bates, R. (2017, July). *Banking on the Future: An Exploration of FinTech and The Consumer Interest*. Retrieved from Consumers International: https://www.consumersinternational.org/media/154710/banking-on-the-future-full-report.pdf

Bayram, A. S. (2018). *Here Are Three Ways Blockchain Can Change Refugees' Lives*. World Economic Forum. Available at: https://www.weforum.org/agenda/2018/06/three-ways-blockchain-change-refugees-lives/

BBC News. (2015). *Why do many Americans mistrust the Federal Reserve?* https://www.bbc.com/news/business-35079495

Bell, D. R., Gallino, S., & Moreno, A. (2014). How to win in an Omni channel world. *MIT Sloan Management Review*, *56*(1), 1–45.

Bellens, J., & Pogson, K. (2017). *As FinTech Evolves, Can Financial Services Innovation Be Compliant?* Retrieved from UK: https://www.ey.com/cn/en/industries/financial-services/ey-as-fintech-evolves-can-financial-services-innovation-be-compliant

Benefit. (2017). *The Benefit Company introduces the National E-Wallet by the 4th of July 2017*. Retrieved from https://www.benefit.bh/events/2017/NationalEWallet.aspx?monthNo=6

Bettinger, A. (1972). FINTECH: A Series of 40 Time Shared Models Used at Manufacturers Hanover Trust Company. *Interfaces*, *2*(4), 62–63.

Bhattacherjee, A. (2001a). Understanding information systems continuance-An expectation-confirmation model-. *Management Information Systems Quarterly, 25*(3), 351–370. doi:10.2307/3250921

Black, J. (2008). *Forms and Paradoxes of Principles Based Regulation.* Academic Press.

Blank, S., & Dorf, B. (2014). *Startup: Entrepreneur manual.* High Books.

Blechschmidt, B. (2018). *Blockchain in Europe: Closing the Strategy Gap.* Cognizant Report. Retrieved from https://www.cognizant.com/blockchain

Blockchain.info. (2017, February). *Total number of transactions.* https://blockchain.info/charts/n-transactions-total?timespan=30days

BlockchainHub. (n.d.). *Smart Contracts.* Available at: https://blockchainhub.net/smart-contracts/

BlockchainI. B. M. (n.d.). Available at, https://www.ibm.com/blockchain/hyperledger/fabric-support

Blockgeeks. (n.d.). *Smart Contracts: The Blockchain Technology That Will Replace Lawyers.* Available at: https://blockgeeks.com/guides/smart-contracts/

Board, F. S. (2017). *Financial Stability Implications from FinTech: Supervisory and Regulatory Issues that Merit Authorities' Attention.* Academic Press.

Bogart W. & Wichadee S., (2015). Exploring Students' Intention to Use LINE for Academic Purposes Based on Technology Acceptance Model. *International Review of Research in Open and Distributed Learning, 16*(3).

Bons, E., Daams, M., Neijnens, E., Ottenheym, D., Segeren, M., & Van der Sommen, G. (n.d.). *Open innovation: The benefits of crowdsourcing.* Tilburg University.

Boustani, N. M. (2020). Traditional Banks and Fintech: Survival, Future and Threats. In *ICT for an Inclusive World* (pp. 345–359). Springer. doi:10.1007/978-3-030-34269-2_24

Bradley Rice, L. J. (2018, February). *Implications of fintech developments for banks and bank supervisors.* Retrieved from Bank for International Settlement: https://www.bis.org/bcbs/publ/d431.pdf

Brummer, C., & Gorfine, D. (2014). *FinTech: Building a 21st-Century Regulator's Toolkit.* Milken Institute – Center for Financial Markets.

Brunsden, J. (2016). *New EU laws legitimize fintech challengers.* https://www.ft.com/content/3803914a-6eba-11e6-a0c9-1365ce54b926

Buckley, R. P., Arner, D., Veidt, R., & Zetzsche, D. (2019). Building Fintech Ecosystems: Regulatory Sandboxes, Innovation Hubs And Beyond. UNSWLRS, 72.

Buckley, R., & Barberise, J. N. (2016). 150 Years of FinTech: An evolutionary analysis. *JASSA The Finsia Journal of Applied Finance, 3.*

Bugrov, D., Dietz, M., & Poppensieker, T. (2017). *A brave new world for global banking.* McKinsey & Company https://www.mckinsey.com/industries/financial-services/our-insights/abrave-new-world-for-global-banking

Bureau, C. F. P. (2016). *Project Catalyst Report: Promoting Consumer-Friendly Innovation.* Retrieved from United States: https://files.consumerfinance.gov/f/documents/102016_cfpb_Project_Catalyst_Report.pdf

Burnmark. (2017). *Digital Wealth.* Retrieved from: https://wealthobjects.com/ templates/protostar/images/Burnmark-April17.pdf

Bushlagh, F., & Zakiq, H. (2015). *Banking Integration and a Course in Improving the Competitiveness of Banks: Case Study of Algeria* (Master's thesis). University of AkliMohandOulhaj, Bouira, Algeria.

Cancian, F. (1967). Stratification and risk-taking: A theory tested on agricultural innovation. *American Sociological Review, 32*(6), 912–927. doi:10.2307/2092845 PMID:5624925

Candra, S. (2014). The service quality of Internet banking and impact to customer satisfaction: A preliminary finding. *International Journal of Applied Engineering Research, 9*(22), 17963–17970.

Cao, X., Yu, L., Liu, Z., Gong, M., & Adeel, L. (2018). Understanding mobile payment users' continuance intention: A trust transfer perspective. *Internet Research, 28*(2), 456–476. doi:10.1108/IntR-11-2016-0359

Carpenter, C. (2017, May). *FinTech, Green Finance, and Developing Countries.* Retrieved from GreenInvest: http://unepinquiry.org/wp-content/uploads/2017/06/Fintech_Green_Finance_and_Developing_Countries-input-paper.pdf

CBB. (2019). *Financial Stability Report.* Retrieved from https://www.cbb.gov.bh/ar/publications/

CBInsights. (2017). *A Wealth Tech World: Mapping Robo-Advisors Around the Globe.* Retrieved from: https://www.cbinsights.com/research/robo-advisor-global-fintech-map/

Central Bank of Bahrain. (2016). *A noticeable increase in the usage of the Electronic Fund Transfer System within a year from launch.* Retrieved from: https://www.cbb.gov.bh/

Central Bank of Bahrain. (2017). *Regulatory Sandbox Framework.* Retrieved from: https://www.cbb.gov.bh/

Chang, Y., Wong, S. F., Lee, H., & Jeong, S. P. (2016, August). What motivates chinese consumers to adopt FinTech services: a regulatory focus theory. In *Proceedings of the 18th annual international conference on electronic commerce: e-commerce in smart connected world* (p. 40). ACM. 10.1145/2971603.2971643

Chen, C. W. (2010). Impact of quality antecedents on taxpayer satisfaction with online tax-filing systems—An empirical study. *Information & Management, 47*(5-6), 308–315. doi:10.1016/j.im.2010.06.005

Chen, L. (2016). From FinTech to Finlife: The case of Fintech Development in China. *China Economic Journal, 9*(3), 225–239. doi:10.1080/17538963.2016.1215057

Chen, L. Y., & Wu, W. N. (2017). An exploration of the factors affecting user satisfaction with mobile payments. *International Journal of Computer Science & Information Technology.*, *9*(3), 97–105. doi:10.5121/ijcsit.2017.9308

Choi, Y., & Sun, L. (2016). Reuse intention of third-party online payments: A focus on the sustainable factors of Alipay. *Sustainability, 8*(2), 147. doi:10.3390u8020147

Christensen, C. M. (2012). Disruptive Innovation Explained/Interviewer: D. Dealov. *The Idea, Harvard Business Review.*

Christensen, C. M. (1997). *The innovator's dilemma: when new technologies cause great firms to fail.* Harvard Business School Press.

Christensen, C. M. (1997). *The Innovator's Dilemma: When New Technologies Cause Great Firms to Fail.* Harvard Business School Press.

Christensen, C. M. (2003). *The innovator's solution: creating and sustaining successful growth.* Harvard Business Press.

Christensen, C. M. (2016). *Disruption in Financial Services/Interviewer: A.* Rise Global, Barclays, New York.

Chuang, L.-M., Liu, C.-C., & Kao, H.-K. (2016). The Adoption of Fintech Service: TAM perspective. *International Journal of Management and Administrative Sciences, 3*(7), 1–75.

Chuen, D. K., & Teo, E. G. (2015). *Emergence of Fintech and the LASIC principles*. doi:. doi:10.2139srn.2668049

Chung, M., & Kim, J. (2016). The internet information and technology research directions based on the fourth industrial revolution. *Transactions on Internet and Information Systems (Seoul)*, *10*(3), 1311–1320.

Chu, P. Y. (2015). An Empirical Assessment of a Modified Technology Acceptance Model. *Journal of Management Information Systems*, 185–204.

CitiGPS. (2015). *Technology at Work*. Available at, https://www.oxfordmartin.ox.ac.uk/ downloads/reports/Citi_GPS_Technology_Work.pdf

Claessens, S., Frost, J., Turner, G. & Zhu, F. (2018, September). FinTech credit markets around the world: size, drivers, and policy issues. *BIS Quarterly Review*.

Cocco, L., Pinna, A., & Marchesi, M. (2017). Banking on Blockchain: Costs Savings Thanks to the Blockchain Technology. *Future Internet*, *9*(3), 25. doi:10.3390/fi9030025

Cockton, G. (2013). *The Encyclopedia of Human-Computer Interaction*. Interaction Design Foundation.

Collins, R. (2016). Blockchain: A new architecture for digital content. *EContent (Wilton, Conn.)*, *39*(8), 22–23.

Comin, D., & Hobijn, B. (2010). An exploration of technology diffusion. *The American Economic Review*, *100*(5), 2031–2059. doi:10.1257/aer.100.5.2031

CommissionS. (2019). *About the SC*. Retrieved from https://www.sc.com.my/about/about-the-sc

Consultancy.eu. (2019). *Global FinTech investment more than doubled to $112 billion*. Retrieved from: https://www.consultancy.eu/news/2390/global-fintech-investment-more-than-doubled-to-112-billion

Cooper, T. (2018). *The Race to Become the World's Leading Leading Islamic Fintech Hub - Raconteur*. Retrieved from: https://www.raconteur.net/finance/race-become-worlds-leading-leading-islamic-fintech-hub

Cortina Lorente, J. J. & Schmukler, S. L. (2018). The FinTech Revolution: A Threat to Global Banking? *World Bank: Research & Policy Briefs Paper*.

Courbe, J. (2016). *Financial Services Technology 2020 and Beyond: Embracing disruption*. Retrieved from Pricewaterhousecoopers: https://www.pwc.com/gx/en/financial-services/assets/pdf/technology2020-and-beyond.pdf

Crane, J., Meyer, L. M., & Fife, E. A. (2018). *Thinking Inside the Sandbox: An Analysis of Regulatory Efforts to Facilitate Financial Innovation*. Retrieved from Washington DC: https://www.regtechlab.io/report-thinking-inside-the-sandbox

Critical Issues to Consider by Small Merchants. (n.d.). *Human Systems Management*, *22*(3), 133–142.

Dahlberg, T., Mallat, N., & Öörni, A. (2003). Consumer acceptance of mobile payment solutions. *mBusiness 2003 – The Second International Conference on Mobile Business*, 211–218.

Dahlberg, T., Mallat, N., Ondrus, J., & Zmijewska, A. (2008). Past, Present and Future of mobile payments research: A literature review. *Electronic Commerce Research and Application*, 165-181.

Daud, A., Farida, N., Andriya, A., & Razak, M. (2018). Impact of customer trust toward loyalty: The mediating role of perceived usefulness and satisfaction. *Journal of Business and Retail Management Research*, *2*(13), 235–241. doi:10.24052/JBRMR/V13IS02/ART-21

Davis F., (1989). Perceived Usefulness, Perceived Ease of Use, and User Acceptance of Information Technology. *MIS Quarterly, September*, *13*(3), 319-340.

Davis, F. D. (1989). Perceived usefulness, perceived ease of use and user acceptance of information technology. *Management Information Systems Quarterly, 13*(3), 319–339. doi:10.2307/249008

de Luna, I. R., Liébana-Cabanillas, F., Sánchez-Fernández, J., & Muñoz-Leiva, F. (2019). Mobile payment is not all the same: The adoption of mobile payment systems depending on the technology applied. *Technological Forecasting and Social Change, 146*, 931–944. doi:10.1016/j.techfore.2018.09.018

Deloitte. (2016). *Disaggregating Fintech: Brighter shades of disruption.* Retrieved from https://www2.deloitte.com/content/dam/Deloitte/us/Documents/financial-services/us-fsi-dis-aggregating-Fintech-brighter-shades-of-disruption.pdf

Deloitte. (2017). *Fintech by numbers.* https://www2.deloitte.com/content/dam/Deloitte/us/Documents/financial-services/us-dcfs-fintech-by-thenumbers-web.pdf

Deloitte. (2017). *Japanese Fintech in the Global Context.* Available at, https://www2.deloitte.com/jp/en/pages/financial-services/articles/bk/jp-fi-fintech-in-japan.html

Deloitte. (2017). *Regulatory Sandbox – Making India a Global Fintech Club.* https://www2.deloitte.com/content/dam/Deloitte/in/Documents/technology-media-telecommunications/intmt-fintech-regulatory-sandbox-web.pdf

Delone, W. H., & McLean, E. R. (2003). The DeLone and McLean model of information systems success: A ten-year update. *Journal of Management Information Systems, 19*(4), 9–30. doi:10.1080/07421222.2003.11045748

Devaraj, S., Kohli, R., & Fan, M. (2002). Antecedents of B2C channel satisfaction and preference: Validating e-commerce metrics. *Information Systems Research, 13*(3), 316–333. doi:10.1287/isre.13.3.316.77

Dewey, J. (2019). *Blockchain & Cryptocurrency Regulation 2019* (1st ed.). Global Legal Group Ltd.

Dickinson, D. (2019). *Digital Banking. Temenos The banking Software Company.* Retrieved from: https://www.temenos.com/wp-content/uploads/2019/08/Digital-Banking-whitepaper-2019-Aug-21.pdf

Dictionary, O. E. (2016). *Definition of Fintech.* Author.

Dictionary, O. L. s. (2019). *Oxford Learner's Dictionary.* Oxford UP.

DIEDC. (2018). *Islamic Fintech Report 2018 Current Landscape & Path Forward.* Dubai Islamic Economy Development Center. Retrieved from: https://www. dinarstandard.com/wp-content/uploads/2018/12/Islamic-Fintech-Report-2018.pdf

DinarStandard. (2018). *Islamic Fintech Report 2018: Current Landscape and Path Forward.* Dubai, UAE: DinarStandard.

DirectiveE. U. (2015). Available at, https://eur-lex.europa.eu/legal-content/EN/TXT/PDF/?uri=CELEX:32015L2366&from=EN

Dorfleitner, G., Hornuf, L., Schmitt, M., & Weber, M. (2017). Definition of Fintech and description of the Fintech industry. In *Fintech in Germany* (pp. 5–10). Springer. doi:10.1007/978-3-319-54666-7_2

Dornelas, J. C. A. (2016). *Empreendedorismo: transformando ideias em negócios. 6.* Atlas.

Douglas, W., & Arner, J. B. (2015, October 20). *The Evolution of FinTech: A New Post-Crisis Paradigm?* Retrieved from University of Hong Kong: https://hub.hku.hk/bitstream/10722/221450/1/Content.pdf

Dourado, E., & Brito, J. (2014). Cryptocurrency. The New Palgrave Dictionary of Economics, Online Edition (S. N. Durlauf & L. E. Blume, Eds.). Academic Press.

Economic Development Board Bahrain. (2017). *Bahrain for Islamic finance.* Retrieved from: https://bahrainedb.com

Economic Development Board Bahrain. (2018). *Bahrain FinTech Bay highlights launch with announcement of startups and founding partners.* Retrieved from: https://bahrainedb.com

Economist. (2015, Oct. 31). *The promise of blockchain.* Author.

Edris, T. A. (1997). Services considered important to business customers and determinants of bank selection in Kuwait: A segmentation analysis. *International Journal of Bank Marketing*, *15*(4), 126–133. doi:10.1108/02652329710189393

El-Gayar, O., Moran, M., & Hawkes, M. (2011). Students' Acceptance of Tablet PCs and Implications for Educational Institutions. *Institutions. Journal of Educational Technology & Society*, *14*(2), 58–70.

Ernst and Young. (2014). *Landscaping UK Fintech.* UK Trade and Investment.

Ernst and Young. (2016). *UK Fintech on the Cutting Edge.* Available at, www.ey.com/Publication/vwLUAssets/EY-UK-FinTech-On-the-cutting-edge/%24FILE/EY-UK-FinTech-On-the-cutting-edge.pdf/

Ernst and Young. (2017). *Fintech Adoption Index 2017.* Available at, www.ey.com/Publication/vwLUAssets/ey-fintech-adoption-index-2017/%24FILE/ey-fintech-adoption-index-2017.pdf

European Central Bank (ECB) (2017). *Guide to assessments of fintech credit institution licence applications.* Banking Supervision. European Central Bank.

EVRY. (2018). *White Paper: PSD2 – Strategic Opportunities Beyond Compliance.* Available at, https://www.evry.com/en/campaigns/white-paper-psd2/

EY. (2019). *Global FinTech Adoption Index 2019.* Retrieved from https://assets.ey.com/content/dam/ey-sites/ey-com/en_gl/topics/banking-and-capital-markets/ey-global-fintech-adoption-index.pdf

Ferreira, A. B. de H. (2010). *Webster's Basic Portuguese Language. 8.* Editora Positivo.

Ferrell, O. C., Fraedich, J., & Ferrell, L. (2014). Business Ethics: Ethical Decision Making and Case (10th ed.). Academic Press.

Fetai, B. (2015). Financial Integration and Financial Development: Does Financial Integration Matter? *European Research Studies Journal*, *18*(2), 97–106. doi:10.35808/ersj/447

Financial Conduct Authority. (2015). *Regulatory Sandbox.* Retrieved from https://www.fca.org.uk/firms/regulatory-sandbox

Financial Conduct Authority. (2016). *Eligibility Criteria.* Retrieved from https://www.fca.org.uk/firms/regulatory-sandbox/prepare-application

Financial Conduct Authority. (2017a). *Regulatory Sandbox Cohort 2.* Retrieved from https://www.fca.org.uk/firms/regulatory-sandbox/cohort-2

Financial Conduct Authority. (2017b). *Regulatory Sandbox Cohort 3.* Retrieved from https://www.fca.org.uk/firms/regulatory-sandbox/cohort-3

Financial Conduct Authority. (2019). *The Impact and Effectiveness of Innovate.* Retrieved from UK: https://www.fca.org.uk/publications/research/impact-and-effectiveness-innovate

Fintech Futures. (2019, August 23). *People's Bank of China to issue fintech development plan.* Retrieved from https://www.fintechfutures.com/2019/08/peoples-bank-of-china-to-issue-fintech-development-plan/

Fintech Futures. (2020, February 26). *The impact of COVID-19 on the Chinese market.* Retrieved from: https://www.fintechfutures.com/2020/02/the-impact-of-covid-19-on-the-chinese-market/

FinTech Innovation Lab. (2018). *Mind the gap: Addressing challenges to FinTech adoption.* Retrieved from Accenture: https://www.accenture.com/t00010101T000000Z__w__/gb-en/_acnmedia/PDF-74/Accenture-FinTech-Challenges-Adoption.pdf

Fintech News Hong Kong. (2019, September 6). *China Lays Out 6 Key Fintech Focus for the Next 3 Years.* Retrieved from https://fintechnews.hk/10032/fintechchina/china-fintech-plan/

Firmansyah, E. A., & Anwar, M. (2019). *Islamic Financial Technology (FinTech): Its challenges and prospect. Advances in Social Science, Education and Humanities Research* (Vol. 216). ASSEHR.

Fong, V. (2017). *Malaysia's Fintech Sandbox Partcipant MoneyMatch Launches Transfer Portal.* Retrieved from https://fintechnews.sg/13658/malaysia/moneymatch-transfer-portal-launch/

Freedman, D., & Nutting, M. (2015). *A Brief History of Crowdfunding Including Rewards, Donation, Debt, and Equity Platforms in the USA.* Retrieved from: https://www.freedman-chicago.com/ec4i/History-of-Crowdfunding.pdf

Fundable. (n.d.). *Crowdfunding101: Types of Crowdfunding. Fundable.* Retrieved from https://www.fundable.com/crowdfunding101/types-of-crowdfunding

Fungáčová, Z., & Weill, L. (2015). Understanding financial inclusion in China. *China Economic Review, 34*, 196–206. doi:10.1016/j.chieco.2014.12.004

Gabor, D., & Brooks, S. (2017). The digital revolution in financial inclusion: International development in the Fintech era. *New Political Economy, 22*(4), 423–436. doi:10.1080/13563467.2017.1259298

Gai, K., Qiu, M., & Sun, X. (2018). A survey on FinTech. *Journal of Network and Computer Applications, 103*, 262–273. doi:10.1016/j.jnca.2017.10.011

Gakman, C. (2019). *Understanding FinTech Categories.* IAN Martin. Retrieved from: https://ianmartin.com/understanding-fintech-categories/

Garriga, M., Arias, M., & Renzis, A. (2018). *Blockchain and Cryptocurrency: A comparative framework of the main Architectural Drivers.* CONF.

Gartrell, J. W. (1981). Cancian. The Innovator's Situation: Upper-Middle-Class Conservatism in Agricultural Communities (Book Review). *Rural Sociology, 46*(2), 342.

Gasser, U., Gassmann, O., Hens, T., Leifer, L., Puschmann, T., & Zhao, L. (2017). *Digital Banking 2025.* Retrieved from: https://xupery.com/wp-content/uploads/2017/08/Digital-Banking-2025.pdf

Gateway, S. (2017). *INFOGRAPH-What are the different types of fintech?* Retrieved from: https://salaamgateway.com/story/infograph-what-are-the-different-types-of-fintech

Gawer, A. (2014). Bridging differing perspectives on technological platforms:Toward an integrative framework. *Research Policy, 43*(7), 1239–1249. doi:10.1016/j.respol.2014.03.006

Gengler, E. B. (2017). Leveraging Blockchain Technology for Corporate Social Responsibility. *Payments Journal.* Available at: https://paymentsjournal.com/leveraging-blockchain-technology-for-corporate-social-responsibility/

Ghai, R., Tyagi, M., & Gupta. (2020). Leveraging Technology for Robust Financial Facilities: A Comparative Assessment of BRICS Nations. In *ICCAKM 2020.* IEEE Xplore.

Gil, A. C. (2008). *Métodos e técnicas de pesquisa social.* Atlas.

Gil, A. C. (2017). *Como elaborar projetos de pesquisa.* Atlas.

Goeller, J. D., & Shureen, C. E. (2016). The top five federal tax issues for FinTech lenders. *Journal of taxation & regulation of Financial Institutions, 30*(1), 5-10.

Goldstein, I., Jiang, W., & Karolyi, G. (2019, May). To FinTech and Beyond. *Review of Financial Studies, 32*(5), 1647–1661. doi:10.1093/rfs/hhz025

Golohvastov, D. V., Pokrovskaia, N. N., & Snisarenko, S. O. (2016). InstitutionalConfidence and Economic Intelligence for the Performance at Macro and Micro Networks. *4th Conf. on Management, Leadership and Governance ICMLG 2016*, 255-263.

Gravelle, H., & Ress, R. (1992). *Microeconomics*. Longman Group Limited.

Gray, A., & Leibrock, M. (2017). *Fintech and Financial Stability Exploring How Technological Innovations Could Impact the Safety and Security of Global Markets*. DTCC Group.

Gray, P. (2020, March 5). China too risky? Do you need a new strategy for your FDI in the face of COVID-19? Academic Press.

Group, F. T. E. (2017). *List Of Approved Participants In Regulatory Sandbox*. Retrieved from https://www.myfteg.com/approved-participants-in-sandbox

Gumussoy, C. A. (2016). Factors affecting users' decision to continue using mobile banking in Turkey. *International Journal of Mobile Communications, 14*(4), 411. doi:10.1504/IJMC.2016.077341

Gurria, A. (2008, January). *Organization for Economic Co-Operation and Development Annual Report*. Retrieved from Organisation for Economic Co-operation and Development: https://www.oecd.org/newsroom/40556222.pdf

H2 Ventures. KPMG and Matchi. (2016). *Fintech 100. Leading Global Fintech innovators, Report 2015*. Retrieved July 31, 2016, from https://www.kpmg.com/FR/fr/IssuesAndInsights/ArticlesPublications/Documents/Etude-Fintech100-2015.pdf

Habib, F., & Ahmad, A. U. F. (2019). Using blockchain and smart contracts for waqf institutions. In Financial Technology and Disruptive Innovation in ASEAN. IGI Global. Doi:10.4018/978-1-5225-9183-2

Haddad, C., & Hornuf, L. (2019). The emergence of the global fintech market: Economic and technological determinants. *Small Business Economics, 53*(1), 81–105. doi:10.100711187-018-9991-x

Hail, P. M. (2015). *Entrepreneurship*. Press University of Coimbra.

Hajkova, D., & Hurnik, J. (2007). Cobb-Douglas Production Function: The Case of a Converging Economy. *Finance a Uver, 57*(9-10), 465–476.

HalalChain. (2018). *Halal-Chain White Paper*. Available at: http://www.halalchain.ae/whitepaper.pdf

Hamid, A. (2001). *Abdulmutallab*. Globalization and Banking Economics. University House.

Hammad, A.-A. T. (2017). *The Integration and Privatization of Banks Part IV*. Commercial Banking Series, University House.

Han, H. (2018). *FinTech in China: An Introduction*. Retrieved from https://medium.com/wharton-fintech/fintech-in-china-an-introduction-6b11abd9cb64

Handro, P, O. (2018). The Role of Customer Experience in Retail Banking and the Rise of Fintech. *Annals- Economy Series*, (1), 175-185.

Hansen, E. (2015). *The Blockchain, Explained*. Available at: https://medium.com/linkreply-blockchain/the-blockchain-explained-3300f4506890

Hansson, S. O. (2005, January). *Decision Theory: A Brief Introduction.* Retrieved from Royal Institute of Technology: https://www.researchgate.net/publication/210642121_Decision_Theory_A_Brief_Introduction

Harrison, R., Jaumandreu, J., Mairesse, J., & Peters, B. (2014). Does innovation stimulate employment? A firm-level analysis using comparable micro-data from four European countries. *International Journal of Industrial Organization, 35*, 29–43. doi:10.1016/j.ijindorg.2014.06.001

Hassan, A. (2014). *The principles of Islamic economic justice and its sources.* Jubilee Australia. Retrieved from https://www.jubileeaustralia.org/page/about/Jubilee%20Islamic%20Economic%20Justice.pdf

Havrylchyk, O. (2018). *Regulatory framework for the loan-based crowdfunding platforms.* OECD. Economic Department Working Papers No. 1513.

Hayashi, Y. (2016). CFPB fines FinTech firm Dwolla over data-security practices. *The Wall Street Journal*, p. C4.

Hebert, C. (2015, June 2). *Ask Clay: The Different Types of Crowdfunding.* Retrieved from Crowdfunidng Hacks: http://crowdfundinghacks.com/different-types-of-crowdfunding/

Hes, A., & Jilkova, P. (2016). Position of Low Cost Banks on the Financial Market in Czech Republic. *European Research Studies, 19*(4), 42–52. doi:10.35808/ersj/579

Hillbom, E., & Tillström, T. (2016). *Applications of Smart Contracts and Smart Property Utilizing Blockchains* (M.Sc. thesis in computer science). Chalmers, University of Technology and University of Gothenburg, Sweden.

Hobbs, J., Grigore, G., & Molesworth, M. (2016). Success in the management of crowdfunding projects in the creative industries. *Internet Research, 26*(1), 146–166. doi:10.1108/IntR-08-2014-0202

Hochstein, M. (2015). *Fintech (the Word, That Is) Evolves.* Accessed 19 October 2016. https://www.americanbanker.com/bankthink/fintech-the-word-that-is-evolves-1077098-1.html

Hochstein, M. (2015a). *Fintech (the Word That Is) Evolves.* Accessed 19 July 2019. https://www.americanbanker.com/bankthink/Fintech-the-word-that-isevolves-1077098-1.html

Hochstein. (2015). *Fintech (the Word, That Is) Evolves.* The American Banker at https://www.americanbanker.com/bankthink/fintech-the-word-that-is-evolves-1077098-1.html

Hollas, J. (2013, December 15). *Blog: Three Types of Equity Crowdfunding.* Retrieved from Equity Net: https://www.equitynet.com/blog/three-types-equity-crowdfunding/

Holliday, S. (2019). *How Insurtech Can Close the Protection Gap in Emerging Markets.* EM Compass Emerging Markets Note 70. Retrieved from: www.ifc.org/thoughtleadership

Holotesch, C. (2018). Understanding Blockchain Opportunities and Challenges. *The 14th International Scientific Conference eLearning and Software for Education.*

Horn, W. (Ed.). (2015). *What is Fintech.* Finnovation. Available at: http://finnovation.com.br/o-que-e-fintech/

Houben, R., & Synyers, A. (2018). *Cryptocurrencies and blockchain: Legal context and implications for financial crime, money laundering and tax evasion. STUDY Requested by the TAX3 committee.* European Parliament. July.

Hung, J.-L., & Luo, B. (2016). FinTech in Taiwan: A case study of a Bank's strategic planning for an investment in a FinTech company. *Hung and Luo Financial Innovation, 2*(1), 2–16. doi:10.118640854-016-0037-6

Hur, D. (2017). Buyer power and supplier relationship commitment: A cognitive evaluation theory perspective. *The Journal of Supply Chain Management, 53*(2), 39–60. doi:10.1111/jscm.12138

Hurst, S. (2016, October 13). *Fintech: FundedByMe Malaysia Debuts Second Equity Crowdfunding Campaign for iTalent Management.* Retrieved from Crowdfund Insider: https://www.crowdfundinsider.com/2016/10/91184-fundedbyme-malaysia-debuts-second-equity-crowdfunding-campaign-italent-management/

Ibn Hubairah, Y. (2009). *Ijma' al-Aimmah al-'Arbaah wa Ikhtilafuhum.* Dar Al-Ola.

Ichikawa, J. J. (2017, March 7). *The Analysis of Knowledge.* Retrieved from Stanford Encyclopedia of Philosophy: https://plato.stanford.edu/entries/knowledge-analysis/

Indiegogo. (2019). *The Essential Guide to Crowdfunding.* Retrieved from: https://learn.indiegogo.com/the-essential-guide-to-crowdfunding/

InnovateFinance. (2017). Available at, https://www.innovatefinance.com/wp-content/uploads/2018/02/2017- vc-fintech-investment-landscape.pdf

InsightsC. B. (2017). Available at, https://www.cbinsights.com/research/google-amazon-microsoft-facebook-ibm-startup-funding/

InsightsC. B. (2018a). Available at, https://www.cbinsights.com/research/report/amazon-across-financial-services-fintech/

InsightsC. B. (2018b). Available at, https://www.cbinsights.com/research/report/fintech-trends-q1-2018/

Insurtech'. (2017). *Investopedia,* accessed March 21, 2017 https://www.investopedia.com/terms/i/insurtech.asp

Intana, M., & Chansa-Ngavej, C. (2010). An extended technology acceptance model for internet banking adoption. *Asian Journal of Management Research, 5*(1).

Inuit Inc. (2017). *The history of money and payments.* https://payments.intuit.com/history-of-money-and-payments

inVerita. (2019). *What is fintech? Uses and Examples in 2019.* Retrieved from: https://becominghuman.ai/what-is-fintech-uses-and-examples-in-2019-f8992d4fd2c2

Investopedia. (2016). *Fintech.* Accessed 19 July 2019. https://www.investopedia.com/terms/f/Fintech.asp

Investopedia. (n.d.). *Smart Contracts.* Available at: https://www.investopedia.com/terms/s/smart-contracts.asp

Ismail, N. (2018, April 17). *The cybersecurity challenges facing emerging fintech startups.* Retrieved from Information Age: https://www.information-age.com/cyber-security-challenges-emerging-fintech-startups-123471506/

Ito, J., Narula, N., & Ali, R. (2017). *The Blockchain Will Do to the Financial System What the Internet Did to Media.* Harvard Business Review, Digital Article. Retrieved from https:// hbr.org/2017/03/the-blockchain-will-do-to-banks-and-law-firms-what-the-internet-did-to-media

Jagtiani, J., & Lemieux, C. (2017). *Fintech Lending: Financial Inclusion, Risk Pricing, and Alternative Information.* FRB of Philadelphia Working Paper.

Jahangir, N., & Begum, N. (2008, January 28). *The role of perceived usefulness, perceived ease of use, security, and privacy, and customer attitude to engender customer adaptation in the context of electronic banking.* Retrieved from African Journal of Business Managemen: https://academicjournals.org/article/article1380536538_Jahangir%2520and%2520%2520Begum.pdf

Jahmani, O. I. (2002). Integration into Jordan: A Field Study on Commercial Banks. Journal of Public Administration, 42(3).

Jamrisko, M., & Lu, W. (2018). *The U.S. Drops Out of the Top 10 in Innovation Ranking.* Bloomberg. Available at, https://www.bloomberg.com/news/articles/2018-01-22/south-korea-tops-global-innovation-ranking-again-as-u-s-falls

Jao, N. (2019, January 31). China's P2P lending sector a 'disaster zone' of fraud: government official. Retrieved from https://technode.com/2019/01/31/china-p2p-disaster-zone/

Jargons, B. (2017, January). *Investment Decision.* Retrieved from Business Jargons: https://businessjargons.com/investment-decision.html

Judge, N. (2017). Research entitled Banking Integration and Acquisitions in Arab Countries. *Journal of Administrative Sciences.*

Juengerkes, B. E. (2016). *Fintechs and Banks – Collaboration is Key.* Wiley. doi:10.1002/9781119218906.ch47

Jun, J., & Yeo, E. (2016). Entry of Fintech Firms and Competition in the Retail Payments Market. *Asia-Pacific Journal of Financial Studies, 45*(2), 159–184. doi:10.1111/ajfs.12126

Juskalian, R. (2018). Inside the Jordan Refugee Camp That Runs on Blockchain. *MIT Technology Review.* Available at: https://www.technologyreview.com/s/610806/inside-the-jordan-refugee-camp-that-runs-on-blockchain/

Juwaheer, T. D., Pudaruth, S., & Ramdin, P. (2012). Factors influencing the adoption of internet banking-A case study of commercial bank in Mauritius. *World Journal of Science. Technology and Sustainable Development, 9*(3), 204–234.

Kagan, J. (2019, May 17). *Financial Technology & Automated Investing.* Retrieved from Investopedia: https://www.investopedia.com/terms/f/fintech.asp

Karagianis, G., Palivos, T., & Papageorgiou, C. (2004). *Variable Elasticity of Substitution and Economic Growth: Theory and Evidence.* Department of Economics, University of Macedonia.

Karina, S. (2012). Inapplicability of Crowdfunding Concerns in The Internet Age and The Jobs Act's Safeguards. *Administrative Law Review, 64*(2), 474–505.

Kasri, N. S. (2017). *Sharī'ah Compliance via Blockchain and Smart Contract – The Case for Islamic Credit Card.* Wahed Invest. Available at: https://journal.wahedinvest.com/Sharī'ah-compliance-via-blockchain-and-smart-contract-the-case-for-islamic-credit-card

Kauffman, R. J., & Ma, D. (2015). Special issue: Contemporary research on payments and cards in the global Fintech revolution. *Electronic Commerce Research and Applications, 14*(5), 261–264. doi:10.1016/j.elerap.2015.09.005

Kaufmann, C., & Weber, R. H. (2010). The Role of Transparency in Financial Regulation. *Journal of International Economic Law, 13*(3), 779–797. doi:10.1093/jiel/jgq037

Kavuri, A. S., & Milne, A. (2019). *Fintech and the Future of Financial Services: What Are the Research Gaps?* Centre for Applied Macroeconomic Analysis. https://papers.ssrn.com/sol3/papers.cfm?abstract_id=3333515

Kenton, W. (2019). *Donation-Based Crowdfunding.* Retrieved from: https://www.investopedia.com/terms/d/donation-based-crowd-funding.asp

Khan. N. (2017). *Smart Contracts - The Future of Islamic Banking.* Academic Press.

Kheong, K. C. (2016). *Publications: Joining The Crowd.* Retrieved from Skrine: https://www.skrine.com/publications/legal-insights/635-joining-the-crowd

Kim, C., Mirusmonov, M., & Lee, I. (2010). An empirical examination of factors influencing the intention to use mobile payment. *Computers in Human Behavior, 26*(3), 310–322. doi:10.1016/j.chb.2009.10.013

Kim, H. K., Lee, M., & Jung, M. (2005). Perceived risk and risk-reduction strategies for high-technology services. *Asia Pacific Advances in Consumer Research, 16*(2), 171–179.

Kim, Y., Park, Y.-J., & Choi, J. (2016). The Adoption of Mobile Payment Services for "Fintech". *International Journal of Applied Engineering Research*, *11*(2), 1058–1061.

Klapper, L., Lusardi, A., & Van Oudheusden, P. (2015). *Financial literacy around the world.* World Bank.

Kleijnen, M., Wetzels, M., & de Ruyter, K. (2004). Consumer acceptance of wireless finance. *Journal of Financial Services Marketing*, *8*(3), 206–217. doi:10.1057/palgrave.fsm.4770120

Klump, R., & de La Grandville, O. (2000). Economic Growth and Elasticity of Substitution. *The American Economic Review*, *90*(1), 282–291. doi:10.1257/aer.90.1.282

Knezevic, D. (2018). Impact of Blockchain Technology Platform in Changing the Financial Sector and Other Industries. *Montenegrin Journal of Economics*, *14*(1), 109–120. doi:10.14254/1800-5845/2018.14-1.8

Knowledge@Wharton. (2019, July 12). *Fintech in China: What Lies Ahead.* Retrieved from https://knowledge.wharton.upenn.edu/article/fintech-china-lies-ahead/

Ko, C. (2017, Apr.). Are FinTech startups eating traditional banks' lunch? *Computerworld.*

Kostin, G. A., Pokrovskaia, N. N., & Ababkova, M. U. (2017). Master-chain as an intellectual governing system for producing and transfer of knowledge. *IEEE II International Conference on Control in Technical Systems (CTS).* 10.1109/CTSYS.2017.8109491

KPMG. (2018). *The Pulse of Fintech 2018. Biannual global analysis of investment in fintech.* KPMG.

KPMG. (2019). *InsurTech: Infrastructure for New Insurance.* KPMG Advisory (China) Limited.

Krejcie, R. V., & Morgan, D. W. (1970). Determining sample size for research activities. *Educational and Psychological Measurement*, *30*(3), 607–610. doi:10.1177/001316447003000308

Kumar, A., Adlakaha, A., & Mukherjee, K. (2018). The effect of perceived security & grievance redressal on continuance intention to use M-wallets in a developing country. -. *International Journal of Bank Marketing*, *36*(7), 1170–1189. doi:10.1108/IJBM-04-2017-0077

Kunigis, A. (2017). *Advantages vs. disadvantages of debt financing.* The Hartford. Retrieved from http://www.thehartford.com/business-playbook/in-depth/debt-financing

Kuppuswamy, V., & Bayus, B. (2017). Crowdfunding Creative Ideas: The Dynamics of Project Backers in Kickstarter. The Economics of Crowdfunding: Startups, Portals, and Investor Behavior. Academic Press.

Kuti, M., Bedő, Z., & Geiszl, D. (2017, December). Equity-based Crowdfundind. *Financial and Economic Review*, *16*(4), 187–200.

Kyryliuk, L. (2019). *What are the different types of Fintech?* Retrieved from: https://www.quora.com/What-are-the-different-types-of-Fintech/answer/Liudmyla-Kyryliuk

Lai, P. (2017). The literature review of technology adoption models and theories for the novelty technology. *Journal of Information Systems and Technology Management*, *14*(1), 21–38. doi:10.4301/S1807-17752017000100002

Lamagna, M. (2018). *This 30-year-old financial term was finally added to the dictionary.* Retrieved from: https://www.marketwatch.com/story/this-finance-related-term-was-just-added-to-the-dictionary-do-you-know-what-it-means-2018-09-05

Lamb & Polverini. (2015). *Assessing risk in digital payments.* Bill & Melinda Gates Foundation.

Lee, C. P., Warkentin, M., & Choi, H. (2004). The role of technological and social factors on the adoption of mobile payment technologies. AMCIS 2004 Proceedings, 333.

Lee, L. (2015, June 11). *Malaysia's Securities Commission allows 6 players to launch equity crowdfunding services.* Deal Street Asia. Retrieved from https://www.dealstreetasia.com/stories/sc-announces-6-equity-crowdfunding-operators-for-malaysia-7680/

Lee, I., & Shin, Y. J. (2018). Fintech: Ecosystem, business models, investment decisions, and challenges. *Business Horizons, 61*(1), 35–46. doi:10.1016/j.bushor.2017.09.003

Leong, C., Tan, B., Xiao, X., Tan, F. T. C., & Sun, Y. (2017). Nurturing a FinTech ecosystem: The case of a youth microloan startup in China. *International Journal of Information Management, 37*(2), 92–97. doi:10.1016/j.ijinfomgt.2016.11.006

Leong, K., & Sung, A. (2018, April). FinTech (Financial Technology): What is It and How to Use Technologies to Create Business Value in Fintech Way? *International Journal of Innovation, Management and Technology, 9*(2), 74–78. doi:10.18178/ijimt.2018.9.2.791

Lim, B., & Low, C. (2019). *Regulatory Sandboxes* (J. Madir, Ed.). Edward Elgar Publishing Limited. doi:10.4337/9781788979023.00028

Lim, W., & Ting, D. (2012). E-shopping: An Analysis of the Technology Acceptance Model. *Modern Applied Science, 6*(6), 4. doi:10.5539/mas.v6n4p49

Lin, L. (2019). *Regulating FinTech: The Case of Singapore.* NUS Law Working Paper Series 2019/028, November 2019, http://law.nus.edu.sg/wps/pdfs/028_2019_Lin%20Lin.pdf

Lin, K. Y., & Lu, H. P. (2011). Why people use social networking sites: An empirical study integrating network externalities and motivation theory. *Computers in Human Behavior, 27*(3), 1152–1161. doi:10.1016/j.chb.2010.12.009

Loonam, M., & O'loughlin, D. (2008). Exploring e-service quality: A study of Irish online banking. *Marketing Intelligence & Planning, 26*(7), 759–780. doi:10.1108/02634500810916708

Lovell, C. A. K. (1973). CES and VES Production Functions in a Cross-Section Context. *Journal of Political Economy, 81*(3), 705–720. doi:10.1086/260066

Lowry, P., B., Wells, T., Moody, G., Humpherys, S., & Kettles, D. (2006). Online Payment Gateways Used to Facilitate E-Commerce Transactions and Improve Risk Management. *Communications of AIS, 17.*

Lutz, A. M. J. B. E. (2015). Investor communication in equity-based crowdfunding: A qualitative empirical study. *Qualitative Research in Financial Market, 7*(3), 309–342. doi:10.1108/QRFM-07-2014-0021

Maçães, M. (2017). *Entrepreneurship, innovation and organizational change. 3.* Actual.

Macht, S. A., & Weatherston, J. (2015). Academic research on crowdfunders: What's been done and what's to come. *Strategic Change, 24*(2), 191–205. doi:10.1002/jsc.2010

Mackenzie, A. (2015). The Fintech Revolution. *London Business School Review, 26*(3), 50–53. doi:10.1111/2057-1615.12059

Madan, K., & Yadav, R. (2016). Behavioural intention to adopt mobile wallet: A developing country perspective. *Journal of Indian Business Research, 8*(3), 227–244. doi:10.1108/JIBR-10-2015-0112

Mai, N., Tuan, N., & Yoshi, T. (2013). Technology Acceptance Model and the Paths to Online Customer Loyalty in an Emerging Market. *Market- Tržište Journal, 25*(2), 231 – 248.

Malaysia, B. N. (2016). *Financial Technology Regulatory Sandbox Framework.* Retrieved from http://www.bnm.gov.my/index.php?ch=57&pg=137&ac=533&bb=file

Malaysia, B. N. (2017). *Financial Stability and Payment Systems Report 2017.* Retrieved from http://www.bnm.gov.my/files/publication/fsps/en/2017/fs2017_book.pdf

Malaysia, B. N. (2018). *Financial Stability and Payments System Report 2018.* Retrieved from Malaysia: http://www.bnm.gov.my/files/publication/fsps/en/2018/fs2018_book.pdf

Mallat, N. (2007). Exporing Consumer Adoption of Mobile Payments. *The Journal of Strategic Information Systems*, 413–432. doi:10.1016/j.jsis.2007.08.001

Manta, O. (2017). New challenges in economic science. LAP LAMBERT Academic Publishing.

Manta, O. (2019). Financial Market Trends, a Local Mission & a Global Vision. LAP LAMBERT Academic Publishing.

Manta, O. (2019). The instrument of globalization for the societal partnership (Sustainable Development Goals UN. *Global Economy Review: A Monthly Journal.* http://iige.co/global-economy-review-a-monthly-journal /

Marr, B. (2018). A Very Brief History of Blockchain Technology Everyone Should Read. *Forbes.* Available at: https://www.forbes.com/sites/bernardmarr/2018/02/16/a-very-brief-history-of-blockchain-technology-everyone-should-read/#5462f7f37bc4

Martell, J. (2018). *Advantages (and Disadvantages) of Fintech-Focused IoT.* Medium. Available at: https://medium.com/@jasonmartell/advantages-and-disadvantages-of-fintech-focused-iot-85aa72a7bd68

Martell, J. (2018, August 20). *Advantages & Disadvantages of FinTech-Focused IoT.* Retrieved from A Medium Corporate: https://medium.com/@jasonmartell/advantages-and-disadvantages-of-fintech-focused-iot-85aa72a7bd68

Matai, A. (2010). *Banking Integration as a Modern Approach.* Administrative and Economic Research, Mohammed Khader Biskra University.

Mavroidis I., Karatrantou A., & Koutsouba M., (2013). Technology Acceptance and Social Presence in Distance Education – A Case Study. *European Journal of Open, Distance and e-Learning, 16*(2).

Mayor, D. G. O., & González, I. A. P. (2017). Fintech: The Future of them servicios financieros. *Revista Española de Capital Riesgo, 1*, 19-28.

McGuinness, C., & Merrey, P. (2017). *KPMG: Value of Fintech.* City of London Corporation.

McKechnie, S., Winklhofer, H., & Ennew, C. (2006). Applying the Technology Acceptance Model to Online Retailing of Financial Services. *International Journal of Retail & Distribution Management, 34*(4/5), 388–410. doi:10.1108/09590550610660297

McKinsey & Company. (n.d.). *FinTechnicolor: The New Picture in Finance.* Available at: https://www.mckinsey.com/~/media/mckinsey/industries/financial%20services/our%20insights/bracing%20for%20seven%20critical%20changes%20as%20fintech%20matures/fintechnicolor-the-new-picture-in-finance.ashx

McKinsey, C. (2018, October). *Global Payment 2018: A dynamic industry continues to break new ground.* Retrieved from Global Banking: https://www.mckinsey.com/~/media/McKinsey/Industries/Financial%20Services/Our%20Insights/Global%20payments%20Expansive%20growth%20targeted%20opportunities/Global-payments-map-2018.ashx

Mercer, C. (2015). *History of PayPal: The history of the biggest online payment system in the world.* From https://www.techworld.com/picture-gallery/e-commerce/history-ofpaypal-1998-now-3630386/

Ministry of Works. (n.d.). *About Us.* Retrieved from https://www.works.gov.bh/English/Pages/home2.aspx

Mitchell, R. B. (1998). Sources of Transparency: Information Systems in International Regimes. *International Studies Quarterly*, *42*(1), 109–130. doi:10.1111/0020-8833.00071

Mohamed. (2005). *Integration and its impact on the financial performance of commercial banks* (PhD thesis). Sudan University of Science and Technology, Khartoum, Sudan.

Mohammad, M. (2020, April 27). *China to consolidate its claim for global leadership post COVID-19 crisis*. Retrieved from https://www.moneycontrol.com/news/business/markets/china-to-consolidate-its-claim-for-global-leadership-post-covid-19-crisis-5190411.html

Mohan, H., Ahmad, N., Kong, O., Yew, C., Liew, J., & Mat, N. (2013). Determinants of the Internet Banking Intention in Malaysia. *American Journal of Economics*, *3*(3).

Moody's: Threat of Cyber Attack on US Utilities cushioned by the likelihood of government support. (2015). https://www.moodys.com/research/Moodys-Threat-of-cyber-attack-on-US-utilities-cushioned-byPR_336640

Morrison, D. E., Kumar, K., Rogers, E. M., & Fliegel, F. C. (1976). Stratification and risk-taking: A further negative replication of Cancian's theory. *American Sociological Review*, *41*(5), 912–919. doi:10.2307/2094742

Mulyani, S. R., Kadarisman, S., & Paramarta, V. (2020). Opportunities and threats of development of financial technologies (Fintech) against competitiveness of banks (at national conventional commercial banks). *Journal of Advanced Research in Dynamical and Control Systems*, *12*(3), 97–110. doi:10.5373/JARDCS/V12I3/20201171

Mun, Y. P., Khalid, H., & Nadarajah, D. (2017). Millennials' Perception on Mobile Payment Services in Malaysia. *4th Information System International Conference 2017, ISICO 2017*.

Nabi, A., & Eide, W. (2011). *Banking Integration in Iraq as a Need for Banking Reform*. Central Bank of Iraq.

Nakamoto, S. (2008). *Bitcoin: A Peer-to-Peer Electronic Cash System*. Available at: https://bitcoin.org/bitcoin.pdf

Nakamoto, S. (2008). *Bitcoin: A peer-to-peer electronic cash system*. Retrieved from: https://bitcoin.org/bitcoin.pdf

Navaretti, G. B., Calzolari, G., Mansilla-Fernandez, J. M., & Pozzolo, A. F. (2017). *Fintech and Banking. Friends or Foes?* Retrieved January 26, 2019, from http://european-economy.eu/wp-content/uploads/2018/01/EE_2.2017-2.pdf

Ng, Y. S. E., Muthukannan, P., Tan, B. & Leong, C. (2017). *FinTech Platform Development: A Revelatory Case Study of a Chinese Microloan Startup*. Academic Press.

Nicoletti & Weis. (2017). *Future of FinTech*. Palgrave Macmillan.

Nicoletti. (2017). *The Future of FinTech*. DOI doi:10.1007/978-3-319-51415-4_1

Nielsen, J. F. (2002). Internet technology and customer linking in Nordic banking. *Internal Journal of Service Banking*, *13*(2), 475–496.

Nieves, E. H., Hernández, G., González, A. G., González, S. R., & Corchado, J. M. (2019). *Fog Computing Architecture for Personalized Recommendation of Banking Products*. Retrieved September 12, 2019 from https://www.sciencedirect.com/science/article/pii/S0957417419306189

Nino, J., L., Langthaler, J., Fabian, M., & Mayorga, J., (2017). *An Overview of FinTechs: Their Benefits and Risks Association of Supervisors of Banks of the Americas*. Academic Press.

Nuamah, P., & Darko, A. (2016). University Students' Perceptions on the Adoption of Electronic Voting. *Global Journal of Interdisciplinary Social Sciences*, *6*(5), 7–13.

OECD. (2017). *Technology and innovation in the insurance sector.* Retrieved from: https://www.oecd.org/pensions/Technology-and-innovation-in-the-insurance-sector.pdf

Oliveira, T., Tomas, M., Babpista, G., & Campos, F. (2016). Mobile Payment: Understanding the determinants of customer adoption and intention to recommend the technology. *Computers in Human Behavior, 61*, 404–414. doi:10.1016/j.chb.2016.03.030

Oliver, R. L. (1980). A cognitive model for the antecedents and consequences of satisfaction. *JMR, Journal of Marketing Research, 17*(4), 460–469. doi:10.1177/002224378001700405

Oliver, R. L. (1997). *Customer satisfaction: A behavioural perspective on the consumer.* McGraw-Hill.

Olsson. (2018). *The Rise and Development of Fintech.* Routledge.

Olushola, T., & Abiola, J. (2017). The Efficacy of Technology Acceptance Model: A Review of Applicable Theoretical Models in Information Technology Researches. *Journal of Research in Business and Management, 4*(11).

Opus. (2018). *Fintech Outlook.* Available at: http://www.opusconsulting.com/wp-content/uploads/fintech-outlook-2018.pdf

Pagani, M., & Schipani, D. (2008). Motivations and barriers to the adoption of 3G mobile multimedia services: An end user perspective in the Italian market. In End-User Computing: Concepts, Methodologies, Tools, and Applications (pp. 2329-2340). IGI Global.

Pagani, M. (2004). Determinants of adoption of third generation mobile multimedia services. *Journal of Interactive Marketing, 18*(3), 46–59. doi:10.1002/dir.20011

Palychata, J. (2016). *Bitcoin: What you didn't know but always wanted to ask.* Available at, http://securities.bnpparibas.com/quintessence/hot-topics/beyond/bitcoin-and-blockchain-what-you.html

Panetta, F. (2018, May 12). *FinTech and Banking: Today and Tomorrow.* Retrieved from Harvard Law School Bicentennial: https://www.bis.org/review/r180515d.pdf

Papadopoulos, A. (2019, January 2). *Most Start-up Friendly Countries in The World, 2019.* Retrieved from https://ceoworld.biz/2019/01/02/most-startup-friendly-countries-in-the-world-2019/

Parasuraman, P. A., & Colby, C. (2001). *Techno-Ready Marketing: How and Why Customers Adopt Technology.* The Free Press.

Pejkovska, M. (2018, April 24). *Potential negative effects of FinTech on the financial services sector.* Retrieved from Helsinki Metropolia University of Applied Sciences: https://www.theseus.fi/bitstream/handle/10024/148416/Maja_Pejkovska_Theseus.pdf?sequence=1&isAllowed=y

Periard, G. (2011). *What is a startup?* http://www.sobreadministracao.com/o-que-e-uma-startup

Pett, J., Kristall, M., & Mack, D. (2017). Opportunity from disruption. *Internal Auditor, 74*(3), 57–60.

Pham, T. T. T., & Ho, J. C. (2014). What are the core drivers in consumer adoption of NFC-based mobile payments?: a proposed research framework. *Management of Engineering & Technology (PICMET), 2014 Portland International Conference*, 3041-3049.

Philip, E., & Zake, S. (2017). The role of user satisfaction in implementing a Business Intelligence System. *South African Journal of Information Management, 1*(19), 1–8.

Pokrovskaia, N. N. (2016). Neuro-communication and reverse rule of payment in the digital economy: the monetary evaluation of experience. In *2th Conf. Technological perspective within the Eurasian space, new markets and economic growth points*. St-Petersburg: Asterion.

Pollari, I., & Raisbeck, M. (2017). *Forging the future: How financial institutions are embracing fintech to evolve and grow*. KPMG Report. Retrieved from: https://assets.kpmg/content/dam/kpmg/xx/pdf/2017/10/forging-the-future-global-fintech-study.pdf

Poon, W. C. (2007). Users' adoption of e-banking services: The Malaysian perspective. *Journal of Business and Industrial Marketing*, *23*(1), 59–69. doi:10.1108/08858620810841498

Prabook. (2016). *Abraham Leon Bettinger*. Accessed 25 October 2016. https://prabook.com/web/person-view.html?profileId=669232

Pritchett, W. (2019). *Insurtech 10: Trends for 2019*. KPMG International Cooperative. Retrieved from: https://assets.kpmg/content/dam/kpmg/xx/pdf/2019/03/insurtech-trends-2019.pdf

Priya, P. K., & Anusha, K. (2019). Fintech Issues and Challenges in India. *International Journal of Recent Technology and Engineering*, *8*(3), 904–908. doi:10.35940/ijrte.C4087.098319

Punch, K. F. (2003). Survey research: The basics. *Sage (Atlanta, Ga.)*.

PwC. (2016). *Financial Services Technology 2020 and Beyond: Embracing Disruption*. Retrieved from PwC: https://www.pwc.com/gx/en/financial-services/assets/pdf/technology2020-and-beyond.pdf

PwC. (2016). *Financial services technology 2020 and beyond: Embracing disruption*. White paper. London: PwC.

PwC. (2016, March). *Blurred lines: How Fintech is shaping financial services*. Available at https://www.pwc.de/de/

PwC. (2017). *Global Fintech Report*. Available at, https://www.pwc.com/gx/en/industries/financial-services/assets/pwc-global-fintech-report-2017.pdf

PwC. (2017a). *Blockchain, A Catalyst for New Approaches in Insurance*. Available at: https://www.pwc.com/gx/en/insurance/assets/blockchain-a-catalyst.pdf

PwC. (2017b). *Global Fintech Report: Redrawing the Lines*. Available at: https://www.pwc.com/gx/en/industries/financial-services/assets/pwc-global-fintech-report-2017.pdf

PwC. (n.d.). *Global Fintech Report: Blurred-Lines*. Available at: https://www.pwc.com/gx/en/industries/financial-services/fintech-survey/blurred-lines.html

Rabbani, M. R., Khan, S., & Thalassinos, E. I. (2020). FinTech, Blockchain and Islamic Finance: An Extensive Literature Review. *International Journal of Economics and Business Administration*, *8*(2), 65–86.

Razzaque, A., & Alalawi, M. (2015). Knowledge Sharing And Positive Emotions In Virtual Communities: The case of the Healthcare sector. In *KS Global Research International Conference on Emerging Trends in Multidisciplinary Research (ETMR-2015)*. Istanbul, Turkey: KS Global Research.

Razzaque, A., Aldahean, E. S., Al-Hashimi, M., Hamdan, A. M., & Musleh, A. (2020). Learning readiness when sharing knowledge while e-learning. *International Journal of Computer Aided Engineering and Technology*.

Razzaque, A., Eldabi, T., & Jalal-Karim, A. (2012). An integrated framework to classify healthcare virtual communities. *European, Mediterranean & Middle Eastern Conference on Information Systems 2012*.

Razzaque, A., Eldabi, T., Jalal-Karim, A., & Karolak, M. (2013). E-Health Collaborative Knowledge management facilitates medical decision making supported by Culture. In *Hawaii International Conference on System Sciences (HICSS-46)*. Grand Wailea Maui, HI: University of Hawai'i at Manoa, IEEE computer society. Retrieved May 1, 2012, from http://www.hicss.hawaii.edu/

Razzaque, A., Hamdan, A., & Cummings, R. (2019). The Propensity to Use FinTech: Input from bankers in the Kingdom of Bahrain. *Journal of Information & Knowledge Management.*

Razzaque, A. (2019). Multicultural teaching-learning model for Western Higher Education Institutions. *International Journal of Electronic Banking*, *2*(1), 358. doi:10.1504/IJEBANK.2019.10022931

Razzaque, A. (2019). Organizational learning through Knowledge sharing in Virtual Communities thru Learner readiness and their Social Capital. In *Implementing Knowledge Management Strategy in the Public Sector*. IGI Global Publications. doi:10.4018/978-1-5225-9639-4.ch008

Razzaque, A. (2019). Virtual learning enriched by social capital and shared knowledge, when moderated by positive emotions. *International Journal of Electronic Banking*, *1*(4), 77–95.

Razzaque, A., Al-Hashimi, M., Hamdan, A. M., Musleh, A., Ahlam Hassan, E. S., Aldahean, B. A., & Reyad, S. (2019). *Learning readiness when sharing knowledge while e-learning*. Option Journal. doi:10.33965/el2019_201909F007

Razzaque, A., & Eldabi, T. (2018). Assessing the impact of Physicians' Virtual Communities on their medical Decision Making quality. In *51st Hawaii International Conference on System Sciences - HICSS-51*. University of Hawaii at Manoa. 10.24251/HICSS.2018.397

Razzaque, A., Eldabi, T., & Jalal-Karim, A. (2012). Knowledge Sharing for Medical Decision-Making in an E-Health Virtual Community of Practice. *2012 Annual Conference of Asian Group for Public Administration (AGPA).*

Razzaque, A., Hamdan, A., & Cummings, R. (2019). *The Propensity to Use FinTech: Input from bankers in the Kingdom of Bahrain. In The International Conference on Intelligent Systems and Data Analytics Applications - ICSDAA 2019.* Jordan University. Retrieved from https://icsdaa.com/

Razzaque, A., & Karolak, M. (2010). Knowledge Management and Electronic Heath Record Facilitate Clinical Support to Improve Healthcare Quality. In *International Conference on E-business, Management and Economics (ICEME 2010).* Hong Kong.: IEEE Press.

Razzaque, A., & Karolak, M. (2011). Building a Knowledge Management System for the e-Health Knowledge Society. *Journal of Economic Development, Management, IT. Finance and Marketing*, *2*(2), 23–40.

Razzaque, A., & Karolak, M. (2013). *Trends and Future Research in innovative and collaborative e-Health. 2013 IIAS-IASIA Joint Congress.* IIAS-IASIA.

Razzaque, A., Mohiuddin, Q., & Jalal-Karim, A. (2011). Semantic Web Based Tacit Knowledge Re-shapes E-Health to improve Healthcare Decision-Support. *The International Conference and Exhibition on Knowledge-Based Business, Industry and Education, Management and Economics (KBIE 2011).*

Rechtman, Y., & O'Callaghan, S. (2014). Understanding the Basics of Crowdfunding. *The CPA Journal*, *84*(11), 30.

Riahi, Y., & Riahi, S. (2018). Big Data and Big Data Analytics: Concepts, Types and Technologies. *International Journal of Research and Engineering*, *5*(9), 524–528. doi:10.21276/ijre.2018.5.9.5

Ries, E. (2012). *The Lean Startup: How current entrepreneurs use continuous innovation to create highly successful businesses*. Paper Moon.

Rihan, K. (2006). *Banking Integration of Banks Operating in Palestine (Evaluation of the Experience of the Integration of Cairo Amman Bank - Islamic Transactions in the Palestinian Islamic Bank).* Presented to the Conference of the Development of the Gaza Strip, Gaza.

Riquelme, H. E., & Rios, R. E. (2010). The moderating effect of gender on the adoption of mobile banking. *International Journal of Bank Marketing, 28*(5), 328–341. doi:10.1108/02652321011064872

Riyadh, E. (2017). *Largest Dedicated Fintech Hub in Mena Region to Launch in Bahrain.* [online] Available at: https://www.bahrainfintechbay.com/single-post/2017/11/06/Largest-Dedicated-Fintech-Hub-in-Mena-Region-to-Launch-in-Bahrain

Rob, M. A., & Opara, E. U. (2003). *Online Credit Card Processing Models.* Academic Press.

Rodrigues, R. (2017). *Brazilian FinTech boom provides new opportunities for investors.* https://www.istoedinheiro.com.br/boom-de-FinTechbrasileirasoferece- novas-oportunidades-para-os-investidores/

Rogers, E. M. (1962). *Diffusion of innovations* (1st ed.). Free Press.

Rogers, E. M. (1995). *Diffusion of Innovations* (4th ed.). Free Press.

Rolfe, A. (2019). *Payments (Cards & Mobile).* Retrieved from Payments Industry Intelligence: https://www.payments-cardsandmobile.com/mobile-Wallet-trends-annual-report-2019/

Romanova, I., & Kudinska, M. (2016). Banking and fintech: A challenge or opportunity? *Contemporary Studies in Economic and Financial Analysis, 98*, 21–35. doi:10.1108/S1569-375920160000098002

Rosemary, E. (2016). *What is FinTech?* https://www.infowester.com/fintech.php

Rosen, S. (1981). The Economics of Superstars. *The American Economic Review, 71*(5), 845–858.

Ryan, C. (2012, May 10). *Navigation: 4 Types of Crowdfunding and What This Means For The Future Of Investment.* Retrieved from Under The Radar: https://utrconf.com/4-types-of-crowdfunding-and-what-this-means-for-the-future-of-investments/

Ryu, H.-S. (2018). *Understanding Benefit and Risk Framework of Fintech Adoption: Comparison of Early Adopters and Late Adopters.* Retrieved from 51st Hawaii International Conference on System Sciences: http://hdl.handle.net/10125/50374

Sahabuddin, M., & Ahmad, A. U. F. (2020). Islamic finance in the fourth industrial revolution: Challenges and opportunities. *International Journal of Islamic Thought.*

Sahni, A. (2019 October 7). *Which Are The Most Successful Fintech Startups In India?* Retrieved from https://inc42.com/features/which-are-the-most-successful-fintech-startups-in-india/

Sangwan, V., Prakash, P., & Singh, S. (2020). Financial technology: A review of extant literature. *Studies in Economics and Finance, 37*(1), 71–88. doi:10.1108/SEF-07-2019-0270

Sathye, M. (1999). Adoption of internet banking by Australian consumers: An empirical investigation. *International Journal of Bank Marketing, 17*(7), 324–339. doi:10.1108/02652329910305689

Sato, R., & Hoffman, F. (1968). Production Functions with Variable Elasticity of Substitution: Some Analysis and Testing. *The Review of Economics and Statistics, 50*(4), 453–460. doi:10.2307/1926813

Saygili, E. E., & Saygili, A. T. (2017b). Contemporary Issues in Enterprise Information Systems: A Critical Review of CSFs in ERP Implementations. In Enterprise Information Systems and the Digitalization of Business Functions (pp. 120-136). IGI Global. doi:10.4018/978-1-5225-2382-6.ch006

Saygili, E. E., Ozturkoglu, Y., & Kocakulah, M. C. (2017a). End users' perceptions of critical success factors in ERP applications. *International Journal of Enterprise Information Systems, 13*(4), 58–75. doi:10.4018/IJEIS.2017100104

Schierz, P. G., Schilke, O., & Wirtz, B. W. (2010). Understanding consumer acceptance of mobile payment services: An empirical analysis. *Electronic Commerce Research and Applications, 9*(3), 209–216. doi:10.1016/j.elerap.2009.07.005

Schilder, A. (2005, April 29). *Compliance and the compliance function in the banks*. Retrieved from Bank for International Settlements: https://www.bis.org/publ/bcbs113.pdf

Schindler, J. (2017). *FinTech and Financial Innovation: Drivers and Depth*. In Finance and Economics Discussion Series 2017-081. Washington, DC: Board of Governors of the Federal Reserve System.

Schneider, L. A., Shaul, M. A. X., & Lascelles, C. K. (2016). Regulatory Priorities for Fintech Firms—and Investors—in the Coming Year. *Journal of Taxation & Regulation of Financial Institutions, 29*(4), 5–14.

Scholtz & Mahmud, (2016). Does Usability Matter? An Analysis of the Impact of Usability on Technology Acceptance in ERP Settings. *Interdisciplinary Journal of Information, Knowledge, and Management, 11.*

Schueffel, P. (2016). Taming the beast: A scientific definition of Fintech. *Journal of Innovation Management, 4*(4), 32–54. doi:10.24840/2183-0606_004.004_0004

Schwab, K. (2016). *The Fourth Industrial Revolution*. Penguin Random House LLC.

Schwienbacher, A. (2007). A theoretical analysis of optimal financing strategies for different types of capital-constrained entrepreneurs. *Journal of Business Venturing, 22*(6), 753–781. doi:10.1016/j.jbusvent.2006.07.003

Schwienbacher, A., & Larralde, B. (2010). *Crowdfunding of small entrepreneurial ventures. Handbook of Entrepreneurial Finance*. Oxford University Press.

Scotland, J. (2012, May 27). *Exploring the Philosophical Underpinnings of Research: Relating Ontology and Epistemology to the Methodology and Methods of the Scientific, Interpretive, and Critical Research Paradigms*. Retrieved from Canadian Center of Science and Education: https://pdfs.semanticscholar.org/f24f/1d16645ee19b0263f4c377d9e086ed277a3c.pdf

Securities Commission Malaysia. (2016). *Equity crowdfunding: List of registered market operators for ECF.* Retrieved from https://www.sc.com.my/digital/equity-crowdfunding/list-of-registered-market-operators-for-ecf/

Seraj, M., & Wong, C. (2014). Impacts of Different Mobile User Interfaces on Student Satisfaction. Learn. *International Journal of Information Management*, (8), 4.

Shah, T., & Jani, S. (2018). *Applications of Blockchain Technology in Banking & Finance*. Retrieved January 26, 2019, from https://www.researchgate.net/publication/327230927_Applications_of_Blockchain_Technology_in_Banking_Finance

Shalaby, M. A. (2003). *Banking Integration as a Tool for Market Access and Enhancing Competitiveness in an Era of Giant Clusters and Entities. Saleh Saleh Kamel Center for Islamic Economics, Al-Azhar University.*

Shen, Y., & Huang, Y. (2016). Introduction to the special issue: Internet finance in China. *China Economic Journal, 9*(3), 221–224. doi:10.1080/17538963.2016.1215058

Shim, Y., & Shin, D.-H. (2016). Analyzing China's Fintech Industry from the Perspective of Actor–Network Theory. *Telecommunications Policy, 40*(2–3), 168–181. doi:10.1016/j.telpol.2015.11.005

Shin, D. H. (2009). Towards an understanding of the consumer acceptance of mobile wallet. *Computers in Human Behavior, 25*(6), 1343–1354. doi:10.1016/j.chb.2009.06.001

Shrier, D., Canale, G., & Pentland, A. (2016). Mobile money & payments: Technology trends. MIT Connection Science's series on financial technology.

Sigar, K. (2012). Fret no more: Inapplicability of crowdfunding concerns in the Internet age and the JOBS Act's safeguards. *Administrative Law Review*, *64*(2), 473–506.

Singapore, F. N. (2017). *Bank Negara Malaysia Approves 3 More Participants for Fintech Sandbox*. Retrieved from https://fintechnews.sg/13686/malaysia/bank-negara-malaysia-fintech-sandbox-approves-3-participants/

Singh, B. (2019). *What the Future of Fintech Looks Like*. Retrieved from: https://www.entrepreneur.com/article/333891

Singh, N., Srivastava, S., & Sinha, N. (2017). Consumer preference & satisfaction of M-wallets: A study on North Indian consumers. *International Journal of Bank Marketing*, *35*(6), 944–965. doi:10.1108/IJBM-06-2016-0086

Slade, E., Williams, M., Dwivedi, Y., & Piercy, N. (2015). Exploring consumer adoption of proximity mobile payments. *Journal of Strategic Marketing*, *23*(3), 209–223. doi:10.1080/0965254X.2014.914075

Smart Service Desk. (n.d.). *About Us*. Retrieved from https://smartservicedesk.com/company.html

Sofia. (2016). *26 FinTech Companies Powering Institutional Investments and Trading*. Let's Talk Payments. Accessed March 24, 2017,https://letstalkpayments.com/26-fintech-companiespowering-institutional-investments-and-trading/

Sokolin, L. (2019). *The Future of Fintech*. Retrieved from: https://www.investopedia.com/the-future-of-fintech-4770491

Sönmez, F. (2018). Technology Acceptance of Business Intelligence and Customer Relationship Management Systems within Institutions Operating in Capital Markets. *International Journal of Academic Research in Business and Social Sciences*, *8*(2), 400–422. doi:10.6007/IJARBSS/v8-i2/3882

Spain Financial Center. (2016). *Eu fintech regulatory framework*. Author.

Srivastav, S. (2019, January 9). *The Fintech Effect: What it Would Mean for Your Business in 2019?* Retrieved from AppInventiv: https://appinventiv.com/blog/impact-of-fintech-on-your-business/

Stark, J. (2018). *Presentation at IIFM Seminar – Fintech, Smart Contracts and Blockchain, Kuala Lumpur*. Available at: https://www.iifm.net/sites/default/files/Session%206%20-%20Fintech%2C%20Smart%20Contracts%20and%20Blockchain%20-%20Nicholas%20Edmondes%20%28Trowers%20%26%20Hamlins%29.pdf

STC. (2019). *VIVA Cash launch*. Retrieved from https://www.stc.com.bh/content/cash_launch

Stefanescu, S. (2004). Solving a non-linear regression model used in the economy. *Economic Studies and Economic Cybernetics Studies and Research, 3*, 59-69.

Sundararajan, A. (2016). *The Sharing Economy: The End of Employment and the Rise of Crowd-Based*. MIT Press.

Swan, M. (2015). *Blockchain: Blueprint for a New Economy*. O'Reilly Media.

Szabo, N. (1997). The idea of smart contracts. In Nick Szabo's Papers and Concise Tutorials. Academic Press.

Szakiel, P. (2018). *What Is Fintech: A Beginner's Guide to Financial Technology in 2019*. Retrieved from: https://learn.g2.com/fintech

Tan, G., Chong, C., Ooi, K., & Chong, Y. (2010). The adoption of online banking in Malaysia: An empirical analysis. *International Journal of Business and Management Science*, *3*, 169.

TC -Toronto Centre, (2017). *FinTech, RegTech and SupTech: What They Mean for Financial Supervision*. Author.

Tech, T. (2017). *CBB teams up with Bahrain FinTech Bay.* Retrieved from: https://www.bahrainfintechbay.com/single-post/2017/12/14/CBB-teams-up-with-Bahrain-FinTech-Bay

Thakor, A. V. (in press). Fintech and banking: What do we know? *Journal of Financial Intermediation.* https://www.sciencedirect.com/science/article/abs/pii/S104295731930049X

The Economic Times. (2018, September 6). *The Jio effect: Consumers have been the absolute winners.* Author.

The Economic Times. (2019, August 30). Retrieved from https://economictimes.indiatimes.com/markets/stocks/news/mega-bank-merger-pnb-obc-and-ubi-to-be-merged-to-form-2nd-largest-bank/articleshow/70909726.cms?from=mdr

The World Bank. (2013). Available at, http://documents.worldbank.org/curated/en/409841468327411701/pdf/840000WP-0Box380crowdfunding 0study00.pdf

The World Economic Forum. (2017). *Beyond Fintech: A Pragmatic Assessment of Disruptive Potential in Financial Services.* Available at: http://www3.weforum.org/docs/Beyond_Fintech_-_A_Pragmatic_Assessment_of_Disruptive_Potential_in_Financial_Services.pdf

Thomas, W., & Malone, J. Y. (1987, June). *Electronic Markets and Electronic Hierarchies.* Retrieved from Communications of the ACM: https://www.researchgate.net/publication/220425850_Electronic_Markets_and_Electronic_Hierarchies

Thomson Reuters (2018). *State of the Global Islamic Economy Report, 2018/19.* Author.

Tidd, J., & Bessant, J. (2015). *Innovation management.* Bookman.

Tonttila, J. (2016). *Reward-Based Crowdfunding.* Thesis Spring 2016 Business and administration Oulu University of Applied Sciences.

Treasury, H. (2011). *A New Approach To Financial Regulation: The Blueprint For Reform.* HM Treasury. Retrieved from https://assets.publishing.service.gov.uk/government/uploads/system/uploads/attachment_data/file/81403/consult_finreg__new_approach_blueprint.pdf

Tschorsch, F., & Scheuermann, B. (2016). Bitcoin and beyond: A technical survey on decentralized digital currencies. *IEEE Communications Surveys and Tutorials, 18*(3), 2084–2123. doi:10.1109/COMST.2016.2535718

UK F. C. A. (2017). *Regulatory Sandbox Lessons Learned Report.* Retrieved from https://www.fca.org.uk/publication/research-and-data/regulatory-sandbox-lessons-learned-report.pdf

Underwood, S. (2015). Blockchain beyond Bitcoin. *Communications of the ACM, 59*(11), 15–17.

UNDP. (2017). *Crowdfunding. Financing Solutions for Sustainable Development.* Retrieved from: https://assets.publishing.service.gov.uk/media/57a08a1540f0b652dd00055c/EoD_HD061_Jul2013_Review_CrowdFunding.pdf

UNHCR. (2018). *Figures at a Glance.* Available at: https://www.unhcr.org/figures-at-a-glance.htm

UNICEF. (2017). *UNICEF to present 'Donercoin' at London Blockchain Week 2017.* Available at: https://un-blockchain.org/2017/01/09/unicef-to-present-donercoin-at-london-blockchain-week-2017/

Valanciene, L., & Jegeleviciute, S. (2013). Valuation of crowdfunding: Benefits and drawback. *Economics and Management, 18*(1), 39–48. doi:10.5755/j01.em.18.1.3713

Vallerand, R. J., & Reid, G. (1984). On the Causal Effects of Perceived Competence on Intrinsic Motivation: A Test of Cognitive Evaluation Theory. *Journal of Sport Psychology, 6*(1), 94–102. doi:10.1123/jsp.6.1.94

Van Alstyne, M. W., Parker, G. G., & Choudary, S. P. (2016). Pipelines, plat-forms, and the new rules of strategy. *Harvard Business Review,* 1–18.

Varga, D. (2017, November). *FinTech, The New Era of Financial Services*. Retrieved from Budapest Management Review: https://core.ac.uk/download/pdf/132273819.pdf

Vasiljeva, T., & Lukanova, K. (2016). Commercial Banks and Fintech Companies in the Digital Transformation: Challenges for the Future. *Journal of Business and Management*, *11*, 25–33.

Venkatesh, V., & Bala, H. (2008). Technology acceptance model 3 and a research agenda on interventions. *Decision Sciences*, *39*(2), 273–315. doi:10.1111/j.1540-5915.2008.00192.x

Venkatesh, V., & Davis, F. (1996). A Model of the Antecedents of Perceived ease of use-: Development and test. *Decision Sciences*, *27*(3), 451–481. doi:10.1111/j.1540-5915.1996.tb01822.x

Venkatesh, V., & Davis, F. D. (2000). A theoretical extension of the technology acceptance model: Four longitudinal field studies. *Management Science*, *46*(2), 186–204. doi:10.1287/mnsc.46.2.186.11926

Venkatesh, V., Davis, F., & Morris, M. G. (2007). Dead or alive? The development, trajectory and future of technology adoption research. *Journal of the Association for Information Systems*, *8*(4), 1. doi:10.17705/1jais.00120

Venkatesh, V., Morris, M. G., Davis, G. B., & Davis, F. D. (2003). User acceptance of information technology: Toward a unified view. *Management Information Systems Quarterly*, *27*(3), 425–478. doi:10.2307/30036540

Venkatesh, V., Thong, J. Y., & Xu, X. (2012). Consumer acceptance and use of information technology: Extending the unified theory of acceptance and use of technology. *Management Information Systems Quarterly*, *36*(1), 157–178. doi:10.2307/41410412

Venture Well. (2016). *Types of crowdfunding and regulations*. Retrieved from https://venturewell.org/types-crowdfunding-regulations/

Vergara, S. C. (2016). *Projetos e Relatórios de Pesquisa em Administração* (16th ed.). Atlas.

Vila, N., & Kurster, I. (2011). Consumer feelings and behaviours towards well-designed websites. *Information & Management*, *48*(4-5), 166–177. doi:10.1016/j.im.2011.04.003

Vives, X. (2017). The impact of FinTech on banking. *European Economy*, (2), 97-105.

Vlasov, V. A. (2017). The Evolution of E-Money. *European Research Studies Journal*, *20*(1), 215–224.

Wamda and Pay Fort. (n.d.). *State of FinTech In Mena Unbundling the financial services industry*. Retrieved from: https://www.difc.ae/download_file/3081/

Wang, L., & Yi, Y. (2012). The impact of use context on mobile payment acceptance: An empirical study in China. In *Advances in computer science and education* (pp. 293–299). Springer. doi:10.1007/978-3-642-27945-4_47

Warschauer, C. L. (1974). The financial programming of the financing companies, credit and investment. *Business Administration Journal*, *14*(1), 33–57.

Webster, I., & Pizalla, J. (2015). *Fintech: Are banks responding appropriately?* Available at: https://www.ey.com/

Wee, R. Y. (2019, March 13). *Which Country Has the Largest Number of Cellphones?* Retrieved from https://www.worldatlas.com/articles/10-countries-with-the-highest-rates-of-cell-phone-subscriptions.html

WomenInFinTech. (2019, May 26). *Understanding the role of women in the emerging industry*. Retrieved from Bahrain Women in FinTech: https://bahrainfintechbay.us10.list-manage.com/track/click?u=ede0050de3961e3f5d090d405&id=741989aef6&e=3d358071f2

World Bank (2018). *Cryptocurrencies and Blockchain.* Europe and Central Asia Economic Update. Office of the Chief Economist. World Bank Group.

World Bank. (2007). *General principles for international remittance services.* Committee on Payment and Settlement Systems. January.

World Bank. (2008). *Finance for All? Policies and Pitfalls in Expanding Access.* The World Bank.

World Bank. (2013). *Global Financial Development Report: Financial Inclusion.* The World Bank.

World Bank. (2015). *World Development Report 2015: Mind, Society, Behaviour.* The World Bank.

World Bank. (2017). *No Poverty. SDG Atlas.* Available at: http://datatopics.worldbank.org/sdgatlas/archive/2017/SDG-01-no-poverty.html

World Fintech Report: 2019-20 – Indepth Analysis for Fintech Sector. (n.d.). Retrieved from https://enterslice.com/learning/wp-content/uploads/ebook/fintech-report-2020.pdf

Wright, C. (2017, November 29). *How Paytm went big on Indian demonetization.* Retrieved from https://www.euromoney.com/article/b15ts6qpxvj51d/how-paytm-went-big-on-indian-demonetization?copyrightInfo=true

Wu, J. H., & Wang, S. C. (2005). What drives mobile commerce?: An empirical evaluation of the revised technology acceptance model. *Information & Management, 42*(5), 719–729. doi:10.1016/j.im.2004.07.001

Xiang, D., Zhang, Y., & Worthington, A. C. (2018, March). Determinants of the Use of FinTech Finance among Chinese Small and Medium-Sized Enterprises. In *2018 IEEE International Symposium on Innovation and Entrepreneurship (TEMS-ISIE)* (pp. 1-10). IEEE. 10.1109/TEMS-ISIE.2018.8478470

Xie, P., & Zou, C. (2013). The Theory of Internet Finance. *Chinese Economy, 8*(2), 1–15.

Yaga, D., Mell, P., Roby, N., & Scarfone, K. (2018). *Blockchain Technology Overview.* . doi:10.6028/NIST.IR.8202

Yaga, D., Mell, P., Roby, N., & Scarfone, K. (2018). *Blockchain Technology Overview.* Draft NISTR 8202. Gaithersburg, MD: National Institute of Science and Technology, U.S. Department of Commerce. https://csrc.nist.gov/CSRC/media/Publications/nistir/8202/draft/documents/nistir8202-draft.pdf

Yang, Z., Jun, M., & Peterson, R. T. (2004). Measuring customer perceived online service quality: Scale development and managerial implications. *International Journal of Operations & Production Management, 24*(11), 1149–1174. doi:10.1108/01443570410563278

Yassine, E.-T., & Abdelkader, M. (2008). The Importance of Banking Integration as a Tool to Enhance the Performance of the Algerian Banking System. *Introduction to the Second International Scientific Conference on the Reform of the Algerian Banking System.*

Young, E. (2019). *Global Fintech Adoption Index.* Retrieved from https://assets.ey.com/content/dam/ey-sites/ey-com/en_gl/topics/banking-and-capital-markets/ey-global-fintech-adoption-index.pdf

Yuan, S., Liu, Y., Liu, J., & Yao, R. (2016). An investigation of user's continuance intention towards mobile banking in China. *Journal of Information Development, 32*(1), 20–34. doi:10.1177/0266666914522140

Yuen, Y. Y., Yeow, H. P., & Lim, N. (2015). Internet banking acceptance in the United State and Malaysia: Cross-cultural examination. *Marketing Intelligence & Planning, 28*(3), 443–448. doi:10.1108/MIP-08-2013-0126

Yusof, E., Fahmy, E., Kashoogie, J., & Anwar Kamal, A. (2009). *Islamic finance: Debt versus equity financing in the light of maqasid al-Shari'ah.* Munich Personal RePEc Archive. Retrieved from https://mpra.ub.uni-muenchen.de/20722/1/MPRA_paper_20722.pdf

Zaideh, M. M. (2006). *The Motivation of Banking Consolidation in Palestine and Its Determinants. Introduction to Master's Degree in Accounting and Finance from the Islamic University.*

Zanjani, N., Edwards, S., Nykvist, S., & Geva, S. (2017). The Important Elements of LMS design that Affect User Engagement with e-learning tools within LMSs in the higher education sector. *Australasian Journal of Educational Technology*, *33*(1).

Zavolokina, L., Dolata, M., & Schwabe, G. (2016). FinTech – What's in a Name? In *Thirty Seventh International Conference on Information Systems* (pp. 1-19). Dublin, Ireland: Association for Information Systems.

Zawya. (2018). *FinTech Consortium and Georgetown university announce strategic partnership for global fintech innovation and education.* Available at: https://www.bahrainfintechbay.com/single-post/2018/04/18/FinTech-Consortium-and-Georgetown-university-announce-strategic-partnership-for-global-fintech-innovation-and-education

Zeithaml, V. A. (1988). Consumer perceptions of price, quality, and value: A means-end model and synthesis of evidence. *Journal of Marketing*, *52*(3), 2–22. doi:10.1177/002224298805200302

Zellner, A., & Ryu, H. (1998). Alternative Functional Forms for Production, Cost and Returns to Scale Functions. *Journal of Applied Econometrics*, *13*(2), 101–127. doi:10.1002/(SICI)1099-1255(199803/04)13:2<101::AID-JAE465>3.0.CO;2-V

Zetzsche, D. A., Buckley, R. P., Barberis, J. N., & Arner, D. W. (2017). From regulatory sandboxes to smart regulation. *Fordham Journal of Corporate & FInancial Law*, *23*, 31–103.

Zhang, L., Liu, Q., & Zhu, J. (2012). A meta-analysis of mobile commerce adoption and the moderating effect of culture. *Computers in Human Behavior*, *28*(5), 1902–1911. doi:10.1016/j.chb.2012.05.008

Zhao, Q., Tsai, P. H., & Wang, J. L. (2019). Improving Financial Service Innovation Strategies for Enhancing China's Banking Industry Competitive Advantage during the Fintech Revolution: A Hybrid MCDM Model. *Sustainability*, *11*(5), 1419. doi:10.3390u11051419

Zha, X., Li, J., & Yan, Y. (2013). Information self-efficacy and information channels: Decision quality and online shopping satisfaction. *Online Information Review*, *37*(6), 872–890. doi:10.1108/OIR-09-2012-0156

Zheng, Y., Zhao, K., & Stylianou, A. (2009). Information Quality and System Quality in Online Communities: An Empirical Investigation. SIGHCI 2009 Proceedings, 8.

Zheng, Z., Xie, S., Dai, H., Chen, X., & Wang, H. (2017). An Overview of Blockchain Technology: Architecture, Consensus, and Future Trends. *IEEE 6th International Congress on Big Data.*

Zheng, Z., Xie, S., Dai, H., Chen, X., & Wang, H. (2017). An Overview of Blockchain Technology: Architecture, Consensus, and Future Trends. *2017 IEEE International Congress on Big Data (BigData Congress),* 557–564.

Zimmerman, J. (2014). *The emergence of responsible digital finance.* Centre for Financial Inclusion. Retrieved August 24, 2016, from https://cfi-blog.org/2014/07/21/the-emergence-of-responsible-digital-finance/

About the Contributors

Yousif Abdullatif Albastaki received a BSc. degree from University of Bahrain, Msc from University of Leeds, UK and a PhD degree from University of Nottingham, UK. Recently he has been appointed as an IT advisor at the Deputy Prime Minster at the Kingdom of Bahrain and previously worked as the Dean of College of IT at the University of Bahrain. Currently he is an associate professor at Ahlia University, Kingdom of Bahrain. His research interests are Neural Networks, genetic algorithms E-Learning, Distance Education and e-government strategies and implementation.

Adel M. Sarea is an Associate Professor of Accounting, he received his PhD in Economics and Muamalat Administration (Accounting) from the Faculty of Economics and Muamalat at the Islamic Science University of Malaysia in 2011. He joined Ahlia University in September 2011 and has been Director of the Ahlia MBA Program since 2013. Dr. Sarea Received the Best Paper Award in 2014 [Emerald Group Publishing, UK]. He conducts research in the areas of Accounting for Islamic Financial Institutions, International Accounting Standards, Financial Reporting, Earning Quality, Earning Management, Intellectual Capital and Accounting Education. Dr Sarea has published more than 40 papers in internationally renowned journals, he is appointed as a recognized PhD supervisor by Brunel University London. He also serves as a member of the editorial boards in a number of international journals. He serves as a Trainer for Accounting for Non-Accountants, Accounting for Islamic Financial Institutions, IFRS and Financial Reporting. Also, he serves as an external evaluator, reviewer and examiner for MBA and Accounting programs locally and internationally.

* * *

Yomna Abdulla is an Assistant Professor at the College of Business Administration, Department of Economics and Finance, University of Bahrain, Kingdom of Bahrain. She holds a PhD in Finance from the University of Manchester, UK. Her research areas of expertise is empirical issues in corporate finance including trade credit, working capital, debt maturity, capital structure and financial policies in public versus private firms. Her current research projects focus on FinTech and cash management policy. Yomna's research papers has appeared in various reputable finance journals.

Abu Umar Faruq Ahmad is currently an Associate Professor of Islamic Finance Law at the Islamic Economics Institute (IEI), King Abdulaziz University, Jeddah, Saudi Arabia. He has about 100 published peer-reviewed refereed journal articles, books, monographs, chapters in edited books, conference proceedings, and other intellectual contributions to his credit on Shari`ah compliance of Islamic banks' products and structures, opportunities and challenges of Islamic finance, case studies of Islamic banks and financial institutions, Islamic insurance and reinsurance, Islamic microfinance, Sukuk, and dispute resolution in Islamic banking and finance, and so on. He has presented over 50 scholarly research papers at international conferences held in the USA, Ireland, Australia, UAE, Saudi Arabia, Turkey, Brunei, Qatar, Sudan, Nigeria, Malaysia, Indonesia, Bangladesh and Pakistan. His current editorial roles include serving as founding editor, senior editor, editorial advisory board member of a plethora of internationally reputed refereed journals including some of those published by Emerald Group Publishing, UK.

Khaliq Ahmad is currently Professor at AACSB accredited Department of Business Administration, College of Business and Economics (CBE), Buraydah, Saudi Arabia, Qassim University, Professor Khaliq Ahmad graduated from AMU Aligarh and obtained his doctrate and master degrees. Before joining academia Dr. Ahmad worked in private sector for five years. Since he joined IIUM 1993 as an academic holding positions such as Deputy Dean, Research Management Centre, Director Graduate School of Management (2005-2008), Dean, Kulliyah (Faculty) of Economics and Management Sciences (2008-2013), and Dean, Office of Corporate Strategy (2013-2015), he is retired in January, 2020. As founding President- ICIFE <https://www.icife.org.my>, and former Dean, Institute of Islamic Banking and Finance (2015-2016), Professor Khaliq steered IIUM's International Institute of Islamic Banking and Finance to be ranked world No.1 in 2015, 2016 by QS Ranking in area of Islamic Banking and Finance for the highest research and publication citation index.

Ebtesam AlAlawi is an Assistance Professor of Human Resource Management (HRM) & Organizational Behavior (OB). She holds a Ph.D. from Brunel University London, UK, Master of Business Administration (MBA) in HRM/OB from the University of Glamorgan, Master of Science in Occupational Health & Safety Management from Brunel University, London, Bachelor of Science in General Nursing from College of Health Sciences (now College of Health & Sports Sciences) the University of Bahrain. She is working as a Director Manager of Pose Consultancy, Bahrain, and part-time assistant professor of Management, HRM and OB at the University of Bahrain- College of Business Administration, and College of Health & Sports Sciences (Teaching Management and Related Courses) Dr. AlAlawi published many papers in leading international accredited journals such as 1- Measuring Occupational Stress among Management Information Systems Workers and Users in the Financial Services Sector: The Case of Bahraini Bankers. International Journal of Scientific and Research Publications, 4(8). 2- Customer Relationship Management: The Application of Data Mining Techniques in the Telecommunications Sector, Journal of Xi'an University of Architecture & Technology, Volume 12, Issue 4, pp 3836-3876 (Scopus indexed). 3- Study of the effects of work-family conflict, family-work conflict, and work-life balance on Saudi female teachers' performance in the public education sector with job satisfaction as a moderator, Journal of International Women's Studies, Accepted for summer 2020 issues. (Scopus Indexed) Ebtesam's research interest is in HRM, OB, Team turnover, Management of occupational health & safety issues, Nursing Management, CRM, Women in Business, Job Stress, and Family Work Conflict.

Adel Ismail Al-Alawi earned his BSc. in Business Information Systems (BIS) from Husson University, Maine, the USA, and MBA in Information Systems from Thomas College, Maine, USA, and holds a Ph.D. in Management Information Systems (MIS) from the University of Leeds, UK, and is Professor of MIS and Management at University of Bahrain (UOB). Previously, on his sabbatical leave, he was Head of Business Department at Royal University for Woman in Bahrain, Dean of School of Business at University College of Bahrain. Prof. Al-Alawi is the founder of the Business Information Systems Department (BIS) and was a Chairperson of the BIS department at the College of Business in UOB and also founders of the College of Information Technology and Head of BIS Department. Adel served UOB for more than 30 years. Adel's research in MIS and management published in several Scopus, WoS indexed journals. Such as Journal of International Women's Studies, Research Journal of Information Technology, Research Journal of Business Management, Issues in Information Systems, Information Technology Journal, Journal of Computer Science, Journal of Knowledge Management, International Journal of Educational Management, Electronic Government: An International Journal (refer https://scholar.google.com/citations?user=v8I-C1oAAAAJ&hl=en). Adel received many awards, such as two awards that were presented to him by HRH, the late Amir Sh. Isa bin Salman Al-Khalifa to recognize and honor outstanding contributions in Academic Excellence in December 1985 and December 1994 during the celebrations of the Education day ceremony in the Kingdom of Bahrain, Excellence in MIS, an award of the Husson University Alumni Association – Maine, US (1993); Judge Award in Bahrain Website Competition – the award given by the King's son Sh. Khalifa bin Hamad Al-Khalifa (2006); award of Appreciation from Bahrain Information Technology Society (BITS) in its 25th Anniversary for providing Leadership and Excellent Services to BITS in furtherance of its objectives (2008); eGovernment Excellence Award - the Award presented by Sh. Ahmed Bin Ateyat Allah Al-Khalifa Minister of Cabinet Affairs (2010); TechNo Disabilities Award for the Recognition of Outstanding Contribution and Academic Advisor -HRH Sh. Khalid bin Hamad Al-Khalifa the King's son (2017), presented the award. Adel is also one of the founders and board members for the Information Systems Audit & Control Association (ISACA, Bahrain Chapter), Bahrain Information Technology Society (BITS), Bahrain Academic Society, and he is the past President of ISACA Bahrain Chapter. The chapter awarded the best innovative chapter in the world (2018). Adel is considered as an MIS Authority in the Kingdom of Bahrain.

Khalid Al-Emadi is an MBA student. He was also working at the Ministry of Works, Bahrain. He is interested in research collaborations.

Ali Al-Hammam is an MBA candidate holding many professional certificates in the Business field such as CPA and CIPA. Form a business practice point of view, I have more than 10 years of banking experience in the Finance department. Two years back I have opened my accounting and consultancy company to provide professional services to the market. In addition, I have provided many business courses and managed several workshops on different topics such as Finance, Budgeting, and Entrepreneurship.

Muwafaq AlKubaisi holds PhD in Operations Research from Lancaster University - UK Holds MSc in Operations Research from Sussex University - UK Works as Associate professor at Bahrain University.

Bahaa Subhi Awwad is Associate Professor of Finance, College of Business and Economy, Computerized Banking and Finance Department, Palestine Technical University-Kadoorie. He has many papers published in regional and international journals that discussed several financial and economic issues . In addition, he has also a reviewer to a number of top international journals. Dr.awwad had more than 10 years of experience in the academic field.

Divij Bahl is a graduate from University of Strathclyde, United Kingdom. He has exposure of 19+ countries in the field of Sales, Marketing, Account Management, Strategy and Products. Since past few years he has been associated with Fintech Industry. He participated in G20 Youth Forum in Germany along with members from other countries. He was shortlisted from the event to present business plan on Mind reading cellphone in front of C Level executives from 140+ countries, at Switzerland G20 Y Summit. He has explored and attained expertise in various domain's whilst working in Europe, Middle East and India. He is now tasting success being a Consultant for a well established Bank. Originally from India, he is a person with global mindset and always open to new ideas and possibilities. To explore more about him simply type his full name Divij Bahl on Google and you will see his name on the top in the results.

Neeta Baporikar is currently Professor (Management) at Harold Pupkewitz Graduate School of Business (HP-GSB), Namibia University of Science and Technology, Namibia. Prior to this, she was Head-Scientific Research, with Ministry of Higher Education CAS-Salalah, Sultanate of Oman, Professor (Strategic Management and Entrepreneurship) at IIIT Pune and BITS India. With more than a decade of experience in the industry, consultancy, and training, she made a lateral switch to research and academics in 1995. Prof Baporikar holds D.Sc. (Management Studies) USA, Ph.D. in Management, the University of Pune INDIA with MBA (Distinction) and Law (Hons.) degrees. Apart from this, she is also an external reviewer, Oman Academic Accreditation Authority, Accredited Management Teacher, Qualified Trainer, Doctoral Guide and Board Member of Academics and Advisory Committee in accredited B-Schools. She has to her credit many conferred doctorates, is international and editorial advisory board member and reviewer for Emerald, IGI, Inderscience refereed journals, published numerous refereed research papers, and authored books in the area of entrepreneurship, strategy, management, and higher education.

Rabab Ebrahim holds a PhD in Finance from University of Bradford, U.K. and is an Assistant Professor at the College of Business Administration, Department of Economics and Finance, University of Bahrain, Kingdom of Bahrain. Her main research interests are in the areas of corporate finance including dividend policy, capital structure, and cash holdings as well as corporate investments.

Tuncay Ercan graduated from Military Academy, Department of Electric-Electronics in 1986. He received his M.S. degree from Ege University, and Ph.D from Dokuz Eylul University in Computer Engineering in 2000 and 2005 respectively. Currently he is an Assistant Professor at Yasar University, Department of Computer Engineering. His research interests include: Advanced Network Technologies, Wireless Ad-hoc and Sensor Networks, Network Security and Forensics, Network modelling.

Ruchika Gupta is a Professor and HOD (Management) at Amity Business School, Amity University Greater Noida Campus. She is having an academic experience of 17 years during which she has played multifaceted role being a teacher, trainer, mentor, and administrator as well. She is holding a Ph.D in commerce with M.Com, MBA(Finance) and M.Sc (Computer Science). She has presented and published business cases and research papers in national and international conferences/ journals and has been granted 33 copyrights. She is also serving as Reviewer, Advisory Board member and Editor of several Indexed Journals.

Farrukh Habib is the Chairman of Leading-Edge Alliance Software Consultant, UAE. Previously, he was a Researcher at International Shariah Research Academy for Islamic Finance (ISRA), a research institute under Central Bank of Malaysia (BNM). He is also the co-editor of ISRA Journal of Islamic Finance (indexed by ESCI and SCOPUS). He is an expert in Shariah (Islamic law), finance and economics.

He is an Advisor, Consultant, Trainer and Researcher by profession with a strong educational background and vast global experience. He is involved in the Islamic FinTech and halal digital economy, focusing on crowdfunding, micro-investments, microfinance, blockchain, smart contracts, tokenized economy, application of artificial intelligence, internet-of-things (IoT), big data, predictive analytics and machine learning in the financial sector. He has contributed in several projects, researches, corporate trainings, workshops and consultation work.

Aimadhuddin Ahmad Kamely is banking practitioner, energetic, passionate banker and highly sociable. He has successfully completed his M.Sc (IBF) from International Institute of Islamic Banking and Finance (IIiBF), International Islamic University Malaysia, Gombak, Kuala Lumpur, Malaysia

Zorah Abu Kassim is an Associate Professor in the Cluster of Business, Open University Malaysia (OUM). Currently, she is seconded to become the Programme Director for MBA Programme at Arab Open University, Bahrain. Previously, she has worked and taught in government and private universities in Malaysia which includes teaching at an Australian University branch campus in Malaysia Her research interests includes strategic marketing, consumer behaviour, consumer NGOs, consumerism and performance of SME's specifically . She has authored numerous publications in reputable journals and has done consultancy work n the area of consumer NGOs.

Maryam Khalid is a PhD student at the University Malaya Law faculty. Previously she practiced as an Islamic financial corporate lawyer in a Malaysian law firm that operates in ASEAN. She has experiences in advising clients on banking product developments and financial regulatory reforms. She pursued her Master of Laws in University of Melbourne and after graduating, she worked as a legal executive in one of the Malaysian Government-linked Trustee Company and also a private company advising for the company's compliance with current laws regarding its commercial operation. Later she embarked on her PhD that revolves on comparative legal study of regulatory sandbox as part of fintech regulation in Malaysia, the UK and Australia.

Gagan Kukreja is currently an Associate Professor of Accounting at Ahlia University Bahrain. He has over 22 years of experience in university teaching, training and research. Dr. Kukreja is a recognised PhD supervisor of Brunel University London, Amity University Noida, India and Lovely Professional University, India. He also serves as a member of the editorial boards in several international referred journals and has presented many research papers in international conferences as well as published many research papers in the field of accounting, auditing and finance in highly ranked journals. His current area of interest is Integrated Reporting, Fintech, Blockchain and Big Data. He can be accessed at gkukreja@ahlia.edu.bh.

Sumathi Kumaraswamy is an Assistant Professor at Collge of Business Administration, University of Bahrain, Bahrain. She holds a Ph.D. in Banking and Finance from Bharthiar University, India. Her research interests include Dividend policies; Portfolio Management and Short term Financial Management.

Sherin Kunhibava is a Senior Lecturer at the University Malaya Law faculty. Her area of expertise is in commercial law and Islamic banking and finance law. Apart from her fifteen years of teaching experience in academia, Dr. Sherin has also worked at Pacific Bank Bhd. and at International Shariah

Research Academy (ISRA). At Pacific Bank BhD she was attached with the legal department. At ISRA she headed research in Islamic banking and finance and was Editor of the ISRA International Journal of Islamic Finance. Dr. Sherin was also for a number of years an Examiner for two external bodies namely the Malaysian Association of Company Secretaries and the Malaysian Institute of Chartered Secretaries and Administrators. Dr. Sherin writes extensively. Her articles on law have appeared in newspapers, magazines, International and local refereed journals. Dr. Sherin has written chapters in a number of prominent books on Islamic finance. Dr. Sherin's latest area of research project has been green banking framework, and regulatory framework for blockchain and fintech.

Rizal Mohd. Nor is currently Assistant Professor at Kulliyah of Information and Communication (KICT) International Islamic University Malaysia, Kuala Lumpur, Malaysia. He teaches FinTech to students of Islamic Banking and Finance at International Institute of Islamic Banking and Finance (IIiBF).

Ebru E. Saygili is an Assistant Professor at the Department of International Trade and Finance, Yasar University. She completed her BA and MBA degrees in Dokuz Eylul University and received her Phd in Celal Bayar University in 2011. She has eight years of working experience in banking sector and she is a CPA under Turkish laws. She has published papers in national and international journals and books about corporate governance, accounting information systems and enterprise resource planning (ERP).

Index

T

U

W

Z

www.ingramcontent.com/pod-product-compliance
Lightning Source LLC
LaVergne TN
LVHW062120300926
849161LV00010B/2503